BUDDHISM
in America

The Official Record of the
Landmark Conference on the
Future of Buddhist Meditative Practices
in the West

Boston • January 17–19, 1997

Contributions by

Bill Aiken (SGI)

Tsultrim Allione

Bhante Gunaratana

Stephen Batchelor

Dai-en Bennage Roshi

Samuel Bercholz

Rick Fields

Issho Fujita

Bernard Tetsugen Glassman

Joan Halifax

Jon Kabat-Zinn

Ron Leifer, M.D.

Judith Lief

Rev. Kobutsu Malone

Peter Muryo Matthiessen

Paul Monshin Naamon

Mu Seong

Wes Nisker

Toni Packer

His Holiness Rizong Rinpoche

Larry Rosenberg

Ven. Samu Sunim

Ven. Seonaidh

Zen Master Soeng Hyang

Miranda Shaw, Ph.D.

Patricia Shelton

Lama Sherab Dorje

Lama Surya Das

Robert A. F. Thurman

Tulku Thondup Rinpoche

Helen Tworkov

Zen Master Wu Kwang

and
Monks and Nuns from the
City of Ten Thousand
Buddhas

BUDDHISM
in America

Compiled by
Al Rapaport
Conference Organizer

Edited by
Brian D. Hotchkiss

Charles E. Tuttle Co., Inc.
Rutland, Vermont • Boston, Massachusetts • Tokyo, Japan

First published in 1998 by Tuttle Publishing, an imprint of Periplus Editions (HK) Ltd., with editorial offices at 153 Milk Street, Boston, Massachusetts 02109.

Library of Congress Catalog Card Number: 98-60244

Distributed by

USA
Charles E. Tuttle Co., Inc.
RR 1 Box 231-5
North Clarendon, VT 05759
Tel: (802) 773-8930
Fax: (802) 773-6993

Japan
Tuttle Shokai Ltd.
1-21-13, Seki
Tama-ku, Kawasaki-shi
Kanagawa-ken 214, Japan
Tel: (044) 833-0225
Fax: (044) 822-0413

Southeast Asia
Berkeley Books Pte. Ltd.
5 Little Road #08-01
Singapore 536983
Tel: (65) 280-3320
Fax: (65) 280-6290

First edition
05 04 03 02 01   01 00 99 98   1 3 5 7 9 10 8 6 4 2

Photograph of Al Rapaport (page xvi)—Ellen M. Augarten.
All other photographs—Judy B. Messer

Text and cover design—Vernon Press, Inc.

Printed in the United States of America

Contents

1. Then and Now: Buddhism Today as Informed by Ancient Asian Practices

2. The Practice: Schools of Buddhism, Methods of Meditation, Monasticism

3. The Path: Buddhist Thought and Practice in Day-to-Day Living and Dying

4. Mindfulness and Compassion: Socially Engaged Buddhism in the West

5. Buddhism in America

And Shakyamuni Buddha said to the goddess Vimala

Twenty-five hundred years after I have passed away into Nirvana,
the Highest Doctrine will become spread
in the country of the red-faced people.

Publisher's Note

Michael Kerber

This book is an encapsulation of what was said at the landmark Buddhism in America Conference (Boston, January 17–19, 1997). Not all conference presentations are included here and those that are have been condensed and edited. In most cases, what you will read are actual excerpts from the presentations. When this was not possible, however, a synopsis has been prepared. For all cases, it is the main focus of each presenter that is included here. Not everything that was said in the presentations could be included in this book—nor should it be. The chapters for each presentation are not authorized renditions of the presenters' teachings. For this, readers and students are advised and urged to refer to the presenters' published books and articles, many of which are listed in the bibliography (pages 565–68). Audio tapes are also available for those seeking a word-for-word record of the conference or of a particular presentation.

The compilation of this book has proved to be an enormous task. Nearly one hundred hours of audio tapes were transcribed, revised, edited, queried, re-edited, and composed into text. All this would not have been possible without the dedication and mindful focus of Brian Hotchkiss, who at all times tried to remain true to the intent of each presenter. One of the challenges was the spelling of terms and names in a variety of Asian languages. No uniform spelling of Buddhist terms has been adopted since the traditions of the presenters are as varied as those from which the words themselves derive. In some cases, spellings could not be verified and we apologize both to presenters and readers for any errors and confusion such instances may cause. We welcome your corrections for subsequent editions.

We also apologize to the presenters if we have misquoted them or if we have deleted elements of their presentations that they consider to be of key importance. Recording the Dharma is not easy, and much is lost in the translation from spoken word to printed page. Fortunately, as the Buddhism in America Conference demonstrated—and as this book hopefully will mirror—dissemination of the Dharma can be.

Introduction

Al Rapaport

Louis Armstrong was once asked to define jazz. He replied, "Man, if you gotta ask, you'll never know."

We encounter a similar dilemma when attempting to define Buddhist meditation. The simple fact is, we must directly experience meditation in order to have any real understanding of its purpose and power. In other words, meditation must be lived to be learned. Time and time again we find this message in the sayings of ancient and modern masters.

With this in mind, I envisioned the Buddhism in America Conference as a forum at which modern-day meditation teachers could present, and attendees could experience, the essence of the Buddhist teachings on life, death, compassion, and enlightenment. This was not meant to be an academic discussion, as many conferences are, but rather an experiential journey through many of the aspects of Buddhism that have been transmitted from East to West. This book serves as a record of these teachings, presented in a very fresh way using modern language.

As a spiritual practice, Buddhism can be traced back to the teachings of Gautama Shakyamuni—or Shakyamuni Buddha as he is known to Buddhist practitioners—who lived over 2,500 years ago in India and Nepal. Shakyamuni Buddha's first teachings, which form the basis for all Buddhist practice, are called the four noble truths.

The first noble truth is that birth, old age, and death produce suffering. The second noble truth tells us that the origin of suffering is craving and attachment. Suffering can be extinguished, however, through the realization and attainment of Nirvana, or the true nature of the mind, according to the third noble truth, while the fourth noble truth, which is of the most importance to meditation practitioners, clearly specifies the path one must take in order to free oneself from suffering.

This path, which Shakyamuni Buddha termed the "noble eightfold path," includes right understanding, right mindedness, right speech, right action, right living, right effort, right attentiveness, and right concentration (or *dhyana* in Sanskrit). The Buddha specifically warned practitioners of this "middle way" not to give themselves up to unhealthy sensual indulgence or to self-mortification and practice of painful austerities.

It is the eighth part of the noble path that gives the most specific direction to those who would follow the way of meditation. In this section, the Buddha teaches that the development of one-pointed concentration leads to understanding the reality of things, and eventually to an ending of all suffering. *Dhyana* actually refers both to focused

Al Rapaport

concentration of the mind and the aspect that we can call "realization" or "rapture," which results from meditation.

In a way, it is amazing that it took 2,500 years for the Buddhist teachings to come to the West, but today, with the advent of modern communications techniques, and aided by a diminishing number of practitioners in Asia, Buddhist meditation methods are being rapidly disseminated throughout the Western world. This has created a historically unique situation, in that techniques from many different countries are now readily available to the modern seeker, who need never enter a monastery and totally dedicate one's life, as was necessary in the past. Of course, the disadvantage inherent in this is that a kind of "spiritual dilletantism" can easily develop for

those who decide to take advantage of the teachings while not following them through to a full understanding.

On the other hand, there is a tendency to immortalize the ancients, to put them on a pedestal that nobody today can attain. However, if we carefully read the sayings and doings of our ancestors in practice, it is easy to see that they were fully human and had many of the same shortcomings we encounter on our own spiritual journeys.

Bearing this in mind in organizing the Buddhism in America Conference, I set out to bring together Western teachers—and some Eastern teachers who have been in the United States for many years—to create an event that showcases the various styles and methods of the practice of Buddhist meditation that have developed here. Representatives from numerous traditions were invited, including those from several different schools of Zen, Ch'an (the Chinese precursor to Zen), Japanese Tendai, Tibetan Buddhism, and Vipassana. Both celibate monks and nuns and working laypeople were invited to be representatives of their various schools, as we wanted to show how varied Buddhist practice has become in the West, and to give an indication of the different ways contemporary teachers deal with the thorny issues raised by meditation.

Indeed, family and work practice has changed the face of modern Buddhist meditation. Several of the workshops at the conference dealt with the differences between monastic and lay methods of practice and how the strengths and weaknesses of each are interfacing in our culture. In America today, few Buddhist-meditation practioners are monks or nuns, and even fewer of those are celibate. Many have relationships, families, and work at jobs outside, in the "real" world, integrating everyday life into their practice and teaching.

There is no question that the line between the monastic and the laity, which was very clear in Asia, is now very blurry. And since virtually all the Buddhist teachings have been transmitted to the West within the last forty years, there has been and will undoubtedly continue to be continued clarification of this issue as monks, nuns, and laypeople strive to find their own "middle path."

Another major change that has occurred since the Dharma has come to the West is the full inclusion of women, and transcripts of talks by several prominent women teachers are included in the following pages. Although the Buddha himself taught that the path of enlightenment could be traveled by anyone, regardless of sex or social status, Buddhist meditation traditions in Asia have historically been celibate and almost exclusively male. Although women practiced in their separate monasteries for centuries, very little was written down about them, as they were often regarded as unimportant.

While many women would argue, with great justification, that the patriarchal model

is still the predominant one in Buddhism, there is no question that tremendous strides have been made in terms of women gaining access to the teachings. Of course, with men and women practicing side by side, the inevitable issue of how to relate within the context of a spiritual practice has arisen. Several talks and workshops at the conference touched on sex, relationship, and intimacy as a path to enlightenment. These focused on treating the inevitable pitfalls that come up when men and women practice side by side as a challenge to develop a different, stronger model for the future.

I'm certain that the next twenty or thirty years will see a further, deeper integration of Buddhist tradition into our culture. The Judeo-Christian perspective will undoubtably be supplemented by other ways of viewing life, death, and the universe in which we live. Buddhist practice and philosophy make too much sense to be ignored by the mainstream forever, and the message of oneness and compassion is one sorely needed in a world that too often turns violent and ugly.

History shows us that Buddhism inevitably exerts a strong influence in the cultures into which it is introduced. It's up to those of us who practice today to determine where we go from here. Hopefully this book will help the reader to deepen his or her own understanding of how to proceed on their path.

I

Then and Now

Buddhism Today as

Informed by

Ancient Asian Practices

Returning to China

AN HISTORIC EXCHANGE BETWEEN EAST AND WEST

Monks and Nuns from the
City of Ten Thousand Buddhas

IN 1962, THE VENERABLE MASTER HSÜAN HUA LEFT HONG KONG to bring the proper Dharma to America and the West. From that time until his death in 1995, the Venerable Master lectured extensively on the major works of the Mahayana Buddhist canon and established the Dharma Realm Buddhist Association, as well as more than twenty Way-places of the Proper Dharma. The City of Ten Thousand Buddhas in Talmage, California, is among these Way-places. In the words of the Venerable Master:

It could be said that the causes and conditions for the establishment of the City of Ten Thousand Buddhas were predetermined limitless eons ago. It was decided then that the Buddhadharma would be propagated to the West at the present time, and that the City of Ten Thousand Buddhas would appear. The City didn't make its appearance by falling from the heavens or welling forth from the earth. Instead, it was built by people. How did they come about? It was done before World War II, during a time of great affluence in America. That's why such a large complex could be built.

In 1974, the Dharma Realm Buddhist Association purchased the some 488 acres of land and the many buildings that had constituted a California state hospital since the 1930s. This association established its headquarters at this remarkable site and has since welcomed all people "with deep and abundant roots of goodness." The twentieth-anniversary of the City's founding was commemorated in part by a publication about the City, which tells us:

The number 10,000 represents infinity. At the City of Ten Thousand Buddhas we do not mind if whole crowds arrive, or if just a few people come. Ten thousand Buddhas now grace the Hall of Ten Thousand Buddhas with their presence, and in the future followers of all the world's religions will grace the City of Ten Thousand Buddhas with their presence.

The Venerable Master set forth the Six Guiding Principles: no fighting—no greed—no seeking—no being selfish—no seeking personal advantage—no lying. Only those who are willing and able to give up the ways of life to which they have become accustomed and to follow the Buddhist precepts find it possible to remain at the City and to give themselves over to the life of the *bhikshu* [monk] or the *bhikshuni* [nun].

Among those who have been ordained as *bhikshu* is Heng Sure, who, along with two other *bhikshus* from the City of Ten Thousand Buddhas, journeyed to the ancient monastery of Lungwasa, at Shanghai (founded 62 CE). They had been invited by Master Mingyang to take part in the ordination of 597 Chinese monks and nuns. This invitation to monks from the West brought about a historic blending of international Dharma. To begin to understand the signifi-

cance of this invitation, Dar Master Petuni Hungwe explained something of why a monk or nun would choose to take on a life of suffering at the City of Ten Thousand Buddhas:

If one wants to become a preeminent individual, one who stands out from the crowd, one must be taking the thing that others cannot bear to take, the suffering that others cannot take. Only through this kind of discipline can one achieve a larger, indestructible body. When one becomes a monk or nun, one must be psychologically prepared to live the holy life in order to be eternally liberated from birth and death and to be freer of the suffering of transmigration forever. Therefore, one cannot be afraid to face any kind of hardship. Talking about suffering, you may feel fear or want to withdraw your interest in leaving the home life. As a matter of fact, from the point of view of Tao, what most people take as happiness is actually the cause of suffering. My experience is that many people find leaving the home life, especially in the City of Ten Thousand Buddhas, to be an experience involving suffering. And that's why leaving the home life is said to be the work of sages. In leaving home to cultivate a way, one must first get rid of grief, eliminate anger, and extinguish delusion. When these three poisons are cleaned out, our wisdom will naturally come forth.

In the City of Ten Thousand Buddhas, a person who has newly left the home life has three years in the novice-training program. He or she has the opportunity to study the precepts and the sutras and share in the community work. When the time for taking full ordination comes, a novice must first undergo a 108-day intensive training program during which they emphasize memorization of the *Vinaya for Daily Use* and the novice *Vinaya,* the Bodhisattva Precepts in the *Brahma Net Sutra,* and either the 250 *bhikshu* precepts or the 348 *bhikshuni* precepts. Only then will they be qualified to receive full ordination, which will establish a foundation for their cultivation. Holding the precepts means stopping all evils and practicing all good deeds. In addition, the Venerable Master summarized the standards of conduct that he himself upheld throughout his life for all his disciples, both the *sangha* members and the laity. The Venerable Master once said if every single member keeps the precept of not touching money, sits in *sangha* meditation, eats one meal a day at noon, wears the precept sash at all times, and upholds the precepts, then the proper Dharma will remain in the world.

The first ordination ceremony in the West occurred in 1972, when the Venerable Master Hua conducted the initial, formal, full ordination ceremony for Buddhist monks and nuns at Gold Mountain Monastery in San Francisco. He invited virtuous elder master to preside for him over the ordination platform. Five monks and one nun received ordination. Subsequent ordination platforms have been held at the Sagely City of Ten Thousand Buddhas in 1976, 1979, 1982, 1989, 1991, 1992, and 1995. Progressively larger numbers of people have received full ordination. Over

two hundred people from countries all over the world were ordained under the Venerable Master.

One of the unique features of the ordination ceremony in the City of Ten Thousand Buddhas has been that distinguished monks from both the Mahayana and the Theravada traditions have been invited to preside with the Venerable Master in conducting monastic ordination ceremonies. The Venerable Master managed to mend a large portion of the two-thousand-year-old rift between the Mahayana and Theravada monastic communities. He encouraged cordial relations between the *sanghas.*

Heng Sure further emphasized this by pointing out that the coming together of the Theravada and Mahayana for an ordination ceremony, as they did at the City of Ten Thousand Buddhas, is something that had not occurred in 2,500 years. In 1982, three masters and seven certifiers took part in such a ceremony. Of them, half came from the traditions practiced in Thailand, Laos, Cambodia, and Sri Lanka, while the others derived their practice from those of China, Vietnam, Japan, Korea, and Tibet. Thus, the importance of the invitation from Master Mingyang becomes especially clear. As Heng Sure said:

Another branch grew on the Buddhist tree when *bhikshus* from America returned to China. I guess this would be a kind of testimony to how far Buddhism has come into this country and put down roots—that the

Chinese *sangha* when they wanted to ordain monks and nuns, came to America looking for masters and certifiers. Outside, I would say this event was a manifestation of an intercultural exchange. The bamboo curtain, in reverse, parted. We went back to China in a religious role; Westerners trained in America and Taiwanese monks who came to America for their training, went back to stand in front of six hundred ordainees from China, men and women who had decided to follow the Buddhist path of renunciation into the *sangha*. There was no special allowance made for the monks from America. We were part of the group, so much so that we were handed the gavel to say, "Yes, you're certified." That's outside. Inside, I have to say there was a magical moment of continuity that involved the precepts that arose from the Buddhist compassion, connecting through a line of men and women from the Buddha's own time, when he first said, "Come, *bhikshus*," and the first five monks came into the *sangha,* right to 1995 and on to the present.

At Lungwasa they have built a luxury hotel right next to the monastery. Buddhism has to make money now in China. So there's one wall dividing the monastery that's been there since 62 CE, with its brand new, plush hotel. There are karaoke bars. There is the Dunhuang Dance Hall. You can send and receive faxes at the international business center and then go down to the gift shop and buy Gucci and Calvin Klein, and as you see the televisions playing commercials from satellite TV in San Francisco. And yet, on the faces of the folks inside the hotel there's the same kind of fatigue and the same kind of searching and frustration that you see in every major airport. Harried; a little burned by the dust; looking and searching; that sense of being off center and of disquiet.

You step through a door and back into the Tang Dynasty. These are the same stones. The wind is blowing. It's drizzling rain. Here are six hundred people on their knees in the cold, their throats hoarse from all the chanting, all the bowing that they've been doing and it's a great shock to see on their faces this beatific glow, this joy and affirmation, full heart. *I am here on my own effort. I know why I'm here. I would not trade myself across that wall for anything.* And the contrast and the paradox between what is suffering and what is pleasure was never so clear to me as in that moment.

Sitting in the presence of all these men who were twice my age, twice my years in precepts, and looking and thinking, *Well, there is a connection.* We were told that in order to get us through the door, Master Mingyang had to make ten calls to Beijing. They said the Earth moved a bit and the door opened so we could come. Somehow it was important for us to be there, I believe, because Master Mingyang genuinely wants the Dharma to transplant into this country, into the West, and so he went out on a limb to certify the certifiers and then to say, "Please carry it on."

So here we were in the holiest hall, the precept platform of the Bodhimanda, taking part in the most sacred and adorned ceremony in all of the Buddhist repertoire. To be able to witness that as an American, bringing, I felt, a kind of an American sense of Dharma, I felt almost as if I was just a function representing all of us, propelled into their midst only through my link with the Master Hsüan Hua, through no virtue of my own, somehow having this job to do, to make a link with the two cultures, but, in that moment, also a link with the buddhas and the bodhisattvas. I had a sense that, as we were doing this, it was not nearly a rite, not nearly a ritual, but that in some sense, having fulfilled the Dharma, the buddhas and bodhisattvas came and said, "Okay, join." And that was profoundly moving. That was what I witnessed. We were connected in that moment to a lineage, to history, to a 2,500-year-old tradition, and to the Triple Jewel, and it was not a myth at that point—initiating new lives into the *sangha* via ancient wisdom teachings that are not forgotten. That was a moment of joy.

It seems that there's not so much new to create in the Dharma. There's a tremendous amount to discover, fields of Dharma, Dharma realms to explore, and the door is very, very wide and it's now open in this country for English speakers, for Spanish speakers, for French speakers, for non-Chinese, non-Asian-language speakers because of the vision of these two elder monks. Dharma Master Hsüan Hua passed away last year. Master Mingyang is not in good health. But men and women whom they brought into the *sangha* are concerned that the Dharma survive in this line, that it not be cut off in this generation.

At the end of his life, when asked by Ananda "While you are in the world, you are our teacher. When you pass on, who will be our teacher?" the Buddha answered "Take the precept as your teacher."

Cultivating Loving-Kindness Through the Slogans of Atisha

Judith Lief

THE LATE VENERABLE CHÖGYAM TRUNGPA RINPOCHE AUTHORIZED his senior student Judith Lief to be a teacher and meditation instructor in the Tibetan Buddhist and Shambhala traditions. Ms. Lief, formerly director of the Naropa Institute in Boulder, Colorado, edited her teacher's *Training the Mind and Cultivating Loving-Kindness.*

At times humorous and at others direct, Ms. Lief warmly invited the participants in her day-long workshop to begin to explore some of the myriad ways of incorporating the Tong Len practice into their individual practices. This particular approach is centered on the fifty-nine slogans of Atisha, an eleventh-century Indian Buddhist scholar who spent the last twelve years of his life in Tibet, where he had a profound effect on that country's practice of Buddhism.

Ms. Lief emphasized that Tong Len practice is not a path one follows instead of a regular sitting practice, but rather it is used as an adjunct to one's sitting practice in order to examine specific elements and issues in life. To set the stage for her work with the slogans of Atisha, Ms. Lief first sketched in important elements of day-to-day sitting practice.

The Tibetan Buddhist tradition incorporates training in what are called three different stages of the path. First there is training in the Hinayana, which, in this context, has to do with working with our own states of mind in a very lonely way—a very rugged and precise way—with a goal of not creating any further confusion or pollution in the world around us. So you could think of it as basic housekeeping: We look at how we live our lives; how our mind works, and how that spreads suffering and confusion in big clouds in all directions; and how we can begin to aim that energy a little bit. The Hinayana stage is also talked about as a narrow path, not narrow in the sense of narrow-mindedness, but as in narrowing down our lives to their more essential points: simplifying how we think, how we live, how we talk, trying to pare down a lot of unnecessary drivel.

The second stage of the path in Tibetan Buddhism is called Mahayana , which means "greater vehicle," or "broad path," or "open way." For example, while it's great progress that we're not polluting the world, we could go further and actually benefit others. We could work in a broader way—more socially, culturally, and interactively with other people. So much of our lives, we're totally interdependent with one another, both humans and nonhumans. We are involved in this intricate web of relationships. So the Mahayana stage is involved with working on the quality of relationship, of developing more skill in how we interact with one another, and on developing more open-heartedness in terms of what we can include in our world. There is a sense of not holding on to a small island of purity—a special spot just for us—but giving up our privacy and our reflex to pull back from a world that is so intense; getting back out in the world and working as a practice, extending the sense of practice further. This, in particular, is where the slogans of Atisha and this quality of mind training fits in the geography of things.

The third stage of the path is called Vajrayana, which is the "indestructible path." *Vajra* also means the "thunderbolt," and can also be referred to as the "diamond path." Here, we go one step further, trying to join what has been learned in the Hinayana and the Mahayana traditions into a much more spontaneous play of energy, making the quality of training seamless; less a project and more a dance of energies.

First, let me talk a little about where instructions associated with the Tong Len practice fit in with the teachings of Buddha. The story that links directly with this kind of teaching concerns the Buddha when he was a young boy. His father was king of a little region and so, of course, had to go through the usual ceremonial cycles and obligations. Ancient India was an agricultural society, so one important ceremony was the annual planting of the first seeds, which begins the cycle of growing food. Everybody was gathered together and, at the climax of the ceremony, using a big, elaborate plow, they plowed the symbolic first furrow, after which all would return to their fields and start planting. The Buddha was there and noticed that, as the blade of the plow went through the ground, the lives of many small creatures were totally disrupted. He saw worms being sliced in two and bugs scurrying out of the way. Things that had been on top were suddenly down below. He saw that just by this simple act, which we all depend on, tremendous suffering was created.

He was so touched in his heart that he removed himself from the ceremony and went and sat under a tree and thought about how our ability to live can be based on creating pain for other beings and that there's seemingly no way to avoid that quality. It is said that years later, when he left his home and embarked on his long spiritual journey and attained a state of awakened mind and heart, that this particular experience had been the seed for his full awakening. It was very simple, the kind of experience that all sorts of children have.

Because of that, it is said that as much as there is a need for insight or knowledge, it is also essential that a path have a heart, which is based on opening your heart to the world and letting it affect you, rather than pulling away from the world. So throughout the Buddhist tradition there is kind of interweaving of these two threads. The development of kindliness or compassion is interwoven with that stream we call wisdom teachings, by which we develop and sharpen our intelligence. Like two wings of a bird, both are necessary for Buddhism to flutter along and fly through space. You could be a very well-intentioned, kind-hearted person, but you couldn't be very helpful if you didn't have any training or knowledge. On the other hand, you could be very philosophically or scientifically advanced, but with no heart connection you're apt to do more harm than good.

Before you can train the mind, you must begin with what is called a taming of the mind. Say you were going to capture a monkey in order to have an act in the circus. Before you start training the monkey to jump through hoops you first have to befriend the monkey and tame it, get it to relate to you. Likewise, if you think of your mind as a monkey, you must first tame your mind, letting it begin to relax and settle a bit. In other words, getting to know ourselves a bit more is really the starting point of a meditation practice. We must first find out who we are, and look in some real precise and deep way at what in ourselves we accept and what we reject and find out what makes us uneasy just being with ourselves. What makes it hard for us just to sit still and be who we are? How can we begin to let our mind relax and settle—to tame our wildness of mind, which is scattered and judgmental and filled with memories, some painful, some pleasurable, filled with all sorts of opinions and ideas and hopes and fears. Taming the mind calls for beginning to create a kind of a space of acceptance and non-struggle.

[The workshop continued with Ms. Lief providing instruction for a basic sitting meditation, demonstrating ways to accommodate the body, concentrate on breath, and loosen the mind's grip on the sitter. This was in preparation for moving into an introduction to working with Tong Len practice and, more specifically, the slogans of Atisha.]

The mind-training school in Tibetan is called *lo jong* and it goes back to Atisha, a famous teacher thoroughly trained in meditation who had heard about this particular teaching of cultivating loving-kindness and training the mind completely. He endured all sorts of hardships in order to find the teacher who knew these mind-training teachings. He traveled from India into Sumatra to find this teacher, Serlingpa, who was the only person with this particular line of teachings. Having done so, he returned to India where he became known for being the originator of these teachings and of the slogans we'll be talking about. The fifty-nine little sayings, or slogans, are traced to Atisha although, in fact, they were not codified into slogans until much later.

Atisha also had a very important role in Tibetan Buddhism. He was one of the teachers who was invited to Tibet. The Indians had many opinions about Tibetans, most of them not very high. Atisha felt trepidation about going up into the wilds of Tibet and teaching these people and he was also worried that he wouldn't have enough challenge to work with his mind-training practice, so he brought along his cook, who was supposed to be very ornery and unpleasant—Atisha needed someone irritating to work with. The story goes that, after being with the Tibetans for a while, he realized that he hadn't really needed to bring anyone along to help on this score. And that's how the mind-training first came to Tibet.

For a long time it was kept very secret, taught only from one teacher to one student, so it wasn't very widely known. But gradually it became more widespread and more useful. In particular Yeshe Chekawa was instrumental in spreading it in Tibet. He was the person who codified it into these slogans because he was struck by the quality of these teachings and wanted to make them more widespread. His brother, who had no interest in a spiritual path, was kind of an impossible character, and he found that it helped him, so he figured it could help almost anybody. He also had a very strong social conscience and worked with outcasts, lepers in particular, so he used this kind of practice in terms of health. Today it is still used in health care and also when working with people in difficult circumstances, such as lepers. Now it's included in all the major lineages of Tibetan Buddhism, and mind training is part of the training of teachers and students.

There are two different components in mind training: the formal meditation practice, which we'll be doing this afternoon, and then the main part of the practice—what you do in your daily life. The benefit of working with these slogans is that you virtually need no time to practice to do them. You can work with the slogans in an ongoing way throughout your life and they become like bits of instantaneous practice that you begin to invite into your life. One may haunt you or pop up in your mind. When you work with these slogans in the midst of activity, an element of practice is always inserted, so if you're a very busy person with some basic sitting practice, but most of the time you're not sitting—you are working or sleeping and doing all those sorts of things— these provide a very skillful way to join that quality of practice in the midst of all those activities.

In the Buddhist tradition, the notion of ego has a quality of holding back at a very fundamental level and of trying to grasp onto things for ourselves. It has a quality of being preoccupied with our own concerns all the time to the exclusion of other people and other events. It's viewing everything through one perspective as though we are the center of the universe and everything else is our environment—that very narrow perception of things—and we create a kind of fortress around ourselves because we're afraid. Deep down we know things aren't as solid as we would like in our world, in ourselves, our thoughts, everything about us. So we create a kind of false security, a false solidity, and then arm ourselves to protect this even though we know deep down that it's not really who we are.

In relationships, for example, we can get to that point where we can't really see the other person as separate from ourselves. We can't bear to let something go, even though it may be to our benefit because it might hurt us. Where we can't change, we get caught in a pattern, even though we know it's destructive, because we're so afraid of losing even a negative identity. We may view ourselves as heroes or as victims, but it's the same kind of energy from this perspective— the energy of ego trying to say, I'm a something and now that I know I'm a something, I'm going to make sure that that something is unthreatened and never changed or never challenged, never dissolves. Got to hold onto it with all my might. This leads to a sense

deep down of deception and a quality of holding, which means that, in a lot of activities in our lives, our energy is blocked because we invest so much into holding ego together and warding off challenges or any chinks in our armor.

So one aspect of this mind training is specifically aimed at trying to loosen that sense of struggle. Ego is fed by struggle. It could even be said that it is a struggle; that we don't feel comfortable if we're not struggling. We feel afraid. We're caught in this realm of struggle, and practice is poking holes in that. I think the blurb for the book [*Training the Mind and Cultivating Loving-Kindness*] said, "This book may be dangerous to your ego." It is said that, no matter what the spiritual tradition or practice—eyes open or closed; elaborate *pujas* or simplicity of *vipassana*— fundamentally it gets down to this real, nitty-gritty point somewhere along the line. Then you are just face to face with this sense of duality, of ego, of cutting off from our world and confronting it, which makes this a powerful practice to try to bring that into the light.

I'll give you an example to show you how egocentric I am. I was reading a little article that said there's a new outbreak of malaria in an area where I'm going to be going soon. Mostly it affects children and old people and people who are very poor and I thought, Ah. Wait a minute. That's great. I'm really happy it's not going to affect me. I'm not a little kid and I'm not really old and I'm not really poor, so I'll be able to get through this. It's that kind of impulse and it comes up over and over again. No matter how we like to think of ourselves, fundamentally it comes down to me—number one, take care of number one, protect number one. One aspect of this teaching works with understanding what this ego is: How does it manifest? How does it affect the way we live our lives? How much do we base on protecting this fortress of self-concern, self-centeredness?

The other side concerns working with two different qualities of compassion. Two terms are referred to here: the practice of *maitri,* a Sanskrit word, which is a sense of friendliness, loving-kindness. Beyond that is the quality of *karuna,* or compassion. How do we open or awaken our friendliness? It is said that we can tap into a kind of natural friendliness and we can start this on the very, very simplest level.

One way that my teacher used to talk about *maitri* was as his fundamental friendliness. He also pointed out that it includes friendliness to ourselves. Many times, especially when people become involved, wanting to be helpful, good persons, they think I'm going to ignore myself. I'm going to try to be nice to everybody else. I don't matter…I'm just little me. Eventually the person burns out and becomes very angry. *Maitri* teaches that if you can't be friendly to yourself, you can't really be fundamentally friendly to other people. So we end up back at the sitting practice we were doing, which is an expression of that same quality of friendliness. In order to accept what comes up in your mind, let the mind rise and fall and not judge so heavily. It requires making an extremely friendly gesture and also beginning

to expose how aggressive and unfriendly we are to ourselves.

Karuna is an unlimited extension of that very same quality. It's that fundamental extending outward of all of that energy of kindness, without limit. Not picking and choosing, just manifesting a natural outflowing of kindliness. The Tibetans have an interesting translation for that. They call it *snying rje,* which means "noble heart." That's how they view the basic translation of the word *compassion,* a nobility of heart.

Therefore, because all of this practice is supposed to lead to inspiration to do good things from a genuine, not a manipulative, motive, the image given for the source of compassionate activity is that of the sun. The nature of the sun is to shine and emanate heat and light. The sun shines on the Earth and causes us to be warm and causes plants to grow, but it's not as though the sun decides to perform a big social-action project and say, "I'm going to help out the Earth. I'm going to do this project where I shine down there and make things grow." It shines naturally and expresses its essence that way. And it doesn't pick and choose. It doesn't say, "I'm only going to shine on this country. I don't like that country. I'm only going to shine on Judy's basil plants. I'm not going to shine on her weeds." It shines on the whole thing. So it's not a project but it produces incredible results. Nobody congratulates the sun. It doesn't really get any awards for its efforts. It doesn't care. It just does what it does and that's supposed to be the goal for you as well: simply expressing what you are—a passionate being who has a quality of awakened heart with which you can connect.

[Here, a participant asked Ms. Lief to share ways in which she uses the slogans of Atisha in her everyday life. She explained that she had memorized them, much as Tibetans do. In programs in which she had participated, several times a day the entire list has been read aloud by a participant. In Tibet, the slogans crop up on small signs everywhere—kitchens and the bathrooms included. The spot in a public area where something annoying had happened could host a sign bearing a particularly appropriate slogan, so that they are often experienced in a humorous way. The resulting proliferation of little notes and chance encounters with them in the course of daily life inevitably assists people with learning them, thinking about them, and putting them to use. She went on to describe another method she uses.]

One way I work with them is just knowing that they sometimes arise at seemingly magically appropriate moments. I have a set of cards, each of which has one of the slogans on it. I keep them on my desk on a little stand, and most days I'll switch to the next slogan. I go through that on kind of a cycle.

You can also work with a single slogan intensively for a long period of time. Then you begin to see there are many levels of understanding for each slogan. They cut a certain momentum of going on and on in our self-centered way. Some people analyze them and study them in some depth, write poems about them, talk about them, interact with other people all working with slogans , which is still another way I have worked with them. But usually the simplest approach is best. Just see the slogan, think about it, and then let it go. You don't try to apply a slogan, thinking What's a slogan for this? It's better just to go through them and if they pop up, it's good, and if they don't that's good, too.

Now I would like to read the fifty-nine slogans for you to hear. Don't worry about what they mean. Let them implant themselves however they do.

1. First train in the preliminaries.
2. Regard all dharmas as dreams.
3. Examine the nature of unborn awareness.
4. Self-liberate even the antidote.
5. Rest in the nature of *alaya,* the essence.
6. In post meditation, be a child of illusion.
7. Sending and taking should be practiced alternately; these two should ride the breath.
8. Three objects, three poisons, and three seeds of virtue.
9. In all activities, train with slogans.
10. Begin the sequence of sending and taking with yourself.
11. When the world is filled with evil, transform all mishaps into the path of *bodhi.*
12. Drive all blames into one.
13. Be grateful to everyone.
14. Seeing confusion as the four *kayas* is unsurpassable *shunyata* protection.
15. Four practices are the best of methods.

16. Whatever you meet unexpectedly, join with meditation.
17. Practice the five strengths, the condensed heart instructions.
18. The Mahayana instruction for ejection of consciousness at death is the five strengths.
19. How you conduct yourself is important.
20. All Dharma agrees at one point.
21. Of the two witnesses, hold the principle one.
22. Always maintain only a joyful mind.
23. If you can practice even when distracted, you are well-trained.
24. Always abide by the three basic principles.
25. Change your attitude but remain natural.
26. Don't talk about injured limbs.
27. Don't ponder others.
28. Work with the greatest defilements first.
29. Abandon any hope of fruition.
30. Abandon poisonous food.
31. Don't be so predictable.
32. Don't malign others.
33. Don't wait in ambush.
34. Don't bring things to a painful point.
35. Don't transfer the ox's load to the cow.
36. Don't try to be the fastest.
37. Don't act with a twist.
38. Don't make gods into demons.
39. Don't seek others' pain as the limbs of your own happiness.
40. All activities should be done with one intention.
41. Correct all wrongs with one intention.
42. Two activities, one at the beginning, one at the end; whichever of the two occurs, be patient.
43. Observe these two even at the risk of your life.
44. Train in the three difficulties.
45. Take on the three principle causes.
46. Pay heed that the three never wane.
47. Keep the three inseparable.
48. Train without bias in all areas. It is crucial always to do this pervasively and whole-heartedly.
49. Always meditate on whatever provokes resentment.
50. Don't be swayed by external circumstances.
51. This time, practice the main points.
52. Don't misinterpret.
53. Don't vacillate.
54. Train whole-heartedly.
55. Liberate yourself by examining and analyzing.
56. Don't wallow in self-pity.
57. Don't be jealous.
58. Don't be frivolous.
59. Don't expect applause.

[After a period of meditation on the slogans and a break for lunch, the workshop reconvened. Ms. Lief began by discussing two types of bodhichitta.]

Bodhichitta is very multifaceted and has been much discussed. The term *bodhi* has the same root as Buddha. It basically means awake, awakened. Not in the sense of not falling asleep but awakened from confusion, awakened from the imprisonment of conflicting emotions, etc.—fully awake, fully alive. *Chitta* is sometimes translated as mind and sometimes as heart, so you could think of it as "mind/heart" or the beating heart of kindness. It has a quality of intelligence but also one of warmth. Mind/heart is the wellspring of your actions. Cultivation and understanding of *bodhichitta* is central in all Buddhism. People do various forms of contemplative practice to develop, express, and understand *bodhichitta,* and training the mind is all about cultivation of *bodhichitta.*

In the Tibetan tradition and others, two types of *bodhichitta* are addressed: One is the ultimate and the other is the relative. Ultimate *bodhichitta* is the quality of wisdom, of unboundedness. "Unfettered mind" would be one way of looking at it; mind not caught up in petty concerns. But it's mind let loose a bit, giving it a quality of vastness and depth. In practice, cultivating ultimate *bodhichitta* holds a sense of reversing an old pattern of trying to deal with our experience by reducing it to manageable size, trying to reduce the intensity of our lives, trying to reduce chaos and confusion The notion of ultimate *bodhichitta* tends more toward letting mind expand, releasing small-mindedness, so that the mind becomes totally unbound. From our fearful point of view, we can say the mind is totally out control. Out of control? What would that be like? According to these teachings, if it was totally out of our control, we'd be much better off, because our controlling reduces light and experience so much that we lose any sense of sacredness and depth.

While most of the slogans of Atisha are involved with work on relative *bodhichitta,* the first six have to do with ultimate *bodhichitta.* The very first slogan—*First train in the preliminaries*—could be called the introduction to all the slogan practices, and it has many different interpretations. At its most basic, it teaches that, in order to do this kind of practice, there needs to be some taming of the mind, some work with basic sitting practice. Also, what's often considered preliminary is looking carefully and honestly at the conditions of our lives, the situation in which we find ourselves, and appreciating that, for some reason, we happen to be in the favorable situation of hearing the teachings of the Buddha and being able to practice them to some degree. We find ourselves in favorable circumstances and thinking that, though we realize that's not always the case. You never know what's going to happen with your life or what you're going to be dealing with, which suggests that if the opportunity arises, you should go with it while it's there.

The second of the ultimate *bodhichitta* slogans is *Regard all dharmas as dreams.* Again, much of this instruction is very relevant to what actually happens when you're on your chair or cushion just sitting. They comprise a form of meditation instruction, or stages of meditation instruction. The term *dharmas,* in this case, just refers to things that we experience. It's not like Dharma, the teachings the of the Buddha, but rather regards what we experience as dreams. What does that mean when you're sitting? For one thing, it means that things are more fluid and loose than we usually think or experience. What arises or dissolves in our mind is constantly changing and not as solid as we would like.

Our mind presents itself to itself as solid

and invincible. But in the meditation practice, just when you think something solid occurs, it dissolves. You try to build up something solid—it dissolves. So there's a sense of seeing how things transform, as in dreams, and seeing how in trying to force situations into real this or that, we miss the fluidity of our experience. It happens all the time when we're dealing with each other. The classic situation is the parent dealing with the child; then the child grows up and comes home and the parent is still living in a time that is ten years earlier. The child has changed and actually is not even perceiving the same universe. Something has solidified and the person hasn't seen the shifting quality of what they're experiencing.

Sometimes you notice that everything seems pretty shifty. Things change, seem insubstantial, seem less solid than they might appear. But who noticed that? What is that perception? The next slogan says *Examine the nature of unborn awareness*—hold coming to the view that everything is shifty as a big accomplishment. Now you begin to see that this series of slogans is progressive; each one is corrective in some way or takes the previous slogan to a higher degree of subtlety.

In this case, when you look at your own mind, you find that your perception is constantly changing and it's also very dreamlike. You're not sure where it is. Where exactly is our mind? Conceptually we may say that it's in the brain, but how do we perceive it? Where does it exist? What is it exactly? What does it mean to be aware of anything? And why is that always changing? One moment we're very aware and the next

minute we bump into the door. Did awareness just go on vacation and then come back? When you perceive something, your perception seems to come out of nowhere and then you forget it and it certainly seems to go somewhere far away. Where does it go? Where does it come from? How do these thoughts arise and how do they build their power?

So you could say the first step is seeing the shifty ground all around us. Then the second slogan suggests that the perception itself is pretty shifty. You never know where it's going to be coming from, what's going to come through your mind at any moment. It's totally unpredictable. Often we haven't a clue. So how does all this work? Who's on first?—the question Who's on first in the ultimate sense. And you look and look and you don't find anyone. That's what this slogan is all about.

So you could think, Well, if that's the case, it doesn't seem much is happening. You may sense a quality of groundlessness in all directions. You can't really count on being able to hold that thought or that relationship or that perception. The whole thing is so insubstantial that it is possible to fall into a trap of nihilism and think Who cares then? It doesn't matter. So what if my thoughts are changing, my mind is all over the place? I don't know what's going on. Can't count on anything.

This leads to the next slogan: *Self-liberate even the antidote.* Here the antidote is that quality of emptiness, that so-what quality in which all the usual props we've relied on aren't working so well. This slogan makes it clear that we should not take that all that seriously either. Self-liberate the antidote means don't dwell on, or wallow in, that understanding of emptiness or groundlessness—*shunyata* or emptiness, openness, unboundedness. Sometimes it's called the sickness of *shunyata*, the sickness of emptiness, which can become an excuse for pulling back from our experience and from other people. We are told to let go of that as well in order to begin to get in touch much, much more with a direct, raw, genuine experience of things. This is what ultimate *bodhichitta* is really about and what sitting should be about.

The next slogan is the heart of the slogans—of the practice instructions: *Rest in the nature of* alaya, *the essence.* You could think of *alaya* as the mind's root; before picking and choosing, before taking sides, before trying to be any particular thing, or experience a particular mood, or have a particular thought. It's more like a storehouse of a mind, the space from which things arise. The same word is in the word *Himalaya,* the mountain range. *Him* means snow, so *Himalaya* could be translated as "the place where the snow is." Since *alaya* is the place where the mind is, the slogan's instruction is simply to rest the mind. Let the mind rest in its own nature and reveal itself, which is a very important point of practice. So we let the mind simplify and simplify and rest and rest and get to that layer of mind we all know and sense but don't fully trust at this point. This is a very deep level that we rely on fundamentally, but it's hidden from us and overladen with so many histories, experiences, story lines, memories, opinions, and

endless thoughts and concepts. We must peel away and peel away to reach a base that has no bias this way or that; one that won't buy into our push-and-pull maneuvering.

The last slogan in the ultimate *bodhichitta* is *In post-meditation, be a child of illusion.* This phrase has three important words. One is post-meditation. Meditation practice is always the other side of the coin of post-meditation practice, and this slogan reminds us that we need to be working with both.

Then the child— the quality of being like a child— is also very important. It has to do with being pointed toward and working with ultimate *bodhichitta;* working to derigidify our mind. What's that like? It's like being a child. In many ways the very open, curious ground that we start off with as children begins to be reduced and defined more and more, and that realm of play of the mind sometimes can become buried as we become adults and take ourselves extremely seriously. Everything is a big deal and if we're going to be spiritual, we get really spiritual. If we want to be successful, we're really successful. Anything we do is serious, whether you are a lawyer or a teacher or a Buddhist practitioner. But this child quality suggests that we relax a little bit to see that there's play in this and to see how seriousness gets in our way. The most terrible thing that happens in religious traditions, in spirituality, is that people don't play. This is carried out by retaining a base of humor and lightness rather than heaviness. It suggests that the spirituality not make everything heavy. There is tremendous humor in how humans live their lives and what comes up in our minds. You could be a famous teacher, sitting on your cushion, thinking about eating a hot dog.

Illusion is the final key word in this slogan. We spin out all sorts of projects and ideas and inspirations, and that's great. You can accomplish a tremendous amount that way. At the same time, you need to realize that they are all like castles built on sand, or visions in the midst of space. Even though we may be working tremendously hard to accomplish something, we remain open to surprise because, chances are, things won't go the way we expect anyway. At the same time, we are still willing to throw ourselves into doing things, not from the illusion of permanence but from the viewpoint of play and simplicity and a basic appreciation of our life.

Of the fifty-nine slogans, six concern ultimate *bodhichitta,* while the other fifty-three are relative. So relative *bodhichitta* is important. Tying it in with our intertwined threads, the thread of friendliness and kindness balances that of wisdom. Literally, relative *bodhichitta* is the quality of heart in practice. It reminds us that practitioners aren't robots. It brings us to let a practice touch us and awaken our heart; letting it begin to remove the thick coverings we put around our heart as protection in the world. If you don't have a heart, you have no juice—no life—in your practice.

The quality of heart goes back to that early story about the young Buddha. That was the fuel for his practice, not some notion that he was going to become a great spiritual teacher, but the quality of heart. He

saw the little creatures and in his heart he felt pain, he felt sadness. He felt touched at how our beings are constantly intertwined with suffering, disappointment, and the upset of the environment all around us. It is said that that is like a saving grace. So this is a practice of digging out that quality of heart, then cultivating and nourishing it; becoming increasingly broad-minded about whom we include in our realm of heart, moving from our little circle of safe people to include others; from our little circle of safe experience to include more.

This is the quality of the Buddhist path, even though people can say they are going to become a "professional" Buddhist, have a Buddhist identity, and make armor out of that. The point is to become a real person who can experience fully what comes up in life. Mindfulness literally means your mind is full. You are fully present, fully aware, and fully connected, all of which contribute to a quality of heart.

[At this point, Ms. Lief instructed the participants in a simple meditation. Each participant brought into focus an individual who had shown them great kindness. From that person, the sitters broadened their view of kindnesses performed throughout the world, even to mother animals caring for their young, so that, ultimately, the "tremendous invisible fuel running through the Earth of some quality of kindness that makes life possible" becomes apparent. This was a preface to her introduction of Tong Len.]

Earlier I talked about mind training, or *lojong.* Within that, the central practice of mind training is called Tong Len. In English it's "exchanging self for others." The Tibetan term literally means "sending and taking," or it could be referred to as relative-*bodhichitta* practice. It is all based on one of the slogans: *Sending and taking should be practiced alternately; these two should ride the breath.*

This practice has many different variations and there are many different contexts in which it is used. In my *sangha,* one of the earlier contexts in which it was used as a practice was, each month, when our community gathered, we brought names of people who were seriously ill and we did a form of this practice. Then it was also introduced as part of our funeral ceremony.

Apart from those limited uses of just one aspect of the practice, Tong Len wasn't introduced in our community until 1978. For a time, it was only introduced to people who had had several years of basic sitting practice. They were required to have taken the bodhisattva vow, which means that only very committed students would include this as part of their practice. Gradually it became a bit more readily available. Sometimes people in intensive, month-long sitting programs would be introduced to Tong Len practice and then it began being used in psychology programs at the Naropa Institute. They also included some training in this for newer students, people without as much background.

Even now, back-and-forth discussion continues as to how useful it is without a really strong sitting practice, and I can't emphasize strongly enough that sitting practice is important. It would be a big mistake to drop the sitting and just do the Tong Len.

On the other hand, I think it's helpful in so many ways to people in the situations we actually encounter, that I feel it's a good thing that it has become more broadly available. Apart from people using this as part of their regular practice, it can also be useful if you are sick yourself, or in dire straights—at a dentist's office, or giving birth, for example. It can have very practical applications in the midst of difficult situations as well.

Tong Len has three stages The first is momentary but important: When you are doing sitting practice and you decide to do Tong Len, there's a moment of transition, which sometimes is described as a flash or an instant or a gap. It is some sense of acknowledging a shift of mind. When you let your mind shift, the actual time is very brief, but it's important not to leave this step out.

Secondly, the actual sending and taking begins. So what do you send and what do you take? Well, in a broad sense, what you're taking in is what you don't want and what you're sending out is what you do want. You're taking in the quality of suffering that you see and sending out kindness or healing energy or well-wishes to others. You take in aspects of aggression, confusion, or ignorance and breathe out gentleness, broad-mindedness, a quality of clarity. If you are taking in narrowness of mind, bigotry, you breathe out acceptance, open-mindedness, etc. Sometimes it is focused in a specific way. For example, if the issue is health, bring in ill health and breathe out healthiness. In sorrow, bring in pain and breathe out a sense of lightness or joyfulness. But generally it's a very simple reversal of our usual approach of hanging on to what we want and getting rid of what we don't want.

One very important thing in Tong Len, especially in our cultural context, is that everybody here is able to do the practice. We all have plenty to breathe out, and in this practice the breathing out and the breathing in are totally even and balanced. The goal is not to become martyrs where we say, Just give me all your pain and I'll just hold onto it and save you. That kind of heroic martyrdom would be a big mistake and wouldn't help anyone very long, That's not the idea. Rather, the aim is a continual flowing in—allowing pain or sorrow to come in—then having strength and gladness or inspiration, or however you perceive it, going out.

In terms of the actual practice, with Tong Len, it's a little different in that it comes in and out through your whole body, all your pores, not just from the lungs Breathing in totally, breathing out totally. We actually breathe through all our body.

So having had that little blip, or flash, however you receive it, then instead of trying to work with particular content right away, we accept that feeling, that visceral feeling of the textures of what we avoid and what we hold, and begin working with the feeling of breathing in a sticky, heavy, and claustrophobic energy and breathing out a sense of lightness and spaciousness, a bright energy. After a little while of doing that, you can work with a particular content.

Usually the best approach for this third stage is to bring to mind something that concerns you, some situation in which you may be involved, someone you know who is suf-fering, whatever is on your mind. It's usually there anyway, so you might as well bring it up and work with that as a more content-particular experience, rather than with just a general sense of things. You should start with something with which you have a personal connection as opposed to something like a world situation. Start with something close to home. That's really helpful in this practice.

So this style of Tong Len is a basic starting point for working intensively with your immediate situation and reversing the usual angle on it. As we practice, we extend that to other people, all different types of people, who are worried about failing something. A student worried about an exam, for example, or someone facing an important job interview. Then we begin to take in that sense of pressure and the lack of confidence, and then breathe out to those people all our sense of strength, of encouragement, of having some light quality about that. Then you begin to send what you have to offer out to all of the people in a similar position and take in from them the understanding that you are not unique, whatever your situation. Millions of other people have experienced the same situation, maybe worse, so you extend it in a broad sense.

That is basically how the practice progresses when you first start. There's that little flash, a period of getting a feeling of that energy, holding it and flipping it around, then working with something immediate, and finally extending that to a bigger view. Each of those steps is important. To manifest enlightened kindness, you must do so in direct encounters, not just in grand schemes. It has to be consistent in your life. You could be a big hero in public life and a schmuck at home. That's not really very good.

The whole nature of Tong Len is based on the idea that everything that comes up is included. If you feel dead in your heart, or cold-hearted, that's okay too. Breathe that in and breathe out a quality of love or open-heartedness. Absolutely everything that comes up is okay. So at this point, no matter what you happen to be working with, try to extend that further to other people, maybe people around you whom you know. Then try, step by step, to go to all the people and other sentient beings who are also suffering and wanting things they can't get, feeling bad, feeling good.

[The workshop concluded with a period of meditation in which the participants experimented with the Tong Len *technique, then asked Ms. Lief questions that arose as a result of this sitting experience.]*

Participant: What do you do to get around the basic resistance to taking in something bad?

Judith Lief: You could breathe in that resistance. Once you start doing Tong Len, you're in a giant trap, because everything feeds it. It's like a hopper. Even if you're totally screwing up the practice, you can't get out of it because you can breathe in, "I'm totally screwing up, there's no way I'm going to do this, this just sucks." Breathe that in and breathe out the Great Bodhisattva Tong Len

person. So it turns and twists in on itself. Once you get into it it becomes very personal very quickly. That's the hard part for us. I generally find it's easier to begin the practice with someone we know who is sick, to breathe out our good intentions to them. But that can get tricky soon because you can think, I'm the helper and I'm helping them and I'm doing this virtuous thing, leading you to another form of fixation in which the sick person becomes something of a prop in your game of trying to be a helper person. But this doesn't let you rest because then you can breathe in or breathe out that sense of being the knight in shining armor dealing with this difficult, sick person, perhaps leading you to breathe in being more selfish.

I think it's important to see this in its broader sense. Otherwise you protect yourself, and the nature of this practice is not to protect yourself. That's the whole point, not protecting yourself from your mind and not protecting good and bad. Ironically, often people have trouble with the good part, the breathing out part.

[In answer to a question concerning the integration of Tong Len *practice into day-to-day life, Ms. Lief emphasized again that:]*

To do it in the context of sitting practice is very good. Sit, and then do some Tong Len, and then sit at the end also. That's what I recommend. I wouldn't recommend doing it if you don't have time to do that. Don't do it at all. If you only have a little time, just do the sitting. If you have a bit more time, you could incorporate some Tong Len practice, and once you do that for a while, try doing it in certain settings, perhaps at the dentist. It's very interesting to do Tong Len in a very specialized way, utilizing it in the midst of some activity that you feel brings out your uptight qualities. Then you have a lot of juice to work with.

The underlying perspective of the whole practice, which is really important, is that the more obstacles, chaos, and difficulties we encounter the better the practice is. You couldn't do this practice if you weren't living a life in which you had to encounter ornery people, or didn't sometimes get sick. Sometimes you're inspired; often you're not inspired at all. Sometimes you feel very warm and others you just close off and don't want to deal with things. If all these things weren't going on, you would have no way of practicing this kind of thing. Tong Len is meant for people who are dealing with the real stuff that we face daily.

So now we have the basic sitting, and the formal sending-and-taking practice. You don't have to make a big deal out of it. It's a form of appreciating and accepting our world. It offers a sense of appreciating our neuroses, difficult circumstances, our incredible wisdom and insight, our courage to be in life fully. We are also courageous to sit, because if you sit, at some point you encounter a lot of things about yourself. You encounter who you are and you dig down to find who you are really—the whole thing, not just some parts. You can accept a little bit of yourself but can you really accept the whole thing? Then can you accept your world and work with that without complaint? Tong Len has a quality of not

complaining. One thing that stands out in certain teachers I've known is a quality of not complaining. For instance, certain Tibetan teachers I know had horrible things happen —their entire country destroyed; they had to become refugees; people who were very wealthy and highly regarded became nobody in little village refugee camps. Even then you don't hear them saying Poor me. I lost my country. I lost all my relatives. They just go on dealing with what comes up in the world, and there's a lot to be said for that. At the same time, it doesn't seem to result from stupidity or denial or pretending nothing happened. It's a Tong Len perspective.

I was talking about Tong Len with one group and a woman in the workshop had read the memoirs of a guard at Auschwitz. She had lost relatives at Auschwitz and had made pilgrimage to Auschwitz. In this journal were incredibly beautiful passages about how the guard had gone on a walk in the woods and was struck by the natural beauty, felt his mind at peace. It sounded like a very sensitive and aesthetically appreciative, eloquently written journal. If you had no idea this person was a guard at Auschwitz, you'd think, Ah, what a sensitive soul, very spiritually inclined, connected with nature and having great insight into himself, etc. At the same time, he's in this hideous situation doing terrible, cruel things to other creatures.

That's the other side: The woman who had read the journal said that that was more chilling to her than almost anything because it's not so simple. We like to say that people who could do horrible things are bad guys, but who knows what it is that makes it possible for people to live in those extreme circumstances—on either side, the bad guys or the good guys. What does that reflect about human nature? There is no room to be arrogant. Who knows what we would do when really motivated, scared to death?

I'm not saying there is no such thing as "the bad guy," just that it's not a good idea to be too smug about who's good and who's bad. Very seldom do we have a whole picture of what's happening in everyone else's life. In the Buddhist tradition, even the worst people were born and were little babies and have some kind of heart. It could be twisted, distorted beyond belief, but it doesn't mean they become nonhuman.

So you can deal with penetrating as deeply as you can. What would make you go against your inclination for kindness? Usually it would be fear.

A fitting conclusion to this gallop through this slogan sampler is the very last slogan. Number fifty-nine is *Don't expect applause.* We've done this whole workshop together, but don't expect anyone to be that impressed that you've done it. You could think Okay, now I'm going to do this great practice. Don't expect anybody is going to say, Wow, you just look transformed. You're so aware; so glowing! They might say, What happened to you this weekend? You sick or something? Generally speaking, that's on the path: not concerning ourselves too much with how we are viewed.

This is closely related to another slogan, which is number twenty-one: *Of the two witnesses, hold the principle one.* This is in your practice. Every one of you is different. You have different backgrounds, different training, different lives, and you can receive teachings and training from all sorts of people, but fundamentally it comes down to you, yourself. You are the only one who knows when you're holding back and when you're not; when you're being genuine or being phony. So don't take anyone's word for anything. You must trust in yourself. Hold the principle witness, because that's the only one who knows fundamentally what's going on. Find that witness and hold it as the principle one.

Buddhist Wisdom in the Light of Quantum Theory

Mu Soeng

UNTIL RECENTLY, MU SOENG HAD BEEN A MONK IN THE KOREAN ZEN TRADITION for eleven years. Today he is Director and a member of the core faculty at the Barre Center for Buddhist Studies, at Barre, Massachusetts. Among his published works are *Thousand Peaks: Korean Zen—Tradition and Teachers* and *Heart Sutra—Ancient Buddhist Wisdom in the Light of Quantum Theory.*

The latter book provided the subject for Mu Soeng's presentation at the Buddhism in America conference. In summing up the aim of the talk, he wrote: "Buddhism was the first 'scientific' religion in the history of mankind. It was the first to offer a systematic investigation of mind and matter—to have a direct understanding, rather than a mediated one—of the nature of reality." Both in his talk and in *Heart Sutra,* this teacher undertakes dealing with issues arising from contemplation of how Buddhist meditative insights developed more than two thousand years ago hold up in the light of modern science. By defining for the session's participants various basic concepts important to Quantum theory and various Buddhist perspectives on the nature of reality, Mu Soeng goes on to examine areas of convergence and divergence between each.

y hope today is to give some sense of what defining aspects of quantum physics have been lately and how they converge with the wisdom tradition of Buddhism. To start, it's important to keep in mind that science and Buddhism are two parallel traditions. I make no suggestion that they are interchangeable, but that they converge at certain points and then diverge again. Their purposes and their functions are quite different and they are entirely two different traditions.

The second thing I want to state is that I'm not trying to make a statement of truth. Even when I present Buddhism, it is not a statement about truth. My hope is to present both quantum physics and Buddhism as two self-investigations through which each one of us has a certain perspective and where you can continue your own investigation into the nature of reality. So it's not about establishing a truth which we can appropriate and then go on and somehow try to transmit and teach to others. From this perspective both Buddhism and science are metaphors and models and we are trying to establish certain models that are helpful for us to look at our own experience.

I would like to look at this whole topic through the *Heart Sutra,* which is one of the central texts of traditional Buddhism. This *Heart Sutra* is a way of looking at how Buddhists have tried to explain or articulate to themselves the nature of their own experience.

I will begin by establishing the theme of emptiness, or *shunyata,* which has been found to be closest to the findings of quan-

tum physics. This Sanskrit word *shunyata* is generally translated as "emptiness" or "nothingness" or "void." However, European languages do not capture the sense of this term. The root verb of this word means to swell up. So the idea is, if you have a boil on your hand, you have a certain shape but inside it's hollow, it's empty. There's nothing in there but there is a shape that's appearing. So when Buddhists talk about *shunyata,* they are talking about it in themselves, that there is this form—appearance—but inside it's empty. If you look at it in its Sanskrit context, it literally simplifies everything to a very large extent.

The issue is appearance versus reality. That's what both the *Heart Sutra* and quantum physics are trying to deal with: the issue of form and emptiness, appearance and reality. One way to understand this concept of *shunyata* is through the concept of zero. In the first century BCE, in India, a grammarian established the whole system of Sanskrit grammar and introduced the concept of zero. Zero represents a position in a space but in itself is empty. However, because of the way it is placed in a certain system, it has a certain function, so it reinforces that system. So if we take 10,000 and all the 0s, they in themselves are empty, but because they are placed in a certain system they establish this 1 in a certain context. We get 10,000 or we get 10 or 100 or 1,000 and can claim that these 0s, if you take this 1 out, have no value in themselves. But because they are placed in this system, they give a certain value sense. Later on, from the Sanskrit grammar, mathematics becomes part of this concept and that's how it came into use.

In Sanskrit, the word *shunya,* out of which shunyata comes, also means "zero." Those who are familiar with the Japanese Zen tradition must have seen the symbol of zero. It symbolizes an empty space that still has a container. This space is contained by this zero; it encloses something but it does not enclose anything at the same time. We cannot talk about nature, what it is containing. And it's the same thing as the swelling: There is an appearance; there is a form, but it does not contain anything that can be directly handled.

One of the problems that science and all the wisdom traditions have found is that when any phenomenon is analyzed by the intellect, the nature of that phenomenon is found to be paradoxical. This is what the mystics have been saying all along when they talk about the infinite. So how do we understand the nature of things? Intellect will take us only so far—and by intellect, I mean the systematic, linear, and analytical way of looking at things—it will take us only so far, but beyond that, things tend to become paradoxical. This was the experience of quantum physicists in the early part of the century and especially physicists like Einstein and Niels Bohr and Werner Heisenberg.

Before the 1920s, science was driven by Newtonian physics or the atomic physics. Before quantum physics scientists tended to analyze the phenomena which were part of the everyday experience. People could talk about light or they could talk about plant life and it was confined to the atomic level. It was part of the everyday experience. Things were not abstract. Science was trying to find its own footing and to engage itself with things that were part of the so-called progressive face of things, how to make life more comfortable, how to make life better. But in the early part of the century, starting with Einstein, the physicists penetrated deep into the subatomic level of reality. This submicroscopic environment we still try to analyze is quite far removed from the everyday involvement to which we are used. It's a level of abstraction that has no direct level of correspondence with our everyday life, but it forces us to look into how we look at the world. The question of the human mind always is How do we perceive reality? And for the longest time, up until quite recently, we looked at the world through our belief system without really having the tools to examine our belief system. The information we had was second-hand or third-hand or fourth-hand, given to us either by the educational system or by the church or by the political system or the social system and that was how the world was. But we never really understood that the world that we knew to be was only a description. We always look at the world through the description that we have received. We never look at the world directly. The function or the engagement of the quantum physicist was to really penetrate deep into the submicroscopic level and to really understand the nature of phenomena, the nature of reality directly, and not through the description.

And this also is precisely the function of the wisdom tradition: We want to understand the world directly and not through description. That's a distinction we always need to keep in mind—Buddhism is not trying to establish a truth. It's not trying to describe the world. It's only pointing to the fact that the world that we normally conceive to be the world is only a description, and description by the nature of things is subject to change.

One of the correspondences that we find here is the uncertainty principle of Werner Heisenberg. According to this principle, the phenomena that is observed changes shape by the very fact of observation. In other words, there is a very intimate link between the observer and the phenomenon that's being observed. This became quite apparent to the physicists when they were looking at the subatomic matter. For the longest time, in Newtonian physics, it was believed that there are certain particles which are irreducible—they cannot be reduced any farther—and these particles were moving around in space according to fixed laws of gravitation. That's how the whole matter came into being, that within each matter scientists thought that they could understand the pattern according to gravitational laws through which the particles would function.

When quantum physics came into its own and went to look at matter at the subatomic level under a microscope, they found that a particle is not stable. A particle could change shape. Sometimes it could appear as particle and sometimes it could appear as waves. As a result of the unpredictability of this phenomenon, quantum physicists developed certain intuitions and some scientists could intuit when the electron is going to appear as wave or as particle. Now, as soon as you put in the element of intuition in science, it's taking us away quite a lot from the way we understand science to function. This is the realm of mysticism.

Five major shifts took place from the old science to the new science. The first two have to do with the our understanding of the nature of phenomena and the other three have to do with the idea of knowledge. Now, in the old paradigm—the Newtonian or the Cartesian way of thinking—the belief held that in any complex system the dynamics of the whole could be understood from the properties of the part. In the new paradigm, the relationship between the part and the whole is reversed. The properties of the part can be understood from the dynamics of the whole, which leads ultimately to the holographic model of the universe. In this way of looking at things, ultimately there are no parts. The relationship between the part and whole is an indivisible relationship. What we call a part is merely a pattern in an inseparable web of relationships.

The second shift is from structure to process. In the old paradigm it was taught that there were basic structures and then there were forces and mechanisms through which these structures interacted with each other and then they gave rise to processes.

In the new paradigm, they have discarded the notion of these structures entirely and insist that they're only processes. Every structure is seen as the manifestation of an underlying process and this web of relationships is essentially dynamic. So if we accept this notion that there are no parts, then there are no structures there. What is left are the dynamics of the relationships.

The first of the remaining three shifts from old to new science is a shift from objective science to epistemic science. In the old paradigm it was believed that the descriptions were objective, in the sense of being independent of the observer, and it was thought that a person could look at a phenomenon and describe very objectively what he or she was actually observing. This was independent of the process of knowledge. In other words, how the observer arrives at a certain set of criteria for knowledge was not really taken into account. The person could say, "Well, this carpet has all these patterns and some are blue and some are gray; some are red," and the person could describe that. So how the person arrived at whether this color is blue or red was not taken into account.

Now, the new paradigm tries to understand the process of knowledge, which is the science of epistemology, and it believes that this process of knowledge has to be included explicitly in the description of what is being observed. At this point there is no consensus in the scientific community as to what this epistemic science could be or should be, but it's in the best of things. It's the on-going process. They are still trying to understand

the nature of knowledge, how it is that we consider something to be knowledge. There are a few lines from a poem by T. S. Eliot that I think are very appropriate to understanding this. They're from "The Rock," and these lines go like this:

Where is the Life we have lost in living?
　　Where is the wisdom we have lost in knowledge?
　　Where is the knowledge we have lost in information?

So I think it's a very appropriate and also perhaps poignant note to what the new paradigm of science is trying to understand: There is information, and there is knowledge, and there is wisdom. I think what we're trying to understand is how can the knowledge that we gain from the new paradigm in science interface with the wisdom tradition that Buddhism has to offer?

In the old science it was believed that there are fundamental laws, fundamental principles, and the basic building blocks of matter that could be understood as such; how certain particles come together in a block and create the basic building blocks of the universe. When the paradigm was shifting in the early part of the century, this way of looking at things could no longer be supported. In the new paradigm, this metaphor is being replaced by that of the network—again, we go to the idea of relationships here. In relationships there is only network.

At this point, perhaps we can talk about what scientists find at the subatomic level. Nowadays there are very powerful electron microscopes and you can take any piece of seemingly solid matter—a piece of wood or a piece of stone or your hand—and put it under a microscope and you can apply the power of the microscope to a thousand times. All the seeming solidity of the materiality that we normally associate with the appearance crumbles. Let me read from *Heart Sutra—Ancient Buddhist Wisdom in the Light of Quantum Theory*:

Somewhere within that emptiness we know is a nucleus. We scan the space and there it is, a tiny dot. At last, there it is. We have discovered something hard and solid, a reference point. But no, as we move closer to the nucleus, it too begins to dissolve. It too is nothing more than an oscillating field, waves of rhythm. Inside the nucleus are other organized fields, protons, neutrons, even the smaller particles, but each of these, upon our approach, also dissolve into pure rhythm.

These days the scientists are looking for quarks, these strange subatomic entities having qualities which you describe with such words as upness, downness, charm, strangeness, truth, beauty, color, and flavor. But no matter. If we could get close enough to these wondrous quarks, they too would dissolve and melt away. They too would have to give up all pretense of solidity, even their speed and relationship would be unclear, leaving them only relationship and pattern vibration.

Of what is the body made? It is made of emptiness and rhythm. At the ultimate heart of the body and the heart of the world there is no solidity. Once again, there is only the dance.

So once we replace this whole metaphor, from basic building blocks to network, what remains is a network of relationships that is a whole unified energy field. We cannot identify two fixed locations because each location is always moving around, but there is an intimate link between one location and the other location. In some experiments, it was found that if an observer were looking at one particle, the other particle with which it was associated, even though it was millions of miles away in the world's terms, would also change shape simply because the observer was focusing on its mate. So we cannot say that there is a direct relationship through time and space as we normally understand it to be. Because of the very fact that the observer is looking at any particular energy field, the entire energy field is being effected.

The last shift that they found was from truth to approximate descriptions. What this means is that truth is not something that is solid, that can be fixed forever, as a reference point. It's not something unchanging. The best that we can hope for is an approximate description and it allows the process of investigation to unfold because then we are not locked into the description and we know its nature to be quite approximate.

People do not experience Buddhism or Christianity or Islam. What people experience is their own experience, and what is the nature of that experience? We are not talking about some truth that has been handed down to us; we're talking about how do we experience our experience? What

Buddhism has been saying for the last 2,500 years is that if we look closely at the nature of experience, it has four distinct parts: There is some element of origination and some of stability; then the process of decay sets in, and then there is dissolution. If you have done some religious practice, you might know this from your own experience. Whether it's parts or feelings or emotions or sensations of the body, they all conform to this one pattern. Most of the time, if we are not paying attention, we are not aware of how they begin, but when the mind has become quiet and we can really cultivate the faculty to investigate, we can find out how a particular thought or feeling begins to take shape. Then there comes a time that it becomes stabilized and dominates the field of our observation. But it does not stay there for very long, and then it begins to lose its intensity and its shape and its contour. The next thing we know, it has changed into something else, it has dissolved.

And this is exactly the process that people find in quantum physics now: All phenomena have the same nature. The time element may be different, so a tree may last for a thousand years, but it is going through the same process as this mind-body system is going through. So this mind-body system may last for fifty or sixty years or seventy years and the mountains or the trees may last a bit longer. But both phenomena are undergoing the same process. If we go to the subatomic level and the energy field, we can't really even talk about these things because when we talk about origination, we talk about something which is solid or something which stabilizes. So what the wisdom tradition is telling us, especially the *Heart Sutra*, is that this is a conventional way of speaking about things, but at the level of the absolute—at the level of *shunyata* or at the energy field—we can't talk about these things, because the energy itself does not subscribe to these patterns.

There are two ways of talking about the relative and the absolute. We can talk about the existential and the metaphysical or we can just talk about it linguistically. So the enterprise of the Buddhist tradition, especially the Zen tradition, is to deconstruct the language in such a way that it forces us not to become engaged with metaphysical speculation and to remain at the level of the existential. That in itself is a paradox—to use the language to deconstruct itself so that one remains at the level of the existential. Whatever the speculations are, if you use terms like the absolute and the relative, they are within the realm of the language. We can never really establish the truth once forever. All we can hope is that it's a working definition or an approximate description that we are using to get where we need to go, and all the Buddhist teachings are not about metaphysical speculation but about suffering and the end of suffering. That's a very existential, psychological, linguistic paradigm.

So this basic teaching of the Buddha gives us the context in which to place our investigation about the nature of our experience. Now we can talk about these things as a pure academic debate and it's not going to lead to the end of suffering. No. Our suffering is to see whether or not this is actually an intimate part of our experience and if we look at suffering, the question that traditionally comes up in Buddhism is where does suffering come from?

I may offer that all our suffering comes from the internal chatter that we have with us, that we carry on with ourselves at all times. It's true of internal chatter with which we construct our world; this is the conditioning of the description that has been given to us and we are talking to ourselves in a certain language which reinforces our idea of the world. It is true that this description that we have created, through a very particular language for ourselves, determines how we see the other world. So the world is never seen directly but through our own filters and these filters are what cause our suffering.

These filters could come in many different shapes, thinking or clinging or whatever the nature of those filters may be, but these filters are created by ourselves, how we talk to ourselves. Basically the purpose of both the wisdom tradition and the meditational tradition is to allow us to disengage from this internal chatter. People have found that in this particular way of looking at things, metaphysical speculation is basically useless. It's a process of investigation. It's not about creating beliefs or ideas or any framework at all. The Zen tradition takes it to the ultimate extreme of trying to linguistically deconstruct the internal chatter and the beliefs and ideas that we might have created for ourselves.

So, given the fact that Buddhism gives us these tools to investigate and ultimately to deconstruct our notions of reality, where do we go from there? How do we spend our time in this world, in this life? Here, perhaps, there is some correspondence with the quantum field. Quanta, the field of quantum, is nothing but energy and information and each of these quanta is affected by the attention and the intention of the observer. So we have been talking about the uncertainty principle and how the very fact of the observer looking at this subatomic matter can change the nature of that matter, how it's going to manifest itself. So attention transforms and intention energizes.

If we look at these two terms in the Buddhist model of the bodhisattva in the Mahayana tradition, the bodhisattva is an embodiment of both attention and intention. Attention is a matter of developing the kind of powers of observation, of investigation, where things are perceived directly, the world is seen as it is, without the filters, and that's the power of attention. When attention is applied to whatever is observed, it transforms. So there is wisdom coming out of applying the attention. The intention that the bodhisattva sets up is to help all beings in the world. If we take it a bit further, the wisdom of the bodhisattva is of *shunyata,* or emptiness. The intention that the bodhisattva sets up is of compassion. This is the ultimate paradox in the Buddhist tradition: Through his wisdom, through the attention that the bodhisattva applies to the world, he or she knows that the world is empty. There are no beings. There are only processes. So each one of us in this room here is a process and the bodhisattva, through his or her wisdom, sees all these beings to be empty.

But at the same time, the bodhisattva cultivates the intention of compassion. So the compassion is not for beings as such, but for their being caught in the world of illusion. It's a very critical understanding, that normally we understand that we are being compassionate to other beings as persons and it becomes quite a dangerous thing to get caught into that because then we are always evaluating ourselves, our performance. The end result of our compassion is whether or not the persons to whom our compassion is directed are being helped by it. But the compassion is not for the beings, it is for the illusion or the delusion, for the ignorance in which the beings are caught.

The tradition of meditation is ultimately to give us the insight into the dynamics of the mind and how we relate to our experience. That's our greatest challenge as human beings because our experience is always changing and we want certain experience to be unchanging, to remain solid for us. But we have no control over the changing nature of the experience. The only thing we can do is establish a new relationship with our experience and the new relationship is to let go, is to be able to see things as they are arising, understand them to be what they are, and then be able to let them go. So ultimately suffering comes from our ignorance about the nature of our relationship to our experience.

[This discussion of suffering and our experience of it brought rise to a question from one of the participants: "If I stub my toe, that's unsatisfactory. If I stub it really bad, maybe I have no attachment to that. Maybe I'm not thinking, 'Oh my God, I don't want to look.' Maybe I look right at it. It looks okay, but it hurts like hell. Is that suffering?" Mu Soeng answered that this goes to the precise point.]

When you stub your toe badly, in that particular moment you can look at the nature of your reaction and that's where suffering begins—how you react to that particular experience. We are not talking about pain, but about our reaction, which can be either suffering or equanimity. So when you actually stub your toe, you can immediately focus on that and you can observe it as pain-pain-pain or throbbing-throbbing-throbbing, whatever the nature of the experience may be. Quantum physics gives us this same opportunity, although we may not be able to do the mathematical formulations. We may not be able to look through the electronic microscopes, but we can give some value to the findings of quantum physics and choose to go along with them, that the world that we know is not solid, it's pure energy. In the field of energy, it's the field of pure potentiality and in potentiality there's both creativity and transformation. I think that's where the two traditions converge: Through the different investigations they come to the same point, that the world being fluid, not being fixed, always being in a flux, things are capable of being changed.

Things can be created and it's always in each moment there is a matter of choice, how we pay attention and how we transform the world that we perceive.

One of the models that's used in quantum physics to describe the nature of the phenomenon world comes from David Boehm. He's one of the most respected physicists of the century and very receptive to Buddhist ideas, and especially working a lot with Krishnamurti. David Boehm has used the example of a geyser, from which he proposes a theory of the implicit and the explicit orders. He proposes that what's seen in the realm of forms, or in the relative realm, is the explicit order. But underlying the explicit order is the implicit order, which is a whole order, not made of parts but rather an indivisible whole. And using the example of the geyser coming out of the water, he proposes that when the water comes out of the geyser, it's an unfolding. This holds true. The shape holds itself together just for a microsecond and then it falls back into the geyser. And so he calls the falling back enfolding. He proposes that the whole universe is made of countless interactions between the unfolding and enfolding, between the implicit and the explicit order. And these lines from the *Heart Sutra*—"Form does not differ from emptiness, emptiness does not differ from form. That which is form is emptiness, that which is emptiness, form"—are best understood through this example of the geyser. What we see in the world is the appearance of the explicit order or just the forms appearing

this way. But as we have been looking at it, none of these forms have self-nature. They cannot sustain themselves. So they appear for a moment just like water rushing out of the geyser and assuming a certain form. But as soon as it appears, it collapses back into that. So things are appearing out of *shunyata* and falling back into *shunyata*. In this sense the *shunyata* is the implicit order and we could use the word energy to describe *shunyata*, keeping in mind that energy is something that quantum physicists cannot comprehend in a direct sense. In the same sense, *shunyata* is not something which can be directly comprehended. We may even go further and say that in the universe there are only forms, there is no emptiness, because emptiness cannot be directly apprehended. If it could be directly apprehended, then it would have to exist as a form. But it can be intuited. So we can intuit that things are appearing out of some base and then they're falling back into that. Another example to use is of the ocean and the waves. The waves appear in the ocean only for a fraction of a second and then they fall back into that. So the water, the great body of water, is a source of the implicit order out of which these forms are appearing and they are collapsing back into that.

Again, we have to remember that in the wisdom tradition, we are not trying to see or observe or somehow appropriate emptiness. We are trying to understand the nature of form and the relationship of form to emptiness, because suffering appears in the realm of forms. So we are trying to understand what forms are and the whole value of interrelationships that created suffering. It's interesting to know what quantum physics has been telling us about the nature of matter and all these kinds of things, but metaphysically, speculation will not help us truly understand what's going on in our own lives.

Going back to the discussion about attention and intention, our nervous system is capable of becoming aware of the energy content of the localized field of quanta. In other words, our attention transforms what is being observed. Through the power of meditation, through the power of attention, it's possible to become aware of the contents of that energy field in a such a way that you affect the whole field. That's what the whole meditation tradition is all about and that's why people in the Buddhist tradition try to become the buddhas, because the buddha is considered to be a person who has become omniscient, who is able to see all of the localized fields of energy in the quantum field and to see the correlations of all those different fields to each other.

One of the later traditions in Indian Buddhism is called the Yogachara tradition. It developed the notion of the *tathagata-garbha,* which literally means the womb of the buddha. The way it is understood is that we have different kinds of consciousness— eyes, ears, nose, tongue, body, and then the mind. Now, these types of consciousness are purely passive forms of consciousness; they just observe what's presented to them. This particular tradition posited a seventh and eighth consciousness. The seventh consciousness they called the discriminating mind, and then the eighth is called the storehouse consciousness. So the model may be visualized something like a funnel that splits, and the discriminative consciousness either likes or dislikes all the information that's being presented. In other words, it's always a reactive consciousness. It's not passive anymore and it's always reacting, too; it's always either pushing over things or it's trying to cling to things. So, as a result of what's happening in this realm, for each reaction there is a seed that's dropping in. Sometimes this is called the seed consciousness. And the nature of our conditioned existence is that through the interaction at one level, we're always dropping seeds into the other.

It is also posited that, at the base of these seeds are some seeds which are pure. These are the seeds that people have cultivated through many, many lifetimes when they have cultivated kindness, compassion, equanimity, loving-kindness, all these positive qualities of the mind. These are the seeds that are always there. The idea is that these seeds are interacting with each other in a very complex way, and each of these seeds contains the totality of this field in itself. That's the holographic model and also the model of the subatomic field. It's not a linear link. It's a field of energy and we can think of it as rather particlelike substances but more as an energy field, which can mend fast, either as wave or particle. So these are the seeds of the Buddha, which, at least in the

Buddhist model, everyone is capable of cultivating and which are already there. Sometimes it's called the buddha-nature, that each one of us has the buddha-nature within ourselves and through attention and intention we can cultivate and give rise to the buddha-nature within ourselves.

In a holographic film, if you take off the film and cut it up into many tiny pieces, each little film will contain the whole film. So in the same sense, each of these seeds in the buddha-nature contain the totality of what's happening here. That's the pure potentiality of the buddha-nature. Just as in the quantum field it is the field of pure potentiality. This also means that everybody in the unified field is a buddha—a very shocking statement to many people. When Mahayana Buddhism declares that you are a little buddha, they do so because they believe that you already contain that seed. And because you are a buddha and everybody else is a buddha, a connection is made if you want to actualize it. It is only through ignorance that we see the separation rather than see the other person as a buddha.

The Unique Teachings of Tibetan Buddhist Meditation and Its Future in the West

Lama Sherab Dorje

TO REFER TO "TIBETAN BUDDHISM," WITH ITS BROAD VARIETY OF PRACTICES, is akin to speaking of Protestantism as a single form of religious expression. The contemporary notion of Tibetan Buddhism is one of elaborate ceremony, art, and architecture, but when one begins to look into Tibetan root forms, it becomes clear that, as Lama Sherab Dorje* points out, "all that is practiced fundamentally comes down to either techniques for calming the mind,...or for discerning the real or having penetrative insight into the nature of mind, into the nature of reality."

In this workshop, Lama Sherab Dorje described and explained aspects of one particular type of visualization meditation, the intent of which is to "[pull] together into its most essential form, the techniques for accomplishing the wisdom and experience of the teacher, who is Guru Rinpoche, the founder of Tibetan Buddhism." He stressed that "this technique is available to help you understand that emptiness is both the starting point and the arriving point of all Buddhist meditation....It emphasizes it at the beginning, it emphasizes it throughout the visualization, and it emphasizes it at the end, as you allow the mind to rest in its nature."

Much of the workshop entailed descriptions of the mandala, which is constructed in the mind and functions as a network of objects of meditation. The visualization process requires commitment and experience, with which one ultimately progresses to the point of realizing Dzogchen, which the lama described as "naturally occurring mind—the highest realization and the ultimate yoga. All qualities of wisdom and enlightenment spring from this understanding."

---

*Biographical information about Lama Sherab Dorje is found in the context of his workshop; see pages 37–38.

I'd like this to be really an experiential workshop, not just adding some more ideas to a large marketplace of ideas that are out there—just another philosophy or theory competing with a lot of other theories and philosophies. I want to give you a sense of how some of the special meditative techniques in Tibetan Buddhism actually work, how they deal with conceptuality and introduce nonconceptuality; how they unify the heart and mind. So I want to share with you in a very informal fashion some experience that I've learned through my years of practice. Hopefully you'll leave here with something that gives you a sense of that which is beyond what you can put in notes on paper or have on tape to listen to later. There is a tradition within Tibet of just informal discussion about meditation that's very colloquial and loose and straightforward and just straight to the point.

I'm going to base this discussion on a particular practice text. I will not be trying to teach you this practice text, which is very profound and elaborate and complex, but just use it as an illustration of some of the different ways meditation can work in the context of visualization practice and so forth. So you'll come away knowing that there are all these different techniques within Tibetan meditation, and these will be just a few of those methods.

The great nineteenth-century Tibetan master Jamgon Kongtrul Lodro Tayay said, as masters in many traditions have said, that all that is practiced fundamentally comes down to either techniques for calming the mind—*shamatha*—or for discerning the real or having penetrative insight into the nature of

mind, into the nature of reality, which is *vipassana*. So that is another theme that will run through this.

I'd like to give you a sense of who I am and how I got here. I was born in Montreal and was introduced to Buddhism when I went to college in New York in the mid-seventies or so. I went on a semester-abroad program to Nepal, and met my teacher, Tulku Urgyen Rinpoche. When I met Tulku Urgyen Rinpoche in Nepal in 1981, I had already been practicing *vipassana* meditation at the Insight Meditation Society and on my own since 1979.

I've also gone back to Nepal many times to live in retreat and to work with my teachers there, and I accomplished a three-year, four-month lama-training retreat in the United States in the tradition of Kalu Rinpoche, another great meditation master. For a time after finishing that retreat, I started to work with meditation groups around North America, translating a lot and getting experience working with people. Then I decided that rather than just continue to do that I'd go back in retreat, and this time in a solitary retreat. You could almost say that I'd finished my B.A. in Tibetan Buddhist studies and I wanted to go into a master's program, a one-year program where I would just focus, developing the techniques that I had learned throughout my years of retreat.

So I went back to Nepal and took a lot of teachings on this particular practice that we'll be working with, from a master who had just recently arrived from Tibet named Lama Pudze, and received empowerments and instructions from Tulku Urgyen. I worked with the ritual masters in the monastery in

Nepal to learn all the different techniques—how to chant and all of the different aspects of the practice—and then I went into a cabin in northern New York and lived there very simply for a year or so, just working exclusively with this to get a very deep experience of it.

After that, while continuing to work with meditation groups and to translate here and there, and to translate the book, *The Mahamudra Teachings of the Supreme Siddhas,* I also decided to expand my experience and to bring what I had learned out into the world by working on some of my interests, developing the other aspects of my being that would be helpful to myself and others.

I went to law school in New York, where I've studied human rights and environmental law and edited some journals. Now I work in Alabama for a famous civil rights judge in the Federal courts. That's a one-year job, and then I'll go back to New York and do some environmental law and a little of this and a little of that. And I should say, another important aspect of my growth and development from what I've learned in meditation is to have my special partner here with me today, my fiancee, who teaches me constantly how to keep my heart open and break through my own barriers.

I would guess a lot of you have the idea that Tibetan Buddhism is this incredibly elaborate, intimidating, inaccessible, overly complex and perhaps even confusing monolithic world. You may ask, How do I get into this in a way that is meaningful? What is all this imagery and ritual about?

It's true that there are thousands and thousands of different traditions of practice in Tibet, and almost all of them incorporate fantastic, elaborate, and complex details of practice. So to present the unique value of this tradition to you in the context of a short workshop, I want to take as kind of a paradigmatic example a short version of the practice that I did in retreat.

This practice is called Tuk Drup Bar Chay Kun Sel in Tibetan, which means "accomplishing the mind of the guru in order to eliminate all obstacles." It alone consists of about thirty or forty volumes of text in Tibetan, and it's a whole universe within itself. Of the actual practice texts, there are four different lengths; the one we'll be working with is the second-shortest, simply called "the essence of enlightened activity." As the title says, it pulls together into its most essential form the techniques for accomplishing the wisdom and experience of the teacher, who is Guru Rinpoche, the founder of Tibetan Buddhism, who composed these teachings.

These teachings arose out of Guru Rinpoche's mind and were left for later generations to discover and to apply. This particular teaching was eventually promulgated by a great master in nineteenth-century Tibet, who was actually blood great-grandfather of my own teacher, Tulku Urgyen Rinpoche, so this is a very close and immediate lineage of teachings.

[Before going into the complexities of the prac-

tice, Lama Sherab Dorje chanted the teachings in Tibetan. He asked the group: "Without forming a lot of ideas, please just listen and try to get an experience of what the recitation of this is like." He then told them he thought they would be surprised by "just how much is packed into what seems like just a few minutes of these noises in a foreign language—how much different meditation wisdom and experience is embedded and locked in to this practice." As he chanted, he explained which aspect of the meditation he was reciting.]

First I chanted the invocation, the seven-line prayer to Guru Rinpoche, which is trying to make the connection to wisdom-mind.... Now I've just recited the verses of refuge, which is common to all Buddhist traditions. This, in particular, is a refuge accompanied by the mind of compassion seeking to attain enlightenment for the sake of all beings, not simply for one's own purposes.... And this section sets into place an environment of protection for the practice that you're about to do, to recognize and dispel inner and outer obstacles so that you can successfully engage in the practice.

This verse is very special. It's a meditation actually, and it expresses the basic or foundational principle of Tantric practice of Tibetan Buddhism, which is that the three bodies of enlightenment and all the deities arise from the ground of mind and that all perfect qualities of wisdom are already present in the nature of mind. So one is requesting that these qualities manifest or be present in an actual form in one's practice. So

one is recognizing at this point that everything one does in practice will be out of an understanding of this basic nature from which all wisdom qualities spring. Instead of having to fabricate something or create something that's not already there, we work within a recognition or understanding of the perfection that is the basic nature and which the practice helps us to recognize.

So what have I just done? Is this a different universe entirely from that of watching-the-breath meditation and *vipassana* meditation? It's not. Let me take you step by step, piece by piece, through the architecture—the transformative architecture—of what I have just built in my mind and in my heart through the process of this recitation. As we go through it, we'll stop at various points and actually try to practice the technique that's being described. I'm going to rely on a very brilliant commentary and instruction text that was written in the nineteenth century in Tibet, so you'll see that this is something that is an authentic part of the tradition, not something concocted in the mind of a Western person in order to translate this into some kind of psychological framework or to turn it into something that it hasn't already been expressed as. There are many commentaries and explanations of elaborate detail about all aspects of the practice. I'm going to focus on just the portion that goes into the methods for meditation itself.

There are three parts to the commentary, and these correspond to body, speech, and mind. For body, there is the instruction on the *mudra*, which is the development stage, which is the creation of the mandala of the deity. For speech, there is the instruction on recitation, and then for mind, there is instruction on the perfection-stage meditation of luminosity.

First, as it says in the root text to the practice, all dharmas ultimately are the indivisible truth, conventional truth, and ultimate truth, which is the superior *dharmakaya*. Through the yoga of great emptiness, the expanse of *dharmata,* the enduring nature of mind is made fully manifest as luminosity, the experience of luminosity. This, too, has three parts. The first part contains what are called the three *samadhis*. And this is very, very crucial. When you first begin to do any kind of visualization practice, you have to begin with a certain experience or understanding of what form is and what emptiness is in order to work with bringing out the pure nature that is already there in the mind rather than to overlay some kind of conceptual fabrication on top of another conceptual fabrication.

[Asking the workshop to begin with a brief period of informal meditation, the lama instructed them to close their eyes, "and just look back in your own mind and see if something is constantly reoccurring in every moment in your mind, which is an image of yourself, an idea of who you are."]

Without interfering with it in any way, just watch that picture of yourself, whether it's in the form of words that you speak to yourself or a visual picture that occurs in the mind, or a feeling of yourself, or a combination of those things. Watch this shifting thing that keeps reasserting itself in every moment, this idea of yourself, and begin to see that this is an idea, this is a concept. It is something that is being reinforced through habit in every moment. It's not something solid or real. In fact, you see it changing from moment to moment. It doesn't correspond to anything you could call reality. It's not like a scientific, perfectly mapped-out picture of your physical makeup.

And you don't see yourself as you see yourself in the mirror. You don't see yourself as you hear your voice when you listen to it on tape, or as other people describe you to yourself. It's just something that you constantly are building up within yourself. See that picture, see what keeps it going. As Tulku Urgyen said, this comes from the force of habit, from grasping or clinging or cherishing oneself.

It's like if you take a flat piece of paper and roll it up again and again and again. Then, even if you try to pull it apart by using a meditation technique to make it flat and open and spacious, the tendency—because it's been rolled up so tightly for so long—is it immediately just springs back into its previous position. That's what the mind does with this concept of self when we open our minds a little bit through meditation. Again, in the next moment, the tendency is to close down and lock into this picture of ourselves.

Another image Tulku Urgyen used is of the hand trying to grasp at space. Our true nature is like space, but habitual tendency is like trying to hold space, to hold it within your hand. Even though you can't hold space within your hand, you can still get your hand locked tight into a fist, which is very hard to let go of.

The basic thing in the beginning is to ask yourself what happens when you work to replace that image of yourself with a different image? As you practice this meditation technique of visualization over that different image more and more, and the more quiet and concentrated your mind becomes, the sharper and clearer a focus that image will become, until you see yourself as that form, as naturally and spontaneously and clearly as you now do your ordinary picture of yourself. But this is not just a different picture of yourself, it is an image that's constituted from an understanding of its fundamental emptiness, its lack of inherent existence or truth as a solid, self-existing, real thing. It comes from a recollection of emptiness rather than a forgetting of emptiness.

One of the basic pitfalls for new practitioners of this form of meditation is that instead of beginning from this understanding of the image of the deity, of a pure wisdom expression, arising from emptiness, we skip over that step, and instead we just replace our customary self-image with kind of a new and shiny self-image—ourself as the practitioner; that's our new image. This is nothing new. Trungpa Rinpoche, one of the first teachers of Tibetan Buddhism in America, talked about this twenty-five years ago when he came here.

But I want to talk about this tendency on a little bit more subtle level. That is, when you begin the visualization practice, as when you begin any practice of Dharma, you can't go about trying to realize egolessness aggressively. You just cannot do it. You cannot force yourself to be a more accomplished being by building up a powerful ego identity of yourself as the dedicated and devout practitioner. Ego is ego, no matter how it is clothed, in Dharma robes or in street clothes or in a business suit.

Open and gentle mind is always born from letting go of an image of yourself, then opening your mind and heart to be aware of and responsive to what is really going on inside you. Every single person I've met in eighteen years of practicing Buddhist meditation who has tried to do a dharmic makeover, let's say, to become the person they think they need to be in order to succeed as a practitioner or as a monk or a nun or as a retreatant, have created, by far, more problems for themselves and for others than they have solved.

So it's very important to remember from the very beginning: Emptiness. Letting go of the idea of being somebody, of being anybody in particular. To leave the mind free. To generate the mandala and the deity. That's the most crucial step. Otherwise, if you're just Sherab Dorje masquerading as Guru Rinpoche, or if you're Norman Posel, which is my Western name, masquerading as Sherab Dorje, you're just overlaying one ego identity on top of another, dressing it up. In Tibetan it is called Dro Dok, which literally means putting on the colorful feathers. You're basing practice on the ego rather than using practice to free up and loosen the ego, to give your mind breathing room.

Another image, which comes from my old friend Lama Yeshe, is you are becoming a tight-ass. You get caught in the constant, self-defeating struggle to change quickly and thoroughly into the person you want to be and think you need to be, which leads to disappointment, heartache, depression, etc.

So practice is not about a deliberate effort to try to become someone new and better. It's relying on the techniques and the transmitted wisdom to give yourself to naturally evolve. Allow your understanding—which is based on the wisdom potential already inside you as your basic nature—to grow and grow. An important point about Tibetan Buddhism is that devotion helps with that, too. Open yourself to relying on something that is beyond your habitual boundaries, beyond your habitual self-identification, to break out, to use the emotional energy as well as the intellectual energy within yourself, to go beyond your limits, the limits of yourself as you've come to define them and to depend on them. When you practice and you find yourself becoming more tolerant, more compassionate, more genuine of devotion, of gratitude to the teachers who've given you these teachings, and you have these qualities growing, these are the true and reliable signs that your practice is working. Trying to crush and suppress the tendencies in yourself that you don't like, causing them to reappear in other forms in other areas of your life, is the sure sign that you are trying to fabricate a new Buddhist identity. So watch yourself. Just watch yourself.

A way to express the idea that perfection is something that's already there at the beginning, and through the practice it becomes manifest, something that you can actualize and see, rather than something that you have to fabricate from some limited conceptual mind, is: When I came in and saw the bookstore that they've set up, early yesterday morning when no talks had been given yet in this conference, I saw that you could order tapes of all of the talks of these wise and brilliant teachers who are gracing us with their presence, even before they'd even spoken a word. That expressed to me a basic confidence in wisdom-mind, because the organizers of the conference knew that the wisdom was already there, it was just a matter of waiting for it to manifest. It will be available for purchase at a reasonable price!

The first of the three *samadhis* is this *samadhi* of *dharmata,* of recognizing emptiness. It's recognizing that all of the Dharmas of *samsara* and Nirvana, all of them, by their very nature, as equanimity, as the unified two truths (conventional truth and ultimate truth) are the *dharmakaya,* are perfection—primordially, originally. They're the nature of enlightenment, the nature of buddhahood. And recognizing this with great confidence and certitude and bringing this very clearly, refreshing it in your mind, is called the *samadhi* of *dharmata,* and that is the starting point for all visualization practice.

Then, there is the *samadhi* of complete appearance, or perfect appearance. Because recognizing that emptiness is the true nature of mind without any deliberate or willful attempt to do so, what naturally springs to mind, again, out of the nature of mind, out of the nature of that understanding, is a referenceless and boundless compassion toward sentient beings, who don't recognize their nature in that way. And just as compassion springs from the recognition of emptiness, so the form of the deity springs from the recognition of emptiness and practice as an expression of compassion, as an expression of the enlightened will to manifest in order to benefit beings, to aid them, to guide them, to help them understand their own true natures. That is the foundation for the appearance of the deity of the wisdom expression in visualization practice.

We've already let go of the usual picture of ourselves. We've meditated on emptiness, we've allowed compassion to arise out of that emptiness. Now we allow our own mind, our own awareness, to appear in the form of a syllable—free, a letter, which is white and clear and stable. So we have an experience of our mind arising in this form. At first it seems awfully odd to see oneself as a syllable. But then, why not? We can see ourselves as anything whatsoever. The mind has boundless capacity to express itself, to appear in any form. There's absolutely no limit to it.

That completes the three *samadhis*. The third one, where the mind appears in the form of a seed syllable, is called the causal

samadhi, because it is like the cause or the seed for the appearance of the full-blown mandala, in which the deities of the mandala are pictured.

The second part is the actual generation of the appearance of the mandala—the external mandala—and the deities of the mandala. There is an explanation here of how different ways to generate the deities out of the seed syllable can work with purifying different kinds of concepts of the self, expressed here as different forms of birth: birth from an egg, birth from a womb, and so forth.

We don't need to go into too much detail about this, but there's one very interesting point that I wanted to bring up. In terms of purifying womb birth, that is, birth as a human being or other sentient being, the text says there is both birth from self and birth from other. The first is birth as one's own child. And the verse is, "Because oneself is all of the previous buddhas, one makes oneself a child of oneself."

What does this mean? "Self" here means *bodhichitta,* the nature of mind, of mind bent on achieving enlightenment. And that, as in that "other born from the self," means all of the buddhas of past, present, and future. Because all enlightened ones are born from that *bodhichitta,* from that mind of enlightenment, that's why it's said that all of the *tathagatas,* all the enlightened ones, are born as the children of that.

Then birth of other, or birth from other, says, "In order for the lineage not to diminish and to continue spontaneously, one's own self is born as the child of the other." This means, because this mind of enlightenment in its nature is primordially enlightened, is primordially the Buddha, by relying on others, such as spiritual friends, guides, and teachers, one's own wisdom essence is in a position to become clear and manifest to one's self. In that way, one's own wisdom-mind actually is born from other, just as previously you could say other is born from oneself.

Now in this context, for this practice, in order to purify birth from the womb (which means to conceive of oneself in the normal fashion as a human being, with all one's frailties, limitations, and so forth), one generates oneself through the ritual of the three *vajras.* This has three parts, the first of which is generation of the external mandala; and then the generation of the deities which dwell within that mandala; and finally, the blessing of the three places. There's one's own body, speech, and mind as being that nature of wisdom body, speech, and mind of the buddhas.

So remember, we had this free syllable before, which was the third *samadhi.* And this seed syllable is just kind of hanging around in space, just floating in this expanse, without any limitation. From it are generated syllables that emanate out from the three and purify all clinging to the reality or solidity of the world, of the environment, of other beings, of everything. As the syllables are withdrawn, they form a protective tent or canopy of *vajras,* which is creating a perfectly locked-in, sealed, and protected environment for the visualization to continue.

Different syllables are emanated out

from the *hri,* and these constitute the mandalas of the five elements from which the physical universe is formed of space, air, fire, water, and earth. On top of those appears Mount Maru, which is the central image of the universe, the iconographic representation of the center of the universe. And on top of that is a syllable *Drung,* which emanates, and this transforms into a wisdom mandala—which is actually the physical, so to speak, because it's all mentally created—and we recognize it as emptiness. But it creates the external palace, the wisdom palace, of the enlightened deity, which is square.

Most of you saw the sand mandala that was painted here. Although it might be hard to recognize as such, that's actually a two-dimensional representation of what is a three-dimensional building or enclosure that has many different features, including gateways and portals and beautiful strings of jewels hanging from the rafters and so forth. This is the dwelling place of the eight buddhas you saw in the center of that mandala. So a structure like that is created at this stage of the meditation, and it says it has all the perfect qualities. When you really do this practice in its full form, then you actually visualize all these in great detail.

Again, through this you are working with your moving mind, your conceptual mind, using it, harnessing it, to develop your concentration, because as your mind is completely absorbed in the process of visualization, it's so busy it has nothing else to do. You are training your mind again and again to be concentrated fully on developing this enlightened picture of the universe.

So there's this great mansion, and in the center of it is an eight-faceted flat jewel, and on top of that, a huge, huge lotus, which has four petals. In the center of that is a throne upheld by lions, on which is another lotus, a flat sun disk, a flat moon disk. And on top of that, that *hri* that one had there all along descends and alights on top of the moon disk in the center. That transforms immediately into the hand emblem of this wisdom family, of this buddha family, which is a *vajra*. Light emanates from that and returns and accomplishes the two benefits. In a globe of brilliant light, one appears as the deity, in its fully complete form.

The form of the deity is an expression of what is primordially beyond liberation or attachment, something that is self-emergent: awareness, wisdom-mind, which is appearing in the form of a physical aspect of a sign of a representation. This goes back to the very first point we discussed. In this case, it's the teacher-guru Padmasambhava in Tibetan, who is white with a red complexion, with one face, two arms, smiling but slightly grimacing at the same time, wearing an empowerment hat on top of his head, on top of one's own head, and wearing the inner garment, the Dharma robe. and the overcoat-type garment, one on top of the other. Right hand in the threatening gesture, holding a five-pointed *vajra,* thrusting it in the air. Left hand is on the lap in the meditation *mudra,* holding a skull cup filled with *amrita,* in which is a vase of the elixir of life, which has a jewel on the top of it, crowning it.

It goes on and on and on in great detail about how he's sitting and on top of his head is the Bodhisattva Chenrezi [the Tibetan form of Avalokiteshvara]. On top of Avalokiteshvara's head is the Buddha Amitayus, who is the lord of this buddha family. On each of the four petals of that huge lotus is another aspect or manifestation of Guru Rinpoche—not separate from Guru Rinpoche, just a different aspect.

One visualizes the one in the front and then on the right and then the one to the rear, the one to the left. And then there was that great eight-sided jewel, the flat jewel that was below that. There are eight more forms of Guru Rinpoche on each of those facets of the jewel, and each of them is a form that is meant to perform a specific kind of enlightened activity for the sake of sentient beings. So, as one goes through, one visualizes all these things.

Then, the actual way to meditate—this is how it actually works. It's easy to say, "Visualize this, visualize that," and generally you will think, How do I do that? My mind won't do that. I'm not used to that. It says, in the beginning, take your time and become accustomed to this. It's something you have to train yourself to do, like anything. You have to follow the signs and indications in order to get to the picture of the mandala. This is really not something that's that difficult or daunting for us to do.

When I came here yesterday, I left Montgomery, Alabama, at about one o'clock in the morning, got in my car, almost dead asleep, followed the sign that said Take Highway 85, it'll get you to Atlanta, just without thinking, just trusting that the whole picture hangs together. There's a world of signs out there. All I have to do is just take my map out, follow the signs, and somehow I'll get to this lectern here today and do what I have to do. So I took Highway 85. And there's a sign for the airport, then there's a sign for the Park-and-Ride. So I left my car at the Park-and-Ride. Then there's a sign where Continental Airlines is, and then the gate number, and then the seat number on the ticket. Then I had to go to this other gate and this other seat number in Newark, and then I had to go to the right belt to get my bags, and had to tell the taxi driver the Plaza Hotel. I have no idea that any of this is really out there; I just have the words on the paper and I'm just putting my trust. And because I can play with the signs and the symbols, I can get to where I need to go.

Visualization practice is just like that. It's just another kind of map—an enlightened map—and it makes a lot more sense. Just getting used to it, we can follow the signs and get to the picture of the mandala, just as we do in our daily lives, take care of all of our other business. So there's nothing really mystical or transcendental or even all that profound about how the mind is capable of doing this.

So, first one should visualize just oneself as the central deity of the mandala, as Guru Rinpoche. Just work on seeing that image clearly, like a rainbow of light. Not something solid, but something that is just light and emptiness. The very best practitioners have been doing this for a long time and can naturally see the whole mandala in an instant without having to make any effort. Those

who have been doing it for a while and aren't used to it see the general form of it and some of the specific details without confusing them or getting mixed up. In the beginning, you have to cultivate the *samadhi,* cultivate your concentration, so you can work on practicing this.

One way to do this is to place an image or an icon with all of the correct details and characteristics in front of you. And having placed it in front of you, focus your mind, your eyes, and your energies single-pointedly on that image. As you work that way, the image will become clearer and you will abandon the thoughts of wild mind and sinking mind, all these meditation faults that you've heard about before will be abandoned as you develop concentration on this image. Just leave your mind in a state of seeing the deity, which is the unification of appearance and emptiness.

As the experience of the quieting and cessation of conceptual mind diminishes, then one's mind becomes calm. One enters a state of *shamatha,* of calm abiding. At times, just allow your mind to rest, your awareness to rest, and just take a break. Sometimes, get really involved in working with all the elaborate and fantastic details of the mandala in order to train yourself. It's just like exercising your mind to its absolute limits to train it.

In every meditation session, you should recite the verses of "The Appearance of the Deity" in their complete form. What I did before, when I was just reciting the text, was actually describing in my mind what the mandala looks like, how the deity appears, all this about the free syllable and the emanation and collection of light, etc., and the fact that it is mere emptiness and appearance. All of that I was actually describing and reminding myself of in the process of meditation.

So one is working with the voice and the energy to recite it. At the same time, one is watching it happen, one is creating that architecture—what I call the transformative architecture—of the mandala, in one's mind, in the process of chanting.

In each session, you should recite the mantra. In each session, you should allow the image of the deity and your own mind to mix inseparably—to become one flavor—so that the deity is not separate from your mind and your mind is not separate from the deity. In each session, through emanation and collection of light, accomplish superb activity. At all times, have the confidence and pride that the deity and one's own mind are not separable. Through doing this, all ordinary grasping and fixation, all clinging to the idea of things as solid and real, all of those things which trap ourselves in our limited picture of the universe of our mind will be blocked, will be eradicated, through what is called this meditation on the complete purity.

This meditation, like everything else, has three parts, which are the clear appearance, the firm confidence, and the recollection of the pure aspects. What the commentary goes on to do here is talk about every one of the details of the mandala—of how it appears—and show how that detail is a representation of an aspect of wisdom-mind, of the quality of enlightenment.

Let me just give you a very small sampling so you can see the beauty and profundity of this language, of this understanding:

So in this way, all phenomena and appearances, everything that comprises the external and internal universe, the container and the contents—that is, the world and beings, the *skandhas, ayatanas,* and *dhatus,* the constituents of all dharmas—all of these things from the very beginning are the complete and perfect bodies and wisdom of the mandala, the great mandala of enlightenment.

They appear as a mandala in their pure form as kind of a network of expressions of wisdom to train every sort of being in a way that is most suitable to that being, to share the Dharma with beings in whatever way is appropriate, to be understanding of an experience of that kind of being.

So that is what the appearance of the mandala actually is and what it does. And it appears clearly like a moon's reflection in water. That is how one should meditate, by focusing one's mind on the general picture and each of the details. If it's difficult to make this picture of the mandala the object of your mental awareness, then you can put a representation of it, a painting or statue or whatever, in front of you, and focus your attention on that. And as you drive away the faults of meditation, like wildness and torpor and so forth, you can foster the understanding of the inseparability of the deity from your mind.

As you get more used to that, you can get into this visualization of the emanation and collection of light, which is called "performing the two benefits": A mantra garland in the center of yourself as the deity emanates light, which makes offerings to all the buddhas of the three times and ten directions, and invokes their blessing and their wisdom and draws it back into oneself, which is called "accomplishing one's own benefit." Then, again light goes outward and goes everywhere in the universe where beings exist, and serves them in whatever way they need on a relative level: food, clothing, health, explanation, education, whatever. On an ultimate level, it serves to share the Dharma with them. All this activity happens through the emanation of light.

Afterward, the light is drawn back in and, instead of a world of suffering and confused sentient beings, through this wisdom activity the whole thing is transformed into a universe-wide mandala of the deity in which all beings appear as Guru Rinpoche. All of their speech is the sound of the mantra of Guru Rinpoche, and all of their thoughts are just the natural expression of the wisdom-mind of Guru Rinpoche. So that is another visualization practice that's done in this context.

Then the "stable pride of the deity" means all of the phenomena of *samsara* and Nirvana are the display of one's own wisdom awareness, and nothing outside that. They don't exist anywhere else; they're not made of anything else. Knowing that, one has a stable pride in oneself as really being ultimately inseparable from, or of the nature of, the deity one is visualizing. You use this image that you create in your mind as a way of

recognizing that it's something that ultimately you don't have to create at all.

Let me describe another way you work with developing the capacity to visualize clearly: working from the inside out or from the outside in. You can start with the very perimeter of the mandala that you visualized, which is this circle of protection that you created in the beginning, and work step by step to see the palace of enlightenment that you created and see every detail. You come to the center of that and see the eight-sided jewel and focus on the details of each of the eight forms of Guru Rinpoche; and then to the four on the lotus; and then to oneself as the central figure as Guru Rinpoche, from head to toe or toe to head; and ultimately into the heart, where a *vajra* is on top of a moon disk. In the center of the *vajra* is the mantra garland, and in the center of that is that minuscule *hri,* which was the cause in the beginning, the seed for the creation of the whole thing; which is always there. That is like the core essence of one's own mind that we generated in the beginning. Once you get to that point, you can just let go of the whole thing and rest in the natural awareness of your mind without having to go further.

When you become more accustomed to this, you can take in the entire sweep and scope of the mandala at once. Or you can move from part of it to part of it. Once you work with these different techniques, there are no rules. You can do whatever your mind needs to do at any point in order to sustain and to improve the meditation. If your mind is moving, you can work with any of these techniques that are designed for moving minds, such as visualizing all these details or doing the emanation and collection of light. If your mind is quiet, then you can just rest on one particular thing, like the free syllable in the center of your heart. If your mind is really in a clear state of meditation, then you can just let the whole picture go, sit quietly, and rest in the nature of your mind. Work with whatever is going on.

So these are techniques that are there for you to use as you see best to help you develop your meditation, your understanding, your wisdom.

The last thing I want to share with you from the text is the meditation on mind itself. Once you've become proficient in the visualization, and your mind is quiet, there are other visualizations that go along with this practice. In fact, if you love detail, you can visualize emanation and collection on the basis of Avalokiteshvara, who is above Guru Rinpoche's head, on the basis of Amitayus, who is on top of Avalokiteshvara's head. There are separate, entire practices to do for each of the twelve manifestations of Guru Rinpoche. There's an activity for what are called the four gatekeepers and the gates of the mandala. There's no limit. None at all.

Third is the instruction on mind. The root text says that, at the end, the whole mandala is dissolved inward, collected inward, into that free syllable in the center of one's heart. By saying "Hung, Hung, Hung," the entire picture that one has created is allowed to dissolve away, including one's own body as Guru Rinpoche, into the *hri* syllable. And that *hri* syllable is also allowed to just vanish, to dissolve away into emptiness, into the luminous natural state of mind. Then, without holding onto the thought that just transpired, in the moment before the next thought arises, just leave mind there without trying to do anything at all, without trying to change anything at all. Just let mind be as it really and naturally is. At that time, whatever manifests in mind, whatever thoughts arise, are just the play or dance or expression of mind-nature itself. Nothing apart from it. Understand all things to be this mind-nature, which penetrates everywhere and ultimately never changes into anything else.

This is the ultimate vehicle of practice, the final understanding, which is called "Dzogchen" in Tibetan, the Great Perfection.* This naturally occurring mind is the highest realization and the ultimate yoga. All qualities of wisdom and enlightenment spring from this understanding. So, at the end, as one dissolves the mandala, again, one says "Hung," three times and through that all appearances dissolve into the mandala.

The first verse I explained was from the root text. Now this is the commentary on it.

The awareness of the present is clear, beyond verbalization, beyond conceptualization. It is

---

* For a discussion of Dzogchen in greater depth, see Lama Surya Das's workshop, "Dzogchen: The Innate Great Perfection," on pages 103–13.

empty in its nature, which is not anything that can be visualized or seen at all. It is clear, spontaneous, and pervaded by compassion. Primordially inseparable from the three bodies of enlightenment. This is not something that can be demarcated, delimited, partitioned. It is like space itself, not something that consciousness can grasp. Not something that exists in any limit of existence or nonexistence.

This is what one just allows one's mind to rest in, as the conclusion or completion of the meditation.

At the end, one would do various dedication prayers in which one shares what one has done in one's own practice, reminding oneself that one is doing this for all beings, not just for oneself.

So all that was in those few lines that I chanted in the very beginning. All that and a lot more. Through this, perhaps we've seen a little bit about how, through visualization practice in Tibetan Buddhism, you can balance conceptuality and nonconceptuality. Of course, there are roles to be played both by critical reason and heartfelt devotion in practice. My point of view is that these accomplish the same thing, like two hands working together. We saw a little bit of what visualization practice does, how it works, how you go about learning it, and how the chanting fits into that.

Again, visualization practice is not a deliberate effort to try to become someone else or to use just the same tired thinking mind to create a different picture. Rather, it is

relying on the techniques of the practice to allow the wisdom that's already within you to have the space to come out. It's something natural. It's not something we're trying to create or fabricate, as the text itself mentions so many times. All these techniques are either ways to help you focus your mind or ways to help you achieve insight into the nature of your mind. There is no technique here that does anything other than that. That's why this is true Buddhist practice.

Faith and devotion, like analysis, help you cut through your old way of seeing things. Use all the energies at your disposal—your speech, your thoughts, your feelings, all of it—to help you break out of the tight web of conditioned ideas that you trap yourself in, that I trap myself in. That concentration is not something you can only do when your mind is quiet.

Concentration means staying on an object so they can work both when the mind is resting and when the mind is moving. With all these techniques that you use in the visualization practice, there's a way to turn any mind state or feeling into an avenue of practice. That is the brilliance of Tibetan Buddhism, that everything can be used as an avenue of practice. Everything becomes helpful. Practice becomes total. Your mind does not have to be in one specific state in order to make the meditation work. Nothing is left out. Everything gets utilized.

The biggest drawback of Tibetan Buddhism? There's too much of it. It's like being handed the key to the Library of Congress and being told, "Go for it." That's why perhaps more than with other Buddhist traditions, you need to have the librarian, you need to have the map on the wall to show you how to get there. You need more guidance because so much is at your disposal. That's why the teacher becomes important and the community becomes important. These are people who've walked the aisles before and know the way.

Gradually, through this form of practice, identification with ordinary mind, with your usual thought patterns and set of self-images, shifts. One replaces ordinary thoughts with thoughts that are grounded in a recognition of the empty nature. Then, through that loosening and that relaxation, one shifts even further to not identifying with any image at all. Images just arise naturally as the expression of mind. But you don't have to make it happen. It just happens. That's the way mind is. Gradually you cease identifying with anything. Just let it all happen. Trust in the self-existing, naturally occurring awareness that is without any center or circumference, which is the true mandala of wisdom-mind.

[A participant asked Lama Sherab Dorje what he thought the average person in America would find appealing about "trying to visualize themselves as some guy wearing strange clothes and a funny hat?"]

Lama Sherab Dorje: Nothing at all. I wouldn't find that appealing. And that's why I kept emphasizing that that's not the point here at all. The point really is that this technique is available to help you understand that emptiness is both the starting point and the arriving point of all Buddhist meditation. This visualization practice is a brilliant technique to help you recognize that. It emphasizes it at the beginning, it emphasizes it throughout the visualization, and it emphasizes it at the end, as you allow the mind to rest in its nature.

This technique is available for people. It uses so much of your being that it's very, very powerful. People who get a taste of what the technique is can appreciate it as a very powerful way to work with what is the understanding within all traditions of Buddhism.

I think it's crucially important to help people understand what is really going on with Tibetan Buddhist meditation, because if it remains at the level of watching a beautiful performance of other people doing their meditation by chanting and dancing and so forth, it's a nice show but ultimately it's not a technique that is very helpful for us. So I personally try to emphasize it. I think in the past people have feared that, although you might work with this with people who are already hard-core, serious Tibetan Buddhist practitioners, that somehow it'll just be too confusing to people who are just interested in Buddhism in general and want to know how this works. I disagree with that completely and think there's a lot more that can be done by people who have experienced the practice to help others understand how valuable it is.

[Noting that there are many different techniques, a member of the workshop asked if one should identify one technique and stick with it,

or select the meditation technique that is best for the individual's practice.]

Lama Sherab Dorje: In all Buddhist practice, you work with developing concentration and focusing or quieting your mind in order to achieve greater insight. So, in a sense, it almost doesn't matter. On the other hand, when you are introduced to something, you may feel that it is working for you. I can work with mind on the basis of this. I can see concentration growing within me because my mind just naturally wants to focus on this, whether it's a candle flame or a statue or the breath within oneself or the picture of the deity that one generates within one's mind.

When you have this kind of visualization practice, it's a smorgasbord. It's the whole thing. So, if you take it like a training course, if you work with a teacher and learn this kind of practice, of which there are thousands, you may feel a close connection to one particular teacher, and it makes sense to work with that person.

[A participant asked if there were more active or physical ways of mandala practice.]

Lama Sherab Dorje: Absolutely. You've seen the sand mandala practice. There is a great tradition of what's called Cham, or "lama dancing," where the mandala is created and visualized in the process of moving as the deity, of seeing oneself as the deity in movement rather than just sitting at rest. When you sit on your cushion and do a visualiza-

tion such as the emanation and collection of light, you don't have to sit there like a statue because this picture that you have is at rest. You are free to move around, stretch your legs, whatever. You're not locked into being this thing. Again, the whole point is to break away from ideas of solidity.

I remember this person asking a lama once, "I'm Vajrayogini and I'm holding this hooked knife up here, and what happens if my hand gets tired holding up this knife, picturing myself as Vajrayogini holding this knife?"

And he says, "Well, put it down! You don't have to hold it up there. There's no rule about that."

So yes, there is a tradition of lama dancing.

And if you've ever heard of the New Year festivals, like Mani Rimdu, where dance performances are put on by lamas, that's exactly what it is. There's one which is the dance of subduing different kinds of obstructing forces and of bringing the teachings of Dharma to Tibet. But all of that internally is a meditation on breaking through obstructing forces in the mind. So the lamas are meditating on that as they're dancing, and the dance becomes an expression of concentration and of wisdom-mind.

[The final questions concerned the use of mandalas that the meditator made for himself or herself and the advisability of embarking upon this practice without a teacher.]

Lama Sherab Dorje: I think there's a tradition of these teachings that comes from the enlightened masters themselves that expresses the kind of architecture or road map of enlightenment; the different expressions of wisdom-mind with different kinds of buddhas. And I do think that there's purpose and wisdom behind those choices.

If you feel capable of duplicating that wisdom as a source of the map that you want to create for yourself, then that's what all these masters who came later did. They created new mandalas and new expressions that came out of their own wisdom understanding. On the other hand, if you're saying,

Can I just work with a bit of this and a bit of that because I like to visualize this deity, or this particular thing resonates with me and I find it helpful? Can I just pick and choose in that sense and not have to do the whole practice like that, I think the answer is yes. Of course. But whether you can take a bit from this mandala and paste it onto that one in a kind of computer-age image, I don't think that would be helpful.

I think it's important to get introduced to a deity with the help of a teacher. It will give you more confidence in that you know really what you're doing.

Medicine Buddha Teachings and Empowerment

His Holiness Rizong Rinpoche

IN LADAKH, INDIA, AT THE AGE OF TWO AND A HALF, Rizong Rinpoche was recognized as the reincarnation of the renowned Tantric master Rizong Tulku. He was placed in the care of highly realized masters in Ladakh, where he studied for a number of years. He then continued his education at Drepung Loseling Monastery in Lhasa, Tibet, until 1959, when the Chinese invasion of Tibet caused him to leave Tibet with the Dalai Lama. In India, he completed his studies, which led to his being named abbot first of Gyud-med Tantric College, then of the Drepung Loseling Monastery that had been established in India. In 1995, His Holiness was appointed Jang-tse Choe-je, second in line to become the Ganden Tri holder, the head of the Galukpa lineage. He recently completed a three-year retreat on the Yamanataka practice, during which he lived in a remote cave in the mountains near Ladakh.

The medicine Buddha represents a buddha's ability to manifest as healing medicine for the benefit of all sentient beings. By receiving this initiation and performing the practice, one may relate with one's latent ability to restore the sense of balance in both body and mind that may have been lost.

Beginning by explaining, by means of a translator, the background and basis for the medicine Buddha practice, His Holiness then presided over the empowerment ceremony, which is rarely given in the West. This Tantric Buddhist empowerment is connected with the embodiment of the healing aspect of enlightened beings called *Vhaisyajairaja guru* or, in Tibetan, *men-la*.

I would like to thank all of you for coming here, and express my delight and happiness to be able to give this empowerment of our medicine Buddha to an audience of such distinguished people in the Buddhist studies and Buddhist practices.

In general, there are many spiritual traditions in the world. Within Buddhism itself, there are many different traditions, based on various interests of the trainees or the students. The Buddha taught many different schools and there are many different philosophical traditions he expounded in India. Similarly, when Buddhism spread in Tibet, the Tibetans accepted its various forms.

Now, among the various forms of Buddhism, I personally don't think there's any particular school that's better than others, because the Buddha taught the various forms of teachings to help people. And he taught to different people the different forms of Buddhism because that will suit them. If the purpose of the teachings is to benefit or help the beings, then we should consider that whatever helps is the legitimate, or the useful, tradition of spiritual practice. Therefore, it would be a mistake to consider that some forms of Buddhism are inferior to other forms. We should not discriminate.

But this is not to say that in each tradition, everybody who practices that form of Buddhism is great. Because in all traditions, we find that some people make mistakes. Some are not able to adhere to the teachings properly, and therefore some mistakes occur in all traditions. But that should not be taken as a reflection of that particular tradition being less important or less effective.

Originally the sole purpose of the Buddhism that developed in India and spread in China or in Tibet was to benefit the sentient beings. Since the teachings were actually taught by the Buddha himself—whether Hinayana teachings, or the Sutrayana form of Mahayana teachings, or the Vajrayana form of Mahayana teachings—there should not be any kind of mistake. But as time passed, certainly there would be some, which is just the nature with any tradition.

As Buddhism is taking its roots in the West—and there are many different traditions flourishing in America, for example—it would be very important that, whatever tradition you follow, you should try to understand it thoroughly and properly. Instead of trying to mix everything together, it would be very important to whatever tradition you are following to understand it very properly; to read and study the original texts, its origins. Particularly, the people involved in translating the teachings, or teaching Buddhism to other people here, should be very careful about translating Buddhism and the specific texts. Also, before you teach you should do a thorough study and also practice.

It took quite a few centuries for Buddhism to take firm roots in Tibet, because in its original phase, there were translators from India as well as Tibetan translators. We had Tibetan translators who studied Indian languages, Indian translators who studied Tibetan languages, and they translated the teachings. As the teachings were translated, they were not satisfied with just one translation. In fact, you'll find there are at least six or seven translations of most major texts, because they might improve with subsequent translations. And so, similarly here, when Buddhism is flourishing, developing, people who are involved in making that flourishing happen should pay particular attention in writing or teaching the authentic principles of Buddhism. Your work will have impact on the future generations. If you don't do a good job, that will mislead in future; if you do a good job, it will be a great benefit for the future generations.

Keeping that in mind, even if you're just reading something, you should also compare it with various other works, and not just be satisfied with one book. In Buddhism, what is important is to examine the teachings that you study. Don't just accept any book, but rather examine. If it makes sense, if it doesn't contradict some of the obvious facts, then you can accept. But without examining, if we just accept the teachings, that wouldn't be very beneficial. The whole of Buddhism is founded on the basis of examination and analysis, and therefore it's important that when we undertake some kind of reading or some kind of practices, we also study and examine and see if it makes sense or not.

Another important factor in practicing or teaching the Dharma is that we have proper motivation. If our motivation is a selfish one, or if it is just to gain some power or respect, and if it is contaminated with worldly concerns, that doesn't quite suit in pursuing the Dharma practice. Whether we are pursuing the studies and the practices for ourselves or to teach others, what is important is that we

should maintain a proper motivation, an altruistic motivation, not to harm others. A motivation such as that, whatever we practice, doesn't just benefit us but also benefits others. Otherwise, if our motivation is very selfish in pursuing the Dharma practice, then we really defeat the purpose of pursuing the Dharma practice. And in many cases we would be strengthening the negative patterns, the negative behaviors, and so forth. So it's very important that we have the proper motivation, the altruistic, positive motivation in pursuing the Dharma practice.

The Buddha himself has said that those who are teaching the Dharma to others should have the proper motivation and understand properly the Dharma that they are teaching to others. While composing the Dharma, it's also important that we have proper motivation. In various teachings, the Buddha mentioned that one's motivation should be free from six faults, and one should have three kinds of positive motivations. These six faults are: It shouldn't be meaningless discourse, nor should it be taught or composed just for the sake of throwing the information out without having any kind of implication of the practice, just for the sake of intellectual understanding. The discourse we teach or compose should not have mistaken content. One should not teach with the motivation of provoking some kind of dispute, whether philosophical, spiritual, or religious; or just to make money. The motivation should not be to deceive others so that one would become important; and it should not be taught or composed without a compassionate attitude toward others.

The three qualities that are important when we teach or compose the Dharma works include that the teachings should have the meaning, the implication, of the practice. It should be something that could be applied in one's practice, that could bring in a transformation. And then, it should be something that would be a remedy for our sufferings or our problems.

Medicine Buddha empowerment is not a major empowerment. In Tantric Buddhism, there are major empowerments and then there are permissory empowerments. The medicine Buddha practice does not have a major empowerment; it's just a permissory empowerment, rather like the blessing empowerment.

The major empowerment is only done in the context of the major Tantric-deity practices, which is unique to Tantric Buddhism. The permissory empowerment, or the permissory ceremonies, are not unique to Tantric Buddhism. For example, this medicine Buddha practice is not exclusively a Tantric practice. It could be done commonly within the context of sutra practice.

The purpose of the empowerment is to empower the students to engage in a specific Tantric practice. The permissory ceremony also is to give permission to the participants in order to engage in that specific practice. For example, in medicine Buddha empowerment, by receiving the permissory blessing, or getting this permissory ceremony, of the medicine Buddha, one is given permission to do the medicine Buddha practice. Thereby, one is linked to the lineage of that particular practice, which is very important for any kind of practice, to have that sort of connection with the lineage. It's considered that our practice will be more effective if we form that connection through the instructions of a master who already belongs to that lineage. Without the permissory empowerment, if we engage in that practice, it may have benefits—certainly there will be benefits of doing any kind of practice—but it will be harder to develop genuine experience. By making that bonding to the lineage, it is considered that it becomes easier for us to develop the actual experience.

The seven medicine Buddha brothers were practitioners at the time before the historical Buddha Shakyamuni became a Buddha, when he became bodhisattva, or first developed a genuine aspiration to become Buddha to benefit all sentient beings. Those seven practitioners (who are called brothers in the sense of being copractitioners), cultivated or made the special aspirational prayers, which became helpful in terms of eliminating the hardships, the sufferings, or particularly disease. People would then be able to engage in practice and develop their practices. Usually you see the medicine Buddhas depicted as eight. Buddha Shakyamuni gave this teaching about the cultivation of the particular aspirational prayers by these seven medicine Buddha brothers at the time of his own cultivation of the *bodhichitta*. When the seven

His Holiness Rizong Rinpoche (left) *and his interpreter*

later manifested as buddhas, with the Buddha they formed the eight medicine Buddhas.

Engaging in the medicine Buddha practice can be more beneficial in restoring and enhancing the health and overcoming disease. Although it is true that all the buddhas have the sole intention of benefitting sentient beings, these seven practitioners, when they first cultivated the *bodhichitta,* made these

specific aspirational prayers that, in future, when there will be so much disease and so many problems, they may be particularly able to help in eliminating that suffering. The present age is known as the Degenerate Age, and there are five kinds of degenerations mentioned in the teachings. In brief, as people's motivations or their minds become more and more polluted with negative emotions and so forth, they also contribute to physical disharmony, physical ailments, etc. So, because of their specific prayer that they be especially helpful when there's so much disease, practicing the medicine Buddha practice now will be very helpful in eliminating our suffering, removing our disease, and bringing our health.

These seven brothers made not just a single prayer; some made twelve prayers, some made eight, and some made four different kinds of prayers. These prayers are mentioned in the extensive medicine Buddha practice by Buddha Shakyamuni himself. There's also another version of the medicine Buddha practice, which was written by the fifth Dalai Lama. In that version, he also mentions briefly the different kinds of prayers that the different medicine Buddhas made.

So those prayers not only help with healing disease, but there are also many prayers included about environmental healing, about protection from natural disasters, and so forth. Many of these seem to confirm the things happening now, particularly concerning environmental pollution and how it affects the beings living in that particular environment. So those prayers seem very much to confirm the situation that we are going through now. Therefore, this practice, with the mantras of the seven medicine Buddhas would be very effective at this time.

In participating in this kind of empowerment, it's important that the participants actively engage in the visualization. This kind of practice requires the firm, active participation of the participants, as the lama instructs. It's also important that we have a firm conviction about the effectiveness of this practice. Although it's true that in order to have a firm belief or to trust our conviction about any kind of practice, we need to examine and understand whether that really makes sense or not. Ideally that's what we should have done, first learn, carefully examine, and then, if it makes sense, we engage in this permissory empowerment.

Therefore, if you have had some experience or contemplation and examination concerning the effectiveness of these practices, that's wonderful. But if not, if you are participating in this ceremony to receive this permissory empowerment, you should still participate in this ceremony by engaging actively with the visualization with firm conviction as well.

There are various evidences that, when these practices are done properly, they help in bringing about healing. When the patients engage in the medicine Buddha practice, or when they request other practitioners to conduct the medicine Buddha practice on their behalf—even those with some kinds of chronic diseases that doctors think are not treatable—in many cases we find that through the practices, people are healed. So it's from those incidences that we can maintain that the medicine Buddha practice is a legitimate, valid practice.

Now, by doing this practice we should not give up the use of medicines. According to Buddhism, there are roughly four different kinds of diseases. Some can be treated just with the medicines, with herbs or chemical medicines. Other diseases actually don't require any kind of chemical or herbal remedy. Another group of diseases can be cured if one takes medicines as well as doing some practice for inner purification. And certain diseases are only cured through the inner practices. In the Tibetan communities, you'll find many people who have been taking medicine for a long time, but the medicine would not work. When they performed the practices, however, the medicines became effective. So sometimes you have to combine the medicine and the practice.

As for environmental crises or the pollutions, natural disasters, and so forth, through actual precautions and prevention of certain pollutions, as well as mentally engaging in some positive mental purification, these prayers certainly help us and prevent various kinds of natural disasters.

[At this point, the lama began the preliminary preparations for the empowerment ceremony, which made up the balance of this session of the conference. First, the translator explained the series of preliminaries the lama performed. Prior to the gathering in this room, the master had, through visualization, cultivated himself as the medicine Buddha. He then symbolically removed hindrances to the empowerment by reciting mantras over certain offering cakes, which then were removed from the room. The master then brought the participants under the protection of the protection wheel, or under the vajra tent of protection. Next, the participants

were instructed concerning basic visualizations they would be called upon to summon forth.]

In the Tantric empowerment or the practices, it's important that we change our perceptions about ourselves, about the environment or the place around ourselves, and also about the lama himself. For the purpose of bringing about that transformation of our mind, we visualize that the lama is the actual medicine Buddha. The place that we are in we visualize as the mandala, or the dimension, or the environment of the medicine Buddha. We also visualize that in the space in front of us, where these offering cakes are placed, instead of the offering cake, we visualize the actual medicine Buddhas invoked and that they are here.

[The participants were then led in reciting a request for the empowerment of the medicine Buddha. This made clear the path to the empowerment, through the Seven-Limb Practice, which consists of (1) prostrations; (2) offerings; (3) disclosing the negative karma; (4) rejoicing in the good qualities of ourselves and others, particularly those of the enlightened beings; (5) requesting the enlightened beings to remain in the world, or the samsara, until samsara ends; (6) requesting them to teach the Dharma to all the sentient beings; and (7) dedicating positive energies for the attainment of buddhahood, so that, thus empowered, all participants can benefit all sentient beings.

The permissory empowerment is an elaborate and colorful rite that requires, as the master had explained, careful and faithful visu-

alizations of a number of elements, culminating in that of the the main medicine Buddha, flanked by Avalokiteshvara and Manjushri, just above the crown of the participant's head. The medicine Buddha, in turn, was surmounted by each of the seven medicine Buddhas in a particular order, one atop the other, each glowing in a specific, jewellike hue. The translator explained in beautiful, poetic detail the appearance of each deity. Once the entire complement was assembled, a process of visualization began: One by one, from the top one down, each figure melted or dissolved into the one below, until, finally, the main medicine Buddha himself dissolved into the letter om located at the heart of the participant, thus making him or her one with all the medicine Buddhas. The ceremony ended with the lama blessing flower garlands, reciting medicine Buddha mantras, and blessing individually each of the participants who had taken part in the empowerment.]

Lama Surya Das speaks with a conference attendee

2

The Practice

Schools of Buddhism,

Methods of Meditation,

Monasticism

The Doctrine and Practice of Anapanasati

FULL AWARENESS WITH BREATH

Larry Rosenberg

THE FOUNDATION OF ANAPANASATI IS SIMPLY THE CLOSE AND DEEP contemplation of that aspect of life that is common to all sentient beings—the breath. If we are living, no matter who we are or what we are doing, we are breathing. *Anapanasati* is the meditation system, taught by the Buddha, in which conscious breathing is used to develop both *shamatha* (serenity) and *vipassana* (liberating insight).

Larry Rosenberg presented *anapanasati* meditation in his workshop at the Buddhism in America conference. His extensive studies, first with J. Krishnamurti and Vimala Thakar, then in Zen with Seung Sahn Su Nim and Katigiri Roshi, led him finally to Vipassana, his practice of which has benefited from studies with Ajahn Maha Boowa, Ajahn Suwat, Ajahn Buddhadasa, and Thich Nhat Hanh. He presently makes contributions to the search for awareness and enlightenment by teaching at the Insight Meditation Society, in Barre, Massachusetts, and at the Cambridge Insight Meditation Center, which he founded, in Cambridge, Massachusetts.

Mr. Rosenberg opened this workshop by asking the participants, during the first four of five minutes, to "just notice your breathing" without concerning themselves about any particular aspect of it; to "breathe gracefully…just notice whatever you notice…see if it can't help you to stay in this very moment." He then told them that they had already begun Anapanasati.

Anapanasati, or breath awareness, is just what it sounds like. The breath is extraordinarily precious and special. In another way, what could be more ordinary? But that's mainly, in this particular sermon of the Buddha, what we contemplate. We contemplate a very, very obvious factor. Each and every one of us is breathing.

I'm going to try to cover in only two hours something that is actually a huge subject. All the teachings of the Buddha, at least in the Theravadan tradition, can be encompassed in this one sermon. I think you may find that the sutra, sometimes called "Full Awareness with Breathing," finally and profoundly doesn't have much to do with breathing at all. It has to do with awareness. And all the different aspects—the different contemplations—that are offered up by the Buddha, are all preparation to learning how to surrender to just this moment, exactly the way it is; to a kind of utter simplicity.

You might say why not just start and do that right now? Many of us would find that difficult. Let me put the sutra in a context. Up until this point, the Buddha had talked incidentally about the role of breath awareness in a number of different talks throughout different sutras. In this one talk, called "Anapanasati," which came toward the end of a three-month retreat, he brought together all that he had said into a comprehensive teaching and described the beauty and value of contemplating the breath. In so doing, he characterized how simple in-and-out breathing can be a gateway to liberation, to clear seeing, to deep insight.

The *Satipatthana-sutra* is a primary teaching of the Buddha. All meditation comes from the four foundations of mindfulness, each foundation of which focuses on a different realm, bringing that realm into clarity. *Anapanasati* is simply that—the four foundations of mindfulness. Those four foundations are the body, of which the breath, of course, is part; feelings; mind formations; and finally, what we can call the lawfulness of it all, or dharmas. This is the foundation of all Buddhist teaching, what we hear a great deal of these days as mindfulness meditation.

Then the question is what to be mindful of? It's whatever is right at hand. It's this body, including the breath. When we say feelings, we mean that, throughout the day, without let-up, the sense organs are picking up things; whatever we're hearing, smelling, touching, etc., feels a certain way. Sometimes it's an immediate reaction we experience as pleasant or as unpleasant or as neither of these, neutral. The third realm would be mind states. If you listen to your mind even a little, you know that the mind is visited by many mind states, by many different guests throughout the day, coming and going. It's coming to know all those visitors. Then finally the fourth in the *Anapanasati sutra* is the "Full-Awareness" or "Breathing Sutra."

We now will look at the very same realms and one of the most obvious things we see, perhaps the most obvious, is that none of it lasts. So we begin to see the law of impermanence at work, out of which comes concepts like emptiness, *anatta*—not-self; and all of that grows quite naturally out of seeing impermanence.

My own interest in this particular sermon of the Buddha came about through contact with a German monk who had been in Burma and Thailand for twenty-five years. We became good friends doing retreats together in the States, and what he was saying was that up until that point, my own understanding of breath awareness as it was used in Buddhist circles was to calm down. I was in Zen for six years and I also did some Tibetan work and so forth, and pretty much every school would suggest that you attend to your breathing, which was usually dealt with as a preliminary device to calm the mind down so that it would become somewhat more concentrated and you could get on with the real work. At that point you would drop the breath and just investigate. What he was saying was that, in real *anapanasati*, the breath, this sermon, was a complete path designed to bring a person from that first moment of ordinary sensitivity to breathing to liberation. It wasn't simply a calming device.

Fine, it went in one ear and out the other. A number of years later I did some practice in Thailand in the Forest tradition there and I worked with Ajahn Buddhadasa, who was a master of this particular approach. After my stay there it was very clear that this was a very profound teaching. The breath was used in a diversity of ways that I was not familiar with until meeting him. Over the years I studied with Thich Nhat

Hanh, another who was quite devoted to this method; and, also from the Forest tradition, a man who taught a different version of it. I read the literature and worked with the living exponents of this, and finally I read the sutra itself (which should have come first), and I fell in love with the teaching because of its utter simplicity. A lot of the way in which I've practiced and the way in which I teach has been influenced by what I learned in Thailand, but of course, inescapably, I've given it my own twist.

There are sixteen contemplations in this sutra; four sets of four. Out of compassion for you, I'm not going to go through all sixteen today, but what I can do is give a sense of some of the main themes and try to make it really concrete and essentially give you a sense of how I use it and how some of the people I've practiced with use it. It ends up that you may find that it's not about the breath at all; it's just finally about our old friend awareness.

One way of approaching these is to recognize that they are not arranged in an accidental way; they actually unfold in a lawful way. Each contemplation leads to the one after it. They are not random; there is some sense to the sequence. (Mainly I use it for exposition because real life is more complex and really just happens and it breaks in upon us, but I find that the exposition can be helpful.)

To begin, we get to know this very simple in-and-out breath. Virtually all Buddhist meditation includes the breath in some form or another. Do you know when you're breathing in; do you know when you're breathing out? You may be surprised to find that you don't because you haven't been paying attention. The breath is used in a sense as a way of learning how to observe ourselves. We start with the simple in-and-out breath and then, as we become more at home with that, just notice what it's like to be breathing. Some might find that you're more inclined to follow the breath at the nose, others at the tummy, some at the chest. I myself don't have a particular locus for attention, I'm just open to the breathing. As you improve your ability to do that—you know when you're breathing in and you know when you're breathing out—can you tell me more about the breath? What's it like? What is the quality of the breath? At first people will say, Well I don't know. What do you mean? But after a while you will see that it's a very, very rich universe of subtlety and refinement and that no two breaths are the same. So the challenge then becomes getting to know this world of the breath. You might begin with an obvious one, like a long breath and a shallow breath; sometimes the breath is deep, sometimes it's not. As you move on, you may also find that sometimes the breath is very fine, like silk or satin, and at other times it's more like burlap or canvas, rough. You might find sometimes it's rapid, sometimes it's slow, and so forth. You won't even have words for a lot of the way the breath is.

Of course, the point of doing this is not to become the world's expert on the different qualities of the breath. You're refining your capacity to pay attention. In fact, you could say you're laying the groundwork for investigation into very deep and important questions about what it means to be human. We're beginning with something very, very ordinary: just the fact that we breathe. As that improves—and I'm actually following the sutra—we're in the body, in that first tetrad, where what we're interested in is coming to know the body, bringing the body itself into focus. If you've gotten to know the breath a little better, you've gotten to know the body better. Not only that, as you begin to follow the breath you begin to experience the whole body, other sensations that we call body. So as you breathe, experience whatever you're feeling in the rest of the body at the same time that you're breathing.

Now here's an important transition for understanding this sutra. Up until now the suggestion to follow the breath is an exclusive attention to the breathing. If your mind goes elsewhere you bring it back, you come back to the breath over and over and over again. In the interpretation that I follow, as you're coming to know the breathing you're also coming to know the body. You begin to see that the breath has a very powerful effect on the body. A sitting could be, for example, as you sit and breathe, notice the life of the body, just as you're breathing. Now something has changed here because we're not limiting our attention to the breathing. The breath is a kind of anchor or gateway into all that is other than breath, but now it's the body. It's not as if you're trying to do two things. As you get more comfortable with it, you come to rest in the breathing. You learn how to hand yourself over to the breath, how to surrender to the breathing.

The instructions would be to breathe naturally, and that in itself is something that has to be learned, oddly enough. You might hear the instructions: Just let the breath flow naturally, if it's a deep breath or a shallow breath it's fine. Don't tamper with it, don't try to shape it in any way. Despite that, as you become more sensitive to the breathing you'll find that you are involved in controlling the breathing. The control can be very, very subtle, but nonetheless we get in there somehow.

Some of it, I think, is a new form of greed that Buddhist teachers are giving you all. That is, before you heard that there was any cash value in all this breath stuff you were just breathing; now you've found out the Buddha got enlightened by it, and for centuries people have used this wonderful technique to go very, very deeply, suddenly the ego wakes up and says Wow, this is important. I want to do this right! Then we're back to square-one, where the ego is trying to breathe properly. But it's observable. Finally, the practice keeps coming back to that—whatever happens is observable.

Little by little we see how we are invested in controlling the breath, whether we know it or not. Perhaps it's a fear, an emotional resistance. As we see this, it starts to go into abeyance, it starts to dissolve, and more and more we are able to just let ourselves sit and breathe. There is a powerful experience that many meditators go

through. The first time it happened to me I was on a retreat and the bell ending the sitting rang. Since I wasn't officially practicing, I was able to just let everything happen, and I experienced what that was like and it was wonderful. It became a little bit easier after that. Once the bell started and we were officially sitting, then the ego, now camouflaged and decked out as a yogi, as a meditator, went back into action. Because that's the problem, isn't it? The problem of meditation is the meditator. We're trying to do it right, get it right, get somewhere, improve ourselves, become better, purer, freer, kinder, more compassionate. Well is that any different from what brought us to the practice? It's for each one of us to find out.

So as you go on you become more intimate with the body. This is the first foundation of mindfulness. The Buddha uses an interesting phrase. He talks about being mindful "of the body, in the body." In the commentaries are many interpretations of what he meant. One says it means that it's just the body; it's just pure body, raw body, a body not dressed up by images or concepts. It means it's just the utter sensation. So we're intimately in a state of nonseparation with that realm of physicality as we sit and breathe. It's a very primitive, simple, raw, innocent, naive kind of seeing. It's just the is-ness of what we call body.

As you sit and breathe, not only is the breath becoming more refined and you are becoming more concentrated, but in this early phase the emphasis is much more on concentration, or training and tranquillity, or serenity, *shamatha*. We're using the breath largely to calm down, to render the mind more stable, so that finally it can become unwavering in it's capacity to pay attention. In the process we're coming to know the physical body. One of the things many of us have found is that the breath is a very powerful conditioner of the body. As you observe the breath, without trying to fix or do anything to it, just by virtue of being conscious—mindful—of the breathing, the quality of the breath changes. As it does, the condition of the body changes. To a certain degree, as the breath goes, so goes the body. As the breath becomes more refined, more fine, more calm, you find that the body starts to relax.

In order to have come as far as where the mind, the breath, and the body start to become as one, they will have started to settle into each other. By virtue of attending to the breathing, then gradually enlarging the scope so that, while you're breathing, you're also aware of the body and bodily life, mind, breath, and body become one and there's a feeling that is palpable in your sitting. The ancient Chinese called it "acquiring a seat." It's spoken of more in the old Ch'an and Zen traditions; the mind, the breath, and the body are unified. The body has become very calm and steady and you now have a sitting posture that is quite stable. You may find that you can sit for longer periods of time. Suddenly the body has become like a tree, planted with deep roots; that's a tremendous aspect in practice. The mind, breath, body becoming one, and your being able to sit in

that kind of stability, is not the end of the journey, but it's a big help if you have to face, just as a tree has to face, storms—the emotional storms—that come up in life. Wouldn't it be helpful if, while investigating fear, the body were planted and stable?

Little by little what clearly happens is that the mind starts to settle down. It becomes more peaceful, more calm, more steady, more pliable, more flexible, whether you call it *samadhi* or *dhyana*, you're learning a new joy that perhaps you didn't have. There are certain joys to a concentrated mind that don't come from the outside. Part of the reason for that is we're learning how, at least temporarily, to let go of the ways in which we identify with all the distractions that tempt us as we attempt to be with the breathing. We begin more and more to just let them be and we're able to be with that breath with more consistency and continuity.

If you were doing this method, very early on you would also be encouraged to keep the breath in mind throughout the day. All authentic Dharma teaching, as far as I can tell, will encourage you to be awake all the time. In effect, I think what does happen is people (not officially) are encouraged to believe that the real practice is happening when they're on sesshin or intensive practice or retreat. Yes, be mindful in all the other postures throughout the day, but it has become a cliché. In interviews, no one asks you about your daily life; that's somehow not part of it. What people want to know about is how the sitting is going. Whenever we look around, the icon is pretty much always the Buddha in the sitting posture; he's not shown with a vacuum cleaner or holding a child, for example. But, in the Buddha's own words, "Mindfulness in all postures," and it's even more detailed than that in the *Satipatthana-sutra*. In short, we pour our whole, undivided attention into whatever we do. That's solid practice. And if sitting is what you do, then you're undivided there.

So what if you leave retreat centers and meditation halls and zendos and Dharma rooms and find yourself in a department store or cooking or wherever else you do find yourself during the week? How does the breath fit in there? If you were going to take on this method to see if it would really be helpful, you would also stay sensitive to the breathing throughout the day. This is tricky because a person can become obsessed with the breathing in the wrong way, making them even more of a misfit than they were before they came to meditation because now they are fixated on the breath.

Let me give you an example. If you're on a subway platform or in an airport, sitting and waiting, you can be with the breath in ways not all that different from being in a meditation hall. Nothing is asked of you. You have to listen for when it's time to board your plane, but you can pretty much just sit and leave the world behind. There are other situations a little bit like that—waiting for an elevator, waiting while a clerk is processing your credit card—and while you're standing there you're not closing your eyes or looking weird, but you're with the breathing. Why?

The important thing is to be awake. The breath is helpful insofar as it helps you do that. If you start using the breath as a way to escape what is happening, that's a misuse of the instructions of the teachings. Here's the beauty of the breath as a method in terms of daily life. It's portable. It's always with you. It's such a beautiful, unassuming process. And it's repetitive, there's nothing you need to do.

You can get to the point where the awareness is grounded in the breathing, but what your attending to is what the situation's intelligence calls for. Following the breath could help you wake up to the fact that, while you're hugging a child, you're still thinking about business, for example. Conscious breathing can cut down on a lot of unnecessary thinking. If you take it on as a practice, the more you do it, the more natural it becomes. The breath starts to become much more vivid, it becomes impossible not to notice the breath. There are times in daily life when we're with the breath in a virtually exclusive way, where nothing is asked of you, such as waiting on a platform of a train station. Other times, a lot is asked of us; things to do with people and without people, physical tasks and so forth. Certain tasks I seem to feel much better about just entering into wholeheartedly, without the breath, but there are also many ways in which conscious breathing enables me to stay awake in the midst of whatever it is I'm trying to do, so it can be done more consciously, more wholeheartedly, more effectively.

One of my most joyful, wonderful meditations is walking—not slow stylized walking—just natural walking. I love to walk and I like to walk rapidly, which is alien at Buddhist meditation centers, but I do it anyway. One of the things I enjoy in life is taking a walk. Just walking naturally, I'm aware of the breathing, I'm aware of the movement; it's one unified field. It's a more comprehensive, panoramic, global kind of attentiveness and I can feel the breath coursing through the body. While walking, notice your breath sensations and after a while you'll see that the awareness is grounded in that conscious breathing and in the movement, and it's a joy to just move. After all, when you contemplate breathing, you're contemplating life and death. If you really are turning over, open to what it is you're contemplating, then you're contemplating life itself.

In fact, in the Theravadan tradition there are what are called *maranasati,* ways of contemplating death—your own death—for very good reasons: to help you get free of it, to allow some of the fears that are latent to wake up, to recognize that you don't have forever, so that you can pour your energy into this life of awareness. One very simple way to do it is to contemplate that your life is literally hanging by a breath. I just breathe in, out, in, out. Well if that circuit ends, I end. So I become increasingly sensitive to how delicate this life is.

That's why it's not simply a skillful means, but can be used to help launch you into a full awareness, at which point you may not be using the breath at all or not using it in such a self-conscious way. I have found for myself and for quite a few other people that

it's a very good way to launch practice; it's a good highway into general awareness because, (1) it's so natural and simple and ordinary; and (2) no one owns it. It's not particularly Buddhist, and there are many people who don't want to deal with anything Buddhist, but they recognize the beauty of awareness and they have nothing against being sensitive to breathing. Other methods, such as mantra or koan, have much more cultural content, whereas the breath is culture-free to begin with.

Getting back into the sutra, we've covered the first four, which have to do with the body, and now we will move on to feelings. Feelings are not emotions as we think of them in Western psychology. It has to do with the quality of pleasant, unpleasant, or neutral in our experience. As the mind gets concentrated, the fifth contemplation is called rapture. In order to get concentrated, we've had to leave all of our obsessions and preoccupations behind—the bills we haven't paid, and so forth. Suddenly we've allowed it to go into abeyance, at least for a little while, and we sink into the breath and suddenly we find ourselves happy. The depth of that absorption can be considerable. When it gets to a certain point, it has a certain excitement and a bit of agitation in it. If you keep getting concentrated, the absorption goes even deeper and you come to what is called *sukha,* happiness or peace, and that's even more fulfilling. I went on one retreat for several months, and experienced extended rapture. If I had to put it into words, it was just endless *Wow!* You get tired of it. You don't get tired of the peace though, at least I don't. So in a sense it graduates or emerges into peace.

These are feelings, dramatic ones, very pleasant ones. We tend to get attached to them. It's natural. It's a wonderful feeling—you want to have it, you want it to last forever, you want to be able to get it back whenever you want. Skillful teachers help us see this. But the point is not to get concentrated or not to experience the joy of a calm and concentrated mind, but to understand what it is. In a sense it's a holiday from the turmoil we've still not dealt with. So at the end of it, if we've not done other things, we would be very, very calm and peaceful, but we'd still be the same calm and peaceful fool that we were before. Eventually what you have to see is the nature of such bliss or peace or rapture. We see that it arises and passes away. That we don't own it. While it's there, by all means enjoy it, but it's not something to stake your life on. It's something with which to nourish yourself, and then, with the strength and refreshment that comes from a calm and concentrated mind, to meet up with yourself once again.

I just mentioned two dramatic feelings, but think of all the different feelings you might have, and while you're sitting and breathing you would feel them and experience them with as undivided an attention as you could. If the feeling was unpleasant, you would experience the unpleasantness of it. Period. As you breathe in and as you breathe out. Now unpleasantness can go from being hardly anything at all to extreme pain, just agony; pleasant can be just a light feeling in the body, light-heartedness, a nice mood in the mind, to extraordinary feelings. Remember, these are not emotions, which are much more complex; they're built up on top of the feelings, in a sense out of them.

[Mr. Rosenberg invited the participants to experience this distinction by concentrating on their breathing and experiencing the feelings that arose from it. After discussing feelings of specific individuals, he brought up another way in which the breath is entailed in Anapanasati.*]*

So we've contemplated, we've become more familiar, more intimate with the body, including the breathing. We've moved into the realm of feelings. Always remember the breathing is accompanying us like a good friend. It's helping do the work of seeing the feelings. For example, we examine feelings in the breathing, but suppose we did it in the body itself. If you were sitting in a retreat context, maybe the body would become very uncomfortable; if you were examining that, the breath is in there with you, breathing in—I'm aware of very sharp pain in the left knee; breathing out—I'm aware of very sharp pain in the left knee. And the breath holds your hand, in a way, until you become really good at observing aversive things or nice things, and it doesn't matter. Whatever is there, you're just able to observe it. So the breath can be an ally, an anchor, in helping to steady your attention.

The final tetrad is all about learning and self-education. This challenge is learning about our mind itself. As you sit and breathe, the mind becomes progressively more fit to pay attention. Now life doesn't unfold so neatly.

In this scheme of exposition, we're looking at the mind itself. Very important here is *klesha*—the tendency of mind to want. It can be the smallest thing, like wanting to open the window because it's too stuffy, but from moment to moment it's not unusual for the mind to want something.

What else does it do? It doesn't want aversion. It hates, or it's resistant to, or it's contracted against, or wants to get away from some form of No. So if it's not trying to envelop, grasp, and pull into itself, it's trying to get away from and push away. Then the third we can call confusion or delusion. Sometimes the mind is just filled with darkness. We know when we're confused. We're ambivalent. We're hesitant. We take two steps forward and one step back and we delay and it's not pleasant.

A very important challenge for us as we sit and breathe is simply to get to know these mind states when they turn up. I'm not saying get rid of greed or wanting or aversion or confusion, but do you know when they are there? Or the flip side, when the mind is generous—free of wanting? It's a lovely feeling to not be wanting anything. Instead, there's no aversion in the mind. Perhaps there's love or affection, but at least there's no aversion. We're not down on anything, at least for a few seconds. Then sometimes the mind is crystal clear. We're not running around in circles or ambivalent or in contradiction. The mind is just radiant and right and it's wonderful.

Of course, if our practice isn't helping us come to some of that wakefulness, we have to look into what we are doing. That's the heart of what we're doing. Let's say you are sitting and breathing and you're not for or against any of these states. As you sit and breathe, what might turn up is, When is he going to shut up? I've heard enough of this. I like the meditation part better.

It's the mind taking stock of itself, and it's not done simply in the formal sitting posture. You're starting to get at the real heart of self-knowing, the self-images that the mind puts up about itself, that it likes or doesn't like. There's also a lot of sorrow in the unexamined mind. So the challenge is to sit and breathe, and to be attentive to the way the mind is in this moment, the particular mood that it's in, etc.

Only in the last four contemplations is wisdom itself taken up. If you were to train the classical way, you would go through all of these contemplations. It's not that you finish them like one was kindergarten and sixteen was Ph.D., then you're done. You might go over it all your life. Then, as you get to know it, particular contemplations might be much more rich for you. You might be drawn to them. You might use them more often.

Had you been training in this classical practice, you would have covered twelve contemplations already. Moving on to thirteen, you would come to, to paraphrase: As the meditator breathes in, he or she sees the impermanence of all formations. That means you could go back through them all and see that no matter what it was, no mind state stays forever. No bodily condition, no feeling stays forever. No breath stays forever.

Now, the learning challenge is to see that transient quality; that if it's the nature of something to arise, then it must fall. If something appears, then it must disappear. It's lawful. Now, probably everyone knows that life is impermanent. That has very little transformative power. One of the main meanings of *vipassana* is "inside into *anitya*," or impermanence. But if you can begin to see impermanence with more depth and sensitivity, it takes you somewhere. Impermanence, in a sense, is shorthand for a lot, because wherever you look, wherever you turn, whether it's whole civilizations or just little us, everything is arising and passing away at a staggering rate. Science, of course, confirms this now. So the challenge here is to begin to see first-hand, in this moment, that to be alive is to be in this state of constant change.

Try self-images, where we identify with notions telling you: I'm a this. No, I'm really a that. As you begin to watch them all, you just look at it, it falls away. You don't try to destroy it. Attention is a flame in itself. As it gets stronger, it just burns up whatever is in its way, and you begin to see that whatever notions you have of yourself are cardboard at best. They're contradictory, they come and go, and they bring an immense amount of suffering because we attach to them.

As for the content, there is a slight shift in the accent of attention. Independent of content, whatever the nature of what it is you attend to, the property of it arises and passes away. This is not so easy for people to do at first. Our mind is not stable enough and it takes it on as just an idea of impermanence and, as such, it's satisfying. The other difficulty comes when you look at your story and begin to see how everything is coming and going. A lot of cherished self-images get shattered, and it's quite painful. But that pain itself is impermanent as well. In short, you begin to learn how to let go and stop identifying with everything as being me or mine. So impermanence leads to seeing the nature of what we attach to.

As you become more intimate with this impermanence itself, not as a piece of knowledge, but as something that's in the marrow of your bones, you see instance after instance of things coming and going. Finally it gets through to you that everything that arises passes away. Whether you call it wisdom or intelligence, what can begin to happen is that a certain ability to let go is enhanced. You become less clinging, grasping. One ancient image for this is like a dye that's fading away on a garment. You begin to see attachments fading away, but they fade away out of intelligence, not out of an ideology. You see that to grasp onto things in a changing world makes no sense.

We learn it primarily out of our own suffering. Any time you're suffering, look at it and see if you aren't holding onto something, attaching to it as being me or mine. As we begin to see this lawfulness, it has a freeing effect. We stop taking our self-images as seriously. We see them as what they are, kind of cartoons. Intelligence starts to set this free. The logic of this teaching is actually rather simple. If you stick your hand in fire, you get burned. Most of us learn not to do that after a while, but so many other things in life are camouflaged. They don't say fire on them. They say far out, fantastic, incredible, and wonderful. And then we grab onto them and that's not what they are. I'm not saying money is suffering; it's that we don't know how to use money. I'm not saying sex is suffering; we don't know how to use the energy. There are so many beautiful things in life that are suffering, because we don't know how to use these energies.

As you begin to see this law and learn that it is really a law and it is not going to be repealed, it helps the letting-go process. Mainly what we let go of more and more is this extraordinary burden that we carry known as me and mine. I remember a cartoon in a Japanese Zen magazine showing a monk walking on a beach He's carrying a bundle, and on the beach behind him are deep craters left by his feet, the tracks he's leaving. He's a little monk with a huge bundle, on which it says, "Me."

So at least we start taking a bit of the ache out of that attachment. We start learning how to lighten up, not as an ideology but as an act more akin to science. You observe. You learn. In that sense, the practice is about listening, looking, and learning. The teachings are signposts. Go this way. Do that. They're very helpful, and they're comforting sometimes, when you don't feel like practicing. They're inspiring before you feel like practicing. Of course, we have to leave all that behind. It's inevitable that the only thing that matters is our first-hand experience and no one can really do that for us. The letting go is the letting go into something quite profound. It would be ridiculous for me to try to tell you what you let go into, but isn't it enough to know what we let go of? Isn't that a big hint as to how our life will be if we are no longer carrying that huge burden?

So how are we lowly laypeople, who are not in monasteries and all the rest, to do this practice? We don't have time to go through sixteen contemplations. Do you have time for two of them? And finally maybe there's just one. A Thai woman, who was virtually blind, spent the last twenty-five years of her life just sitting in her blindness and meditating. She was a laywoman and she sat there and people came and learned from her extraordinary, simple, direct, concrete wisdom. She called it the condensed method, which is basically all sixteen steps condensed into two. It's really Shamatha-vipassana. Calm and concentrate the mind on the breath. When the mind settles down a bit and feels more concentrated, the mind is less perturbable. You have a quieter seat. The mind is more planted. Then sit and loosen your grip on the breath. In other words, your first step is exclusively attending to the breathing. Now, loosen your grip on the breath and the awareness that's grounded in conscious breathing is now aware of whatever's there.

It's on the way to what some call choiceless awareness or free attention, or what some people in Buddhist traditions called *shikantaza*.

So just as we've learned to surrender to the breath and feelings, the body, bodily conditions, and different mind states, the challenge comes: Can we come to rest in the breathing and form that as a gateway into all that is other than breath? Just sit and let life come to us. It's training and learning how to be ourselves. I'm dealing with the formal sitting practice, now. You're just sitting smack in the midst of your experience. Now finally, from this point of view, is the breath so special? It's happening anyway—in, out, in, out. No matter what else is going on, there it is. So it can be helpful for the awareness to be grounded in that conscious breathing, but now you're aware of whatever is there. Then you allow everything to roam freely. You sit and have no designs on how things are supposed to be. What you're surrendering to is yourself. You soon may find that you don't like what turns up, but you're sitting and breathing and what you're aware of is the arising and passing away, the emptiness of it all. When you're awake to what's happening, you see that everything arises and passes away and it lacks self. It's not really a self, it's just what it is. Perhaps the mind spins out, appropriates it, and makes me or mine out of it. We see that and we're off the Dharma track, but we can get back on, which is attentiveness. The breath is helping us.

Say you're sitting and breathing and fear comes up. Here the breath can be helpful, because it often helps us vivify life. It helps us stay anchored when we might be pulled off course easily. At least until we learn how to make friends with it, fear is not something we want to be with. So if you listen to the instructions, the challenge is to allow fear to flower, to blossom. Then the challenge can be leaving behind all we've ever learned. That won't help us now. It's seeing it with a fresh mind and beginning to see that fear is an energy on the move. If we're really attentive, it's just fear, and it comes and it goes.

When we *say* we're being mindful, we're not. In real mindfulness there are no concepts. It's preconceptual. Mindfulness is not for or against anything. It's just the clear, beautiful mirror. But typically, when we're mindful at the beginning, we're entangled in our psyche to some degree. So the mindfulness is colored by our likes and dislikes and unresolved stuff. All of that can be purified, too, and that's how the mind gets purified.

Finally, there's another little step, an important one. It is self-consciousness of being the meditator, being the observer, being the mindful one. It's an improvement and certainly will help you, even if you don't go beyond that. But there's a dualism; there's self-consciousness about being the one who's observing the fear. Then the challenge of our practice is to enter into communion with the fear. I'm intentionally using positive words like flower, blossom, communion, because the energy that's trapped in states like fear is immense. And we waste that energy in avoiding it; there is no escape from it, but we try. We suppress it, we deny it, we take our mind off it, we delay. If you added up that energy, it would be a piece of cake just to direct it toward the fear and get it over with, and just look at it. But instead, our energy is fear. With reeducating and perhaps with the help of others—of friends, teachers, a community of people practicing together—the day comes when you can look eyeball to eyeball at the fear and there's no separation. It's just fear. If the attention vacillates even a wee bit, suddenly what jumps in is that self-consciousness and identification and self-pity. That can be observed, too.

Remember that I'm depicting a particular method that comes out of a particular sermon of the Buddha, in which conscious breathing is used to help accomplish all this. But please understand, you don't have to use the breath to help you do this. Finally the two steps becomes just one step, where *samadhi* and *prajna*—concentration and wisdom—fuse, and there's just a very, very attentive mind, keenly interested in what's happening to it and seeing deeply into it and, of course, freeing itself.

[*Having finished explaining this condensed method, Mr. Rosenberg suggested that some may question the need for the more elaborate process. In answer, he briefly described his own spiritual path.*]

My first teacher was J. Krishnamurti, an extraordinarily wonderful teacher and person. I feel fortunate that he was my first teacher and that I maintained my connection with him throughout his life. He threw away all this stuff. What he counted on was the urgency of our need to become sane as citizens of this planet on which we have this magnificent technology that is just drowning out wisdom.

He started with a very simple, extraordinarily mature and ripe teaching. He really listened and watched, but he offered no help. He counted on the urgency and the joy of learning, which for many of us has been compromised and destroyed. What could be a more powerful motivation than learning? We see it in children, and all of us in this room know this. I hope we still have those moments when we really learn something for ourselves—fresh, not what X, Y, or Z said.

When I met him, I was already wounded emotionally from getting a Ph.D. and being in the academy. On paper I was quite successful, but inwardly I was impoverished. So I'm happy that I met him and he got me off to a very good start. After a year or so, I did a Zen retreat and then was in Zen for five years in Japan and Korea, which really helped me understand what he was talking about. Now I feel I've come full circle. I started off not relying on any method. I think that reflects my nature: I like things simple and natural, but I did koans and mantras and all of it. I've been through the mill.

In Anapanasati, however, people already are breathing. For most of us, it's not a big deal. It's not complex. And then, little by little, it ripens into the capacity to pay attention and to learn and to free ourselves by ourselves from what we've learned. To me, that's the heart of the Buddha's message.

Vipassana Tranquillity Meditation

Bhante Henepola Gunaratana

BORN IN A SMALL VILLAGE IN SRI LANKA, BHANTE GUNARATANA was ordained a Buddhist monk at the age of twelve. After receiving his basic Buddhist education, he then, at age twenty, was given higher ordination, and he received his advanced education from Vidyalankara College in Kelaniya and the Buddhist Missionary College of the Mahabodhi Society in Colombo. His missionary work in India was devoted to serving the Harijana, or "untouchable," people in Sanchi, Delhi, and Bombay. In Malaysia, where he was a missionary for ten years, he became religious advisor to a number of Buddhist organizations and teacher at several schools.

At the invitation of the Sasana Sevaka Society, Bhante Gunaratana came to the United States in 1968 to serve as honorary general secretary of the Buddhist Vihara Society in Washington, D.C., which named him its president in 1980. During that time, he earned his B.A., M.A., and Ph.D. in philosophy from American University, where he has since taught courses on Buddhism and where he has been Buddhist chaplain since 1973. His teaching has also taken him to Georgetown and Bucknell universities and the University of Maryland, and he has lectured widely in academic settings in the United States, Canada, Europe, Australia, and New Zealand. He is the author of numerous articles as well as three books, the most recent of which is *The Jhana and Mindfulness in Plain English*. Bhante Gunaratana is now president of the Bhavana Society in West Virginia.

In his workshop on Vipassana, or insight, meditation, Bhante Gunaratana taught ways to use the breath to focus attention and develop an ever-increasing awareness of the inner workings of the mind. Then, through the tools of insight meditation, he showed how we can begin to "tear down the screen of delusions through which we normally view the world."

M y plan is to talk on meditation, first tranquillity meditation, then *vipassana* meditation. I have always had to refer to Buddhist tradition, since we learn about *shamatha-vipassana*. In the Buddhist teaching, these two are almost inseparable, *shamatha-vipassana* and *vipassana,* and therefore when we talk on meditation we have to talk on both.

My approach to *shamatha* meditation is very traditional. I'm trying to present it in a very simple and concise way to show that relationship between tranquillity meditation and insight meditation.* Also I like to start with a practical aspect of tranquillity meditation rather than theories. A practical aspect of tranquillity meditation is that it begins naturally and necessarily with our practice. For tranquillity meditation, you need a very quiet place, steady posture, and a very simple subject. Forty subjects for tranquillity meditation have been recommended in texts, some of them are good for *vipassana*-tranquillity meditation as well. But all meditation in Buddhist tradition begins with breathing, so essential, important, without which nothing can be possible in our life. Therefore one assumes a comfortable place to sit, in a comfortable posture, with less noise, and sits there comfortably and starts paying total attention to the breathing.

Now, total attention is absolutely necessary for both tranquillity meditation and insight meditation. Without paying attention

<hr>

*Throughout this text, *shamatha* meditation refers to tranquillity meditation, and *vipassana* meditation refers to insight meditation.

to something, that thing does not exist in our mind. It is that simple. If something does not exist, how can we use it as an object of our meditation? Therefore, in order to start with any meditation, with the *vipassana* or tranquillity, we have to become aware of what exists. To know what exists, we have to pay attention, and that is why Buddha referred to *manasikarya.* In Pali, *manasi* means "in the mind"; *karya* means "putting," "keeping," or "making"—*making it possible in the mind.* In other words, the mind becomes aware of certain things. *Manasikarya:* putting in mind. Only when we put something in mind, do all mental objects somehow arise. All mental objects arise in the mind only when we pay attention to the object, to that particular object.

Now, paying attention—total, undivided, 100 percent, not 99.99 percent attention, 100 percent attention—alone is not enough. You know, even animals pay attention to things. You may have noticed when a cat wants to catch prey it has to pay total attention, otherwise the prey will run away. The cat has to pay attention to its own movement not to disturb the object. A crane that wants to catch a fish has to pay total attention, very quietly standing. So even ordinary animals pay total attention. That is not attention that we want to have; it is not enough. A cat and a crane may not pay attention with the other necessary component.

The other necessary component for meditation—tranquillity as well as insight—is mindful attention; paying attention with the origin or with the root. There are six roots in our mind. Out of them we have to select the necessary roots to pay attention to something. Out of these six roots, three are considered to be unwholesome and three wholesome. So we do not want to pay attention to something with unwholesome roots. Even an animal can pay attention to something with unwholesome roots.

Greed, hatred, and confusion are unwholesome roots. When we pay attention with greed, which is clinging or craving, we may get absorbed in the object, but we will be totally lopsided. We will not see the object exactly as it is because the moment the mind is affected by greed it is confused, prejudiced, and therefore, with that prejudiced, confused mind, you cannot see things. Moreover, when there is confusion we will not see the things as they really are. The second unwholesome root is hatred. When there is hatred, we cannot see objects as they really are. Greed is the diametrically opposite mental factor to mental concentration. Therefore, with these unwholesome roots we cannot see objects as they are.

We have to have wholesome roots when we pay attention to something. Wholesome roots are nongreed, nonhatred, nondelusion. Nongreed means generosity. In meditation, generosity has a very specific, deep, profound meaning. Generosity ordinarily is understood to be giving away material things, but in meditation generosity means letting go of things that happen in our mind during meditation. When somebody comes to meditation we ask the person to let go of things. The person begins to get confused thinking, How can I let go of my house, my wife, my children, my husband, my property,

my bank account, and all possessions and wealth that I have accumulated all these years at the expense of my health? How can I let go of all this? What it really means is that we have to let go of *things,* not *everything.* If you try to let go of everything at the beginning-of-meditation stage, it would simply be throwing away the baby with the bath water. There are certain things we have to keep and certain things we have to let go of. When we pay total mindful attention we begin to see what we should let go of and what we should not let go of. We should let go of all those things that hinder or obstruct our progress.

What is there to let go of? Greed, hatred, delusion, jealousy, anger, tension, worry, anxiety—these psychic irritants should be let go of. Don't pay attention to them. Don't get carried away with them. Just make a mental awareness and let go of them. Nongreed is generosity, nonhatred is loving-kindness, nonconfusion is wisdom. So we can say generosity, loving-kindness, and wisdom are the positive roots; greed, hatred, and illusion are negative roots.

And then, what to keep in the mind? Those things that are wholesome, supporting our practice. If we gain a little bit of concentration, we must maintain it, support it, sustain it. If we become energetic, we support it, sustain it, cultivate it. If we have a little faith in our practice, we maintain it. Don't let go of it. If we gain a little wisdom, insight, don't let go of it. Cultivate it. Similarly, there are many such beautiful, important mental factors that arise, even in the initial stage of meditation. Don't let go of those beautiful things. Cultivate them. Pay attention to them.

Stay with them. All other negative things we should let go of.

The third component of both insight and tranquillity meditation is to remember all these things. With this we begin the practice. When we begin the practice with these things, bringing our mind back again and again, over and over again to our breathing. Breathing is the wonderful object: pure, clean, without any religious connotation, ethnic connotation, geographical connotation. All living things breathe and therefore we accept it and we take it as our primary object of meditation all the time.

I'm going to explain how we gain progress in tranquillity meditation with that background. We keep paying attention to it over and over again but of course the mind drifts away. We don't know very much about our breath. Although we have been breathing from the day we were born, we do not know very much about our breath. Only when we start paying attention to our breath do many things that are unknown to us begin to unfold in the breath, and we keep paying attention to it. First we take a few deep breaths to notice the expansion and contraction of our body, and the state of breathing, and so forth. This is the tranquillity meditation method, although we use breath for both. We begin to see the mind coming closer and closer and closer to the breath. At the beginning, mind is like a wild monkey. After some time it becomes a tame monkey. So it comes closer and closer and closer to our breath. At this initial stage, our mind becomes relaxed, body becomes relaxed,

and consequently we may feel sleepy, drowsy, so we have to overcome this. This is one of the things that we have to let go of. We have to let go of the sleepiness and drowsiness. What should we do?

When we are sleepy and drowsy, it is as though we are in a prison. When you are in a prison, you don't know what is happening outside the prison walls. You are confined to the four walls. Similarly, when we are sleepy, drowsy, it's so pleasing, so comfortable, overwhelmingly pleasant and we succumb to it. It is almost impossible to proceed when sleepiness comes. The head becomes very heavy; body becomes very heavy. You know the English words are very beautiful, sloth and torpor, everything is slow. And everything in our mind and body slows down to the degree not favored in a positive way, to the negative; it becomes so slow that we fall asleep. There has to be an energizing factor at that time.

To energize the mind we have to do several things, and these are all recommended by the Buddha. One, very strongly recommended, is to pinch our earlobes with our index finger and our thumb, very hard. Hard enough that we will feel the pinch. That wakes us up. Second, take a deep breath, hold it as long as you can, and breathe out slowly. Do this exercise as many times as necessary in order to overcome sleepiness. When you do this, your body warms up, you even begin to perspire, and that takes care of your sleepiness. Third, Buddha recommended to get up and do walking meditation. Fourth, get up and wash your face with cold water. If that doesn't work, Buddha recommended visualizing an extremely bright light. Develop the perception of light.

If none of these works, go and have a nap and come back. That is going to slow down your practice but, if you had a bad night, did not have good sleep, are very tired physically, or have a lot of food in the stomach—maybe the night before that you had gone to a party and spent all night there, or you had a lot of dreams—all these things, many, many things, can affect your meditation. That is why people who are very serious in meditation have to learn to be disciplined, restrained, *vinaya*, morality—all these come in very handy and useful when we try to practice meditation.

What happens when you overcome sleepiness? Your mind becomes energetic, active; not overly active or energetic, but sufficiently energetic that you won't feel sleepy. This is why the practice builds up our own strength. This is self-evident. We don't need somebody to tell us what will happen next. And Buddha said, when this lethargic stage of mind disappears, you don't have to wish, Ah, let me have confidence. Confidence arises. As a result of your overcoming sleepiness, drowsiness, and becoming energetic from your own practice, you gain confidence in your practice. You gain confidence in the method. You gain confidence in the result. You gain confidence in your own ability. Prior to that you might have felt you are a very lousy, lazy, useless person who can never meditate, but when you take the initiative and start to practice you begin to see the result. Of course the practice has to be very committed, honest, sincere, not doing it just

to please somebody. With the commitment, you start the practice and then you see this initial result. Confidence arises in yourself.

When confidence arises, your doubt fades away. Doubt is like traveling in a desert. When you are in a desert you don't know where you go. There are no road signs, nobody to ask, no roads, nothing. And that state will disappear when you gain confidence. That is your ability to see what is ahead of you. That is called inner confidence coming from clarity. The mind becomes clear.

Of course, in meditation one thing that inevitably happens is the mind becomes clearer and clearer and clearer, and that is one of the five purposes that Buddha mentioned. For the purification of beings, we meditate. So when the mind becomes clear, confidence arises and doubt fades away. When doubt fades away, confidence arises and you become joyful. Joy arises. Naturally, when you are confident, you begin to see two sides. Are you disappointed? Sad? No, you will be joyful. And that joy arises by degrees. At the beginning a very faint degree of joy, and then it slowly builds up. What happens when joy arises? Your resentment, disappointment, anger fade away and you gain happiness.

Now joy and happiness are not one and the same thing. Joy is arising in anticipation of something. Happiness arises when that thing is accomplished. Before accomplishment there will arise joy.

It is very much again like traveling in the desert. When you travel in a desert you are very tired, hungry, thirsty, full of worries, you don't know where you go. You are right in the middle of a desert, and all of a sudden you see somebody coming toward you with red hair, red clothes, red body, fresh face, energetic, walking toward you with a smiling face. You say to this person, "Sir, I'm also traveling in the same desert, but look at me. I'm weary, tired, hungry, thirsty, full of worries, and no joy." Then the person tells you, "Sir, I just happened to see an oasis in the desert. I jumped into it, drank plenty of water, swam in it, ate lotus roots and lotus buds, and spent lots of time on it, and came out relaxed and walking with red hair, red clothes, red body, and smiling face. Refreshed myself, I'm walking." Hearing that, you will be joyful. You become hopeful and joyful, and then you think, Ah, let me try that. So you pick up more energy and continue to walk in the same direction that this man came from, and you see the oasis. As soon as you see it, without taking off your clothes you jump into it and you swim as much as you want, drink plenty of water, eat from lotus buds and lotus roots, lotus leaves. This is an oasis in the middle of a desert! Then you come to the bank, come to the beach of the oasis, and stretching your hands and legs you say, "Ah, what happiness." Joy arises in anticipation of something; happiness arises when you have accomplished, fulfilled what you have anticipated.

So when joy arises, your resentment or anger fades away. Disappointment fades away. When happiness arises your restlessness and worry fades away. In the past you were full of worries and you were restless, then you accomplished something by diving into the oasis and drinking water and so forth, and you accomplished it. Prior to that,

what you had was anticipation. When you hear this man's story, in anticipation of what you are going to see, you become joyful. You become joyful anticipating an oasis.

Happiness is not a kind of excitement. When you are excited, you become restless. When you accomplish something your mind becomes settled down, more calm, relaxed. With that happy, relaxed, calm state of mind you proceed with the practice, then you gain concentration. When you gain concentration, whatever doubt you have fades away.

When you gain concentration your mind is pliable, relaxed, elastic, and full of happiness. That state is the state where you gain concentration, and with that concentrated state of mind, you focus your mind on the object. When you focus your mind on the object with a concentrated state of mind, you see the object exactly as it is. And that is why the Buddha said "Concentrated mind can see things exactly as they are."

Now this is a very beautiful way of gaining concentration. We call this concentration *method,* and with that concentrated state of mind, we focus our mind on objects to gain insight. That is what is sometimes called "insight preceded by concentration."

Now concentrated mind can see things exactly as they are. Don't we normally see things as they are? When we see so many people around us, we should see them as they are. When we look around us we see walls, light, various colors, and so forth as they are. Friends, what we see with our naked eyes or what we hear with our naked ears, what we smell with our naked nose, what we taste, what we touch, and what we

A conference attendee in deep meditation

think normally is not what these things really are. We do not see, hear, smell, taste, touch things exactly as they are, and that is where *vipassana*—tranquillity—meditation comes in.

Now so far we have explained what tranquillity meditation does: As the term itself suggests, it tranquilizes the mind. Not tranquilizing like taking drugs or drinks, which may provide a certain amount of relaxation. What you gain from meditation is not that

kind of tranquillity or that kind of relaxation, but tranquillity and relaxation with clarity of mind. With that clear state of mind we begin to see things as they really are. We normally see things superficially, therefore we want to cultivate insight using this tranquillity, using this concentration.

Insight meditation is more subtle, deep, and profound. We use this concentration just like using concentrated force. When we say we want to see things exactly as they are, generally people think: Of course we see things as they are. We see white as white, black as black, tall as tall, fat as fat, slim as slim, what else? Anything that our eyes catch, we see as it is. But insight meditation penetrates that object more deeply. When we say *penetrates the object more deeply,* do we mean our mind can penetrate through this bell? No. Can our mind penetrate walls? No. Then what do we mean? What do we penetrate? We penetrate ourselves. Our eyes are extroverted, always outside. Ears go outside. Mind always goes outside bringing information all the time and filling our mind with information. Filling our mind with sensations. Filling our mind with visual objects. We do not pay attention to ourselves.

This concentrated state of mind that we gain Buddha described in such beautiful terms. He said that this mind, when it is concentrated, is pure, purely white—not the white of the skin—nobody has pure-white skin—*pure white.* Stainless; no psychic irritants, mind is completely free from psychic irritants. It is pliable, steady, imperturbable. Just imagine when you have that kind of mind how powerful that mind is. With that powerful state of mind we focus on ourselves, not on external things. However, when we focus that mind on ourselves, we begin to see us exactly as we are. This so-called solid body is no longer solid. It is porous; big holes are there. Microbes living on our skin we can see—all the millions of microbes we kill when we apply soap, when we take a bath, we kill them, and we can see them with the concentrated state of mind. Every one of the trillions of cells in this body

is dancing and we can see them. They are not static, they all are in a state of flux, moving, changing, never remaining the same for two consecutive moments.

Then what happens? We see our *form*—f-o-r-m—form, as f-o-a-m—*foam.* It's coming as a huge bundle of bubbles, and then it disappears. We are no longer solid. Solidity is a superficial appearance, it is not solid. That's true. If you take a very powerful microscopic lens and wear it and look at your skin, you will see the pores, changes.

I remember once, at the Smithsonian Museum, they showed a beautiful movie about going out into space. Somebody is lying down on a beach and somebody focused a powerful lens and took pictures and put it up on the screen and we saw that it is very true. Scientifically you can prove that this body is porous, changing every atosecond—an atosecond is one billionth of a billionth of a second. The body is changing, every cell is changing. We can feel it when we pay total mindful attention with a concentrated state of mind. Mindful attention itself is very powerful. Just imagine when this mindful attention is combined with concentration! That mindful state of mind can see this body exactly as it is, and that is what it means to see things as they really are.

Then we pay attention to our feelings. Our feelings, Buddha said, are like bubbles. Feelings are bubbling all the time, just like when you cook something in a pot, you only see bubbles appearing and disappearing. And that we feel, that we experience when we pay total mindful, concentrated attention to our feelings.

And then our perception is like a mirage. Actually a mirage appears to us to be real. When a vehicle is driving in front of us and we are several hundred yards away, we can see the shadow of that vehicle in the mirage, and it appears to be real, but when we get closer it is no longer there. It is a visual deception. And our perception is like that. When we get into a very heated argument and get upset with one another, then we say, "Oh, that is your perception. That is not real, that is just your perception." Ordinarily we don't think that way. You've got to get angry to think or say that. With our perception we do not perceive things as they really are. Look at ourselves: We all perceive ourselves as solid, strong, six-feet or five-feet tall, this way or that way. But we are all changing. Then *sankhara*—another untranslatable word, but some people translate it as "conditioned things." I don't think of it as conditioned things. *Sankhara* is condition*al;* that which conditions things. That which is conditioned is called *sankhata* in Pali. So these two terms are confusedly used. However, *sankhara* means all mental activities, in one sense, but it also means that all of everything in the universe is *sankhara.* Everything!

But I was explaining the five aggregates, and we had come to *sankhara,* mental activities, which I compare to one English word: *onion.* Onion has "on" and "on," with "i" in the middle. All of our *sankharas* are going on and on and on with "I" in the middle. Every *sankhara,* every mental activity, is generated, originated, produced, and caused by "I." In the past, it was going on and on and on because of the "I"; in the future it will go on

and on and on because of the "I." "I" is trapped in this *sankhara,* in this continuous, on-going process. When we peel the onion layer by layer, eventually we don't see anything we can call a core, heart. Similarly, when we analyze or look at our *sankharas,* all mental activities, and try to go to the origin of them, there is no single core, origin, or one single entity. What we see is an ever-changing process that can go on and on and on because I is there. The moment the concept of I stops or is brought to an end, the process of continuation stops. No more *sankharas.* When one comes to the end of *sankhara,* we are known as "one who has reached the end of doing." He has nothing else to do. Buddha said that individual has done what has to be done. We can reach that state only when we get rid of this notion of I by seeing our mental activities exactly as they are, with concentrated mindful attention.

The last of these aggregates is consciousness. Buddha said, "Consciousness is exactly like magic." Suppose there is a magic show and one of you wanted to see exactly how this person performs this magic. You go behind the stage and hide yourself behind the screen and watch this person. He will come with his stick in his hand, hat on his head, and he'll take the hat and show everybody it is empty, nothing in it. He takes it back, puts his hand in it, turns it around, blows, and takes out a pigeon. Standing behind the screen and looking through that hole, you will see what this person does. He has an empty hat and the pigeon in his pocket. He is so fast that he can deceive everybody and create a pigeon.

When you come out of hiding, your friends will be sitting in the audience and ask you, "Have you seen the magic?"

"He did no magic. There is no magic," you say.

Then your friends will think: Ah, my poor friend. He's so confused he has not seen magic that all of us have seen.

And you will think: How deceived my friends are. How foolish and gullible they are, that they think that this is something real.

This word *gullible* is also a beautiful Pali word. It is used in English in a very good sense, but, in Pali it means "swallow bait." You swallow the bait. Any bait that I give you, you swallow it, and I fool you to my direction. So many people gullibly swallow anything and think, This is real. When we practice *vipassana,* we cannot be cheated, we cannot be deceived. You will see the reality of yourself. When you see the reality of yourself then, as the Buddha said, you see yourself exactly as you are—your body, your feelings, your perceptions, your thoughts, your consciousness. Then you compare them with those of others. Ordinarily we compare ourselves: How much money we have, what is my bank account, what is my height, what is my color, what are my possessions, what is my relationship with other people? How about so-and-so's height, color, situation, position, and so forth? So we always do this kind of comparison. But when we practice *vipassana* meditation, we also compare ourselves with others. How? These so-called *my* form, feelings, perception, thoughts, and consciousness are no more different from other's forms, feelings, perceptions, thoughts, and conscious-

nesses. Their forms, feelings, perceptions, thoughts, and consciousnesses are not different from mine. We all are made up of the same material, the same elements. We are no different. We all are the same. We all are in the same boat traveling in the same *sankhara,* going through the same problems, experiencing the same suffering. We are no different. And that is why Buddha said, "Comparing oneself with others, one abstains from doing wrong things to others." That, of course, goes along with the biblical "Golden Rule," and Buddha said that six hundred years before Jesus Christ said it.

[Bhante Gunaratana completed this presentation by inviting the participants to join him in sitting meditation. He began with the "Loving-Kindness Meditation," inviting any who knew it to join him in reciting it. He next directed the practice by explaining his breath-centered focus, an excerpt of which follows.]

With these beautiful thoughts of loving-kindness in mind we begin our practice. At this point, we may take three deep breaths to notice the sensation of breathing. When we breathe in and out, we notice the expansion and contraction of our gut area, abdominal area, and chest area. Noticing these three places of expansion and contraction, breathe deeply three times and then breathe nor-mally, letting the breath flow in and out freely, effortlessly, and pay total, undivided, mindful attention to your breathing. In order to gain a degree of concentration, you may pay attention to the point where the breath touches, as you breathe in and out—the tip of your nose, or rims of your nostrils, or upper lips, or inside the nose between the eyes. Once you've found it, pay total, undi-vided, mindful atten-tion to the breathing, noticing inhaling as inhaling, exhaling as exhaling. Notice the beginning, middle, and end of each inhaling and each exhaling: inhaling, exhaling; begin-ning, middle, end of inhaling; pause; begin-ning, middle, end of exhaling; and pause. These are the points or events that occur repeatedly as we breathe in and out.

If these seem to be too many things to notice, they are too many only if we try to verbalize or conceptualize. If you do not ver-balize or conceptualize, you can notice all of them when you pay total, undivided, mindful attention, because they all happen in succes-sion. Without concept and without words, simply pay attention.

At the beginning that will be difficult because from the moment we learn words and concepts to this moment, we have been trained to verbalize and conceptualize clearly. Temporarily we have to suspend that training and pay total, mindful attention to the occur-rences of breath. That keeps your mind fully occupied on the breath, and then the mind begins to see very wonderful and marvelous things in the breath. Relaxed breath is noticed as relaxed breath, Shallow breath as shallow breath, short breath as short breath, long breath as long breath. No two breaths

can be breathed twice. Each breath is totally individual and independent of the others and they appear and then disappear.

Along with the breath, whatever sensa-tions or feelings arise change as the breath changes. Feeling is neatly, tightly connected with the breath. Every perception related to the breath and its feeling also changes as the breath and feeling changes. Every thought related to the breath changes as the breath, feeling, and perception change. Every state of consciousness along with the thought, breath, feeling, and perception changes. We can sim-ply notice them, become fully aware of them, and all we have to do is keep paying atten-tion to them. Words, concepts, and ideas can get in our way and interrupt the flow of awareness. We want to keep the mind in the present moment. The words also can inter-rupt the awareness of the present moment. We have to interrupt the flow in order to verbalize something or conceptualize some-thing. When we verbalize, what we would want to notice would no longer be there. It slowly slips under the word, like undercur-rent; it passes away very quickly when we try to verbalize. Therefore, what we verbalize may not be what we experience in the pres-ent moment, but what has already happened.

There's no meditation without wisdom, no wisdom without meditation. One who has poor wisdom and meditates is close to peace and emancipation.

Shikan–
Calming the Mind,
Discerning the Real

Paul Monshin Naamon

TENDAI IS ONE OF THE MOST SYNCRETIC FORMS OF BUDDHISM. For example, the word *Tendai* is the Japanese word for the Chinese *T'ien-t'ai*. Unlike many other schools, whose beliefs, practices, and characteristics change greatly as they cross national or cultural boundaries, Tendai and T'ien-t'ai remain nearly identical doctrinally. In addition, Tendai is the root of most modern schools of Buddhism in Japan, including Soto and Rinzai Zen, Jodo-shu, Jodo-shi-shu, and Nichiren.

Shikan, the basis of Tendai methods, is the Japanese form of *Chih-kuan,* which in turn is Chinese for *Shamatha-vipassana.* This practice combines tranquillity meditation and insight meditation by following a ten-step process, first calming the mind and body, then progressing to attain insight into Buddhist teachings. In his workshops,* Paul Monshin Naamon provided a sketch of the early history of T'ien-t'ai/Tendai and then discussed in more depth the underlying concepts and principals of *shikan.* He also directed meditations that demonstrated the basic elements of *shikan* practice.

Mr. Naamon is Abbot of the Karuna Tendai Dharma Center at Canaan, New York. He has been a practicing Buddhist for more than twenty-five years, during which time his six years of formal training for Shokke-Tokudo (priest's ordination) was with Masao Shoshin Ichishima in Japan. as well as at Taisho University, and Sensoji and Tamonin temples.

---

* Mr. Naamon led two sessions at the conference. In one, he dealt with the historical background of Tendai and he shared his insights regarding contemporary Buddhism in the West. The other, longer session was devoted to the practice of *shikan.* The text that follows is drawn from both sessions. A brief history of Tendai precedes Mr. Naamon's introduction to the practice of *shikan.*

Tendai was established in Japan by a fellow named Saicho who lived from 767 to 822. This was the Heian era in Japan, just after the Nara period, during which the three major schools of Japanese Buddhism were Kegon, Hosso, and Sanron. Those three schools primarily viewed themselves as what today we would call Hinayana schools. Saicho really brought Mahayana Buddhism to the fore in Japan.

The practices at that time in Japan had been brought primarily by Chinese monks, and Japanese people, being to a large extent ethnocentric, would never have permitted a Chinese monk to establish a school. In order to get the initiations and to recognize the authority necessary to create a school and to create the teachings, Saicho went back to China, where he stayed for a matter of nine or ten months. While there he received initiations in the Ox-Head school of Zen, Soto, and Rinzai Zen; he had also studied Mikkyo, or esoteric Buddhism, in which he received a number of initiations; and he was ordained into the platform of the *Lotus Sutra,* T'ien-t'ai Buddhism. T'ien-t'ai is located a little bit south of Shanghai.

In China in the sixth century was a fellow named Chih-i (to the Chinese, Chi-che), who was not really the founder of T'ien-t'ai Buddhism, but rather, one of its popularizers. He is certainly the most notable patriarch and the one that we remember primarily when we look at our history books. His original training was that of a Zen master. I have a real affinity for Chih-i because the difficulty he had was that he thought sitting was great,

but he also kept saying Is this all there is? I've been practicing now for nearly thirty years and I had reached a point in my Zen practice where I kept saying This is great, but is this all there is? It's not a disparagement of Zen at all, it's a recognition that each of us has to find a path that resonates within us. Not that there is a right path or a wrong path but that there are lots of different paths —which one do we choose to take? Some Zen practitioners say This is great and I don't need anything else, and that's good. So Chih-i began doing lots of stuff. He was the first person who really systematized Buddhist teachings to a large extent. You can blame Chih-i for a lot of the eight these and ten those and twelve this and four of this and five of that.

He taught six basic types of meditations. The first one, which we sometimes overlook, is repentance. Many Buddhists don't realize that repentance is a necessary element. It's an essential aspect and there's a meditation on repentance. Essentially, repentance in it's most simplified form says that I recognize that I have developed bad karma through my body, speech, and mind and I now repent them all. That's a very basic repentance. There's also *zazen,* sitting Zen; and he felt that *kinhin,* or walking meditation, is very important as well. Chanting was very important to Chih-i, as was the use of visualizations as a part of meditation. The six senses became important because he felt that *samadhi* does not just take place on the cushion, it takes place while we're chopping potatoes, it takes place while we're getting out of the way of the ox in the middle of the road, it takes place during all sorts of mundane activities. It's an opportunity for *samadhi,* it's an opportunity to calm the mind and to develop that.

So we see from a historical perspective that, at the time of Chih-i, Mikkyo or these esoteric practices were not explicitly done, though one might infer that in fact they were there. We do have some evidence that even in the sixth century some esoteric practices were taking place. It comes down now to what do we call esoteric practices. We think of the *mudra* and mantra as the primary elements of esoteric practice, but we see some of those at the time of Chih-i.

Perhaps most important for the later development of Buddhism in Japan was Chih-i's reliance upon the *Lotus Sutra,* which had been translated earlier, but really came to the fore as an important piece of spiritual literature at that period of time.

Saicho brought T'ien-t'ai—Tendai is just the transliteration of that word—back to Japan around 800, and it became state Buddhism. At the time, the three major schools were Hosso, Sanron, and Kegon, and a fourth school, Ritsu, also developed at this time. Previously Hosso, Kegon, and Sanron each had three scholars who would go to the ordination platform. Three monks each— nine a year—were the only priests permitted in Japan. We have more in this hotel than all of Japan had in 800. And so when Saicho changed that form of state Buddhism, they reduced the other three schools to two each and they gave a couple to Tendai and

Ritsu, maintaining a total of nine all together. This is important because historically Buddhist priests had always mucked about in politics, to say the least. One of the reasons that Nara Buddhism fell was because the priests were mucking around a bit too much and the emperors not only became alarmed, but almost became overrun by priests. After this the priests were still mucking about, but they moved them from Nara to Kyoto so they couldn't muck about to quite the same extent. This is right around 823.

As I mentioned before, what Saicho did was not necessarily original. *Lotus Sutra* had already been in Japan. Mythologically it's attributed to Prince Shotoku, which is around the fifth century. Mikkyo had already been there, all of these other things were already there, but he was putting it together. As a matter of fact the person who had first brought Mikkyo to Japan was a Sanron priest, whose practices got incorporated within Shugendo, and this is as early as the sixth century. These were mountain monks. My suspicion is that Saicho may have actually been exposed to these practices when he was a young monk on Mount Hiei, which is where he had practiced. Later Mount Hiei became the sacred mountain of Tendai and the guardian for the city of Kyoto, until the Kamakura era, which was the twelfth century.

Now the successor to Saicho really fleshed out what Saicho brought. He brought a format that later was fleshed out by Ennin and Enchin. Others later made the *Lotus Sutra* more important. Two real aspects that became much more important after Saicho emphasized them were, first, a reliance upon the *Lotus Sutra.* Before that in Japan other sutra were used, including the *Lotus,* which had never been a very important sutra. Now the *Lotus Sutra* is unarguably the foundation of modern Japanese literature. The most repeated sutra in Japan is the *Heart Sutra,* but the most influential is certainly the *Lotus Sutra.* In art, in literature, in music—tomes and tomes exist about how influential the *Lotus Sutra* is in Japanese history.

The other thing that was very important were the meditation methods that he brought with him, which include meditation methods not only of Chih-i through T'ien-t'ai, but also the some that we find in Mikkyo, mandala meditations for instance.

There was another character at the same time named Kukai who was a Shingon priest. And Kukai in Shingon is referred to as Tomitsu, which literally means "primarily Mikkyo," primarily this idea of esoteric practices. And Tendai was not Tomitsu, it was Tamitsu, which would be loosely translated "with Mikkyo practices." Today, many Buddhologists really look at Shingon as being an esoteric school and they don't recognize that Tendai is also a Vajrayana school.

During the Heian era, from about 754 to about 1100, lots of changes occurred, and right at that interface between the Heian to the Kamakura eras, around 1100, we see something very important happening to Japanese Buddhism. Until this time, Buddhism in Japan was the Buddhism of the aristocracy. It was the Buddhism of the elite, not a Buddhism of the people.

As a matter of fact, one of the reasons Mikkyo was done is because Taoism became very strong once it had been introduced into Japan. This idea that Taoist priests could maneuver the elements—hell, they could make it rain when you had a dry period! They could make the floods go away!—Mikkyo could do this. All you had to do was a few *mudra* and mantra and he would make the flood waters go away. Because in China, as in Japan, the emperor was not just somebody who lived high on the hog. If you had a flood and the flood waters didn't go away, they were going to find another emperor because the emperor was a descendant of the gods and you had the wrong one if you had too many floods. This wasn't just mumbo-jumbo, these were life-and-death activities.

And so during this period around 1100 we see the flourishing of new sects in Japan. The elements had all been there but they didn't have leaders, or at least they didn't have leaders that are identifiable today. But this period saw a fluorescence of popular Buddhism, of Buddhism of the masses. Honen (1133–1212) founded the Jodo school; Shinran (1173–1262) began Jodo-shin-shu; and Nichiren (1220–82) instituted his offshoot. What distinguished this Buddhism from the Tendai that had gone before—the Buddhism of Shingon, the Buddhism of Kegon, the Buddhism of Sanron and Hosso and Ritsu and several others? Salvation.

In addition, it was something that everybody could do. If you were rich and you were part of the aristocracy you could go to a fire *puja,* you could go to a *goma* ritual. You could go to see the priests do these things and you could get somebody to do it for you. You could essentially contact somebody and say "Could you send that priest over. I'm having trouble with my rice fields." Farmers couldn't do that. If farmers had difficulty, what were they going to do? They couldn't call the local priest—there was no local priest. It became, primarily through the use of chants if we look at Jodo-shu and *nembutsu, Namu Amida butsu,* devotional practices. You don't have to sit on a cushion for ages to learn how to do it, you can learn to recite it, it's very simple, and you can do it. And you are essentially empowering your life! Nichiren, NAMO HO RENGE KYO, the same thing. You're providing a means for people to take part in these activities. Up to this time, Buddhism was something that everybody said, "Oh, I've got to be nice to the monk because he might off me if I'm not looking carefully." You know , this was really a problem because at that time some of the monks were running around with swords.

So you have this idea of salvation. If you believe in Amida, you can have salvation. As a matter of fact you go to a world called Jodo—"pure land." Pure Land Buddhism was a very powerful school in China and was not new to Japan, but it had not been introduced to the Japanese population as a whole. It was up to Saicho, and later his disciples, to introduce it into Japan.

Additionally during this time, some of these characters, specifically Nichiren, really posed a threat to the status quo. Can you imagine being a shogun and all of a sudden having your form of Buddhism (which by the twelfth century had actually become Zen Buddhism) be supplanted by a group of people chanting *Namu Amida butsu Namu Amida butsu Namu Amida butsu Namu Amida butsu* —and they really believe it! It's one thing to do it but it's another thing to believe it. As a result, Nichiren, who was not blameless in this whole affair, was banished to Sado Island. Shinran and Honen were not persecuted to the same degree because they weren't trying to foment revolt the way Nichiren did.

So, many Tendai priests were breaking away and forming sects that were of the people. And there were other schools—Eisai founded Rinzai Zen; and Dogen's disciples founded Soto Zen—about the same time, but these were not popular schools. They served the purposes of the samurai, the warrior caste. We have the emperor: He or she is above the caste system. Then we have the warrior caste, which we refer to as the samurai. Then we have the farmers, the merchants, and the craftsman, and then the untouchables, and others. The samurai caste really latched onto Zen, which was never a popular school either, even though Soto Zen today is probably the second most populous school in Japan, Jodo-shin-shu being the most populous school.

Shamatha-Vipassana Meditation

Sometimes I think, within the Tendai tradition, we get involved in what happened after the fifteen century and forget what happened back in the sixth century in China, which was really important. The practice we're going to do really reflects that tradition today. Then, we're going to connect that to what happened in China, which is a more esoteric tradition. Now by esoteric, we mean the use of *mudra* and mantra. In the seventh century, an Indian pundit and a Chinese scholar went to Tibet to try to convince the Tibetans what they should be doing, so this dual tradition arose in sixth-century China and in seventh-century Tibet of the study of the *vipassana* and *shamatha* together. *Shamatha* is the portion that we refer to as "calming the mind" and *vipassana* is the portion we refer to as "discerning the real." Many of you know Shamatha by virtue of Soto Zen practice and *shikantaza*—just sitting—as a form of Shamatha practice. Vipassana involves meditations into self.

Chih-i, the founder of T'ien-t'ai Buddhism, writes that Chih-kuan [Shamatha-vipassana] is a reliable method of provoking full awakening. By inference, he was saying that if you just do one, you're not going to get it. Now, Shakyamuni Buddha spoke eighty-four thousand lectures, and if he did that many, he had to assume that different people had different needs at different times, so I'm not going to go so far as to say that Chih-kuan is the only way to go, but it's certainly a very useful method. Chih-i wrote that *shamatha* unties the bonds of the mind and *vipassana* roots out delusion. What you see here is a duality: You've got to let things go before you can root out the delusion. He

also wrote that *shamatha* nourishes mind and senses, whereas *vipassana* is the art of developing spiritual faculties.

Chih-i had practiced Ch'an previous to founding his own school and he felt that practicing Shamatha in China at that time developed a sense of ego. The people were supposed to be getting rid of ego, but in fact they were developing ego. He also felt that Vipassana developed arrogance, the reason being that Vipassana was practiced by *arhats*—individuals who went into a monastic existence, separated themselves from society, and studied "for their own benefit." Whereas the Mayahanists, and specifically those who were practicing Shamatha, reportedly were doing it for other people. Therefore, Chih-i felt it was very arrogant to say, essentially, I got mine.

By doing *shamatha,* you're concentrating, you're calming the mind; "concentration-contemplation" is another term for Shamatha-vipassana. Calming the mind leads you to a place where you can deal with things like anger, conceit, or craving much more easily. Discerning the real is a more specific way of dealing with things once you realize that's your problem. First you need to know you've got a problem, and then you have to have something to work with it. So sitting, calming the mind, gives you the idea—Hey, I've got this craving always coming about; or I've always got this conceit, I'm always comparing myself to this other monk over here. What's going on? It's great that you find it out, but what are you going to do with it? Vipassana is what you're going to do with it.

The *Lotus Sutra* tells us that, taken together, Shamatha-vipassana is seen as two wheels of a chariot that carries the Buddha. If one wheel falls off, you're going to have a big problem. One of the very basic ideas of this is that you have to have a balance. It doesn't mean that you have to spend twenty-four minutes on this one and twenty-four minutes on that one, but over time you have to balance out these two. Otherwise, you're going to fall off your chariot.

Chih-i offers ten essential steps—which are important in meditation—to the path. First you have to create a favorable condition. By favorable condition he means that it's difficult to sit if there's a kid screaming around the house. It's difficult to sit if you're uncomfortable. (I don't mean because your legs hurt a little bit. I mean if your condition is truly uncomfortable—you're poor; you don't have enough to eat; you're not warm enough in your home; other people in your family are suffering.) Creating a favorable condition is necessary to follow the path. We sometimes overlook that aspect of it. How do we nurture the spirit if all around us things are falling apart?

The second essential step is to rebuke all desires. That does not mean that we go out and become monks and nuns. It means that we recognize what the desires are and we take those desires and work with them. Sometimes it's more important to use it as a tool than it is just to walk away from it. It's a little bit different now than in the society of China in 700. We look at our desires today, at what our favorable conditions are today.

We have to reinterpret that for what we're going through. These texts were written twelve hundred years ago and say, "Do this," which was great twelve hundred years ago, but twelve hundred years ago they didn't have to put up with traffic jams. They might have had to put up with an emperor who was going to behead them, but that's a different sort of problem. We have to find solutions to *our* problems, not enact the solutions to *their* problems.

The third thing is to remove all encumbrances, which means that we have to let go of the fact that we have a goal. What an idea! Having a goal is an encumbrance to this whole process. It is essential that we let go of that. Somebody recently asked me "How long do I have to sit before I reach enlightenment?" We have to remove that encumbrance—the fact that there is no goal in it. One of my *sangha* members said to me "Why should I come and sit on my butt for an hour in a cold zendo if I don't have a goal?" In this case we have to look back to Dogen, who said "Sit because you sit."

The fourth thing is to regulate food, sleep, body, breath, and our meditations. We have to regulate ourselves to a certain degree. Somehow, when we talk about meditation, we forget this stuff, but it's because sometimes the basic level is where we have to go back to.

The fifth thing is to conduct ourselves with dignity. What a concept. We can talk about moral precepts. We can talk about ethics. Conduct yourself with dignity. The ethics and the moral constructs will come along with it. By dignity, I mean not just the way you hold your body, but doing things that will bring credit upon yourself, upon your family, upon your nation. Doing things that reflect the values you would choose to espouse. And, of course, practicing mindfulness. Right now, mindfulness is the hot topic in Buddhism. Thich Nhat Hanh is a wonderful, wonderful monk and he's made that sort of a common denominator for American stress reduction—to be mindful. It really comes from a sixth-century construct. One of the meditations Chih-i talked about specifically was the meditation of living: How we cut the onion is as important as what we do on the cushion; being mindful when we are scolding the children is perhaps more important than what we do on the cushion, because it's affecting other sentient beings.

Sixth, manifest good qualities: Basically live up to your own expectations of morality and ethics, etc.

Then, recognize Mara, which means recognize when the evil arises within us. Recognize when that seed of anger begins to sprout so you can then control it in some way. In the Western construct, we talk about evil as we talk about God—it's the other. In Buddhism, we talk about evil as we talk about Buddha—it's the inside. So evil does not arise out there, evil arises in here, and that is where we have to approach it. We have to say, Wait a second, I'm getting pissed. What am I going to do about it? Instead of getting pissed and then two hours later realizing you slammed your fist into the car, broke the dashboard and your hand, and

now everybody is upset. That's Mara—recognition of that evil that's fomenting within us.

Now these are all progressive. Eighth, we have to heal ourself, both physically and psychically. Healing ourself also means that we have to recognize our limitations. Through these things, we will eventually reach enlightenment.

Meditating on the cushion is just one aspect of meditation. It's the cushion practice. Just saying I'm going to be mindful is great, but it may not necessarily give us the tools to do it. So taking off the cushion into your life it a wonderful cycle. You sit on the cushion, you calm the mind, you discern the real, you take that into your life, you take that to your children, you take that to your family, you take that to your employer, you take that to your coworkers, you take that to the bus driver, and then you sit on the cushion and you take all those things with you in a very real fashion and work with that and just keep building and building and building.

Awakening can come suddenly. Awakening can come gradually. Awakening can come through the secret methods and awakening can come through the combination. History tells us that awakening comes suddenly to very, very few. Awakening comes gradually to some. Awakening comes by secret methods to others. Awakening comes to most by a combination of these methods. But awakening does not just mean feeling good about oneself; awakening means taking this into the world, and how we do this is an essential practice.

How does all this fit into esoteric practices? Esoteric practices essentially are the use of the body, speech, and mind. When we're sitting in *shamatha,* doing *shikantaza,* we're just sitting. We're calming the mind. We recognize that something is happening Sometimes we need a little boost, as Ichishima Sensei said, "Sometimes to get to the moon, you need a rocket." So sometimes we get to the moon through transcendental processes, but most of us need a rocket, and these esoteric traditions are, to a certain extent, using a rocket.

Within Tendai we use mandalas. To be quite candid, in Japan Tendai priests do not sit around the temple all day looking at mandalas in meditation. They are running around doing funerals and memorial services and things that priests do everywhere. But mandalas are very useful tools, and only that. They're tools for focusing the mind and for transforming ourselves into the characteristics of those deities and beings that lie within the mandala.

[In answer to the question "Is a mandala supposed to have power in it?" Mr. Naamon responded:]

All the power from anything comes from within us. It's not an objective, outside element. The things you view from this tradition are things that you view to have power, but they're invested with the power that you are creating. It's not the statue that has the power. The mandala itself is an arrangement of energy forces, which is powerful. But the power to you is power that you invest into it, and the power you receive from it in the interaction with the mandala.

[Mr. Naamon continued by discussing five classic meditations, one appropriate for each of the five poisons.]

Once you've reached a calm mind, then what do you do with it? Once you've determined that it's craving that keeps popping up or it's conceit that keeps popping up, it will change. Today it's craving, tomorrow it's conceit. These are the five poisons: distraction, anger, craving, conceit, and spiritual ignorance. For distraction the meditation really is mindful breathing—Shamatha practice. So the first one is to watch the breath coming in and the breath going out, to calm the breathing, to feel the harmony within oneself and within those around us.

When you're sitting, you are not trying to go within your shell. What you're trying to do is say, "I recognize that that noise is there, but it's there, it's not here." By going into your breath, you're recognizing the noise, but allowing it to be there instead of here. When we have emotions and feelings that are damaging, we can look at them and say, "Yes, that anger is there and it's part of my reaction to a situation, but *I'm* not anger. It's the emotion that is anger and I've got to let go of this anger."

Then, anger: You're driving down the street and somebody pulls in front of you. You lay on that horn and, in that situation, what happens? You get really upset. Your blood pressure is increasing. Your heart rate is going off the wall. The person in the car is saying "Why the hell is that guy honking at me?" They didn't even realize that they pulled out in front of you; they wouldn't have done it if they had seen you. What's happening is the anger is affecting you. It has no effect on that person, unless you ram their car, and recognizing that that anger is just something that's arising within us and something we can let go of is really important.

Here we have to be very careful. Don't confuse this with creating a situation and justifying your reaction to another person by saying, "Hey, that's their problem." That's a consequence of taking this to an extreme and not recognizing the difference between true anger and using anger as a justification. I've heard people who have been sitting for a period of time, perhaps when a relationship is going sour, say to the other person, "Well, I'm beyond feeling like that." That's repression and you don't want to repress it, you want to let go of it. There's a difference. Just be aware that some people can use that as a justification for other actions. The way we get through anger, the way we treat anger is very important. You breathe in the suffering of others and you breathe out compassion.

This is where the Vipassana and esoteric practices really begin to mix. We start with a mother, picturing our mother when she was pregnant. It's the middle of August and it's hot and sticky and you're very pregnant and no matter where you sit, you can't get comfortable. No matter how you lay on the bed, you can't get comfortable. Or it's the middle of winter and you're cold and your coat

doesn't fit around you. The object is to visualize this like it's in front of you. To visualize your mother; visualize your birth. What suffering! The suffering and the joy that happen simultaneously, I'm sure, but there was still suffering involved in that; and imagine getting up at two in the morning with this little screaming brat and you want to sleep. My God, do we owe our mothers an incredible thanks for taking care of us and not tossing us out the window. You just keep going with that. Every time you breathe that image in, you breathe out compassion.

Start with your mother, then go on to your father. Go on to your Uncle Fred, your Aunt Frances, etc., until you reach the point in these meditations where now your dealing with that S.O.B. you work with who keeps putting work on your desk because he or she doesn't want to do it and you recognize that there's nothing you can do about this person's habits. You recognize their suffering. How insecure that person must feel because they have to have you do their work. How afraid they must be that their boss is going to find out that you're doing the work for them. Can you picture the scenarios? Every time you breathe that image in, you breathe out a feeling of compassion. That's dealing with anger. You're learning to transform this experience of objectification of anger into something useful. If you do it for a while, you will see a change in your relationship with people and, hopefully, their relationship with you.

People probably have most trouble with anger and craving. The meditation for craving is contemplation of the ten stages of the corpse. This is a magnificent meditation. It's the first meditation I do every morning. Contemplation on the ten stages of the corpse is both the easiest contemplation and the most difficult contemplation you can do.

When you do this meditation, picture your body laying on a funeral bier and people coming up to it. You're up in the corner of the room looking down upon yourself and you see your best friend crying over your body. You see your spouse and recognize the difficulties in their life as a result of your dying. You recognize that you feel liberated. You see your body being taken to the crematorium and you see your body beginning to dissolve in flame. You see the flames coming up and consuming your body and you picture the flames going up and the ashes that remain. You keep visualizing this until finally, all that remains is a very fine ash and you recognize that that's all there is, but you're still there.

One of my favorite meditations is one in which I'm on a mountain top and I picture birds coming along and picking at my flesh until I see the bones underneath it. Then I see the bones bleaching in the sun and I see the bones over time dissolving into nothingness. You go out that day and recognize what a marvelous gift we have in this life.

[A man asked how this sort of meditation worked for a food craving, suggesting it could be seen as "I'm going to die anyway, why not just eat the cake."]

Paul Monshin Naamon: I'm not saying this is a weight-control method. For the cake it's more useful to picture the cake rotting. In terms of spiritual practice, the visualization leads us to recognize that this bag of bones is only that, a bag of bones. Our spirit continues through this.

At hospice, at any given time I probably have somewhere in the vicinity of twenty patients and of those twenty people, most will be dead within three to four months. Some will be dead next week. You can see how it would change my relationship to those people, but believe me, it also changes my relationship with people who are perfectly well; that are walking around and having a great time and wondering how many potato chips they should buy for the Super Bowl.

This is profound, to recognize the limitations we have within the corporeal stuff here. And it's a very useful meditation for craving, because craving, ultimately, is attachment to this body and a feeling that this body is who we are. Craving itself is not who we are.

[A woman asked how to disentangle the idea of craving from being the goal of sitting. She referred to "a deep craving" in herself, that arises due to an illness. "I see a deep craving in myself and...a desire to heal," she said.]

Paul Monshin Naamon: Well, because you want to be healthy does not necessarily imply craving. Craving is something like "I really want that Ferrari or that Porsche." Being healthy is recognizing that you would like to feel better. That's why all of us are doing this: At some level we want to feel better. It may not necessarily be physical, it could be psychological, there's no difference. This is not a goal if you recognize that it may not happen, and you do it anyway.

The meditation for conceit is the meditation of six elements: earth, fire, water, air, heavens, and consciousness. In this situation, to get over the idea of conceit, you begin by dealing with earth. You picture your body as just elements of the earth—just components of potassium and calcium, things that are in the dirt. Then you visualize the fact that your flesh is made of water. You picture your bodily fluids and recognize that they are really water. Fire: Picture your lungs, picture the respiration process, which is actually a very slow combustion process, and picture this going on as a way of recognizing what conceit is.

Conceit is: "I'm the center of the universe...and you're not. I'm better than you are because I'm the center of the universe." To get away from that, we have to recognize that I'm the same as you. The only difference is I'm occupying this space and you're occupying that space. But there's no difference in us. We each have such a level of interconnectedness that we cannot separate. Once we get down to the elements, literally the elements, of earth and fire and water, we can begin to work through those.

Usually people who are conceited don't recognize it, so this is one that almost has to be given to you by a teacher. That's a difficult one to recognize in ourselves sometimes. If we do enough Shamatha meditation it might come to that point.

The fifth one is spiritual ignorance, and that's a meditation on the Wheel of Life, which is the wheel that shows the various stages through existence and the various realms of existence. In this case, you just place it in front of you and visualize the first step and meditate on it a while, then visualize the next step and meditate on it. We do this because sometimes spiritual ignorance comes from the fact that we somehow feel we're above all this. To me, the most spiritually ignorant individual is a fifteen-year-old. They're going to live forever, they're the smartest person in the world, nothing else counts, and they're probably the most spiritually ignorant. It's a wonderful-terrible stage to be in; wonderful because it's transitional. So, for spiritual ignorance, we take on the process of recognizing that we have somehow to deal with the lot that we have—the cycle of birth, illness, old age, and death.

[In preparation for the directed meditation that followed, Mr. Naamon led the participants in the Zen form of prostration, then in a repentance, during which each person repeated: "Over many thousands of lifetimes, I have created negative karma through ignorance, anger, and greed. These actions were produced by my body, speech, and mind. I now repent them all."

Mr. Naamon then acknowledged that, to many of the participants, the repentance may have seemed uncomfortably like an element of a religion they have left behind. He explained:]

I think it's important to recognize that some of you have run, not walked, from organized religion, and a repentance sounds a lot like a confession. Repentance in this case is not to God, it's to others. And it's about yourself, and it's to yourself. It's not a repentance because somebody's going to forgive you; it's a repentance as purification. If you're going to do these practices, you have to be purified. This is a form of purification and it's a form of letting go. It's a form of recognition that I'm the one who does it to myself. I'm not doing it against God. She may not even hear me. I'm doing it to myself, through my body, speech, and actions. And it's to bring that home every time and to purify oneself by saying, "Today I'm going to try not to do it again." We will—that's part of *samsara*—but we're not going to do it as much today as we did it yesterday.

[Observing that "Buddhism is wonderful in many senses. For one, every single day we reinvent ourselves and transcend our body like none other," Mr. Naamon then led the workshop in the first of two directed meditations. To begin, everyone repeated the seed syllable ram three times.]

This is a preliminary to sitting in Shamatha. We will sit quietly and, when you hear that *ram*, repeat it with me. When you feel that, as opposed to hear it, allow that sound to penetrate. The vibration it creates is what is relevant. Allow your mind to dissolve into the sound. Feel the resonance through your body. If you have a thought, allow it to drop away. Experience only the vibrations.

[Before moving on to the second meditation, the participants rose and stood quietly while Mr. Naamon explained that:]

One of the differences in this form of Shamatha is that you are alive with your eyes, ears, nose, and taste. Smell the incense. Feel the breeze against your face. Recognize the energy of the people that surround you. Just stand silently.

[The second meditation was a seated visualization, after which the participants were directed in a number of physical motions and shiatsu hand massages. The visualization follows.]

In your life there has been someone with whom you have been very close, whom you love and cherish. Visualize that person as they were the best day that you knew them. Visualize some of the time that you may have hurt them with your words, your actions, or with your thoughts, and visualize the effect it had on that person. As you breathe in, breathe in their pain and suffering in the color red. Visualize that pain and suffering coming down the front of your body into a place just below your navel, between your navel and your genitals. Within that sphere is a Sanskrit letter *vam*. Visualize their suffering coming in. As you breathe in, visualize that color and their suffering coursing into your body. As you breathe out, visualize a crystalline white light coming up the back of your body. That sphere has turned to white and you see a letter *ram*. The white light of compassion goes out the top of your head and infuses that person with loving-kindness and compassion. Continue the meditation, breathing in suffering in the color red, breathing out compassion in the color white.

[Hands in the gassho mudra, all repeated three times:]

Sentient beings are numberless.
I vow to save them.
Desires are inexhaustible.
I vow to put an end to them.
The dharmas are boundless.
I vow to master them.
The Buddha way is unsurpassable.
I vow to attain it.

[Having been sitting in seiza when completing the last meditation, one of the last questions of the workshop was: "When you're a bodhisattva, do your legs stop hurting?"]

Paul Monshin Naamon: Yes, if you're sitting long enough, but you know, when you're just beginning, you've got that pain as a remembrance of what suffering is. I don't mean this facetiously. I mean it very truly. It's a way to connect you with your life. Meditation is not to escape your life, meditation is to fully engage your life. If your legs hurt, you're fully engaged. Sometimes your nose is going to itch or your cheek is going to itch or your head is going to itch. It's your ego. Your ego is saying "Yo, I'm still here. Pay attention to me. I need attention. You're off in this never-never land again". Don't scratch it. Ignore your ego. Let it go. It will go away. If the house is on fire, respond to it, but if it's only your nose itching, go ahead.

Dzogchen

THE INNATE GREAT PERFECTION

Lama Surya Das

DZOGCHEN, ALSO CALLED ATIYOGAYANA, the ninth of the nine *yanas*, is considered the "consummate path of Buddhism" by many followers of Tibetan Buddhist practices. It is said to have been the definitive and most secret of the teachings of Shakyamuni Buddha. For centuries, this secrecy was encouraged and maintained by Tibetan Buddhist teachers and practitioners, which resulted in its wider dispersal in Western Buddhist circles being relatively recent.

Lama Surya Das* has been an avid practitioner of Dzogchen meditation for some time. He believes that its emphasis on the inherent presence of purity of mind and its flexibility in terms of practice make it particularly well suited to the lives and needs of contemporary Americans. As he says, "This is really the luminous heart of the Dharma. Not the forms, not the culture, you don't have to sit on the floor, you don't have to have Japanese wall hangings. We pray, we meditate with our hearts and minds, not only with our legs."

Bringing his ideas into a broader, Western context, the lama continued: "What we are doing is *sangha*-making. Bringing Buddhist community, Dharma community, spiritual connection beyond our little ghetto, or the New Age ghetto, or the countercultural ghetto, and into society. As the Dalai Lama said, 'Contribute to others. Don't try to convert them.' Wherever we find ourselves, take it on, this bodhisattva work. Bringing Dharma values, or truth and love, or wisdom and compassion into our program and sharing it with others, so it does, if it is meant to, spread. It is not we who do it; it happens by itself. And if we can contribute to creating a space or context or facilitation, it happens by itself."

---

*Biographical information about Lama Surya Das is included with "We Are All Buddhas," page 202.

The common ground or the core of spiritual life is its application, its practice, its actualization. Not just studying, and thinking, and talking, and theorizing about it, but its actual application or practice, bringing it into our lives, applying it in life. My own teachers in the East, the great lamas of the last generation, always say that we are all Buddhist by nature. It is only temporary obscurations like ignorance, duality, greed, anger, and so on, that veil that fact, that keep it from our eyes. We are all Buddhist by nature, some sleeping buddhas, some awakened buddhas, but buddhas by nature. That is the gospel of Buddhism. Actually, the gospel means "good news." The good news of the Dharma is that we all have this within us, not only potentially, which is one way of seeing it, but also, it *is* us. All beings are endowed with buddha-nature.

But, this leads to a certain misconception, like buddha-nature is a needle in a haystack; in there somewhere—we have to find it. The fact is all beings *are* buddha-nature, and nothing but. It's not just a needle in a haystack, it's every needle of hay in the entire stack and even the ground it is on, all the way down. So, with that holistic understanding, with that kind of awakening, that enlightened vision, we start to see things in a different light. Not just, we have to go far away to find something that we don't have, or we have to get something that we don't have from some catalog or some guru or buy it or bottle it or get it or we can't get it or it's too late to get, but we can get in another life.

We are all buddhas by nature. And not

Buddhists. I gave a weekend seminar and after I my usual spiel, and group meditation, and some chanting, a lovely old lady came up who was wearing a lovely silver cross, so I could guess that she was a Christian type of lady. Yet there she was and she said, very openly, "I loved what you had to say, but, why did you say in the beginning that we are all Buddhists? I'm not a Buddhist." "No," I reminded her, "I said we are all *buddhas*." And why become Buddhists when the point is to become buddhas? Of course, if becoming a Buddhist or being a Buddhist or a Dharmaist or Dharma-farmer or whatever new word we are going to have to coin, helps you be more of a buddha, be more of a Christ, be more sane and loving and true, then good. Whatever it takes. But, if it doesn't, who needs it? So, we believe in contributing and not just trying to convert.

One of the best contributions we can make, I feel, is to be able to embody this in a way that resonates with others. Every little good deed counts, a lot. In the way of recognizing our own buddha-nature, that is what the whole path is about.

The entire Buddhist experience or Dharma experience comes out of one thing and one thing only: the enlightenment experience. That is why everybody talks about the Buddha. We don't care about Buddha the man. We respect him, he was a man like everyone else, and we respect everyone, or try to. But, the enlightenment experience, the possibility of enlightened experience, it all comes from that and that is something that we participate in, too. It is part of us.

It is a path, it is a way. We can do it. It is

a do-it-yourself Dharma, as the Buddha said. His last words: "Work out your salvation with diligence." Don't look for Buddha to come back and send light rays. Don't look for somebody else to do it for you. Of course, others can help, but don't look elsewhere. It is all within. It is the path. It *is* the way. It is the way it happens. That is the good news, that anybody can do it and that we all participate in that. The enlightened experience is not just something that the Buddha had, it is something we all participate in, and this "great perfection" that the Dzogchen teachings talk about is not a Tibetan philosophy, it is not some kind of Oriental philosophy. It is not something that only the Dalai Lama can meditate on or practice, or for that matter, Lama Surya Das, or Lama Pajama or whoever. These teachings refer to and introduce the great perfection that is our own innate great perfection. Natural wholeness and completeness, our untrammeled spiritual nature, our purity and naturity of heart. The core of basic goodness.

So, the whole practice and path and the way of being comes out of this reality, this enlightenment, this truth. It shows up in our lives, not just because we are Buddhist, or because we meditate. We all participate in that. Who here hasn't experienced that for one moment in their life? Not just in meditating. A moment of completeness, of wholeness, of being totally at peace, at oneness. Who hasn't experienced that? That is why we say we all participate in it.

This isn't something that we can only have after doing ten or twenty years of meditation or prayer. This isn't just for monks and nuns. This is for all, all who want it, all who choose it. This great perfection—another translation is "great wholeness," "great completeness"—is beyond notions of perfect and imperfect. It includes imperfection. It includes everything. It is the way things are. It is a natural state. That is truth according to Buddhism of every school. How it is.

That is why we talk about seeing clearly. When we say wisdom it sounds like something hard to define. "Seeing clearly," "seeing things"—that doesn't just mean with the mind. Knowing things as they are, as they are right now. Not receiving some dogma, belief from the past, not blind faith. But, finding out for ourselves and seeing clearly. Penetrating with discernment and awareness, knowing things as they are and how they function.

So this great perfection teaching introduces the fact that we are all buddhas by nature, that there is no other buddha to worship. Of course we can learn from others, or we can teach others; we can share with others. But the Buddha is within each of us and is the nature of each of us. Again, even calling it "buddha" sounds too foreign, sounds like something we have to import from the Orient.

Contemporary Dharma is and has to be, and what we are all involved in, and why I think Dzogchen teaching is particularly so precious and valuable, is that it's the luminous heart of the Dharma that we care about, not just the cultural forms. Whether we sit on the floor or in a chair, with or without pants. Whether we chant or don't chant. Whether we chant in Tibetan or Sanskrit or Pali or Japanese, or we chant in

English or French or whatever our language is. Or speak from our heart with our own original heartfelt prayers—that's what counts. The authenticity of it. Not just, did they do it exactly the same before? But, is it authentic for you, now?

Of course, if we want to really follow in the footsteps of the masters of old, that's the key. Not just to follow in their exact footsteps —maybe your feet are shaped differently; maybe you only have one foot or three feet—but to seek what they sought and to find what they found. They found it in their way and we are finding it in our way. This luminous heart of the Dharma can take many forms. You can do it in a chair, you can do it at work, you can do it in family life. You don't have to be in a monastery. (Of course, you may also be able to do it in a monastery. That is a good incubator for these things.) You can do it at retreat, like Jon [Kabat-Zinn] said, after the eleventh day of his one-month retreat, he realized there is actually something going on here that has traditionally been in a monastery or in retreat; a silent, intensive, res-idential, monastic retreat. But what if you take that month and spread it out over thirty months—one day a month. That would be interesting. Then we could do it without leav-ing our families and our jobs. Or sixty half-days a month for two years. Or one or two hours a day for five years.

I am going to make a radical statement: Integration is more important than just try-ing to do it all at once in one day, or one week, or one month. That thirty days, one day a week, I think, will change your life as much or more than thirty days in a row. Because what happens when you go back after the thirty days? That is the problem, that is the challenge. Of course, a really intense experience changes your whole per-spective, and I advocate retreats. But, let's not forget the other side—integration. Bring it into daily life. Otherwise we learn something special when we go and we come back and how do we do it every day. That is a big challenge for us in the West today.

These great-perfection teachings say this is something for every moment; this moment is pivotal. There is no other moment to be concerned about. It is not about prolonging our meditation. It's about quality, attention, awareness, presence, not quantity. It's about being totally present right now, at any given moment. Quality not quantity. So in the Dzogchen tradition, we don't stress duration. We try to have many short, vivid moments or minutes of wakefulness and we keep refreshing it.

Gary Snyder, the great, wonderful American poet ecologist, anthropologist, and bodhisattva and Buddhist teacher, always says, "Five minutes in the morning and five minutes at night, that is what counts." Even if you sit for half an hour, an hour, still it's the real minutes that count. You choose, you find. How do you get those five minutes? But it's not about five minutes, it's about the second, the instant. That is why I mentioned at the beginning that it said in the Dzogchen Tantra, One moment of total awareness is one moment of perfect enlightenment. Perfect freedom and enlightenment. Not later, after you've built up enough moments, like an investment plan, to retire on. One moment, but to have that moment, continuity and practice definitely help.

Let's not overlook this moment, what we're doing right now. Not wait for something like next year's retreat, or some other time after the kids go to college that we can go to a meditation retreat or wait until Sunday to go to church. Every day is for the real churchgoing.

In Dzogchen, if we bring it back to every moment, and of course then try to enhance that or expand that, how do we do that? We do that by the practice called "seeing through" or "cutting through." In Dzogchen practice, the main practice is seeing through.

Dzogchen has been called an advanced teaching. It is something only a few yogis and mystics in Tibet and India practiced. It is not so well known in the West, although it is coming out now. There are many teachers teaching it. We've talked about the common ground, the basis, the origin of all Buddhism —all Dharma is enlightenment or an enlightening experience. The truth and the realization of it. In Dzogchen, we work with that directly. Not waiting many lifetimes or years to try to get there, but to realize that it is here and we can access it and it is our own true nature. We have to look into that directly.

That is why in the meditation I asked you to turn your mind toward itself as a kind of way of short-circuiting many of our dualistic subject-and-object mental processes. The eye cannot see itself and all that. But, if you have a mirror, guess what. The eye can see itself. So the meditation is like this kind of mirror. It is a skillful means to help us better see and know our "true self," as Buddhism calls "not self." True nature. Beyond our selfness. Self with a big S, or *anatta*, "not-self" in Pali. A transpersonal being.

Whenever you hear about enlightenment or satori, it only has one meaning: awakening. Waking up to what is, not building some new thing. That is why it doesn't take very long. Of course, it might take a long time, but it's in the moment. It happens when it is ripe. Practice helps us ripen it. Facilitate the conditions for it to happen so that we can get out of the way and it can show up any time, even right here. That is why a Robert Aitken Roshi said, "You can't produce enlightenment. Enlightenment satori happens as if by accident. But, practice makes you more accident prone." You have to show up to win. You have to be present to win. As in, *it* is always here; *we* are usually elsewhere. So bring ourselves back, whether you call it mindfulness or collectedness, recollectiveness, presence and awareness, centering prayer, holy waiting, attending on presence. It will come down to something that is not far. We may feel far from it, but it is never far from us. That is why the Dzogchen teaching keeps coming back to the idea of the innate great perfection.

We talked about all being buddhas by nature, some are sleeping buddhas, some are wakened buddhas, therefore our only task is to awaken. Our only spiritual task is to awaken. Whatever we do in the spiritual life, it needs to help us in that direction. Otherwise, it is very secondary, or worse. To awaken, to recognize who and what we are, that's the meaning of satori, of awakening, of enlightenment, of *bodhi.* Buddha means "the one who woke up." Awaken from the dream of delusion. That is recognizing reality. Recognizing your own true nature. That is the meaning of enlightenment. How do we wake up? How do we realize who and what we really are? That is the challenge of the path, if we like what the Buddha said or embodied. He teaches, he points the way, it is up to us to travel it or to walk it—or in America probably to run it.

The Dzogchen practice is about recognizing the wholeness and completeness that we all know to be there. Again, I am putting it to you: Is there anybody here who doesn't know it to be there? Who hasn't experienced it for at least one moment in this dreamlike existence? That moment of complete peace and fullness. Where nothing was missing. Where you were there. We all resonate with that. Maybe it happened to us when we were children, maybe it happened to us in bed, maybe it happened to us by accident in nature, maybe it happened to us in a moment of crisis, maybe it happened to us in a spiritual environment, a church or a meditation room. But don't we all resonate with that and know it to be true?

So then how do we live that more fully? Experience that more fully? That is the challenge; that's the way. To cut through or see through. That is the main meditation practice of Dzogchen (*khredgs chod* in Tibet, there is

no easy way to translate it). Let's just call it cutting through, or seeing through, as in seeing through the veil of illusions, seeing what is right there. As my own teacher Kalu Rinpoche said, "You are what you are seeking. You are the Buddha. You are it." Then why don't we know it? What would it take to know it? To awaken, to recognize who and what we are. To go beyond ourselves and to realize we are not who we think we are. To be as if nothing, then we are everything, one with everything. That is another meaning of "buddha." It is cutting through, or seeing through. It is piercing this veil of illusion or of dualism, the separation of dualism, self and other, you and I, good and bad. It is beyond meditation. The joy of being.

So, Dzogchen, I think, is a teaching for our times. Many traditional lamas from Tibet have said that because it is a formless awareness practice, it doesn't need a lot of studies, sutra memorization, foreign languages, fancy initiations or empowerments, monastic vows. It is something for those of sharp faculties who want to cut right to the chase. It is called a teaching for our times. We see how our times are, we understand.

We don't have time, like they did in the East, to memorize all the prayers for the first ten or fifteen years in the monastery, and then to hand-copy them all for another few years. Then to memorize the scriptures and then discuss and debate from what you memorize and then, after thirty years, to meditate. Who has time for that? We want to get right to the point, so we seize on meditation or yoga or some technique, which is good. That's only part of the whole cornucopia of rich awakening practices, but at least we get something that is real and put it into practice and find the results for ourselves; confirm what the teachings say to be true. That is another meaning of enlightenment: "confirming it for ourselves," or awakening; enlightening experiences. We have confirmed it for ourselves. We have seen things as they are. It is no longer just a rumor or something to believe in. Because, as the Buddha said, "Don't believe in it just because the Buddha said it. Don't believe it just because the scriptures say it. Don't believe it just because the elders say it or just because everybody else says it or because it is written down." Check it out for yourself. Find out if it is true, if it is conducive to the good, the wholesome, and the rest, and *then* adopt it. Otherwise leave it and go. I think that is a good touchstone for us all.

These Dzogchen teachings are something any of us can practice without learning all about Tibetan Buddhism and all kinds of esoteric things. It is very luminous, clear. There is a lot of experiential instruction about it—meditation masters, little tips and pointers that speak English. We call it the *pith* instructions in Tibetan. In other words, it is not just the curriculum of all the 84,000 Buddhist teachings in the scriptures. It is very experientially guided tips and pointers, teachings between teacher and student. That is why teachers often emphasize this as important. You get the parentlike guidance, where somebody tells you where it's at; you don't just have to learn about everything and find

your way. You actually have a guide who has been there who can show you some of the shortcuts and pitfalls.

I have a lot of faith and delightedness and gratitude also that this has come to me and our way. I hope you, too, can enjoy it and take it up. You can read about Dzogchen in some books like the *Tibetan Book of Living and Dying,* by Sogyal Rinpoche, some books by Tulku Thondup Rinpoche, Tarthang Tulku, and other people. Or in my book with my teacher, *The Natural Great Perfection.* You can learn about it by going to meditation days or retreats. You can also seek teachers and teachings and see what works. I think that is the essence of the way—to find *your* way. A very genuine, authentic way to awaken the mind and open the heart at the same time. To realize the wisdom and compassion that is the heart of Buddhism. Wisdom and compassion or truth and love, which are inseparable.

[A participant asked for suggestions of ways to learn more about whether Dzogchen might be appropriate for her, to which Lama Surya Das answered:]

I traveled the world to find it. That is always an option. You came all the way here, so this is a good start. You are doing it. What did Jon Kabat-Zinn quote from T. S. Eliot? "Not found because not sought for." Not found because it is impossible to find; not found because not sought for. Seek and you shall find. There is no shortage of it. The Dharma gates are many. Travel a little, find something like this weekend. You follow your heart, you follow your nose, you sniff around. You make a few mistakes, but you also hit a few jackpots. I have total confidence in you and your buddha-nature. You are working this out. Be fearless, bold. Enjoy it. Go to the teachers and ask for what you want. There is an ancient Buddhist tradition that we try to follow. The Buddha said, "Don't teach unless asked." Don't missionarize, don't try to convert. Only go where you are invited. Go and ask. Otherwise you might not even recognize a Dzogchen master when you see one. They can be very themselves, very ordinary. Ask. Seek. Knock. Storm the gates of heaven, whatever image fits you. Walk slowly and you will soon arrive.

[Another participant explained that he had been searching for a supportive community of practitioners for more than twenty years. He observed that "…perhaps one of the dark sides in stripping the imported cultural characteristics of Buddhism is that it can reblend imperceptibly into the environment without support for our individual practice. In other words, we become an all-too-characteristic American individually." The lama agreed, explaining further that:]

The danger in individualism is not that you are individuated, grown-up adults who can take care of themselves, but it's the ego of individualism; selfishness and egocentrism.

Maybe you need to start your own community, even if it is small or just two people, so it's something that fits you. That's

what I did. That's what the Buddha did. That's what the Vipassana people did. That's how it happens. There are a lot of institutions around, and there are a lot of new forms of community around. If those don't fit you, maybe you need to be a *sangha*-maker and a pioneer and a leader yourself. Or maybe you're not the kind of person that likes or flourishes living in community. Just like some people don't flourish in family life, they want to be a bachelor or a monastic or a priest or something else.

Don't expect too much from outside. In one way, we take refuge in the *sangha* and it is good and nice and important to go to places and see what is there for us. If we don't feel there is something there for us, keep seeking until you find something that is here for you. Part of your question suggested that we in the West threw out all of the traditional forms and now we don't have anything. That is not the case. There are a lot of very traditional places you can go and do it just like it has always been done.

[A participant whose practice put particular attention on paying close attention to every body sense, emotion, and so on, asked how Dzogchen includes body sensations.]

Lama Surya Das: That is a good question. First of all, Vipassana doesn't just deal with body sensations. It is taught that the Buddhist path is a training path. In the beginning you train very meticulously, you concentrate, you focus, you attend to the four foundations, the mindful body, feelings, mind formations,

Dharma, and so on. For that you might concentrate on breathing and focusing, even getting superfocused, as in *dhyana,* is very helpful. That is just a means to gain more wisdom and insight, which means being less fixated and meticulous and more spacious and open and flowing. Meticulous meditation goes more into a more panoramic awareness, like choiceless awareness. It is a progression. If you can practice when you are concentrated, when your mind is stabilized, when you can be present, then you don't need to concentrate on one thing. You can be with, or aware of, whatever comes up, that is the one thing every moment. But that takes a little training.

Participant: So instead of focusing meticulously on the twinge in my stomach, I could just become more spacious and the twinge is irrelevant.

Lama Surya Das: The twinge is just part of the whole parade. Of course, if you are going to work on specific things, then that is a different kind of phase of the practice. It could be more purifying meditation or healing mediation or therapeutic mediation. You're analyzing things and how they fit together. But with Dzogchen, the openness and awareness meditation, we are not dealing with the particular furniture in the room. Instead it is like blowing out the ceiling and the walls and just enjoying the spaciousness, where everything has room just to fit. Physical or mental sensations, or noise outside, everything is part of the meditation,

because the meditation is just awareness or a way of being. It is not something you have to do. So, what is the difference if you are aware of the twinge in your stomach, the sensation in your nostril, the sound in your ear, or the memory in your mind? It's just mind moments of awareness.

[When asked to expand upon the differences between Dzogchen meditation and traditional Tibetan Buddhist meditation, Surya Das first sketched out some of the basic elements of such Tibetan traditions as Theravadan Buddhism.]

The main practice in Dzogchen is the *khregs chod,* the cutting through or seeing through; the openness and awareness practice. We talked about Theravadan Buddhism, which has been transmitted from the past and has been transformed in the West into Vipassana. At the heart of that is choiceless-awareness meditation. Not breathing, not *metta,* not Theravadan anything. Choiceless awareness.

Theravadan Buddhism has a lot of circles—all kinds of things, statues and walking around stupas—but in the middle of it is the heart of the Dharma; awareness. Not even awareness meditation. *Awareness.* Attention. Zen also has outer and inner circles of clothes and rituals and whatnot. But its center is "not to," as the sixth patriarch said. That is the choiceless, open awareness we are talking about. A little further out of that circle is practice using koans, which help you get back to this "not to." Or *shikantaza,* just sitting, helps you get back to the not to. Or chanting and studying the *Heart Sutra,* which says not this, not that, not that, not that, not that. The heart of it, the sacred not, the big middle, the not. We are getting there, this is the real truth, right here, this thing.

Tibetan Buddhism looks like, and almost is, an impenetrable jungle to us outside. Let me explain a little more about Tibetan Buddhism: In the outer circle are all the temples and iconic psychedelia and colors and people and tulkus and hierarchies. Then you get a little bit closer into the center—meditation practices, a hundred thousand prostrations, a hundred thousand mantras, offerings, and debating, etc. Monasticism brings us further toward the center; then visualizations and so on, getting more to the center; concentration, inside practice. Yes, they do Vipassana and *samadhi,* even in Tibet. Getting more and more to the center, all Tibetan Buddhists agree the formless essence, the luminous heart of Dharma is Dzogchen and *mahamudra.* This isn't just my school that says this, it is how it evolved and how it is explained by the commentators. The Dalai Lamas practice Dzogchen and would agree with this.

So this can be explained in terms of the three *yanas:* Hinayana, Mahayana, Vajrayana, *Yana* means "vehicle." Then, you can explain this also in six tantric *yanas* until you get, all in all, nine *yanas,* the ninth of which is called Atiyana, or Atiyogayana, and that is Dzogchen. *Ati* means "peak," *yoga* means "union" or "oneness," *yana* means "vehicle." It is the consummate. It is the way you arrive. It is the center. It is not just the top, it's the middle. You can think of it as a pyramid. Also you can think of it as circling toward the center and arriving where you begin in your true nature, your source; your luminous, enlightened nature. All of these things in Tibetan Buddhism have different kinds of practices.

From the point of view of the nine *yanas,* or the three *yanas,* climbing the spiritual mountain, this is the progressive, the sutra, way of looking at it. You develop the seed of buddhahood—*bodhichitta,* the seed. Water it. Get the flowers of enlightenment eventually. That is the sutra vehicle.

The tantric vehicle is more nondual. You start at the center, which is where we are anyway. If you can be there, you don't need to go out. If you are there, you don't need to train. But who is there? Who can be there all the time? So maybe you need to go out a little and do a little formal practice, maybe you need to go out a lot. Maybe you need to ordain as a monk or nun for ten or twenty years so you get full-time training to help you stay home where you belong.

Dzogchen takes a little different approach. Rather than climbing up from below, as in the sutra way, we call it swooping down from above, the tantric way. Actually, the best practice is to climb up from below while having a bigger picture, the view from above. Climb up from below according to your capacity, according to your inclinations. Some people like altars, and bowing, and rituals, and some don't. That is not contradictory to this. We practice climbing the footpath, developing our buddha-nature to the full blossoming of it developmentally, while keeping in mind the bigger picture that there is nowhere to go. That there is here. This is the nondual, tantra view.

In Dzogchen is the whole thing, but there is a kind of progression: view, meditation, and action. It is the ground basis. The fundamentals: the path of practice, and the fruit, or the result—enlightenment. From the view comes a different kind of meditation practice that is more effortless, more *being* oriented than *doing* oriented. From that comes a different kind of conduct or activity in life. From the ground of how things actually are, we develop on the path to the fruit. That is the developmental model within Dzogchen itself. We are seekers, we are not just Buddha sitting under the bodhi tree. Blissed out, nothing left to do. We need to come from the ground of buddha-nature, develop it on the path, and realize the fruit. Then we realize these are all one. The fruit is actually the ground. So it is really a circle. Ground, path, and fruit. View, meditation, and action.

Finally, within Dzogchen itself are actually a lot of different practices and sections. First you practice Rushen to discern the difference between mind and awareness or finite mind and pure transpersonal awareness. Mind and *rigpa* in Tibetan. Then you practice *khregs chod,* the cutting through that opens awareness. Then you practice *thod brgal.* That is the progression of practice.

The Legs of Jin Shan, The Incense of Kao Min

CH'AN BUDDHIST PRACTICE IN THE UNITED STATES

Monks and Nuns from the City of Ten Thousand Buddhas

DURING THE SIXTH AND SEVENTH CENTURIES, Ch'an Buddhism was developing in China. Its origins stem from a blending of Dhyana Buddhism, brought from India by Bodhidharma, and Taoism, one of the two religions native to China. It wasn't until the twelfth century that these teachings found their Japanese counterpart in Zen, which is the Japanese rendering of the word *ch'an*.

Venerable Master Hsüan Hua, Dharma-heir of the 120-year-old Hsu Yun ("Empty Cloud"), was the nineteenth generational patriarch of the Wei-yang Ch'an School lineage. Master Hua spent thirty years making great contributions to the propagation of Mahayana Buddhism in the West.* Through his work, the rich heritage of Ch'an teachings began to be better known and studied in the United States. His founding of the Sagely City of Ten Thousand Buddhas was among the many spiritual gifts he gave to this country, and today it is the largest Buddhist monastery in North America.

Bhikshus and *bhikshunis* from this monastery, many of whom learned the practice of Ch'an directly from Master Hua himself, presented an introduction to some of the basic concepts and practice of this venerable tradition. They were led by Heng Sure, a disciple of the Venerable Master.

---

*See "Returning to China: An Historic Exchange Between East and West," pages 2–6, for further information about Master Hua and the City of Ten Thousand Buddhas.

Homage to the bodhisattva who contemplates the sounds of the world, sounds of misery, sounds of joy, and all kinds of sounds. When we can put those sounds in our mouths and put volumes of compassion of light in our hearts, then that energy is part of us and we'll be in harmony of body and mind.

The Buddhist door is very broad and wide and certainly some of the common denominators are found in the practice of Ch'an. Ch'an is the Chinese pronunciation of the word *dhyana*, which is the foundation of the Japanese word *Zen*. So as soon as you enter the study of Buddhism, right away you become a linguist and a multiculturalist and you have to come face to face with this multi-layered, multi-cultural texture, this tapestry that is the Buddhadharma. So now it becomes American and what do we call it? Well, our playbill said Ch'an and the same dharma, the same mind-ground dharma is being taught next door as Zen and probably around the corner as Dhyana.

Bob Thurman* talked about ripping open that layer of nasty stuff that covers the heart. They call it breaking through the barrel of black lacquer. That's an analogy for the ignorance that covers our mind. If we are possessors of the buddha-nature, why don't we know that? How come people can still push my buttons, and how come I can see forms that attract my eye and hear sounds that hook my ear. If I'm already completely in touch with all of reality, why do I narrow it

down with my false thoughts and attachments? It's because of that ignorance. And ignorance is nothing but thoughts; it's made from the mind as well, but it's thoughts that congeal and harden over habit, over lifetimes. To get rid of it takes more than just thinking. It takes the power of something equally strong to eradicate, to break open, to rub away, that "black lacquer barrel."

A teacher in this century who did that work was a monk who's name was Hsü Yun—"Empty Cloud." People considered him a sage and his disciples numbered in the thousands and tens of thousands. He passed away in 1957 at age 120 and he was the teacher who passed on the Dharma to our teacher, Master Hsüan Hua. The stories are told of him because of the lengths he went to in order to break through that ignorance.

One story tells of the time he became enlightened. Enlightenment sounds like a goal, something that we want to own and possess, and being a society that is usually able to buy or to invent what we want, we tend to focus on the goal. We come to meditation because we want to get enlightened. Well, Master Hsü Yun, despite his good start and all his ability to renounce and the fact that he was pure his whole life—he was married to two wives, but he and his wives had a compact whereby they were able to remain pure—even with this incredible start it still took him, I think, fifty-six years including a pilgrimage of three steps, one bow, from Mount Puto in the Eastern Ocean, all the way to Wutai Shan, which is in the far west, three thousand miles, bowing once every three steps, nearly dying twice. Still not enlightened; still not awakened to his original

*See Robert Thurman's keynote address, "Toward an American Buddhism," pages 450-468.

nature. Master Hsü Yun was famous for doing things like crossing his legs in June and then uncrossing them in July, sitting for an entire month before he would get down off his seat. He really single-handedly revitalized the Ch'an school in China.

So Master Hsü Yun was on Gold Mountain and he heard the word that the Kao Min Monastery was going to have a Ch'an session. In China, Ch'an sessions were quite lengthy events. You would sit for sometimes a week straight through, sometimes two weeks, sometimes three weeks in a row. This was a three-week Ch'an session, twenty-one days. They started at 2:30 A.M. and would go around the clock until midnight. Then, after two and a half hours' rest, they'd get up again and start. He heard that this was going to happen and so he set off down the mountain, planning to go to Kao Min Monastery, which is 100 or 120 miles away. None of the other monks with him could leave at that time, so they all gave him their entrance fee and said, "Please sign us up. We'll show up later."

So he set off down the mountain and he walked alongside the river. It was in spring and the rivers were running high; he was walking fast and walking at night, and he stepped off the bank and fell into the water and found himself bobbing downstream, bumping into rocks, snagging on branches, being dunked in the whirlpools. He washed downstream for two days until he ran into a fisherman's net. The fisherman hauled out this large fish and, sure enough, here was Master Hsü Yun in the net. He pulled him onto the bank more dead than alive.

The fisherman went to the nearest monastery and said, "I've caught a monk and he's too big. I can't throw him back and also I can't legally sell him. So what do I do?" A monk came and said, "That's Master Hsü Yun. My God, he's almost dead. Quick!" And so they took him into the monastery and he recovered after a day and he said, "I've got to get to Kao Min. They already gave me the entrance fee and I can't be late or they'll miss out too." They said, "We'll carry you." He said, "No, no, I'll get there myself." So he stumbled on to the monastery.

Now the custom in the monasteries was that Ch'an sessions were open to the public; anyone can come. When a monk with real virtue, someone who had a reputation or a lot of cultivation would show up, they'd say You're going to be the proctor of this session. You're going to be the abbot of this session. This is always the way. The Ch'an monasteries were really severe. This was just the way people did it. If you refused, you had to be beaten. Why? Because nobody wanted to be the administrator. Everyone wanted to sit, not go around and check up on the other people and waste your time. Since no one wanted to accept, they had to make the rule. If you refused, you were beaten with the incense board, the famous stick.

So Master Hsü Yun said, "I don't think I can be the administrator." And they said, "Ah, well, of course you realize you're going to have to be disciplined." He didn't want their pity. He didn't want to make an exception for himself and say, "I fell in the river. I'm half dead," because they probably wouldn't let him join. He didn't say anything and they said, "All right, well, if you don't want to serve…" and they beat him with the incense board. More insult, more injury.

At this point he started to bleed. They say he bled from every orifice and people said, "My God, what's wrong?" But Master Hsü Yun said, "Never mind. Just save me a spot on the bench." So they propped him up on the bench and he crossed his legs in full lotus and he sat. The first week passed this way and, bit by bit, his strength returned and he was able to sit upright.

He was pushed to the limit. His physical strength was exhausted. He was hungry. He had recovered from this ordeal, and he had been beaten in the bargain. So all of his merit and virtue, all of the work that he had done in his cultivation, in these fifty-four years, now started to come to a head and he really bore down. You could say he had nothing left. There was no other reason for false thinking or attachment. So he really was able to put his body down and he sat still and concentrated.

At the start of the second week, a kind of a radiance began to emit from Master Hsü Yun's body and he started to keep a journal. He wrote that there was one night when he suddenly felt that all of empty space somehow became solid, then broke apart. He said space and form are not different, and he said he could see through the wall of the monastery. He saw the verger, one of the other administrators, urinating in the urinal out back. He saw boats passing by on the river. The next morning he asked the verger, "Last night at two o'clock, after the last sit, did you go out to relieve nature?"

And he said, "Yes, I did. How did you know?"

Well, he went right back to his seat and at this point the other monks, including the one who had attended to him after he had been fished out of the river arrived at the monastery and they said, "Look, there's Master Hsü Yun sitting in full lotus there. We thought he would be in the infirmary. What is he doing here? He almost drowned." And the monks, who had administered the beating, said, "What? Why didn't he say so? Don't you know we almost beat him silly with the incense board?" At this point, they all said, "Please, venerable master, just sit still. You are our honored guest. You don't have to do anything but meditate. Just keep working. We're very pleased that you've come."

By that point, everybody was watching him because, by rights, he should have been laid out in the hospital. But there he was, determined to push on no matter what. It was the custom in the Ch'an monasteries that at night, maybe the last two sits that come around, they pour tea and a server, probably one of the novices, comes around and fills everybody's tea cup. So two nights into the last week, with another five days to go, Master Hsü Yun stuck out his hand for his tea cup and the server missed the cup and poured the hot water onto his hand. His cup dropped and went *ching!* and his mind opened and he was awakened, enlightened.

He said all of the work from his childhood, when he fled schooling and went out in the mountains to eat pine nuts and drink stream water, all of the work that he had done by resisting his father's desire for progeny and staying pure in his relationships, all of the work of leaving home and doing the pilgrimage was not one part wasted. Not the slightest part did he regret. He said "To think that in this life I almost missed it again," and lifetime upon lifetime of effort came to a head at that moment and he wrote two poems to commemorate the experience.

The cup fell to the ground.
The water scalded my hand.
The cup shattered with an echoing sound.
Empty space broke apart and my mad mind came to rest right there.

Burnt my hand.
Busted my cup.
Family's gone.
Good words are hard to find.
The flowers, the trees, the earth itself are all sweet and full beneath the sun.
The mountains, the rivers, the earth itself, are just the dust come one, are just the Buddha.

He wrote his own commentary in which he tells: "If I hadn't fallen in the river, if I hadn't almost died, if they hadn't beaten me, my ignorance would have grabbed me. It would have kept me in the dark. I had to go through every single step of that in order to be up against the wall to the point where all things could be set aside, there was nothing left." So his work came ripe at that point.

Now, is it always that hard? Does it have to be that forbidding? I really don't know. We don't have that many stories of people who actually did that work to success, but there is

one. Master Hsü Yun had 120 years. So when he was 60, he was still a sprout.

Master Hsü Yun went on to be beaten to death at age 112 and then come back to life, strangely enough. The Communists came and beat him, thinking that he was hiding gold in the monastery. They beat him to death for three days until his body was pulverized and his disciples set him on the bed and started to recite the Buddha's name. Two days later they heard, "Uuuhhhh. Ooohhh. Sit me up."

The story he told was that he went to the Tushita heaven and met with Maitreya bodhisattva who was speaking Dharma and who said, "What are you doing here? Your work's not over. Go back. You have more to do." Master Hsü Yun said, "I've had it. I'm through. Let me stay."

"No, no, no. You have more years to teach. You have to go back."

"Ooohhh, sit me up on the damn bed." So there he was.

One of our Dharma masters said it takes a lot of difficulty to break through. Maybe not necessarily. Maybe our ignorance is already very thin. Who knows? Nonetheless, the process is the same.

[The bhikshus and bhikshunis now led the participants in a period of meditation. In preparation for this, a bhikshuni counseled them to remove their preconceptions about what their bodies were able to do and not to do. She then went to various participants to help them assume a full lotus position, countering every excuse or objection with good-natured cajoling.

Later she explained that "this posture is designed for very, very long sitting.... The longer you sit, the deeper you samadhi, the more living beings you may be able to save."

Next she explained the positioning of the hands in this posture: the right hand in the left with the thumb tips together. This closes the four limbs so that the sitter becomes very aware of him- or herself. Each sitter then places their tongue on the roof of their mouth, just behind the hard pallet. The bhikshuni explained this in terms of the meridians and channels in our body. The two major channels, the ren and the do, go down the front and the back of the body. One is yin, the other yang. The major function of the tongue placement is closing the two meridians, a vital element in closing the system.

The next element concerns the eyes, which are to be focused in such a way as to permit imagining a line from the nose to the mouth to the heart to a star about one inch directly behind the navel. The energy line focuses there. Finally the sitter takes notice now of their spine, trying to maintain a straight spine with the head right between the shoulders and sitting front to back also between the shoulders.

A bhiksu called the posture "geometrical," in that the base is triangular and the overall posture is rectangular. He went on to observe, "…that bodies enjoy sitting in lotus. Your body thanks you after a while. There's a lot of wisdom in the body and there are ancient molds or templates that, when we touch them, the body remembers and knows them."

Positioned, the group sat in meditative posture, after which Heng Sure continued.]

Often that experience will be very humbling because we realize one thing: We're not in charge of our minds. It may continue for some time, the discovery that meditation's not so easy. That's a positive conclusion; a negative conclusion would be, I can't do it. I'm not a good meditator. I'm out of here. I'm going to watch TV instead. The reality is, I think, that the mind is very much like a sponge and everything we put in front of it, from the last comic strip to the last TV show, to the last bit of anger, is all in it. The mind soaks up whatever we present to the eyes, ears, nose, tongue, and body and what we have done for the last fifteen, twenty, fifty years and maybe the last lifetimes. It's all planted in different corners of your brain.

From the time when we first take breath until the time we breathe our last, our six senses are constantly engaging, going out with the eyes to see the latest sights. Now, if we're driving on the freeway, that's very useful. But often we're simply feeding our eyes things because of habit. The eyes are constantly scanning. Not only that, they're scanning for things we like to see and avoiding things we hate to see. There's always this discriminating going on, the consciousness behind those eyes. Nice sight, bad sight, like that, hate that. Really busy. All that is in there and it all made tracks on the fundamentally bright mirror of the mind.

Ears are always moving out picking up sounds. If you want to test it, have your mom call and have her say your name. The sound of your name spoken by your mother is one of the first things you hear. It's a very deep, atavistic, primal sound. Our minds move when we hear these sounds. We also hear the key of certain voices. We reject other voices. They produce physical responses in us based on our emotional key to those sounds. More and more research suggests also that smells trigger memory. We associate smells with places and states we're in. These are not shallow. They are very deeply tied in to our six senses and the mind contains all these traces, all these scratches and values and tracks are all there in the mind.

So when you sit and tie up the body so it can't wiggle around, when we tie up the mind, tie up the eyes, bring the ears in and take all that energy and bring it back and physiologically shut the body down, all of that outward moving and grasping and absorbing slows and quiets and the contents of what we have done up to that moment when we last sat start to arise and the sponge squeezes, the garbage can starts to tip over, and all this stuff comes out. That's what's on our mind.

When we sit, it's up for review. It's as though we go down into our own cave library, garbage can, museum, whatever you have, and all this stuff starts to come up. I did a period of intense inner work for two years and nine months in silence when I was a pilgrim and that was all I did. I didn't talk. I had a vow of silence and I worked from early in the morning until late at night. I was bowing, as a matter of fact, and simply doing that, only that, all day for nearly three years and I was astounded that every pop music song I had ever heard was in there and played

back, every note intact, just as if I had punched a button and all the tapes played back. Every argument I'd ever had, especially the ones with my parents, all came back as if they had erupted in my mind. It came back and the fear surrounding it all played back and was gone, only later to come back again. Bit by bit it starts to fall quiet and then, maybe because your own garbage has been washed clean, you go deeper.

This is a healthy, normal mind. I recall one Ch'an session, Master Hsüan Hua asked:

Why do we tell you not to speak falsely? Why do we tell you not to tell lies?

You've often heard that the mind in Ch'an is not defiled by a single speck of dust, right? It's that pure, just like a great, perfect mirror. Well, let's call it an ocean, an ocean without waves. What a wonderful image. You tell one lie, one hundred waves on the mind form. One lie stirs up a hundred waves. When will your mind be clear again so you can see what's on your mind? You tell me when the hundred waves die down. You throw a stone in that pond and bloop! All those waves. How many lies did I tell today? Well, if I were counting, I could probably come up with a couple of falsehoods, exaggerations. Now two hundred, three hundred, four hundred, all those waves fighting. How many have I told this year? I have a choppy pond that I'm trying to make still.

So if we have killed or stolen or lied or misused sex, lusted, broken my marriage or betrayed other people, those are always on the mind. Broken precepts. Intoxication. We want a still, clear pond. If we toss in alcohol, dope smoke, or whatever chemical, then that's in there too and it's distorted, it's broken, it's smudged, it's smoke-filled. Get the smoke out of here so I can see what's on my mind.

These five precepts were spoken by the Buddha, very pragmatic, very practical. The Buddha wanted everybody to experience this experience as fast as possible, so he provided the short-cut: Avoid these things; they mess the mind over.

We're talking about looking inside. What do we need? If we have lead a dissolute life, we find out that's what's there. That's why I asked how many had a very tranquil experience. Maybe we have some sages—I hope so, the more the better—but until that time, until we do this more and get the flavor of Ch'an, the joy of stillness, the concentration that comes, the efficacy and the efficiency in our daily life, from driving a car to remembering the names of our students. That all comes from doing this stuff of meditation.

The more we do it and get that flavor, we think, How do I enhance that? That's when it starts to influence our lifestyle. You think, I could probably give up an hour of TV and sit still. I could probably give up shouting at my mother. Then the meditation gets much more still, much more serene. Things work out.

The use of wisdom, you could say, is when a situation arises and we see right through it and don't move. The pattern's clear. That's nothing more than emotion. That's fear. That person is snapping at me,

attacking because they're afraid. That's their affliction. Okay, that's fear. Don't be afraid. Cut through. You don't have to move. You remove the cause of the fear and the entire situation subsides. You've seen that pattern coming out again. You don't have to move. It's just clear seeing. You see patterns develop and identify them within yourself because you are still, you are quiet. It is nothing more than the mind used through joy, fear, anger, sorrow, happiness, desire.

So this comes from a pure lifestyle. When you change your habits to enhance the meditation, the meditation allows the mind to be still. You can reflect accurately any situation that arises. Precepts, *samadhi*, and wisdom all start to connect. Bit by bit meditation becomes such a joy, taking the pressure off our minds, which are cluttered with junk, with memories, with the sensations of the lunch we ate and the cool wind outside and the phone call from home last night. When we can sit and be still, then all those things find their own priorities. The important things rise. The unimportant things disappear and our six senses begin slowly starting to get quiet and pure and sharp.

Then, if we can continue and really work hard, there is a time when, in our sitting, we can see how sight connects with eye and the consciousness discriminates. Sound connects with the ear. There's a point where they actually do touch and if our *samadhi* is able to be a witness to that happening, then there's a liberation that generally happens when the six senses and the six sense organs take their own sphere and realize where they're rising from. In the words that we use to interpret and name and distance ourselves and classify and categorize, the left brain function is always naming and forming. When that becomes a movement that we detect because our mind is so quiet, a genuine, deep joy can happen. In Buddhists it happens when words and names start to lose their hold on the mind and there's a door where these things all move.

What about the realm behind the six senses? Where do the six senses come from? Would it be all black? Would it be some terrifying black hole? The sutras say it's not only not terrifying, it's a joyful, beautiful, crystallike world of limitless, boundless, Dharma treasures called the Dharma realm, the realm where logic and consciousness don't rule. Dharma rules, principles, the principles of the Dharma that the Buddha explained in the sutras are all there brightly lit, perfectly arrayed like jewels. That's the Dharma realm and there's a door to it that can be our consciousness right this instant if we had the requisite skills and purity. Ch'an is the door to that, among others.

But all you can do is point to that, do you homework in the sutras, and then sit long. Bit by bit, that can become your realm. There were masters in the past, from the T'ang dynasty and before, who spoke from that place.

Why are monasteries so white and so bare? Because we don't want anything adding to the noise. There's enough noise inside already. Let's calm down that noise, let it gradually subside without picking up more colors and sounds.

In the world, it seems that pleasure and joy come from a higher quality of stimulation. You keep upping the ante in the kind of noise, the kind of flavor on the tongue. Add a little bit more sauce, something different. When we sit, the six senses can be quiet. They can be still and then all that stuff that has eventually to sort itself out, does. If we don't find it, we die again, come back with those same seeds planted, another round, another chance to sort out the garbage. Will we do it? Maybe in many, many lifetimes.

So I would say treat your body kindly and keep to the middle. If you can cross your legs for five minutes without them falling off, give them five minutes. Then sit in the way that you can because it allows you to sit. The important thing is mind. The body isn't here.

[A participant was interested in hearing about some of the similarities and differences between Ch'an and Zen.]

There is definitely a cultural overlay every time Buddhism jumps a culture. America will have its own. The Zen ritual was characterized by someone with the word *militaristic,* and part of that is a Japanese approach to religion. The Ch'an approach is a little more easygoing. The Japanese style tends to be formal. It's very much a function of Japanese geography, the fact that there is not that much space and you have to do things in a tight, small area.

Bowing to the zafu is not something we do. They bow to the cushion in Japan. The idea behind this is gratitude. That is a ritual that we did not pick up. We sit for three weeks every winter and we keep the old style. The first sit is at 3:00 A.M. and we sit for sixty minutes with twenty minutes walking. There's a five-minute pause while you rub the stiffness out and bring the mind back to a different way of clarity. Everyone stands and then walks for twenty minutes and the walking is fairly brisk. The idea is to walk and bring the circulation back and to exercise and stretch. Then we go around the pads for about four or five minutes and then everyone stops and sits again. Another stick of incense and we sit. That's the only ritual we have. Usually we sit facing the wall. Other times I've done it where you sit facing in or facing the Buddha. We used to do our Ch'an sessions with men on one side and women on the other side of the big hall. Recently they've separated into different monasteries.

One big difference might be that in Ch'an you're very much on your own. I think in the Japanese tradition there's often someone watching over the hall. No one is watching over you during the Ch'an, so each person is sitting in their own space.

I hope that your sitting practice brings you stillness, an empty garbage can, and all of that capacity to contain the Dharma realm and real compassion. We didn't get to talk about empathy but it's part of Kuan-yin Bodhisattva's great compassion and it is also part of our own great compassion. It's a natural force. It arises from real wisdom. If you can't see through to the sameness of all living beings, you can't really be impartially, equally compassionate. As long as we set up likes and dislikes, it will be based on ego.

Maybe we could take one thought and give away all the merit and virtue of our cultivation today and share it with others. This is a very wonderful part of a practice called transference. All the goodness and merit and virtue we create from our work, we share with the entire universe, all living beings. And to whatever end you would prefer, maybe your own health, maybe someone in your family to recover from illness. Maybe AIDS could disappear, rather large, maybe you'd like wars to end or simply someone in your family to be in more harmony inside. Whatever kind of wish you might have, you can transfer it to that end. And I'm going to put my palms together and recite in English the translation of the verse and then we'll chant in Chinese.

May all this merit and virtue adoring the Buddha's pure lands, above, repaying the four kinds of kindness, below, rescuing those from the three evil residents. If there are those who hear and see of what we do, may they all bring for us the bodhi resolve. When this life comes to an end, may we be reborn in the land of ultimate bliss.

Introduction to Shikantaza

Issho Fujita

DOGEN ZENJI (1200–53) TRAVELED FROM HIS NATIVE JAPAN TO CHINA, where he experienced profound enlightenment during his studies with Master T'ien-T'ung Ju-ching. This Ch'an master transmitted the seal of confirmation in the lineage of the Soto school of Ch'an to Dogen, who, when he returned to Kyoto, brought the tradition of the Soto school, which he fostered through his teachings and writings.

Principal among the teachings of Soto Zen is the emphasis on *shikantaza*, which literally means "just sitting." Zen Master Dogen strongly emphasized it as "the true gate to the Buddhadharma." In the words of Issho Fujita, "in *shikantaza* we just sit, with the body/mind aimed at maintaining correct *zazen* posture. It is a practice of such subtlety and depth that it is essential to undertake it with proper understanding."

Born in Japan in 1954, Issho Fujita has been the resident priest of Valley Zendo in Charlemont, Massachusetts, since 1987. Prior to devoting his life to Zen practice, he had pursued academic studies in developmental psychology, aikido, and Chinese medicine, which he left when he entered Antaiji temple. He was ordained in the tradition of Dogen Zenji, Kodo Sawaki Roshi (1880–1965), and Kosho Uchiyama Roshi (b. 1911).

Mr. Fujita's gentle wit and warm manner is apparent throughout this workshop, during which he presented the participants with some of the concepts underlying the practice of *shikantaza*, basic information about proper *zazen* sitting posture, and his ideas about related concerns that were raised by individual participants.

Early in the workshop, Mr. Fujita discussed the way in which both Kodo Sawaki Roshi and Kosho Uchiyama Roshi characterized the *shikantaza* practice: While the former said "just do zazen," his disciple put it more colloquially—"Aim at the correct *zazen* posture with your flesh and bones and leave everything up to it." As Mr. Fujita, phrased it:

In a sense, Sawaki Roshi and Uchiyama Roshi are the example of people who wasted their whole lives, in *zazen*. They encounter *zazen*—or *zazen* encountered them—then *zazen* grabbed them and they led a life in which they are glared at by *zazen,* scolded by *zazen,* obstructed by *zazen,* proved by *zazen.*

I entered Antaiji and what I have learned there through *zazen* practice was not the technique or method to make myself happy, to contour my mind, or to attain and maintain a certain state of consciousness which I want to have, but a kind of attitude toward life, an attitude like this—this is a quotation from Sawaki Roshi's sayings. "In life there are rainy days, windy days, stormy days, but whatever happens, just settle myself in *zazen.*"

Before giving basic instruction in *shikantaza,* Mr. Fujita explained the meaning of *zazen*. In Japanese, *za* means "sitting" or "form," and *zen* is the Japanese pronunciation of Ch'an, which, in turn, is the Chinese word for the Sanskrit *Dhyana*—"thinking" or "one-pointedness." Stemming from these words, his definition of *zazen* is "sit in a certain way with certain quality." He then proceeded with a basic instruction:

If I tried to give a detailed instruction, it would make many, many pages because if I check out all the part of the body, I have to say something. Eyes, facial expression, shoul-

der, and so on. It's kind of endless. But I can make it shorter, one sentence. "Sit upright." Uchiyama Roshi said that doing correct *zazen* means taking the correct posture and entrusting everything to it.

But what is a correct posture? What does it mean by entrusting everything to it? We have to understand that. Some people think just sitting sounds great. That's fine, but if we lack basic understanding of the practice, easily we color that practice with our prejudice or preoccupation, preference, and partial understanding, and so on. So practice is very simple but we are very complicated beings. We complicate it.

He contrasted *shikantaza* with other types of meditation by noting that:

"Most of the meditation people have two types of instruction: Body sit and mind meditate. Meditate on a visual image, mantra, physical sensation, breath, etc. In contrast to that, in *shikantaza,* we sit with body and mind together and mind does not engage in anything else. So it's sitting plus zero. All sitting. "Okay, so I sit, then what should I do next?" No next. That's what Sawaki said, "Just do *zazen,* that's all." He never said sit and then do something else. He said sit and do not add anything else to it. So it's a little bit misleading to use the word meditation. That's why I prefer to use *zazen* or *shikantaza.*

Quoting Dogen—"Have a full lotus posture of your body, and a full lotus posture in your mind; have a full lotus posture in a state where body and mind drop off"—Mr. Fujita explained that this "means when we sit in a full lotus posture, fully with body and mind, when whole body and mind completely become zazen, we should call it zazen, not body and mind." Going further, he used the metaphor of making a doll with clay: "When you finish making that doll, you don't call it 'clay,' you call it 'doll.'" So body and mind become completely transformed into zazen.

Dogen also said, "The lotus posture is an upright body, upright mind, and upright body-mind." This prompted Mr. Fujita to observe that "usually we are more interested in what to do with mind than posture." He explained that this arises primarily because we are conditioned to grant such emphasis to mind and its place in our lives. "But it's not everything. When you are completely, deeply sleeping, you are there, but your mode of being is very, very different. We are more interested in what to do with the mind, because it's I. I want to do something."

Contrary to this tendency, Dogen said, "In our zazen, it is of primary importance to sit in the correct posture. That comes first." To do this, it is extremely important to arrange for a good outer and inner environment for zazen—"quiet, clean, neat, not too bright, not too dark, not too hot, not too cold, etc. In short, an atmosphere that supports our doing zazen. We are surrounded by noise and busy schedule and environmental crisis, etc. We are not sitting in a vacuum. We are sitting in concrete, socioeconomic or historical conditions, situations that we have to work with. That's a part of zazen."

Mr. Fujita discussed some of the most basic elements contributing to good inner environment. For example, diet must be taken into account, as it is not good either to eat too much or to be hungry, which leads to certain rules regarding how to eat and what to eat. Sleep is also important. "We modern people think that sleeping does not produce anything. No benefit. But the quality of your work is dependent on the quality of your sleep." So sleeping well is good practice. These are just two of the fundamental elements, but, as Mr. Fujita noted, "every trivial thing in everyday life" supports your practice.

Cushions and their placement are another important part of the instruction for sitting, which led into the description of the posture for shikantaza practice.

Lay down a large, flat cushion facing the wall. Facing the wall is a tradition of the Soto Zen but it came from Bodhidharma. Rinzai people sit facing each other. On this flat cushion, set the round cushion. Sit on the round cushion and fold your legs. This is the most difficult part. Sit in the full lotus or half lotus, because it's the most stable posture for sitting and both knees and the base of your spine form equilateral triangle and support your weight evenly. Without this, I have to force myself to sit upright. The pelvis and lumbar spine can have a good position to support the upper torso in good alignment with gravity. I think the zazen is something of how to relate with gravity or how to connect ourselves with the center of the Earth—not doing it in your intellectual mind, but with your whole body. Meditation, we tend to focus on our conscious level of the mind, but zazen is more than that, more than mind, organs. Because sitting this way, each organ returns to its own natural position. There's no tension like this, just with gravity. Because in the process of evolution, we acquired this upright posture. We only have an upright posture as a normal posture. So thinking about why we sit this way gives me a lot of questions about that kind of issue, our relationship with gravity, how to connect ourselves with the center of the Earth. I think this is a very spiritual question because we never get out of gravity. That still not may be possible, but usually we are in the ground.

Sit upright. Straighten your back, keep your neck straight, and pull in your chin. This kind of good posture can be described as neck free. Most of us fail to connect the neck or head properly to the torso, which means there are two centers of gravity. Neck free, head forward and up. Back lengthen and widen. Don't hold your posture with unnecessary muscle tension. Sit with balance, not with tension.

Zazen is not a competition with another person, how beautifully you can sit, compared to another person, how long you can sit without moving. No. Sawaki Roshi said "*Zazen* is self, is doing self by self. No room for other person." For us to sit with balance, we need a correct posture. We sit like a tripod. Open your chest naturally and relax in your shoulders. Not too much, not too little, is a key phrase for all parts of the body. Most of us tend to use our body too much or too little. We are not sensitive enough to our body.

We need a sharp, alert sensitivity and we think the muscle is like a tool to move, but especially in sitting, muscle is a sensory organ.

Issho Fujita in discussion after his workshop

If muscle gets tense, we become numb or dull; we cannot be sensitive. That's why we relax. Relax doesn't mean dull. Relaxation is very important, so we have to find the middle way to naturalness in *zazen* posture. When we sit upright, we tend to make our abdomen stiff and tight, but it should be opposite. We have too much tension and that creates a kind of contraction with the muscle in your abdomen. But this muscle has to be loosened. Not only in the surface but deep inside. Actually, when we relax a deep muscle in the abdomen, our back naturally lengthens. You have to experience it by trial and error. The center of gravity gets lower and you feel more grounded because the muscle loosens, the organs sink, and breathing becomes deeper.

Close your mouth without leaving an air pocket and put your tongue against the upper pallet but don't do it too much. Project the top of your head as if it were going to pierce the ceiling. Just try to kiss the ceiling with top of your head. You have to create the very fine but clear central axis along your spine.

And we are not a stone. We are alive.

Always there is some resilience, moving clockwise within a certain range. First, you have to feel that center axis and then try to maintain, but it's always moving—very, very subtle, small.

Make an oval with your hand, four fingers overlapping and both thumbs slightly touching each other. You have beautiful, powerful, and symmetrical oval; put it on your foot, somewhere you feel comfortable. Don't keep lifting it up. Just rest it without collapsing this hand posture. This is called hand *mudra,* but our whole body should be *mudra.*

I'm explaining the posture part by part, but it's like a jigsaw puzzle. You have to make it into one consistent picture. So when I talk about hand, I actually talk about whole body. We sit as an organic system. Bodies are very finely connected, one organism, so you cannot sit properly if you have bad hand posture, if you had a bad connection with your head and torso, you can't sit. Everything should be connected, integrated.

Keep your eyes naturally open and drop your line of vision slightly. This is a big difference from other meditation. Some people say I prefer to close my eyes. Easy to focus. But we don't have to focus on anything. And also we are not cultivating our ability to focus on one object. *Shikantaza* is the opposite—we can see, but we are not looking at something. Everything should be described in a passive way: Things are seen; sounds are heard; thoughts are thought. You are not watching. You are not listening. You are not thinking. But sound comes in, sights come in, and thoughts pop up and go away; sensation too.

You become transparent in a sense. So for that purpose, we have to keep our eyes open. And in my experience, this is helpful to monitor my posture. With eyes closed I have a bad habit of using my body.

Mr. Fujita provided a few pointers for sitting having to do with facial expression, breathing patterns, and the like. This was followed by a period of sitting, after which he took the opportunity to make a number of observations about the practice and it components. He noted the natural tendency to try to obtain "the perfect posture," explaining that there is not a perfect posture and that "we cultivate many, many things without intention. The learning is happening outside of your awareness or consciousness. Our consciousness has a boundary and outside of this, many, many things are happening. So what we can experience is a very tiny part of the whole picture. *Zazen* is, I think, making that kind of whole picture again."

He also addressed a common concern about what to do if a thought presents itself, interrupting the process, a situation he referred to as "getting off."

It's a whole work of the body and mind. If we start thinking of something else, a tiny thought changes everything. As soon as you start to think of something or feel drowsy, it collapses and this hand form disappears and your breathing becomes irregular, shallow, and so on. So we watch ourselves to maintain that center axis and quality of the breath, not judging. We know if we're off, just to come back. So if you're thinking Why did I get off, I should not get off, or if you start blaming yourself—*off, off, off, off*—but simply come back. You don't have to analyze why. It's not a matter of this is better than this. Just simply come back and that's a practice. So it's not a matter of success or failure. This should be clear when you practice *shikantaza*.

Zazen is not thinking, nor is it sleeping. Mind has to be alert and to be together with body, which is sitting and breathing. But this does not mean that you have to suppress the thought or thought has to cease entirely to occur. As far as we are alive, thoughts occur. In the same way, we have in-breath and out-breath. If you think in-breath is better than out-breath, you keep breathing in, in, in, you die. Life is always in and out, off and come back, off and come back. The brain creates thought because it's necessary for us to survive. It's useful. But the problem is we don't know how to use that useful tool. We are used by tools. It's happened in many, many different forms because it's so powerful and we are not mature enough to use that tool effectively. That's why we need this kind of meditation.

Our attitude toward thought during *zazen* is not to chase after thoughts nor turn them away. Do not become caught up by them or struggle with them. Just leave them alone. Just awaken from destruction, which is thinking, or dullness, which is drowsiness, and return to the right posture moment by moment. Uchiyama Roshi described this attitude as "letting go of thought" or "releasing your grip on thought." But if you try to do it

with your mind, you're clenching your thought. We are doing it with the body, with bone and flesh. And we tend to solve the problem caused by thought. It's like giving fuel to the fire.

He explained that the *shikantaza* approach to this sort of problem is based on the understanding of the nature of thought. Behind *shikantaza* is an understanding of how we are living, the cause of our problem, and how to solve it. The Soto tradition doesn't include koan practice as a mainstream aspect of its practice. Rather it is comprised of two others: "One is sitting, hopefully with a colleague or fellows; and the other is studying, including intellectual understanding of the scriptures or listening to lectures, Dharma talks, and so on. We need both." Mr. Fujita illustrated this with a poetic visual image:

Imagine a high mountain, like Mount Fuji or Everest, and then at certain height are clouds and under this level the air is circulating because of the dynamics of the weather. But above these heights, always sunshine. Under this, rain, snow, lightning, twister, and so on. For most of us, this is the world, this is everything. This is called "life-death" in Buddhism. For us, for "I," this is everything, because that's all we can see, all we can experience. But that does not mean there is no realm above this height. And to quote from Zen words, "the big sky does not prevent clouds from flying freely."

That should be our attitude toward it all.

Thought is like a cloud and the sky, all the weather belongs to parts of the sky. So *zazen* practice is not going usually where it is raining. We'd get wet. We want to go somewhere else on the same plane, on the same ground. So we try to find the place where we keep comfortable on the ground, assuming that this is the whole world and only that's reality.

But reality is more than our perception, and whether we know it or not, there always is this above; we are simply blind. We are ignorant and this zone is always out of our perception. *Zazen* is not an effort to find a good spot under this level, nor try to leave this world for the other level, but knowing this is the reality. Sawaki Roshi described *zazen* this way: standing on the top of the high mountain and not being disturbed by the weather down there.

So this *shikantaza* attitude is: It's raining. We know it's a temporary rain. There's no rain forever. Rain turns into sunshine, but sunshine turns into rain. Based on this wisdom, we can have a different way of living under the rain. We'd get wet but we'd get wet knowing it's temporary rain and we can find the more constructive or meaningful way of being wet. It's a very big difference. Both get wet but very differently. So we need a capacity to allow them to happen, to let them be there.

While most of the workshop focused on sitting practice, Mr. Fujita pointed out the importance of recognizing that "practice in the midst of daily life, and the effort to cultivate the body and mind to fit *shikantaza* practice, transforms us gradually without knowing where or what is happening." He also established that "we have to arrange daily life in a certain way so that we can practice properly. There's a kind of mutual relationship between sitting practice and the rest of your life. You have to organize twenty-four hours and you have to be creative to establish your own style." He emphasized the importance of having a teacher or guide who can provide assistance in developing such a style and practice, "because there are some pitfalls, and grief, and poisonous snakes, and so on. If you have that kind of guide, you can avoid that kind of thing. But if you don't, you have to walk anyway, so you should walk by yourself. The teacher is just a tool. Uchiyama Roshi said being a teacher is a role: 'Our true teacher is *zazen*. If you dedicate yourself sincerely, wholeheartedly to *zazen*, *zazen* guides you. Make your *zazen* a good guide by practicing sincerely, wholeheartedly.'"

Mr. Fujita next addressed the issue of the human tendency to separate out aspects of our lives, rather than viewing the life holistically, organically, as a whole. He quoted a beautiful passage from Dogen Zenji's principal work, the *Shobo-genzo*:

"A fish swims in the ocean and no matter how far it swims, there is no end to the water. A bird flies in the sky and no matter how far it flies, there is no end to the air. However, the fish and the birds have never left their element. When their activity is large, their field is large. When their need is small, their field is small. Thus, each of them totally covers its full range and each of them totally experiences its realm. If the bird leaves the air, it will die at once. If the fish leaves the water, it will die at once."

I think he's not talking about birds or fish. He's talking about ourselves. When we think of fish, we only think of fish, but if it's a real fish, a live fish, it should be in the water. Fish and water make up a unit, but in our concept of thinking, we abstract fish out of the water and then we think this is a fish and try to know about a fish in this context. We think of ourselves in that way.

This "I" feels a strong necessity to survive in this kind of context. There's a gap in the deep part of our psyche between our self and the world. Actually, fish never left the water but we live as if we are fish out of the water. That's why we feel choked. We need something. We are thirsty for it, but we never left. We cannot be left. So *zazen* is simply a simple way to realize we are fish in the water and swim freely, hopefully, joyfully. We don't have to choke ourselves.

Mr. Fujita touched upon the role of *kinhin*— Zen walking between periods of sitting— establishing that it is "not the break after *zazen*; it's a part of *zazen*." He briefly described elements of this aspect of practice, explaining that "each step is arrival. We are not going somewhere else. Each step is completion and then the next step is completely new."

A man in the workshop mentioned that, due to trouble with his eyes, he was unable to lower his eyes without his head locking in a certain position. Mr. Fujita returned to the importance of a more holistic outlook that approaches the entire body and the meditation posture as an interrelated system. Thus, when one "fixes" one part, other parts automatically also become fixed, thereby throwing off other aspects of the posture and body. He went on to say that:

Many people quit *shikantaza* practice in the middle of it, saying it's too difficult or it's completely different from what they expected. But I think it's a pity, because that's a good starting point. If you said: "*Shikantaza* is too difficult. It doesn't fit me. I should look for some other practice." That means you are setting a standard. You are here and judging— this is no good, this is no good. But our relationship with *shikantaza* should be all positive. *Shikantaza* is checking ourselves, checking myself. So that's a chance to transform our attitude toward the things.

I was like that when I just started. I met my teacher at Antaiji. I said, "*Shikantaza* practice is very, very difficult and high-level, like graduate school level. I'm just a beginner like a kindergarten level. And so what do you think of this idea: I go to Rinzai monastery, start from counting breath, and pass some koans, and get some kind of first *kensho*, and prepare myself for *shikantaza*. How about it?" He said, "No. *Shikantaza* practice must not be practiced like a grafting method. If you want to do *shikantaza*, practice from the beginning to end. Once you get the habit of practice and meditation this way, and the longer you practice, the more difficult it is to change.

"The second reason is difficulties, frustration and pain, doubt, those names I keep saying are very, very valuable to cultivate your *shikantaza* practice. We think, perfect *shikantaza* practice, but before that we have to pass those things. So the more you suffer, the better. But you have to be ready for it, otherwise you quit." So he gave me great advice at the beginning, because I could interpret my frustration and doubt, my difficulties in that way.

In Dogen there's the archery metaphor: You fail one hundred times and you make it the hundred-first time. The question: Does this hundred-first-time success have no relationship with hundred-times failure? No. Because of these hundred failures, this success. Of course, it's sometimes so difficult to just sit and also many, many questions present themselves. What am I doing besides just warming up the cushion? And my colleague and other people have nice social status and are having a nice time and I'm doing the pain or boredom. But in that way, I experience that kind of metamorphosis of shedding my old things. So my attitude toward life changed. Everything becomes material for the practice.

A participant asked why Mr. Fujita thought it important to work with a companion or group. "In the relationship I manifest myself in a very different way. If I practice, I have my own image. But among the other people, I manifest the face which I never see," he explained.

The final question to Mr. Fujita was if he still has a teacher. He answered that his teacher is in Japan and they communicate by letter. He closed the workshop by offering his ideas about the teacher-student relationship and its role in practice.

The teacher exists only when there is a student. So instead of trying to find a good teacher, be a good student and a good teacher will be there.

My teacher not only teaches, but we collaborate to have that kind of relationship. I know he's just an ordinary person, but more experienced. He himself sat I think thirty years or so, so I can learn from him. Uchiyama Roshi sat, I think, more than fifty years. He said, "Issho, time is very crucial. Sitting is like making whiskey. Put in grain under certain conditions and just wait and then slowly fermentation happens. *Zazen*'s the same. Just normal, ordinary. Simply sit regularly for long time. Sit ten years, then ten years, then ten years."

When I decided to go into Antaiji, I visited Uchiyama Roshi, who gave me advice. He said, "Only one thing"—and this is to everybody—"be quiet and throw away your standard or yardstick to measure what is good and what is bad and sit there for ten years. That's advice. And if you like to listen to the next one, come ten years later."

Don't Know
Is Closest to It

Zen Master Wu Kwang
(Richard Shrobe Soensa)

THE SOURCE FOR ZEN MASTER WU KWANG'S TITLE IS A BRIEF STORY, with which he began this workshop. At the time of the Sixth Patriarch, a monk named Hui-jang came to call, and the patriarch asked Hui-jang, Where are you coming from? Hui-jang said, "I've come from Song Sahn Mountain." The patriarch asked, "What is this thing that comes from Song Sahn Mountain." Hui-jang couldn't answer, but was left with a big question. So he went back to Song Sahn Mountain and sat in meditation for eight years. Then he had an awakening and came back to the patriarch and said, "To call it a thing is not correct, so don't know is closest to it."

This workshop was punctuated by a number of such parables that assist in gaining a basic positioning in relation to some of the thorny paradoxes and meditation points that stem from Zen Buddhism. The one element they have in common is their ultimate goal of approaching the concept of "don't know," which is fundamental to Zen. Focusing on the Kong-an approach to meditation, Zen Master Wu Kwang used both illustrative narrative and sitting meditation to demonstrate the importance and inherent release of recognizing that uncertainty is a strong and positive place through which one may strive to attain enlightenment.

Zen Master Wu Kwang (Richard Shrobe Soensa) is guiding teacher of Chogye International Zen Center in New York. Having begun practicing in 1966, he was given *inka* (certification) as a Zen teacher by his teacher, Seung Sahn Soen SaNim, in 1984. He received Dharma transmission in 1993. Wu Kwang is a lay teacher as well as a psychotherapist and trainer of Gestalt therapy. His first book is entitled *Open Mouth Already a Mistake*.

At the time of Bodhidharma's coming to China, he first stopped in the south of China and had an audience with Emperor Wu of the small kingdom of Liang. Emperor Wu was a devout Buddhist and he had sponsored the building of many temples as well as the ordination ceremonies of many monks and nuns. He had studied the teachings quite extensively, both in terms of philosophy and the scriptures of Buddhism. So when Bodhidharma arrived, the emperor said to him, "I've built many temples and supported many monks. What kind of merit did I gain from all this?" And Bodhidharma said, "No merit."

The emperor was a little bit taken aback because the gist of Buddhism in China at that time was that you did all these good actions to build up merit for positive rebirth, so he asked Bodhidharma, "What is the highest meaning of the Holy Truths?" According to the Buddhism the emperor had studied—a system called Two Truths—there is an absolute truth that says that it is nonexistent. Then there is a conventional truth, which says it is not nonexistent. Perfect integration of these two was considered a deeply esoteric piece of business and, according to the philosophical schools, the highest meaning of the Holy Truths. When the emperor asked this question, Bodhidharma said, "No holiness is clear like space."

The emperor again wasn't expecting that kind of answer, and he asked, "Who is this facing me?" and Bodhidharma answered, "Don't know."

That is the first historical reference to don't know in the Zen tradition. At that moment, when Bodhidharma said, "don't know," he "revealed his gall bladder," as the old Zen masters say—he very intimately showed his true, simple, unadulterated, essential being. The emperor looked puzzled and didn't understand, and felt disconcerted, so at that moment the emperor also got a little taste of the don't know in his not understanding. Of course, in that not understanding, not knowing is an intimate meeting of the two of them, face to face, eyebrow to eyebrow, mind to mind, heart to heart. It's like that for us, too. When you completely don't know and don't hold your ideas, and your opinions, and your conceptions, and your conditions, and you meet the other, at that moment there is true intimacy. But at first it can be a little disconcerting because it doesn't feel safe. We are not with our usual props at that moment.

Just as Bodhidharma responded "Don't know" to "Who is facing me?" when we ask ourselves Who is it who sits down here? Who is it who stands up? Who is it who walks? Who is it who talks? Who is it who eats a meal? Who is it who interacts with their fellow human beings? Who is it who makes love? Who is it who gets angry? Who is that? When we ask that question sincerely, of course, we already know who it is—it's us. There's no one else here. But exactly what is the nature of this existence that we keep pointing to with this word I? What is that? What am I? When you look into that, then you become intimate with yourself. The name for that intimacy is don't know. The substance of that intimacy is also don't know, and out of that meeting the other, which in some sense is not truly another, also becomes a possibility.

So the emperor didn't understand and felt disconcerted. Bodhidharma left, crossed the river and went north to the Shao-lin temple, where he sat facing the wall for nine years. But Bodhidharma had obviously penetrated the emperor in some way and this disconcertedness was fermenting inside him, Later he brought up the matter with his first minister, who asked, "Doesn't your majesty know who that monk was?" The emperor very sincerely said, "No, I don't know." So the minister said he is the Mahasattva Bodhisattva Avalokiteshvara, transmitting the buddha-mind seal. Mahasattva Bodhisattva Avalokiteshvara means "the great enlightened being of compassionate energy."

Now, why is this don't know Bodhidharma Avalokiteshvara? In China they call Avalokiteshvara "Kuan-yin," in Korea they say "Kwan Seum Boso", in Japan "Kanzeon Butsu," but the names are all the same, and in those countries this bodhisattva's being of great compassion, this universal energy being represented as great compassion, is pictured in female form. The meaning of the Japanese word *kanzeon* is "hearer or perceiver of the world's sounds"; "the one who hears the cries or sounds of the world." The one who perceives sound universally is an expression of compassionate energy manifesting greatly. If you are talking, talking, talking to yourself, you can't hear anything, And why are we talking to ourselves? Usually to sustain our

own version of reality. That's a big problem. So, when you return to this don't know place, then true listening, true hearing is a pregnant possibility and can spontaneously emerge. My teacher, Zen Master Seung Sahn, told a story about a friend who was a Quaker teacher. This teacher had a student who asked, "Do you talk to God?"

The teacher said, "Yes, I talk to God."

"Does God talk back to you?"

"Yes, God talks back to me."

So, the student said, "Would you ask God how come he never talks to me, because I keep talking to him."

The minister said, "Okay, I'll do that for you." Later they had a second meeting and the student again asked the minister, "Did you ask God why he doesn't talk to me?" and the minister said, "Yes."

"Well, what did he say?"

"God said I kept trying to get you, but your line was continuously busy."

If our line is continuously busy, there is no possibility of transmitting and receiving, of listening and hearing, of call and response, which is very much at the basis of compassionate activity.

So the emperor heard that this was the great bodhisattva Avalokiteshvara transmitting the mind seal and he felt regretful and wanted to call him back. But the first minister said, "Your majesty, don't say that you will call him back, because even if the whole kingdom would go after him he will not return."

When you enter and become intimate with this point of don't know, of not knowing, that's a dangerous place, because from one perspective there is no returning after that. On the other hand, there's a poem by T'aigo, the great Korean Zen master who lived in the 1300s. He wrote about the Sixth Patriarch's journey, enlightenment, and transmission:

When he heard the Diamond Sutra, his eyes were switched around. [There was an immediate revolution.] *Because he venerated the Dharma, he didn't fear the journey.* [The Sixth Patriarch was living in the south of China and the Fifth Patriarch was way in the north, so he had a long journey. But there is, of course, an inner meaning to not fearing the journey.] *When he got to Huang Mei, the patriarch was getting old. / Plum blossoms, white willows so green. / We can all sympathize with the time he spent on the treadmill.*

When the Sixth Patriarch got to the Fifth Patriarch's place, the Fifth Patriarch said to him, *What have you come seeking?* And he said, *I don't seek anything, I only want to become buddha.* So the Fifth Patriarch chided him for that kind of response. He said, *How can you monkeys from the south become buddha, you have no buddha-nature?* The Sixth Patriarch was not daunted by this at all, and he said, *As far as space goes, there is north and south, but in the buddha-nature there is no such thing.* The Fifth Patriarch realized that there was something outstanding about this man, but also knowing the politics at the monastery and the petty jealousies, he decided he would send him to the rice-pounding shed as a layworker in the temple. The Sixth Patriarch spent eight months in the rice shed pounding rice on a treadmill. The Sixth Patriarch kept pounding the rice, so this line in the poem says, *We can sympathize with all the time he spent on the treadmill, but for him the rice had already been ripe a long time.* The Fifth Patriarch came to him in the middle of the night and transmitted the Dharma. Because of the situation in the monastery, the Sixth Patriarch's life was hanging by a thread, so he crossed the river and fled.

Now, here's the last line: *Who could know at that time that he was happy to leave?* From one perspective, when you enter this don't know place, there is no turning back. That's dangerous and perhaps some fear can arise. On the other hand, there may be a feeling of relief and a recognition that coming and going are not really coming and going, and that what you had where you were, you take with you in some form. *Who could know at that time that he was happy to leave?*

In Providence Zen Center, on the wall in one of the hallways, is a hanging that has a Chinese calligraphy poem with a little translation on the side, which says:

Buddha went to Snow Mountain
sat six years
don't know
without thinking, full universe.

I particularly like the last line. *Without thinking, full universe.* When you touch this mind of not knowing, then clear seeing emerges, clear hearing emerges, clear sensing emerges, clear action emerges. So, the sky is blue emerges, the grass is green emerges, the wall is white emerges, the carpet is red emerges. One by one, each thing fully and completely emerges and the experience is, without thinking, complete universe, full universe.

That's the good news. Buddhist Enlightenment Day comes in December, according to tradition—the eighth day of the twelfth month—so we always celebrate it in December according to our calendar. Of course, that is just around Christmas time. In the Christian tradition it says the angel appeared and said "I bring you good tidings." But here it doesn't say anything about an angel appearing. It says, "Without thinking, full universe." That's Zen Buddhism's good news.

A recent newsletter of the Providence Zen Center has a transcription of a talk given by my Dharma-brother Zen Master Dae Kwang Sanim, in which he said there are two sutras that every Zen student should study, practice, and take to heart. The first one is called the "Cookie-Cutter Sutra." If you open a box of animal crackers and lay all the cookies out on the table, you will see that the forms and shapes are all different. monkeys appear, kangaroos appear, giraffes, lions, tigers, bears all appear. But if you go to the factory where the cookies are cut, you will see that there is only one dough that all of these various forms and shapes are punched out from. So likewise all of us— men, women, human beings, animals, the sky, the earth, the rocks, the water, the distant stars, the sun, the moon—are all essentially punched out from one don't know sub-

stance. That means that the many are the one and the one is the many.

There is a second point in that sutra, lest we reduce everything to just a lump of dough. This second point is, because I manifest as a gorilla, you can manifest as a bear; because you manifest as a bear, I can manifest as a gorilla. Because you have beauty inside, I can share in that in some way, and because I have ugliness inside you also have to take some part of that and share in its responsibility. That means that the individuality and uniqueness of each of us—and of each particular color and shape and form in the vivid array of creative activity of this universe as it manifests in all of us—is all interdependent. Because we all share something universal, what is in you is in me, and what is in me is in you, without our ever having to lose our particular shape, our particular form, and our particular place. If you glimpse that, then you have a moment of enlightened view.

The second sutra that Zen Master Dae Kwang Sanim said all Zen students should take to heart and practice and study is the "Nike-Commercial Sutra." It's only one line: "Just do it." Here's my commentary on the Nike-Commercial commentary: [HIT]* Just do it. When you do something completely, wholeheartedly, without holding back, at that time your function of the moment and your essential don't know substance are all there. So function and substance, what appears and

---

*During his talk, Zen Master Wu Kwang occasionally used the traditional HIT—the sound of stick against wood or palm against floor—to cut off discriminative thinking.

what is never visible, all manifest together in that "just completely do it" activity.

An old Korean Zen Master said, "When you say 'don't know,' you've already hit the nail on the head." That means, the very first time that you even hit this don't know— *What am I? Don't know*—at that moment you've already hit the nail on the head. You've already touched something that you can rely on, that you can have confidence in, and that you can trust in. At that moment, the mind of faith emerges.

Bodhichitta, the thought toward enlightenment, is the initial moment of faith. So when you say "don't know," at that moment you've already hit the nail on the head. That's called the initial moment of inspiration. An old master said, "The initial moment of inspiration is already enlightenment." When you say "don't know" and have hit the nail on the head, faith mind appears, simultaneously enlightenment mind appears. Faith mind appears, enlightenment mind appears, practice mind appears. The Sixth Patriarch, in the *Platform Sutra,* said, "The Zen of our schools is *samadhi* and *prajna* together, like the two wings of a bird." *Samadhi* means "stability," "deep meditation," "quiescence"; *prajna* means "to see clearly," "wisdom"—see clearly, hear clearly, perceive clearly. He said that because the usual view toward practice had been that you first practice meditation and the power *mitas* of generosity, doing good actions, compassion, etc., and then you get wisdom.

But the Sixth Patriarch said, "No, it's like the candle flame and its light. The candle flame steadily burning is quiescent Zen; sitting Zen, *samadhi*. The radiating light is the light of wisdom shining into the world. Those two are not separate." So when you say "don't know," already you've hit the nail on the head. At that moment you already attain faith, practice, enlightenment. Then, like having a baby in your arms, you have to continually walk with it and nurture it, and nurture it, and nurture it. Now we come to the actual title of this workshop.

The last Zen school to emerge in China was the Fa-yen school. The Koreans pronounce his name not Fa-yen, but Peop An, and the Japanese call him Hogen. When Fa-yen was still a student, not yet a Zen master, he was traveling around on pilgrimage. Monks at that time wouldn't stay very long in one place but would go from place to place, calling on different teachers and staying in different assemblies and journeying; they were referred to as cloud-and-water monks. It was a practice of nonattachment, in a certain sense. So Fa-yen came to the temple of Ti-ts'ang, who asked, "Where are you coming from?"

And Fa-yen said, "I have been on pilgrimage."

"And where will you go when you leave here?"

"I'll resume my pilgrimage."

Master Ti-ts'ang said, "Oh, that's wonderful. But tell me, what is the essential meaning of your pilgrimage?"

Fa-yen was taken aback and just blurted out "I don't know," and Ti-ts'ang, the master of the temple, said "Don't know is closest to it." Another translation of that line is "Not knowing is nearest"; and a third translation is, "Don't know is most intimate." So closest to it, nearest, most intimate—they all point toward the same meaning.

The story says that, at that moment, Fa-yen had a small awakening and decided to stay at this temple to let his perception get more certain. He stayed for some time, then one day announced to the master, "Tomorrow I'll be leaving to continue on with my pilgrimage."

Zen Master Ti-ts'ang said, "Do you think you are ready to go yet?"

Fa-yen said, "Yes, of course."

So the master said, "Let me ask you one question, just to check. All of you monks are very fond of repeating the saying, 'the three worlds are mind alone, and the ten thousand phenomena are all just recognition.' You see those big boulders over there in the garden? Well, are they inside your mind or outside your mind?"

Fa-yen immediately said, "They are inside my mind. How could anything be outside?"

Then the master said, "Well, you'd better get a good night's sleep because it's going to be difficult traveling with all those rocks inside your head."

That is a very important sentence, I think. What is the need for a traveling monk to carry rocks inside his head? For what reason would a traveler carry rocks inside his head? If we sincerely look, we will see that we also all are carrying some fairly substantive rocks inside our minds at times. *My* opinions, *my* conceptions, holding *my* condition, attaching to *my* version of the way

things are, etc. Essentially, it's all a fabrication. It's all a construction that we make.

When my teacher first came to this country, his English was extremely limited so he used to teach through very short slogans that he would concoct out of the limited English that he knew. One of his slogans was, "Don't make anything, don't hold anything, don't attach to anything." *Don't make anything* is very important. We are all always constructing rocks inside our heads and fabricating a story around them to substantiate their solidity and their existence. Essentially it's based on a need to secure our own ground, which is fear-based. Sometimes even the ideas are quite grand.

Someone I know told me a story a while ago. She said, "You know my tendency to immediately jump to the last chapter of some event? Well, there was this guy whom I had known for quite some time and we had been friends for a while and I knew his family but we had never been intimately involved. His family was quite wealthy and they owned a big mansion. But one thing led to another and somehow I found myself getting into bed with this guy and making love with him. That wasn't a problem, because that's what I wanted to do at that moment, but when we had finished and were just lying there I began at lightning speed to fabricate a whole story and I had a picture in my mind that we were already married, and that such and such was going on, and I said to myself, 'We've inherited the mansion.' In the next moment, I woke up to what I was fabricating and realized the sheets are white and I'm lying next to this guy who I don't really know too well yet." So, what need does a traveler have to put rocks inside of his head?

Again Fa-yen realized that he was not as enlightened as he thought and he unpacked his bags and decided to stay longer. Each day he came to present his views to Master Ti-ts'ang, who would just say to him, "The Buddhadharma is not like that. That is not the living truth of Buddhism." So Fa-yen would go back and practice more. The next day he would come with something else and again the master would say, "The Buddhadharma is not like that. That is not the living truth of the Buddhadharma." So this went on for over a month, day in and day out. Finally Fa-yen came and said, "I have completely exhausted everything. I don't understand anything." Then the master said, "Yes. That not understanding already contains the sun, the moon, the stars, and the rocks in the garden." Fa-yen's mind opened up.

[Master Wu Kwang here invited the participants to take part in a half-hour meditation. After giving brief instructions regarding posture, position, breathing, etc., he continued to direct the meditation as follows:]

Ask yourself this question: What am I? Ask the question a few times. What am I? If you ask it with sincerity, before long you'll come to a place where you recognize all your ideas about I-ness don't fully satisfy the question What am I? and you'll come to the point

expressed by these two words: Don't know. What am I? Don't know.

[After this meditation, Master Wu Kwang elaborated on the meaning of don't know.]

Because there is no knowing, there are no eyes, no ears, no nose, no tongue, no body, no mind—no knowing. If you grab that point, then, according to the Heart Sutra, no eyes, no ears, no nose, no tongue, no body, no mind means just clear seeing, just clear hearing, just clear tasting, just clear smelling, just clear perceiving, moment by moment by moment. If you manifest that openness— "clear like space" the old Zen masters said, meaning like a mirror—it clearly reflects just what comes in front and remains radiant and bright just as it is. So seeing is there spontaneously, hearing is there spontaneously, sensing is there spontaneously, recognition is there spontaneously.

Then how do we use that mind? Our life is always situational. We always find ourselves in a context. The context of this moment is not the context of the previous moment. And the situation of the next moment is not the situation of this moment. In old times in China, Layman Pang, who was a great Zen adept, said, "My miraculous attainment is when I'm hungry I eat, and when I'm tired I sleep." That means, if I am completely attuned and intimate with myself from this point, then I respond appropriately to the situation. Layman Pang only mentioned two situations—when I'm hungry I eat, and when I'm tired sleep—but one might infer a third, which is vitally important, especially in these times: If someone *else* is hungry, then what?

Being attuned to the moment, the situation, and the context is not only about me. If someone else is hungry, then what? Obviously, give them some food. Of course, there are many kinds of hunger—physical hunger, emotional hunger, mental hunger, spiritual hunger, etc.—and many kinds of food. In the training of Zen, especially in the Kong-an tradition, there are various kinds of questions that are used to refine the clear perception coming from [HIT] into the world, both in terms of the subjective and the objective sides of the pole. That doesn't mean we divide the world into subject and object, it means that, in this unified context in which we find ourselves, there is a subjective and an objective polarity. When I'm hungry I eat and when I'm tired I sleep. That is taking care of the subject. When someone else is hungry, give them some food, is responding to the objective side. What do you see? What do you perceive? How does it move you in the moment? If you are holding too much of selfhood and I-ness, then you cannot respond freely and clearly to the call and the moment.

Ananda, who was the cousin of the Buddha, asked Mahakashyapa, the Buddha's successor, "When Shakyamuni Buddha transmitted to you the Dharma robe and the bowl, which were signs of the transmission, did he give you something else as well?"

Mahakashyapa just called out "Ananda."

Ananda, without thinking, responded, "Yes, sir."

Then Mahakashyapa said, "Take down the flagpole in front of the gate." (At that time, in India, when a Dharma speech was to be given, a pennant was hoisted in front of the temple. Then when the Dharma speech was over and everyone went about their business, the pennant was taken down.) "Cut down the flagpole. That means the complete Dharma has now been revealed, so what need do we have for the flagpole any longer? Cut it down. Because I called, you answered. Because you're there to answer, I can call."

That's called the ability to respond. The ability to respond means the response ability. If you have the ability to respond and have the response ability then, of course, you have responsibility. Here's a traditional *kong-an* about responsibility:

One day great Zen Master Nan-ch'üan heard the monks of the eastern hall and the western hall in his monastery in the courtyard arguing over a cat. "This is our cat. No, no, this is our cat." But these were all monks, who are supposed to be free of petty attachment, and of possessiveness, and of I, my, and me. Nan-ch'üan heard all this and came out of his room and grabbed hold of the cat. He picked it up in one hand, then he took out his precept's knife in the other hand.

"If any of you give me one word of Zen, then I can save this cat," he said. One word of Zen doesn't necessarily mean literally one word. It means, show me your true Zen spirit as connected with the situation of this moment. Give me one word of Zen—give me the final word of Zen—show me that you perceive your correct situation, your correct function, and your correct relationship just now.

"If you can, I can save this cat. If not, I have to kill it." No one came forward. No one presented anything. No verbal answer. No demonstration answer. Nothing. All just stood there. So, finally, Nan-ch'üan killed the cat.

Later in the day his number-one disciple, Chao-chou, returned from outside the monastery. He hadn't been there all the time this went on, so Nan-ch'üan told him all that had happened previously. Chao-chou took off his shoe, put it on his head, and began to walk out of the room.

Nan-ch'üan said, "Oh, if you had been there at that time I could have saved the cat," which means, you know what to do now, and you would have known what to do then.

So the question for Zen students is, if you were there at that time, what could you do? If you enter deeply into that, then you will be able to manifest the mind of compassion and of great love, and of great responsibility and obligation.

[A participant returned to Hui-neng's story from the Platform Sutra and his experience pounding rice. "One of my teachers once said that the eight months of rice polishing weren't only a result of the politics. Because all of the rice was ripe, there was a lot of chaff, and most of us, whether eight years or eighty years, would blow the chaff away. I wondered if you could speak about that process. Perhaps there is some ripening, but there is still endless work, and that chaff polishing was very important. And when the Patriarch came down and asked,

'Is the rice polished yet?' 'Yes.' But how can any of us say yes?"]

Zen Master Wu Kwang: In fact, in the first chapter of the *Platform Sutra,* when the Sixth Patriarch tells this story, I think it says, "The Fifth Patriarch came to the rice-polishing shed and he said, 'Is the rice ready,' and the Sixth Patriarch answered, 'Ready for long time, but waiting to be sifted.'" I mentioned earlier this spontaneous emergence of faith, enlightenment, practice. In the Soto tradition, for example, Dogen Zenji said, "Just sitting is itself the manifestation of enlightenment or buddha-nature." In the Lin-chi tradition, some masters said, The minute you pick up the *kong-an,* already that is enlightened mind. It's just that you don't realize it at that moment. So it's not that after working on this *kong-an* for umpteen years, all of a sudden something is going to emerge that wasn't there from the beginning.

But there is the issue of cultivation and of on-going refinement. In the sutra tradition, you see that example brought to the foreground in the *Hua-yen Sutra.* In the very last book there is a long story about a young pilgrim named Sudana, who wants to learn how to practice the way of the bodhisattva, how to practice the way of enlightened wisdom and enlightened compassion and activity. So he meets the great bodhisattva Manjushri, who is the symbolic representation of fundamental wisdom. Manjushri first gives Sudana some teaching and stirs up in him a moment of inspiration, he gives rise to the *bodhichitta,* to the thought of enlightenment, moment of enlightenment. After that, Sudana doesn't ask anymore about enlightenment, but he says, "How is one to practice the way of the bodhisattva?" They didn't talk about enlightenment after that, just *How is one to practice the way of the bodhisattva?* That means that enlightenment stands on its own but practice is not letting your habitual energies obscure that self-existing fact.

Manjushri then sends him on a pilgrimage—in the sutra it says he sends him "south," which has the connotation of moving toward openness and clarity. He calls on fifty or so teachers. He comes to each one of these teachers asking, "Please teach me the way to practice the way of the bodhisattva." Each gives him some teaching, and he has some other experience with them, and then at the very end of the chapter that particular teacher always says: "I only know this small portion. How can I know the vastness of the great bodhisattva way? Now you should go and call on X, Y, or Z, and they will teach you such and such." These teachers are not all typical representations of holy beings—they are not all monks and nuns with halos. There are laymen, laywomen, children, prostitutes, fishermen, salesmen, etc. Other teachers he meets are demons, goddesses, and beings like that. There is a vast array of teachers in different forms, the meaning of which is that the teaching in compassionate and skillful activity is always present in the world if you can just open up and listen to it and respond to it.

So he goes through all the various teachers and there is a refinement going on. If you're a great scholar of this sutra, you understand that each of these teachers is picking up concretely on something that has been taught earlier in the sutra, and these rather abstract concepts are all being embodied in a very practical, human form, although one that is sometimes slightly fantastic. At the very end, he is directed to three more teachers, and these are the main teachers in the whole sequence. He's directed first to Maitreya, whose name actually means "loving-kindness." (According to Buddhist mythology and legend, Maitreya is the Buddha to be, who is just waiting to be born and emerge from the Tushita Heaven.) Maitreya once again extols the virtues of this initial inspirational mind of enlightened thought. Then Maitreya is in a huge tower called the Tower of the Adornments of Vairochana. (Vairochana is the Buddha of Infinite Light, and infinite light represents both some unifying principle and also the differentiation of all the array of colors in the universe shining forth.) Maitreya snaps his fingers and the door to the tower opens. That means wake up. At that moment the door opens. Then the door closes behind Sudana as he moves into the tower, which means essentially that there is no opening, no closing, no before, no after, no delusion, no enlightenment, everything returns to the source before any ideas like that.

Inside, he sees that the space of the tower is as vast as space. That means that the tower represents the real nature of the universe. There are many dazzling jewels and lights and pennants and streamers, all of which are representative of the various compassionate activities shining forth in the world. But that is not enough; the sutra is very ornate. So inside this one tower filled with all these things are infinite numbers of exactly the same tower, all as vast as space. Within each one of these towers is the whole panorama of everything that was in all the other towers, and yet each tower never loses its own unique position and its own place and never obstructs or hinders or interferes with any of the other towers. Sudana experiences this and goes into a very deep state and attains a kind of unimpeded liberation, until Maitreya snaps his fingers and Sudana awakens and is sent back to Manjushri. That's a very important point. Manjushri was his very first teacher. The meaning is, the place where you embark from is not separate from the place of your destination. The cause of your embarkation is not different from the result. There is some identifying principle between cause and effect and beginning and end.

Manjushri again gives some teaching but the gist of all this teaching, although the sutra does not use this phrase, is that Manjushri taps him on the head and essentially says *Always keep this beginner's mind.* That's the source of the phrase "Zen mind, beginner's mind." Sudana finally finds himself with the great bodhisattva of skillful action Samantabhadra and he perceives that all the buddhas in the universe, in every atom and every millisecond, are already enlightened, and that the principles of universal good and of skillful action are already present in the universe. That means perpetual practice goes on endlessly.

So there is always some rice and some chaff, but the chaff is fundamentally not different from the rice, and chaff doesn't necessarily have to be thrown away. Trungpa Rinpoche used to have a saying: "Shit makes good fertilizer."

Intimacy as a
Path to Enlightenment

Miranda Shaw, Ph.D.

IN CONTEMPORARY AMERICAN LIFE, TERMS LIKE "intimacy," "sexuality," "interdependence," and "relationship" often take on an unwanted edge. They can seem to shake an invisible finger of blame in our faces. In part, this may be due to a too-readily adopted double-standard of false moralizing combined with a fast-paced modern-day existence that permits little time for grappling with such potentially thorny aspects of life as relationship and intimacy. Seldom, it seems, do contemporary Western individuals turn to ages-old religious and philosophical underpinnings for counsel in developing and maintaining relationship, in all its multifaceted complexity.

Tantric Buddhism offers methods whereby an intimate relationship can become a path to fully embodied enlightenment. This path configures the healing journey of men and women in complementary ways to meet their differing psychological needs in the process of becoming whole. Together the partners seek to make their daily interactions, intimacy, and erotic experience occasions for spiritual growth and psychological healing.

Miranda Shaw, Ph.D., is on the faculty of the University of Richmond in Virginia. She has devoted herself to research into the survival of women's ancient spiritual traditions in the Himalayas, focusing on the embodied practices of sacred sexuality and sacred dance. As a pioneer in research into numerous aspects of Tantric Buddhism, she has demonstrated the historical primacy of women in the development of these practices, as she documents in *Passionate Enlightenment: Women in Tantric Buddhism.* Dr. Shaw's forthcoming book, *Her Waves of Bliss: Buddhist Goddesses of India, Tibet, and Nepal,* develops this still further, demonstrating through works of ancient to modern Tantric art the central role of women in Tantric practice and the manner in which men complement the female energy and the harmony that then can arise.

The journey that brought me to you today is part of a search started many years ago for a religious tradition in which women did not fare as badly as they do in the Western tradition in which I was raised. I was looking for a religious tradition that would nurture and enrich my emerging sense of femaleness as positive, not as a religious liability. What first attracted me to Tantric Buddhism was the amazing female images that I encountered in the art. I saw women pulsating with energy, leaping and flying, unfettered by clothing, dancing joyfully without shame or fear, clothed only in their billowing hair, in ornaments made of flowers or bone. I saw their eyes blazing with passion, ecstasy, ferocious intensity. They appeared to revel in their femaleness, in glory, in freedom of every kind.

I wondered what kind of women can have given rise to such images, so I looked into the literature on Tantric Buddhism to see what information was available, and I found the same opinion repeated in work after work with very little variation. These opinions also express an interpretation of Tantric relationships. To give just a few examples:

The chief role of women in the Tantric cult is to act as the female partner of the male adepts.

In Tantrism, woman is means, an alien object without possibility of mutuality or real communication.

The goal of Tantric practice is to destroy the female.

And this one by a very important Jungian, Mircea Eliade:

The role played by girls of low caste and courtesans in the Tantric orgies is well-known. The more depraved and debauched the woman, the more fit she is for the rite.

Then, finally, one from the formerly leading Tantric scholar, who was also a Jesuit priest:

The women's presence was essential to the performance of the Tantric rites...[so he noticed that much] and their activities generally are so obscene as to earn them quite properly the name witch.

Now, according to this theory, if the women themselves were downtrodden, exploited, then it follows that the female images bore no relationship to women in the movement, and that these powerful female images were designed by men with no relationship to the actual women. Then scholars draw upon Jung and Freud (that great friend of women) to theorize that these female images symbolize male psychic processes and drives. We are asked to believe that women did not think of themselves when they looked at these naked, anatomically correct, female images, and that men did not think of them either.

When I compared these descriptions to the actual images that I was looking at, I simply could not believe them. I realized that when these Western scholars looked at these women— who are beautiful, sensuous, erotically alive—they could not imagine that they were also disciplined, spiritual and, in fact, enlightened. So I wondered, if I did some research on Tantric Buddhism, might I find something different. Many people assured me that I would not, but when I looked at the women in the paintings, their eyes gripped mine, just riveted me, and called me and said, "Look for us. You'll find us. We're here." That summons really led me on a journey that turned out to be much longer than I anticipated, as journeys this profound sometimes do.

Their summons carried me through the hardships of research, such as looking for texts in tropical heat in Calcutta; searching for yogini temples in the jungles in Orissa; and reading manuscripts in an unheated hermitage in the Himalayas, the place that has the coldest winter in the world; and passing unscathed through the labyrinth of academe.

In *Passionate Enlightenment*, I presented my discoveries that women had a major role in the founding of Tantric Buddhism, and although Tantra represents a very ancient form of spirituality, when we look at the emergence of Tantric Buddhism in the seventh and eighth centuries, it can be traced to circles of women gathering together in the countryside, which has shaped Tantra in important ways.

These women gathered in remote locations where they wouldn't be disturbed—in forest clearings, in cremation grounds where bodies are burned and generally no one goes after twilight, and also in yogini temples. The yogini temples of India are circular and have no roofs or doors. Therefore, they're open to the sky and they're open to

be used by women day or night. The entryway is small and low, like the entrance to a womb, and the walls are just high enough that no one can see what's going on inside. If you read descriptions of these temples currently, you will hear that they are not used anymore. That is because the anthropologists do not go there at midnight on the full moon. (Don't tell them. Don't let out the secret, but it is a living tradition. They are still in use.)

The women assembled in nonhierarchical circles to feast together, practice yoga and meditation, and inspire one another with sacred dance and song. One of their practices was to pass around a sacred bowl, made of a skull, filled with sacramental wine. When each women received the bowl, she offered a song expressing her insights into ultimate reality. I found collections of some of these songs, which give a wonderful taste of these gatherings, three of which follow:

Who speaks the sound of an echo?
Who paints the image in a mirror?
Where are the spectacles in a dream?
Nowhere at all. That's the nature of mind.

KYE HO, wonderful, when someone experiences reality, the whole sky cannot contain her bliss.
Can you express that? Then speak.
I have seen what is utterly invisible.

KYE HO, wonderful, this spontaneous wellspring of great, ecstatic wisdom.
Without realization, one cannot describe it.
After realization, why speak?

Taste it and you're struck dumb, speechless.

Male Tantrics, or yogis, were very anxious to gain admittance to their gatherings, these circles, because if the women deemed a man qualified to attend, they would initiate him and teach him their Tantric lore. Many of the early, now classical, Tantric texts emanating from this period go into great detail about how to locate these gatherings and then how to approach them, how to gain admittance, and the behavior and decorum that would show the proper honor when they did enter. Sometimes each woman would bring a male companion to the circle to feast and do yoga. These men apprenticed themselves to women and accepted the women's teachings as their own, adding their own insights along the way. A list of the famous male Tantrics who attended these feasts is, in essence, a "Who's Who" of the so-called founding fathers of Tantric Buddhism.

Now, the significance of these origins is that Tantra initially represented a women's philosophy, and that has shaped it in profound ways. The female founders of Tantric Buddhism prize their femaleness and they embrace the body, the senses, the emotions, as sources of knowledge and power. Those sources of wisdom had been devalued in some of the previous traditions of Buddhism, which were emphasizing other aspects of being as important on the path. So the women pioneered this new, embodied spirituality. Their goal was to be inwardly disciplined and outwardly untamable; to be erotically alive and totally free. Tantric annals are filled with their legendary attainments, and

their teachings and practices form the core of Tibetan Buddhism and Nepalese Buddhism as living traditions today.

I feel that Tantric Buddhism is highly relevant for us today because Tantrics seek to attain enlightenment in the midst of life, of work, of intimacy, relationships. Tantra offers many methods whereby couples can use their daily life as well as their intimacy and their erotic life as sources of psychological growth and spiritual insight. Further, the female founders of Tantric Buddhism configured the healing journey of men and women in different and complementary ways in order to meet what they considered their differing psychological needs in the journey to becoming whole.

One of the most fundamental features of Tantra is that Tantra is a spiritual orientation in which it is necessary to honor women. This honor is built into every aspect of Tantric relationships, although it has different implications for men and for women. To begin with, women must learn to honor themselves. The female images that initially brought me to the research have played a central role in women's spiritual lives over the centuries as objects of meditation and yogic transformation. They portray enlightenment in female form, or what we would call goddesses. They are the cornerstone of women's journey of self-empowerment. Using the artistic images as a point of departure, a woman develops a vivid mental image of her divine counterpart in order to awaken those divine qualities within herself. So she understands that image to represent her potential for enlightenment, her inherent sacredness.

Sometimes the meditation takes a physical form as well. The woman may don the ornaments of the deity and dance, evoking the presence of the goddess within herself, bodying forth the presence of the goddess through her movement. This sacred dance form may be practiced as a solitary meditation or in a ritual context. One aspect that really hasn't come to the West yet is the original sacred dance form that was associated with it. When I studied it in Nepal, it supplied this missing piece of what this full embodiment of deity is supposed to represent. I foresee in the future of Buddhism in America, this exploring the implications of that full embodiment and the transmission of that dance form.

Women on the Tantric path seek to develop a quality known as divine pride, which comes from discovering one's sacred female essence. This confidence is qualitatively different from ignorance. It is not based on a sense of deficiency, or compensation for self-hatred, or a desire to be better than others, to dominate others, but rather it is a source of self-esteem that comes from deep within one's own being, that makes it unnecessary for a woman to seek outer sources of approval. This is very important for the integrity of one's path, and also so that she will not give in to a sense of self-doubt or inadequacy, which can be fatal to spiritual progress.

[Editor's note: A sizable portion of this day-long workshop consisted of a slide show that presented works of Tantric sculpture and painting, from ancient times to contemporary. These images provided points of departure for Dr. Shaw to describe and explain the characteristics of Tantric deities and devotees. While these descriptions were vivid and eloquent, since these images could not be reproduced here, only the basic essence of the spoken text is included. Interested readers are referred to Dr. Shaw's books for illustrations and in-depth explication.]

A female buddha is the color of the sky, symbolizing her unlimited capacity to understand reality. Her awareness is as vast as the sky, encompassing all of reality, for she has transcended ego-centered existence. As is typical of Tantric goddesses, she is naked and dances in a dynamic pose that reveals the body in all its female glory. She wears only delicate ornaments of women's manufacture made of flowers and of carved bone. These ornaments do not require wealth, but only the knowledge of how to make them, which women transmitted among themselves. They also represent the nondualistic outlook needed to be able to work with the human bone. The third eye on her forehead indicates her omniscience. Her gaze is concentrated and focused. Her eyes are not averted or demurely downcast. She does not offer herself as a passive object of observation, evaluation, or even appreciation. Rather, she stares straight ahead with piercing one-pointedness, gripping the eyes of the viewer, challenging engagement.

Tantric goddesses generally dance upon a corpse, which represents the former self that is left behind on the journey to enlighten-ment. Psychological wholeness involves losses and death of the unenlightened aspects of the self so the enlightened essence can emerge. This is not an image of conquest per se.

Tantric goddesses are known by the generic names of yogini and *dakini*. Yogini means "female practitioner of yoga," or a "spiritually advanced female." *Dakini* derives from a verb meaning "to fly," so it can be translated most literally as "a women who flies," which refers to her spiritual attain-ments. The flight of a *dakini* is a flight of free-dom—freedom from social restraints and freedom that comes from knowing ultimate reality. This can also be translated as "sky dancers" or as "women who dance in space." Sometimes dakinis literally dance in space. Since the the sky is their special preserve, Tantric practitioners and adepts watch the sky for their messages, signs, and manifesta-tions.

The curved knife is one of the main *dakini* symbols. It is a small, handheld knife with a curved blade rounded like a woman's body, like a crescent moon. Women use it not as a weapon against others, but as a knife that cuts away illusion and conquers problems. In her imagination, a woman places the source of her emotional pain in the skull bowl. With her knife, she pulverizes it into atoms, returning it to its original form as a dance of energy, a play of light, merely a momentary illusion. Thus, with her knife she transforms pain and negativity into a sublime, blissful nectar which she then drinks from her skull cup and also may offer to her part-

ner. One of the ultimate things we have to offer one another is our joy, of course.

Both women and goddesses are called *dakinis* because, in this world view, there is no clear-cut dividing line between the human and the divine. Deities represent the divine potentiality of all humans, where a human who has attained enlightenment is seen as a deity in living form.

Machig Labdrönme's biography recounts that, while receiving teachings with her com-panions, she left the group and was gone all night. When the teacher and her friends searched for her the next morning, they found her "sitting in a tree, naked, free from habitual neuroses, beyond shame, free from embarrassment." The teacher pronounced that the others had received the words of the teachings, but that Machig Labdrönme had received the essence. Having displayed her enlightenment in this and may other ways, she went on to become a very impor-tant teacher, guru, and founding figure, which is why her portraits are made to this day.

Simhamukha is the lion-faced female buddha. Spiritual wholeness includes the abil-ity to commune with other living creatures, including animals. This motif also refers to women's rituals in which they are able to disidentify with humanness and to experi-ence life as another life form. The head of a wild cat symbolizes the cauldron of a raw power that a woman can tap within her own being. A woman on the spiritual path may at times manifest a feline ferocity as she becomes untamable by the standards of con-ventional reality or develops a ruthless intolerance of anything that would detract her from her goals. Her mouth is drawn in a perpetual roar of fury. Her body is black, the color of wrath. Her face is white with the lightning, laser light of clarity that shines at the heart of anger. She never surrenders her stance of outrage against anyone and anything who would transgress against her sovereignty of being. A yogini cannot let anything stand between her and her experience of ultimate reality. The staff, which represents that she is not celibate, is the symbol that indicates that the being in question has integrated their eroticism into their spiritual path and that they have a consort tucked away somewhere for when they need him.

The main female buddha is Vajrayogini, which means "adamantine yogini" or, in a sense, "the yogini whose attainments are diamondlike, irreducible," "the supreme yogini." Red is the prototypically female color in India—the color of the life force, the blood of birth, menstrual blood, and the fire of spiritual transformation. This life force is known as *shakti* and it is regarded as female. Vajrayo-gini's glowing red body signifies this primal female essence. Her long hair streams behind her, rippling with the intensity of her energy and her fiery wisdom bursts around her in flames. Vajrayogini has a wide-eyed, fearless expression for she is truly a fearless goddess. She embodies the ability to face reality directly, never flinching, never turning away, and always finding a reason to celebrate, to rejoice, to dance. In this characteristic stance, she raises and drinks from her skull bowl, made from a human skull. This

shows that nothing deters her ability to fully taste and enjoy life, not even the fact that life's feast is sometimes served in something that looks like death.

Vajrayogini personifies the feminine energy pulsating at the heart of reality. What does her iconography tell us about reality? When we see her dancing red as fire, red as rubies, red as blood, we are to understand that this energy, the essence of the world, is blissful, radiant, and pure and that it can be encountered directly in a naked, dancing, female body. Vajrayogini is always identified in museum catalogs and actually in a lot of contemporary books by Western scholars and practitioners as the consort or wife of a male buddha. This is not true. She is a sovereign deity, who often appears without him and with her female retinue. The opposite is, in fact, true: He rarely appears without her, which has been the case from the earliest origins of Tantric iconography. Seeing an image like this calls a woman to reenliven her spirit and her body to gain full access to all the energies and capacities of her being, which is the Tantric definition of wholeness.

The "sky-bound" or "space" Vajrayogini is shown in a leaping pose that indicates that she has transcended worldliness. She is not bound by conventional reality. She doesn't linger at any point of attachment and doesn't get frozen in any one frame of reference. She leaps beyond every form of bondage and illusion. Her awareness is dynamic, ever-flowing, and always keeping up with the present moment.

Female Tantrics get the skulls for these cups from people who don't need them anymore, often from a departed friend or a departed teacher. After they are deceased, they take the skull, cut off the top, scrape it out, clean it, sun bleach it, etc. Human bone remains shiny for a very long time so it's actually like ivory, a very beautiful natural substance.

The space yogini image epitomizes the Tantric understanding of femaleness. A women on this path does not have to deny, repress, or devalue her femaleness, or pursue a masculine, androgynous, or a so-called gender-transcendent ideal. No sense of shame or impurity attaches to the female body; rather, she displays her most characteristically female and sacred part, offering it to receive admiration, honor, and worship, expressing total affirmation, total celebration.

Passion and sexuality are energies that can be used on the path to enlightenment. They are in no way inconsistent with the wisdom and insight that a woman can attain. This motif beautifully illustrates women's capacity for wholeness, our ability to integrate our sensuality, sexuality, and spirituality.

[A participant asked Dr. Shaw why such images are not viewed as images of conquest of female over male.]

In the case of the goddess Kali, who wears the heads of male demons, that's a very explicit image of conquest. But she's the supreme goddess, the object of devotion, not an object of identification as these [images of Vajrayogini] are. Kali's work is

bringing order to the universe. She conquers that which is alienated from the divine, which is symbolized by maleness. Male heads and male animals are always sacrificed to her, which demonstrates her capacity to transform them into a more enlightened state. That represents that process she constantly carries on of integrating back into the divine powers, so it is actually a different motif. It is an image of conquest but informed by a very spiritual understanding, not as a kind of battle or in an external sense.

A sculpture from above a pillar on an Indian temple shows a woman framed by lotus petals; the lotus stem then passes through her body, likening her body to a lotus, which is a symbol of purity in Indian culture, and expressing in particular that her vulva has the purity and beauty of that transcendent flower. Female sexual fluid is believed to contain a concentration of *shakti,* the female life force. Here her sexual fluid is flowing into the temple walls, enhancing their purity and sacredness.

These sculptures from Orissa, about tenth century, help to understand the relationship of the Tantric symbolism to the rest of the culture. These are motifs found on a temple where practices of both an exoteric, or devotional, nature and an esoteric and Tantric nature would take place. These symbols would be shared by both, demonstrating that this is continuous with the whole cultural realm in which it occurs.

Here, the yoni—the vulva or female sexual organ—itself is the altar, the place of offerings. This part of the female body is considered to be the original altar in ancient Indian texts. It is the most sacred object in the visible world and, hence, the place most worthy of offerings and worship, so the altar shape that you now see in India is simply a geometric abstraction of this form, which is understood as the template of the altar.

The interpretations of women in Tantric Buddhism that I cited at the beginning all focused upon the women's relationship with men and their sexual subservience to men. I believe this interpretation represents prevailing views of sexuality in our culture, which simply accords primacy to male sexuality, around which female sexuality is somehow supposed to be constellated or configured. In the Tantric view, a woman's body exists solely to serve her as a vehicle of her pleasure, knowledge, power, and joy. A woman on the Tantric path seeks not only to accept her femaleness, but to savor and revel in it.

The Vajrayogini in her severed-headed form was originally introduced by a woman named Laksminkhara, a princess in India who had had a very good education and did spiritual practices and also had some Tantric training. She was betrothed to a king in another country, but she did not like her husband-to-be. He wasn't Buddhist, he was very uncouth, and he brought her these skins of a deer that he killed as his tribute to her. She was horrified by this and so she ran away into the forest and pretended to be mad. She started going naked and letting her hair down. She got caked with mud and leaves. If anyone came up to her, she pretended she was insane, so she was obviously

unmarriageable. Having severed all ties with both her family and her family-to-be, she used this time as an intensive meditation retreat. She spent several years in her meditation, by which she attained a visionary state in which this female buddha revealed herself in this form. The name of this form of Vajrayogini is simply Chinnamundah or severed-headed goddess.

This has been a favorite object of meditation for women over the centuries. The meditator identifies with her and envisions herself as taking a sword or knife and cutting off her own head, triumphantly waving it aloft. Three streams of blood issue from her neck. Two go into the mouths of two yoginis at her sides, and one goes into the mouth of her own head. Male interpreters always stress how gory and repulsive this image is, which is not surprising. Who but a woman would appreciate this viscerally direct symbol of nourishment in which streams of life-giving liquid flow from a woman's body? Clearly, this image is based on a female experience of embodiment.

Although the severed head refers on one level to biological nourishment, on a deeper level it locates the source of spiritual sustenance in a woman's body, expressing that a woman can tap a never-ending stream of energy within herself and direct that energy to the life of her mind and to the accomplishment of her life's purpose. Rather than being a gory image of beheading, this is actually an image of self-sufficiency. When she has tapped that inner source of emotional sustenance—the roots of her psychological wholeness—she can share that energy with other women and teach them how to discover it within themselves. However, the primary stream feeds herself, signaling that when she directs that energy to other people, such as her disciples or her partner, she does so voluntarily and without sacrificing her own needs and spiritual growth. On another level of symbolism, the severed-headed female buddha is the need to cut off dualistic thinking at the root if one is to attain a level of direct knowing.

In this work, the severed-headed Vajrayogini and the two yoginis are standing on a copulating couple. The women are on the top, which symbolizes that it is this *shakti* in the body of the goddess that passes into the world through the act of conception—that that's a divine spark of life. And the woman of the couple is on top not only because that is the more predominant motif in the Tantric world view, but because that spark passes into the woman and then through the woman into the world.

The Tantric journey takes one beyond what Buddhism regards as derivative, socially constructed emotions—such as guilt, boredom, sadness, loneliness, resentment, and self-pity —to the primal passions blazing at the core of the psyche: fear, anger, jealousy, greed, hatred, selfish lust. For most people, the passions are a cause of suffering, but it is possible to learn to ride that energy as if it were a galloping horse or a tidal wave and to revel in the intrinsic pleasure of its surging power. The passions then become a source of energy to use however one chooses, to

meditate, create, heal, or go through daily life with impeccability, clarity, and compassion.

So we see in these images the self-understanding and self-empowerment of the women of Tantric Buddhism. They affirm themselves absolutely as women, as embodiments of goddesses, as sexual beings, and as spiritual seekers.

I found many passages that describe the ideal Tantric yogini (basically what Tantric yoginis are about) and also stories of actual yoginis. These descriptions are taken from both types of passages. For example, female Tantric practitioners celebrate women who are physically strong and mentally strong, women who speak the truth fearlessly, who love to argue and pick fights, who anger easily and never back down in an argument, women who have extreme mood swings, and who laugh and cry easily, maybe laugh one minute, cry the next, who are proud and arrogant, who are aggressive and domineering, who are fearless and who revel in their ferocity, who are powerful and who *delight* in their power; women who are proud of their strength, who are untamed and, who revel in their untamability.

Further, when I looked at the actions of such women, one of the first things I noticed is that there are no external constraints of any kind on their behavior or on their speech. They speak their minds without restraint. They are never encouraged to develop qualities that would appeal to or meet with the approval of men.

Women teach one another freely. They act as self-appointed teachers and guides of men as well. We see this in many stories where a man is minding his own business and a Tantric yogini happens by and notices that he was in need of some impromptu spiritual advice, so she just delivers it to him on the spot and continues on her merry way. Sometimes it was just a sharp rebuke aimed at, perhaps, a self-inflated image of himself. Or sometimes it was a poem or a song that she made up on the spot. Sometimes a gesture or totally unexpected action would shock him to awareness or put him back in direct touch with reality.

The way one of these women functioned is seen in the case of the life of Luipa, who later became a founder. He was a prince destined to take over his father's kingdom, but he did not want all the work. He initially set out to be a yogi—basically, living off the offerings of others was what first drew him to live as a beggar—but he also became serious about spiritual practice. He had done a lot of Tantric meditation and thought that he was above reproach in his meditation. He *was* very advanced, but he had not attained the supreme state.

One day he went to beg at a wine shop and, unbeknownst to him, the owner was a yogini—in fact, a highly realized Tantric guru. With her clairvoyant vision she perceived that he had this small knot of royal pride in his heart, that he still thought he was above some things, so she saw that he was clinging to this dualism of purity/impurity. Instead of giving something from the menu, she gave

him a bowl of moldy leftovers, which Luipa threw into the street. He yelled at her, "How dare you serve garbage to a yogi." And she said, "How can a connoisseur attain enlightenment?"

This accuracy of her insight stunned him and he saw that she was pointing out the one obstacle that he had to overcome in order to attain enlightenment. So he decided to go somewhere he would confront something that's considered very impure and repulsive. He went to live on the river bank and to eat a diet usually reserved for dogs and scavenging animals—fish entrails from the place where the fish were gutted. The fisherwomen saw him there eating the fish entrails and they named him Luipa, "fish eater." Through this practice, Luipa attained a state of uninterrupted bliss. He experienced this diet as no different from ambrosial nectar. This story is generally told as Luipa's story, but it is regarded as her story as well.

In another case, Kantalipa was a yogi who lived by the side of the road as a very lowly tailor. He took rags he found and stitched them into cloth, which was how he made his living as a yogi, meditating. One day he stabbed his finger while he was sewing and cried out in pain. A yogini just happened to be strolling by and she thought, "Oh, look, this fellow is still clinging to the idea of seeking comfort for himself and cherishing himself." So she made up a song for him on the spot. She sang,

Envision the rags you pick and stitch as empty space.

See your needle as mindfulness and knowledge.
Thread this needle with compassion.
Stitch new clothing for all sentient beings.

When he heard this, a floodgate of compassion opened in his heart and he started laughing and shouting, "Look at this wonderful cloth I've sewn," and they both started rolling and laughing in the dust by the side of the road. He became her disciple and she gave him the higher Tantric initiation and led him to enlightenment. So these women are, in essence, self-styled gurus, devising whatever lesson or initiation was needed on a particular occasion. This was before the institutionalization of Tantric Buddhism, in which a more formal initiation structure now prevails.

One of these self-styled yoginis is Yambu, who lived in Nepal in a little temple that had a statue of the Buddha. She didn't wear any clothes and she didn't own anything. If people made offerings to her, she ate that; if they didn't, she ate garbage. And she sat on this Buddhist statue, her legs open in that posture you see, always smiling and laughing. One of her disciples brought his friend to her. He could instantly see that she was a very enlightened woman, so he asked her to receive initiation and she said, "If you want to be my disciple, first you have to give everything away." He got rid of all his possessions and he came back to her and she picked up a clump of dirt and spat on it and threw it at him and said, "All right, now you're initiated." When that happened, he immediately went into a very deep meditative state.

The Tantric biographies really bear out the empowerment of women that is reflected in the images and that has been true of the yoginis that I have met as well. Their spiritual life is very inner-directed, very self-directed, and I've never met more assertive, confident women than these yoginis. They're really not practicing for anyone other than themselves and the enlightenment of all sentient beings. But they do not configure their lives for their relationship with their partners or their families, which benefit from *their* development of enlightenment, the *shakti* that they channel, the bliss that they radiate.

Honoring women is central to a man's Tantric path. A man's relationship to women in general, and to his female companion in particular, assumes central importance because it is considered to be the measure of his ability to embrace and participate in life fully. It's the measure of the fact that he is on this path of participation. It's not an ascetic path or a path of withdrawal. His relationship with his companion is considered to be the guide that teaches him to dance with all the energies of life and to honor the life force that surges through her and then pulsates throughout the universe.

For a man, coming to see the inherent sacredness of women is a way for him also to purify his vision, to come to see the inherent sacredness of all phenomena and of all beings. It's also a way for him to refine his emotions, to move his emotions from cruder expressions—perhaps of domination, denigration, exploitation—to the subtler range of respect, honor, and celebration. If he does have a tendency to those cruder expressions, it can be either from his own past lifetimes or the way he's been socialized in this lifetime. It is necessary for him to uproot any tendency he may have to objectify his partner or introduce any kind of dynamic of manipulation or of making demands upon her, because that can set forth a struggle that will deplete her energetically and also deprive him of the energy he needs to attain enlightenment, the energy that's to be created and built in this relationship. So his task is to learn to interweave his energy with that of a woman so that, together, they can build this pattern of harmony, interdependence, and wholeness with one another that will then radiate out and permeate their family, their community, the cosmos.

Tantra really does see what a man and woman can accomplish together on a cosmic scale; that, as they become more enlightened together and attain enlightenment, they then become sacred beings in the center of this sacred universe. The bliss they have awakened, the wisdom they have awakened, radiates out and fills the cosmos and can be passed on to other people. Even though they're accomplishing it together, they see it very much in relationship to the whole of which they are a part.

The Tantric world view is somewhat essentialist philosophically. They see that some things about male and female are almost irreducible differences. They feel that women have a certain relationship to the life force, which is to be a channel of that life force or *shakti,* that bliss, into the world. But men's psychology is seen as more open to being formed or constructed by the society, that men can go either way.

One of the words used for men on the Tantric paths is "hero," which refers to the heroic quality of the Tantric path as one on which you face every aspect of the psyche, working with all your emotions. It also refers to the heroism of seeking self-mastery and discipline in the midst of life, in the midst of relationship; and it refers as well to his whole relationship to life, which is not in any sense as a user or as abuser, but as an upholder, a supporter, a celebrater, a participator. This is seen as the heroic stance a man on the Tantric path must take or has chosen.

[A participant asked if both male and female are seen as having an equal amount of self-awareness and an equal amount of external awareness in the Tantric view.]

Miranda Shaw: In Buddhism, no two people would ever be seen to have the precise same amount of awareness. It's not a question of male versus female, of who has more awareness. But women who have a more advanced state than the men, have that as their spiritual credential; the insight they've attained is their spiritual credential. There's no authenticating, authorizing body to which they have to go and there's no male hierarchy from which they have to gain approval. They're not told, "Oh, you're a woman, then you can't attain this. If you've attained it, you can't teach it, can't initiate." This did happen later in the monastic system in Tibet, although not in the yogic system. This concerns me because we've received Tantra in America, for the most part, through the monastic system of Tibet.

[A participant raise the issue of sexual relationships in Tibetan Buddhism, in particular between monks or teachers and students.]

I think, in the past, people have tended to see sexual relationships with spiritual teachers as more or less Tantric. Just because you have a spiritual teacher doesn't mean you're practicing Tantra. I have met some of these Tibetan teachers who have had relationships with their female disciples, or with women who were not disciples, and there was nothing Tantric involved. I discussed it with the woman involved, and in some cases I was able to interview the man about his understanding relative to Tantra. There was no Tantra from beginning to end, except the fact that, because he was a Tibetan Buddhist practitioner, there was some assumption that it must be Tantric. In a few cases, these people had no knowledge of Tantra whatsoever.

So that is actually one of the reasons I wrote my book. I flushed these people out. This is a cloak they're hiding behind. There's a cloak of secrecy in Tantra that's meant to be there to protect the sacredness of that realm from those who are not prepared or even suited temperamentally to be there. But there's also another cloak of secrecy of lack of information about which people can hide. That I sought to remove.

The word *tantra* means "weaving" and this refers to the fact that Tantra is a path on which every aspect of daily life, relationship, and erotic intimacy is woven into the path to enlightenment. Tantric partners seek to interweave their energies and use their combined energies to attain enlightenment.

In textual descriptions of sacred union, the female partner is always the one who takes the initiative. She approaches him, she embraces him, she raises her lips to kiss him, and she initiates union. This is often described in very poetic terms, for example, one text says Vajrayogini wraps her arms around him like a "red-dawn cloud embraces a lapis lazuli mountain." Again, it shows that she's the one who's moving, embracing. Retaining the right of initiative is a way to assure that the woman's actions emanate from her own motives and primary purpose, which is to attain enlightenment. So you can see that this is not a dynamic of domination, but a blissful and mutually satisfying process protected by the aegis of female initiative.

In a Tantric text that records a conversation between Vajrayogini and her consort, she emerges as a great champion of women. She closely identifies with women and insists, "Wherever in the world a female body is seen, that should be recognized as my holy body." She goes on to say that, since all women and female beings in the universe are her embodiments, they should be respected, honored, and served without exception: "I am identical to the bodies of all women and there is no way that I could be worshipped except by the worship of women." Her partner asks her how a man should worship her.

She replies that he should regard his female companion as a living goddess and thus should prostrate to her, and circumambulate her, and make her his religious refuge. He should give her clothing, incense, flowers, lamps, perfume, and sacramental meat and wine. In their daily interactions he should rub her feet, cook for her, feed her, and wait until she has eaten to partake of her leftovers, as a symbolic gesture. He should regard every substance discharged by her body as pure and should be willing to sip sexual fluid and blood from her vulva and to lick any part of her body if requested to do so. He must satisfy her sexually, cultivating his erotic repertoire, taking special care to incorporate the female superior position.

In one text I read, the writer said, "And why, you may ask, should you do the female superior position? To attain buddhahood, of course." The man should never verbally or even mentally criticize her: "He should always speak with pleasant words and give a woman what she wants." This becomes his prayer of aspiration: "I must practice devotion to women, until I realize the essence of enlightenment."

In addition to outward expressions of devotion, the man must have a devotional attitude. A negative or derogatory attitude toward a female companion is expressly forbidden. A man seeking enlightenment on this path is warned never to abandon, forsake, or even criticize women. One text states that even if a man has been accumulating merit or good karma for a thousand lifetimes, it will all be wiped out by a single instant of criticism of a woman. A passage on this theme says, "One must not strike a woman, not even with a flower, not even if she commits a hundred misdeeds."

In the following text, Vajrayogini's consort, Chanda Maharoshina, joins her in her strong advocacy on behalf of women. He agrees to punish those who transgress against women and assures her that he keeps his sword and noose at the ready as he scouts for men who fail to pay homage to women so he can slash the scoundrels to pieces.

Mother, daughter, sister, niece, and any other female relative as well as a female musician, priestess, sweeper, dancer, washerwoman, and prostitute, holy woman, yogini, and ascetic as well. These he should serve in the proper way without making any distinction. If he makes a distinction, I will be provoked and slay the practitioner and throw him into the lowest hell and threaten him with sword and noose. Nor will he attain enlightenment in this world or the next.

Chanda Maharoshina apparently feels very strongly about this because he repeatedly warns a man seeking enlightenment on this path never to abandon, forsake, or even criticize women.

The buddhas command that you must serve a delightful woman who will uphold you. A man who violates this is foolish and will not attain enlightenment. On this path women must not be abandoned. Never abandon women. Heed the Buddha's words. If you do otherwise, that transgression will land you in hell.

So Vajrayogini has a very supportive boyfriend, and I feel like his references to hell are metaphorical ways to say that, if men do not honor women, this world is going to turn into a hell.

Clearly Vajrayogini is a strong supporter and champion of women but she does not promote this philosophy at the expense of men. For a man to show honor and worship to a woman is simply a way to refine his emotions and to purify his vision, which is essential for him to attain enlightenment. For the woman, the man's worship supports her in her effort to uncover her innate divinity, and that would support the psychological path that she's on and her inner growth. But a woman on this path does not seek to dominate or exploit the man or crush him into submissive service. In Vajrayogini's vision of ideal relationships, the women who embody her presence in the world are to dispense kindness, happiness, bliss, insight, and *shakti,* or spiritual nourishment, helping men to overcome whatever alienates or distances them from ultimate truth. A woman can provide insights and energy that a man needs to attain enlightenment, but she does so completely freely, not out of duty, obligation, or coercion. Women on this path are never required to do anything to assist men, or to meet the approval, or gain legitimacy in the eyes, of men. They are enjoined only to pursue their primary purpose, which is to attain enlightenment. Even in the midst of an enraptured embrace, both partners seek to maintain their mindfulness and meditative focus. It is

the supreme test of their ability to remain free from neurotic attachment.

Men and women on this path seek to create relationships devoted to their mutual enlightenment. I've come to believe that one of the reasons that the man has to pay homage to the woman, while the woman does not have to show any particular deference to the man, is to symbolize concretely that their relationship will be devoted to enlightenment. That is, it will not be centered upon the unenlightened ego needs of either person. His expressions of reverence betoken that he understands that her purpose for being in the relationship is to attain enlightenment. It symbolizes that he will not try to enlist her energies in the support of his physical, emotional, psychological, or even spiritual well-being; that is, he will not enlist them against her will or attempt to take them from her. This frees the woman psychologically from the depletion that takes place when involved in a dynamic of struggle or any kind of coercion. Freed from that dynamic of domination, her energy is able to flow in a much stronger way, which increases the amount of energy that both partners have available to obtain enlightenment.

This is not to say that men intrinsically have the tendency to dominate, but that their psychology is more open; they have that potential more than women. Women's relationship to the life force is pretty well set. She is a channel of the life force into the world. She can create life, she can bear life, and the *shakti* flows through her body in a more powerful way because of that. But the man has a choice, and the culture has a choice as to how men will be raised, what their relationship will be to the life force. So, according to this, male psychology is much more up for grabs—they can be raised to be abusers, haters, destroyers of life, and it's much more difficult to turn women into that. But men can also be raised to be supporters of life, defenders, celebraters, enjoyers of life. So Tantric Buddhism is paying very conscious attention to how this male psychology is configured. On this path, men will be heroes who have chosen to embrace life, dance with light, and all that that entails, participate in life and all that that entails.

The final stage of ritual worship begins with the man's offering of himself and the giving of sexual pleasure. Vajrayogini insists that sexual satisfaction be part of her worship. This is the ultimate method of worshipping the female partner and is sometimes described as worshipping the female organ, which is referred to directly as a vulva and also indirectly as a lotus or even a stainless lotus of light. The lotus is a Buddhist symbol of purity and enlightenment and thus is a natural symbol for the vulva. The female buddha promises her approval and blessings to a man who honors her vulva.

Ah ho, I will bestow supreme success on one who ritually worships my lotus, bearer of all bliss. A wise one unites calmly and with patient application to the requisite activities in the lotus.

The Tantric texts list many types of skills somewhat akin to the *Kama-shastra* and the listing of different positions and oral talents and other things he would have to employ.

Vajrayogini describes how this Tantric worship is to proceed. A yogi and yogini should seclude themselves in a hermitage to practice together. After gazing at each other and attaining single-minded concentration, the woman should address the man, affirming that he is her son and husband, brother and father, and claiming that for seven lifetimes he has been her servant and slave, purchased by her and owned by her. He in turn should fall at her feet, press his palms together in a gesture of reverence, and declare his devotion and humble servitude to her, asking her to grace him with a loving glance. She will then draw him to her and kiss him, direct his mouth to between her thighs and pinch and embrace him playfully. She guides him in how to make the offering of pleasure to her:

Constantly take refuge at my feet, my dear. Be gracious, beloved, and give me pleasure with your diamond scepter. Look at my three-petaled lotus, its center adorned with a stamen. It is a buddha paradise adorned with a red buddha, a cosmic mother who bestows bliss and tranquillity on the passionate. Abandon all conceptual thought and unite with my reclining form. Place my feet upon your shoulders and look me up and down. Make the fully awakened scepter enter the opening in the center of the lotus. Move a hundred thousand times in my three-petaled lotus of swollen flesh. Placing one's scepter there, offer pleasure to her mind. Wind, inner wind, my lotus is the unexcelled. Aroused by the tip of the diamond scepter, it is red as a *bandhuka* flower.

In this robust passage, a female buddha demands pleasure for her embodiments— human women—and alternates between referring to the woman in the third person as someone else and in the first person as herself. This identification is an important part of the man's and woman's visualization during this process. Instructions specify that the man should be free from lust and maintain a clear, nonconceptual state of mind. He is instructed not to end the worship until she is fully satisfied, then he is allowed to pause and revive himself with food and wine and meat. But he has to serve her first and let her eat first. Selfish pleasure-seeking is out of the question for him because he must serve and please his goddess. I think we can see now why there's so much emphasis on the self-mastery, self-control, centeredness, and mindfulness of the male from this description.

The offering of pleasure is not an end in itself, but a basis or a point of departure for the advanced Tantric yoga that uses the bliss of union as a basis for meditation. Different meditations and yogas may be done. According to the Tantric theory of conception, the moment of conception occurs when the drop of male fluid, the drop of female fluid, and a drop of bliss, a spark of bliss, unite together and a child is conceived.

Then the whole thing is described as how the child takes shape in the womb. But that bliss in the child is considered to be the spark of the divine—according to Tantra, bliss is the basis of human nature. That's our core and that's what we're trying to get back to. This is why pleasure and sexuality is a bridge to get back to it: That's our link with that bliss, that cosmic, original bliss, which is why they do not reject sexuality as something very spiritual.

Sahajayogini Cinta is one of the major founders of the sexual yogas, one of the main designers. She had a prominent teaching career and wrote a text that was very influential in the seventh century. When Tantra was transmitted to Tibet, her text was one of the seven key texts that they said contained the core of the Tantric teachings. Three of those seven texts were by women.

Sahajayogini Cinta came from the dancer-courtesan class, by virtue of which she had a very good education. Further, at the feet of her guru she received philosophical training and for a time she was a successful businesswoman who imported wine for the king's table. Later in life she adopted a simpler and freer way of life, which many Tantric practitioners choose to do, and she found a spiritual companion, moved to a small village, had a daughter, and subsisted by herding pigs and gathering wood.

The story of what happened when she met her disciple Padmavajra is telling. Padmavajra, a Buddhist scholar, was a very skilled public speaker. On one occasion a wood-gathering woman attended one of his public discourses and she would alternately laugh and cry throughout his lecture. Afterward she went up to him and said, "Would you like to know why I was laughing and crying during your talk?" And he said, "I certainly would." And she said, "Well, I was laughing because I was enjoying your exquisite speaking style, and I was crying because you don't know what you're talking about."

She directed Padmavajra to seek out a guru in a little village north of there, on a pig farm. However, when the aspirant found the man living on the farm, he barely noticed him. Instead, he became fascinated by Sahajayogini Cinta. She gave her total attention to every task. Her every action was impeccable, dancelike, graceful, communicating a deep immersion in reality, and he realized that watching her move was more profound than listening to any philosophical discourse. So, when he begged her to accept him as her disciple, she beat him off with a stick and drove him away saying, "How can a low-caste woman like me be a guru?" But he wasn't to be put off that easily and that night he slept in their pigpen. While he was sleeping, some of the pigs got into his knapsack and chewed up his books. In the morning, he was furious about this and started stomping around and shouting. Sahajayogini was deeply impressed by this and said, "So you're not so perfect after all. Maybe I can teach you." She accepted him as her disciple and transmitted to him the teachings on bliss. He actually became so delightful that Sahajayogini's daughter accepted him as her consort and

they went back to the capitol together... another happy ending.

The teaching on bliss that Sahajayogini taught to him was the Tantric yoga of transforming the bliss of erotic union into enlightened awareness. In this practice, the ardor of passion becomes the fire that consumes ignorance, both metaphorically and literally. Through the practice, the practitioners actually fuel this inner fire, which then becomes a kind of bonfire into which they feed their ignorance, their dualistic thought constructions, their concepts of the world. Sahajayogini transmitted these teachings to her daughter, to several male disciples, and to hundreds of female disciples. The description of the text she wrote describes how, on the occasion she was addressing an assembly of women,

...the spontaneous, jewellike yogini entered the cosmic, indestructible concentration that instantly confers the powerful energy of the truth of reality that is without error and arises from a realization of ultimate truth.

So this is the source of her authority to teach, that she had this power of meditation that enabled her to see reality without error and distortion. And that's the only authentication that was needed in that context. This entire teaching on the inner yoga, or on the sexual yoga, said, "This teaching, a honeyed stream rich with the glory of bliss, flowed forth from her blossoming lotus face without hesitancy."

In this work, Sahajayogini portrays buddhas as capable of feeling and responding to passion. "Seeing a delightful woman who was enlightenment spontaneously appearing in human form, a buddha gazes with passion and playfulness and a desire for pleasure and bliss arises." So unlike other Buddhist traditions, which describe buddhas or characterize buddhas as passionless, in the Tantric view and in her view here, she presents buddhas as capable of feeling and responding to passion. She refers to gazing, which is a very important stage in Tantric practice. In the initial stage of practice, through gazing at one another, the couple attunes their energy to one another. In the process of gazing, different visualizations can be used. First, simply gazing into one another's eyes and attuning and centering on this moment; next, calming, as one does in any meditative practice, centering; and then they may, in addition, do a visualization. In this practice the man is envisioned as a male buddha, the female is envisioned as a female buddha, and the stages of love-making become buddha deeds.

So seeing one another as a buddha can play out in several ways. In one, they may envision themselves in the forms of buddha couples. For example, if they want to, the man can visualize the woman, especially at this point, as having the appearance of Vajrayogini, with the red face, the third eye, and the ornaments. She can envision him as Chakasamvara, dark blue and with his characteristic expression. The other way to visualize it is to look at that person as they are and to see them as a male buddha and as a female buddha, as they are; to see that embodiment as the expression of buddhahood. So part of the expression is looking

deep within their eyes on an even more subtle level at which you're actually attempting to see them as they really are, as a male and a female buddha, so that you can perceive that buddhahood within.

Since the man and woman are visible embodiments of buddhahood, their feelings of mutual attraction and desire have a transcendent aspect. In this tradition, desire and attraction are seen as religious impulses—they're lured, invited by the transcendent states that they will experience with that person. Ultimately, they are drawn by the fact that they will attain these nondual states together. Cultivating bliss is then one of the main purposes of the union that they will undertake. So, in order to cultivate bliss, each of the five senses is engaged and satisfied—sight by gazing, hearing by sweet words, smell by perfume, touch by rubbing with scent and embracing, massaging with scent and embracing, and taste by kissing. In her own words, Sahajayogini gives instructions for this practice:

Then with gentle and sincere speech, he takes her into his heart. Rubbing her with heavy scent, he satisfies his mind by inhaling the lingering fragrance. Having experienced that and obtained bliss and pleasure equal to one hundred vases of nectar, they embrace without hesitation, experiencing different nuances of bliss. The female lover, gazing with desire, utters sweet words like drops of honey. She unites with him, moving the lotus that brings a rain of pleasure. The innermost self, intent upon its purpose, should remain mentally concentrated while engaging in the different styles of kissing for the sake of the singular taste, and engages in all the specialties of lovemaking like biting, piercing, and so forth. Then, having generated intense bliss, they scratch each other gently with their fingernails from time to time in order to dispel delusion.

So here, in order to remind each other to maintain clarity and prevent a descent to drowsiness or ordinary passion, the lovers scratch each other with their fingernails to remind each other this is meditation.

Then, as Sahajayogini sees it, the yoga of union is perfect for overcoming dualisms of ordinary consciousness because it removes ego boundaries and temporarily lifts that sense of subject/object, in which we're continually engaged, by which we're continually bound. She says:

In stages, because of the taste of desire, one ceases to know who is the other and what has happened to oneself. The lovers experience an inexpressible bliss that they never experienced before. Both of them, the man and the woman, are bound by a stream of concepts that are born from, and arise from, the mind. As long as they are united, the minds of both will not remember anything else, but will be mindful only of pleasure. Hissing passionately, both, without being distracted by anything else, will attain abundant, unsurpassable pleasure and increase that. They awaken from the darkness of ignorance by enjoying the wealth of the activities of bliss and then develop an increased bliss and pleasure. Human pleasure, which possesses identifiable characteristics, is

that very thing that, when it's characteristics are removed, turns into spiritual ecstasy free from conceptual thought, the very essence of self-arising wisdom.

She's saying that this activity provides an opportunity for one-pointed concentration and for maintaining a nonconceptual state of mind. If the partners can remain on that point and not start to elaborate on it, not descend into conceptuality, they can remain in that nondual state and feel the pleasure of that, and then increase the pleasure, and then when the pleasure has reached a certain state, use that as the object of meditation. The pleasure itself is not the goal, but developing that quality of pleasure, of bliss, is the purpose of that activity.

It is necessary that both partners have a stable meditation practice before starting this practice. In other words, this is not the time to begin to develop mindfulness. It is an opportunity to deepen mindfulness and nondual awareness in the midst of an activity that normally causes great attachment and great loss of mindfulness.

To complete her teaching on this, Sahajayogini explains that the enlightenment that is then attained through the body will be expressed through the body. An enlightened person can engage in all the moods and behaviors that they did formerly, but now they will be spontaneous and liberated and liberating. The inner state of spiritual ecstasy will naturally express itself in an unbroken stream of compassionate, liberative activities. All bodily expressions will become pure, dancelike, and sacred.

All bodily movements that are fashioned spontaneously from enlightened mind, pure in essence, become sacred gestures. Whatever is spoken becomes sacred speech. Activities that are graceful, heroic, terrifying, compassionate, furious, and peaceful, and passion, anger, pride, greed, and envy, all these things without exception, are the perfected forms of pure, self-illuminating wisdom. A skillful one who has the capacity to use all these patterns of energy as inherently pure has the great accomplishments of supreme buddhahood in the palm of their hand.

This teaching of Sahajayogini expresses one of the central themes of Tantra, that the body and sexuality provide a means to attain enlightenment and they then participate in the expression of enlightenment. Once the bliss is generated by union, it can be used as the basis for more advanced forms of meditation and inner yogas, of which there are quite a variety.

Now Kundalini yoga in the Hindu context—inner-heat yoga or *vajra* body practice in the Buddhist context—are sometimes called perfection stage. This practice is predicated on the belief in a subtle network of veins or energy pathways throughout the body that carry a subtle energy or a subtle wind, whose quality and movements are determined by a person's thoughts, feelings, and habitual responses to life. According to Tantra, there is one basic energy, but it can be used for procreation, sexuality, creativity, or spiritual growth. Most people simply allow that energy to move in their body in an undi-rected and chaotic manner, but the inner yogas offer specific ways of channeling that energy. The goal of the practice is to concentrate the energy in the central pathway of the body, which is very, very close to the spine that runs vertically through the body. When the energy can be concentrated in the central channel, it is accompanied and made possible by nondual states of awareness.

I find that the way this yoga is generally presented in Western-language sources, it is rather male oriented, and the anatomy of the male *vajra* body is what is described. However, the yogini Tantras devote considerable attention to the inner female anatomy and yoga processes also. For example, in the visualization that supports this yoga, the woman envisions her sexual organ as the mandala, the jeweled palace in the center of a buddha field, or in the center of a buddha land. This palace has no set dimensions because it is a measureless mansion on the visionary plane of experience. The center of the mandala radiates out from the cervix, or innermost point of the vulva, but the form and size of the envisioned mandala will vary depending upon the specific meditation. For example, in the case of the Chakasamvara mandala, the center of the mandala will be Vajrayogini and Chakasamvara in union, surrounded by the twenty-four yogi and yogini couples, all of whom have names and different colors and are feasting in the presence of Chakasamvara and Vajrayogini. In the visualization, each partner visualizes the deities in the center of the mandala uniting and generating bliss and generating drops of nectar that then is rained upon the yogis and yogi-nis in their retinue, and from there, onto all sentient beings throughout the universe. They envision their union as filling the universe with bliss, joy, and cosmic satisfaction.

At times this mandala will be as tiny as a mustard seed and at other times the mandala will be imagined as expanding beyond the body to embrace the world and all living beings in the perfection of this celestial environment. Regardless of the precise meditation, the mandala itself is made of purity, bliss, and wisdom. In the woman, the location of this is what we call the cervix. In the man, the corresponding location is the tip of the diamond scepter. So those two parts are brought into juxtaposition during this meditation. The man assists the woman in her inner yoga by moving the veins in the lotus, "waking them up," and drawing the woman's attention to the lower end of the central channel, helping her concentrate energy at that point where the energy will be drawn into the central channel.

This practice is actually based on a very precise understanding of female anatomy. Normally the cervix is not adjacent to the tip of the spinal column, but during excitation the size and also the location of the female organ changes. It actually rises and becomes adjacent to the tip of the spine. If you look at Western anatomy books, which I did to try to find Western names for these parts of the anatomy, for the veins articulated in the Tantra texts, it's just a void. There are just big, empty spaces in our anatomy books. In the Tantric view, this is a very precise nexus of

veins and it's all visualized as the buddha and the mandala. Stimulating that nexus of veins helps the woman unify her sensations, concentrate her attention at the point near the lower opening of the central channel. Similarly for the man, that is considered to be the lower end or that which is linked to the lower end of his central channel. The man must be careful to incite arousal without detracting from her mindfulness, a challenge to both erotic and yogic virtuosity—another reason why it's important that both should be practitioners.

As the yoga proceeds, man and woman mingle or release and absorb just a few drops of their sexual fluids, which again assumes a certain mastery over that process. Then they visualize themselves absorbing those drops, that mixture. The mixture is referred to as a blend of white drops and red drops, the red being the female, the white the male. It doesn't refer to their physical color. Instead, it refers to, in her case, its permeation with *shakti;* in his case its permeation with the elements that become the white part of the body, the male essence.

They've already been harmonizing their energy in many ways, through the gazing, through the embracing, through the uniting, and now through drawing the attention to this part of the body. So this symbolizes, in meditational form, the exchange that's taking place. This is the point where they consciously and voluntarily absorb the concretized essence of that partner's energy. So it's a very profound practice, because you're absorbing something that carries that person's karmic imprint into your central channel. For them, this would be an ultimate kind of union or ultimate combination, but the purpose of doing it is that you add the quality as well as the quantity of the partner's energy to your own. Therefore, it makes possible the attainment of meditational states and insights that are difficult to attain on one's own.

This exchange of fluids on the physical level really accompanies the exchange of breath and subtle energy that's been taking place on the psychic level. When that energy is absorbed into this central channel or located in the central channel, they start this internal process of combustion, each on their own. They now can direct their combined energy in specific ways to produce even more subtle states of bliss and insight. There is a Tantric saying that it is impossible to attain enlightenment without a consort.

At this point in the process, the partners really start focusing on the inner yoga that's taking place. Having used pleasure as a point of departure, they each draw their inner wind or breath into the central channel, which is ultimately what the offering of this act represents. That is, they're offering each other the yogic experiences that this has made possible. The partners will revel in the intoxication of the sensations of bliss that are spreading through the body. One of the terms used for this is "soaring in the sky." That sense of very subtle states of bliss, an inner intoxication, and very sublime sensations, of course, is a new opportunity for descent into loss of mindfulness and into attachment. The more pleasure you feel, the

more tendency there is to attach. So this attainment of these very rarefied sensations of soaring in the sky, is the signal to begin meditating on emptiness. In this way, the bliss of union is combined with the understanding of emptiness.

At this stage, the yogi and yogini must relinquish attachment to the pleasure and meditate on everything, including their bliss, as devoid of intrinsic reality. In this equation, emptiness means that the other person, myself, and even the bliss have substantial reality, and therefore there's nothing to hold onto—nothing to cling onto—as a point of attachment. If you allow yourself to construct or to hold on to a point of attachment at that point, it will prevent the even more subtle realizations that will follow. The point is to take that bliss and meditate on the emptiness of that. One method that is recommended is to meditate that your partner is no more real than a mirage. This is so you do not fall into the conceptual trap of thinking that that person has caused your bliss, because the bliss that you are feeling is the capacity of your own mind.

At any point you're feeling attachment, you can use your understanding of emptiness or use this technique of thinking of it as a mirage to dissolve any point of your attachment. Simply dissolve it into the sky, this expanse of skylike awareness, and let your awareness become very skylike. This final step, if it can be successfully completed, will put both partners in contact with the primordial nature of their own minds, which is vast, spacious, pure awareness. They'll experience that level of vastness of their own being and realize that everything, including their mind, is clear, pure, and spacious. like the sky.

[*A participant remarked that "it seems that the stability of meditation among partners would require some preliminary understanding of emptiness."*]

Miranda Shaw: Some study of emptiness is a very important part of the prerequisite for this. When I was seeking these teachings, one of the things the teachers I approached were most interested in was my background in the philosophy of emptiness. They did not simply ask if I had studied emptiness, but how many years, and what texts had I read, and what philosophies had I studied and that kind of question. Because when you bring emptiness into the equation, you're talking about different analytic or conceptual techniques for deconstructing the contents of ordinary awareness. The central insight of emptiness—the absence of intrinsic reality, the absence of permanence, fixity, stability anywhere in phenomenal reality—is a very important understanding to have going into this practice.

Another type of visualization that can be done when at that point in doing the yoga, of mingling those drops, and then starting to perform the inner yoga, is that the partners can visualize in their central channel, at about the level of the navel, a flame. As they absorb the energy, they can make that flame very hot and form an inner fire. While they're doing this practice, they can visualize themselves as a male and female buddha in union,

in the midst of their retinue, in their castle, in the midst of the entire world and the expanse of space. In their minds they go to the outer edges of space and gather the space in the celestial bodies and bring them in and feed them into the fire so that the celestial bodies are dissolved. Then they go out and gather in the other planetary bodies until they get to this Earth and they start gathering the entire Earth, feeding the Earth and all beings into that fire until it's just them in their celestial mansion. And then they take all the basic building blocks of thought—earth, air, fire, and water—into the bonfire and burn them. Then they take every kind of dualistic thinking, all different conceptual categories, and put those into the fire and burn them. Then they take the very thought of dualism and put it into the fire. Next they take the very thought of self, the existence of self, and put it into the fire and burn it. Then they put the walls of their celestial mansion into the fire and burn them, until, finally, they dissolve themselves into the fire and become this pure flame of enlightened awareness. The text I read asks What do they do next? It says that out of that pure awareness and that pure enlightened state, they generate buddha bodies for the enlightenment of all sentient beings, of course.

In this process, as one is burning these things, there's actually the physical process of their being combusted. It's a tangible process. You put in your concepts first, and your attachments. This is something that's a little different for each person, the attachments you've built up over thousands of lifetimes. Since those are built-in, you actually feel, physically, experientially, and perceptually, the clearing of your consciousness. The clearing of your perceptions, the purification of your vision as you feel this burning off. So even though I'm describing it in a very abstract way, it's something that, when it's happening, would be tangible. That's called the inner-fire offering.

The intimacy envisioned in Tantra is really a very ultimate kind of intimacy, which is why the choice in partner is so important. Some of the bases for choice would be spiritual qualities that you recognize in that person, certainly former practices that they had done, their religious knowledge, and one of the main keys is their sincere intent to approach the relationship in this way, because if you have someone who doesn't, then you're processing everything.

Compassionate motivation is also very important for Tantric practice because that is the understanding that you're undertaking this practice for the enlightenment of all sentient beings and, therefore, this would include refraining from harming any others in the process and also the intent to help others through the process, liberate, gladden, inspire, delight, and amaze others through the process. The practice is sometimes called *karmamudra* practice, partly because of a belief that the partner will be brought to you by your karma, either through your own preparedness or through karma of having shared other lifetimes together, but there must be this karmic link to practice together. The choice of partner is so important because you are, in essence, entrusting your spiritual destinies to one another—you're mixing your breaths, you're mixing your fluids, you're mixing your thoughts and your emotions, and actually you're literally mixing your karma.

This also happens in ordinary relationships, but the difference, I think, is like that between swimming in the ocean or injecting salt water into your veins. You are literally injecting this person's karma into your subtle pathways, so it's much more intense. You will begin to merge at a very intimate kind of psychic level. On the positive side, the couple will attune to one another's hearts, minds, and bodies in a very subtle way. They may begin to dream the same dreams, to share memories, at times to feel the other person's thoughts and emotions. This is one of the reasons that Tantric texts always say that two people should be at roughly the same level of spiritual development because whichever person is of a greater level of spiritual development will end up processing the other person's karma and negativity and become almost like a garbage incinerator for the other person. You'll be injecting into your system all this karma that they haven't purified at all, and then you must deal with it because it's in you now.

Sometimes a Tantric partnership can be temporary. People may come together to accomplish a certain goal, a certain meditative attainment, to do a retreat of a certain amount of time together, maybe six weeks, a month, a year, two years. One does hear of that, but more often such relationships tend to be permanent because of the rarity of finding a person with whom one can do these practices. Once you get to the point where you're doing them together, there's a tendency to remain with that person and keep going deeper and deeper and deeper instead of starting with another person. One of the terms that's used in the Tantric texts is you're not attached to that person, but you're *transcendentally attached,* and it's a very clear distinction. You're transcendentally grateful for the generosity at a fundamental level that happens in a relationship like this, and you are also grateful to have someone who can work with their emotions in that way.

Sometimes people ask about multiple partners at the same time. I think it's very necessary to be absolutely honest with a partner on this point because, if you were to consort with another person, you would be bringing that person's energy into the practice that you're doing. It's absolutely unfair to inflict that upon someone. They have to have a choice whether or not they want to deal with that person's energy or engage at all with that person's energy.

[A question raised the issue of whether or not a Tantric relationship could also be a "romantic" relationship.]

Miranda Shaw: I'm not really clear in my mind even what my definition of romance would be. The thing that I think is very romantic in Tantric relationships is that the partners are actually creating this visionary universe that they enter together. It's a very poetic universe because they're envisioning the same deities, they have this elaborate vocabulary for what they're doing, and an

understanding of what they're doing. Then there's this kind of exaltation of their relationship, which, in a way, can be very romantic. In that sense I do think it's romantic, but it's a kind of transcendental romanticism, because it's not devoid of romanticism at all.

Participant: But it's a true love relationship.

Miranda Shaw: Yes. I think for those for whom that is love, that is definitely true love. They use the word *raga,* which is passion, desire, attachment, love, for the affection that they have for each other, but they call it *maharaga,* which means great passion or love, transcendent passion, love, desire, and that is seen as a requirement for practicing Tantra. Tantra is for passionate people, people who have a lot of desire. It's not for everyone. It's for those who have this quality in abundance and want to use it on the spiritual path.

Previously I described a few yogic methods, but Tantra also offers ways of working with the emotions in an on-going way in a relationship. This is another way the relationship becomes the focus of spiritual practice in daily life. As we all know, relationships can provide us with many opportunities to confront some of our more vivid and challenging emotions, and so they also provide us with rather direct access to the deep contents of our psyche. Normally this makes relationships a major source of pain in life. On the Tantric path, these deep emotions are seen as opportunities for growth if one knows how to work with them.

This way of working with the emotions is predicated upon the Buddhist view of the self as a stream of energies that has no core. Buddhists see the self at any moment as a process, a pattern of energy, that is reconfigured at the next moment, and there's nothing in there that's stable or that links them. So there's no owner of the emotions; when an emotion happens, it's rising and falling in empty space. It's like a cloud in the sky, returning to the sky. The emotional practice is also predicated upon the Tantric view of the emotions, which is quite different from other Buddhist traditions. One Tantric insight into the emotions is that they are on-going. The emotional life will not stop and there's no sense in trying to repress it or trying not to have the emotions. According to Tantra, the emotions are part of the richness of life; they ornament life.

There is in Tantra a sense of really trusting this instinctive nature, trusting the self on the level of the passions, almost at the universal level of the very primal states of, for example, passion, or a very pure state of anger. You see a pure, white-hot state of hatred—something more universal than the little kind of whiny, staticky surface type. In Tantra, they tend to trust that level of emotional life and to see it as valuable. Also, in Tantra they see passion as the greatest virtue. They see the capacity for emotional intensity as the greatest virtue one can bring to bear in Tantric practice. They're not saying it's for everyone, but in Tantric practice, your passion is your fuel.

According to Tantra, emotions are simply patterns of energy—neither pure nor impure. They are no more good or bad than an atom or a photon is good or bad. Therefore, if emotions are just energy, they are simply a play of energy and ultimately it's all the same energy that's configuring in different ways. When an emotion first arises, there is a blissful quality to the energy and a kind of clarity to that energy. But then we start getting in on the act and interpreting that energy event. We put a label on it. Then we start judging that emotion. Should I be having this emotion? Should I not? And we're off and running, adding all these emotions and concepts and *this* interpretation is what causes the suffering, not the energy, not the emotion itself, according to Tantra. It is necessary to either refrain from interpreting the emotions or to remove the interpretations that we have naturally imposed. This is the on-going work of Tantric Buddhism in a relationship.

In this process, each person takes total, absolute responsibility for his or her own emotions, for processing and for transforming them. This is very different from ordinary relationships, in which one person might say, "You made me feel...." You didn't make that person feel that way. Each person comes to the relationship with their own habitual emotional patterns and predisposition to relieve familiar forms of emotional pain. You've acted one way with the person in one relationship and they love it. It drives the next person crazy. You are not causing that. Their own mind is causing their reactions to what you do. Your own mind is causing your reactions to what they do.

You have to get to that very basic level where you're actually acknowledging that these emotions are arising without specific reference to the present moment. Then, if you do superimpose those emotions on the present moment and say it's caused by this moment, you simply intensify the emotional pain, because you're then in the situation that's causing the pain. So each person works with their ongoing stream and with deconstructing these emotions, seeing that the causes of the emotions are not objective.

You have to deconstruct the three poles or three aspects of interpreting that emotion. First, you say that you are the owner of the emotion, that you are the subject of the emotion that you have to deconstruct. Then you have to deconstruct your label of the emotion. And finally you have to deconstruct the object or cause of that emotion. Various methods can be used to do that. You can deconstruct that that person has caused your emotion: Just think of some other situation in which a person acting precisely that way would not cause pain. For example, if someone is criticizing too much and it's bothering you, imagine if that person was on their deathbed and they were criticizing. Would it hurt me, would it bother me if they were criticizing me? Or imagine that you didn't speak their language—just these little waves hitting my eardrums. What do they mean? You can imagine you just came in with some very sad news, and you know the minute you share it they're going to be devastated, and you don't care what they say. You just deconstruct that they're causing your pain.

Then you can deconstruct the interpretation of the emotion. Instead of interrogating the emotion intellectually and saying what quality it is, simply feel the emotion and remove your interpretation. Rather than thinking, I feel angry, simply try to feel it as an energy. The problem is labeling the emotion. It doesn't help to say Maybe this isn't anger; maybe it's something else. At this point it's better just to relinquish that whole conceptual process and just try to feel that energy and feel how it is without a label. You'd be surprised how much less painful it is.

Then the other idea you have to deconstruct is the idea of yourself as the *owner* of the emotion. Simply see that the emotion is not something separate from you that you own, but merely the process that's happening at that moment, without a center, without a core. That, of course, you'll be familiar with from your previous Buddhist meditation, which you now apply to your emotional life.

If you're deconstructing your emotions in this way, it's very important to be in a conscious relationship, because when you have an emotion you want to deconstruct, you have to have the space to withdraw a little bit and do that work without the other person's projections on you—"Why do you feel angry when I say that?" You also need that space in order not to have the other person take it personally. That takes a lot of detachment from self. If you see the other person turning colors over in the corner, working with their anger, and think it reflects on you in any way, you have to detach and say, "That's what they're doing, they're working with this." You're both acknowledging that ultimately that is true, even though something that person did triggered that habitual response in you, which may have been present for many lifetimes. This becomes even more important in the Tantric relationship. As you generate fire in the inner channel, you will actually be working with the heart center or the heart chakra, which is considered the seat in the body of the deepest fears, the deepest hatreds, from many lifetimes. Therefore, untying the knots of the heart chakra, or melting those bonds through the inner fire, is considered part of the very important work that is done in Tantra. If you untie a knot in the heart, you may feel a hatred or a fear from ten lifetimes ago. It's going to come out and you've got to have the ability to work with that emotion and not to superimpose it on the present relationship.

Because one feels these emotions when flushing out and opening the heart chakra, it's very important at that time to have this clear, sacred space of trust in which to work to release those emotions and to know absolutely that that person didn't cause that.

[Dr. Shaw was asked to clarify further the point she had made earlier considering the distinctions between primary and secondary-derivative emotions in Tantra.]

According to Buddhism, the more trivial emotions would be things like boredom, resentment, self-pity, loneliness, and guilt. Those emotions are considered to be derivative because there is something deeper behind them. When you label what you're feeling as boredom, for example, there's actually something deeper behind that emotion: If you're bored with what's happening at the present moment, someplace within you you are resisting or rejecting that reality that surrounds you at that moment. It's like a hard spot on your consciousness, a place where it's rubbing, so there's a negativity there. In other words, we think of boredom as an absence of stimulation or excitement, but really there's a resistance to what's happening, then an impatience. Is it fear? Is it anger? Anger can make you bored. But just to look behind the emotions that are not what they call the primary emotions—fear, hatred, selfish lust, jealously, and the desire to ignore some things completely, what they call ignorance. If it's not one of those five, then according to the Tantra, it is a less primary emotion. It doesn't carry that energy in all it's intensity and quality. If you can deconstruct the boredom, it will dissolve, or you might get in touch with the deeper energies behind it, if it's masking something else.

All of these passions have bliss and clarity at their core because it is an experience. According to the Tantra, all experiences are blissful at the core if we can stay on that point. If you deconstruct fear, for example, there is simply an emotion happening. There is an energy event that, according to Tantric Buddhism, has a blissful quality. Some people watch scary movies just to enjoy the pleasure of fear. It's a pattern of energy that gets your blood racing. But there is also an unenlightened element in fear, the feeling of being threatened and thinking that you can be threatened on any level.

Perhaps "awakeness" is a better way to refer to this than "bliss" or "clarity." Bill T. Jones says that when you know that your life will come to an end at some point, every emotion that you feel is pleasure. He says everything that happens to him, he says how great to be here and experience that, which is a very Tantric attitude. He said, "It's all great because I'm still here."*

[A final discussion began when a participant mentioned a Buddhist sculpture in the Museum of Fine Arts, Boston, of a yogini and her consort, which is described as though the yogini is gazing upward at the male figure in awe.]

Miranda Shaw: Go to any museum and this is very pervasive. Vajrayogini's name won't even be given. It's always "Chakasamvara and his

wife" or "a female buddha." I want to know who performed the marriage ceremony!

According to Tantric interpretation, Shakyamuni Buddha attained enlightenment through the practices of bliss, just as all Buddhists do, and his consort was Gopa, his queen. They show him in union with Gopa and then, in the text, they tell that he left the palace in order to demonstrate the path of renunciation for those people who would benefit from that path. But he did the practices required for that enlightenment, which is the generation of bliss through union with the consort, before he left the palace. They got around that. Isn't that fascinating?

They said when he walked on the banks of the Nairanjana River and sat under the bodhi tree, that was simply an illusion for those who would be liberated by that illusion because a buddha is a person who can generate whatever illusion is necessary to liberate sentient beings. Therefore may all beings be enlightened by the liberative displays of the dance.

Maybe that can be our final wish: May beings be enlightened by the infinite liberative displays of the dance of the buddhas, male and female. And may you all attain buddhahood in this lifetime in the present body.

---

* Editor's note: Choreographer and dancer Bill T. Jones's partner Arnie Zane died of AIDS-related causes. More recently, Mr. Jones was diagnosed with the same disease. In 1994 he created a major dance work entitled "Still/HERE," which deals with living with AIDS and the emotional complexity that brings into play.

Deep Agnosticism

A Secular Vision
of Dharma Practice

Stephen Batchelor

IN CONTEMPORARY PARLANCE, "AGNOSTICISM" IS ALL TOO OFTEN CONFUSED WITH "ATHEISM." It has taken on something of a patina of thoughtlessness, or lack of belief, rather than being seen as the belief system it was for T. H. Huxley, who coined the term. As Stephen Batchelor points out, however, the word *agnostic* comes from the Greek *agnosis*—"not knowing." It suggests the ultimate unknowability of the nature of things. Rather than being a slinking away from belief, it is, as he says, "as demanding as any religious, philosophical, or moral creed...[and] requires the same degree of commitment, the same degree of integrity, to take that kind of stance." Seen in this light, agnosticism provides an apt means of investigating the contemporary practice of Buddhism, which Mr. Batchelor likens to a "deep agnosticism."

Mr. Batchelor's interest in the ways in which Buddhist thought and practice are engaging with modern, secular, and democratic societies makes him an especially appropriate person to introduce this material. Born in England, he left at the age of eighteen to receive a traditional Buddhist education in monastic communities in India, Switzerland, Germany, and South Korea. His primary teachers were Geshe Ngawang Dhargyey, Geshe Rabten, and Kusan Pangjang Sunim. In 1985, however, he disrobed, married, and returned to England, where he lives today. Currently he is Director of Studies at Sharpham College for Buddhist Studies and Contemporary Enquiry, a guiding teacher at Gaia House Center and the Barn Farming Retreat Centre, and Buddhist chaplain at Channings Wood Prison. Along with important books of his origination—*Alone with Others, The Faith to Doubt, The Awakening of the West,* and the recently published *Buddhism Without Beliefs*—he has published a number of translations from Tibetan, including Shantideva's *Badhicaryavatara* (Guide to the Bodhisattva's Way of Life) and is presently working on a study and translation of the writings of Nagarjuna.

What I want to talk about today is an idea called deep agnosticism and this is the outcome of many years of reflection. I certainly don't see it as some kind of position, certainly not a final or dogmatic position, but, in a purely personal sense, a step along the way to trying to understand what my own relationship is with the teachings of the Buddha as a European/Westerner. I discover as I grow older a reconnection with the roots of my own culture. Maybe many of us of my generation were drawn to Buddhism as a kind of act of defiance, a kind of rebelliousness against what we viscerally disliked—often for rather naïve, adolescent, and idealistic reasons—in our own culture and we saw Buddhism, or at least I saw Buddhism, as a kind of vindication of that dissent.

But as the years have gone by, I've found that this denial of one's roots, this denial of one's cultural upbringing, is not actually possible to sustain. If one seeks to sustain it, one often ends up as a kind of mock Tibetan or pseudo-Japanese. Although I have tried to do that on occasion, dressing up in all of the appropriate regalia, more than that I feel it to be still seeking to find an identity outside that of my own culture. It's, as Freud might say, impossible to repress these things. They simply come out in other ways.

What I found in myself though, when I say returning to my cultural roots, is not some rediscovery of Christianity. In fact, I was brought up outside an explicitly Christian culture. I never went to church. I was excused by my family from attendance at religious assemblies at school and so on. What I reconnect with, therefore, is not

what we would call the religious traditions of the West, but rather the humanistic, secular, agnostic culture, which I feel a very, very deep sympathy with. And I feel that this attempt to create dialogues between Buddhism and the West often seems to assume the essentially religious nature of such a dialogue. So we have Christian-Buddhist dialogs and so on. So in recovering my roots, I'm also recovering, as it were, a nonreligious identity which finds itself at odds with much of how Buddhism is implicitly or explicitly presented as a religion.

Now, of all the terms I've just listed—"humanist," "secularist," "agnostic," and so on—the term *agnostic* seems to me the vein with the greatest possibility to mine something out. Most of you are probably unaware that the term is only very recently coined. It didn't exist before about 1888 and it was coined by a man called Thomas Huxley, T. H. Huxley, the biologist, who was a very staunch defender of Darwin in the latter part of the nineteenth century and a very radical critic of the church and religion. Also, we note that Huxley coined this term somewhat as a joke, tongue-in-cheek.

He belonged to a philosophical circle in London and found that he was unable to identify, as all the other members of the circle were able, with an -ism, with an identity —as a Christian, as a materialist, as a whatever, a thingamabob. So he thought about this and said, Well, what generic term would best describe where I stand? And he came up with the term agnostic, "in order that," he rather jokingly says in his essay on the subject, "I could have a tail like all the other foxes." So we don't want to take this term agnosticism too seriously. There's already an irony at the beginnings of its usage.

Of course, we can trace historically, way before Huxley, something that we might now call an agnostic position. It would go back, in fact, to the Greek Protagoras, I think is how it's normally traced, and it would go through people like David Hume and so on. But Huxley is the person who coined the term.

Now, once he'd somewhat jokingly come up with this idea, he recognized, Ah, this seems to actually have some mileage. And he started to define it, to really look into what it meant for him. *Agnosis* is constructed from the Greek—"not knowing," "not know," *a gnosis*—which Huxley contrasted to *gnosis*, not in the sense of the early Gnostics, but gnosis in the sense of those traditions that claimed that they have some kind of privileged knowledge and then declaim that as their religion or their philosophical position.

Now, interestingly, Huxley describes agnosticism as being as demanding as any religious, philosophical, or moral creed. In other words, it requires the same degree of commitment, the same degree of integrity, to take that kind of stance. But he distinguishes it from a creed and describes it as a method. The kind of method he had in mind in many ways underpins the kind of attitude that would underpin what he saw as the scientific approach. He saw it in two ways: On the one hand, this method requires taking one's reason as far as it will go; and on the other hand, it requires not accepting something as true unless it can somehow be demonstrated. In other words, it's a commitment to rea-

son but also a refusal to accept anything as true unless it is somehow demonstrable in one's own experience, either empirically (I think that's probably what he had in mind), or perhaps experientially.

Here we have very clear parallels with many elements of the Buddhist tradition. When I was training as a Tibetan Buddhist monk, my practice was actually very much about the cultivation of rational inquiry. One of the great sort of unacknowledged riches in the Buddhist tradition is that tradition of rational investigation, the tradition of logic, of epistemology, which, for many Buddhists, immediately evokes, "Uuaah!" But I think the often rather romantic, anti-intellectual perception of Buddhism is one that then conceals from us the richness of its own rational traditions and the power of ideas and reason. And of course, whether or not that commitment to reason is found in all Buddhist traditions, nonetheless the second criterion of Huxley—not to accept something as true unless it's demonstrable—is certainly the case in all Buddhist traditions and often that is what is appealing to people about the Buddhist path, that it presents a process of practice that claims to result in demonstrable changes in one's own life, in one's understanding, something that one can actually witness and experience for oneself. It's demonstrable.

Huxley even described agnosticism as the agnostic faith, in other words, giving the kind of seriousness and commitment that you would normally reserve for religion. It's also striking that, within fifteen years of Huxley coining the term agnosticism, it was already being applied to Buddhism. Now, we have to put that into an historical perspective. The first Englishman, effectively the first European, to become a Buddhist monk, a *bhikkhu,* was a man called Allan Bennett. He was actually a close colleague of a somewhat notorious figure called Aleister Crowley, who described Bennett as "the kindest man I have ever known." Bennett left for Burma, where he became a *bhikkhu* in 1901, and then he took the name Ananda Metleya. Bennett was the first European to take the robe in the whole of Buddhist history. Remember that that's 2,450 years, at that point, to actually engage with a non-European or let's say non-Middle East-based tradition. That is a very, very important break with this conviction of Europe to embody the supreme philosophical, rational, and cultural tradition of the world; and this was still in a time when colonialism was at its peak. So it's a very radical break. In one of the very first Buddhist magazines ever issued in English, Bennett spoke of Buddhism in 1905 as "exactly coincidental in its fundamental ideas with the modern agnostic philosophy of the West."

Now, why would this young man have adopted this term? I suspect that one of the key sources he would have drawn on would be the *Culamalunkya Sutta* in the Pali canon. It's number 63 in the *Majjhimanikaya.* The Buddha is speaking:

Suppose, Malyunkyaputta, a man were wounded by an arrow thickly smeared with poison, and his friends and companions brought a surgeon to treat him. The man would say, "I will not let the surgeon pull out the arrow until I know the name and the clan of the man who wounded me, whether the bow that wounded me was a longbow or a crossbow, whether the arrow that wounded me was hoof-tipped or curved or barbed." And all this would still not be known to that man and meanwhile he would die. So too, Malyunkyaputta, if anyone should say, "I will not lead the noble life under the Buddha until the Buddha declares to me whether the world is eternal or not eternal, finite or infinite, whether the soul is the same as or different from the body, whether or not an awakened one continues or ceases to exist after death." That would still remain undeclared by the Buddha and meanwhile that person would die.

What's striking about this passage is it brings together two key features of the Pali tradition. On the one hand, the primarily pragmatic nature of the Buddhist practice, of the Buddhist path: It's about doing something to resolve a dilemma that's with you here and now. That's the primary concern, praxis. Secondly it illustrates a very distinct agnostic bent. In other words, I think a fairly reasonable interpretation of that passage would be that what the Buddha was concerned with was not the kinds of questions that would generally fall under the heading of religious belief: Where did the universe come from? Where is it going? What happens to the Buddha after death? Are the mind and the body the same or different?

As Buddhist tradition has developed, it's interesting to note that the extent to which it becomes a religious institution is that degree to which answers to these questions tend to be supplied. One will find in many of the later Buddhist traditions, and even the later versions of the earlier traditions, quite clear views on many of these unanswered questions. It seems to me that as we look at Buddhism historically, we find that it continuously loses its agnostic dimension by becoming institutionalized as a religion, with all the usual dogmatic systems of belief that religions have.

This is actually not an idea of my own. This comes from a very good study by a man called Trevor Ling, who talks of Buddhism as actually degrading into a religion from a civilization. I would argue rather than Buddhism initially being a civilization, it was a culture that embraced all elements of human life, which I think is already very implicit in the structure of the eightfold path. But as the vitality of that tradition declines, or when it becomes co-opted, often by secular powers, political powers, it tends to become institutionalized as what we would describe as a religion. So if you go to any Asian country today, you will certainly find religion. If you go to a temple in Bangkok or in Lhasa or in Kyoto, you will find something that is quite definitely religious. There's devotion, there are priests, belief systems, dogmas, etc.

This, of course, has led to Buddhism, as it comes into the West being automatically regarded as a religion. The very term Buddhism which, remember, is a Western concoction—there's not really any exact Asian term that corresponds to the English

term Buddhism, that I know of—the -ism word automatically puts it into a camp of a belief system of some kind: a position, a stance, a view. It suggests that it's a creed to be lined up alongside other creeds. It's another set of beliefs about the nature of reality that we cannot really know by other means than through faith. What that identification of Buddhism as a religion does is to distort and to obscure the encounter of the Dharma with secular culture.

The word *secular,* I've noticed, in many Buddhist writings is often used quite spontaneously as a negative term. "In this materialist, secular world," for example. It's difficult to find secular being used in a positive sense. But what does secular mean? The word literally goes back to the root, meaning "of this world." Secular has to do with a concern for the matters of this world. That would apply to someone who is simply concerned with maximizing greed and pleasure, true. But surely it would also apply to someone who, let's say, is committed to social justice in just as much the same way.

As a Tibetan monk, I was taught for many, many years that if I practiced for the sake of this world, I would not actually be practicing the Dharma. If you crave this world, this life, you are not a Dharma person. You're not really doing the right thing. Now, there is a sense in which one can see that as a perfectly legitimate point of view, but it does tend to postpone any kind of action or any kind of practice that would be concerned primarily with the state of the world we find ourselves in.

Another problem is that the word *agnostic* also has lost its potency. People often confuse agnostic with atheist. An "agnostic atheist," you often hear in the same breath. When people say they're agnostic—even if they know that it means that they do not claim to know certain things—very often today that goes hand in hand with an attitude of actually not caring about certain things. It's a kind of careless: "I don't care. I don't really want to know. I don't know what to think about those sort of things." It's a dismissive denial in some way.

So modern agnosticism has kind of degraded into a skepticism, a cynicism that we find so much in the world today. It's certainly lost the kind of confidence, what Huxley called the "faith," that underpinned it initially. At the same time, we find that the agnostic dimension in Buddhism has also been somewhat lost, that that cutting edge you find in the Pali discourses, you find in Madhyamika philosophy, you find in the Zen koans, those things too have lapsed into kinds of philosophies or forms of meditation, but that radical, cutting edge is gone.

Now, it seems to me that an agnostic Buddhist would not regard the Dharma as a source from which we can derive answers to the questions of where the universe is going, where the universe came from, the nature of the universe, the difference between the mind and the body, and so on. In this sense, an agnostic Buddhist would not be a believer with claims to revealed information about supernatural or paranormal phenomena and in this sense would not be religious.

I found recently that saying to myself, "I'm not a religious person," has a curiously liberating effect. It's liberating in my own case, perhaps, because at least it's truthful. I think I spent a lot of time pretending to be religious and I really don't believe that one has to be religious or a religious person to practice the Dharma. One of the features about religion is that it has very much to do with providing metaphors of consolation. Religions offer a consolation in the face of birth and death by offering the promise of survival after physical death, offering some sense of reward if one behaves in a certain way; and one finds this in Christianity as much as in Buddhism. They offer a kind of psychological security that's achieved by making an act of faith.

Now, I wouldn't want to be so narrow-minded as to exclude the consolatory dimension of Buddhism. It certainly, in a social and a cultural sense in Asia and also in the West, provides that, and that's a perfectly good thing. But I'm personally not interested in that. To me, the Buddhist teachings are not consolatory—they're confrontative. They're not about telling us stories that appease our anguish, but they're about telling us truths. It's about truth telling. It's not about painting a more attractive picture of life somewhere else. And they start, of course, with the primary recognition: Life is painful; there is suffering; there is *duhkha*. That's where the business begins, not with the promise of some salvation and an afterlife.

But I think we need to take this one step further. This kind of agnosticism is not based on disinterest. It's not based on saying, "I just don't really care about the great matter of birth and death." It's recognizing that, *I do not know* in a very passionate way, in a passionate sense, where, perhaps we find our deepest integrity as human beings. So it's not just something that one would periodically reflect upon, but really something that one brings to heart, that I do not really know where I did come from. I do not really know where I am going. I do not really know what will happen after death. The only honest stance I can take toward the doctrine of rebirth is to say I just do not know, and to rest in this do not know or, as Seung Sahn calls it, this "don't-know mind." It's a very different order of don't know from the more superficial skepticism or cynicism of much modern agnosticism.

It's this process of stripping away consolatory illusions by holding true to this kind of not knowing that leads to what I would call deep agnosticism. For me, Buddhism is the practice of deep agnosticism. Let's now look at what we mean here by "deep." To me this is getting right to the heart of what Dharma practice might be about. Let me illustrate this with the very first koan of the *Blue Cliff Record* (and this is from the Cleary translation):

Emperor Wu of Liang asked the great master Bodhidharma, "What is the highest meaning of the holy truths?" Bodhidharma said, "Empty. No holiness." The emperor said, "Who's facing me?" Bodhidharma replied, "I don't know."

I don't think it's accidental that that's the first case in what is one of the major collections of koans in China and, as you can see, it much confirms the kind of don't know. But this kind of don't know brings the notion of agnosticism down to another depth, what we might call a contemplative or a meditative depth. Deep agnostic metaphors are also found in such terms in Ch'an Zen as *wu shin,* no mind; *wu nien,* no thought. Again, it's easy to think that no mind, no thought is about sort of blanking out but, as any Zen teacher will tell you, that's nonsense. It's far more challenging than that. It's about literally getting down to our primary state as beings who do not know.

It's also interesting that we can take this not knowing as a link, a bridge between the Zen tradition and the Indo-Tibetan Mahayana tradition of the Madhyamika philosophy. I don't know is likewise suggestive of no self and emptiness. So if we apply this notion of don't know to Bodhidharma's case, by honestly inquiring into his self-identity, Bodhidharma could perhaps find nothing he could ultimately take hold of and say, "Yes, that's me. There it is. I've got it. I've realized it." Instead, he discovers the ultimate unfindability of himself, and by implication the ultimate unfindability of everything and everyone else as well.

This gives us a clue. It's not that there's literally don't-know mind. If you try to understand the nature of anything in the deepest sense, you will not be able to arrive at any fixed view that defines it as this or that, as some kind of essence, as some kind of substance, as some kind of thing. In his public lectures, the Dalai Lama uses a quaint expression in colloquial Tibetan, which literally means "there is no finger-pointing place" or, as we would say in English, there is nothing you can put your finger on. This doesn't imply that the thing in question doesn't exist at all, it simply exposes the fallacy of a deeply felt, almost instinctive assumption that our self or our mind or anything else must be secured in some kind of permanent, quasi-metaphysical base. So if we follow the analysis of Madhyamika philosophy into inquiring into the nature of self, the nature of mind, or anything, we find that ultimately there's nothing we can point to and say, That is what the thing really is. There is no "nugget" of essential identity or self-identity to which a person or a flower, anyone, or anything, is reducible.

And yet, this is not a denial of the uniqueness of a person, or the uniqueness of a flower, or the uniqueness of anything. The the uniqueness of things is totally compatible with the idea of their emptiness, of their lacking some kind of self-nature. What this insight into the unfindability of something in an ultimate sense reveals is that things are what they are, people are who they are. I am who I am. Not because there's something in me, a kind of blueprint or code, an essence of any kind, but that things are what they are in their unique way because of the unrepeatable matrix of contingencies, conditions, causes, conceptual, linguistic frameworks. My uniqueness is because of the unique trajectory of my choices of my life in contradistinction to the unique trajectory of yours.

This is just another way of saying how emptiness and interdependence are the same. Things are empty because they are complex, because they are what they are out of a set of myriad relationships. And this is the central philosophic truth of Buddhism— not just a philosophical truth, but something that through meditation practice can be demonstrated. One can realize that.

Whether we follow the Tibetan analytical approach or the approach of asking a Zen koan such as *What is this?* this kind of meditative inquiry leads to a mind that becomes more still and clear. In other words, this kind of investigation is a meditative or a contemplative investigation. This deep agnosticism is not just a stance, but it is an attitude that can be cultivated through practice, through stilling and focusing the mind on the question and it is another commonality between Tibetan and Zen analysis. It's sometimes assumed that as the mind becomes more still and clear, then the nature of reality becomes somehow more self-evident, more obvious, more clear cut, but that doesn't seem to be the case. In fact, because it seems the more our experience of life becomes vivid and clear, it also becomes more mysterious and perplexing. We must have had this experience just by doing a simple kind of awareness practice, just sitting still, watching the breath and listening to sounds or watching the play of light on a wall in front of you. As the mind becomes still, it might be a bit boring initially, but one passes through that boredom into an encounter with the world in an increasingly unfamiliar way. Let's face it, we define our fixed sense of self by constructing a world that appears to reflect and to confirm that static center of our own identity. If we express this in more emotional language, we end up constructing psychologically a reality in which we *can* be bored, and that, I think, is a very tragic thing. We live in this utterly extraordinary world that has taken billions of years to evolve, enormously complex, profoundly beautiful, and yet we find ourselves sitting around not knowing what to do. We find ourselves feeling bored, tired, waiting for something exciting to happen, like the next episode of our favorite soap opera. We fail to encounter the utterly astonishing nature of our experience and as soon as we witness our life as astonishing, we immediately find ourselves back with a world that poses a question—the world *is* a question. It is something that we are unable to contain within the categories and confines of a world that would be designed for the security of my ego.

So as one's perplexity and questioning become stabilized in the stillness of meditation, one comes to inhabit a world that is mysterious, and in a very real sense, magical, in the lived sense, not in some sort of ideological sense.

But this is not where the practice ends. Emptiness is not the end of the process. That's not what it's about finally. That is just a halfway point, because what we discover in this open, but nonetheless ambiguous, space of not knowing, of perplexity, of mystery, of emptiness, of astonishment, is we also dis-

cover the origins of imagination and creativity, two subjects which we rarely hear anything much about in traditional Buddhism. I don't even know if there is a word for imagination in traditional Buddhist terms.

This leads us into another area. For me, one of the great doctrines of Mahayana Buddhism is the notion of the three *kayas*, the notion of the buddha bodies, the *Dharmakaya, Sambhogakaya*, and *Nirmanakaya*. That points to that idea that the Buddha is not just someone who's had an incredible mystical experience, whose mind has become liberated from craving, who's totally there in the emptiness of reality. But the Buddha is also this being who spontaneously and compassionately manifests and is embodied in the world. (*Nirmanakaya* would be the technical word.)

If we go back to the traditional story of the Buddha's awakening, we have this strange period of about six weeks after the awakening under the bodhi tree where the Buddha just sort of hangs out around the tree and effectively hesitates. In the Pali texts it says that he didn't want to get involved in the vexation of teaching, in the vexation of the world. And it takes a god—in this case, Brahma Sahampati—to say basically, "Come on, Sunshine, there's something to do out there." *That* prompted him then to get up and leave.

If we think about this process, it is quite comparable to the process of artistic creation. When we're faced with the task of articulating a deep, intuitive vision, whether it be in words or in clay or in paint, we might find ourselves in a very comparable state of intense trepidation. This is something one finds (at least I've found very much in my Zen training): When one really gets into the core of asking a question like, What is this? one gets to a point of stillness; but at the same time, one hits up against a tremendous resistance to pursue the inquiry further. There's something very threatening about asking questions at that level of depth. Usually we become very prone to fantasy, daydreams, drowsiness, and so on, and this perhaps is somewhat similar to the experience a writer may have, when you're trying to really communicate something that's important to you and all you have in front of you is a blank sheet of paper or an empty computer screen. You so easily become caught up in compulsions to tidy your desk, to clean up your books, reorder them, do something you would never do like Hoover the room, dust the room, whatever. Although that's, in a sense, somewhat comical, it points to how there is this reluctance to encounter an unknown and a reluctance to encounter and to engage in expression, in creatively generating something that has never quite been said or thought or imaged in that way before. This is what creation is about—bringing into being something that did not exist before. So creativity is that dimension of ourselves that takes the risk of stating what has not yet been stated.

Of course, religious institutions are not terribly keen on that. Religious institutions are very much about controlling the imagination. The imagination is threatening. The imag-ination is a very deep way of owning your own experience and articulating it in a way that is true to that experience. So when we sit in meditation, we also sit on the threshold of the imagination and I personally feel that the Buddha's genius lay in his imagination. I don't swallow the kind of stereotyped picture of the awakening or the enlightenment—that he was sitting beneath this tree and then, all of a sudden, *ka-pow!* and the four noble truths sort of appeared in letters of fire in the sky, one, two, three, four. Okay, got it. I don't honestly think we can put that into words. It seems to me that the awakening did not actually become real until the Buddha had to stammer it out to his former companions in Sarnath.

In other words, awakening is not a state. Enlightenment is not a state. It's not some kind of inward mystical event in which everything suddenly becomes articulated for you. But rather it is the first step in a process for which perhaps there is not an end. Now, religious institutions like to think that they have got the end product. If you listen to the polemic—you know, "the ultimate teaching of the Buddha," "the final teaching of the Buddha," "the original teaching of the Buddha," "the quickest teaching of the Buddha," etc.—this is all about laying claim to some kind of truth, which appears in definition to be static. The task, then, of the tradition becomes that of preservation rather than that of creation.

I think one of the great things that Western consciousness can bring to the Buddhist tradition is historical awareness, the recognition of historical contingency. The different Buddhist traditions, different Buddhist expressions, are all contingent upon the cultural, social, economic, political circumstances that prevailed at the time that they were first stated. So from an historical perspective, the wheel of the Dharma didn't just turn once, twice, or three times depending on your tradition, but it's actually turning through time. It's like a wheel that's moving along with the unfolding of history. It's a process. It's something that's continuously challenged by every new situation it encounters.

We are in a situation that's very different to that of Asia, to any of the former situations in Asia, and we talk very much of the creation of a Western Buddhism. Very dangerous idea. How much of that is yet another attempt to freeze Buddhism into another religious, dogmatic, institutional form?

[A man said that "there has been a tendency for some traditions to look at other traditions in Buddhism and say, 'No, that's not the real thing.'" He went on to say "that what we are doing is not really Buddhism anymore. It's something else." He asked Mr. Batchelor if his intent was to suggest that what has been called "Buddhism," be it in India, Tibet, China, Japan, and other places, is now "something else [we're calling] 'agnosticism.'"]

Stephen Batchelor: It's clearly differentiable from agnosticism. That's why I would preface it with "deep." And certainly it's got nothing to do with critiquing any particular tradition of practice. I guess it has to do with what we might call *samma dittthi* [Pali] or *yangdag pa'i*

tawa [Tibetan], usually horribly translated as "right view." "Authentic vision," perhaps. It's the basic sort of *weltanschaung,* or basic sort of paradigm within which we understand, interpret, and make sense of the practice. It's really that paradigm that shifts with different cultures.

There are two dangers: One is that, if we're too loose in our adherence to the integrity of the Buddhist tradition, then all these practices and philosophies and psychologies could easily just get absorbed into other fields. So a bit of it could be drawn into psychotherapy; a bit could be drawn into contemplative Christianity; a bit might help postmodern philosophy, etc. But the actual integrity of the tradition is then dissolved, which clearly I wouldn't want to do.

On the other hand, if we're too rigidly adherent to the Asian cultural forms, then the chances are that Buddhism will remain a kind of marginal cultural artifact of interest to eccentric people like us, but not really have much impact on the world in which we live. So it's about somehow finding a middle way between the two.

[The next question took the ideas discussed farther, positing that institutionalizing Buddhism gets static and that it's a constant tendency to want to freeze things. "I would say that aside from the cultural tendencies, it's a parallel, individualistic tendency to freeze because [change is] so scary. It has to do with clinging. It has to do with grasping."]

Stephen Batchelor: Since Buddhism has as two of its primary axioms "Everything changes" and "Nothing is self"—nothing is substantially frozen and real—it strikes me as paradoxical that the very tradition that states that rarely applies those perceptions to itself. The idea that the Karma Kagyu tradition changes or the Galukpa or the Soto Zen traditions change is not really up for grabs, in a sort of metaphysical way.

I think Buddhism has to be subjected to the very critique that Buddhism applies to everything else, that's it's not some *thing*. We like to think there's some sort of thing, some sort of essential Buddhism, that doesn't change.

Let's say we lined up in this room and put a Tibetan Nyingma yogi here, a Japanese Pure Land priest here, and a Sri Lankan *bhikkhu* here, and we ask them What do you teach? I think we'd get three very different answers. One of the great richnesses of Buddhism is it's fantastic diversity and yet what's interesting is that each of those traditions would actually be very reluctant to celebrate diversity. Instead, diversity is seen as a kind of pyramidical structure. We're at the top and the other guys are okay, they're good, but they don't quite make the grade. To me, that betrays a certain commitment to essentialism, a certain attachment to some sort of frozen image of who I am, of what the tradition is. That is something we need to really question, I think, because the whole identity of Buddhism is bound up in that issue.

[Pointing out that he perceived Mr. Batchelor to be "dichotomizing" by using such phrases as "at odds," a man remarked that an important

component of Buddhism for him "is the idea of oneness, of the unity of everything." He also mentioned that he would like to see develop what one could call "Buddhist humanism," which would "force us to take a look at the humanistic aspects of Buddhism a little more closely."]

Stephen Batchelor: I actually have some difficulty with this term *oneness*. I'm not aware of any term, at least in Tibetan, that corresponds to this and I don't see that term valued and celebrated as it often is in contemporary writings on Buddhism. The very notion of interrelatedness and emptiness presupposes difference. You cannot have relationship without difference. If everything were one, there could be no relationship. So I think we need to be careful to be able to preserve a valuing and a celebration of difference, and philosophically a necessity of difference, without slipping into a kind of frozen dualism.

Buddhism is very critical of dualism, but dualism is actually a denial of relationship. Dualism basically could be described as, my relation to you or the world might be *I'm* one thing, *that* is another thing, and ne'er the twain shall meet. We are separated from each other. We are separated from the environment by an unbridgeable gulf. There is total opposition.

Buddhism is not saying that we need to dissolve all sense of difference and opposition and enter into a kind of mystical, oceanic oneness in which all sense of differentiation is gone. That, as far as I'm aware, is not the traditional Buddhist view. It's far more about replacing dualism with a kind of relational awareness. That rather than me being utterly opposite and at odds with you, I stand always in a relationship with you, even if that be a relationship of opposition or a relationship of love. But that difference is what makes it possible.

Although I did mention at the beginning of my talk my reconnection with the humanist tradition, I'm not sure that Buddhism is humanist, in fact. I think a more comparable term would be something like "sentient-beingist." The Buddha always speaks of *sattva* —all sentient beings. I think the Buddhist concern for the world is far more than a concern for human life. It's a concern for all that lives and breathes and has consciousness and awareness, and perhaps beyond that, too. So although the Buddhist tradition is a human tradition, created by human beings, it's a valuing of human potential— there's absolutely no question of that—I'm slightly nervous about identifying it with humanism.

[*Another participant, further addressing issues of carrying on Buddhist traditions in the West, noted that everything he has read about Buddhism "was somehow transmitted down through somebody who was 'within' the traditional orthodox Buddhist religion. Everything I've gotten, I've gotten out of that." While he didn't consider himself to be part of any particular group or sect, "I do have a great deal of thanks for those people who carry on those traditions."*]

Stephen Batchelor: The danger of seeking to move toward some kind of Western or agnostic or humanistic Buddhism, or whatever, is that that might feed into a kind of devaluing of Asian cultures, which I think would be not the way to go. There's also a danger, of course, of identifying Buddhism with the Asian cultural force, but, on the other hand, we could say that Buddhism has the great virtue of spreading diverse cultural forms through the world. For many of us, what we know of Tibetan culture, for example, or Japanese culture, comes through our interest in Buddhism. That actually brings us into other people's realities. It brings us into other ways of aesthetic appreciation. It introduces us to other ways of thinking about the world, other forms of society, and that's immensely enriching.

I don't actually like the idea of Western Buddhism. I think it's a horrible notion as well as a very outdated notion. It presupposes West/East—again, a standard dualism and one that reflects, in fact, a kind of imperial, colonial bias. Of course, it's a purely arbitrary distinction. Where do you draw the line? It may be useful as a sort of generic generalization, but it potentially preserves a cultural arrogance. Is there actually such a thing as an essential Buddhism that is separate from these cultures? I don't think there is.

The Dharma finds its form not because there's some essential dharma that then dresses up in Tibetan robes or Japanese robes. What the Dharma is, in that historical instant, is that particular manifestation, and it needs to be respected as such. I think it's falling into precisely the trap that Buddhism warns against if we think there's some kind of "essential dharma" hidden in there somewhere. Take off these Tibetan robes and we'll find it. That's nonsense. It's like the peeling of the onion: You peel away the culture, there's actually nothing there. Or like the analysis of the self: I think I'm in here somewhere. I peel away all the bits, there's nothing there. So Buddhism is configured out of cultural structures and that's a much more complex and difficult way to look at it than the often-repeated one about Buddhism inside culture, outside. I don't think it's as simple as that.

Since I've sort of ceased practicing within the Tibetan tradition, I've actually become much more engaged with Tibetan politics, writing guidebooks to Tibet, and so on, which has led me to an appreciation of Tibetan culture I probably didn't have when I was actually in the tradition.

Participant: Using the example of pieces of paper and computer screens being blank, you talked about our reluctance to encounter things that we don't know; to avoid them, Hoover them. What can you say further about that in terms of getting past that? I do much better with computer screens and pieces of paper. Can you just say more about that and whatever thoughts you have about how to practice with that reluctance or avoidance.

Stephen Batchelor: For me, a lot of this has to do with coming back again and again to the question Why the hell am I sitting here? What am I doing this for? It's so easy when you adopt any kind of practice that initially it can be inspirational, it can be invigorating, it can be challenging, it can be provocative. But,

like anything human beings learn to do, it can so easily become mechanical and routine. I think that's actually in the bigger picture one of the ways in which we deal with the real challenge of sitting, is to routine-ize sitting, is to routine-ize practice, make it into a routine practice. And this often leads to an experience of I don't feel my meditation's really going anywhere anymore, or I don't seem to be able to do anything about these wandering fantasies and thoughts that I have. And if it's likewise about avoidance, if you notice you're getting caught up in strategies of evasion, it seems that in a weird way we come to the practice with a very authentic question. And yet so easily that question becomes, as it were, compromised or somehow shifted from a living question into a set of theoretical inquiries about what emptiness means.

So to deal with avoidance, to deal with compulsive distraction, to deal with routine-ization—to ask oneself why am I sitting here? In the Tibetan tradition, a practice that I've always found extremely helpful is the meditation on death. To sit there and to reflect on the fact that the only thing that's certain in life is that I'm going to die. Everything else is uncertain, and that one certain thing that's going to happen could happen at any time. It's totally uncertain as to when it will occur and that paradox of certainty and uncertainty serves to focus the mind extremely well. If we could really touch a felt sense of the certainty of death and the uncertainty of its time, that, I think, can reawaken an authenticity of the question of what our practice is really about.

Again, that practice too, that reflection too, can become routine-ized. You can't get out of the routine-izing loop, but it seems to me a way of perhaps, you know, you're halfway through a sitting, perhaps, and you notice this kind of repetitive, habitual sort of thing that's set in, just stop—stop looking at the breath, asking a koan, and just stop. Be aware of the fact that you're sitting there and ask yourself why. In other words, question. Keep the question at the heart of the thing and then I think it'll work.

[Opening what Mr. Batchelor called a subject for a whole other lecture, a man asked how the concept of reincarnation fit within the idea of deep agnosticism.]

Stephen Batchelor: That's one thing I have a very agnostic view about. I don't personally believe that you have to hold any belief in reincarnation to practice Buddhism. To me, reincarnation is a very good example of a metaphor of consolation. Traditionally, reincarnation is actually what you're trying to *escape* from. It's very ironic that Westerners actually think that reincarnation is something to look forward to, because it's actually what the Buddha was trying to get you out of. But, even if you see it in a very traditional Buddhist way, nonetheless it is containing death within the confines of what the human brain can imagine. It's much more comforting to know that, when I die, I might even go to Hell, but at least I'll know where I'm going. But to me, that denies death of its dignity. It denies death of its mystery. It

denies death as the profound unknown of our lives, to which we are inexorably headed.

["I feel that the presentation that you gave was a magnificent presentation of the prajna *side of Buddhism, the wisdom side of Buddhism," a participant said. What concerned this man, however, was that he didn't feel that compassion, "the Mahayana balance, which is so crucial to my love of Buddhism," had been addressed here. He further related compassion to the creative aspects of meditation, which Mr. Batchelor had discussed.*

Agreeing this was a good point, Mr. Batchelor elaborated.]

The reference I did make to compassion was when I said that the awakening only really happened when the Buddha stammered out his understanding to others. That, of course, is the act of compassion. So creation—bringing something into existence that has not existed before—is bringing something into the world. One does not do that just for one's own egoistic satisfaction. As soon as I say something, or you say something, or you write something, or I write something, or paint something, it becomes public; it becomes instantiated in the shared world that we inhabit together.

The agnostic dimension, I think, and the secular dimension also, brings the attention back primarily to practice as a response to the situation we live in now, with others, not to some future life. That is very much about compassion. Had I gone on to develop my ideas about community, the kind of community that we would perhaps envisage from this perspective, that would necessarily bring in forming the kinds of relationships that would support a practice. So, in the realization, if I were to tease out the implications of this kind of perspective, it would come more and more to reflecting on the actual concrete forms that Buddhism might take in terms of community, of teacher-student relations, of *sangha* relations—in terms of responding not just to the questions of how does Buddhism survive, but the questions of how do we address the issue of suffering in our world.

To go back to your question, my own vision would be that I would look to a kind of Buddhism that would be small scale, that would be community centered; one that would be socially engaged. And I can't really conceive of what an authentic Buddhism for me would be without those dimensions.

Watering from the Deep Well

LOOKING AT PERCEPTIONS OF MONASTICISM

Dai-en Bennage Roshi

THIS CONFERENCE DRAMATICALLY EXEMPLIFIED THE VAST RANGE of practices, approaches, and concepts traditionally supported under the wide umbrella of Buddhism. But one issue in particular seemed to present itself in a majority of the workshops and seminars—the disparity between the traditional prescriptions for gaining enlightenment and the more individually determined ways of seeking enlightenment. In "Watering from the Deep Well," Dai-en Bennage demonstrated how she has melded her fifteen years of monastic life in a Japanese Zen monastery with her current life in Pennsylvania, where she teaches, runs retreats, cares for her mother, and works as a spiritual counselor with men in a maximum-security prison.

Dai-en Bennage began Rinzai training in Tokyo as a lay student of Zen Master Omori Sogen Rotaishi. When he became ill, she entered the priesthood of Soto Zen, training primarily at Aichi Semmon Nisodo, a women's monastery. In 1984, she received Dharma transmission and Zuise; her roshi certification was granted in 1990, at which time she moved to France, where she studied with Ven. Thich Nhat Hanh ways of teaching to students in English. The following year, she returned to the United States. She is translator of *Zen Seeds*, the only one of the fourteen books by her teacher, Abbess Aoyama Shundo Roshi, to have been translated into English to date.

In this country, she continues to be a monk, but finds herself questioning what that now means, in an American context rather than that of a Japanese monastery. Her practice consists of many elements—aiding her mother; working with well-to-do college students in a private college in central Pennsylvania; leading retreats; and working with prisoners.

Noting that, for full practice, many Japanese Zen training temples have very strict requirements for their students, she explains that her "greatest desire upon returning to the United States has been to be able to offer *zazen* to all who inquire." In presenting this to those who attended this session, she looked at a series of questions: How can the Buddhadharma be offered freely and accurately if its source—the deep well associated with monasticism—is not protected, maintained, and nourished? What is Zen monasticism? From what set of values are non-Asian ordainees practicing? How can the deepest of the teachings be truly carried on so as to be accurately available to others over centuries to come?

Dai-en Bennage Roshi began to deal with the deep well of monasticism by looking at what it means to be a monk. She described the wall decoration of clouds painted behind a giant statue of the Buddha at Byodo-in, a temple south of Kyoto that was built in the 900s. This painting was made to depict paradise on Earth at that time:

On these clouds are seated bodhisattvas playing heavenly instruments. One that caught my eye and my heart has a ninth-century version of the accordion on two sticks—a wonderful image of the awakened way. How do we get music? We pull the accordion out and it goes *waaaah,* and when the *waaaah* is gone, we have to push it back in again. When we cease moving our hands, there is only silence.

Our practice [she went on to say] is to deal with all of the contradictions that are in this life. I like to feel that monks are full-timers, whatever the circumstances or the outer form may be. In many ways I look like a monk to you, with the shaved head and all of these robes, and yet the way my practice is manifesting in this country I'm not really sure if it's monastic or not.

Citing a Chinese proverb—"We can change the city, but we cannot change the well"—she broached the subject of to whom it is appropriate to offer training. "We have so many manifestations of this practice," she said, recalling that:

The late Katageri Roshi said in the book by Natalie Goldberg, *The Long Quiet Highway,* "I want hairdressers to come and do *zazen,* I want truck drivers to come and do *zazen.*" We haven't begun to pierce the multi-layers of our society and have this practice be available for as many people as it needs to be.

How do we take care of that well, and how do we make it accessible to others? In the very beginning pages of *Zen Seeds,* Abbess Aoyama Shundo Roshi talks about how things flow: The rivers flow, but the mountains also flow, and houses flow. We lose a sense of that until we're up in the attic and take out a box of old letters or old clothes and we see the patina of age and realize that, of course, everything flows. Yet we tend to see things in time segments.

In our own society, which is so into ontological individualism, we see things only within what is labeled our "life span." In many countries in the world, things are not mea-

Two of the many Buddhist nuns in attendance

sured that way. You may have seen a beautiful scroll of bamboo: a stroke; and then the sideline; another stroke; another short cut off; another smaller stroke, another cut off; the different segments of the bamboo. One sees oneself as one segment of bamboo in an endlessly growing bamboo stalk, so that there must be a carrying over from before me, to me, to after me, and on. So we should look with very great gladness and joy at all of the wonderful new expressions that the path of awakeness is taking now. Yet equally we have to find ways to keep the well viable, to keep the well clean, to keep the well flowing. That's not the easy part to see because it runs so slowly.

Before moving on from this inquiry into passing on the Buddhadharma, Dai-en Bennage Roshi emphasized that, "if we really do what it

is we want to have done, people will see and, even without thinking, they will follow." She told the audience that for the first twenty years of her adult life, she had been a classical-ballet dancer, and she used a story from the world of ballet to illustrate her point:

Just recently I have found myself looking back to the traditions I came from and see how some of my teachers and peers have used dance. I had a tape of Jacques d'Amboise talking to the Press Club, and he said that once he reached his mature level as a dancer, he felt the great need to share his teaching with students, young people in the inner cities. So he took his own pocket money and hired a pianist, a friend, and they'd take cabs all over New York City to the various inner schools and say to the principal "We'll offer ballet lessons every day at the lunch hour for free, if you like." He did that until he couldn't pay for the pianist any more, and he had to take a tape recorder. After about two years, Lincoln Kirstein, the financial head of the New York City Ballet Company, said, "Well, Jacques, you look pretty serious with this and it looks like it's getting difficult, so here's two thousand dollars for now. See how far it will stretch for what you need to do and then maybe come back to me."

Her next question—What is Zen monasticism, really?—was prefaced with the caveat that she could only speak with authority on the Soto Zen tradition. "Our rules are very similar to the Chinese rules," she said, "but as Buddhism moved from China to Korea and Japan, it took on the set of values, the climates that are of the country. That is happening again as we just begin to become established in this country." The issue of appearance and its effect upon others—students, outsiders, etc.—was addressed.

I ask my students, "Could you hear my message better if I had hair and a denim skirt?" Some say, "We're used to you the way you are." Others say, "Well, if you want. It doesn't really make any difference." So, I haven't had any strong pull one way or the other.

Just yesterday, however, my student came to pick me up at the airport and, walking toward the car, someone stopped and asked what I represented. Was I Amish? I said, "No, I'm a Zen monk." They said, "I don't know exactly what that means, but it just looks wonderful, and I'm happy to see it today."

Another person who was deeply effected by seeing the roshi in her robes was a woman in an airport, who asked, "May I please touch your sleeve. I just have the feeling it will be good luck, because you are someone who is living according to some rules that are bigger than yourself." She told of a personal experience in Japan in which "the sight of a monk made a very big difference."

After three and a half years of training with a Rinzai master who became so ill I could not continue with him, I took a pilgrimage around the island of Shikoku. That takes about six weeks to walk.

I didn't start out in a very good mood because I wanted to go with the shaved head and robes like another woman practitioner had done under Omori Roshi. He said, "You still make mistakes in the *Heart Sutra,* and so if someone stops you as a monk to recite the sutra, our name will be on your hat and it is not only a mark on your practice but on ours as well. So, please, just go as a pilgrim and enjoy the flowers." I took that in a very cynical way; I was miffed.

The first day I rode because the caretakers of temple number one were worried about me, huffing and puffing, not used to hiking with something on my back. They told the next person coming along, who happened to be a Shinto priest, "Please give poor foreigner a ride." My teacher had said, "You may ride to one temple and then say goodbye and thank that person. Then, if someone else offers you a ride, that is alright, but don't ride from temple to temple." Well, I was miffed and the Shinto priest said "The first twelve are so close together, why don't I just take you to all of them?" I said alright. So, we drove to each of these temples.

At temple thirteen you may stay overnight and the next day take a longer ride to temple fourteen. You get up very early and participate in the Shingon sect's tradition, the goma, the fire rituals, and then you set off just about at dawn. Well, we drove due east and, suddenly, up this hill I could see the dark silhouette of a monk doing the pilgrimage backwards, from temple eighty-eight around to temple one. He was at temple thirteen. My whole being just stopped. I said to the driver, "Thank you very much for your help, I'm getting out right here." I began to open the door and he pulled over in a hurry.

"Are you alright?"

"I'm fine. I've got it now. I'm fine. Thank you very much."

"Are you going to be able to walk this?"

"I'm fine."

Just the sight of a monk was like that. What are you doing on this pilgrimage? Are you going to do it or not? And so I set out and passed the monk, and we gasshoed, and he kept going. You should see the pace of someone walking for five and a half weeks. Later the Shinto man came back and said, "Are you really going to be alright?"

I said, "If you want to help, leave me two notes somewhere—don't say where—at the other temples, and they will be a kind of help to draw me along."

So just the sight of a monk can sometimes be a lesson.

Next Roshi looked at what it means to be a Buddhist monk, saying that a monk is someone who "has come to learn, although we keep forgetting, that living life is getting what Shakespeare wrote, 'Fair is foul, and foul is fair / Loss is gain and gain is loss.' What looks like a loss in this world, is a gain in the world of the absolute and vice versa."

Discussing what might be termed "qualifications," she reiterated the traditional idea that it takes ten years to make a monk, twenty years to make a teacher, and thirty years to make a master. She also quoted Charlotte Joko Beck...

who says some interesting things about transformation—"Over a long period of time, life gets *us* to do what *it* wants." Is that not another way of finding a monk? She speaks of "*thy*

will be done." What is the "thy" if it doesn't mean just what's outside of this little conception of self? But we keep forgetting.

An example of the call for one to step beyond the ego and individualism that can afflict most of us, brought this point home:

A student of mine recently came for a sesshin. She brought some squares of cornbread to eat on the long drive to our center. It wasn't enough for the number of people we had for the last meal before the sesshin started, but I had some mix for cornbread so I said, "If we have that too, and you warm that up we'll have enough for everybody with the soup this evening." We have two kitchens—one in the zendo and one at my mother's next door, so I began to make the cornbread in the zendo oven and when I went over to my mother's kitchen to see if things were lined up I saw that the other oven was on. I said, "Well, I've already started the muffins in the zendo oven."

My student said, "I decided to warm them up here."

"Why couldn't you use the same oven for warming up your muffins?" I asked.

She said, "I wasn't there. I'm here."

So she was bringing the practice to her personal level instead of going out to where the need was. For a moment she forgot, and that's a very important part of our practice.

Another student, who practiced a long time in the Korean tradition, said someone once asked a teacher, "What's the difference between a practitioner and a teacher?" The reply was, "The teacher corrects his or her mistakes faster." It's not that we don't have them, but that we remember that we forget.

Looking at her next question—From what set of values are non-Asian ordainees practicing?—Roshi said that, many times, when she had made a suggestion to a student, they had responded that that was "too Asian" or "too Japanese" for them to consider. This made her think of another example from the world of dance. She told of a videotape about Rudolf Nureyev that she had seen, recalling in particular an interview with the great dancer—"a wonderful part that's a Dharma lesson.

He's just by himself, framed by the screen, telling about when he had just left the Soviet Union and he went immediately to George Balanchine, who had also been a Russian emigré, and said "I want to dance in your company."

Balanchine said "Well, my ballets are very dry. We don't have any of these romantic *pas de deux*. I don't know that you would be happy there. Go away, get rid of your princes, and then we'll see."

So Nureyev went to Europe and danced in smaller companies that had Balanchine's works in their repertoire. Sixteen years later he went to Balanchine, and Balanchine said, "Welcome."

Now is this any different than what is asked of us as serious Zen practitioners?

She completed her talk on the values held by non-Asian ordainees by contrasting the way in which Americans are given a back-

ground in which to practice: "no obstacles; no guard-rails."

When I was a teen, I didn't want to pay any attention to those signs in the middle of the road. Fifty miles an hour for the dotted lines and the NO PASSING signs. Now that I'm much older, I am so grateful. At night, the white stripe along the righthand side of the road keeps me from going off.

We don't have a lot of signs in our country's values. Our practice requires us to be more than our country does; when we get vague on that we see how quickly we're in trouble.

How can the very deepest of the teachings be carried over into the future? This final question brought her discussion around to BUDDHA–L, an Internet newsgroup concerning Buddhism, which she referred to as "another way to try to practice with equilibrium." Part of this equilibrium is between Buddhist academia and those "in the meditator field." She said:

We need to practice openness as much as possible, not close down on those within our own groups; not close down on those in other groups. Sometimes messages make it very difficult for dialogue.

One academician said he had visited a number of Zen centers intending to make a book on what's going on. He took a photograph of some books in one center and was asked not to, which made me wonder if Buddhist academicians and Buddhist meditators use books differently? We might. I have a feeling that meditators use books because they grab at our guts and they change our whole lives, and I have to ask myself, Does this also happen for academicians in Buddhism?

Roshi also mused about the possibility that the medium may affect the way in which the message is received and understood. "When oral teachings are available in paperback, sometimes something happens."

There's a story about a Japanese woman who had a very good knack for healing people. She uttered a particular statement and people went away healed. Now the Japanese language is full of homonyms—words that sound alike. So one day a monk came by and heard about her. He went to see her and to see how she was with people who needed help. He heard her phrase and said, "You're saying, 'Wheat and barley so be it. Wheat and barley so be it.'" And what happened to the woman healer? She could no longer heal.

Asked to comment on differences, conflicts perhaps, that Roshi may have noticed between the method and manner of her own training and that of American-ordained monks and priests. The roshi said she couldn't make a comparison, since she had just lived one way in Japan.

I have been back in the United States six years now, and I have been trying to follow the same pattern as I did in Japan. It's worked out and there have been some tests for that. I am caregiver to my mother who lives next door and I also work with six prison *sanghas* and some wealthy college students. So, I have a rather full range in which to deal with.

John Daido Loori had a very good article that asks Why are monks relevant? In one way we're useless in this world, for this world's values. We're also marginal. He quotes Thomas Merton who said, the marginal person, the monastic, the displaced person, the prisoner, all of these people live in the presence of death. If you cannot forget about that too much or for too long, that will help you keep on track.

A young man, who used to come from time to time, returned recently. He looked quite rattled because someone that he knew quite well was murdered. Because the young man has seen the shadow of his own possible death, he's back into practice much more seriously than before. So to the extent that we do not forget that, too much or for too long, to that extent will we be real with our practice.

Whatever number of precepts we take, they feel like a conflict, they feel like a constriction. When I first read the Vinaya, it was the driest law book I had ever come upon. But when my training took me from a women's setting to a men's setting—twenty-eight male monks and me—we lived that Vinaya every day. And it became the livingest, most vibrant, real document. It just switched like that because I lived it instead of reading it. It has to be real to us; it has to speak to us at a gut level. But it takes death, it takes something, to turn us around.

If you want to do volunteer work, if your students want to do volunteer work, get them into maximum-security prison. Men are there—women too, but I haven't had a doorway into a women's prison—inmates are there thirty years to multiple life. Over half of them are lifers in the one that I go to. They are my teachers. They *live* a life sentence. They help me not forget. We need to find something in our daily life, with our family, whatever, that keeps us remembering the bottom line. Whatever form it takes, I think is secondary. To find the *upaya,* the skillful means, to know the bottom line, is the most helpful thing that I know of.

When asked to say something about her understanding about relationship, marriage, and parenting, Roshi allowed that she could only speak as a caregiver to her mother. "It's been very helpful that she has now taken the precepts, too," she remarked.

It is even a stronger tie than familial. But not everyone has relatives that will take the precepts, but can we not hold them in our hearts as though they have all the dormant potentiality for that? Always ask ourselves, What is required right here and right now in the Dharma? That helps stretch us beyond the boundaries of personal interest.

I saw my mother and that she needed help, and I had no agenda made up for how my help was to be called upon. I didn't say, This is my big call, and I'm going to do this kind of work in America. I said, I will let the Dharma call me. So it's prisons that have called me and it was my mother living next door that called me.

Also there's bodhisattva work. I never had children and so it seems the bodhisattva said, "Well, Dai-en, can you take care of your students? How about some "Home work?" I use the term *Home work* in a special way: It means work that gets us to our true home. It doesn't mean school work. Let's see if you can take care of your mother and your students and that will be your Home-work assignment.

Sometimes I feel impatient. I've got faxes coming in, things to be translated into Japanese; I'm going 78 rpm. Then I have to go and prepare a meal and I find my mother going at 33⅓ and just want to say "Speed up." It doesn't work.

So there is the Dharma lesson. Get flexible. Take the wheels out of gear, come and blend. Drop all your faxes and things. So, wherever we feel a button pushed, can we gassho to that? That's our secret bodhisattva that has our present Home work assignment right here for us. That's fair is foul, and foul is fair. Anything that pushes your buttons, gassho to it—that's your built-in teacher.

Focusing on the teaching

3

The Path

Buddhist Thought and Practice

in Day-to-Day Living and Dying

We Are All Buddhas

THE JOY OF MEDITATION AND THE NATURAL GREAT PERFECTION

Lama Surya Das

FIRST INTRODUCED TO BUDDHIST PRACTICE at a Zen center in Rochester, New York, in the 1970s, Lama Surya Das has since ranged the world in his pursuit of enlightenment. He is an authorized American lama in the Tibetan Buddhist Order and has spent more than twelve years in the Himalayas, twice completing the traditional three-year, three-month Nyingma meditation retreat. He founded the Dzogchen Foundation, based in Cambridge, Massachusetts, and, with the Dalai Lama, the Western Buddhist Teachers Conference. Surya Das is also a poet, translator, and storyteller. Among his publications are *The Snow Lion's Turquoise Mane: 155 Wisdom Tales from Tibet, The Natural Great Perfection: Dzogchen Teachings and Vajra Songs by Nyoshul Khenpo,* and *The Facts of Life from a Buddhist Perspective.*

Lama Surya Das presented two workshops and a keynote talk at the Buddhism in America conference, all of which drew upon his practice of the Dzogchen tradition of Tibetan Buddhism and revolved around the evolving understanding and embracing of Buddhist practice and attitudes toward living in 1990s America. The workshops included periods of directed meditation as well as lively Dharma talks about various aspects of leading the life of a buddha in our contemporary world. During one meditation Surya Das defined Dzogchen as "the innate Great Perfection, or the Great Completeness, a Tibetan teaching about how to awaken the native, natural, organic buddha within each of us," which he often characterized as "you-ddha" nature.

Inviting participants in "We Are All Buddhas" to "open all of your inner doors and windows, and awareness, like fresh air, will flow through," he began in the traditional fashion with an invocation of "all the enlightened ones, all the buddhas, bodhisattvas, Dharma protectors," etc. This was followed by chanting of the Mantra of Great Compassion. In this atmosphere of meditation and awareness, Surya Das began.

W e are all Buddhas by nature. Only momentary obscurations, veils of illusion, of ignorance, cover that fact, keep us from our true selves, our true nature, so-called buddha-nature. Even to call it "buddha," though, is to make it too foreign, like we have to import it from Japan or Tibet or somewhere.

Buddha nature is not *Buddha*. It's our true nature. It's you. It's *you*-ddha nature. American buddha-nature. Natural, organic, home-grown buddha-nature. It's the ground, even before we grow anything. It's earth. It's even below the earth. It's our source, not just where we're going to. It's where we are, it's where we're coming from. That's why we call it "the buddha within," or "buddha-nature." This is the ancient, timeless teaching of the Dharma of Buddhism, of the scriptures, the sutras. And even beyond Buddhism, we can find it in the mystics of all traditions, the sages of all the ages speak of it in perennial philosophy, whatever language is used. So we call it buddha-nature, which means your own true nature. Your own great completeness and wholeness. Nirvana within, not just nirvanic peace on the far shore; you have to build a huge bridge to get there. But the buddha within: Don't miss her! The sacred feminine energy in all of us, male and female; that's Tara, that's Kuan-yin. That's the female buddha.

Dzogchen comes out of the Tibetan tradition and it refers directly to our own perfect and complete nature. We only have to recognize this. That's why my own guru, my own teacher, Kalu Rinpoche, always used to say,

"We're all buddhas by nature. We only have to recognize that fact." Awaken to that fact. Realize that fact. That's enlightenment. That's awakening. That's self-realization. That's satori. That's a spiritual breakthrough. All these terms have the same meaning: recognizing our true nature, awakening to that fact. Not that we need to get something elsewhere. It's more like a muscle; maybe we haven't been using it, so it's a little flabby. It's a little forgotten. We all have the muscle of awareness, of buddha-nature. We only have to use it, to firm it up, to recognize it.

So this practice comes from that outlook of the great perfection of things just as they are. Of seeing clearly the truth or, as Buddhism defines the truth, things just as they are. And meditation is the best way to do that. Meditation is not a trance or hypnosis. It's not dropping out or avoiding. It may be a way to come closer to others and to the world, to really be intimate with everything, rather than separating ourselves from it and from others, being afraid, hiding behind our ego barrier, and so on. Meditation is the best way to awaken and to know ourselves. And meditation has many forms, not just quiet, seated meditation, although that is the one application that all use. But then the rest of the programs are also there—walking meditation, chanting meditation, eating meditation, visualization or prayer or mantra meditation, breathing meditation, kundalini or energy meditation, and so on.

But the common denominator is always awareness, attention, clear seeing, awakening. So these teachings, these practices, have been called "the luminous heart of the

Dharma," "the naked essential," "the essential-ized practice," for which we don't need a lot of special learning. We don't need to memorize the scriptures as is sometimes done in traditional monasteries. We don't necessarily need to study foreign languages like Pali or Sanskrit or Tibetan or Japanese. We don't need fancy initiations. We don't need to take up monasticism. We don't need to leave our home, our family, and our work.

We may need to let go a little bit of something in order for something else to come up or fit in. It may be helpful to simplify a little, simplify our lives, simplify our minds, slow down, but we don't need a lot of external changes in order to awaken within. When Thoreau said, a hundred fifty years ago, "I don't trust the people who change their clothes; I trust the people who change their hearts and minds for the better," he meant I don't trust the people that change their outer garb into holy garb. I trust the people that change their hearts and minds into holy hearts and minds. This is an inner work, the wisdom work. It's something for each of us, if we choose to take up ourselves. As the Buddha said, "Be a lamp unto yourself. I only point the way. You walk it yourself."

I think that's very doable. It's something we can do today, even here and now. In our speedy, technological, postmodern society, still we can do it. The luminous essence of the Dharma can take place in many forms, even here in this hotel. So this is the joy of awakening, of spiritual life. It always is here with us. We may feel far from it, but it's never far from us.

[Since much of this workshop was in question-and-answer format, Lama Surya Das frequently changed direction to respond to specific questions. One such question concerned making a beginning at Buddhist practice, its methods and means. He answered with a long list of possibilities, from reading books and magazines to seeing which aspects attract you and which "turn you off," to tapes, correspondence courses, lectures, and meditation retreats. He recommended talking to people involved in the practice, especially teachers, noting that "you don't have to have just one teacher. One can learn from many different teachers." He then made a distinction between the outer work he had just described and the inner, or spiritual, work involved:]

Somebody once said the first half of the spiritual life is kind of the honeymoon phase, but then you get down to the real work. So life is not just a spiritual path and not just a honeymoon. There's real work. There are valleys to go through; lows as well as highs, twists and turns. But it was one of the best times of my life, and I made some very good friends among other practitioners, the monks and nuns, teachers, friends, and supporters.

[A participant mentioned that, while liking the techniques of Dzogchen and feeling that the practice was helping, she was feeling a resistance to it, partially arising from the seeming need of ritual. She asked Lama Surya Das if his "brand of Dzogchen" is less ritualized.]

That's the idea of the Westernizing or the

Americanization—the naturalization—of the Dharma. And Dzogchen, I think, has a very good shot at doing that, because it doesn't depend on all those esoteric things.

I'm teaching as much as I can in a way that we Americans can practice, without the ritual training and the dogma or the theology or the cosmology or the cultural aspects. Because the Dharma is not a culture. There is, of course, Buddhist culture and Asian culture around it, but the luminous heart of the Dharma is truth. It's clear seeing. It's love and sanity. So contemporary Dharma has to relate to that fact.

In my books, I explain things, and also integrate what I call the three great traditions—for simplicity's sake Vipassana, Zen, and Mahamudra Dzogchen—the three great practicing traditions that we've inherited here in America from the whole Buddhist feast table in the East. Be a lamp unto yourself and walk the path, and also honor the resistance. Maybe it's your karma to resist that and not to do guru yoga but to do something else. There are many different gateways to the Dharma.

[A participant carried the earlier question farther, by asking if, though "we are not necessarily raised in the dogma and the ritualized tradition, there is a concern ever about losing that and too loosely approaching the Dharma. In other words, Americanizing the Dharma so that Americans, as we have a tendency to do, massage it to fit us instead of us fitting it."]

Lama Surya Das: That's one of the main questions about preservation and authenticity on one hand, and adaptation and authenticity on the other hand. And that has to happen from transmission—from where we learned it and received it—into a process of some transformation in order for people to learn it and receive it and practice it. This is traditional; it has happened from the moment the Buddha got up from his meditation or taught the first people. It started being "translated." Translated into words to fit the people in India at that time, and then it moved to Sri Lanka, Thailand, and it looked a certain way. Then in Tibet or China or Japan or Southeast Asia or Korea—it looks different when you begin integrating native beliefs and customs. So Buddhism contributes to and changes the culture it enters, hopefully for the better. But it is also informed and changed by the culture it enters.

Of course, all the common elements are there: ethics, meditation, wisdom. But this is a natural, traditional process. The question is, How well is it happening? How clear are we about it? What's our intention and motivation? Not just for those teaching it and bringing it, but for practitioners, too. What's our intention and motivation in practicing it? Is it just a new fad that we want to get with so we can talk about it at cocktail parties? Or show how smart we are? So is that part of our bag? Or are we really seeking the answer to our deepest questions and doubts, existential questions and doubts in life, the life-and-death questions that we all face? And that's going to determine a lot of how it turns out. We want to be very careful and attentive and conscientious about this.

What's going to happen really depends on us, so I'm just going to pass the buck back to you. It really depends on you. And the other future buddhas of America. I'm sure you know from just being together here for two hours that I have a lot of confidence and even delight in the fact that Buddhism is here. Many forms of Buddhism—many American Buddhisms—monastic Buddhism, traditional Buddhism, academic Buddhism; also lay Buddhism; just meditational Buddhism. All kinds of possibilities. There's a very Westernized, New Age kind of Buddhism and very traditional Forest Buddhism. There's a Forest Monastery in California that is very traditional. They don't eat after noon, they wear robes, shave their heads, and the rest, just like in Thailand, following the same rules. So all these things are there for us to pick up, according to our needs and wishes, and that's going to define the new Dharma. For whatever our American karma requires and produces, there is a contemporary American Dharma.

Buddhism is also dying out in the East, because of communism taking over in China, and other reasons. So it's very important, if we love the Dharma, to revive it or fan the flame here in the West, or wherever we are. Some of us have even been invited to teach back in the East. Suil teaches in Japan and Korea at her monastery, and I've been invited to teach in Bhutan. I also have taught in Nepal. Some of my friends do that because, in the West we

have religious freedom; in some of those countries they don't.

Dharma, Buddhism has really arrived here, both in theory and in practice. It's a very exciting development. For example, since you're a woman, you have a much better place in the Dharma here in America than you would in the East. In that way, American Buddhism might even be better for you. Half the teachers in the West are women, which is very far from the case in the East.

[A lawyer raised the issue of right livelihood, which is causing him some concern. The focus of his work is environmental preservation and in the course of this work he is in a position to do harm to the careers and lives of government officials and others who may be doing harm to the environment. (He noted, however, that since he began practicing Buddhism he has found that he is more effective at this work.) He asked if this work and what it required of him was consistent with Buddhist practice.

After explaining that right livelihood is one of the steps to enlightenment on the eightfold path taught by the Buddha, Lama Surya Das allowed that "if you're really clear and conscientious, if you're really honest with yourself, it's very difficult to find anything that is totally right and totally wrong. We each have to draw the line for ourselves. Does smoking cigarettes send you to the devil or not? Only you know. It's hard to say who knows, if one's self doesn't know." This led him to mention engaged Buddhism.]

I think it's important that we are engaged Buddhists, not "enraged Buddhists," and we do it in a loving and compassionate fashion. Then we can expose the lies and hypocrisies of those who are destroying the environment. But it's tricky business, because it does play right into our violence and aggression, egotism, and all the rest. That's why the Buddha always said that the touchstone is to ask Is it really conducive to the good of the whole and also to your own spiritual development? Or is this making you more reactive or aggressive or proud of yourself?

[Another participant explained that she has difficulty in letting practice be a part of her life. For a period of time it may become a pattern, then she may "fall asleep for a week or two," which leads to stopping altogether. She wondered if there is a resistance to enlightenment or to feeling good. Lama Surya Das referred this question to his colleague Suil.Her response suggested that the questioner could begin by reframing resistance. Rather than trying to get rid of it, she could…]

…find a way to work with that resistance. That moment of resistance has a lot of energy so rather than trying to push it away, use that resistance to go deeper into yourself, to come home to yourself. Remember that meditation is not just sitting on your cushion. Think of your whole life as a meditation, and the moments that you take to sit are just remembering to return home. If you're agitated, get up, maybe walk around. Rather than trying to do something else, just

be with what is. Be in the moment. There isn't really anything better that we can do than turn the mind back toward itself.

[One participant brought up the question of passion and feeling passionately. She said, "I study a lot of literature and some of the readings refer to passion as a mental poison. Living in the present moment, I'm a very passionate person."]

Lama Surya Das: Classical Buddhism talks about the *kleshas,* the conflicting emotions or the passions, as a mental poison. But in later evolutions of Buddhism, like Mahayana Buddhism, Tantric Buddhism, which use everything as part of the path, passion takes on another character. There's a lot of energy in it. It's like a wave. Does the wave drown you, or do you say Surf's up, let's go? If you're a skillful spiritual warrior, if you're brave and fearless, and you can risk that and use the great wind of the passions and learn to sail with it.…A skillful sailor isn't just driven by the wind. You can tack, and even tack into the wind, using the wind's power to go in the direction you choose. So Tantric Buddhism and Tantric Hinduism and other forms of practice are very insightful and broadminded about this question.

Since I'm talking about our joy of meditation and so on, I also talked about being more intimate with things, not getting away from them, withdrawing, avoiding. But the bigger perspective of entering totally, even being one with everything is different from the more narrow approach of the danger of these virulent emotions, passions, habits, and attachments. It could be a razor's edge or a slippery slope. We don't want to rationalize and fool ourselves and end up alcoholic or sexaholic or just thoughtaholic. There are other ways of learning about these things. Dealing with the passions could be seen as passion for enlightenment, passion for truth, passion to awaken and serve others. Enthusiasm is a kind of passion, isn't it?

Passion can also be your strength. *Bodhichitta,* aspiration for enlightenment, is a passionate thing. The bodhisattva has six transcendental virtues or six practices, and the fourth one is energy or effort, enthusiasm—passion.

[*Karma was an issue for a participant who had recently read* The Jew and the Lotus, *a book that deals with Judaism and Buddhism. In her words, "the book brought up the idea that karma means that the Tibetans have somehow brought their exile upon themselves…and the Jews brought the Holocaust on themselves because of their karma.…Could you clear up my confusion?"*]

Lama Surya Das: What karma really means is conditioning. Habituation. Cause and effect. It's not just destiny. Of course, we also have free will. It's a combination of both of those. We're free to work with our karma now. Your karma is to live wherever you live. My karma is to live where I live. But also we have a choice. For example, one day you decided to move there, and then in some other year you might move again. So it's a

mixture of destiny or predestination and free will. The dividing line is in the present moment. That's where we can catch ourself. Like the wind blowing us, that's the wind of karma. The wind is blowing, our habits, our propensities, the ruts we're in from conditioning: karma. But how we sail with the wind right now, how we use the tiller and the rudder and the sails, makes all the difference.

So one reason that thinking about karma is very helpful is that we may take responsibility for our own experience in that it depends on how we relate to things. If an Eskimo was in the back of this room, they'd wonder why it's so hot. But if somebody in the back of the room were from Central America, they'd probably say, Why is it so cold in here? So how we relate to it determines a lot of how we experience the world and our existence. That's karma.

That means we're responsible for what happens to us, but we shouldn't stretch that too far. Because it's also talking about cause and effect, and interdependence, connections. It's not just what happens to you now, but it goes back…back…back. Many causes and effects conspiring and connecting. Cause and effect implies that it continues into the past, before your birth, because you can't find any sort of effect that wasn't caused by something.

The questions of the Holocaust and the Tibetan exile, these are group karma. But they also are the world's karma and it's not just those two groups that experience this kind of suffering. It's going on right now with the Palestinians and the Azerbaijanis and the

Rwandans. It's a karma of our times. The refugee office is one of the biggest things in the UN because of that. We like social mobility, but we hate displacement and refugees. The two go together. In the old days in Tibet or Europe, nobody went from one valley to another, ever. But now we're so mobile that naturally people are displaced. So it has a plus side and a minus side and all kinds of variations.

I think that the point of karma is to understand that nobody else is causing us suffering. Let's not talk about the Holocaust. That's too big. Let's talk about why you get whatever you get—angry or lustful or guilty. You may say to your boyfriend, Why do you make me angry? According to Buddhist understanding, enlightened vision, or the law of karma, nothing can *make* you anything if you don't have those seeds inside of you. Your boyfriend's activity doesn't make somebody else angry, it makes you angry. So you have that inside of you. You care about him, you know him, you're invested in the relationship. Somebody else sees him acting like an idiot and they just laugh. They don't get angry.

So nobody can make us angry. Nobody can make us do anything, karmically speaking. Mastery is within us, and in fact, we're already inherently free. This is a free expression, actually. We can be as free or as conditioned as we like, if we really look into the situation. We have karma to be a man or a woman, an American or a German, a this or a that, but that's also fairly fluid, especially if you look in the bigger sense. We're not exactly who we think we are.

My teacher would say, "Even negative karma has one positive aspect. It can be worked with. It can be transformed." This is why we were saying be with whatever is, honor the resistance, there is also something there for us. The stumbling block can become a stepping stone. Sometimes we get a real lemon, but we might be able to make lemonade out of it. So karma can be purified, transformed, expiated, worked with, transcended, and so on. You can even be one with your karma; then you don't have to do anything about it, because there's no you, there's just the karmic connections rolling on. No separate you; just karmic phenomena and numina.

[Several participants who were relatively new to Buddhist study and practice raised questions having to do with becoming better connected with other Buddhists, working with teachers, and related issues. This was particularly true for people from more rural areas. A woman from Kansas, who has read numerous books and magazines on the subject but did not know of organizations in proximity to her home, voiced her frustration: "I read about it and I see it on the Internet, but it's not the same as being with people." Surya Das agreed fully, referring to the Sangha Jewel, the importance of community. Another participant quipped that "You can get to Oz from Kansas!" which the lama quickly embraced:]

That's right! You don't even have to get there—you *are* there! When Dorothy comes to the wizard and finally meets him behind the screen, and there's really no great wizard, she says to him something like, "How can I get back to Kansas?" Do you remember how she got back? Somebody pointed out to her that she already had the magic shoes; all she had to do was click her heels. She always had the shoes on, but she didn't know how to use them. So earlier, when we were talking about Dzogchen, we pointed out or introduced you to your true nature or your true buddha-nature. You're already *in* Kansas! You don't have to get there! That's where teachers and teaching and spiritual friends and the mirror of practice, of looking inward, come in. You're interested in the path? Don't look at enlightenment, look at the path. Look at your feet. Where your feet are on the path, that's where the goal is, right there, right now. You've got the shoes. Just click them. Three times.

(It's important to remember these stories for the oral tradition of American Buddhism.)

[As had the morning portion of this workshop, the afternoon session began with a guided meditation. Lama Surya Das focused the final few moments of this meditation on the six senses and the Buddha's teaching "In seeing there is just seeing, no one seeing and nothing separate seen. In hearing there is just hearing; no one hearing it and nothing separate heard."]

When we talk about the joy of meditation, the joy of awakening, remember what the Buddha said, that if you practice like this, if you have an open heart, if you practice loving wisdom and compassion, loving-kindness,

that twelve great benefits will ensue. (He says this in the *Metta-sutra,* the Loving-Kindness Scripture.) Your face will be clear and radiant. Your sleep will be clear. Your health will be good. Your dreams will be pure. You will be happier in this life and the next. You will be surrounded by loving friends and companions. You'll find the Dharma almost wherever you look, and so on.

Although being a skeptical, rational American intellectual-agnostic type, always doubting, questioning everything unless I could find it out for myself, I find that these teachings actually are true. Somehow, as we move along the path, as we get deeper and deeper into that wisdom tradition, we find out it's all too true, and our life can become quite different, transformed, without going elsewhere, without throwing away all that we know. It might take some inner letting go or transformation, or even sacrifice. We may have to simplify or empty out something, let go of something from our life if we want something else to fit in or come in. But we can really find all that we seek right here. In fact, that's the teaching—*it* is always here; *we* are usually elsewhere. That's the problem. That's why the *Mahayana Sutra* says, nirvana and some sorrow are inseparable; wisdom and illusion inseparable; bondage and freedom inseparable. All opposites inseparable. A radical concept, isn't it?

How to become what we really are already? That's a koan, a conundrum. How to become what we are. That's the path. That's why it may not take as long as we think to get from here to here. But sometimes you have to go around the whole world in order to come back to the point of origin and know it as if for the first time, as T. S. Eliot said.

So as we open to the Dharma, as the fullness of being, or the joy of meditation, or the spirit of awakening starts to happen and starts to carry us, we don't have to carry it all the time. We don't always have to do something strenuous, arduous, explicitly religious and so on. We start to integrate the Dharma into everyday life. As our wisdom grows, we start to be able to be wise enough to practice ethics and meditation in every aspect of life, so that every aspect of life includes those three things: wisdom, ethics, and meditation, the three trainings of the eightfold path of Buddhism.

We can apply that to work, we can apply that to relationships, we can apply that to parenting, we can apply it to farming, we can apply it to lawyering, we can apply it to whatever we do. In fact, we must, if we so choose. Having taken on this wisdom work, committed ourselves to awakening or to truth, to liberation of all, to the end of suffering and delusion, having taken the bodhisattva vow, then we must get on with it and bring it into every aspect of our life. Otherwise, how could it be complete enlightenment? Or, more basically, how could it be a spiritual life? It'll just be a spiritual Sunday, from 10:00–11:00.

But what about all the other hours of the week? Bringing it into everyday life is really the challenge. First, learning something. As we say in Tibetan Buddhism, first hearing, learning; second, contemplating or reflecting on it; and third, meditating and experiencing it. Not just jumping into meditation—sitting down, closing our eyes, crossing our eyes, crossing our legs, crossing our fingers, hoping to get enlightened—but what are we really trying to do? If we haven't learned how, if we don't know which direction to head, maybe all of our efforts are running in the wrong direction, climbing a ladder that's on the wrong wall. So it's good to learn a little, question a little, inquire, investigate, find out. Then contemplate, reflect on it, internalize it; so that then we can really meditate or experience it for ourselves. That's the threefold process to go through. Then we can really develop, from intellectual knowledge or understanding, the spiritual experience, to deep, profound experience. And from that, develop even more deeply to self-realization and liberation.

For that, we have theory and practice. Theory helps us practice, and the practice helps us understand the theory. Otherwise it's just like throwing rocks in the dark, hoping we're going to hit something. Dogen Zenji said, "To study the Dharma is to study yourself." Study, in this case, means to penetrate, to practice. To study the Dharma is to study yourself. Not to study somebody in front of the room or somebody in the past, or study some books, but to look in the mirror of the Dharma to know yourself better. Then he went on: "To study yourself is to forget yourself, to transcend yourself, to go beyond yourself." The third line, and the most hard to fathom, is, "To go beyond yourself is to be one or intimate with all things."

To study the Dharma is to study yourself; to study yourself is to forget or transcend yourself; to transcend yourself is to become one with all things. That's the direction: beyond ourselves, realizing our greater, transpersonal, buddha-selves, and ultimately becoming one with all and everyone. This is very, very doable, practical. It's a tried-and-true path. It's not something that we have to try to make up each time. There are living exemplars, living teachers who embody it and we can read about them and meet their wisdom-mind and know for ourselves that what they're saying could be true. If it resonates with our inner heart's intuition, that's all we need to know. We don't need to know that somebody else approved it or gave it the stamp of approval. That's why the Buddha said in the *Kalama Sutra*, the scripture given to the tribe of the Kalamas, "Don't believe in what I say just because the Buddha says it. Don't believe in anything just because it's said by scriptures, by elders, in holy books. Only believe it if you taste it, test it for yourself, and it's conducive to the good and the true and the wholesome. Otherwise, let it go."

So I think that's really a good touchstone for Western Dharma students today. Not just to accept received wisdom, belief systems, dogma, and so on, but to remember these wise words—not because the Buddha said it, but because I think they're wise: to find out for ourselves, not to take anybody else's word for it. Otherwise it's just rumors from the past. We can confirm it for our-

selves, and that's one meaning of the word enlightenment. Some people use the word confirmation to translate this word. It means you've confirmed the truth for yourself. Then you speak with the Buddha's authority. You speak with enlightened vision because you've confirmed it for yourself. That's the whole purpose of the Dharma, to help you confirm it for yourself. Then it's self-authenticating.

Then you get great, joyous confidence—passion, to use the word we heard today—conviction, not just belief or faith. Not just blind faith, but unshakable faith born of conviction. The faith that you can just let go and the world won't collapse, that you're actually on the ground. Life is not a high-wire act. We're on the ground here. We don't always have to be on our toes, keeping our back guarded. We're safe. We hear the phrase, "save all beings." All beings are safe already. Just stop bugging them! Stop exploiting them, seeing them as objects. Save the whales. You know, the whales are safe. *We're* not safe. We're the ones that make it dangerous for them.

So as we go along the path, this starts unfolding from within, the fullness, like a joyous groundswell! And I think that that's happening here in the West today. Some of you said you live in places where there are no Dharma centers, well you can find the Dharma everywhere, once you know what you're looking for. Every leaf, every raindrop, every bird, every piece of litter on the ground radiates truth and immediacy.

Personally, since I've been in this my whole adult life, I feel like I live in a Buddhist nation. That's something you might think about also bringing into your life…or "joining." There are no membership fees. So just let yourself know when you join and you're a member.

[A participant's question brought the Dharma dialogue around to issues of death and dying. Lama Surya Das asked Suil to address the question.]

Suil: Buddhism actually addresses death a lot. This moment is precious because it is going to pass on; it will die into the next one. There is never a denial of death in the Buddhist tradition. We all know people that have died. We know that we're going to die. In the moment, we are not aware of it, perhaps, but we all know that, yes, this human body will die. What Buddhism addresses, I think, very deeply is that part that does not die. What is that part that does not die? This body, is this me? This thought that I'm having at this moment, can I hold onto that as being me? What is it that can transcend the body, the thoughts of the moment? What is it that does not die? A lot of the Buddhist practices bring us back into that moment of realization.

Lama Surya Das: I think we all know that we're going to die, but do we really believe it? My mind doesn't know what that would mean. If you really check, it's hard to believe. What does it mean? And it's helpful sometimes to keep the notion of mortality or tenuousness, impermanence with us. Keep that

awareness, be mindful of it, because it helps us prioritize what we're doing now, and how and with whom, knowing we won't be here forever, they won't be here forever, and so on. We're fooling ourselves if we're waiting for a better day or another time or a different somebody, a different teacher, a different student, a different teaching, a different something. You're just killing time and deadening yourself if you're waiting. And not to get morbid, but death comes without warning sometimes, and then it's a little late to do what we wish we had done. The Himalayan yogi and poet Milarepa said, "The only thing I accomplished in my life is I can die without any regrets. Done is what had to be done."

[Lama Surya Das led the workshop in another period of meditation and chanting, after which he summed up the day.]

It occurs to me to point out that often when we Westerners take up Buddhist practice, oriental practice, we're first attracted by meditation or yoga, some technique or some practice. Or we might be attracted by a guru or some other piece of the whole Dharma cornucopia. Then, being Westerners, we're very technique-oriented; we want one-minute buddha, instant enlightenment. Just add hot water. Not only that, I don't have time to boil it, so have it on a timer, so when the alarm clock goes off, the water's already boiled and it's pouring into our cup and being funneled into our mouth.

But in the spiritual life, since we want a little more than just an hour of buzz, it's more like we're looking for an everlasting fulfillment, which might take more than a minute or two. And we don't want to mistake this for just an intellectual pursuit. We hear these words meditation, mindfulness, mind, clarity, wisdom, enlightenment, realization, awareness. It all sounds very mental—like enlightenment from the eyebrows up. What about the rest of our whole being. It has to be grounded. Heaven and earth have to join in us, with our feet on the ground and maybe our heads in the clouds. Grounded, opening heart as well as awakening mind. Warming up as well as getting very sharp and clear. A sharp sort of wisdom is nice, but how about the soft touch with which to use it?

So wisdom and compassion always go together like the two wings of a bird. As the bird can't fly with only one wing, the bodhisattva wings to enlightenment soars on the wings of wisdom and compassion. Wisdom or truth. Emptiness, wisdom, and compassion. Love. Ethics. Virtue. Heart and mind. Body and soul. Bringing this all together. Rational and intuitive, male and female, yin and yang. Bringing it together in us. Joining heaven and earth. Non-dual. Right here, and now. That's why the Japanese Zen Master Hakuin sang in the "Song of Zazen," "This very land is the pure land. This very body, the body of Buddha." *This very land is a pure land:* He didn't mean Japan, he meant where we are, where we think we are. *This very body is the body of Buddha:* He didn't mean just his body, he meant this body. Any body. Anybody. You. Not just Buddha, as we said before, but you-ddha.

So I think it's incumbent upon us to look deeper outward and inward. Simplify. Slow down enough and attend. Pay attention. Be present enough. Like at Bingo, you have to be present to win. Some Buddhist teachers say you have to be absent to win, but I'll say you have to be present to win. You have to show up, and our practice is showing up. Every day we show up on the path. We show up, we sit on the meditation cushion, we light up our candles, we show up and we dress the children for school. We show up and we work at our livelihood. Hopefully it's a fairly right-on livelihood, as the Buddha taught. We show up. We may not be the perfect best at it, but we show up, we do our best. The bodhisattvas do their best and let go. Whatever happens, happens. Keep doing our best and let go. Whatever happens, happens. Not worry so much about outcomes, but know what to do and how to do it. That's doing our best. And let go; whatever happens, happens.

We can't control the universe. In fact, it's totally out of control, as you may have noticed. So we just do it. Practice is perfect. Sitting is sitting buddha. Masters have said Speaking is speaking buddha; chanting is chanting buddha; breathing is breathing buddha; sleeping is sleeping buddha. Even when we don't know we're buddha, we're buddha. We just have to awaken to that fact. We're all buddhas by nature, as the sutra says. We only have to awaken to that fact. Of course, some of us are sleeping, snoring buddhas. Some of us are awakened, eloquent buddhas. But still buddhas. And beyond buddhas—true self;

true being; authentic. That's where our wheels get some traction on the spiritual path. Right now, in authenticness. Being ourselves. Being true to ourselves and not just our habits or our personae, but our deeper, deepest self; perfectly pure-hearted self.

So as we look into these things, as we share in these things, I don't think we need to worry about what's going to happen. It's happening. We don't need to worry when we're going to have the big bang of enlightenment. It's happening every moment. We already missed it. So forget it. It's happening. All we have to do is wake up to it and keep showing up. So I think rather than having some higher ambitions, we can just keep showing up and let the show go on, and delight in it.

Being Free
and Enjoying Life

Robert A. F. Thurman, Ph.D.

IN SEVENTH TO EIGHTH–CENTURY INDIA, THERE LIVED A MONK NAMED SHANTIDEVA, who was affiliated with the Madhyamika school of Mahayana Buddhism. Today, he is best known for having written two important Buddhist texts, one of which, the *Bodhicharyavatara,* is still used as a teaching text in Tibetan Buddhism. In the "Great Compassion" section of this book, Shantideva presents what is considered the precept on compassion passed down by the Bodhissatva Manjushri:

All the suffering that occurs in this world, comes from wishing your own happiness. And all the happiness that occurs in this world comes from wishing others' happiness.

Robert Thurman used this single verse as the cornerstone for his entire workshop. Using examples and images from contemporary everyday life and peppering the talk with a jovial, down-to-earth humor, Prof. Thurman held the participants' alert attention as he showed what is a seemingly simple—but undeniably arduous—path human beings may follow to happiness in its most basic, perhaps least often–enjoyed form.

A professor of Indo-Tibetan studies at Columbia University, where he holds the Jey Tsong Khapa Chair in the Department of Religion and heads the American Institute of Buddhism, Prof. Thurman is among the most widely known and respected Buddhist scholars in North America. He has translated a number of Tibetan Buddhist texts, some of which are included in his *Essential Tibetan Buddhism.* He has also published such books as *Tsong Khapa's Speech of Gold in the Essence of True Eloquence* and *Wisdom and Compassion: The Sacred Art of Tibet.* Presently he is collaborating with His Holiness the Dalai Lama in writing *The Tibetan Book of Inner Science.*

Here we are, and we're supposed to be free and enjoy life. My wife told me that I should tell you how I do it—I simply work all the time. I don't even know I'm alive. So naturally, I enjoy it. And I'm just happy as a lark working 17 hours a day, 7 days a week, 30 days a month, 365 days a year. And even practically when I sleep. I'm not that good in dream yoga yet, but as soon as I can get my dream yoga going, then I'll be working while I'm sleeping. So that's the secret—Confessions of a Buddhist Workaholic.

I guess it's the American way, working all the time. I was a monk for a couple of years, and monks are supposed to be leading a spiritual life. But we worked all the time as monks. I studied, worked, meditated. Up at 4:00 A.M. Totally working all the time.

But someone told me that the most important factor for heart disease in this country is not overwork. The most important factor predictive of when someone in their late twenties or thirties will have their heart attack, or if they will have one, is whether they *like* their work. People who don't like their work often die of heart attacks. And you know when they tend to have the most heart attacks? Monday mornings!

My whole subject today is one verse in Shantideva, a preposterous verse in the *Bodhicharyavatara* (Guide to the Bodhisattva Way of Life). You should all read that book and try not to be offended by Shantideva's more graphic descriptions when he's trying to be offensive. The Buddhists have the meditation of offensiveness. The great thing about it is that it is offensive and talks about how the body is a bag of shit. Describes lovemaking as two bladders lying one on top of another. It's a real turn-off, that one. But it's supposed to be a turn-off. It's for people who are trying to control their horniness. And it works! Try to get through those parts of the Shantideva, which are hard. And then really, really dwell on little things in that book that are just incredible. *Shanti* means "peace," and *deva* means "god;" *Shantideva* means "god of peace." His vow was that anyone who would ever hear his name in the future would feel peaceful just hearing his name. Shantideva.

There's one verse in the "Exchange of Self and Others" section—the "Great Compassion" section—that is one of the essential precepts in his book, and that is considered *the* precept on compassion teaching from Manjushri. In Tibetan tradition there are two major living lineages of compassion. (Of course, there are infinite numbers, but they're counting two special ones that are in a sort of live historical lineage.) One is from a *sangha* from the Bodhisattva Maitreya, and the other is from the Bodhisattva Manjushri, through Shantideva's book. He says:

All the suffering that comes in this world, that occurs in this world, comes from wishing your own happiness. And all the happiness that occurs in this world comes from wishing others' happiness.

This is the entire topic of my talk today, because that's kind of a preposterous claim.

In America, with the whole idea of not being a martyr and sticking up for yourself and being liberated, don't we think that sort of smacks of Christian self-flagellation, or something like that? *All suffering comes from wishing your own happiness. And all happiness comes from wishing others' happiness.*

Don't you think that's strange? Do you expect that from Buddhism? You don't want that from Buddhism. We come for Buddhism to break free of all of these oppressive cultural ideas and to find our own true happiness. Don't we? Didn't we? Did we find happiness? Haven't a lot of people found a lot of happiness from Buddhism? Did you find it? Is Shantideva describing what you found?

Now we must keep it clear. He doesn't say that the source of suffering is gaining your own happiness. He says the source of suffering is wishing your own happiness. When we wish our own happiness, we are not usually helping other people. In other words, if you accept Shantideva's argument that you would only be happy when you wish other's happiness, then you would forget about wishing your own happiness because you'd be wishing others' happiness. You'd then be wishing *their* happiness; you would work for their happiness. In the process of working for their happiness, you would become happy, he's saying.

Then, the more happy you become, maybe the less you'd be interested in your happiness. Because you just were happy. When is the one time that you were most unhappy? It is when you are evaluating your condition. People ask me sometimes, "How are you?" Sometimes I say "Fine," but then sometimes I'll add, "If I don't think much about it."

In other words, let's keep clear between gaining and wishing. (Of course, it creates a paradox, which Buddhism takes from life, which is so paradoxical.) You get into sneakily trying to get happy by not thinking about yourself getting happy. And then you're helping others to be happy, and sneakily thinking "Aren't I nice?" But actually you're getting more happy, and the one thing you want to try not to let your mind do is turn into wanting to get happy out of making them happy. Then you really make them happy and you get happy too. The minute you start thinking "how happy did I get," *forget it!*

[*A woman posited that, in order to work for, seek, or wish someone else to be happy, one must have at least a modicum of one's own happiness. "Definitely," Prof. Thurman agreed. "Therefore, when you really wish to make them happy, you realize, 'Well, but I can't when I'm so miserable all the time. The first thing I have to do is to shake this misery.'"*

The participant continued by bringing in the idea of separateness, which brought Prof. Thurman up short. "Shantideva didn't say that. Although he does say earlier, in the eighth chapter..."]

Oh, it's such a brilliant thing. All of his most important things that are written, the whole book really, is a debate between his good mind and his bad mind; his selfish mind and his intelligent mind. And the selfish one is always chiming in: "Well, why should I accept or why should I embrace the suffering of others? Why should I take that on?" Which, in Buddhism, is what compassion means— the sensitivity to the suffering of others and the will to help them become free of it. Then his sensible mind, his normal, egocentric mind, says, "Why should I open up to their suffering? Then I'll be so much more miserable." And Shantideva says,

But when it is realized that all beings are but the limbs of one life, then I will naturally feel other beings' happiness, and that will be an ocean of joy.

Which isn't quite an answer, but it's a nice statement. So he does say a little about non-separateness, but even limbs are different limbs.

[Another participant asked "Is wishing yourself happiness the same as wishing to eliminate suffering or duhkha?" Prof. Thurman agreed that it was. The man continued his question by saying that "wishing yourself happiness is why you start on the path."]

Robert Thurman: In a way that's right. Then you start practice, and by wishing yourself happiness when you're starting, you then focus on how miserable you are. And then you want to get rid of that misery and you engage in getting rid of that misery. When you first started engaging in getting rid of that misery, are you usually happy? People

Professor Thurman makes a point

who are just starting usually are more miserable, I think. Then when is it they start to lighten up? What may have happened? Maybe they become a little more resigned about their misery? Maybe they forget about themselves a little more? Maybe they notice how miserable other people are, maybe even more than they? They get distracted. So something happens in that process of starting the path.

This is a very important thing we need to correct. The first noble truth is not the main noble truth. Just because it's first it's not the main one. Buddha was joined by many other people, but Buddha said everything is miserable, in Buddha's time. He was not making a big announcement. Everybody staggering around in their usual stupor in Vedic India said, "Eh, this is all misery," Right. Yes. No one was the slightest bit flipped out by hearing that. So maybe this was a big thing in the 1950s—Ronald Reagan, pasted-smile America....We're all fine.

So *duhkha* is nothing. It's really not a big deal, in the sense that everybody knows about *duhkha*. The big teaching of the Buddha, the big announcement, was the third noble truth: freedom. And that is freedom from suffering—happiness, in other words. He clearly expounds it, as he gets on with the Dharma, as happiness, everywhere, in Pali sutras as well as everywhere else. Nirvana is the supreme happiness. It's everywhere. His name is Sugata, which means Sukhumgata, the one who achieved *sukha,* bliss. It doesn't mean "blessed one," as those theistic people translate badly. Nobody blessed him! He is blissful. *Sukha* means "bliss." He's the blissful one! He is not miserable, because he forgot about himself. He realized Shantideva's statement.

Coming back to this very important point, awareness of *duhkha* is simply putting one's normal existence into context of the kind of happiness one could have, and then recognizing that it is, relatively speaking, *duhkha,* and therefore getting happy. That's why Buddhism was always popular, because people got happy very quickly when they dealt with it. We need this new emphasis on Buddhism. We've got to get out of this gloom-bag business. Although it was useful as an *upaya,* I think, as an art, in attracting people brought up in absolutely miserable Protestant societies, such as myself. It was good that *duhkha* was there; it made us feel virtuous, all of us Protestants and neo-

Protestants and pseudo-Protestants here in America. But it's now safe, perhaps, for us to recognize that Buddhism is a method of having more fun. Having *real* fun. Don't you think that's safe?

I was on a trip in Bhutan recently, teaching the three principles of the path to a group, going over the first path the way Manjushri taught it in that text—what they used to translate as "renunciation," there, which is *niryana,* then there's compassion, *bodhichitta,* spirit of enlightenment; and then there's wisdom. Those are the three main principles of the exoteric path.

Now the first one, *niryana,* which means "departing;" "escaping" literally. (It doesn't really mean renunciation. It means escaping.) *Niryana* means getting out, and it means really getting out from home to homelessness. It has to do with monasticism, and that's why they translated it renunciation. I translated it as "transcendence." And I didn't really realize until that time of going through it, after having gone through it for over thirty years, maybe a hundred times, maybe several hundred, that the achievement of what they call true transcendence, to achieve the first part of all of that that focuses on *duhkha,* impermanence, impurity, offensiveness, death, and all of the sort of negative sides of ordinary living. All of that is methodology aimed at making you feel more sorry for yourself. What does it mean to be sorry for yourself? It means to take pity on yourself. And what does it mean to take pity on yourself? It means to have compassion for yourself.

So the recognition of *duhkha* means that

you realize that what you have been pretending to yourself is pleasurable, is, relatively speaking, miserable. For example, "When I get another dollar, or when somebody says something to me, or when I get a house, or when I get a possession, or when I get to have this momentary pleasure—then I'm going to be so happy. And if I get more of them, I'll be so happy. Therefore, I must put myself through tremendous effort to get more of these pleasures and things. Because they're so good."

So *duhkha* sensitization is just a connoisseur's type of discarding that type of pleasure, because it isn't really good enough. Rather than just rubbing your nose in how miserable everything is, it's recognizing that there are really unmiserable things. That they can be achieved. That they can be experienced. And therefore, giving up these things simply means giving up. It's like fasting because of the really delicious chocolate cake you're going to have at night. So you don't eat normal supper because you know there's this great chocolate-mousse parfait cake waiting for you. That's a little bit different context.

So that bears on what someone said, that you first have to have this compassion for yourself. To excuse yourself. What is it we're insisting on, and what have we foisted upon ourselves? When we go to school and are brought up, what do we normally foist upon ourselves? That we should make money. That we should have good relationships. We should have possessions. We should be famous. We should be strong. We

should be healthy. There are a lot of things we feel we *should* be. We should live a long time. We should have a good burial plot somewhere—all the things we think we need—and in thinking that we need them, we do what? We go to Harvard. We go to prep school. We learn mathematics. We go into business. We fire our friends. We rob the bank. And we worry all the time, and we have a miserable life, basically, thinking that those are going to be great things.

So, if we feel sorry for ourselves and realize, Here I am, a person, a human being, who has an incredible embodiment in so far as it's incredibly capable of...what? Why do we have this weird body? Why don't we have four eyes? Or another two or three arms? Or measure nine feet tall? We're all just sitting around like it was normal, but why do we look like this, with these two arms that sort of flap like this? They don't fly well. And they only reach back this far, unless I become a yogi. Why?

[In answer to this questions, several participants offered hesitant ideas. A woman suggested that our "eyes are in the front so that we can have connection." Prof. Thurman asked "...where we can have connection? What do you mean by that?" "For love," she replied.

"So we have love and compassion. Why is it that we are designed to have love and compassion. Did God do it? Or the mad scientist? Or Henry Kissinger? Why do we have that? Why do we need it? Why doesn't every animal have this form?"

Another participant offered evolution as

the explanation, to which Prof. Thurman rejoined: "But what kind of evolution? Spiritual evolution? And what does that mean? Think about the mammal form. Why aren't all beings mammals? What is the thing that mammals do that is really amazing?" "Talk," someone else offered.

"Yes, we talk," Prof. Thurman agreed.]

But how did we get to talk? Could we have talked if we ate each other the minute we saw each other? We would not have had much conversation. We'd just glump and burp, that'd be it. In order to talk, we had to have a slight pause before consumption, so we hung out together first. And then in the hanging-out time, we talked. But not only that; there's this other weird thing: The young, the new embodiments, are generated inside the body of the other being, so you talk about all being one. And only the mammal conceives the young inside the more-intelligent half of the species. They're more intelligent because they know that the membrane, the surface of the skin, is not the difference between self and other (although they keep forgetting it, I think). But they inherently know that because they have the rude awakening one day. The thinking your own happiness that Shantideva refers to is, of course, not just a sitting around and having a committee meeting and deciding, well, now I'm going to think about my happiness, wish my own happiness. Wishing my own happiness is a constant mental habit which is known as the "I, I, I, me, me, mine habit." I'm this and I'm that and I'm the other. Or as my old Mongolian

teacher used to say, the basic refrain, the deepest note in that is, "I'm the one."

But then, the more intelligent members of the mammalian group, the females are going around, "I'm the one, I'm the one." And then one day this little voice they hear from inside themselves says, "Forget you. *I'm* the one!" And then suddenly they hated strawberries all their lives and they're eating pounds and gallons of strawberries. Because the little one says, "I want strawberries."

[A participant asked how Prof. Thurman, a man, can "have the same awareness."]

Robert Thurman: Well, that's why men have a hard time—they're always trying to crawl in there in some form or another, and they're never cured from that until they can remember their previous lives when they were women, luckily. Otherwise it's breast feeding envy, womb envy, every other kind of envy; running around trying to pretend that that little thing of theirs is so great. Meanwhile, they feel totally left out, and they tend to be more easily deluded and insane and demented.

I trust everyone has had the experience of their brain lighting up with joy. But of course, there's nothing compared to the joy of the Buddha's brain. The Buddha's brain was so illuminated with joy that he grew an extra piece of brain. He had that "umbrella" of brain on the top of his head, because the thousand-petaled chakra (or the thirty-two-petaled chakra, or whatever it is) opened.

And all the sensitivity in the brain was available to the Buddha. Western art historians say it was a hairdo or something like the fashion style in Kashmir. But that's nonsense. The Buddha's head was like that to symbolize that no one can see the top of the Buddha's head because the top of the Buddha's head is just open to the joy of the cosmos. It's like a great, giant funnel of energy, and the brain is feeling all of that.

Shantideva would say that people who would argue "Well, I'm happier when I do this and do that," don't answer to that, and it's true. It also goes for when I realize *duhkha,* then I want to get out of the *duhkha.* That's a healthy thing—that starts me on the path—so that doesn't bring misery. That's a good argument. But the point is that you couldn't realize that easily except that you're human, and you couldn't have become human except that the human body itself is the evolutionary result of having wished the happiness of other beings, in the previous life forms.

We all are humans because we were the crocodile who was really, finally sick of not being able to give or get a massage. And we said, "No more of this crocodile stuff. I'm sick of it. All I get to do is bite. And I never got a massage because I'm too scaly. And also my fellow crocodiles are too creepy and the way they do it, it's like fingernails on a blackboard." So that being was reborn with a softer skin, with other beings who had massage-capable appendages—that is our form. Receiving each other is to be born within ourselves. You know, luckily some men can

remember their previous lives, or even if they can't remember them, they know intellectually by understanding the karma of former and future lives and the common sense pattern of life in sensible societies, with good science traditions, unlike ours. They know that they've been mothers many times. And in fact, all of you have been in my womb in some life. And I've been in every one of your wombs....Oh, excuse me. Now we're terrified. We wouldn't want to bleed on each other—and we shouldn't, given the plague that's around, but in the old days we all had the same one bloodstream, once, in some previous life. We simply don't remember.

From the Buddhist point of view, therefore, the human embodiment, with its capacity for joy, is the product of having wished the happiness of others. The mammal is the life form that has developed a sensitivity, the ability, to imagine the nature. The redundancy of the brain is because of its need for imagination. And we simulate reality with our brain; the forebrain simulates reality. This isn't to say that they think so that they can practice hunting and go out and catch a dinosaur. The simulating of reality is that we can imagine *being* each other. So I can feel like what it feels like to be you and to interact with you and to imagine how you're feeling when you're interacting. That's a human capacity—to put yourself "in the other fellow's shoes" is the American version, the male chauvinist–type version—to put yourself in another person's place so you can feel how they feel. We're capable of that.

This is Shantideva's way of answering

that. When a human being may do something even to improve that quality of joy by
recognizing that habitual, driven inferior
methodology of gaining happiness based on
cultural ideas of what happiness is (owning a
house or whatever) is just not good enough.
The humans who seek enlightenment are
the humans who realize it's just not good
enough to go through life using eight percent
of your brain. Because then you'll just die,
and when you die, if you don't have control
of the rest of your brain, you might be
reborn with a brain that is only eight percent
relatively, which would be some lower mammal or lower animal form.

That's one way of overcoming the
debate to *all happiness comes from wishing
the happiness of others; and all suffering comes
from wishing your own happiness.*

*[A man raised a question related to the length
of time human beings have been on earth,
which resulted in a minor controversy among
participants. Prof. Thurman resolved it by noting
that it was irrelevant to the previous discussion,
"because there are so many millions of other
planets on which there's life, with human
beings. So whatever they say about this one, it
doesn't even matter."]*

We come from another place. There are
millions of other planets, which our so-
called scientists are getting pretty cool
about now—that there must be life on
other planets. (Although they're looking for
a petrified germ on Mars.) But from
Buddhist science, this is in millions of different planets with billions of different life

forms on them, and humans are always
around. Humans and gods and all kinds of
other inconceivable forms.

For example, that question about where
all the people coming on this planet are
coming from—that the population has
exploded—well, they could be coming from
animal forms, they could be coming from
other planets. That's not a problem. If everyone was killed on this planet with one huge
nuclear holocaust now, today, we would all
be reborn immediately in other places. We'd
be back in another hotel somewhere, worrying about the same problems. We wouldn't
get out of any of our traps. In fact, it would
be much, much worse, because many of us
in the confusion and the chaos and the panic
would think that it would be better to be a
crocodile, and we'd be back there in the
massageless world of crocodiles. That's the
Buddhist view. Contemporary science is not
open to that because they're still backward.

The basic Buddhist view is that that life
is beginningless—not just a long time, but
beginningless. That's really key. Beginningless.
There was never a time we *weren't* around,
in other words. The chicken and egg problem
is neatly finessed, because there was always
another egg and a chicken. There was no
beginning. There's no Big Bang, big beginning,
big "where'd it all come from" thing. It's
solved or finessed by beginninglessness,
which is a very powerful idea.

When I was a young monk, about three
or four months into it, beginninglessness suddenly hit me in the most incredible way. It
was really, really pleasant. I was walking
somewhere to buy something for the monks

at the store. I was striding along as I had for twenty-two years at that point, rushing after something, and suddenly this thought of beginninglessness just came into my mind. At the same time, I felt as if I'd lost my motor. I had felt like I'd had something like an outboard motor sticking out of my coccyx, and I'd been—*Vrroom*—running through life. Or like something was pushing me at the base of the spine, pushing me along. Then I realized I'd always been pushed along like that, and I realized somehow that there was no first starting to anything; any process I was engaged in never had a first starting, had always been going on. Suddenly, it made me feel less hurried and less pushed. It was as though the background of whatever was in the back of my mind, my sense of back structure just dissolved.

I still went and bought the milk at the store, but I had a really relaxed way of strolling, realizing that I could go any different direction. So beginninglessness is an incredibly liberating insight. It frees you from this dreadful thing we're all conditioned to, that we came from somewhere, which comes from the monotheistic myth and the sense of patriarchy in the family and the sort of memory that you were created first at birth and you didn't exist prior to your birth. Then it's sort of analogized in our still-backward, materialistic science by this insane Big Bang mathematical thing, where all of life came out of a fist-sized—*human* fist-sized—lump of matter.

So this is the thing—the being free—this is Buddha's freedom. There are four aspects of the third noble truth—each noble truth has four aspects; in other words, four ways of thinking about it. The third one has four aspects, all having to do with the fact that, even at the time that he taught that, just as today, it is an effort for people to actually conceive of being free of suffering. Does anyone seriously imagine or want to go out and tell their brother-in-law, "I'm going to really be free of suffering...forever"? Or do we really think of it in our mind? Do we really aim at such a goal, even we who are Buddhists? Do we really aim for nirvana, unless we redefine nirvana in some way?

[*A participant responded that he could imagine the possibilities, which led to a question-and-answer cycle during which Prof. Thurman tried to help the man get closer to an experiential understanding of what nirvana may be. The professor explained: "When I say what does it mean, I mean aesthetically, graphically. What would that feel like? Are you imagining it as a feeling, or imagining it just as an idea, as a description?"*

Still the man maintained that he could only "imagine it as a possibility" and Prof. Thurman asked him: "What feeling do you like most of all?" The participant progressed from "one great massage" to "I begin to imagine something that is increasingly expansive."

"So that's the highest joy you ever tasted, and you're imagining something beyond that, then?" the professor asked.

"I don't have a form beyond what I currently imagine," the man replied.

"Well, why don't you work on that," Prof. Thurman suggested. "Buddhism has the aspect of working on that." He recommended that his

audience read the Mahaprajnaparamita Sutra *(Great Prajna Transcendent Wisdom Sutra).]*

Robert Thurman: In all Mahayana sutras, the Buddha invariably does something before he even says anything about anything. It is a complete mind-blower, imagination-blower. For example, at the beginning of the *Mahaprajnaparamita Sutra,* he sticks out his tongue. And Buddha has a tongue from lifetimes and lifetimes of doing yogas and different things, his tongue can touch the hairline at the top of his forehead. And it spreads out and can cover his whole face. It's very flexible—and large—Buddha's tongue.

But somebody asks him about wisdom and he sticks out his tongue, and from this tongue, a ray of light comes out, and this light goes *buzzz,* it goes all over. Of course, everyone is transfixed by this light, and the light spreads beyond them (there are tens of thousands of people in the audience), and it spreads everywhere. Suddenly, all of them on the band of this light, this jewel-net of Indra, can see millions of other planets with other beings on them. And those other planets have assemblies where there are buddhas, just like Shakyamuni Buddha, who are also sticking out their tongues, and the light is also going in and out of their tongues. So this transcendent wisdom teaching is being taught everywhere, simultaneously throughout the multiverse. But the beginning of the teaching is the blasting open of the imagination by that vision. Which is like a special effect, basically. They all see this, even the dumb ones in the audience, every single person suddenly sees multidimensional vision in every direction.

So was there a being called the Buddha who is capable of such special effects without Industrial Light and Magic? Who knows. But there was a being capable of imagining that and writing it. And there were beings capable of painting it on temple walls and cave walls and frescoes, etc., in different parts of Asia, although much of it was destroyed by unimaginative Muslims later.

The point is, that part of that teaching— which has been neglected in the West— is this powerful, imaginative teaching. To be really able to get the third noble truth, the first thing one has to do (the reason he taught them like that) is to conceive of it to the point where you can taste it. Then you really want it; and you don't really want it unless you can taste it; and you don't taste it unless you can imagine it; and you can't imagine unless you work on imagining it. When you've been someone who has been making widgets all their life, or who has been brought up in a culture where everybody is just supposed to figure out which widget they're fated to make by some sort of mechanistic, authoritarian destiny, and then go and make that widget, then there's no question of freedom.

Even political freedom just means I'm paid more for my widget. I get a salary. There's no question of total freedom, from death, from pain, from everything. From the body, from the mind. And certainly no total freedom as bliss; or bliss being not just some other bliss. And all worldly blisses are dirty and something awful. But bliss means every kind of bliss that can be imagined multiplied a millionfold.

In Tantra, we get it—in Tibet and in India. Tantric art shows Buddha as a male-female in union. But they're not satisfied with just an ordinary union, so they sprout extra hands and arms and legs, and extra everything, to be more intertwined. The imaginative element is very important.

At the beginning of the *Vimalakirti* [*Vimalakirtinirdesha Sutra*], the Buddha is teaching about the pure land, the buddha land, saying, "What is the buddha land? Buddha land is the land of pure generosity. In the buddha land, even the ground is made of generosity of beings. And every being is made of generosity. In that land, all the beings, their only motivation is to give things to each other, in the buddhaverse." So we're all taking off our shirts and throwing them at each other. Emptying our wallets for each other. We'd be having a food fight, a money fight, a clothing fight. The whole universe is like that. Basically he describes a land opposite to our land, in which everybody's hiding their wallet, keeping their things. They have a better one than the next person. Don't take my thing! Perhaps somebody lost their glove. You may think of the misery of this poor person who left their glove. That's all. Therefore, everyone feels poor no matter how rich they are, because they think someone wants to take it away from them. Buddha land is the opposite. Everyone only wants to give everything away to others.

When the Buddha says that, Shariputra, the great wise Shariputra, foremost wise disciple, is thinking to himself, This guy's supposed to be a buddha, and he says that a buddha who was a generous bodhisattva over billions of lives, infinite numbers of lives, when they are buddha, their buddhaland is a land of total generosity, and only beings are born in that land who are beings of total generosity. It's a land where everyone is divesting of everything to everyone. So everyone is actually very wealthy, having all of everyone else's wealth coming toward them as they are divesting themselves of it. It's a land of constant abundance, therefore, because we're all giving everything to each other.

"And that's what this land should be," said Shariputra, "but this land is this pile of carp. Everybody's hiding their treasures and hoarding. People are poor. So he must have been a terrible bodhisattva, this Shakyamuni. He must not have been generous. Because his land sucks."

So then Buddha says, "Shariputra, were you having some negative thoughts about my land?" "Well, yes. It doesn't look that great." Then the Buddha said, "Well, it doesn't look that great because it's *your* view. Your attitude is not great, so you can't see the way it really is." And then God, Brahma, came and scolded Shariputra a little more, in that particular sutra. Then the Buddha put his foot on the ground and said, "But take a look, Shariputra," and he touched the ground with his toe. When he did, Shariputra and everyone suddenly saw that the whole land was made of jewels. And everyone's body was made of jewel plasma. The air was filled with jewel energy, and there was ecstatic, exquisite wealth. Everyone in that place saw it like that. They saw it as perfect, actually; the whole land as absolutely perfect. Nothing out of place in the entire land. And every being who was there, and every form that they were was exactly right where they needed to be to expand themselves toward infinite joy with the sort of optimal efficiency. And it's described in the sutra as everyone perceived themselves as seated on a jeweled lotus with a jeweled body, etc.

Then he says to Shariputra, "Well, how does it look now?" "Oh, it's great," Shariputra says. Then the Buddha pulls his toe off and picks up his foot again, and it looks ordinary to him. This kind of vision is in every Mahayana sutra.

We don't have this vision. We're stuck in ordinary reality. We think that the reality that we are brought up with—material reality—is the only real reality. One time I thought I was just sort of a hot-shot Buddhist. I'd been a monk for some years. I'd meditated, I'd studied, I'd learned languages, and I thought I was so great. So one time, I was meditating or something on a retreat, after maybe ten years in the Dharma, and my teacher comes upon me, he looks at me, and says, "Ah, it's nice that you're meditating, but you'll never attain enlightenment. It's really too bad."

I said, "What do you mean? What are you talking about? I'm sure there's more, but I've had a taste of this and that. Come on, give me a break."

"No, no, you can't attain enlightenment."

"Well, why not? What are you saying?" I asked.

He said, "Because enlightenment is something that you attain with your mind, and you're certain that you don't have a mind. Since you don't even have a mind, how would it become enlightened?"

"What do you mean, I don't have a mind? I know I have a…"

"No, no," he says. "You don't think you have mind."

I thought about that one. And I thought about that one. And I read a little more about our current scientists, studied a little more about them, and I recognized that the way we're brought up, we don't really have minds.

After we die, we're nothing. That means the innermost core of consciousness, of subjectivity, of ourselves, a sense of ourself as a real being, as an aware being, is an illusion. It's an illusion produced by scrazzling wetware, the brain. And it's scrazzling away in different rays and neurons and axions and serotonin uptakes and downtakes, and outtakes and intakes, all zipping around. Then it's creating the illusion by the aggregation of all of that that *I'm me,* that *I'm here,* that *I'm aware.* But as soon as all the brain scrazzling stops, that's no more, that illusion. So there's no mind, really. It's an epiphenomenon of the brain.

That's how we're brought up, therefore we don't believe that if we fell out the window that we could hover and come back in if we wanted to badly enough. That if someone was running over our loved one, that we could just will them to stop or to miss or to come out of the way. We don't believe that we could. And we hear about some *siddha* who did this, some adept, and we think that's a premodern, primitive folk tale. It's hagiography and childish, primitive ideas, and since we think that way, it simply couldn't happen to us.

When you say the mind, whose mind? Buddhism is not idealistic in the sense of a solipsistic idealism. Buddhism is not a subjective idealism. Buddhism is an intersubjective idealism. Your mind is some sort of a concrete external reality to my mind. And there are many other minds; and then there are all the buddhas' minds. So the world is not just created out of any one mind, but *minds,* and minds also do not exist without bodies. So minds and bodies are always interactive in the Buddhist world view. But sometimes it's useful to talk about mind as a separate key thing.

What my teacher meant in that case, in that context, however, is that our materialistic upbringing is so thorough that we are given a very strong discredibility toward our own mind. We don't really believe we have a mind power or will power that can overcome what we think are material realities. That's deeply, unconsciously ingrained in us. He was trying to tell me that I was looking for, working for, some sort of transformation in my own understanding that would transform my whole being, but I basically had relegated my understanding to a place where it had no power over my being; where the being is all just matter and material arrangements.

I see quite a few meditative people who have a certain view of meditation, a rather over-narrow view I would say. They say, "Oh, Buddhism is not some sort of understanding. You can't learn about it. There's nothing to study or think about, because only by meditating can you have some sort of experiential change. What you understand doesn't change your experience." Whereas, from the Buddhist point of view, your understanding is what shapes your meditation. It's what shapes your whole life. Your view of reality is what determines how you will experience reality; your view is a form of understanding. Becoming enlightened is a changing of your view; developing a holistic view that incorporates especially the view of other beings—a multiperspectival view.

Buddhism is irrelevant to scientific people—materialistic, scientistic people. They think it's irrelevant. I, myself, think Buddhism has a scientific tradition superior to the modern scientific traditions. It has a superior form of medicine in most respects, except surgery. They have a superior knowledge of the psyche and how it works. They have a superior form of physics. They knew long ago there was no indivisible particle, which was only recently discovered by these other guys with the machines. Their scientific traditions are basically more intelligent, and they emphasize particularly what they call the inner science, the science of the psyche. But that's a very idiosyncratic opinion of mine. Not many people share that opinion.

[A participant broached the subject of the relationship between beauty and pain or sadness, suggesting that "beauty is just the beginning of terror." Referring to Peter Matthiessen's keynote

address,* she continued, "I would go so far as to say that [Matthiessen] was implying not that we need to recognize the unhappiness and the shadow and the dark side, that the dark side is, in fact, truth—absolutely inextricable from what we recognize as being truth, something that's warm and fuzzy. And that true happiness is exhilaration beyond both."]

Robert Thurman: I wouldn't knock warm and fuzzy either, not in this weather. Then there's this horrible stuff, the pain and whatever, and there's something beyond both of those. But is that thing that is beyond both of them neither of them? Isn't that thing that's beyond both of them, in fact, real beauty and real bliss and real happiness? Isn't that what real happiness means? What [Matthiessen] means, of course, is nirvana, which is real happiness. In other words, real happiness is unafraid of terror, I would certainly agree. Total bliss is the sort of expansive thing that is completely unearthly as far as our normal, habitual scale of pleasure and pain goes. It is such that pain is unnoticed.

For example, sometimes people are so happy they don't even feel something unpleasant that happens. Later they notice they have a wound or they stepped on something, but they didn't even feel it at the time. Unfortunately, of course, other emotions can also dampen sensation in a certain way, too. People can become so enraged that they don't notice they've gotten shot until later. That also could happen.

---

* See Peter Matthiessen's "The Coming of Age of American Zen," pages 396–406.

There is a kind of intensity of experience that changes the normal parameters of what's pleasant or unpleasant, yes; but is that unpleasant? No. Or is it neither pleasant nor unpleasant? No, it's pleasant, actually. At least the Buddha said it is pleasant. In some quarters of Buddhism, it's called bliss, void indivisible. And it's not afraid of death, of course. The *mahasiddhas,* in Tantra, used to live in charnel grounds, which, in India, is where dead bodies are thrown. They wouldn't kill anybody for bones, but they would take bones from the ground and make jewelry out of them, wonderful ornaments that they would wear. They purposely dwelled where everyone else thinks the shadow side and the terrible thing is, in order to show that they had an ecstasy and a bliss that was unfazed by that. Not to show that that happiness is boring and warm and fuzzy, and terror is groovier, but to show us that there is a bliss beyond the normal cycle. What we think of as normal happiness is called in Buddhism "the suffering of change," and normal misery is called "the suffering of suffering." Nirvanic bliss is free of such sufferings.

If you're asking how I account for the fact that human beings in Western culture like tragedies so much, I account for that as a register of how miserable they are. Tragedy is a kind of theatrical transposition of sacrifice, and sacrifice is an ancient religious ritual where they kill some animal, or some human being a little earlier—not just the Aztecs, everybody, every culture. Someone gets killed—and you *don't!* Therefore, you enjoy that, because you're so miserable. It's the mere clinging onto life; if some overlord didn't come and chop off your head that day, it's a relief. And our culture's like that.

In India, of the eight or nine major aesthetic moods they have in theater, tragedy is only one of them. And it's not the big one like it is in the West. Actually, tragedy is where compassion can be born. On the other hand, in the Buddhist sense, if you use it well, instead of just being glad that you're not the one who's getting it, you feel compassion for the being who gets it, the Hamlet or the Macbeth. Then, by feeling that compassion, you develop compassion.

[Referring specifically to the place of work in her life, a woman asked Prof. Thurman to talk about the struggle with the grasping people may fall into when they think they want or need something in order to be happy.]

Robert Thurman: To come back to Shantideva, after that verse, he writes that a buddha is a being defined as one who only lives for the sake of others. That is the definition of a buddha in Mahayana: a being who doesn't even need to breathe. I need to breathe, for example. I want my breath, my oxygen. But a buddha technically doesn't need to breathe that way. They only draw breath— and maintain a form that has to draw breath —in order to benefit others. This means that even their autonomic nervous system is no longer grasping in a certain way, which is why they're so open and happy.

That then, brings us to the point that the Dalai Lama something makes. He says, If you want to be selfish, stop being a stupid selfish. Be a wise selfish. And realize that

you'll fulfill your self-interests when you fulfill others' interests by sharing their burdens and helping them, being loving to others, and compassionate and kind to them, and so forth. That way you'll be happy. Even right away, you become more happy.

In relationship to grasping and not grasping, what you're saying on some small scale is: If I want to be happy, and I have imagined the possibility of really being happy, and I don't allow myself to be depressed by people's pretense that they know that nobody's happy—"Oh, nobody can have this," or "That's impossible," or "No, that's unrealistic"—and I'm not deterred by that, then I realize that, I notice and analyze when I am happy, and when I analyze when I am happy, I notice that it is when I am not worried about how happy I am. When I'm focused on some other people rather than on myself, when I'm not evaluating where I am and what I've got, that's when I feel unhappy. So when I notice that, then, in order to make myself happy, I forget about making myself happy. It's a thing I begin to learn to do, like any skill. When you learn to ride a bicycle, it's when you're secure on the bicycle that you no longer worry about falling off.

That's what *mahayana* means. It doesn't mean that it's not renunciative or its teachings aren't transcendence-oriented, mediating on *duhkha*. Mahayanists do that. But the *mahayana* means that the orientation, the goal, is for everyone simultaneously. You don't entertain the notion that you can't effect the liberation of others. You realize that your happiness makes them happy, so you want to be happy for their sake, because then you can always make people happy when you're happy. And when you're depressed and miserable, then nothing you do will make them happy.

[A participant asked if, "in our crashing around to...get happiness, nirvana, is it more the whip or the carrot?" She continued by saying that sometimes in meditation, we may catch a glimpse of where we think we are headed, but is that more an enticement or a prod? The same question, turned on its head, was asked regarding suffering, which Prof. Thurman answered by asking "isn't suffering itself imagination too? Aren't we imagining suffering when we're suffering?" He continued:]

Imagination is mobilized and involved in that, which we see when, for example, we use mindfulness over pain. Then you realize how you're constructing the pain. But actually, imagination is routinely imagining the bad things also. In other words, I think that the emphasis should be on imagination of freedom, and I think that the one hope of humanity is that we all have a better time.

The people who are really dangerous on this planet are those who are more miserable. They don't mind dying or killing, therefore, and they don't think they're doing anybody a big disservice when they kill them, because they think life sucks. They're very devil-may-care about getting killed themselves, because they don't enjoy their lives. I think, in particular, the societies where they're most cruel to women are like that, as

are most potentially violent societies, because they're not having a good time; they're very miserable. Therefore, they're quick to jump into some military action or to become a martyr and blow up a million people, strap bombs to their head, ears, anything. They have no pleasure in life, basically, and they don't allow anybody to give them pleasure or to have any pleasure. Then they become very dangerous to everybody.

I think our society is a very dangerous society. It's very isolated from us. We don't realize how dangerous we actually are. But it is we who have an incredible bunch of nuclear weapons still, spending billions of dollars on them; incredible delivery systems; incredible chemical gases and nerve gases and things that are just staggering, in big cans tumbling all over each other in the desert. Just our normal industrial production, pollution, waste, and exploitation, we're incredibly dangerous, our society. And the sectors of the people who still actively pursue those things that are dangerous and are crushing to many other people are those who are most miserable, having least fun. They may show themselves off, they may wear Rolex watches, but they don't even enjoy the feel of the Rolex watch on their wrist.

So, I think that a *major* yoga should be the yoga of trying to discover the possibility of some sort of relief, pleasure, happiness, what have you. Part of that, of course, is being aware of what isn't really pleasurable. The *duhkha* first truth is called a "noble" truth because Buddha is admitting that it is not true for normal people. It is not true that everything is suffering for a normal person to whom he is talking. He knows that. He said it's a *noble* truth. It's true for a noble person. And he redefined noble to mean not just upper class, but to mean a person who has developed a higher kind of sensitivity by realizing selflessness; realizing the emptiness, the voidness of the self, and therefore feeling the feelings of other beings.

Those people, who we are taking as normal, we are armored against. We don't really feel it as a suffering, or we may even think it's a pleasure. To them it's pain. The analogy is a grain of sand on the palm of your hand doesn't hurt you; inside your eye, it hurts. The noble person's sensitivity is like the inside of your eye. So *duhkha* is not just going and trying to find some misery, and saying, "I'm so miserable." It is actually analyzing what I normally think of as happiness, and being aware that it isn't really happy, and dropping the pretension to myself about it. It's really more an analytical and technical thing than deciding to go out and embrace some suffering.

As recorded by his monastic followers in what they think of as the earlier, or at least the most monastic, the most conservative, sector of Buddhism, the Buddha said: "Come, monks, go to the four directions. Proclaim to everyone the door to nirvana is open. Everyone can go and become free of suffering. I see that this is possible. I became so free. It is possible for people to do it." He didn't say, "Go and proclaim everything is suffering."

[Inspired by the foregoing, a participant mentioned that the blending of the Protestant ethic into Buddhism in the West has brought people to feel, often, that they are not supposed to do yoga and feel this phenomenal bliss.]

Robert Thurman: That's right. Protestant ethic in Buddhism has said, "Ah, *duhkha*, great! It agrees with us: We are all miserable. At last!"

I was brought up in a basically nice family, not really bad. I didn't ever believe in God. I always thought he was a mean guy, being so nasty to his kid. I just innately had that feeling. (My mother told me I kicked over the baptismal font, even as an infant.) I never liked tragedies. I always thought they were incredibly boring. I insist on happy endings in all movies and books.

So which lightning bolt is going to hit me, and what's wrong? I'm waiting for something awful to happen, because we are conditioned like that. But we should work against that conditioning, and we should not take Buddhism as reinforcing that conditioning.

[Another question had to do with the role of God in causing suffering.]

Robert Thurman: Buddha doesn't think God created people. Buddha thinks people created themselves by their past actions. Human beings in particular have a very wonderful embodiment, he felt—that they themselves earned a very high evolutionary position. You made your own beautiful human body. Now, you borrowed genes from your parents in this particular lifetime. but you were able to appreciate their genes because you had evolved to the point where you saw the beauty of that particular form. Which doesn't look that great to a cockroach. We are human and have cultivated this very high degree of sensitivity relative to many other life forms, and yet we haven't gone to the level as the gods, who are too happy, actually. Buddha believed that the gods had become a little bit too happy in a superficial way, so that they were a little unaware of the kinds of problems that could occur to them later. They're more deluded than we are—more hypnotized by their ordinary activities. That was his view of the gods.

[A final participant brought up the question of whether Buddha felt that people were supposed to have pain and suffering.]

Robert Thurman: No, he doesn't feel people are supposed to have pain and suffering. He feels that pain and suffering are attendant upon all embodied beings who are driven by ignorance and compulsive energies and emotions. It's necessary for them, but there is a form of life that is free of ignorance, that is constituted by wisdom, driven by wisdom or released by wisdom, and capable of creativity, free of compulsion. That kind of existence has no suffering and is joyful always, blissful always, no matter what. Even in the midst of hell, it can be blissful. Even in the midst of the searing flame, this level of existence can be blissful. He perceived that to be, and that is the goal of evolution.

Whether they're consciously aware that they're in such a state, all beings are struggling for real, reliable happiness. The human being has reached the closest condition to that state, and therefore, the human life form is immensely valuable for the beings who have it—because they're closest—and for others, too, because once human beings become buddhas, then they can do so much for other beings.

That is what the Buddha said. He didn't say that you *have* to have suffering, but that as long as you are still under the spell of ignorance, you *will* have suffering. You'll feel free and then you'll suffer again. And since it's possible for you to become completely free of suffering by releasing yourself from the spell of ignorance, then you should recognize that even the partial relief is still not relief enough, and it is still suffering, relative to the released state of joy. And that's what the truth of suffering, its real drive, is: It's to give up questing for palliative solutions when there's a real cure. He's not denying that it's a palliative to cool yourself when you're too hot, but the key is to achieve a state where you're blissful whether you're hot or cold. It's a different quality of joy than the kind that is always afraid of losing itself. This is a joy that is never afraid of anything.

Meditation—
Moment to Moment

Toni Packer

AS THE HUMAN MIND QUESTS FOR CONCRETE THOUGHTS AND IMAGES, even in the midst of medita-tion, to which to relate, it is all to easy too let culturally and personally conditioned ideas and concerns replace the ultimate reality that can be apprehended just by observing, being. In her workshop on meditation, Toni Packer returned again and again to the simultaneous need and danger in allowing thought, or brainwork, to overcome the mind's and body's capability to step aside and permit whatever is of the moment be what it is and nothing more.

Born in Berlin in 1927, the daughter of a Jewish mother and Gentile father, Ms. Packer and her family survived World War II in Leipzig. After being relocated to the American occupation zone, she moved to Switzerland, where she met an American student, whom she married and accompanied back to the United States. Searching to answer fundamental questions that arose during the Hitler years, she studied psychology, anthropology, and sociology at the University of Buffalo. This search ultimately led her in 1967 to the Rochester Zen Center, where she became a disciple of Roshi Philip Kapleau. She provided psychological counseling for his students in the early 1970s and began to share his teaching duties in 1976. In 1981, he placed her in charge of all teaching at the center.

For some time, however, she had had serious doubts about the hierarchical organization, prescribed formality, and unquestioned authoritarian teacher-student relationship so often asso-ciated with established religious traditions. Ms. Packer's encounter with the work of J. Krishna-murti in the middle 1970s had a profound effect on her, eventually bringing her to resolve her increasing doubts about organized religion. She resigned from the Rochester Zen Center and joined with friends to found the Genesee Valley Zen Center, later renamed Springwater

Center for Meditative Inquiry and Retreats, which is nonsectarian and unaffiliated with any particular tradition.

Ms. Packer conducts silent retreats at Springwater throughout the year as well as semiannually in Germany, annually in California, and biannually in Sweden and the Netherlands. Her publications include *The Work of This Moment*, *The Light of Discovery*, *Seeing Without Knowing*, and *What Is Meditative Inquiry?* as well as numerous articles.

Easing the assembled participants gently into a quiet, meditative frame of mind, Ms. Packer began this workshop by holding up for examination a basic assumption: "We're here." Then saying, "Or are we?" This simple pair of questions brought her to remark that "a question is asked, and from time immemorial this brain is programmed to supply answers, for better or worse."

As something akin to a leitmotif, the concept of the interaction of the brain and of thought with the reality of the moment reoccurred throughout the workshop, bringing the participants up short as they tried to suspend any interference from past or future, and just dwell in the present. Ms. Packer asked:

Can we become aware of how we're living and talking about things, about ourselves, about each other, about our meditation practice, or Buddhism, or Hinduism, or Christianity, or ecumenicalness? We are brought up and nurtured in living in thinking about ourselves and each other, which seems so real because a single thought, conscious or unconscious, sets this whole organism into motion—glandular, organic, physical, muscular. One single unfrightening thought, and the body is alive with what we call fear or anxiety. It's real, we think. It's not just thought. People are often very resistant to hearing "This is just thought." It's not a good remark to make to anybody, because it isn't just thought, it's the whole organism, single and collective, participating in thoughts, creating thoughts; affecting and infecting each other with thought/feeling/emotions. With very little awareness.

She drew a distinction between thought and emotion, allowing that thoughts may be positive or negative, but the emotions—how we feel about the thoughts—are neither positive nor negative. They are just what they are, so are feelings, sensations. "But thought: Thinking about it, making it into story-line, creates the world we live in."

Ms. Packer explained that the material presented in the workshop "is not presented as something to be followed, believed, made into dogma, formula, even though that's what the brain wants and does all the time. Whatever is said is just an offering to look freshly, now this moment. It's always *now, this moment*, that looking takes place, it doesn't take place in the future." This led her back to the idea of present-moment attention and the banishing of thought for the time. Just then, a person entered the room, allowing the door latch to click as the door closed.

Opening? That's the door. Or is it? What if we didn't say *door*? Is that possible: To hear clicking and, even though words come up to describe it and know it and associate it with judgments and other clickings, is it possible to listen again and *not* know? To listen for the second time, as for the first time? And whatever else is going on, these are not words, the words come later—maybe a fraction, a minifraction of a second later—but at first is the perception. Then the word, the knowing, which is so needed by this conditioned organism. To be "in the know" has survival value, but it comes a split second later, after the perception.

But the question remains. Is it possible to hear without knowing? Listen without knowing? Look without knowing? Even though the brain is sputtering, giving all kinds of labels? That is also happening now, and it may become clearer and clearer that the instantaneousness of being is not the knowing. It is free of that. The moment the knowing sets in, there are complications.

So, what am I? What are you? What are we? This whole thing we call *the* world, what is all of that without knowing? When the images and the volumes of knowledge we have stored in the brain or the libraries about it, when all of that is seen to be just that, but not the real thing. We couldn't negotiate one moment of our daily practical living without knowing, having learned this leads to that. Yet is there a place, or a no-place, for not knowing—being without knowing?

Using the abstract question "What am I?" Ms. Packer observed that this brings to mind the many different answers we all have to that query. Ideas jump up based on the images we have of ourselves…

from what kind of tag we wear, what costumes we wear, whether we sit in front of a group or in the group; whether we're good at it or not so good at it. Ten thousand identities of what we are and we have tremendous investment in them. We can't fathom this investment most of the time, until the image gets questioned or hurt. Somebody doesn't take us for what we want to be taken. Crosses our ways, ridicules us, insults us, and what happens? Can there be a moment of perceiving without knowing, or is the reaction so powerful to defend, to protect, to rationalize, to counterattack? This is how images manifest themselves indirectly.

So is that a good question to let sit there: What am I without the images? Or does it immediately instill the yearning to be without images? The question works well when it illuminates all the imagery in which we live and move. And still that question is there: Is there anything beyond these images, this story about myself? Because the images all are coherently ordered into a story, remembered scenes. There must be some place in the brain that coordinates and makes past memories into a coherent sequence, which then is believed to be this continuous "me" or "I."

See, all of this is not just giving facts and information to be accepted and stored and remembered and given back to someone else. Instead, it's an invitation to look—Is this really so? Am I really just a series of coherent, or at times not-so-coherent, images? Is there anything else? Is that all?

This led to a fresh point of departure: *I don't know.* Ms. Packer observed that "A true 'I don't know' opens up to looking and listening anew, and an 'I don't know' that is sort of resigned, or maybe has a little hope that I will know sometime, or a big hope, or an 'I know if I only consult the right experts, the right books,'—those are openings, tracks to get onto. But to truly *not know* and open up to wondering, can that be one's life, moment to moment?" She continued:

Somebody said something that got me all upset. Do I know why he said this or why I'm upset? I don't really. I have quick answers to it but I don't know. And in this not knowing maybe our relationship can reveal itself in a new way—how we bump into each other inadvertently, and yet think we do it on purpose. He did this or she did this to me; she meant to do that. We think this way all the time, that we're all purposeful, intentional agents; little entities with a steering mechanism inside. That we have choices. We have choice to go with awareness or choice to go with the drive, the habit.

First, we have to become aware of how beholden we are to the idea that we have choice. There would be no hope if we human beings didn't have a choice. But what is it we mean when we say "I choose"? There may indeed be a moment of attention when it's very clear what's going on, very clear that there is an almost overriding desire to go with a habit. But how does it come about that awareness remains and the habit subsides, or that there is going with a habit? How does this happen? And what is going on in choosing such a marvelous meditative inquiry?

Having provided so many points of departure for discussion, Ms. Packer devoted the balance of the session to working with participants' questions. One person asked "Can we really talk about the present at all?" He pointed out that, "if I try to find that present, it's gone. It isn't there. And if the present isn't there, then the past and future aren't there either. Because they can't be there without present to depend on....Something's going on, but the 'I' can't see it." Ms. Packer rephrased the question as:

Can the "I" really experience a present? Of course not. "I" is thinking and imaging. The "I" itself is a chain of memories and thoughts and ideas, and being in the present is one of them.

But let us ask it this way: Is it possible to see the limitations of the words we use and not lose it? Be here even though the words *being here* don't capture it, and not get thrown off by thinking, "Oh, I just said 'being here.' Now that doesn't make any sense because I feel I'm here." Then you've lost it; a thought process has taken over. The thought arises— Okay, I'm here now—so see it as a thought, which cannot capture the whole thing.

Another question concerned the distinction between knowing and perceiving, and the sequence in which they occur.

A very heavy set of knowing can affect our perceptions. Talking about it meditatively, the main question of interest is, Is it possible to perceive purely, seeing that the knowing is something else? It's a process that can become transparent interiorly and need not be related to affecting the perception.

Say you are observing something and seemingly there is a perception simultaneously with knowing about it. Can there be a fine discernment that the perception is not the knowing about it? That these are two different processes? Or are they so merged with each other that one perceives through what one knows? It may be difficult, but not impossible, to discern. Different physical processes are involved in pure perception and interpreted perception. Something is conducted differently through the organism when knowing is involved, and it is very marvelous that this can become transparent. This is not without significance because so much of what we think, we believe to be true. We think that thought tells us the truth about the world. It may not.

A question about the wellspring of thoughts that may present themselves during sitting meditation brought Ms. Packer to wonder about the importance of understanding the source. She went on to demonstrate how such a question can ultimately lead one to a point of not knowing.

There probably are all kinds of new theories about where thoughts come from, because one can represent that line of thinking. You can think right now of your home. The memory will generate thoughts or images about your house. But I don't have that memory of your house, so no thoughts are generated in my mind because this memory doesn't exist for me.

Is the memory all located in this brain that generates these thoughts, or are thoughts in the air? There are lots of thoughts, ideas, and even scientific theories that thoughts are in nonlocal fields, which suggests, for example, that kids and adults learn through computers more and more quickly because something is in the air that we are touching. So there is storage somewhere of these masses of thoughts that we manifest. It's a collective affair manifested by human beings, who are also collective.

"Okay," you say, "That's all fine, but I want to know really where these thoughts come from. Where do the fields come from? Where does everything come from?" Then you have to sit with that question and *not know*, because as long as you know, this thing is spinning in a limited, possibly very interesting and theory-producing way. Then you sit because you can't fathom where thoughts come from and your question is not being filled with answers. The answer is let go. There is just nothing there. Emptiness… wholeness… openness. And then, suddenly, a thought: Have I got it now? So where did that come from? A moment ago there was nothing and now there is a thought about myself, or somebody else. Then watch this. Either the thought takes over and starts spinning a network, or it's seen and subsides again and there is nothing.

Asked about the expectation of awareness—expecting yourself to extend your moments or instances of attention—Ms. Packer suggested that this is an opportunity to watch one's expectation and wanting of greater awareness spaciously, and to listen to it spaciously, which we usually don't do. Instead, we almost reflexively go with the expectation, "imagining how it would be if I was more aware, or what I can do to get there. That fills the mind and body." She continued by bringing into focus some of the physiological aspects of expectation and the effects on them of simple awareness.

The fact that the heart may be pounding in expectation is just a physical response to the thought of getting more this or that, but it doesn't mean that there is something to be expected. The fact that the body responds so faithfully to a thought, manifesting fear or agitation, doesn't mean that what is expected or feared is real. But the brain assumes that there must be something to be expected, or something to be afraid of!

If you can really, totally be with whatever the body is manifesting and have no conclusion about it—not know it, but *be* that—wonder of wonders, it begins to abate, because there's no new input of thoughts about what could happen. That is meditative listening or attending. Without knowing.

A woman asked Ms. Packer to address issues of effort and progression; the seeking and desire for change, development, and improvement.

One has lived through so much stuff—repetitively, time and time again—and there comes a moment when one wonders, Do I have to keep going through this, or is there a different way? At a time like this, one hears or reads about it, somebody tells you about it, and in a very "natural" way, one wants that new way of being. It's now all very understandable and observable; not to be condemned. But as you sit down, in a place like this, a retreat, a sesshin, whatever, provided you're being left alone, can you just sit with all this wanting and expecting and feeling I ought to make an effort, and just listen to it? At the thought of effort, the body already begins to tense, the muscles tighten, and you listen to that. You attend to it. You have this tremendous space and quietness to let all of this come into full bloom, beholding it nonjudgmentally. Not going with the effort toward something, but allowing the energy of watching or perceiving gather in just being here with what's happening, what's unfolding.

And this is the case not just in a quiet sitting, certainly. These things then pop up in your daily life, when you notice you have your hands tensed as you're working on the computer or cutting a carrot. So you catch yourself: Why all this tension? But once you notice it, you can relax. If you don't notice it, the habit just runs. But now you've noticed it, and you will notice it more often.

Inadvertently thinking "it has to be like this" is our biggest hindrance. We assume, or it is assumed, that the way we operate and the way other people operate is the way it has to be. But you've already wondered whether it has to be like that. That's a marvelous step to take. And when you come upon a habit, wonder "does it have to be like that?" But don't immediately answer. You have to be quiet and watch it; allow something else to take the place of habitually reacting.

A participant remarked that, in sitting meditation, regardless of how she approaches it, "and as deep as I go in my meditation, I don't think I've ever lost the sense of somebody" being present.

Toni Packer: Yes. This sense of existence, of somebody being there, is very, very, very deep. Lately I've been reading in a different tradition, which is really nice to do because all the words are turned upside down—the self is not what the self is here. The writer's practice is just to have people follow this *I am* to the very ground, to its very source. Because that is the most obstinate thing. I don't mean that like "I am obstinate;" but there are people who sit so, with no thought in the mind, and there is still a shadow of me-ness there. Well, what is that? Is that again a quick reflection? Am I here? And not necessarily I *am* here, but *am* I here? connected with some fear that I may not be here. So that shadow may be held in place by, among other things, clinging to having to exist as something. If that fear isn't there, there is no shadow of this observer, but there is everything just as it is, revealing itself.

Participant: Is it possible to live in the world like that? Or can you have that just when you meditate?

Toni Packer: Is it possible to live in the world and not have a shadow of me-ness?

Very difficult. Very difficult! Everything appeals to the me to be somebody, to respond in habitual ways, to defend. And yet, there is a shadow of an observer there that sees all that. An awareness that can really be intelligently learning about all of this stuff that we've been talking about.

Participant: But I'd like to get rid of the observer, and I don't know how to do that. I'm observing what's going on. I'm observing my thoughts. I'm observing my attachments.

Toni Packer: But you're not doing it, it's just becoming transparent. There's no one there who's observing it. That's a thought—a very, very deeply ingrained, habitual, commonly shared thought—I'm observing this. If you say that observation is going on, that's clearer. You don't confuse yourself then. But if you say, "No, wait a minute; I am the observer," then you have something to look at—the fear of not being anybody, or fear of disappearing.

Participant: But there is somehow a difference with different people. In your presence I experience a loving kind of transmission. If there was an angry person sitting in your chair, I'd be experiencing something different. How do you explain that?

Toni Packer: I don't have to explain it—you said it—it is so. It's amazing how we feel we get one step farther if we explain it. All that's needed is to observe it, and now you've observed it, you keep observing it, and maybe some real wisdom is growing about how we affect each other with moods and all kinds of states. There's some contagion. Somebody used the words "contact *samadhi*." You're with somebody who's in *samadhi*, and you feel as though you're almost in it, too. Of course, to watch thoughts can be very inspirational and masquerade for the real thing. You can think, Oh, I'm with a person and I'm getting a transmission, and the thoughts themselves ignite you. Then, when you question that and look again and let the thoughts wither, maybe a calmer state of just being there ensues.

When a man asked Ms. Packer for her thoughts on the "progression or the evolution of compassion," she responded that she doesn't think in terms of development. What she finds more interesting are such questions as: Is there compassion now? If not, why not? She pointed out a disparity in the ways people think about others.

Toni Packer: When a crime happens, some people will say, "Well, I could forgive anything else but that. This is just so heinous." Of course, that blocks compassion. But, if you hear about something or see something in yourself, to wonder how come these emotions and drives and urges arise in the human being? What makes it possible for us to do to each other what we do? You really grapple with this. You want to find out. Then you're not on the fault-finding and blame-assigning and hating trip, but trying to find out. The whole panorama of human on-goings is the macrocosm for it in oneself, and out of understanding it in oneself and

understanding it in each other, comes compassion.

A woman whose father had died recently recounted an experience that had taken place a few days before his passing on. "It was on his deathbed, at home, and we were talking. Our eyes met and that glimpse of selfing fell away: He wasn't he and I wasn't I, and something transcended and then we went right back into this moment, and it was very powerful." She went on to explain that, from the time of his funeral, all her assumptions and ideas about what is real came into question. She explained how "powerful and bad" it was for her that "someone you've known for forty-one years doesn't exist on this planet anymore, in the form that I had known."

Ms. Packer asked her about the moment she had described, where there was no selfing: "At that moment, was he even your father?" The participant responded that he wasn't, and that was fine. Ms. Packer brought the discussion back to the idea of not knowing and the value there is in recognizing this.

I could say this is what he is right now, but does this become a comforting thought? Or is it a living truth? Or I could say, What part of your father is most oppressing? The one in the casket; the one on the deathbed? And before he was born, what was your father? Particularly when something like this hits us, we are so overpowered by our thoughts and the story that evolves out of them.

On the last day of a retreat, I read old and contemporary masters and poems. There's a beautiful poem by Mary Oliver about Boston

University Hospital, and a couple of times when I read it I choked up. My husband is ill and that poem about somebody dying just made me choke. I don't read it right now because I don't want to choke up. Maybe the next time I would read it, I wouldn't choke up, I don't know. But without that poem, where's the choking? Where are the tears? I'm not saying tears are necessary. A lot of upset with the death of somebody very close is linked to the fear of one's own death. How will I die? Will it be a painful, drawn-out death? Will I not see the beautiful sunrises over the hills anymore?

And yet, if you do quiet meditation, and the meditation has this twofold aspect, one part is to illuminate the heavily conditioned organism so that, with attention, it is made somehow transparent or permeable—one aspect is to come upon that and begin to notice it. The other aspect is that in which all of this takes place, which is something not to be explained or described in words. It's been called one's last emptiness, darkness, light, whatever. When that is there, there is no fear of passing away, of coming and going, because coming and going is what's happening, but it's all happening in this other vast space of no limitation, no hatred, no attachment, no fear—no individuality, to which we cling for dear life and which brings us all our sorrows. So that's why it's so important to come upon that oneself so you don't need the comforting words of anyone.

A woman brought up the question of what she termed "formal training" as opposed to "stumbling along on my own." She explained that she had been on retreats and experienced various people's ideas, "but the teachings for me have been life experiences... what arises in life becomes my teacher."

Ms Packer responded that, "If this is how it works for you, then so be it," and she briefly described her work with and without teachers. The woman clarified that the "transmission of knowledge and such seems to me a very formal way." But, she concluded, "there is a possibility all of us learn the same truth through different paths."

We learn the truth *in spite of* different paths. Because the truth has nothing to do with a path. This truth is not caused by a path and waking up to it. Who knows why there's waking up. It's the miracle of humanity, of the universe, that there is such a thing as waking up to the truth. The Buddha kept saying something akin to "there is the unconditioned and because it is unconditioned, it cannot be conditioned." Unconditioned means not conditionable, not subject to cause and effect. Everything we do—hurting each other and then retaliating or forgiving—is all cause and effect. But the clarity of insight has no cause and no effect. If you say something degrading to me, and there is complete listening to what you're saying, what's going on, and what's happening here, the body may want to tighten, to fight back. Or if there is complete openness of listening, then what you're saying does not become the cause of an effect here. We're the results of everything that's ever happened, so why pick out one thing and say this was the cause of that? Everything is the cause of everything and everything is the effect of everything. If you think, Can my teacher be the seeing of a leaf swirling to the ground, well, of course, at this moment there is awareness—that's the teach-er—and the leaf was just revealed.

A man raised a question about the array of methods in Buddhism, pointing out that Ms. Packer does not really advocate even one method. She agreed that she is not, "and yet we work. We look, just like we did today. Awareness happens. In spite of anything we do, it does happen." She told of a man who had come to see her at Springwater:

He was a steelworker, quite a coarse-looking person, and I've never seen him since and I'd never seen him before. He said that he hadn't talked much about this experience since the Vietnam War. At the time it happened, he had mentioned it to his comrades and they just laughed at him. His wife didn't understand. But it had come up again and he wanted somebody to talk to about it.

So here he was in the Vietnam War. There was a certain particularly dangerous, Viet Cong–infested hill to be taken. His commander was chosen to do that and they had to volunteer for it. Nobody volunteered, so people were called out by name and his name was called. He says, "You cannot imagine how I felt. My knees hardly held me up as I walked up to the helicopter. I was so afraid." Then sitting in that helicopter, looking for that hill, he said something happened. Every bit of fear, everything, dropped away and there was just nothing but love and openness. (I don't remember what words he used.) And he said, "We didn't even find that hill. It didn't exist." Coming back, he was filled with wanting to tell this to people and they all thought he was odd, something had snapped in him.

Maybe this thing happened because he was facing death. Maybe everything dropped away, and when everything drops away, including all the paths—and every good teacher of every good tradition says this is what has to ultimately happen, the whole thing dropping away including the I am or the Buddha or what you will—then what's there is there in all simplicity.

Breaking Out of the Shell of Self

INSIGHT MEDITATION AND DEEP-ECOLOGY PRACTICE

Wes Nisker

IN VIPASSANA MEDITATION, ONE STRIVES TO GAIN INSIGHT based in "mindfulness." Wes Nisker devoted his day-long workshop to guiding the participants through basic meditations centered on the traditional Buddhist four foundations of mindfulness—body and breath; sensations; mind states; and consciousness and the objects of consciousness. Interspersed with guided meditation were Dharma talks that provided a rudimentary philosophical structure for understanding Buddhism, a structure aligned closely with what Mr. Nisker terms "deep ecology"—

the understanding of ourselves as imbedded in nature, as no different from the world; understanding *our* nature *as* nature. By developing the skill of mindfulness, we are able to use it to explore and experience our deepest identities and truest nature. As we come to know ourselves as part of the wider web of evolution—both of earth life and cosmic forces—our lives gain new perspective and meaning, and we begin to find relief from the suffering of a separate, disconnected self.

Stating that he doesn't think of himself "in any way as a guru," he said he is, rather, a "spiritual friend," someone who "may be a few steps ahead along the path and can turn back and say, 'Look out, there's a rut or a barrier there.'" Besides being a Buddhist meditation teacher, philosopher, and journalist, his steps have brought him to be an affiliate of Spirit Rock Meditation Center and a faculty member at the University of California Extension Division and at Esalen Institute. He is founder and co-editor of the Buddhist journal *The Inquiring Mind* and author of *Crazy Wisdom* and *If You Don't Like the News, Go out and Make Some of Your Own.*

It's a very exciting time and I think Buddhist practices are really answering a deep hunger in our culture for connection. Somehow we have all gotten lost in a world of our own. There's no one to blame for this. The development of consciousness seems to have produced an extreme degree of individualism and it's become pathological. We now go about our lives believing and behaving as though we are independent, we have complete control over what we do and our destiny, our future; that we are separate, that we have no connection to the world, to nature, to each other. It's ironic because our science—our wisdom tradition in the West really; how we have gone about investigating ourselves and reality through various disciplines of science—is telling us in the most amazing ways how deeply connected we are. How there is not one thing that you can pick out that is independently existing, or separate from everything else.

The question is, How do we experience that? How do we make it a part of our being? We can understand it intellectually. You can go into a room of scientists and the physicists will tell you how everything is made of quarks and leptons and gluons and you are composed of the same subatomic reality as that. And the biologist will tell you how your being was created through genetic evolution and how you really are completely a part of all of life; the history of all of life is your biography. You can understand all this, agree with it, and then walk away, believing again in your completely separate world.

The genius of what the Buddha taught was actual methodology, techniques, to shift your identity; to shift your understanding of your identity. The Buddha taught a lot about identity and who we really are, and that was the key to his teaching. The key to liberation in the Buddhist cosmology, is seeing through the illusion of separateness and the illusion of self that we carry. He emphasized in seeing this, looking at how things arise, how they are created. He had a principle, a law, called dependent co-arising, or dependent origination, which really is looking at how things arise in relationship, how no thing exists separately. And he said, if you see this law, if you understand causality, you will understand all of the Dharma because you will see that there is no separate self—it is an illusion—and once you see that there is no separate self, you begin to lose your attachment to it and thereby begin to ease your suffering. By seeing your true nature, you begin to ease your suffering, and that is the core of the Buddhist teaching. He said I teach about what causes suffering and I teach about what relieves suffering, the end of suffering.

Vipassana, or insight meditation, comes from the Theravada Buddhist tradition. Theravada means "the way of the elders," and the Theravada tradition originated in India, Burma, Sri Lanka, Thailand, and is based on the earliest written record we have of what the Buddha taught, which is called the Pali canon, Pali being the language that the Buddha spoke. It's considered the original discourses of the Buddha. There are many texts that have followed that and have given commentary on those discourses.

Most of the practices in the Theravada tradition, and the *vipassana* meditation practices we will be doing, come from one discourse of the Buddha, the *Satipatthana-sutra*, which is the sutra on the development and cultivation of the quality of mindfulness, *sati* meaning "insight," which is based on this quality of mind called "mindfulness."

Mindfulness is a quality we all possess, though most of us don't know that we have it or how to use it. I remember when I first sat down to meditate in India, in 1970, and I had gotten a good college degree and I had been through some Freudian therapy, and some Jungian therapy, and a little Gestalt out in San Francisco, and in all of these processes, this education, and even the psychology I had studied, I had never been shown that there was this other way to look at myself and to look at my own mental processes. Suddenly I was offered this gear in the mind, this mental attitude that allowed me to look at myself in a completely different way, and by cultivating this mindfulness, this factor of mind, I was able to understand myself in a completely different way and alleviate a lot of my difficult patterns of emotion, thought, and behavior. I really began to see that I was not who I thought I was, to lose my self.

That's why they call it a practice of self-liberation. The core of all spiritual practice and of all the perennial wisdom is asking the question Who am I? In this technique we investigate it through this quality of mindfulness, of being as objective as possible about ourselves, almost like a scientist. The question Who am I is really what we're going to be asking.

Some Zen masters put the question in very colorful ways. They say "Who is it that's

dragging this corpse around?" "Who is it that goes in and out of these sixth-sense doors?" Socrates, the guy who started Western philosophy, said "Know thyself," and that was a turning point in the history of consciousness, when Socrates began to examine the thought process. To ask ourselves: What is it of our mind, of our body, that is really ours, that we own? What of this experience that you have that you call by your name or that you call "I," or "mine," or "me," what do you really own?

In some ways it's a process of deconstruction. You go in, and look, and ask this question, not so much in an intellectual way, but almost in an experiential way. That's where mindfulness begins to work it's magic. It focuses your mind, it gathers your energy, and it gives you a place to rest your mind and look around. You kind of have a platform. You pick an object—in our case the breath, which is central to many of the Buddhist practices in all traditions. The breath is a fairly neutral object unless you're sick and have a cold or you're gasping and wheezing. You intend to rest the attention, rest the mind, on the breath and then see what happens, and you begin to see how things happen in your psyche completely independently of anybody willing them; completely independent of a "you" behind it all. And you begin to see what of all of this phenomena can I call "I," "me," or "mine"? Also, with this mindfulness you explore the body. Where does this body come from? What is it? What is it composed of? How did it appear here? In the West with our scientific and intellectual development, which is a great blessing, a wonderful tool, we have gone outward to examine these questions (and we've done a pretty marvelous job of it), but to see what science sees looking at somebody else's body or mind, if you see it in your own mind, has the power of transformation for you. It becomes experiential, cellular; it becomes wisdom rather than knowledge. That's the difference.

There are four foundations of mindfulness, four places to investigate: the body and breath is the first one and the sensations make up the second one—sensations actually being the nervous system, the sentience that we have as sentient beings. The third is mind states, emotions, the limbic system you might call it, and the fourth is consciousness and all of the objects of consciousness—the psyche and all of its productions in thought and thinking and ideas and concepts. You can really see this progression, and the way it's described in the sutra is almost as a progression, an evolutionary journey. It's really touching the basic aspects of your identity: touching in to body and breath; touching in to the nervous system, the sensations, emotional brain, emotional life. And then the consciousness, the identity factors that we call and experience as uniquely human. You can see it as an evolutionary journey where we can actually sort of regress. We can go way back and begin to touch the most basic elements of what we call "I" and what makes up this existence.

Sometimes mindfulness has been called "the witness" or "the higher self." That's what it's often called in Christian traditions—the

higher self or the witness, the observing power of the mind. Higher self I kind of shy away from because it has a feeling of judgment in it. (This is my higher self and everything it's looking at is my lower self.) But witness is a useful metaphor for mindfulness. Mindfulness is a kind of bare attention to what is actually present in awareness; bare attention in the sense that you are not interfering with it, you are not adding anything to it. For instance, right now you can be aware of your body posture, just the way it is. Just be aware of it, without identifying with it, or identifying it as I, me, or mine. It just happens to be the way your body was set when I told you to look, without adding any kind of emotional value to it, without getting attached to it or lost in it, in other words keeping the mind steady and even—balanced—you look at what is present in awareness. The quality of bare attention, noninterfering awareness.

I advise people when practicing mindfulness to develop a tender mindfulness; a real, accepting, almost bemused kind of observer quality to your mindfulness, a curiosity—like "Okay, let's see what's going on in here. Let's see what this is." Looking at yourself with that kind of quality. One thing at which many Asian teachers who come over here to teach Westerners are amazed is how self-critical we are and how we are continually beating ourselves up. The Dalai Lama was in a conference with a bunch of Western psychologists and somebody raised the issue of low self-esteem. He said, "What's that?" He worked with his translator and they tried to figure it out, but apparently they didn't feel that in the same way, they didn't feel the need to even label it. It didn't have a name in the Tibetan vocabulary. So when we try to be mindful, often, if we have a difficult time—and chances are if you haven't done this practice a lot you will have a difficult time, because it's not something that we're used to—usually we get lost in our experience. We are completely mind*less*. And even though it's difficult, one of the great lessons of this practice is when you start to do it and see how difficult it is, you realize how much of our lives we go through completely asleep or completely mindless, lost, being pulled by this and by that, by reactions, by patterns, by old stuff. So have a tenderness to your mindfulness.

This is one of the great lessons of this practice and one of the great contributions that Buddhism can make to us: We share a common moment of evolution—we share a common level of awareness and consciousness—and we're all just trying to wake up. The reason your mind may have difficulty being awake is not your fault. It's not anybody's fault. The Tibetans have a great saying: "Roll all blames into one." Just one sticky, yucky ball of blame and, you know, blame it on the Big Bang. Why not? If you really want to get down to causes....So how it all was intended to come out is exactly this moment's experience.

[Mr. Nisker began the first meditation, which arises from the first of the four foundations, the body and breath. Starting with the breath—the air element—he said, "Each single breath

expresses your intimacy with the world, your interdependence as you exchange nutrients with the plants."

Next he asked the participants to become aware of any other movements they may feel in their bodies—"any kinds of sensation: tingling, itching, flashing in the head," etc. He brought their attention to the heartbeat.

To bring the attention to the earth element, Mr. Nisker asked the participants to "become aware, very simply, of your posture, your body and its solidity, its shape, the solidness inside of it. Feeling your legs and your buttocks on the ground or on the chair, become aware of the earth below supporting the structure and supporting you." Again demonstrating each person's interconnectedness with nature, he pointed out that "the earth is holding you, even when you walk. You are not on the earth, but have grown up out of the earth. Your body is composed of all of the same elements that are found in the earth. The earth is inside you.

Moving to the water element, he brought their awareness to "the fleshiness of your limbs or your belly, feeling the liquid inside you. Pointing out that 80 to 90 percent of our body is water, he continued that this "is the composition of the oceans. We are sea water that splashed up on shore and walked away."

Finally, for the fire element, the workshop was directed to "feel the warmth of your body inside as it radiates around the surface of your skin. This heat we feel is created by the warm air that we breathe, by the food that we eat that has synthesized the sun's fires. The heat we can feel in our bodies connects us directly to our sun, the solar system."

After the period of meditation, Mr. Nisker noted that "this meditation on breath and on the four elements in the body is indeed classical Buddhist practice and comes directly from the Satipatthana-sutra. It can be framed with our modern scientific awareness because what we are finding corroborates in many specific and very interesting ways what the Buddha was teaching."

A participant asked if, in doing this meditation on his own, he would go through the four elements in his body, as they had during the directed meditation.]

You can guide yourself through it any time you want. It's a very wonderful meditation to remind you of your basic identity. To really touch again all those elements that are feeding you, that give you life. They're wonderful meditations because they really bring us into the body. And they break out of that shell of self because the self really lives in the thoughts, in the identity with thoughts. When you're with the breath, when you're with the heartbeat, when you're with your bones, when you're with your blood, you're with what we all share, with the commonality.

But the Vipassana practice we do as the on-going basic practice takes the breath as the primary object, so that your intention is to be with the breath, and then to be aware of whatever else appears in awareness, whatever else arises. You rest in the breath, then investigate from there, but your exploration happens from the breath. The breath is the anchor. It's not like you push other stuff away. When thoughts arise, or sensations, or feel-

ings, or emotions, you experience them. You just notice them, experience them. You can name them or label them. Whatever appears in your awareness you would notice with that kind of bare attention of mindfulness, and after it no longer was grabbing your attention you would come back to the breath.

But in this meditation that I just guided you through, we changed the object. It was the breath, then the heartbeat, the bones, and the liquidity, so the primary object changed. Different meditations have different primary objects, but with the primary object, whatever else appears, you try to hold it with as much equanimity or balance of mind as possible. In other words, including it.

What the breath does is breathe. What the mind does is think. It's not bad or good. Where we get in trouble is when we identify with it or when we grasp onto it; when we try to hold onto it or fight it. When we begin to see it as just what minds do, it's no problem. As a friend of mine says so beautifully, "No self? No problem."

[A member of the workshop brought up an issue related to posture and physical discomfort it may result in during lengthy meditations. "This comes from centuries of Protestantism," he said. "I expect that if I shift a muscle some guy is going to come and whack me with a stick." He asked, "When you are aware of that, do you then try to say 'I'm just not going to give in to that muscular need to shift'? Or do you go ahead and shift and get comfortable and get back to the business at hand?"]

Wes Nisker: You do different things at different times. Sometimes you'll want to sit and make a vow: I'm not going to move. You're just going to sit for forty minutes and do a practice and, when the pain comes, you experience the pain and work with the pain. It's a wonderful practice to actually work with pain, to push the edge of it, explore it, see what's at the heart of it. See how much of the pain is your tensing around and wanting it to go away. Ordinarily in our lives we push pain away. We try to mask it; we divert ourselves. So using the vow and the almost inevitable arising of soreness in the legs can be a way of actually working with pain. Other times you may have another object in your meditation or another thing you want to explore, and you'll want to sit where the pain is not going to be prevalent. So at different times it's good to sit with it and it's good to let it go.

Pain can be very concentrating. It's easy to get lost in the thoughts when you're working with the breath because the breath is fairly neutral. When the leg starts hurting and the pain is there, it's hard to be focused on anything else. Working with holding the pain with a balance of mind, without pushing or without tension, you can really get a sense of what the quality of mindfulness can be like and how it can work. As Jon Kabat-Zinn teaches, and a lot of people now are teaching, this particular practice is a way of dealing with pain and with stress.

The wonderful thing about Buddhism in America is that we have available to us all of these wonderful practices and ways of talking about the Dharma that we can draw on. And while it's important to work with one particular practice that really speaks to you or that feels comfortable with you, within that one tradition there's usually a set of practices. You learn these different techniques and then you have them as tools and can apply them. You can guide your own practice.

There are times when you're going to want to work with more spaciousness of mind, if you're feeling really constricted; or times when you need to sharpen your concentration, and you have another technique for that. So you have all of these tools you really can apply yourself. It's good to have a teacher to guide you, but you can do a lot of the guidance on your own. I think it's important at some point to choose a tradition. It's skillful means to choose one and go with it. But within the different traditions there are different practices you do at different times in your spiritual life. Also, you may want to do a very basic practice when you're advanced, but what you learn as you go, you keep as a tool you can always use when you feel you need it.

We're dilettantes here in America, anyway, and having all this available to us can be dangerous. If you're switching practices because it seems really hard, then question it again. But you have to look really deep—you have to question very deeply—why you might want to switch.

The second foundation is sensation, and the Buddha gives a whole section of his teaching to sensations because they are where our experience really starts. The moment of contact at the level where a sensation is felt, and felt as either pleasant or unpleasant or neutral, is when our whole range of experience begins. So the Buddha told us to become aware of experience on the sensation level. He said that's where you can begin to find your freedom.

Ordinarily we feel a sensation that is pleasant, unpleasant, or neutral, and we immediately start grasping after it or pushing it away. The reaction is so built in that you really don't have a choice. The closer you are to your own sensations—to being aware of how your own sensations work; feeling them, and becoming familiar with them—the sooner you can have a freedom of choice as to whether desire arises or aversion arises. You actually can have a choice as to how you're going to react to the sensation.

In Danny Goleman's new book, *Emotional Intelligence,* he describes what the neuroscientists are discovering and how emotion begins without freedom of choice. Our brain is built so that we don't really get to choose, the emotional center bypasses what we call the higher centers (the intellect and what we think of as our free will) and reaction starts before we are even aware of it. The meditation on the sensation brings us down into a level where we can become more in charge of our own emotional behavior, our own reactions to things.

We will work with a technique that is sometimes called sweeping. It's basically a body scan. We use the same quality of mindfulness, but instead of the primary object of

our meditation being the breath, the movement of breath, the experience of breath, the primary object is whatever sensations we feel as we scan our awareness through the entire body. Again, the idea is to be with whatever sensations appear—we're not trying to create anything or get rid of anything —but whatever sensations are felt, just notice them. You can even give them that little label or note: It could be heat, it could be tingling, it could be soreness, it could be tension, the qualities that sensation can take on. It's a simple, bare attention to whatever is present as we move through the body. It really is a meditation on our nervous system; what brings us pleasure and pain. It is sort of the membrane between us and the world.

[As with the previous meditation, the members first brought awareness to rest in the breath, the anchor to all the techniques with which Mr. Nisker would work. As he said, "Whenever we get in trouble, or get too lost, or find ourselves really out of sorts, come back to the breath. Just being with the breath for a few minutes can bring us back to ourselves and remind us of that gear of mindfulness."

He then directed the participants to bring awareness to the very top of their heads.]

With a very balanced, bare attention, explore the top of your head and whatever sensations you feel there. Very slowly, almost as if water was being poured over the top of your head, very slowly, evenly begin to move your awareness down over your forehead, the back of your head and the sides of your head feeling whatever sensations are present.... Try to cover all the parts of the body, every inch of the body. Let your body scan be as complete as possible, perhaps even noticing what is inside, any sensations you feel on the inside.... If the awareness seems to get stuck in one place you can move it along, letting the breath give the awareness a bit of a push.

[Upon reaching the soles of the feet in the scan, Mr. Nisker then directed them to return the awareness back to the top of the head and moved down through the body in a second scan, which helps to develop a pattern that can be repeated each time they scan the body.]

If you find that it's more useful to go down the front part of your body and then go back and do the back part of your body, that's fine, but do it the same way each time. If you find that the mind has been distracted, bring it back to the place where it left off scanning. If one particular area of the body has a particular kind of sensation—pain or pleasant tingling—you might want to explore it just a little bit longer. Let your attention just rest there for a little while, experiencing it, perhaps noticing if there's any kind of emotional tone that appears as you're on that part of the body. Then move on and continue to scan. As you scan through the body, simply being aware of sensations, sense that you are exploring this process of life that goes on within you and without you—all of the cellular, molecular, and atomic changes continually going on. As you continue to

scan, see if you can sharpen the focus of your awareness, taking it deeper; feeling the subtlest sensations that exist both inside and on the surface of your body.

The scanning technique has a number of benefits. It's quite an active way of developing very strong concentration. It gives the mind something very active to do, and yet it's not something that you're creating with your mind. It is naturally occurring and going on all the time. Again it's a way of becoming familiar and intimate with this process that goes on usually beneath our conscious awareness. Just by touching it, just by experiencing it and bringing it into consciousness, we shift our identity out of the psyche and into physicality, into natural processes.

It's also a very powerful meditation on *anitya,* which means "impermanence"—one of the factors that the Buddha taught. If you focus on impermanence, the continually changing nature of all things, you will no longer be able to grasp so tightly, trying to hold on to anything. You will see that everything is in process and has no self-existence, in the sense that it's all disappearing. It's all in a continual process of change, alteration, transformation.

I started meditating in India in 1970, with a teacher who just taught this practice. I studied this practice of scanning the body for almost five years and it's very powerful if you use it and work with it in a retreat setting. The body begins to dissolve. You sit down and close your eyes and there's no solidity there. You can actually experience the molecular changes going on at every moment.

Mind and body are not two. We think of them often as two, but whatever is in the mind is in the body. Often where we're stuck appears as a body sensation as easily as it appears as a conscious thought. When sweeping through the body, some people will hit a certain place where suddenly they're lost in thought, and it seems like every time they go through the body there's one place where they get distracted. When they go back and focus on that place they find that there's some kind of deep feeling underneath there; some kind of emotion attached to that place in the body. Just by being in the body and focusing on that—putting the attention there without desire to get rid of it or to create anything—it begins to heal in some way the whole mind–body structure, the whole mind–body process.

What we're doing is really exploring. We're asking Who am I? We're going in and asking it in a kind of experiential way on the level of body, and now on the level of sensations and the process. You're not trying to change anything. You're just noticing, and that's really the deep healing that comes from this practice. We don't create those tensions: I'm going to include the good in my life and exclude the bad. That's completely unrealistic and gets us into so much tension in our lives. So much of our suffering comes from not looking at the facts, that there is no such life as just the good and not the bad. That's what the Buddha's first noble truth is really about: This is the nature of existence—it is unsatis-

factory. You may come to a moment of satisfaction but the next moment is going to be a moment of dissatisfaction. There's no way out of that; it's the human condition.

In beginning to work with that and to hold difficulty, pain, and discomfort—even the discomfort of our posture—you begin to realize how hard it is to sit in one position. Ordinarily you go through a day constantly shifting and moving your body around, trying to get comfortable. When you sit, you realize that this is the nature of the body. It gets uncomfortable all the time.

This is also a really good practice if you find it hard to stay with the breath as an object and you find your mind getting scattered, give it more to work with and use this process as giving it something more to do; engaging it.

[Before breaking for lunch, Mr. Nisker shared his thoughts about what Western culture may contribute to Buddhism as it takes a stronger hold.]

I think that Buddhism, as it travels the world, starting in India, it combines with the particular elements or qualities of the different countries that it lands in. So, in China it combined with Taoism and it became nature-based. And in Tibet it combined with the Bön religion, the mountain religion, and became a kind of shamanistic Buddhism. As Buddhism comes to the West, we are going to offer it the language and techniques of science, which is really our genius. I think that together they are going to create a powerful new Buddhism.

[Throughout the workshop, Mr. Nisker interspersed his Dharma talks and directed meditations with readings from a variety of sources
that directed the audience's attention to specific aspects of Buddhist thought in general as
well as to particular elements of practice. The
authors and poets included a wide range, from
D. H. Lawrence, Gary Snyder, and Mary Oliver
to Jack Kerouac and Daniel Goleman. An article in Time magazine—"Oedipus Schmedipus:
The Fault, Dear Sigmund, May Be in Our
Genes"—dealt with recent genetic research
from which the writer suggested he finds
"proof of what one has suspected all along:
Fear, dread, worry, pessimism, anxiety, and
other neurotic traits are all normal" (i.e., genetically determined). Mr. Nisker commented on
this as follows:]

The Buddha said that this body is not mine
or anybody else's. It arises due to past
causes, and for now it should be felt and
experienced. Not only our neurosis, but the
structure of our body is encoded in our
genes. Every little gene is actually an encyclo-
pedia of the entire rest of our body—a phenomenal piece of information there in those
little genes. But when you think about your
body, where it comes from and what we
now know about evolution, I think it's pretty
widely accepted as the case that it comes
from all those little adaptations, over the millions and millions of years, that create this
body, this mind, all of it we inherited. We
have somehow gotten into this belief that
we are self-created. It's a kind of delusional
state that we ordinarily take ourselves to be

in. What we ordinarily consider ourselves is a
complete delusion.

In many Buddhist traditions, when you begin
a ceremony, meditation session, or a retreat,
you call on the ancestors. You invoke all the
names of the people who have kept the
practices alive, and really when you think
about it, it's quite amazing that this teaching
that started 2,500 years ago is still so vital
and relevant to everyone who takes it on. It's
not a kind of knowledge that was useful at
one moment in history and now seems
archaic, but it seems very pertinent to our
lives today. So, as a Western Buddhist, I like
to call on our ancestors, who are the
Beatniks. Myself and many of my contempo-
raries who started practicing Buddhism in
the 1960s and 1970s, really drew on the
Beatnik poets and artists who first started
talking about the Dharma and these teachers; bringing words like karma and Dharma
into modern usage, along with Alan Watts
who was sort of on the Beatnik fringe. They
are the ones who really got me interested,
who showed that there was a way, outside
of our Western tradition, to experience life,
to know life and to understand it, that it was
very unique. The Beatniks were often misun-
derstood, and still are, as having been like
juvenile delinquents, but they were really on
a spiritual quest. It got a little mixed up in
there with their search for kicks and highs,
but they were after the ultimate high.

I wrote this down at an exhibition about
the Beatniks. They had a glass case with
some of Jack Kerouac's notebooks, where he

used to scribble his thoughts and his ideas. He studied Buddhism by going to the San Jose Library and reading everything under Buddhism that was there. Now, forty years later, there are practices and centers everywhere, but there weren't just forty years ago. He never quite got the sitting down too well. I copied this little excerpt from one of his notebooks.

I breathe in ignorance with wisdom breath but I breathe out golden-mind essence with compassion breath. Gently, evenly, deliberately and peacefully, I fumigate the universe with mind-essence.

[A piece called "Old Wood Rat's Stinky House," from Gary Snyder's Mountains and Rivers Without End, *brought Mr. Nisker to make the following observation.]*

That wonderful, big perspective is something that I found in Buddhism that I had never found in the Western traditions that I was taught or that I grew up in. There's a way in which we are given to conceive of this world as a singly, specially created entity—this particular universe; this life we're given as a single life. You get this one time to get it all right as a separate individual and then you get damned for eternity or you get salvation for eternity. What a burden that is.

Science is now exploding the narrow sense we have of what life is about, at least in our tradition. It is just vast beyond all our imagination, all our abilities to conceive. The Hubble telescope has been sending back pic-

tures of the cosmos—a little, nickel-sized piece of the sky, a picture of it—and they found two hundred million galaxies in one little area of the sky. Unbelievable vastness. What does that do to our conception of this little life that we have come to believe in?

The Buddhist cosmology is vast. It's huge, it's enormous. There are world-systems after world-systems. It's not one universe, it's another universe and another universe. The Dalai Lama was asked "Is there a Big Bang in Tibetan Buddhist cosmology?" He said, "Yes, bang, bang, bang—many bangs, many universes." The Buddha said we've been here so many times that everybody has been everybody else's relative. You've been my mother, my daughter, and that if we really understood that and knew that we would treat each other that way.

The first meditation we're going to do this afternoon has to do with mind states, the third foundation of mindfulness. It's really about feelings, emotions, tendencies of mind, and in order to work with them and begin to learn how to hold them in the context of this practice, in the context of mindfulness, we will attempt to actually evoke some emotions, draw them up out of the wellspring of our repertoire.

We all do carry the same repertoire of emotions. The basic ones—fear, sorrow, love—are pretty much everybody's, and we all have variations on them and put our personal story on them, but we all carry them all within us. They are part of the structure of being human, a part of our being.

It's interesting to look at the way our mind works and to notice, when you get lost in thought, when you're meditating, or even when, in your ordinary life, you find you've been working over something and it's all sort of in conscious thought form, to actually stop, close the eyes, go into the body, and feel what the emotion is underneath it. What is the engine that's driving it? Almost any thought you have, underneath it you can find some basic human feeling that is driving it. Most often it has something to do with fear.

Most of our thinking life is planning life, planning mind, trying to figure out what this environment right here is about, and how I fit into it, and why I feel insecure here, etc. It's all very, very primal stuff. And then we add all this sophisticated flowering of story on it, which is not bad; that's what we do with it. But when we forget about what's underneath it, when we lose touch with what's underneath it, we're dealing on this story level of who we are and we become very lost in it. When you drop down and touch the engines that are behind all this thinking, it's very, very liberating, because it's primal fear, primal anxiety, that you can feel. It is not yours, you don't own it, it's just there. It's part of being alive and of what one single organism that's concerned about its survival goes through. So part of going through and touching the emotional level of our being is really powerful practice.

[The third meditation also began as the participants brought their attention to whatever experience or sensations they might have with the breath. Mr. Nisker asked them then to check to see "if there's any feeling present, flavor of the mind, flavor of the heart, that is present within you this moment."]

Any kind of restlessness, any kind of anxiety. Perhaps there's a warmth or a joy. Whatever flavor or tone, emotional tone is present, see if you can experience it within your body. Where is it held? How does it feel? If you have trouble finding any particular emotional tone at this moment, recall some event, situation, difficulty, or happiness that you were having with a particular person. Visualize that person or situation and let the emotion associated with it arise into your heart, to your mind, into your body. Let yourself fill up completely with this feeling, holding it, touching it, saying yes to it, accepting it.

The key to working with emotional states in this practice is to say yes to them without letting them identify you or becoming identified with them. Anger, sadness, anxiety are all human qualities that arise at different times in all of us. To allow them, but not to allow them to identify us is the key.

[A woman mentioned that, at first, she had some discomfort with the emotions that arose in her. Toward the end of the meditation, however, she was better able to withdraw her resistance and let them arise.]

Wes Nisker: The minute you try to deny them and push them away, they stay there anyway. Often it creates a kind of unconscious conflict and tension in us that is never resolved because we try to push it away. This is walking that line between opening and not saying this is mine, or not identifying with it, but yet not pushing it away. So we're not repressing and we're not getting carried away by it. It's a powerful thing to do to say yes to what arises. The practice is not about getting rid of your personality or getting rid of any of these emotions that may arise, it's just not taking them quite so personally. When you start to get into the practice, your personality becomes like your pet. It comes up and you feed it and you keep it on a leash most of the time. Sometimes you let it go. It's what you've been given to take care of, but you don't really own it. It's just a little variation you're playing on the common themes of being human.

[This prompted another participant to bring up issues of attachment. He referred to being with a friend whose father had recently died. On the one hand, he empathized with her grief, while on the other he recognized that it was necessary to detach from the idea of the person who had died... "but then you start intellectualizing the whole process and you're not even grieving at all. You're thinking about it. You're analyzing it." He said that the "confusion between the viscera and the nonattachment to it is just confounding."]

Wes Nisker: I don't think there's really a conflict there. You go through a human existence and you grieve. That is part of the conditions that you're given. You have no choice over it. You grieve, you love, you hurt, all of it.

You die. It all is there at the beginning. To see it as not my grief but as the grief of being human gives it a space to live in. We don't drown in it. People that I've known that have done a lot of practice will go through grieving or intense emotions, but they always have a sense that there's a wider sense of acceptance of what this is. It's not quite so personal and individualized.

There was once a mother who came to the Buddha. She'd just lost her son and she said, "I can't go on. I'm going to kill myself. Can you help me at all?" He said, "Go to the village and go to a house and bring me back a mustard seed from a family who hasn't suffered a loss like this." Of course, she can't find anyone who hasn't suffered a loss like this, and she comes back to him, still very sad, but she has some other lightness about her because she has seen the universality of what she is going through.

It's putting it in a context. There are schools of Buddhism, teachers, who would be much harsher about it and say, What did you expect from life? This is the way it is. This is why you should become detached and independent of what happens in the world, so you don't grieve, and you don't go up and down, and you aren't tossed about by the events of the world. I don't think it's useful. It's kind of superhuman and some people would go for it, but I think there's a balance, a middle way.

In the first foundation of mindfulness on the body, the Buddha includes meditation on death and a number of times in the sutras he says to his disciples that, of all the mindfulness meditations that I teach, the mediation on death is supreme. In the sutra he teaches that the monks should take themselves to the charnel grounds, the place where they burn the bodies, and there they should sit and look upon the corpses. They should watch the disfiguration and decay of the corpses, then see them burning and watch, contemplating that they too have a body like this, and this is the inevitable end of that body. It's something our culture really tries to hide from us and it does a fairly effective job. As I'm beginning to get older and my friends are starting to die, it's a bit of a shock. There's no preparation for it. We really try to hide death away. Some of the Tibetan monks eat out of bowls made out of human skulls. It's like taking life, with death right there behind it.

The Buddha also gives comtemplations where you actually meditate on death. I think it's a really powerful, wonderful thing to do. It's like the Zen saying: Die before you die. Then when you die, you won't have to die. You've already done it.

Organic life transforms itself. It organizes itself in the most complex, wondrous way and then it decays, and it dies, and if there's any lesson that you need to know about the fact that your body is not yours, just try telling it when you would like it to die. It does its own thing. Apparently some of us are born with certain genes that are going to create a disease that's going to kill us when we're fifty, and some of us are going to go on longer.

Wes Nisker addressing a workshop

The Buddha, from the *Majjhima Nikaya:*

Did you ever see in the world a man or a woman eighty, ninety, or one hundred years old, frail, crooked as a gable roof, bent down, resting on crutches, with tottering steps, infirm, youth long since fled, with broken teeth, scanty hair or none, wrinkled, blotched limbs? Did the thought never come to you that you are also subject to the same decay, that you cannot escape it?

Did you ever see in the world a man or woman who, being sick, afflicted, and grievously ill, had to wallow in his own filth, was lifted up by some, put to bed by others? Did the thought never come to you that you are also subject to the same disease, that you cannot escape it?

Did you ever see in the world the corpse

of a man or a woman, one or two or three days after death, swollen up, blue-black in color, full of corruption? And did the thought never come to you that you are also subject to death and that you cannot escape it?

The Buddha didn't want us to turn away from any of the facts of life and especially not the end of life.

[After reestablishing a focus on the breath, Mr. Nisker led the group in this meditation on death.]

Closing your eyes, bring your attention to the breath, feeling the breath breathing you, the universe breathing you. Each breath is a gift; experience it, the energy that it brings into the body. Feel the heartbeat, the blood being circulated around the body.

Feeling this process of life inside of you, imagine or recognize that the muscle of your heart will grow weak, the muscle of your diaphragm will begin to wear out. Even if you don't die by any of the other numerous ways that you might, someday you will no longer be taking in energy. Energy will no longer be pumped to your limbs, to your brain. Without oxygen, the fuel of your life, your body will begin to grow cold. Imagine yourself perhaps lying down or, even as we sit here, not being able to move any of your limbs. If death came at this particular moment, all of your plans, your worries, all of that ephemeral thought would float away, would fade away like a radio receiver losing its power.

All of the story, this precious identity, all of your loved ones—all would disappear. If you were to die at this moment, at this time, what would you regret? What do you feel yourself missing or lacking? What do you feel sorrow about as you imagine your death at this moment? If you can fully imagine yourself dying at this moment, what emotion appears? Is it sadness? Is it fear? Perhaps you feel relief. There is an up-side—no more struggling with gravity; no more demands to feed this being, to keep the fuel going in. No more effort to keep the masks, the persona, in place. They're coming to pick up your corpse and take you to the hospital.

Bring the awareness slowly back into the breath and the heartbeat and the warmth of your body, the sense of aliveness that is present in this moment. Simply to be fully in this moment of aliveness.

[Mr. Nisker read several Japanese death poems written by samurai warriors, Zen masters, and others, all of which demonstrated an equanimity in the face of death that most Westerners would likely find inconceivable. A member of the workshop, who had recently spent two months in India, said that he was struck by Mr. Nisker's remark concerning the way that we in the West have pushed death away from us. He remarked that the experience had shown him "how hidden we are from the concept of impermanence in the West. When you go to a place like India you're overwhelmed by impermanence, decay, transition, bodies burning, and you can never get away from it.... You can't build a foundation of the paradigms that we have in the West to

sustain yourself in India, because every time you try to use the old paradigms....somebody hauls a body across in front you....Every time I started to get grounded, for some reason I'd have to go by where they burned the bodies, and you would see the embers at night....In the West, we even cover the mound of dirt with Astroturf at the grave sites."

This brought Mr. Nisker to the last element of his Dharma talk—the interconnections between our culture and the way we perceive the self.]

The understanding of self that we have has been culturally and historically constructed. It's brought us great benefits and a lot of material comforts, so that we even have the ability to mask some of the realities of impermanence and death. But the down-side is that we don't face them and we somehow don't incorporate them into our belief system or our lives.

The way people felt about being a person, being a human being in different times and in different cultures, didn't always feel like we feel about being a self. That's really interesting to contemplate and understand because then you begin to realize that the self you carry around with you is not self-created. It really is a product of history, a product of culture.

In *The Origin of Consciousness in the Breakdown of the Bicameral Mind,* Julian Jaynes describes how he studied the texts and literature from different cultures. He came to the conclusion that, in early Greece, around 1000 BCE, the notion of free will did

not exist. What they heard in their minds, their thought process, their decision-making process, they thought was literally the voice of the gods. He cites various examples of how people really believed that the gods were what were directing everyone's fate and thought process. It's hard for us to imagine what that was like.

Abraham, perhaps, is another example. Abraham thinks God is saying, "Kill your son," and he believes so much that whatever this god who is in charge of everything decides is right, he's willing to go and sacrifice his son. We can't imagine that kind of belief in an outside agency, in some external agent having that kind of effect, that kind of influence on our lives. It's just unimaginable to us.

I think that how much freedom you think you have goes along with how much self you believe in, how much you believe you are self-created. The more decisions you think you make without any external influences or conditions, the more you think you are separate from the world. The more independent you think you are, the more you think you're separate.

About five hundred years after *The Iliad,* you see in Greek civilization Socrates, Plato, Aristotle saying—and this is their great revelation—We control it. We can control all the contents of our own minds. And that may have been what launched the great fallacy of Western civilization. I sometimes think the planet is split in half, each half representing one hemisphere of the brain. We got the left hemisphere of the brain and they [Asia] got the right hemisphere of the brain. At that very same time period, Lao-tzu was in China and the Buddha was in India. They were looking inward for understanding, knowledge, wisdom, and they saw that they didn't control the functions of their mind, while Socrates and Plato were saying, We control them. Both were right, and wrong. Neither was fully right and neither was fully wrong, I think it's safe to say.

It was that sense that I can create my own reality that began really to separate us from the universe. In Christianity there's the idea of an individual soul that gets eternal salvation or damnation, while in the Old Testament there's much more of a sense of the tribal thing happening. Things happen to "the people." There are individuals that are doing the leading, but the people are saved. It's very much a communal thing and then it becomes an individual soul that gets saved.

The modern self, the one that we carry around with us today, has its roots back then, but it was really born in the Enlightenment era, in the fifteenth, sixteenth, seventeenth centuries, when there was a shift of consciousness. It was an emergent consciousness that somehow became so enamored of its own self, its own newly found powers and ability to reason and dissect reality, that the individual became further separated from the world. The Enlightenment thinkers started saying, We have power. God doesn't have power. The Church doesn't know what's right and wrong. We can decide what's right and wrong for ourselves. This mind is really so wonderful and independent it can manipulate the world. The world doesn't have mind.

Matter doesn't have mind. The individual mind is all-powerful, can really manipulate truth, can manipulate matter. Soul, spirit, was taken out of the world.

The kind of fascination with the self, the individualism, that we are living with, perhaps to an even more extreme degree, may have been born in Europe but I think has been fully developed here in America, the land of personalized license plates. This is where we have given it full reign.

It's interesting, too, to think that the self that was born in the Enlightenment era was raised alongside of capitalism. At the same time that that self was being born, the whole feudal system and all the old roles were breaking down. Before the Modern era, people didn't decide what job they were going to have or what religion they would prefer or would meet their own personal convictions. They didn't choose spouses. They didn't choose jobs. They didn't choose social classes. You're born. That's that. There's no sense of personal autonomy that we have now. Then, here in America, you could really create your own identity. You could create your own social class if you were tough enough and strong enough and you could create your own upward mobility. You could really re-create yourself. That was the belief.

A historian studied advice manuals, pamphlets, and magazine articles that, up until the end of the 1800s, had emphasized character. That was the quality that defined an individual. A person of character was a sort of Victorian ideal, someone who had forbearance, was upstanding, moral, and soft-spoken. Around the end of the 1800s the emphasis shifted from the word *character* to the word *personality.* "Personality" was used for someone that had a kind of flamboyance, could charm other people, and was independent of what they added to the community in terms of utilitarian value, the jobs they did. What was important about them was just how they presented themselves. And the whole idea that you could create your personality, that you could actually work on it and develop at least a facade, whether it was true or not, all those ideas of how independent you are, of how much of a separate self you are, how much that has changed over time and how now it seems like we are really lost in a world of our own. The sense is that we act, behave, think, and do everything disconnected from the world, disconnected from the past, from other people, from the sunlight, from the water. There's this really fragmented sense.

I think what's really important is not to condemn it. It's not anybody's fault. Perhaps it goes with a certain movement of evolutionary history. The self comes with lots of benefits. It's certainly given us a sense of our own personal power and freedom, that we could actually do this practice and become enlightened or lose our sense of individuality. Our individuality gives us the sense that we could actually lose our individuality. That is not to be condemned, but to understand that so much of who we think we are and how it feels to be ourselves, is culturally created, is culturally, historically determined.

Don't take it so personally—that's really the message of Buddhism. I think that, if we truly take the understanding that we have here at the end of the twentieth century and translate it, make it personal, make it real, we start to come to that place of not taking this personal existence so personally. We look at ourselves in the mirror of our culture and we can see the distortion, that something is vitally wrong, and there is a hunger for connection and reconnection. I know of no better way than through this particular kind of practice. You don't have to call it Buddhist. You don't have to call it meditation, if you don't want to. But going inside and experiencing, on the level of experience, on the level that brings it into a deep, cellular kind of awareness, and going in over and over again to do that is what it requires. It's not a habit you suddenly understand—Oh, yeah. I'm not really independent. I'm connected to everything I see and everything that came before me. You have to go and learn that lesson almost on a daily basis, like you would practice the piano, so that it becomes more and more the reality that you live with.

Gary Snyder has a wonderful statement about meditation:

Wisdom is the intuitive knowledge of the mind of love and clarity that lies beneath one's ego-driven anxieties and aggressions. Meditation is going into that mind to see it for yourself over and over again until it becomes the mind you live in.

That's why we call it a practice, because

you're never done. What you're working with really is the whole of history, the whole of evolution as it brought you to this moment when you're working with practice.

Robert Thurman says Buddhist meditation is an evolutionary sport. I think that's a great definition because you're working with the moment that you arrive in this life and what you're offered is the chance to see if you can evolve your own consciousness; if that's at all possible. We may not ever know the amount of freedom we actually have in any given moment, but I think we greatly exaggerate the amount we do have. Whatever amount we have, I think that to apply it to seeing clearly how much we don't have is really our task and a joyous task.

There's a lot of call in the world of environmentalism for saving the planet not so that humans can keep living, but really to understand that we *are* nature and our destructiveness is the destructiveness of life. We're a part of it and to separate ourselves and say somehow that we're different or more valuable is absurd. The problem is how to give people the experience of that, aside from being in the wilderness for months and experiencing it on a life-and-death level. I think that Buddhist meditation practices can give us a sense of our embeddedness in the natural world. Using these practices can give us a real sense of not-separateness, a real sense of connectedness.

It's all natural. The concrete is made out of sand and seashells and the plastic is made out of forests that disappeared. I think people who put out plastic products should put on the side, *All natural*. Our language shows

how removed we are when a winter snow-storm is a "natural disaster," but we don't talk about our wars as natural disasters. That's in a different category, as if what we do is somehow removed from natural.

[The final meditation—on sound—was introduced as being a particularly good practice to do outdoors. Mr. Nisker pointed out that "meditating on sound is a wonderful way to create a kind of spaciousness in the mind, a kind of all-encompassing state of mind. It's a good practice to have in your tool kit when you're really feeling like you want to open up to the world."]

Buddhism is really about life. Practice is about all of life. There are really two prongs to Buddhism: You can see one as an existential practice, a practice of just sitting and being present with what is—it's not about doing anything. The other is a more active, investigative aspect of the practice: What is this? Who is this sitting? It's a little more looking. It's coming into the moment. This meditation on sound is more of an existential, open-to-the-world-and-just-sit-there practice.

Bring your attention to a sense of hearing without feeling the need to name or identify any sound. Simply let the sounds, the waves, play across your sense of hearing, noticing how it's continually changing. Sound is a continual flow that you cannot stop. No resting in any moment of sound. It just keeps moving. With sound, it's easy to get a sense of receiving. Just let your ears be open. There's nothing else you need to do.

Now sense or visualize that the edge of

your awareness reaches out to touch the farthest sound you can hear, creating a vast space of consciousness. Knowing that your hearing connects you to the source of the farthest sounds that you can hear, your awareness is that vast and expansive. Staying with the sounds, let the edges of your awareness dissolve so that the space of mind becomes as big as the sky, open, holding onto nothing, accepting everything. The farthest sound you can hear and beyond, and into this vast sky of mind thoughts arise and float through. You can feel the breath in the center. Everything appears and disappears, liberating itself. Can you see that awareness, too, arises in this space?

You have a lifetime left to work with these meditation techniques and it'll probably take you that long to perfect them. They're wonderful and I recommend that you try this at home—every day. Choose a practice that you want to work with, that feels good to you, and work with it. Remember that you are doing it for all of us, because you are all of us; that the level of consciousness that you achieve, the amount of wakefulness that you achieve, is really ours. We inherit it commonly, the level that we're stuck with at this point in history and what we pass on is also in common. It's not easy work, but it is the only way I know to really break out of the suffering and to begin to heal ourselves, and heal the extremes of our culture, and perhaps make it a little easier, the world, life.

Acculturation or Innovation

MEDITATION AND RITUAL PRACTICE IN AMERICAN BUDDHISM

Ven. Samu Sunim

AN ISSUE FREQUENTLY RAISED AT THE CONFERENCE was the validity of late-twentieth-century Americans adopting age-old Asian rituals and ceremonies. Each dialogue revealed an array of approaches and beliefs, from the imperative of maintaining strict adherence to traditional practice to the feeling that ancient practices from foreign cultures alienate and deter Western practitioners from their spiritual path.

Ven. Samu Sunim's description of this workshop is a cogently encompasses this potentially divisive issue: "The largest and most flourishing Buddhist movements in America today are ethnic movements represented by Asian Buddhist immigrants under the leadership of charismatic or missionary-style monks. Ethnic Buddhists are generally tradition-minded, support monastic Buddhism, and engage in ritual and devotional practice as their main cultivation. However, the most visible and perhaps most important form of Buddhism in America is the development of English-speaking Western Buddhist groups. They are liberal-minded, practice meditation, and promote lay Buddhism. They represent a new brand of Buddhism. As a foreign religion, Buddhism faces major challenges in the West. Therefore, it is crucial to understand Buddhist traditions correctly and to discover the contemporary in the Buddhist teachings in order to respond appropriately to the needs of changing times and to formulate a Buddhist vision that transcends cultures."

Dharma successor to Zen Master Solgbong Sunim, Ven. Samu Sunim came to North America from his native South Korea in 1967. Following a three-year solo retreat, he began teaching Zen meditation in Toronto. He is president of the Buddhist Society for Compassionate Wisdom and founding teacher and Zen Master of the society's three temples in Toronto, Ann Arbor, and Chicago, and of a growing *sangha* in Mexico City. He also serves on the International Advisory Board of the Council for a Parliament of the World's Religions.

I'd like to give you the four personal daily cultivations that are like meditation in action. The first is *hapchang* practice. *Hapchang* is a Korean word for *anjali* in Sanskrit, or *gassho* in Japanese.

Hapchang and the three prostrations are very basic Buddhist practice. In all Buddhist traditions they do these. Each of us has these two sides, positive and negative—strength and weakness—so we bring these two together. You know sometimes people try to reject their negative side or fight it, but you can never fight it, you can never win. Your negative side is also yours and is employable, so we have to bring these two together.

There are three basic *hapchangs* and I will just do one. In this *hapchang* you bring two hands together, palm to palm; right thumb, covering the left, is held vertically in front of your nose. And this is called a "*hapchang* of a sincere heart." It helps to say it out loud: "*hapchang* of a sincere heart." So everyone has a sincere heart. It's your buddha nature, so you can always rely on that.

Hapchang practice is also the practice of waking up. You have to raise your hands up and then you pay more attention and you become more attentive, more mindful. Mindfulness is meditation in action, so it will wake you up. And you can do morning *hapchang* practice upon waking up and also in the evening or preferably before your bedtime.

Three years ago there was statistical information published in the newspapers that a lot of Americans have trouble enjoying a good night's sleep. We live in a business world and that can be a big problem if you miss sleep. So at the end of the day, just before you retire, you sit up and do *hapchang* practice in order to close the day peacefully and in reconciliation.

We do live in a very stressful society, so even in the span of a single day a lot of things can happen, both pleasant and unpleasant. All these things get stored away in your psyche and then you retire, so no wonder you cannot enjoy a good sleep. Then, when you wake up, you are still confused and then you have to rush to go to work. So then days and months pass and people fall apart and depend on chemical solutions to go through the day.

So Buddhists practice this *hapchang* when they are young. You do *hapchang* practice and bring the two sides together, your buddha side, your liberated side. Sometimes they come into conflict, like your enlightened side wants to go to a Buddhist monastery and your unenlightened side wants to go to a bordello or something like that. So you bring these two sides together with *hapchang* practice. To end the day peacefully will take about one or two minutes. If you do that, your mind wakes up and you can sit for five minutes before you retire, and that's very good.

Also, if you are so inclined, since your mind is awake, you can keep a journal and that's also a good habit. Then you retire and you can have a good sleep and when you wake up the following morning your mind is fresh to face another day. It's a very simple liberating technique coming from Buddhism or Indian custom, but you have to do it.

Ven. Samu Sunim

Now, the three prostrations. Buddhists always do three prostrations when they come to the temple—to Buddha, Dharma, and *sangha;* to the three jewels. But it also implies the threefold training: That's moral discipline, and meditation or some other concentration, and then unfoldment of wisdom. So it always reminds you of these threefold trainings.

Meditation is based on this threefold training, so that when you sit, the moral discipline is the pure heart. Purification takes place as a kind of a side effect and you develop a single heart. So single mind and pure heart. The three prostrations are not just honoring the three jewels, but also it reminds you of the threefold training. When we ring the bell we ring it three times at the

beginning of meditation. It's threefold training.

Then there is also three jewels practice, like Buddha, Dharma, and *sangha*. So once a day, preferably in the morning, you can do Buddha practice, and then in midday or early afternoon you can do Dharma practice, and in late afternoon you can do *sangha* practice. But you should, at least once a day, do Buddha practice, once a day do Dharma practice, and once a day do *sangha* practice.

Buddha practice is waking up. For instance, when something fails or when something breaks down, our first reaction is to blame someone else or the government—the bad guy. But then it occurs to you at a little-bit-more-advanced stage to blame yourself—I'm responsible for this, it's my fault. But a still better attitude is waking up and seeing that it's both yourself and other people. So it's waking up.

Dharma practice is like wisdom practice, always something you can learn. There is the old proverb that if you have the company of three people, someone out of the three will become your teacher. There is always something to learn, so try to find wisdom from ordinary things. That's Dharma practice.

Sangha practice is always trying to do something once a day for yourself and for others. Something like picking up trash on the street. There is always something you can do, you know, just simple friendship or kindness. So those are Buddha, Dharma, and *sangha* practice.

And then there's the six *paramitas,* also called the six perfections. The first, or *dana, paramita* is "May I be generous and helpful." *Shila-paramita,* "May I be pure and virtuous," is the second. And then *kshanti-paramita* is "May I be patient, energetic, and persevering." This is called the practice of virtues and merits.

Kusan Sunim, the late Korean Zen Master, had a method to promote the six *paramitas* among his followers. He would say Monday is *dana-paramita* day—May I be generous and helpful. Then Tuesday is the second *paramita*—May I be pure and virtuous—and so on. So it helps to have something on which you can focus each day for Dharma practice.

Then there is this *gatha* practice, which kind of comes from monastic practice. *Gatha* are short Dharma verses. We have a book for

everyday *gatha.* Robert Aitken Roshi of the Diamond Sangha put out this wonderful book called *The Dragon Who Never Sleeps.* In it he writes, "Waking up in the morning, I vow with all beings to flow with each moment of the day and rejoice being among the living." Also, "When the doctor pokes here and there, I vow with all beings to consider my cellular structure will all come apart soon enough."

You can even make up your own practices. This one is a purifying practice that comes from the *Avatamsaka Sutra* (Thomas Cleary's translation): "When I see flowing water, I vow with all beings to develop a wholesome will and wash away the stains of delusion." So that's the *gatha* practice, and you can have an early morning *gatha* practice and midmorning *gatha* practice and then you can come up with your own Dharma verse when your tension rises or when stress arises or when you have difficulty dealing with your boss or coworkers or something.

Now, regarding meditation practice, I usually say you should do five minutes for a minimum practice, because people lead a very complex life, so if I tell them to do thirty-minute meditations, then they really struggle with those thirty minutes. Sometimes people get really insistent about meditation practice and say, "Sunim, I can do one hour of meditation practice every day or every morning and every evening," and then I tell myself internally, This guy's not going to last very long.

It's a wisdom practice, a minimum practice, so you start always with the minimum —five minutes—then, no matter how busy you are, you still have five minutes. Because if you have ten minutes or fifteen minutes or twenty minutes you can always sit more.

Having said that, a little discipline is important. An English Christian theologian who studied Zen for many years put out this book, *Into Every Household a Little Zen Should Flow.* It's an interesting title. So you can always use a little Zen discipline, which would help. That means, if you wake up around 6:30 or 7:00, then give yourself about fifteen minutes to worship. Also it's a very good idea to go briefly outside, even in cold winter, to do a little bit of stretching. And then you come back in and have a big glass of spring water or cold water. That's called the Buddhist philosophy of drinking a big glass of water and being able to forget all your ills. It's also very good for your body.

Then it's also good to do the thirty-six prostrations; then your body-mind settles. Sometimes even five minutes, depending on the kind of work you do. If you are a lawyer or an academic, then already your head is busy trying to organize the day. Or if you have young children running around, so you are not in the space of mind to sit still quietly, then you should do prostrations. It helps your body-mind to settle.

You do *hapchang* practice before the meal and recite the meal grace to develop a grateful heart, which is very important. I usually give the three foundation stones and one of them is gratitude. So always make sure you start out the day with a grateful heart. It will make a big difference.

Healing breath is breathing out, but you have to get in the habit of that, you have to breathe out on purpose. We breathe in and out all the time mechanically, but you really have to breathe out, like deep breathing. You breathe out through the open mouth and breathe in through the nose, and make a sound. If you make sound, then it helps psychologically; then you are doing something. For instance, when you develop resentment or ill feelings or hatred or whatever, or when you get upset, instead of trying to cling or hold on to that, you breathe out.

So it's a letting-go practice and it's very helpful. It so happens that in Michigan the schoolchildren are so restless and so scattered they just cannot concentrate on their studies. So some teachers got together to try to find ways in which they can help these kids to come down and concentrate on what they are studying. They came out with this idea: They would start the class with a breathing exercise, just to help them calm down. Then the parents found out that these are a kind of yoga or meditation and they came out with such an uproar, it's simply breathing out, but they had to stop it So, it's good to do early morning healing breath, and midmorning and early afternoon, three or five times a day. That's building good habits.

Now there is also the practice of having power movements. Traditional Buddhism has all these techniques to help you at every stage. Actually, there is a *gatha* mantra of enjoying a good bowel movement. It goes something like this: You go to the outhouse and sit down and then recite this *gatha* and the mantra and it says, "After great push, and after that great let go. And great joy and happiness prevails." They repeat it three times and it's each stage of having a bowel movement, and how to wipe your bum nicely. If you go and visit a Korean-temple outhouse or bathroom there is this plaque, which says PAVILION FOR RELEASING YOUR ANXIETY. It's quite a feeling.

The Zen experience has four qualities: It's intimate, it's immediate, it's spontaneous, and obvious. And the bowel movement has all that. It's a Zen experience—always direct and authentic experience that is prior to your thoughts and before your concepts arise and before emotions appear. So that's very important in Zen sitting. And scholars try to write about the experience of having a bowel movement, but the best thing is for you to go and have one.

Now I'll go over these life cycles, and this would be very helpful for people doing Buddhist ministry, like a priest or monk. It's blessing or honoring newborn babies as future buddhas and bodhisattvas. This is very very important. For instance, celebration of a buddha's birthday, like a baby buddha, the whole concept is that in the Dharma practice it says how human birth—being born in the human body—is a very precious experience. That's the first one.

One Buddhist environmentalist said that it would be more precious to be born as an alligator because there are too many human beings. But I think the one reason for this saying is human beings can wake up and help themselves and others. So it's a blessing to people who have newborn babies.

They can bring their newborn babies on a proper day and then it's like a sacred offering to the great tradition of wisdom and compassion. Then the temple priest comes and gives blessings, holding his hand on the head. It's like a prediction—You will become buddha; you are destined to become buddha—and to help them discover their original mind.

Buddha's birthday is the best day, of course. We always have a children's service in our temple. Then we have refuge-taking on Buddha's birthday at the end of the children's service. So these are children who are able to recite after the temple priest, maybe three-, four-, and five-year-olds. At fifteen years or older they can take the five precepts, or at least the first precept. There are people who are reluctant to take all five precepts because they are afraid of breaking them, but at least you can give them the first precept, which is the most important and is about nonviolence: "At least in this lifetime I renounce all violence, all hatred, and engaging in all abusive activities." The positive side is to practice love and compassion.

On your birthday, it is a good thing to express your gratitude or your indebtedness, not only to your relatives and parents, but to your friends. We are all indebted to all for being alive and for being born as well. So instead of having your friends bring gifts to you, you give gifts to express your gratitude. That makes more sense, and then you have the temple priest teach a little Dharma to make your birthday more meaningful. That's the basic spirit and you can come up with your own structure.

There is also a self-purification or repentance ceremony, and this is very, very important. We all make mistakes, so how to renew ourselves, and prevent ourselves from retrogressing, and to go forward? This has not taken root in American *sangha*.

The Buddhist wedding is called a flower wedding ceremony, for the engaged or betrothed couple pledge themselves to their marriage through the exchange of flowers. This customary ceremony is based on an instant that took place in one of Shakyamuni Buddha's previous lives.

In this previous life, before he became a buddha, Shakyamuni Buddha was known as Megha, a spiritual seeker and wandering mendicant monk. After completing his study with his teacher in the Himalayas, he came down from the mountains and was visiting towns and villages, begging alms in order to pay his teacher the tuition that he owed. When he entered the city of Dipavati, he found that the whole city was bedecked with flowers and banners. People were in a festive mood and he wondered what holiday or festival this might be. Just then a young, attractive, Brahmin girl came along, and she had a water jug and seven lotus flowers in her hands. He asked her, "Is there a festival in the city today?"

She replied with these verses:

You cannot, young man, be a native of this place.
A stranger from another city you must be.
You do not know that there is coming to this town

The Benefactor of the World, the Bringer of the Light!
Dipankara, the leader of the world....
He, a greatly famous Buddha,
Is drawing near. To honor him this city
Is decked in gay and festive garb.

Megha asked her to sell him five lotus flowers so that he, too, could honor the coming buddha. She agreed to sell the flowers on the condition that in all future lives he would take her as his wife.

Megha said, "My heart is set on supreme enlightenment. How can I think of marriage?"

She answered, "No need to desist from your quest. I shall not hinder you."

So Megha consented, and said, "In exchange for those lotuses, I take you for my wife. I will be able to worship Dipankara, the Lord, and continue to strive for supreme enlightenment."

"A sublime joy and exaltation had taken hold of his body when he had heard the maiden speak of the Buddha." (This is quoted from *Buddhist Scriptures,* translated by Edward Conze.)

Mindful of this instant, the engaged couple exchange flowers and marry each other as spiritual companions. Aside from their significance in the above story, the flowers have a further natural symbolism. The period of one's wedding is compared with the flowering season of the plant kingdom. Following, the flowers and leaves come out and fruits are born after the wedding. Children are born in due course and the husband and wife become parents. So the cycle turns and the wheel of life moves on.

Now, there are three parts to this Buddhist wedding. The first part is procession: The bride and groom carry candle lights and then they offer the candles on the altar and they burn incense and offer a bowl of tea. Then I, as the officiating priest, lead the three refuges, and then I give the five precepts to serve as ethical guidelines for their shared life together. If they don't want to, I just do one precept—at least to renounce violence, because of domestic violence, to honor each other. So spiritual partnership is very emphasized.

Then, after having taken the precepts, we ask them to greet their parents and parents-in-law to express their gratitude. The parents always love that, so they go and express their gratitude for raising them up and all those things. And that's the end of the first part.

The second part is exchanging flowers. The bride gives five stems to the groom and the groom gives two stems, and they hold the flowers together and then they sing music that goes with it. The officiating priest then will take the flowers and offer them to the altar, to the Buddha.

And then ceremonial bows. They perform one ceremonial bow that sort of embraces the whole universe in their marriage. That means that they'll be taking care of all beings in the universe as spiritual companions, and then also mutual respect, mutual love, and mutual care is emphasized in this ceremony.

They then take their written vows; they can come up with their own vows, but we have three simple vows. Then they exchange gifts over a bowl of pure water, which is the water of life. Then they hold each other's hands in blessing, and that's the end of the second part.

I declare them as fully married husband and wife, and if there's something to be signed, the documents can be signed, and I invite parents or relatives or friends to come forward and give congratulatory remarks. And then they kiss each other if they like. This is so erotic that usually you don't do that in front of the altar, not in traditional Buddhist societies.

That's the short version of a Buddhist wedding. And then on the proper occasion I bring the ceremony to a close by reciting Buddha's *Golden Chain of Love*.

Relationship and Intimacy as Path

Tsultrim Allione

PRACTICING RIGHT RELATIONSHIP IS PERHAPS THE GREATEST CHALLENGE contemporary Western Buddhists face as they continue to develop a *sangha*. In her keynote address, Tsultrim Allione spoke at many levels, from the personal to the global. She explored relationship and intimacy as a part of practice and posited ways they can become a path to liberation. Bringing to bear a wide spectrum of traditions, from the basic precepts of Buddhism and Tantric teachings, to poems by Rumi and the slogans of Atisha, she looked at the choices one must make and how they can assist us on this path. As she noted, "From the choices of simplicity and renunciation, to expansive love and understanding of egolessness, to the transformation of the poisons into wisdom in Vajrayana, at every turn of the path we meet ourselves in relationship."

Born and raised in New England, Tsultrim Allione developed an interest in Buddhism at an early age through her grandmother, who was a professor of philosophy. She has been practicing Tibetan Buddhism for more than twenty-eight years. In the late 1960s, she traveled in India and Nepal, where she was ordained and lived as a Tibetan nun for several years. During this time, she received teaching from Kalu Rinpoche, Sapchu Rinpoche, Dudjom Rinpoche, Dilgo Khentse Rinpoche, Khamtrul Rinpoche, as well as her principal teacher, Apho Rinpoche. Taking heed of the call to give birth to a child, she left the monastic life and returned to America, where she joined the faculty of Naropa Institute in 1976. In 1993, she founded Tara Mandala, a retreat center in Colorado. For the last fifteen years, she has studied with Namkhai Norbu Rinpoche and teaches under his guidance. She is the author of *Women of Wisdom,* the biographies of six Tibetan women teachers and an exploration of the feminine in Buddhism and woman's spiritual quest.

L ast winter I was in retreat in my cabin in Colorado, which is way up on a ridge, and you can see for hundreds of miles from this place. I was thinking about what to talk about here, and I was reading a book of Rumi poems. I want to read you the poem that inspired me to choose this topic of relationship as path.

When you are with everyone but me,
    you are with no one.
When you are with no one but me,
    you are with everyone.
Instead of being so bound up with everyone,
    be everyone.
When you become that many,
    you are nothing, empty.

To me, that poem is about relationship in practice. So I decided at that moment to speak about relationship. In thinking about what makes us unique as a Western *sangha* I realized that one of the main differences that we have from the Eastern *sangha* is we are a lay *sangha* that's giving birth to a monastic *sangha*. In India it was the other way around —it was a monastic *sangha* that gave birth to a lay *sangha*. And, in fact, we are predominantly a lay community, so we are naturally concerned about, and relating to, each other very intimately and sometimes with great difficulty.

I was also thinking about the whole Earth, the fact that in 1961 there were 3.2 billion people on the Earth, and now there are 5.5 billion people on the Earth. So it's almost doubled. By the year 2000, 20 percent of the life forms now extant on Earth could be extinct. We are in intimate relationship with all life. I want to talk about our intimate relationship as we normally think of intimate relationship, but also intimate relationship in terms of us being in relationship with all life. Because there are so many of us, it's getting so crowded, we are forced to be in relationship with everyone.

In the Rumi poem, when it says, *When you are with everyone but me, you are with no one,* to me, that *me* is the vast presence— and also the minute presence of intimacy. When we're not there with that other— which is vast presence and also our intimate relationship with each other— there's no connection; there's no awareness of interconnectedness. *When you are with no one but me, you are with everyone.* When we focus and stop grasping, the whole universe is one. *When you become that many, you are nothing, empty.* In that focus of being really present with each other, we are empty.

I read this poem and got very inspired, and I wrote the blurb for the talk. I was up there all alone in a blizzard and it all made perfect sense. Then my partner, David, came up. And we got in a big argument. So I thought, Oh, no! I think I'd better change my subject! And then I thought, it's really not about being perfect. It's not about having the perfect relationship. It's really about being able to see relationship as a mirror and as an opportunity to practice. In some way, the irritation is the path. The irritation triggers us back into awareness, turns the mind around. I realized that it's really not about the perfect couple disappearing into the sunset. It's really about becoming present with each other.

There was a time, when I was a nun in Nepal and I was way up in the mountains with Lama Zopa, and another woman was there, and there was also Lama Zopa's sister. Now Lama Zopa is a monk, and this woman was flirting with him. This was really irritating his sister, so she stopped making good tea for this woman. She was giving her less and less milk, and less and less potatoes when we ate. Up there, you can't go to a cafe, so she was completely dependent on the sister, who kept decreasing her rations. Finally she went to Lama Zopa and she said, "You know, this is really a problem. I can't stand your sister. You've got to talk to her about giving me more milk in my tea, and more potatoes," which was all we ate. And he said, "Well, you know, I'm really not your teacher here. She is."

So in that spirit, I think all of our problems with each other are really our greatest teachers, and sometimes, when it goes well, we could get lost in the God realm. The image that came to me when I was thinking about relationship was an oyster; that the two sides of the oyster are like the two people in the relationship. The grit that comes into the oyster, that has to be digested, is everything that happens in our lives together. And sometimes we manage to make a pearl, but we only make a pearl through the grit.

There was an early Tantric teacher called Suraha. He was a monk, and eventually he left monastic life. He was told to find a teacher who was an arrowsmith woman in the marketplace. He went from one arrowsmith to the other, trying to figure out who

this teacher would be. Eventually he found a woman who was incredibly intent on her arrow, unwavering, so he approached her and said, "Excuse me, are you an arrowsmith?" She looked at him, and she said, "My dear young man, the Buddha's teaching can be known through symbols and actions, not through words and books."

So he began to live with her and study with her, and at a certain point in their relationship he asked her if she would make some radish curry. She said, "Sure, I'll make you radish curry." And he said, "Well, while you make it, I'm going to go meditate for a little while." Well, he meditated for twelve years. When he came out of meditation, he asked about the radish curry—those were the first words out of his mouth!—and she said, "You sit in *samadhi* for twelve years without getting up, and now you want radish curry, as if it was even still in season!" So he said, "Okay, if you won't make me radish curry, I'll go to the mountains and mediate." To which she said, "Simply removing your body from the world is not true renunciation. Real renunciation is when your mind abandons frivolous and absorbing thoughts. If you're still attached to radish curry, what's the point of going to the mountains?"

What greater teachers do we have than our intimate relationships? Our partners, children, parents, ex-husbands, ex-wives, our students, our bosses, our colleagues. When you really think about it, who is it that you really learn from? There's a Dzogchen phrase that means to return existence to its original condition, which is turning the flow of being everyone *but* me around into pure, relaxed presence.

So how can relationship turn the mind around, grind the grit into a pearl?

And what does accepting relationship as path have to do with us as practitioners?

And what does it do with what effect we have on the world?

These were my questions, so I decided, as I always do, I had to look at my own experience, because nothing's real if it's not from your own experience. I thought about my life, becoming a nun when I was twenty-two. At that time I had complete freedom to practice, no problems with relationship, ecstatic experiences, no anger, no jealousy. But I had a problem with passion, which is why I'm not a nun anymore. At that point, it just kept bubbling up. As I turned twenty-six, it was getting extreme, and I thought, This couldn't be good; I don't think I should keep doing this. So I went to my teacher, Apho Rinpoche, a wonderful mountain yogi who has four children, and I said to him, "Rinpoche, I keep dreaming about babies." And he said, "All nuns should have babies." I said, "Rinpoche, I don't know how much longer I should keep being a nun." And he said, "It depends how much longer you can stand it," and then he started laughing, and he laughed so hard he started drooling. Then he sort of was rolling around in his bed! And so I started laughing, and then we were both laughing and rolling around on the bed. I gave back my vows the next day.

What happened next was, I got pregnant, almost immediately. This baby that I had been dreaming about, arrived. I knew I was pregnant because I thought I might be and a friend of mine said, "Does the world look completely different?" I said, "Yes, it does." And she said, "I think you're pregnant." Then all those emotions I thought I didn't have anymore, like anger, jealousy, depression, all started to come up again. And I started to do very bizarre things. I broke an egg into the frying pan and the yolk broke, and I burst into tears and threw the frying pan across the room. Now, this was completely out of character; I felt like everything was completely out of control.

I had no time to practice once my first baby came, and I ended up having four children in five years. I calculated once that I had seven years without a full night's sleep because of one of them coming into bed. During that time, only what I had deeply understood stayed with me. All the theory was out the window. I kept trying to get back to my cushion. I kept trying to say, "I've got to practice! I've got to practice!" But I couldn't get there. It was just impossible. From morning until I collapsed at night, on and on it went.

In this process of having four children, the last two were twins. My second twin, at two and a half months, died of sudden infant-death syndrome. When my teacher, Nahmkhai Norbu Rinpoche, came to do the funeral he went in and did some things, put some mandalas and put some sand from a sand mandala on her body and so on. She was in the morgue at the hospital in Italy, where I was living. Then he came outside. This would be the last time I would see her body before she went away, and I was completely full of emotion. I threw my arms around him, weeping, and he just stood there, and it was almost like when I threw my arms around him, his shoulders dropped down and he relaxed; he relaxed completely. Instead of holding me back, which was what I expected, I had this completely unexpected response from him, and in that moment the world turned around—that experience of existence returning to its original condition.

I felt my mind go out and become totally vast; and I saw this event as a little blip in history, and I thought of all the other women all over the world who had lost babies, and how much more protected I was from this experience than most, because of living in the West. And I realized that at every moment, we have a choice. There's a word in Sanskrit which means "coemergent." This means that, at any moment, we have a choice. Do we go with attachment, with ignorance, with passion? Or do we make that slight shift and go into vastness and rest in our true nature? That extreme experience with him, when I was probably in the most extreme moment of all the ways that human beings can get tied up, was so intense that it broke completely for a moment.

Another time, when I was giving birth to my daughter, I remembered the story of Naropa and Tilopa. Naropa was Tilopa's stu-

dent, and one time Tilopa told Naropa to jump off a tower. When he jumped off and was all squished on the ground, Tilopa came up to him and said, "Believing in an 'I' will always cause pain and suffering." So I remembered this as I was in labor, and I stayed in that level. The way I saw it at the time was there were these waves of pain, and I was staying right here, just slightly ahead of the wave, not grasping on to that belief in an 'I.'

This winter, when I was in the cabin, one day I got into a funk, a depression (as you can in a retreat), that seems to come out of nowhere and get very solid very quickly. So I decided I'd go out for a walk, try to work this out with a walk. I ended up going way, way down. My cabin's way, way up, so going way down you have to go way back up afterward. After I went way down, it didn't get any better, and then I was walking up and I was thinking, Why did I go way, way down? Now I have to go way, way up again. And it didn't help, so by the time I got to the top, I was in exactly the same state as I had been when I'd gone way, way down.

So I looked at this wall in front of me, and suddenly I remembered that I could make a very slight shift. And I did; I just dropped it. I just shifted into that coemergent wisdom, which is always there, just dropped this whole thought thing that I was in. It was like a sort of hunk. It was almost like sidestepping it, and suddenly there was a huge vastness in front of me. And the word that came to me means "great space" in Tibetan.

Sometimes in relationship, things are not as they should be, and we get the feeling this is not as I want it to be. I was reminded of this this Christmas. We went to Ecuador, and on the airplane they show a video of Ecuador—all these really beautiful rain forests and mountains and so on. And I thought, Wow, this is really an incredible place, and I was in that experience. It was like looking at the pictures of the Bahamas in the magazines. Then we got there, and we were in the rain forest, and there were five different kinds of ants that could bite you, and these humongous mosquitoes. So we were sort of covered with mosquitoes, boiling hot, and trying to understand the interrelationship of all things.

I think relationship's like that—we keep looking for the video version, but we keep getting dysentery. Sometimes there's too much grit in the oyster; sometimes there's too many bites, and a relationship ends. But that's part of the path, too. We can't always make a pearl, and that teaches us impermanence and grasping.

A lama I know was married and he split up with his wife, and I said, "Why did you split up?" I thought, Now, how could a lama get divorced? And he said, "We weren't generating *bodhichitta* anymore." *Bodhichitta* is the thought toward *bodhi,* expansiveness in our hearts. So when we're not generating *bodhichitta* anymore, it doesn't make sense to stay together. But even when we're separating, it's important to hold the essence.

Some friends were getting divorced, or they thought they were, and a friend said to them, "You know, I have one piece of advice to give you, and that is to talk to each other for a half-hour every day. During that time, what I want you to do is just hold a vision of your partner's essence. Talk about anything you want, but try to keep holding that vision of that person's buddha-nature, that awakened being that you saw when you fell in love." They ended up staying together, but I think even if we don't stay together, if we can keep holding each other in that way, no matter what happens, that's still practice; that's still path.

When I thought about how I hold relationship as practice, the way that I decided that I really try to hold it is with the three vows, and the three robes that Guru Rinpoche wears—the robes of the Hinayana, the Mahayana, and the Vajrayana. The Hinayana is the path of renunciation, which is mindfulness and not causing harm, holding to vows and precepts, which, in the West, sometimes we think we're beyond; that precepts are sort of like the Catholic Church or the Methodist Church or the Commandments, that they're not important. But they are important. They're really the base. Then the Mahayana, the training of the mind—the first is the taming of the mind—the training of the mind in emptiness and compassion. And finally, the Vajrayana, which is the experience of the continuity of luminosity; the transformation of poisons into path. The image of the peacock is used, that the poisons actually become the path.

So the first one, the renunciation of harming the other, means renunciation of harmful action. The Tibetan word means "hindering" and is usually translated as "sin" or "negative action." But Norbu Rinpoche said it actually means "hindering," and what it's hindering is our experience of our true nature.

The first thing that happens when we fall in love is we become incredibly insecure because we're so close to what we yearn for. We're so close, and we want it so much, that we can become violent. Murder happens in that space. The precepts create a container in which that incredible insecurity finds some kind of space to be in, and to develop from there. So the first precept of not killing is not only not to murder each other, but also not to kill each other's freedom, each other's creativity, each other's inspiration; to allow each other to be independent. That can be a very subtle thing, not to kill, especially when we're feeling so insecure.

The second precept is not to lie; speak the truth, even when it's hard. At one point in my relationship with David, he started keeping a diary, and he was really careful that I never see this diary. He actually would take it everywhere with him. Of course, I was incredibly curious about what was in that diary. As it developed, the longer this went on, the more distance came between us, until we were practically at the point of breaking up, and he was writing more and more in his diary. What was happening was, he wasn't telling me the truth, and he was writing all about his doubts and about his thoughts about his ex-wife. Finally, we were

in Bali and we were in this little house in this place we called the Asylum, and I said to him, "You have to tell me what's in that diary." At that moment, a bird hit the glass of our house in the Asylum and fell to the ground. I had just said, "I feel like there's a wall between us; a glass wall between us," and this bird hit. So we stayed up all night and he read me the entire diary, and then we got incredibly close. He had thought he was protecting me. He thought he was being kind to me by not telling me all these things. But it was a way of lying, and it created a wedge between us. If we don't tell the truth, we can't really be intimate. We can function, but we can't really be intimate.

Then, not stealing. What does that really mean? Not taking what is not given. To me that's about grasping; it's about grasping onto someone else. In the extreme, in relationship, this ends up being that we cut our partner off from their friends. In abusive relationship, this is the first move; you cut the other person off from their friends. You steal them.

The next-to-last one is not to take intoxicants, or the way I understand it is not to become intoxicated, which doesn't mean not to have a glass of wine, but that you don't lose it. You don't become drunk. Some people interpret it more strictly as not taking any intoxicants. If we look at the statistics of violence and alcohol in relationship, it's obvious why we shouldn't get drunk or stoned, and it's also because it numbs us. It creates a distorted version of what's happening.

As for the last one—sexual misconduct—one time somebody said, "Well, you know, having the same partner is like having the same thing for dinner every night. It's just not interesting." But that's not the way I see it. What I see is that through holding to one person, the entire universe opens up. There is a vast multiplicity when we focus. When we really are completely with somebody— you can be in a monogamous relationship and not really be there—but if you're really there, it's huge, vast, contains everything. It also creates stability in the family, creates trust and peace in the relationship. Sexual misconduct, sexual abuse, can create incredible professional and social damage. We've also seen this within Buddhism. Think about what pain this has caused in Buddhism in America, this simple precept. Seemingly simple and so difficult to keep.

So the precepts create a container like the oyster shell, and within that container, we can, as Bernie [Tetsugen Glassman] would say, we can cook. We have to have the pot. We can't just put everything on the stove. We have to create the container. Once we have the container, we can begin to develop compassion and begin to move out to others. Once we have the container of mindfulness and the precepts, then we can begin to experience interdependence—which is the opposite of codependence—opening of the heart, through being able to settle down and make friends with ourselves and each other.

Then we begin to train—that's the second path. All events, no matter what happens, are seen as opportunities to practice, and the principle is of opening to big mind. This isn't

about a reference to me, it's about a reference away from me. Compassion in Buddhism is based on the experience of emptiness, and that's really different than compassion as seen in other kinds of practice.

Back to the Rumi poem: It says that not being bound up with everyone, we can begin to notice what's around us with compassion and with an open heart. I have a friend who lives in the Bronx, in a terrible neighborhood, just incredible. She told me one time that she'd stopped looking, because she just couldn't take it anymore.

I told her the story about the birth of Tara. That Avalokiteshvara, when he reached enlightenment, was very, very, very deep within his practice and within himself. He reached enlightenment, and he turned around and because of his enlightenment, he could see everyone. It would be like I was looking out here and I could see all of you. I could actually see all of your pain. It was so intense that he began to cry, and they say that out of the tear he shed, Tara was born. So Tara is the witness of the pain.

So I said to my friend, "Why don't you try just being present." One of the bodhisattva vows is you don't turn away from pain. She said she would try it. I said, "You don't have to feel like you necessarily have to fix it. Just try to be with it." So she came back to me after a couple of weeks, and she started talking, and she started crying, and she said, "I am so full of love. I am so full of compassion. I don't know what's happened to me. But all I've been doing is just looking, just being open."

I live in a very small town in Colorado and I was asked to be on a panel with a Catholic minister, an Episcopalian minister, and myself, to talk about what we believe happens after death and how to counsel families. An Episcopalian minister was there, who was very round and sort of pink-cheeked and jovial, and when it came his turn to speak, he said, "You know, I used to go in to families when somebody was dying, and I would go in and I would hope for a conversion. I would counsel them according to my beliefs. And it never really worked. It never really felt right to me. So lately what I've been practicing,"—and he said *practicing* —"is a ministry of presence. All I do when I go in is I'm just there. I'm just as present as I can be with everyone that's there, and I feel so relaxed, and it makes them feel relaxed. And then I can actually function. Instead of going in to fix it, I'm just present." I think that it's not that we wouldn't fix it or do something, but first we have to drop our agenda, and I think that's really what compassion is about in Buddhism. Stephen Levine says "the pool of tears becomes the ocean of compassion." I think we have to open our hearts. The poem says, *When you become that many, you are nothing, empty.* So when we actually come together, we're empty.

The word that comes to me about this path is "beholding." Be holding. That's being present and holding. How many of us have ever actually been held? Who's held you? Who's *beheld* you? Who have you *beheld*? Simply being and holding. So powerful and so simple, yet why do we avoid it? Why are

we always trying to get away from that? I think that it's about losing territory, we feel if we really open up we're going to lose our territory.

In the Mahayana, there are slogans, which Judy Lief talked about on Friday.* Slogans are about training the mind, and they're really wonderful. These are slogans of Atisha that also John Kuntro has written about and Ken McCloud also translated a book about that. One of my favorite ones is, *Don't be so predictable.* Ever say that to your partner? Dave starts to push one of my buttons and I start to react, and then I remember, *Don't be so predictable,* and then I shift. So the slogans are kind of like little trigger words that turn you in the middle, at that moment of coemergence, when you could make either one choice or another. A slogan comes up, and you shift.

There's another one that I think is really good for relationship: *Don't wait in ambush.* Have you ever waited in ambush? It's like you wait until he's really down, and that point you've been trying to make is so clearly exposed, that thing you've been trying to fix. This is the moment to move in, make your point. He's on the ground, laid out. But, then you remember, *Don't wait in ambush,* and you shift, and suddenly you don't do it—you don't attack—and this huge space opens up where you can actually be together.

There's another one, which is, *Don't transfer the ox's load onto the cow.* What that

*See "Cultivating Loving-Kindness Through the Slogans of Atisha," pages 7–23.

means is, don't take your problems or myproblems and put them on your partner or your kids, or your mother, or your ex-husband, or your ex-wife. You actually hold your load, and take it, and hold it as yours. So if you're in a bad mood, you don't take it out on somebody else.

The whole thing about Dharma is it actually changes what we do. It turns the mind around. We don't do what comes most easily, usually. There's some kind of effort, even if it's very slight, and that's what awareness is about, that shift. This process takes place internally. Like when you don't wait in ambush, your friend, or your child, or your partner may never know that you didn't attack. You might want to tell them...but you don't necessarily have to tell them for it to work.

There's another Rumi poem about a guy who's in love, and he goes to the doctor. He went to the doctor because he was in love; I don't know why exactly.

And he said, "I feel lost. Blind with love. What should I do?"

And the doctor said, "Give up owning things, being somebody. Quit existing."

When we quit existing, we return to our original condition: relaxation and love.

So compassion is like that liquid that makes the pearl. Pearls are actually made out of slime and minerals, so compassion is like that slimy stuff that we feed each other with. That actually creates the links, like the white stuff that creates the links and the synapses of the nerves. It wraps itself around the sand, wraps itself, and just keeps wrapping and wrapping and wrapping until the grit is a pearl.

In the Vajrayana, which is historically the most nonmonastic of the traditions—it arose as a protest movement from the seventh to the twelfth century—there was an interesting joining of ancient goddess worship and Buddhism, the Shakta tradition. What happened was that Buddhism was brought back into the marketplace, back home, back into the ghetto, and the practitioners had interesting names, like Fish-Gut Eater; the Royal Hedonist; the Senile Weaver; the Compulsive Liar; the Wise Washerman; the Dog Lover; the Blacksmith; the Enlightened Moron; or the Rejuvenated Dotard. This was about taking whatever was your worst thing, or whatever your work was, and turning it into practice. For example, there was a blacksmith, and the guru said to the blacksmith:

Transform your daily task into an internal meditation. Pumping the two arms—the righthand side of the central channel—and the lefthand side—to ignite the coals of conceptual thought lying in the hearth (which is the central channel). Kindle the flame of knowledge and awareness. The result is the immaculate *Dharmakaya*.

The blacksmith was given this as his practice, and after six years horseshoes started coming out of the fire by themselves.

So it's alchemy. It's about turning mindlessness into magic. I was thinking, Well, how would that apply now to us? And I was thinking about computers, and the whole experience of losing work. I've lost days of work—it was there and then it was totally gone—so what has been incredibly complex becomes incredibly gone. Tantra's an immersion in the poisons, into senses and sexuality; living together like Saraha and the arrow-smith woman; long-term practice as a couple, together; sexuality feasting. It's really about discipline and not license, it's about holding those experiences so that when you come together sexually there's a visualization of each other as luminous buddhas, maybe red or blue. There's a transformation of that experience through visualization. Opening to the divine, first seeing it externally and then gradually it comes closer and closer until it's internal. Until the divine is oneself.

My favorite of the Tantric teachers is a woman named Sahajayoginicinta (Spontaneous Jewellike Yogini). She said something that I think is so incredible: "At the core of our being is bliss." And she said that this happens, that at the moment of conception, the male and female generative fluids come together, and there is a ball of bliss that creates the new life, and that that ball of bliss stays in the heart throughout our lives. As we enact being male or female and coming together in sexual union, what we're really looking for is returning to that bliss, which is our true nature. That's why the whole sex thing is so pervasive. We can't get rid of it. It just goes through everything. It's not about procreation, it's not even about lust. It's about trying to go home. She says it like this: "In order that one may realize one's

inner self, which is spontaneous, naturally pure, and nondual, the inner self manifests here as man and woman. One's own self, created by nature, enacts reality through bodily expressions."

So bliss is our core. In sexuality, there's something really happening. When we meet with our eyes and with our bodies, we focus completely and we lose the sense of me and you. Have you ever made love and there's not me and there's not you? You don't know whose is what's? The five senses come together. There's the sense of taste, of touch, everything is there—sight, hearing—and it's union. It's not subject and object. At that one-pointedness, which is probably about the easiest one-pointedness for us to achieve, or it's the one that we're most interested in getting to, what happens when we really get there, according to Sahajayogini-cinta, is that we return to our heart essence, and seeking stops. Thus the world is transformed into an enactment of bliss, and from that we begin to go out with compassion. It's like something is fundamentally healed in that moment.

There's a joke a lama told me about a monk who was celibate for his whole life until he got pretty old, and then he got into a relationship. The next day his friend saw him and he was crying, and he said, "Oh, yeah, I'm really sorry. You broke your vows . . . terrible." And he said, "Well, that's actually not why I'm crying. I'm crying because I waited so long." That's not to put down celibacy, because I think it's an incredibly powerful path, but what happens is like discovering that we're a fish in the ocean.

This can also happen within ourselves, with what I call self-seeding; the experience of that union in the heart, through the raising of the female and the lowering of the masculine into the heart. So this doesn't necessarily have to come with somebody else, but with somebody else is the one that we're usually more interested in.

All these three practices that I've talked about today are about turning the mind to presence, returning home, coming back to our original nature, which is, first, the taming of the mind through mindfulness; then, holding the container of the precepts, and training the mind, turning to each other with an open heart within that space, taking the sand and weaving it into a pearl; and then, the transformation of the poisons into the pearl through recognizing the inner pearlness of each grain of sand.

The Meeting of Minds

STUDENT-TEACHER RELATIONSHIP IN BUDDHISM

Samuel Bercholz

IN *THE MYTH OF FREEDOM*, CHÖGYAM TRUNGPA RINPOCHE WRITES: "We could say that discipline and devotion are like the two wings of a bird. Without both of them together, there is no way to relate to the spiritual friend, teacher, or warrior. And without a spiritual friend, there is no way to realize the teachings."

The notion of teacher, spiritual friend, or guru presents an enormous challenge to those who encounter the Buddhist teachings. The prospect of entering a relationship with a genuine spiritual teacher has given rise to every conceivable human emotion, from gratitude, respect, love, even desire, to fear, anger, ambition, and hatred. In this workshop, Samuel Bercholz raised issues with which nearly every student and teacher is apt to have found themselves grappling. Confronting problems like respect and loyalty and their lack, the difference between loyalty and devotion, the dangers of sycophantism, the difficulties introduced by ego, among others, this workshop was characterized by the give and take of dialogue among Mr. Bercholz and the participants. Posing questions like "So what?" and insisting on the importance of "Don't trust" as a cornerstone of contemporary Buddhist searching, Mr. Bercholz encouraged lively discussion that often led to new understanding of this pivotal relationship on many a Buddhist's path.

Mr. Bercholz is a student of Chögyam Trungpa Rinpoche. As founder and editor-in-chief of Shambhala Publications, he is particularly well qualified to present the Kagyü and Nyingma teachings of Tibetan Buddhism as well as the Shambhala teachings, which he has done throughout North America and Europe. He is coeditor of *Entering the Stream: An Introduction to the Buddha and His Teachings*.

The whole idea of meeting of minds is an interesting one. Actually, when I agreed to sit up here in front of all of you I must have been in an altered state because I thought it was a good idea at the time. Maybe it's still a good idea, because for better or for worse we get to meet our minds, we get to meet our hearts here, together. But why would we want to do that? Why would we come to a thing like this?

Why do we need this Buddhadharma? Those of us who are Catholics can experience the Mass and go to church. We can actually have a genuine experience. We can become contemplative and everything is there. There is no reason to go anywhere else. Those of us who are Jews, same thing; Protestants, same thing; Muslims, same thing. Those of us who are atheist, same thing. Everything is there, if we'd like to look. So what is it that attracts us to Buddhadharma? It may be that we have met somebody that impresses us. Or we've met some teaching in a book that impresses. So there is something that Buddhadharma has to offer America, offer the world, and that is something quite extraordinary, quite simple, and quite powerful. It's simply Buddhadharma, the teachings of awake, of wakefulness.

If one wishes to make a connection with that awake, there are different ways to do it. We do it by reading, we do it by talking to our friends, but there seems to be one essential factor for most people and that's meeting somebody—another human being, an actual person—who has taken this path and gone forward with it. We can call this person a teacher, but every teacher is also a student because they have made the same journey we would like to make. That's the humanness of the situation. There are many levels of teacher just in terms of our relationship. A teacher can be someone who simply shows us what to do; gives us meditation instruction. How do I work with my mind? That's 100 percent worthwhile. That's the simplest form of teacher—teacher as elder. Someone who has gone before; someone who has done the practice and because they have done the practice they can impart it to you and teach it to you in the way that it's been imparted and taught since the time of the Buddha.

But then something else might happen, you might actually want to go a little further and maybe your teacher becomes a friend. There is loneliness in the path of meditation. One is alone and that's a wonderful thing; that's part of the discovery we have when we practice meditation, the sense of being alone. Meeting someone who also knows that they're alone is an interesting prospect because a communication can happen there. So, especially in Mahayana Buddhism, there is the idea of *kalyanamitra,* or spiritual friend. Truly someone who cares about you because they care enough to share their path with you and you care enough to share your path with them.

The interesting thing in Buddhism is that the relationship between the so-called student and the so-called teacher is a two-way street. There is no one-way situation; if it's one-way, it's totally blocked and it's a fantasy. If we just make somebody into a god, we might as well not be practitioners of Buddhadharma because Buddhadharma historically is a reaction against gods in some way.

So the relationship between ourself as someone who might want to pursue the truth—Buddhadharma, the truth of awake—and a teacher is an interesting one. A good teacher is human. It's tough to have a teacher who is a god. It's tough to have a teacher who is dead. It's tough to have a teacher who is yourself. Not to say that you can't have a teacher who is yourself, or you can't have a teacher who is gone, but it's best if that relationship is one person to another person.

The spiritual friend, *kalyanamitra,* that happens by coincidence, by good auspiciousness. If you go searching, you probably won't find it. If you do, it might be questionable. That's a warning. If you meet it, that's something quite different. It just happens. There you are and either there is a meeting of minds or there's not. It's quite simple. There is the first glimpse and in that first glimpse all the potential is there. But the thing about spiritual friends is that they are human. They eat, they defecate, they sleep, they do ordinary things just like we do. They might be a monk, they might be a nun, but I'll guarantee you they do all those things. Doesn't make any difference if it's a nun, monk, Eastern person, Western person; there is no typecast spiritual friend. Spiritual friend is what you meet on the path. It's a very intimate relationship. It's almost at the level of lover. Not to say that you have to make love with that person—in fact, that can be a problem. But it might not be a problem either, whatever the karma of that situation might be. I know that

is very controversial and very politically incorrect to say, but this is the human realm we are talking about and it's all about human things.

It's said in the Buddhist teachings that the best place to obtain enlightenment is in the human realm, our realm; that it's extremely difficult in any other realm. That's why this life as a human being is so precious. This is the life that we have, this is the life that's been given to us. Here we are in these bodies, here we are, we've heard Dharma, we've heard the words "Buddhadharma," we even have some interest—our mind goes in that direction. Each one of us here is the embodiment physically, psychologically, genetically of every one of our parents, grandparents, all the people who have gone before us. Our parents worked hard to create their life. Their parents went through all sorts of hardships. We can go back to beginningless time and each one of our ancestors worked hard in this world, did all kinds of things in this world; good things, bad things, made sacrifices, were foolish; all kinds of amazing, extraordinary things; all sorts of amazing, horrible things. Each one of us is the child of all that has gone before us and that's an extraordinary event.

It's said in certain aspects of the Buddhist teachings that every sentient being that you meet has been your mother. Not only that, you have been their mother, because if they've been your mother, it logically comes to pass that probably there has been the other situation as well. Here we are and we have our mother, our father, their mothers, their fathers, etc. We are the embodiment of all that, and this precious human birth is here in the moment. It's what's with us, and I think that is good news, that mixed with the awake is the seed of helping this world. It's not enough to help ourselves.

Each one of us could easily make a relationship with a spiritual friend. And we could have a great time with our spiritual friend. We could learn a lot from our spiritual friend. In fact, we could be a benefit to our spiritual friend because it's part of the spiritual friend's vow that they relate to other people. We could be all happy little students with teachers and then happy little teachers with students. So what? The problem we have in America is this: So what? Buddhism has been here for a very short time; Buddhadharma has been here for a very short time, and we can make it part of our comfort, we can make it part of our discomfort. But really, so what? I'd like to ask you this question: So what? So what if you meet a spiritual friend and your mind meets? So what if you have great discoveries and great meditation experience? So what?

[In posing the question, So what? Mr. Bercholz had most of the participants stymied. Several answered that they could not answer, that words were not sufficient. Of those who ventured an answer, all agreed it is an important, far-reaching question.

One woman presented her quandary by saying, "We're here in our human bodies and the best possible thing we can do with our human bodies is practice the Dharma for the benefit of everyone, so we can all become enlightened, so we can all stop all this crap that's going on. I mean that is the key, that is how we do it, unless I'm going to be spontaneously enlightened, which would be great. The teacher-student relationship is essential and spiritual friends are essential; friends period are essential. I don't even understand, So what?"

Another participant admitted "that the question really resonates so deeply with me. I feel the fact that within a world, within our society, we have to grapple with so much ugliness and so much violence and so much racism and sexism and ecological disaster and destruction and so forth. I think that previous to the exposure that we've had in the West to Dharma, it was very easy for us to simply blame other people—they're evil, we're right; they're bad, we're good, and so forth. I think that we've finally reached a point where we are capable of getting beyond that. So in terms of the So what? the getting beyond is our development of our own self-awareness so we've stopped throwing out all this garbage onto the rest of humanity. But we simply own our own feelings, we own our own emotional circumstances, and it's as though the Dharma offers a spiritual path to doing just that."

Mr. Bercholz responded by saying:]

I think it comes down to domestic situation, which is really how we live our lives. If you meet the mind of a teacher, that's wonderful, but there is a bigger issue, which is a domestic issue. If you're meeting the mind of a teacher, it's very domestic. If your teacher is idealized, there's a problem. If your relationship with other human beings is idealized, there's a problem. Our idealism is a problem. Nothing works until it's domestic, until it's you and I. That is the heart of the meeting of minds, it's real, it's human, it's one-to-one, and it's more than just devotion.

Another quality that's not talked about all that much in Buddhism is loyalty. You meet a teacher, you go through the honeymoon period, you think your teacher is the cat's meow, best thing you ever met. All of sudden you find out that your teacher is human, they have a penis or a vagina, they may have a liver even. They're human. They have human desire. They're human. They're just like you. Ooops! There's a problem. All of a sudden, if they're human, do you turn against them? It happens all the time. You're with your husband, your wife, your lover; you've got the honeymoon. All of a sudden, honeymoon's over, there you are, two human beings. Time for divorce? Where is the loyalty factor?

To whom maybe isn't a question here. I think we have a really interesting problem in our society. Excuse my French, but what burns my ass is that sometimes in the name of Buddhadharma we take the same social problem and shout about it in the name of Buddhadharma. I think that's unfair to the Buddhadharma. I think what we need, what will make Buddhadharma effective for us, for our students, for our teachers, for our friends, for anyone whom we encounter, will be if it has some social connection at the human level that we can't just toss away.

You know, we live in this so-called disposable society. We can dispose of anything. The level of garbage—whether it's physical, psychological, spiritual—is huge. We live in the age of materialism. That materialism is physical. That materialism is the materialism of our minds; wanting something, wanting to be better, wanting to be this or that. We live in the age of materialism of our spiritual values, because often we want something from our spirituality. We want something from our families, we want something from our friends, we want something from our teachers, we want something from our students. If it doesn't meet our expectations, we're just willing to toss it away. Now, that's a mess because there's garbage everywhere.

[This raised the question of the appropriateness of comparing the husband-wife relationship with that of the teacher and student. "When you spoke of the honeymoon period, the husband and wife getting together and then suddenly realizing they're human, you also spoke of the teacher and the student having a honeymoon period and realizing they're human. But the difference is that there is not an equal relationship with the student and the teacher. The issue sometimes is exploitation—it's part of being a human—and sometimes the concern of the student is Am I going to be exploited? How does one deal with that?"

Asking the participant if he had ever been married and finding out that he presently is, Mr. Bercholz asked him to explain "what the big difference is."

The man responded: "The only difference is that my wife and I are not always on the same level. But it shifts, and we're supposed to be on the same level, so when it comes to an argument or discussion we always have that as a lodestar that we can orient ourselves to."

Mr. Bercholz replied, "If you're foolish enough to have a relationship with a teacher that isn't like that, then you have a problem. Why would you make the student-teacher relationship any different than that?"

In answer, the participant explained that he perceived a teacher to be someone with wisdom to impart, someone at a higher level than himself. And with that perceived status came the potential to misuse the relationship with the student.

Quoting the Zen saying, "Never put anyone's hat above your own," Mr. Bercholz rejoined that "every teacher that exists in this world is somebody's student. If they're not, be careful." The questioner then recognized that "it's always my own individual responsibility to sort things out and figure it out myself."]

Samuel Bercholz: Buddhism is not a religion of salvation—even for Pure Land Buddhists, who can be extremely pure and are wonderful people. But still it's up to them to see the Buddha. Whether you practice or you just have devotion doesn't make much difference. It's still up to you. I don't differentiate practices because there are many different ways to attain enlightenment. It's not all the same for each of us. That is the wonderful thing about the Buddhadharma, there are so many different approaches—one that will work for anybody. But it's still up to you.

[The discussion reminded a participant of the teacher who admonised, "If you see the Buddha on the road, kill him." Mr. Bercholz observed that could be likened to "killing your concept," and asked the questioner his impression of that. He replied: "I don't think it has to do exactly with concepts. I think it's related to what you've already said. That we shouldn't deify a principle or a person. That we need to accept whatever it is for what it is."

The next question was the first of several during the session that turned upon the issue of misconduct by a teacher: "When the teacher does things that aren't appropriate, that's your teacher and you are trusting in him. You know they can back it up with Dharma, and you don't know because you are learning all this. How do you know the guidelines?"]

Samuel Bercholz: It's all eyes open. I think that's where loyalty comes in, because it's easy to react. Student-teacher relationship is a two-way relationship. It is not a one-way relationship. When it is a one-way relationship, that has nothing to do with Buddhadharma. From Buddhadharma's point of view, the only relationships are two-way relationships. The teacher has a responsibility, but the student has the same responsibility. Now if you make mistakes, good for you. But how many times do you have to make them? Sometimes you have to make them two, three, a thousand, ten thousand, a hundred thousand, five hundred thousand times, but one day you don't have to do that again.

The relationship with the teacher is quite a powerful situation and if you are just a yes man or a yes woman to the teacher, you are doing the teacher a disservice more than the teacher is doing you a disservice by being an idiot. This relationship in Buddhadharma is extremely important. It has to be a two-way relationship. It is a combination of ultimate surrendering and ultimately not trusting.

[The next question continued to address the issue of loyalty between student and teacher. "Would you say something about the relationship between fearlessness and loyalty? Particularly in a student-teacher relationship, there is a sacred trust, especially when the teacher is guiding you. You have to have faith in yourself as well as in that teacher. So how are loyalty and fearlessness balanced, or how do they come into that sacred trust?"]

Samuel Bercholz: You hit the nail on the head. Loyalty and fear go hand in hand. It's all about fear, in fact. What I mean is, Who *are* you? I don't have a clue. If I want to find out who you are, I have to approach you. I have to actually encounter you. This is at the human level. There's a lot of fear. Again, it's the same thing: We could have a nice little relationship. You could be my teacher because you're obviously a wise woman. You could teach me a lot, I'm sure. But who are you? Who am I?

Fear goes along with nihilism because, if we really fear, we will materialize, empiricize, make everything solid. Everything has to be solid, because once it goes out of that realm we're in the woo-woo realm and there is a lot of fear about that. Now loyalty is an interesting thing. When two people meet and actually become friends, one can be

devoted to the other and the other can be devoted to the other, but the long-term issue is, What are we doing in this world? That requires a loyalty to take it further than just simple devotion. It's not really even a spiritual issue, it's a social issue. Okay, we've met. What do we do with this?

[Mr. Bercholz's response prompted another participant to raise the issue of misconduct in the teacher-student relationship. She posed it in terms of trust and the potential abuse of that trust: "We all know that [the person positioning themselves as teacher] is why the student puts their faith and their trust in the teacher. To me it follows that the teacher does not abuse that setting. I think this can place the student in danger, such as [of] sexual overture toward the student [by the teacher]."

Mr. Bercholz observed that "it happens all the time and the problem is that the person who calls himself a teacher is a human being. Even though you can make a rule—No teacher will sleep with any student—as soon as you make that rule it's going to be more enticing, because of the taboo."

The woman who posed the original question asked: "Is it taboo because it's understood to make sense? Or is it taboo because somebody else said it is and we don't understand why?"]

Samuel Bercholz: It always takes two people to have a sexual relationship. If the teacher is foolish and the student is foolish, that's their foolishness. There will be repercussions from that foolishness. I know it's politically correct to think that the teacher is the only responsible person, but every teacher is a student, no matter what they say.

[A participant raised a pragmatic question that clearly had been on the minds of a number of participants: "If you go to [a meditation] center and you study and you listen to somebody for two hours, I don't see where there is time for this meeting of equals."

Mr. Bercholz responded that "a meeting of minds first of all happens outside of time. You go to a place and hang out there for a few thousand years, then it's time to go to the next place. But how do you know if it's been a few thousand years or just a week? You have to ask yourself that question. When it's time to move on, you move on if you haven't made a connection. But it's not about shopping; this is not like going to the supermarket."

The response clarified the issue for the questioner, who came back with, "but do you keep going when . . . there's one person that is doing all the talking and one doing all the listening?"]

Samuel Bercholz: Well, that's no meeting of minds is it? But it might happen that way, too, who knows? There's no set formula: If you do such and such, and such and such, the next thing is going to happen. There is no set formula like that. If there was, we could all follow the formula and all be enlightened. But there is no formula. There is auspicious coincidence, and when it happens you'll know it; probably when you've stopped looking. The only way to stop looking is by starting.

[The next participant's question drew on a widely shared experience in teacher-student relationships. She explained that she had had teachers with whom she felt no rapport, where she felt like she was asking "Who are you? What is this?" With no answer forthcoming, she had ended the relationship. Other situations were examples of a meeting of minds, in which case, she said, "the loyalty, the devotion, the humanness, and the two-way interaction always follow. . . . Do you think that's wrong, that I would have a teacher [for whom I have absolutely no] respect or loyalty?"]

Samuel Bercholz: I think you are speaking from very basic intelligence. If you bow to the wrong thing, you are just stupid. I think that it's very important when you bow, that you're bowing to something you respect. The way to know that is that something you respect always bows back. I'm not just talking about physical things. That's the whole issue of meeting of mind. It is never one-way; if it's one-way, run as quickly as you can run.

[A question raised an issue that goes to the heart of the teacher-student relationship in Buddhism. Saying that he had only had one teacher, and that because the teacher had moved away after a year and half, "since then whatever I have been able to accomplish for myself has not been in terms of people, . . . but it's ideas. Those are my teachers as such. Whether it's in print or whether it's words, and even there for good or for ill, I discriminate: . . . That's an intelligent idea that I can agree with; or that's kind of dumb."]

Samuel Bercholz: You bring up a very good point: The teacher, the spiritual friend, that person you feel close to is just a representative, at their best, of things as they are. They are giving you back something that is, in fact, yours. What happens is whatever presents itself, and that is no different than the teacher. All the sounds of this world—everything that we encounter—become the teacher.

I had a great love affair with a teacher. Great devotion, an absolutely wonderful teacher. Someone who cared about me. I cared about him. We fought. We had a great time together. We drank together. We ran around together. We meditated together and it was extraordinary. We loved each other, we hated each other. Every possible thing. It was a very difficult relationship because I was always watching to see if he would make a mistake. I was always watching to see if he would say one thing and do another thing.

Then this person died. But the person died even before they died. They sort of disappeared for a while and there I was looking at a body that was supposedly my teacher. Was the body my teacher? Interesting question. Of course the body is my teacher, but because my teacher was sick, the speech was gone. But it was extraordinary being in this room with this person who couldn't talk and was quite ill. Still the mind of the teacher was right there, maybe more than ever. Maybe I could actually hear clearer when my teacher couldn't speak. Then my teacher passed away. But here I am, I'm sitting here, I look at you, I still feel my teacher here. But is it that body; is it you; is it the sound from the next room? Doesn't make any difference.

There's more to it. Teacher-student relationship begins at the human realm and is quite simple, but it is not anything separate from what is already within. Buddhism has an interesting view: Buddha is there; awake is there. The crap we've collected just has to fall away and there it is. Now, the crap falling away may be difficult because, over numerous lifetimes, whether we believe in them or not, we have convinced ourselves that we exist to some sort of separate entity. We have all kinds of storylines about who we are. Maybe those can fall away. I don't know if that goes along with your view.

[A participant observed that, perhaps in American Buddhism "the notion of teacher . . . appears to be a much more flexible term than [that] used by people in the past."]

Samuel Bercholz: I would disagree. I think the human situation of student and teacher is out of time and place and out of culture. It's a human situation. I think the only big difference between America and the introduction of Buddhism here and it's introduction in the past is it's not being presented through the royal court, because we don't have a court.

Now, democracy also presents an interesting question. I don't think you can have a democratic Buddhism. I don't think you can have a socialist Buddhism. I don't think you can have an imperial Buddhism. I don't think that's what it's about. It still is the same as it ever was. The Buddha gave up his princeship and went on his journey. The only reason the Buddha taught is because someone asked. I don't think the Buddha would ever have taught unless someone asked. It's simply that human thing. There is awake. People experience awake. Someone sees it and they ask how do you work that. It's a human-level situation.

But also there are all kinds of bodhisattvas and buddhas that exist in a subtler realm. That we can't see them may be part of our human problem. The skillful means of the teachers who have gone before us, who have been able to see, have provided skillful means for us to see those things. There are buddhas and bodhisattvas—countless, numberless, existing in all sorts of realms—that we don't even have a clue about that are immediately accessible to us if we have the eyes to see or want to see. Or we can just call that mythology. Fine. Closed case. But it's extraordinary what there is in this world. We have our five senses, our six senses, our seven senses, or our eight senses, depending on how you want to count them. There are limitless experiences and limitless pure fields of buddhas. I believe in a hierarchy, but it's not about trying to put me down. The hierarchy of buddhas and bodhisattvas that exist in these subtle realms are all calling "Welcome." And that to me is a real hierarchy. It's about opening, bigger and bigger, and wider and wider. That's a different way of looking at hierarchy.

[A participant ventured several ideas that touched on the attributes of the teacher as prescribed in various texts. This led to issues of lineage and the passing of Buddhist precepts from one person to the next.]

Participant: *I think each level of practice [in the three yanas] has its associated texts and in those texts it specifically states and specifies qualities, attributes of a teacher. And there are specific requirements to be able to teach. So things are not quite as wild as perhaps they might seem. When we speak of the very highest teachings, then perhaps we could say the relationship between the teacher and the student is one in which the minds meet. There has been preparation and when we are really at a very close level with a teacher, anything can happen, but that's in a specific area. There are very many checks and balances that show that that kind of thing should remain in that area. When Dr. Jon Kabat-Zinn teaches mindfulness meditation, he is working at one level of Buddhism [for] which there is a specific technique that is taught and he is a teacher of that technique. He's not proposing himself as a guru. When we speak truly about the mind meeting the mind we are speaking about something that is, obviously, more subtle and if the teacher doesn't have a realization—if the teacher does not have a profound understanding and knowledge of his own mind—that teacher can't show you that because they don't have it. . . . But if they really have it, then you can meet there.*

We know the historical stories of wild behavior, but within that context that behavior is appropriate. Outside that context we have to exercise great care [regarding] what we are becoming involved in. I think, in the sense of lineage—that's to say that one teacher has talked to another teacher who teaches to another teacher who teaches to another teacher—we've seen downfalls in the sangha.

They're unfortunate, but we're learning from them. But generally speaking, that lineage continuity has been our protection, our insurance, our insulation. It has been our guarantee of the authenticity of the teachings we are receiving and our guarantee that when we enter the space with somebody who is going to present where we are going into a completely free and open danger zone, we know that we are within a context which has a history, even though we try and transcend all that."

Samuel Bercholz: Lineage is the human quality that everything that we have been talking about has been passed on from one person to another. There is some problem in American Buddhism that we think we can toss off China, we can toss off Japan, we can toss of Tibet, we can toss off Sri Lanka, and so on. If we do that, if we don't respect that these teachings came from a particular place, from very particular people—real people; human beings—we get ourselves in trouble. If an American Buddhism is created that doesn't keep it's roots, we're all going to be in a lot of trouble. That's a whole issue of racism that's subtle, but it's real. That's just a little warning because we're human beings.

If we're not Japanese, there's a problem if we try to become Japanese and take on Japaneseness or Chineseness or Tibetaneseness or Sri Lankaneseness or Vietnameseness. We're in trouble if we try to change our cultural being. In the same way, we're in trouble if we don't acknowledge that our teachers come from some *place* and it's a real thing that was passed to them that

came from somebody else that came from somebody else directly from the buddhas. Lineage is direct and, in fact, it is the safeguard, but not a stupid one.

I still say, because my teachers always say, Do not trust. If you are going to trust, trust that, but still do not trust. It goes together. If you trust your idea of what lineage is, then you're in trouble. I think each of us is in trouble if we make a homemade lineage. Lineage isn't homemade. It's real. It's about real human beings. It's not abstract.

[Toward the end of the session, the discussion came back to the issues of loyalty and of abuse of the teacher-student relationship. "Is loyalty being awake so that you question, you don't trust, and then, in a teaching situation, [if] a teacher does something that you find inappropriate, . . . does loyalty go? Is it that, whatever happens, because you find your mind has met with this person, who is inspired, then your loyalty continues even when something very inappropriate or wrong happens?"]

Samuel Bercholz: It's interesting that loyalty comes up in that context, because that is not what I was talking about at all. But, it probably is connected. The way I've been talking about loyalty isn't just loyalty to a person. It's loyalty to the fact that we have a whole world of people and if we just create garbage continuously, we're being disloyal to this world. If we toss away our wife, if we toss away our teacher, if we toss away our husband, if we toss away our boyfriend, if we toss away our garbage, if we're not taking care of those situations, just because we may have a temporary or long-term aversion to them, something happens in our society. Loyalty is being loyal to the reality that we are in this together. And the "we" is an interesting we. It includes the teacher, it includes your family, it includes other human beings, it includes sentient beings. Loyalty here is not just a simple thing about setting up your little world with your teacher. There is a bigger issue, and it's connected with fear. It is difficult to be loyal because we're afraid. It's much easier to hide.

What it comes down to is, if you have a relationship with someone where you've had a mind-to-mind meeting, not saying yes always. In fact, probably it's rarely saying yes. A meeting of mind is not just saying yes, it's a *meeting*. But it's not being always combative. If you take it down to a person-to-person thing, it's very domestic. Loyalty is cleaning up the dishes. Loyalty in the house is as simple as being willing to clean up your own mess.

[Another participant expressed her concerns this way: "If you have the teacher, you have the meeting of the minds, . . . and the teacher did things that were not on the list of approved things. Would the loyal and fearless way to handle it be to address your teacher and say 'Look, this is what I find to be uncomfortable.' and just talk about it and tell them basically what you see the misconduct to be and . . . where you don't feel it's a correct teaching relationship?"]

Samuel Bercholz: That's up to you. I can't tell you. Sometimes it's about confronting, some-times it's about offering support, sometimes it's about being angry, sometimes it's about being kind. Loyalty always comes from kindness, but kindness has many different faces.

I had a very interesting teacher, a very traditional person. One day I was called into his office and he was extraordinarily angry. I was extraordinarily afraid because he was extraordinarily angry. He shouted at the top of his lungs to me "You've become a yes man. I don't need you anymore if you are going to do that." I was shocked because that's what I thought he wanted, and so my teacher was very kind because I am a very stupid person.

[Another discussion concerned the interplay between awareness and the idea of Don't trust. As a participant phrased it, "You say awareness is a key. Don't trust has something of a negative connotation. That's what you're there for, to learn awareness."]

Samuel Bercholz: A friend of mine quoted a poem. This is not the poem, but its message is Don't trust, but be friendly. Don't trust, but be kind. Don't trust, but be open. Don't trust, don't trust. It's an incantation and you can chant it over and over if you like. You have to not trust, and in the not trusting maybe you can actually trust, but you still can't trust, but you can be friendly. You can be cheerful.

That is the horrible truth of all this: It is a lonely journey that each of us has. It is a lonely journey; we are each on our own. We can meet each other and we are blessed by the three jewels of the Buddha, the Dharma, and the *sangha*. That's a wonderful thing if one can surrender to that, but even in the surrendering we don't toss away intelligence.

Participant: *Where does self-trust come into all this?*

Samuel Bercholz: Interesting thing for a Buddhist to ask. I think there is no self-trust. It's awareness.

Participant: *And loyalty must be a two-way street as well?*

Samuel Bercholz: One hundred percent a two-way street because there is no loyalty if it isn't two-way. Loyalty one way is worthless.

[The session ended as a questioner proposed a way to think of loyalty—"Do the right thing."]

Samuel Bercholz: It's do the right thing and it's up to you what the right thing is. But there is a whole world that you have to think of. If you do the right thing and it's wrong for everybody else, I doubt that it's the right thing.

Buddha Born among the Celts

Ven. Seonaidh (John A. Perks)

THE BUDDHISM IN AMERICA CONFERENCE PRESENTED A BROAD SPECTRUM of approaches to Buddhism and to practice, primarily those deriving from Asian roots. It also represented a wide variety of nationalities and ethnicities, but nearly all of the Western speakers were North Americans, and most of those were from the United States. One prominent exception was the Venerable Seonaidh, who is temporary lineage holder of the Celtic Buddhist lineage, which was conferred upon him by his teacher Chögyam Trungpa Rinpoche, whom Ven. Seonaidh credits with bringing the Buddhist teachings of Tibet to the West. (As he states in his biography, Trungpa Rinpoche "gave the 'Celtic' transmission to his servant....Reluctantly, John Perks took the ball and crawled.")

Ven. Seonaidh, born John A. Perks in 1934, was brought up in the nature-centered Wicca tradition by his mother. His training in personal service made it possible for him to become butler for Chögyam Trungpa Rinpoche in 1975, and he lived and traveled with Trungpa for eight years. Presently he is butler to Senator Rockefeller in Washington, D.C.

He began his talk noting that "there's some kind of transmission taking place here, and it's transmission from the Buddha, before the Buddha." He also noted that "communication is just telling stories. We tell stories to each other about how it is—It's cold outside or it's hot. Did you experience that? Was that real? That kind of thing." Then Ven. Seonaidh began "to talk about this story of this Buddhist lineage that we all belong to."

His first topic was reincarnation, "because the Celts believed when you die, you just go to another place....When the tribe was in difficulty, the head Celt would be expected to go into the next world to work things out. So they would give him the old threefold death thing—stran-

gle, hit in the head (thunder), and drowning"
to send him into the next world to work on
the problems existing in the tribe.

What the Buddha said was, The self that you
are, or this collection of things that you are,
does not reincarnate. Which makes this present situation enormously vibrant because
each one of you is extremely special, only
going to be here for this impermanent session. Interesting, ain't it? That's what the
Buddha said—the self does not reincarnate.

So anytime you go somewhere and
somebody says, "Well, it's really okay, because
I'm going to come back as president of CBS,"
or "Hey, I was Tutankhamen—I remember
past lives," [recall that] if you hang onto past
lives' vision, then visions become visions of
Mara, which are illusions.

Much of Ven. Seonaidh's talk centered on his
years with his teacher Chögyam Trungpa
Rinpoche:

I was his butler, or I thought I was. And I lived
in his house and I did all this butler service
and I figured early on, Well, I'll figure this guy
out and I'll be able to put him into my conceptual pigeonhole,… and once I get him figured out, hey, I'm safe. I freaked out because
there wasn't anything there. I thought I
almost had it—I thought I almost had him
figured—and there was nothing there. There
was nothing there that I could grab hold of.
His habitual pattern, that didn't exist. Here
was an entity that wasn't even human, really.
It certainly wasn't male and female.

I used to go into the bathroom with him
every day—we had a ritual—and he'd take off
his kimono and stand there. He had a Tibetan
kind of smell, which is kind of like wood soap
and a horse's saddle. And his pubic hair was
very straight and it kind of hung and no hair
here. But then it would change—his body
used to change—and the more it changed
when we walked into the bathroom to do the
shower ritual, the more I freaked out.

He would look in the mirror and he
would say, "What's the matter, Johnny?" This
wasn't a human being. He was a *mahasiddha,*
emperor *mahasiddha,* but not even that. I'd
met a lot of beings, animals, humans, and
things. This was nothing that I had ever
encountered before.

To help a participant who asked what he
meant by saying Trungpa Rinpoche's body
changed, Ven. Seonaidh explained that a
teacher, especially when one is the teacher's
butler, has you "pay attention to small details:
how to put a knife down, how to put a fork
down, peppers and salts and glasses and
things like that. From that knowledge you
start to be able to apply it to everything
around you."

When you walk into a room, all of a sudden
you realize you're smelling something. If you
go out into the park, all of a sudden things
look different. That's the way you're trained,
paying attention to small details. When you
pay attention to tiny, small details, you
become sensitive to your surroundings. It's
basic ecology. So the change was my percep-

tion, absolutely. I was the one freaking out. That was my perception.

"Trungpa Rinpoche would destroy spirituality. Trungpa Rinpoche was the destroyer of illusions," said the speaker. "He never stopped, not for one second." The teacher clearly saw the Western need to derive practice from sources that fit life as the practitioner knew it, rather than to search out arcane rituals from other cultures. Ven. Seonaidh told three stories related to this.

Trungpa Rinpoche would always say, "What are you? What *are* you?"

Well, I thought I was a butler. Try again. He said, "Well, Johnny, why don't you start a Robert Burns club?"

And I said, "Robert Burns club? Alright, I'll start a Robert Burns club."

"Let's go and buy some kilts, Johnny."

There he is, Trungpa Rinpoche, in his kilt, going to the Robert Burns Club.

"We'll make haggas. We'll play bagpipes. We'll sing 'Auld Lang Syne.'"

So we did that. We got all the *sangha* members who thought they were Celtic and had this big, Celtic dinner where everybody got absolutely sloshed on scotch.

Trungpa Rinpoche drank all the time. I asked my friend Douglas Tenet, "Why do you think he drank like that?"

"Because he couldn't drink more" he said.

A long time ago I spoke to Lame Deer, who was a Sioux medicine man. He said, "You know, it's awfully funny, you white guys, you

come out here, you put feathers in your hair, or you go to Tibet and you put on Tibetan robes. Why don't you just do your own thing?"

I said, "I don't know what our own thing is."

He said, "Well, you better find out."

I met an Irish washerwoman the other day who was a wearing a Japanese dress and she said, "Would you like to come to hell with me?"

She cleans up this place where the people are in cages. It's a place up a river somewhere. It's called Sing Sing. And it's doing ecology, cleaning up shit in Sing Sing.

The mythology talks about going into the underworld, the hell realms, and you clean up the hell realms. And first, when I got the invitation, I thought, Nay. Then I said, Well, why not? Let's do it. Let's do it for ecology. Let's do it for Celtic ecology. Let's do it for human ecology. Let's do it for the ecology of the planet. We don't need more stuff. We don't need more illusions.

You know, the Buddha said, This is what you do. You sit on this cushion and you breathe out and you follow your breath. Meditation instruction. Simple, isn't it? That's all you do. If you have a thought, just label it "thought."

The motto of the Celtic Buddhist lineage is something the Buddha said when somebody came along and asked him, If you could sum the whole thing up in a nutshell, what is the whole teaching? And the Buddha said, Sure, it's this: Nothing whatever should be clung to. If you understand that, you understand the whole of Buddhism. That's it. Nothing whatever should be clung to. There's nothing there. Thoughts arise in your mind, they are magnified, and they develop, and you think you have to act, but basically there's nothing happening there.

Duhkha is roughly translated as "suffering," and you have to actually be sick of *duhkha,* but suffering is not a good word for *duhkha* because *duhkha* also means bliss or pleasure or anything that comes up. And the Buddha said, That's what we want you to be free of. I want you to be free of *duhkha* and this is how you do it. You meditate. You have to practice.

You actually have to discipline yourself to sit down on the cushion and work with yourself. You have to be enormously disciplined to do that. You actually have to believe in life, the ecology of life, the ecology of yourself. You don't have to keep beating yourself into the ground. You can become enlightened. It's not tremendously hard. Gradually you can see your own mind and how it works because eventually it slows up a little bit so you can get a glimpse of it going past.

What was that?

That was my mind.

So that's a discipline. The other discipline is jumping off the cliff and giving yourself to it totally. You cannot, in Celtic Buddhism anyway, be a Celtic Buddhist unless you're willing to jump off a cliff and give yourself totally to it. There are not half-measures here. It has to be absolute total commitment because we can't play around anymore. It

actually doesn't matter if it's Christianity or Buddhism or being a Sufi. You have to give yourself.

I run into a lot of students and they say, "I started to do prostrations and then I got busy and then I, you know....And then Trungpa Rinpoche slept with a lot of people and he drank a lot and I can't really go along with that and, you know, the other thing is the teacher insulted me. Can you believe that? He insulted me. Me, me, me, me, me. He made me angry. Actually, personally, he made me angry. He insulted me all the time. He kept insulting me. Bang, insulting me, my intelligence."

Students do that. They say, "It hurt, it hurt, it hurt." And it hurts. Sure it does. But you get back down there and sit on the cushion, or you do the prostrations. The Buddha did it.

An obvious connection between the concerns of his childhood practice of Wicca and his Buddhist practice today is the deeply held devotion to nature, in all its permutations. The necessity of such strongly held connection is apparent in his frequent references to "ecology."

"I have a lot of friends that are animals," he said, "and they're really pissed off and they say, 'We've been waiting around for you human beings to become enlightened for centuries, and we're very patient.' My dog is very patient with me and it sits and looks at me sometimes and I know it's saying, 'When are you going to get it together? You keep looking up there, waiting for the spaceships to land. We're already here. Here we are.'"

Coming back to one aspect of the discussion of each person's need to develop a life based upon a practice that is appropriate to who that person is, Ven. Seonaidh mentioned that he had once asked Trungpa Rinpoche how the Trungpa lineage started:

He said, "Well, there were three idiots sitting by the bank of the river and one of them started the lineage. Why don't you try starting a lineage, Johnny? You're an idiot too."

Why not? You know, if you've ever read a Carlos Castaneda book, Don Juan says, "Jump off this cliff." And then Castaneda spends the next two books asking everybody, "Did I really jump off this cliff?"

A member of the audience mentioned that Castaneda also misses the point when he tries "to figure out where the hell Don Juan went when he jumped off the cliff."

"That's right. *Shunyata,*" responded Ven. Seonaidh. "The word *shunyata* is "a means of voidness," "the void," "being void of self." When we feel that the I or the self or the me or mine has been taken away, we all of a sudden feel groundlessness. Holy shit, there's nothing there!

Another participant said, "I somehow need to understand about Rinpoche's drinking—why he literally drank himself to death and what purpose as a teacher he has served.

Ven. Seonaidh recalled that a friend of his had said, "Trungpa drank when he couldn't drink anymore." Now, when he went to Japan, he sat in a sushi house and ate 108 pieces of sushi and threw it all up."

A lot of people say to me, "I want to be a Buddhist because I want peace of mind. I want to send out waves of peace to tigers so they won't eat me."

When I open the shrine-room door, it's full of crocodiles and they're all eating each other and they say, "You want to sit in there?" Yes, go and sit in there.

Sing Sing is full of crocodiles and they're all eating each other. The ecologist goes in with a bat and hits them on the head and says, "Sit!" Whack! "Sit!" Whack!

Energy! Trungpa Rinpoche energy. Energy of the lineage. It exists, it's here now, that energy.

People say to me, "Well, Trungpa slept with a lot of ladies." Well, it's true, he did. And because I lived in the house, I used to ask the women, "Well, what was it like? I mean, was it like *Kama-sutra*—you hang on the ceiling?"

And they said, "Nothing happened. We sat on the bed and read comic books."

Once we were walking down the street and saw a massage parlor. He said, "Come on, Johnny, let's go in."

We'd go in, lay on the bed. Girls in little miniskirts. I'm listening next door. He's giving them meditation instruction. And when he leaves they're saying, "Oh, thank you, thank you." We go into a topless place and a girl in a G-string runs up and says, "Oh, Rinpoche, Rinpoche, I took level one!"

Energy, see. Willing to engage anybody, anytime, anything, any energy—willing to engage. This guy lives off energy.

So, yes, that's Buddhism. The Buddha walked around India. He didn't sit on a big chair like this and give lectures and say, Hey, crawl up here and kiss my feet. He talked to people. He said, "What's your experience of life? Tell me, tell me."

Other teachers came and said, "Well, I've heard you talk and I don't agree."

He said, "Well, tell me. What is it?"

Energy. You want to be a Buddhist—Celtic Buddhist—it's all energy.

Trungpa Rinpoche said, "In Ireland we're going to have to have shrine rooms with padded walls because everybody's going to be fighting here and drinking. They're going to be using their Celtic energy, the basic Celtic energy that you have, the Celtic people have.

"You don't have to go out and play with the American Indians. You don't have to go to Tibet and play with the Tibetans. When you have your own lineage, then they'll come and play with you. Then the Tibetans will come here and want to study Celtic Buddhism." That's what Trungpa said.

On another day, he said, "Well, I guess we'll have to send people over to Tibet to teach them Buddhism, because they all wear protection cords and little amulets. And they pray to statues of the Buddha. That's not Buddhism. Buddhism is the living lineage that lives all the time."

Scrubbing the floor, cleaning up Sing. Your responsibility, our responsibility, practice, practice, practice.

When a participant asked for his thoughts on her attraction to a variety of lineages, Ven. Seonaidh said it was like buying a car—"You go and pay your money, buy a car, get in, and drive it and it's a lemon. But you're stuck with it."

He recalled that Trungpa Rinpoche said anybody could be your teacher. "You have to give what you think you want up. Give up your search and jump off the cliff and then you're stuck with it." Kukkuripa, the *mahasiddha,* found this dog and lived in a cave with the dog. He found it on the road and they were stuck with each other. He got enlightened through being stuck with that dog for twelve years in a cave, living with this dog.

When a participant later asked, "What about the teacher that turns out to be a lemon?" Ven. Seonaidh responded that he didn't have personal experience of that situation. "I grabbed hold of Trungpa Rinpoche and I didn't let go, and he wouldn't let me go either, until he finally said, "Get out." I went for it. I saw this guy and I said, This guy's got something and I want it.

I'll tell you another story. We're in the middle of India, driving in a taxi. Trungpa Rinpoche throws my passport and my money out the window, and he says, "Stay here and start a *dharmadhatu.*"

I don't even speak Bengali. I don't have any money. I don't have a passport. They drive off down the road. Of course, they came back a couple of hours later and laughed a lot. But eventually he did it, dumped me out there.

A member of the audience asked if the speaker wished to comment on "Celtic spirituality's closeness to nature and the elements." Ven. Seonaidh showed them a picture of a "Celtic Buddhist *dorje,*" which he compared to a picture of a Buddhist one, and this is a meteorite that fell in Africa

This is Celtic Buddhist *dorje.* It came from somewhere in the universe. Long traveler. This person traveled a long way. I know because we've spent some time together and it tells me stories about the universe. It tells me stories. If you practice whatever practice you do—be it sitting meditation or deity yoga or Chöd or any of those practices—then you become sensitized and then an oak tree starts to say, "Hey."

You say, "What?"

Maybe it's not actually in English-verbal or even Gaelic-verbal tongue, but there's some reality between you. There's some ecology between you, between the dog or the tree or the lamppost. And then all of a sud-den, you're in love, but you don't have an object to stick it onto. You're just in love. Walking down the street, I fell in love with this lamppost. You can't take it home. You can't do anything about it. You're just in love.

That's the relationship between Celtic Buddhist lineage and the environment around it. The Celtic Buddhist is in love, without attachment, to the environment. An attachment without the senses. The senses don't come up and grasp the object. They don't even come up and identify it at some point. You can't identify what it is that you're looking at. It's just this thing is just here, this energy form. Maybe not even form. So you can't grab it. Nothing grabs it because there's nothing there to grab hold of. That's the practice. That's how you relate to the environment. I was brought up actually with that tradition.

It doesn't hurt to make offerings. There are a few simple practices. When you leave a room, if you've been staying in a room for many days, you can just bow and say thank you. Now, you're not saying thank you to anything in particular, you're just saying thank you. It's an offering. Thank you. That's all.

The Great Question
of Life and Death

Zen Master Soeng Hyang
(Barbara Rhodes)

THE CONCEPT OF "DON'T KNOW" AND THE CULTIVATION OF DON'T-KNOW MIND were frequent topics during the conference. Whether a speaker dealt with the ancient practices in India or Tibet or teachings by contemporary masters, this theme recurred again and again. At the beginning of her workshop, Zen Master Soeng Hyang gave a wonderful example of how Korean Zen Master Seung Sahn, who came to the United States in 1972, evidenced don't-know mind:

[Zen Master Seung Sahn] had been living in Japan for seven years and was flying from Tokyo to Los Angeles. There is a very large Korean community in Los Angeles and he didn't want to teach Koreans; he wanted to teach Americans because he wanted to teach Zen and most Korean people don't like Zen that much, they're more interested in more devotional Buddhism. So he asked "Where is a good place to go in the United States where I can teach Zen?" He had no idea. The person he was sitting next to happened to be a professor from the University of Rhode Island, a Korean man, and he said "Oh, Providence is a wonderful city. You should come to Providence." Just from that one exchange Seung Sahn decided to come to Providence.

Zen Master Barbara Rhodes was living in Providence at the time, and became his student, studying with him from 1972 on. Having received transmission from Zen Master Seung Sahn in 1992, she is his Dharma heir. Along with him, she was a founder of the Providence Zen Center.

Most of her talk, however, drew primarily on her work as a registered nurse and as a caregiver at Hospice Care of Rhode Island. Telling of her experience with people who are sick and dying, she sketched out a kind of map of the day-to-day life of compassion and attention that many Buddhists lead, beginning with the example of her teacher's determination of where he would go to live and teach in the United States.

That don't-know mind my teacher had in the airplane—just accepting the first city someone mentioned to him—is something we really stress in our practice: The mind is just receptive. By using the term *don't know* with your meditation, you're actually giving of the busy consciousness that likes to think in terms of opposites: good/bad, right/wrong, expensive/cheap, high and low—it cuts that off and all you say to your consciousness is "don't know." It's not a negative message; it's just saying "Relax. let go, just don't know."

Another way to describe it will be, Just don't preconceive, don't have an idea—only don't know. So for beginning meditation we teach to breathe in clear mind, and the exhalation phrase is "don't know."

[Referring to Patricia Shelton's workshop "The Great Work of Life and Death,"* she reiterated that Ms. Shelton's "main point [is] it's not this special, magical technique to be with someone [who is dying]. She said the two main points were to be attentive and to be with the person; to be of one, to be connected."]

So obviously it's not just with someone who is physically leaving their body, but it's about every moment to be attentive and to be connected. That's the whole point of Buddhism. It's so very very simple.

And the whole point of the enlightenment experience is to viscerally get that— that we ultimately were never separated. It's just an illusion that we think that we're

---

*Excerpted on pages 364–72.

the only one in the room, and it's a sad illness—you can use the word *disease*. It makes us very uneasy to be under that illusion and yet it's ingrained very deeply into us. So when we do finally recognize that that's our illness and can intelligently find ways of working with it, then that's it. Doing *don't know* and just letting go and spending some time every day meditating or doing some practice is what will free us and open us up to our opportunities and to our own innate intelligence and our ability to get out of that trap of our ego-centeredness.

[She emphasized that there is no one "right" or "wrong" way of doing this. Using the wearing of robes as an example, she noted that "sometimes wearing a robe can really turn people off," but her teacher advised her to keep the robes as a sign to someone in need of learning to meditate that here is a person who can help. She explained that, since she has always worked as a registered nurse, and for the last eleven or twelve years has been doing hospice work, she doesn't wear her Buddhist robe to work. Nonetheless, the challenge remains "finding skillful ways of integrating your wisdom into your everyday life....Somehow we want to practice; we want to find ways of honing in and getting a deeper experience of that egolessness."

From this, she described ways in which she has integrated these two elements of her life— "how my practice has helped me in my work and helped me with working with people."]

I was called out to a family where the person was at the end of her life. I had heard that this family was having a lot of trouble.

There were two daughters, probably in their fifties, and they were very, very worried about their mother, thinking she was uncomfortable and very anxious. So I came into their home, and they were running around; two TVs were on, and the patient was lying in her bed. One daughter said "I don't know what we should do. I don't think she's comfortable, I think she's scared," etc. It was all a projection that they were uncomfortable and scared. The patient had cardiac disease, she was at the end of her life with heart failure, so she had no pain, she just had a dying heart, which is probably one of the easiest ways to die, as long as you're not having a lot of trouble breathing, which she wasn't.

The first thing I said was "I don't think your mother's uncomfortable. Let's sit with her for a minute and just see." One of the daughters couldn't handle it, but the other daughter sat with me. I sat on the patient's bed and started to breathe with the patient, just the same pace as the patient. I asked if we could turn off the TV sets. (It's basic stuff like this that sometimes we might think is obvious, like seeing if it can be a little quieter, that we need to remember.) We turned off the TVs and sat there.

What was so amazing is that I didn't tell the daughter to do anything. She just followed my example. I think we sat for maybe forty-five minutes or an hour, just breathing, and finally the patient passed on. She exhaled, and didn't inhale again. This was one of the first times I felt an incredible embrace; a wonderful loving-kindness thing come and lift her out of the room and embrace us at the same time.

I don't always sit and breathe with my patients. I don't always have the skill or the know-how to set that up, and it's not always that easy, especially coming in and never having met the family. But that time it worked out so beautifully. I wasn't sure if I should say anything, but after about a minute had passed, after she had stopped breathing, we were just sitting there quietly, and I glanced over at the patient's daughter and I said, "Did you feel that?" and she said "Oh, did I!" It was wonderful.

As I humbly say, I haven't had that happen that much in my hospice work, I think because I haven't slowed down enough and haven't been able to know the skills and the techniques. But it's not magic. It's just attentiveness and it's connecting with the breath. That's exactly what we're trying to do with our sitting when we sit in most meditations, particularly Zen meditation—to be attentive, to be awake, and to connect with your breath.

[Zen Master Soeng Hyang went on to explain the importance for her of connecting with the breath and incorporating don't know into daily routine. "There are certain activities where you can't consciously connect with your breath. It would be inappropriate, distracting. But don't know is portable and can be taken into everyday life without even calling on the trained you at all."]

The words don't know also imply a question. If you think Don't know, sometimes you might ask "don't know what?" A very powerful part of the Korean Zen tradition is to use doubt in your practice. Not doubt in a negative way, but that you realize that there is a big question and that all of us as human beings have questions. To ask What am I? or What is this? or How is it just now? can really help you let go of your own personal agenda and to open up to this moment.

We encourage students, when they're driving for example, to ask How is it just now. What is this? The words disappear after awhile and it's a state of mind of inquiry and looking into; asking rather than assuming. It doesn't just mean that you have to say "The white line is on the left and I've got to turn in 5.3 miles"—it's not a compulsive, obsessive type of thinking. It's a very wide How is it just now? You could be attentive to the driving and at the same time be connecting to a much deeper metaphysical question.

That's what I really wanted to stress: Zen practice isn't just about sitting, it's about learning to realize that every moment the teaching is there and there's an opportunity to open up. You're not waiting for some event. This *is* the event—just now, this moment.

One of the things my teacher said about living in the Zen center is that you live with people you didn't choose as your housemates. They just came, and so you learn very quickly to, we say, put down your condition, your opinion, your situation. I don't mean to strip yourself of all fun, but to start to learn to let go of your personal opinion, your conditioning, and your situation, and to act with others and be with others. So the power of living in community that way comes from being forced to do it. The more you are able just to go with it and be with it, then you

enjoy the community. But if you keep saying "Well I like this and I like that and I don't like that," then you suffer a lot.

[Before working with questions from the audience, Zen Master Zen Master Soeng Hyang told a story about a Korean monk that illustrated the importance of attentiveness.]

In Korea, sometimes there would be a lot of orphans, especially after a war, and sometimes Buddhist temples would take the little boys or little girls, and they'd grow up in the temple. (They shave their heads and wear little monk's clothes and go to school.) So a little boy was raised from the age of three or four in a Zen temple. This little boy was very, very bright. He started learning the sutras when he was only about seven or eight and memorized them. By the time he was fourteen or fifteen, he knew more than a lot of sutra masters knew, and he could teach and recite and talk about these sutras. He got bored with that and decided he wanted to practice Zen, so he started to sit Zen and do long retreats, and he was really good at that. He started a koan practice and was good at that. He was good at everything.

When he was still fairly young, an old master came to visit the temple. He was very old and a little bit senile and he would come back and forth to the temple pretty often. So at one point, they asked this little boy to attend him. The boy took really good care of him for about two weeks and helped him bathe and helped him with getting his clothes clean and helped him with his meals. He was a wonderful attendant.

When the old man left, the little monk walked him to the gate and the old monk said, "You've been so great to me I want to give you a present." Back then they didn't have Hershey Bars or gum, but he was hoping for something like that. But the old man said "If you ever need me, when you get old—you might be caught in a jam or some awful situation—you just face the East and bow three times. I'll come to you and help you." Now to this little boy, being very bright and having studied a lot of Buddhism already, that sounded kind of hokey, but he was polite and said "Thank you very much. That's wonderful," and walked away, disappointed.

The years went by and finally, by the time he was nineteen or so, he decided to be a hermit and go up into the mountains and just sit on his own. He went off to the mountains and found a nice cave or a hermitage and sat facing a wall for many years. People brought him rice and helped support his practice, and he got quite a reputation for having steadfastness with his Zen meditation. He'd been so wonderful even before he started doing these retreats that people started to imagine that this guy must be amazing, and he became quite famous. By the time he was twenty-seven or so he was very highly respected.

When the main Buddhist teacher in Korea died, they needed to find a replacement. Because this particular monk had such an incredible reputation, the head of Korea wanted him to become the national teacher. They went and asked him and he said "Oh no. I would never want to do that." Then the president said "Go and ask him again. We have to have this person as our national teacher." So they asked him a second time, and he said "No, no, no! I'd never want to do that." They asked him a third time, and out of politeness (you're not supposed to refuse a third time when you're asked something that important), he finally agreed to become the national teacher.

Here's this man who is used to living in a cave or hermitage out in the middle of nowhere, who had been raised as an orphan in a temple, and who was used to a very austere, simple life, and all of a sudden he's in the capital city, given brocade robes and silk sheets, an attendant and a personal surgeon, etc. And he had a whole lecture circuit that he needed to do. It turned out he was a beautiful orator, he gave wonderful and appropriate talks. He'd know the audience and he was more than they could have dreamed for a national teacher.

This man had had such wonderful karma all his life. Everything had gone his way. But one night he was going to sleep and his right thigh, just above his knee, began to itch. Now he had never had any body problems—he was still only twenty-eight or twenty-nine. It was pretty annoying but he was able to fall asleep. When he woke up in the morning it was even itchier, so he pulled up his silk pajamas and looked at his leg and there was a big, round, red rash on his thigh. He thought, This is funny, but he ignored it and went off to do his thing that day, working hard and teaching and meditating and doing whatever he had to do.

That night, as he was going to bed, it itched even more, but he was able to get to sleep. When he woke up in the morning, he heard this funny noise—it was like a sniffing noise—that sounded like it was coming from underneath his sheets and so he pulled them back, pulled up his pajamas, and looked at his leg. Now, not only was there a round rash, but a nose was placed right in the middle of that circle. A nose on his leg! So he took his bath, got dressed really fast, and just distracted himself. He couldn't deal with it so he did his work and did it well, but he really had to focus to keep from thinking about the nose, which kept sniffing.

Again he went to bed and woke up in the morning, hoping the nose was gone, but when he looked down at his leg, not only was there this nose, but also two black, beady eyes staring up at him—very unfriendly eyes—right above the nose, where they belong. He did the same thing he had done the day before: He got to work. (That's what we're taught. Just focus, be attentive, breathe, and that's what he did.) He did all that and did it well. He came home exhausted, went to bed, and went to sleep.

The next morning, he got up and heard profanities coming from underneath the sheet. Guess what had appeared—a mouth; the worst part—and, just like the eyes, it was not a friendly mouth. It was very abusive, insulting, angry, and started calling him all kinds of nasty things. Now, he had been a good little kid and had never been called anything like this before. Anything you can think of that was nasty, this mouth said to him, and

some of them were very personal insults. This was just too much this time, so he called his surgeon in and said "This is embarrassing, but I've got to show you what I've got on my leg."

Now in those days the surgeon wasn't going to start inquiring how he had gotten this face on his leg. This was the national teacher, so the surgeon was very polite. He immediately prepared his operating room and did a skin graft. He removed the face and grafted and put herbs and salves on the leg and wrapped it with some bandages and said "That's it. We won't mention it again."

The master went to rest in his room and within minutes the face ate its way through the bandages and said, "You can't get rid of me like that!" and was even more angry. The surgeon was called again and he removed it again, and it popped through again immediately, so that wasn't going to work. So, for the first time in his life this man was really upset. He couldn't give a lecture that day. He couldn't override it and carry on with his day and be clear and attentive and breathe. It wasn't working any more.

Just as in our lives certain things might hit us, we may feel like we've plateaued—"I can handle this"—and that's just the time when another grain of sand comes in or you receive some new teaching in your life, that was his day. This was new and this was something he didn't know how to handle.

As you can guess, he went outside, faced the East, and bowed three times. He never thought he would do that, but he was desperate. He didn't know what to do. So lo and behold, the old monk showed up.

"How can I help you? I'm here for you. what do you need?"

The master told him what had happened and sheepishly pulled up his pants and showed him the face. The monk said "Oh, that's nothing. We can deal with that." He gave him directions to go to a certain mountain, and in three days he would get to a stream that has a particular water.

"Bring a bowl and you can just scoop the water up from that stream and pour it on your leg. The face will disappear and that will be it. Nothing else will be heard of it."

He decided to do that and told his disciples that he was going to do a six-day pilgrimage; that he needed some time to himself. So he set off on the trip and the whole way the face was screaming and yelling at him, insulting him and calling him every name in the book in a very loud voice, but he just kept walking and walking and walking and focusing and focusing and focusing on getting to that mountain. He got there and found the stream, got out his bowl, and started to scoop the water into the bowl and the face said, "Wait a minute. Stop!" He stopped, and the face said, "Look at me."

So he pulled up his pants leg and looked right at the face, and the face said, "You know, the whole time I've been here" (and by then he'd been there for five or six days) "you've never once asked me who I am or what I am. Not once. You've just hoped I would go away and distracted yourself and never asked me who I was."

The master knew that was true and so he said "Who are you? What is this?"

So the face told him. He was a friend of the monk's from two lifetimes back. "Don't you remember me? We were best friends."

The face on the leg was the son of a general and the Zen master was the son of a king. There had been a big war, a big national upheaval, and the son of the general had to go off to war while the other young man had to stay home and help his father with the kingdom. While the son of the general was gone, the prince fell in love with his best friend's girlfriend, and after three years, the prince married the girl and took her away from his best friend.

When the son of the general finally came back from war he found out he had lost his girlfriend to his best friend. He was full of rage and revenge and tried to kill the prince. He ended up being imprisoned and never got the revenge; he just got punished even more, being put in prison for trying to kill the prince. So it was a very bad incarnation for this poor son of the general. When he died, he didn't forgive his friend at all and was filled with unresolved anger. He explained to the Zen master that, in his next life, "I tried to find you to have my revenge and to kill you, but I could never find you. You became a very strong practitioner of Buddhism so I couldn't find you." (If you practice hard you lose a lot of your own personal stuff and you become one with the situation, you become one with everything, and so you don't have I, my, me.)

So the face said, "You got so clear so quickly that I never could find you during your last life. But this life, a little ego appeared. You were giving a Dharma talk one day to five hundred people and, as you were talking, for just a second, you noticed how everybody loved your talk. Everybody was responding and smiling and getting it, and for a minute you had this idea of 'I'm a pretty good teacher. Look at these people.' Just for a second the thought went by, 'These people like me. This job of mine is working out.'"

So in that little ten-second span of thinking, the face on the leg found him. He said, "There he is. There's the ego." The ego appeared—the "I" appeared. The face said, "At that moment I landed on your thigh and that's when your itch started."

The zen master listened to this face giving him this teaching and he did recognize him and said, "I know you, you were my friend." He looked at the face and he apologized for his past actions. He remembered, he apologized, he said, "I'm so sorry."

The face accepted his apology and said, "Okay. That's all I wanted." He had never said he was sorry when he was the prince and they never came to that place where they completed it. So, when the face accepted the apology, it just faded off and was gone. There was no need to pour the water on it, to use the magic, it just disappeared. The magic was the clarity of recognizing the mistake and the clarity of accepting the apology. That's how simple it is.

So often with Zen we'll say, "I call you. You answer. It already appeared." There it is. You're hungry, I give you food, it already appeared. So you're dying, we breathe

together, it already appears. It's not deeply hidden, it's not complicated, it's not esoteric; it's about attentiveness, just being present. And if, when the face had started itching, he had asked that simple question, "What is this, how is it just now?" it might never have had the nose.

What a metaphor for our personal lives. Just because it's different, just because it's strange or threatening, just because it's not familiar, then that's more than ever the time to ask *What is it? How is it just now? What am I?* Just be with it. It's hard when it's not familiar; that's when it's the hardest to be open. It's not just when we happen to be with someone who's ill or someone who's about to leave their body, but all the time, there's that opportunity, that itch, where we need to be with whomever we're with or with whatever situation we're with, and not back off and be intimidated or have some discriminating consciousness about it.

[A participant asked how the story would have changed had the master been aware at the moment that the ego had arisen during his talk.]

We call it a mistake, but we all transgress. Even the Buddha transgressed. It's not about being perfect, and I think that's why a lot of us give up on our practice, because we think it's about perfection. But it's really about seeing your mistake more quickly; your depth of being attentive and noticing when there's an itch or when there's something a little bit off.

[Leaving the story, another member of the audience asked Zen Master Soeng Hyang how far one would take the response to What is this?*]*

That's the whole point. You don't want to analyze, you just want to notice this moment. How is it *just now?*

Let's say you're a psychotherapist working with a patient. You'd be doing What is this? How is it just now? while you listen. Obviously you're digging into the dynamic, the body movements, the facial expression, the tone of voice, the actual words that are said. There's a lot going on when you're talking to someone. If they say something that is particularly honest, you're going to note that. It depends on what you're doing in that moment. Sometimes it might be somewhat complicated. Then from your memory bank you have to remember what the circumstances of that client's life were. That's all just normal human intelligence that we all have.

Again, sometimes people think Zen means you don't think, but it means that you think very clearly. You stop distorting. If you're a math teacher explaining some complicated calculus thing on the blackboard, you're thinking. But you also need to be turning around and looking at the thirty students or so, seeing what is the quotient of people who are getting it to those who aren't. Are you going too fast? Are you going too slow? Do you need to break them into groups? A clear mind can help any occupation because it's about attentiveness and asking How is it just now?

[Another member of the group referred to identification with the body. Having noticed how frequently she looked in the mirror during a recent retreat, it suddenly struck her "how really attached, how into one's body, face," one becomes. She then related how, while watching her father dying from cancer, it became so clear that "the body is just a shell." She concluded that she could "understand why I'm attached— I've been conditioned since Day One to be very attached to this body. How do you work with that attachment the more you see clearly, and yet still feel attached?"]

It's not about attachment or nonattachment. It's about What are you doing just now? It's about What's the point? Often with practice you have to have a vow and you have to have a direction. So in our practice we have these four great vows:

Sentient beings are numberless. I vow to save them all.
Delusions are endless. I vow to cut through them all.
The teachings are infinite. I vow to learn them all.
The Buddha way is inconceivable. I vow to attain it.

Sentient beings are numberless. I vow to save them all. What does that mean? That's not some moralistic thing that you have to do because you have a human body. That has to be something that you feel in your heart— you actually perceive that sentient beings are numberless and then have the sense that I would like to vow to save them all. That's a lofty pursuit, but why not?

Then, *Delusions are endless. I vow to cut through them all.* One of the questions is What's a delusion and what's not a delusion? That will keep you going for a while. Sometimes we think we were on the ball and we weren't. Again that's where seeing your mistake more quickly comes in. You just apologize, hopefully the apology is accepted, and then the karma is over. Next, *the teachings are infinite, but I'll learn all of them.* That'll keep you busy, too.

And then, *the buddha way is inconceivable. I vow to attain it.* Inconceivable Buddha has nothing to do with religion. *Buddha* means "wake up;" I vow to wake up. It's inconceivable to be completely awake, but I'll do it. So if you have those vows and say them at least once a day—not just out loud, but embrace them—it doesn't matter if you look in the mirror or not.

About a year ago, I had done hospice work all day, and it had been more difficult than usual. I remember coming home, thinking, That was hard and I wonder if I did as well as I could have done. But I was brushing my teeth and happened to look in the mirror and saw these really bright, clear eyes looking back at me. I was kind of surprised; I hadn't looked at myself all day. It was so affirming: You know, you work really hard and you did a good job today. It was like I had to give myself a pat on the back because there was nobody else to do it. I think it was very appropriate I did that.

So I don't think it's always wrong to look

in the mirror, but if you look in the mirror, look in the mirror 100 percent. What do you see? And then when you see someone die, look at that 100 percent. What do you see?

[A question from a man in the group concerning the dichotomy between the "one" and the "other" brought Zen Master Soeng Hyang to use a koan to elucidate her point. She noted that, "we use koan practice a lot in our tradition to cut through the dichotomy so that you see the interrelationship and the connectedness.... You don't even want one; you don't want to have that idea." Pointing to a cup of water next to her, she demonstrated the use of this koan:]

If you call this a cup of water, I'll say you're attached to labeling, to name and form. And if you say it's not a cup of water, I'll say you're attached to emptiness, to negating—attached to the void. So you can't say it's not a glass of water and you also can't say it is a glass of water.

That's uncomfortable sometimes. You're sitting in front of the teacher and so don't call it a glass of water and don't say it isn't one. What is it? Don't know. We always encourage the don't know; we say "So only go out and sit with the don't know, with the stuck mind." If we were in an active koan practice at a retreat, then I would say, "The next time you come in I'm going to ask you again about the cup." It's not punitive or one-upmanship, it's just about: look at it; look at it and try again next time. Then you have homework. You go out, and sit on the mat, and think: Hmm, she's going to ask me again about this cup of water. I can't call it a cup of water. Also I can't say it's not a cup of water. What do I call it? That might be uncomfortable, but it's also very spacious because you actually stumped your ego. You stumped your intellect.

But there is a beautiful answer and that's what I love about koan practices. Even the above-average person wouldn't answer a good koan the first time. That's what makes it a koan, you're not supposed to be able to answer it the first time. You have to break through it, to really chew on it and digest it, we often say.

The first thing we teach a student is to do primary point; to go like this [sharp hand-clap]. That's primary point. You're asked is it a cup or not and you hit the floor or slap your hands. You know you have to be there, but if you're sitting three feet in front of your teacher and they ask is it a cup or not, the first thing you get to do is hit the floor really hard. In our tradition we do that so that you have a second to keep your *chi*, keep your energy, in your center, in your gut. You don't think right away. It's like, if you were walking underneath scaffolding and someone inadvertently hit something and all of a sudden a pile of bricks is going to land on your head, you would, without thinking, protect your skull. You're not going to die from scraped-up arms, but you could die if you're hit really hard with a brick. So you would—if you were awake—protect your head without thinking, and that's what this [handclap] becomes. So this is protection from cognitive thinking, like the everyday opposite thinking.

You learn how, just immediately, to go [handclap] so your mind is still empty. This is the thing about standing on the edge of a cliff with koan practice. It takes a lot of guts (literally staying centered in your guts), and it takes a lot of faith and trust in your intuitiveness. Usually, if you're asked something, you want to use your brain.

I've seen many students do that and then, *boom!* They automatically answer the koan and wonder Where did that come from? That's where it comes out that we're already buddha. We already intuitively know our correct relationship and our correct situation, our correct function. We just get in the way of ourselves all the time. The koans get in the way of you on purpose, like a homeo-pathic remedy: They give you the disease—thinking—to see if you can fight back.

[The session continued with the answering of this koan by members of the audience. A few attempts were made before the correct one, which isn't readily "transcribed" into text, was revealed.

During these attempts, some laughter ensued, which led the discussion to the role of humor in practice and the reasons for laughter. One participant observed that she had been to teachings where the teachers talked about tragic events and "they start to giggle! It has always perplexed me, until it seemed to be that what they were giggling at was the absolute magic and beauty that's taking place in the whole process."]

Zen Master Soeng Hyang: Maybe that's why

they giggle; maybe it's not. You have to understand your own giggle, become one with it. That's what I like about Zen, it's not some theory about giggling, it's about Why am I giggling? What's my giggle? That's what's important. And that's what I love about the koan practice. It doesn't depend on your knowing the answer; you've got to know the question. What's the question? What's the point? What's my issue?

I did a long retreat several years ago. I was in the woods for a hundred days, just sitting in a nice cabin. I had my food, water, and wood supply. I had everything I needed, except what I wanted was company. I was lonely. I'm a people person so I kept feeling like I was lonely, and I couldn't pretend that away. It was kind of like the face on the leg. Finally I started to think What is it that feels lonely? What is this loneliness? Not up here [pointing to her head], but to be with the loneliness. How is it just now?

So when I went with the loneliness, I started to ask "What is it that feels lonely?" Not *who* is it, because I didn't want to personalize it as much, or say that I've always been lonely, but more like just *what* is it that feels lonely? What is *that*? And guess what happened: I visited it and it wasn't lonely anymore. I wasn't feeling intimidated or judging it, I just asked "What feels lonely?" [and the answer came back] "Oh, thanks. I'm not lonely anymore. You came over and you visited me." Visit the giggle. Be with it.

[*A woman asked if the question just discussed—"What is it that feels lonely?"—is doing the same thing that some traditions do when they label the feeling? Zen Master Soeng Hyang made a distinction, in that what she had done was to turn it into a koan, a question.*

The final issue of this workshop concerned integrating practice into daily life. A woman presented her dilemma as one in which she frequently tells herself she can't possibly reach her goal in practice because, "In the Zen tradition as I understand it, time on the cushion is really indispensable.... What frequently happens to me, in a very busy, lay-based life, is that that doesn't happen; or it happens on such a marginal level that I don't really have a chance to develop it. And it seems as though, in this country, we are accommodating ourselves so easily to that—that it's lay-based and that... we can't sit on the cushion, so we do it other ways." Zen Master Soeng Hyang responded to this by first telling another story.]

Zen Master Soeng Hyang: Well there's a story of a person in India who was so low class that he wasn't even an Untouchable. But since there was a small group of people that ate beef, there were also some cow killers. That was the worst of the worst, that they would kill these cows, but he was born into that system: His grandfather and father had done it. He had to take a big sledgehammer and hit the cow right between the eyes and bring the cow down. That was his job, but that was not this person's nature. He hated it. But in this system there was no way out and his father and grandfather made him do it and the system made him do it. So he did it.

But in his mind he loved the cow, so he would do it the best he could so that the cow wouldn't suffer. He got really good at doing it so that that cow didn't know what hit it. Sometimes people would miss and have to do it two or three times to finish the cow off, but this guy never missed. So he focused, focused, focused and attained this supreme enlightenment doing this.

He wasn't a Buddhist, but this is a good story to show that it doesn't matter what you do when you do it 100 percent. I'm not a sitter. I'm a mover, so I do the prostrations and I do a lot of chanting and I do my Nordic Trak in the morning and that's my nature. That's what makes me feel better in the morning. I do sit—I go to retreats and I sit a couple times a month—but in my daily life I would rather be bowing or chanting than sitting.

But I think that we can't have that excuse. We have to know that the real instructions are *Just do it.* Own it, embrace it, believe in yourself, and don't make any excuses. If you make a mistake, say "I'm sorry" (if you need an apology, ask for it), and go through life that way.

[The session ended with several minutes of the chant KWAN SEUM BOSAL, which means "perceive world sound" in Korean. Zen Master Soeng Hyang explained that to "perceive world sound is to hear the cries of the universe."]

To listen—whether we're looking at ourself in the mirror, or we're looking at someone we're with as they're taking their last breaths, or picking up a glass of water. No matter what we're doing, we want to listen to it, be in correct relationship to it, and become one with it. Perceive world sound, hear the cries of the universe, hear the laughter of the universe. Just listen.

The repetition and doing it together to become one with the vibrations is very therapeutic. Even in a few minutes you can feel how that takes you out of your opposite thinking, your dichotomy mind, and you can just become one with the vibrations; that's the whole point. Buddhist practice isn't complicated, it's about attentiveness and becoming one and that's it.

[After chanting, Zen Master Soeng Hyang closed with this suggestion for the audience:]

I trust that all of us will stop the ideas and forget about what I said today and forget about anything you heard this weekend and just trust yourself and become one with your own experience and believe that. The more we're awake, the more we can believe it so that if someone says to you "That's not true" you can say "Not enough? You have a problem? " And it's a wonderful feeling not to defend yourself but to stand your ground; trust that you're standing in your ground.

The Healing Power of Mind

Tulku Thondup Rinpoche

AT THE AGE OF FOUR, TULKU THONDUP RINPOCHE WAS RECOGNIZED as the incarnation of Kome Khenpo, a celebrated scholar and adept of Dodrupchen Monastery, a famous institution of learning of the Nyingma school of Tibetan Buddhism. When he left Golok, his birthplace, in eastern Tibet, Tulku Thondup went to study at Dodrupchen Monastery, where he became a *vajracharya*. During his twenty-two years in India, he taught at Lucknow and Visva Bharati universities. In 1980 he moved to the United States as a visiting scholar at Harvard University in Cambridge, Massachusetts. Still living in Cambridge, Tulku Thondup is presently engaged in translation and writing on Tibetan Buddhism, the teaching of the Nyingma school in particular, under the auspices of Buddhayana, an organization dedicated to Tibetan Buddhist studies. He has published more than ten original Tibetan Buddhist works and translations.

Tulku Thondup's book *The Healing Power of Mind: Simple Meditation Exercises for Health, Well-Being, and Enlightenment* was published in 1996. At the beginning of this workshop, Rinpoche characterized the exercises as "healing the person as a whole—the body, the mind, and everyday life—through the power of mind." Grounded in principles and methods of Buddhist meditation, this work deals primarily with conceptual mind rather than enlightened mind, making it appropriate for use in a secular context. Explaining that there are two kinds of teachings in Buddhism, which he likened to two sides of the same coin, he drew a distinction between teachings peculiar to Buddhism or to Asian culture, which entail unique images, names, expressions, disciplines, etc., and those that fit in with many languages and contexts: "The most important aspect of Buddhism, the overwhelming aspect of Buddhism, is a universal teaching or way of approaching whatever meditation or discipline we pursue." He then presented the goal of this session, as well as his book, as "not necessarily to realize that enlightened nature, or enlightened mind, that is our true nature, but to have a more healthy, peaceful, joyful, conceptual mind."

The session began with Tulku Thondup defining a number of terms or concepts that underpin the meditation approach he addressed. First, he asked "What is healing?"

There are many kinds of healing. Generally we think healing means that if we have a sickness in our body, someone says something, someone touches us, and we will be cured. That is one of the aspects of healing, but the most important aspect is to have peace, joy, strength in our mind. If we have that in our mind, then we will have it in our body, and then every aspect of our life, every movement of life, will become an expression of peace, joy, and strength.

Peace is a creation of the mind, a concept created by mind, and it is experience filled by the mind. That's very important. If there is no mind, how can you have peace? Through meditation, through right way of thinking, right way of behaving, even a general awareness of peace, joy, strength in us is the main aspect of the healing process.

These answers led to the question, "If the mind is so important, what is mind?" Rinpoche answered with a metaphor: "Mind is the puppeteer. Mind says, "Oh, I need to go…" and the body says, "Okay, we'll go wherever

you want to go." The body and mental objects are puppets, but most of us have lost that concept. We have forgotten and have become puppets of external phenomenon." This led to a basic distinction between two types of mind—conceptual and enlightened.

Conceptual mind is the surface of the mind. It is a stream of consciousness that thinks, sees, and feels mental objects through intellectual or emotional thoughts. For example, when we see an object, the liking and disliking, being happy or unhappy, all these cycles begin. The Buddhist term "grasping at self" means mentally grasping at an object as a truly existing entity. If you grasp at something as a truly existing entity, you become dualistic, which leads to discriminations, then to disliking and liking, and then you will have pain and joy, etc. Then the cycle increases, the cycle karma starts, the pain and the excitement start, and a never-ending cycle evolves.

Enlightened mind is the true nature of the mind. A buddha has realized the true nature of the mind, enlightened mind. So when Buddha sees this watch, he sees a watch, but his mind is not grasping at this as a truly existing entity. It doesn't break into the subjective-objective duality, which means you won't have all the other mental discriminations mentally, you won't follow the liking and disliking or the hatred and the desire, etc., and then pain and sorrow won't come.

Having made these distinctions, he explained that his goal is to describe and demonstrate how to have a more healthy, peaceful, joyful, conceptual mind; a positive dualistic mind, which will lead to a joyful, healthy body and relationships as well as to prepare the way for a person to "be helpful to others."

"Then why am I bringing in this enlightened mind?" he put forth. Tulku Thondup explained that, while this work concentrates on aspects of everyday life that stem from conceptual mind, "it is very important to know that we are fundamentally on a good ground; we are good people. If we have that understanding, if we have that belief, then we will have to improve the conceptual, ordinary level of mind and life."

The crux of the issue concerns regaining a center in our lives. "If we have peace and joy and strength in our mind, then what happens?" Rinpoche asked. We will then "become self."

At present we have lost our center, the core of life. We are only puppets of external situations. If we have a peace and joy and strength, we will find our own center and our own core. Then we will become the puppeteer, not the puppet, and we can transform our everyday life. We can heal the sicknesses and the difficulties we experience in our body.

And not only that, if we have a peace and joy, then we have a good relationship with people. I have witnessed many people who are sick, dying, have a smile in their face and peace in their face. Not because of their physical health, but because of their mental peace. We all know of many people who are healthy, handsome, beautiful, rich, but many of them

are suicidal because there's no peace, there's no joy, there's no strength in their mind.

Before beginning the directed meditation, Rinpoche discussed the four tools of healing:
1. Form
2. Thoughts, names, expressions, words
3. Feeling
4. Believing

He defined form as "mental visualizations, imaginations, images." Many people are reticent, even unable, to use visualizations initially, but Rinpoche put this in the context of everyday experience: "If you think about your home, you immediately see your kitchen, your coffee pot in your mind, and that is visualization, imagination. Most of us, whatever we think, always think with the image. We have this treasure of imagery capacity, so we should use it to our advantage, which means using positive images— the healing-technique images.

As for words, names, or thoughts, Rinpoche pointed out that we always impose labels. "When you see a friend, you think, This is a friend. If we just see an image, it doesn't make much difference. But we always talk in our mind. Always we dialogue. We are always thinking, talking, and when we see things we use names, labels. This is something we have with us all the time, so use it as a positive tool."

In healing, he pointed out, the third tool— feeling—is very important.

If you don't have a feeling, images and names

stay in one place. Of course, they make a big impact, but when you feel, it comes into the core of our mind and our body.

For example, in your mental image, if you see a flower, you *think* Oh, this is a beautiful flower. But don't just think about or visualize the flower and the beauty of the flower, but *feel* the freshness, the calmness, the color, the moisture, the light, the blossoming of the flower. Again, mind is thinking. Let it feel too, then it becomes really effective. When negative images, negative concepts arise, try not to feel. But for positive images and feelings, then you have to feel it if you want to make a big impact.

Once you bring feeling into the experience, it is important to utilize the final tool, believing, in order to obtain the most lasting results. Without belief, the good derived from the earlier tools can be discarded simply by subscribing to such a notion as "It won't work." Rinpoche noted that we:

always find a way to reject, to cut off, to throw away. But if you have faith—bring in believing, trusting: Yes, this *is* a beautiful flower. Then feel the beauty of the flower bringing peace and joy and strength in you; believe it has the power to bring healing in you and you are healed. If you believe in it, it becomes a hundred times more powerful. But if you don't believe in it, if you reject it, minimize it, you will destroy everything you have got.

Finally, Tulku Thondup looked briefly at the three types of results these healing exercises

and meditations may have. First, many sicknesses and diseases, whether having to do with our physical or mental health or the well-being of our relationships can be healed completely through such meditation. Then, though we cannot heal many things, this practice will help to ease the problems. Lastly, the result Rinpoche suggested may be the most important of the three is that the peace, joy, and strength in our mind "will bring the strength to tolerate [those things that cannot be healed], and that is even more powerful."

Meditation

Rinpoche led the participants in a simple meditation. He began by working to develop an awareness of the body. If they were feeling uncomfortable, he instructed the meditators to visualize a dark cloud in the part of their body that was experiencing the discomfort.

See it. Feel it. Feel that this image holds the feeling of anxiety, the source of anxiety, and the image of anxiety. Then take a deep breath, and with the out-going breath, expel that dark cloud. It comes out through your mouth and comes out totally, completely with out-going breath. See the dark cloud in front of you in the sky. And then the dark cloud slowly, slowly moves away, floating away through the sky, slowly, slowly, like a bird slowly flying away. See it flying away toward far horizon. Feel the distance—it's going away, farther and farther. As much as it goes away, you become free—freer and freer —from the anxieties.

Having established this freedom from anxiety, he told the participants that they must scan the body noticing that it is made of bones, flesh, arteries, organs, all wrapped in skin. "We are not seeing the body as ugly or as beautiful, but as it is." He told them to bring as much information as they know to each part. "If you don't know much, don't worry about it, but as much as you know, just think about the structure of the head, the materials of the head."

As they continued this progressive scanning, they were asked to "see that body's not just made of bones, flesh, etc., but it is made of billions and billions of cells."

Tulku Thondup Rinpoche

Again, look at the whole body. It is a heap of cells. It is a statue of cells, a structure of cells. Billions of them. Not just one, two, ten, hundred, but an infinite number. Billions of cells. Now, think that, according to Buddhism, the elements are there—earth, fire, air, and water, and so each cell is made of four elements and all the cells are cells of light. See our bodies made of cells of light, billions of cells of light. Colorful, beautiful, immaterial. The upper body is made of billions of cells of light, colorful, bright.

Now, again look at the head and look at the forehead between the eyebrows. There are many hundreds of thousands of cells of light between the eyebrows. Choose one cell—this cell is a cell of light, bright, colorful—and enter into that cell. It is as if you were entering outer space, into the vast openness. The cell is made of light, beautiful, colorful, peaceful; filled with warmth. It is

not cold, but is warm. Feel the blissfulness, joyfulness in this cell of light and see and feel the boundlessness. If we try to find end of sky, we won't find it. In the same way, the cell is infinite, boundless. Enjoy that beautiful and peaceful and joyful cell. Now see that our head is made of billions of these cells. Cells of same kind. Vast, boundless, beautiful cells.

Now and then, if you feel uncomfortable, or feel suffocated, do the same exercise that we did before, visualizing that anxiety in the form of a dark cloud, expelling that with outgoing breath.

Now see that you are breathing. See and feel that the breathing is not coming from the stomach or through the respiratory system, but every cell is breathing, from the top of the head to the soles of the feet. All cells, these vast, boundless cells, are all breathing. The cells are not just breathing air, but they're breathing energies—the energies of warmth, blissfulness, and strength. As we breathe, every cell is sending energies to other cells and receiving energies. When we exhale, the cells are sending healing energies. And when we inhale, each cell is receiving the healing energies. Waves of energy. Waves of heat. Waves of bliss. Waves of power.

The waves are moving with the sound. There are no movements without sound and no sound without movement. Waves coming from every cell of the body, from the head to the soles of the feet. Sound of AH—the source of all the sounds. According to Buddhist and Indian wisdom, all the sounds come from AH, and AH is the basis of all the sound. But AH doesn't convey any conceptual messages, only openness, emptiness, unborn nature. If someone is a nonbeliever, still AH can be expression of a simple syllable.

The meditation continued with chanting led by Rinpoche, who advised that the "lower voice has more power."

Now think and feel that the sound—the waves of energy—is not coming through the respiratory system, through the vocal system, but is coming out directly, bursting out of every pore of the body.

We chant slowly, in low voice. We don't chant loudly. Just hear the sound coming from all the cells of the body, with the waves of energy—coming out, bursting out of every pore of the body. We hear the sound coming, but not through the vocal system. Now think that the waves of energy coming out from every pore of our bodies, are filling the whole

universe. We are sharing the healing energies through the whole universe, every being in the whole universe.

Understand that every being in the whole universe is made up of individual cells, and every cell is a cell of light. The whole universe is made up of atoms, and every atom is made of light. So the whole universe is transformed into universal light, universal healing energies, universal waves of healing energies with warmth, bliss, and power.

Now, look back at your body. What it is feeling? Maybe peacefulness, or warmth, blissful, maybe spaciousness, strength. Each person might be feeling differently. See what your main feeling is. See it, recognize it, and enjoy it. That particular feeling. If it is spacious feeling, enjoy the spaciousness of it. If it is blissful, feel that blissfulness. Enjoy it openly, not grasping at it.

Now meditate on oneness. That means whatever you're feeling, recognize that feeling and feel that. And then just don't think anything more. Rest there. Relax there, without any thinking. Let everything go. Just relax there without more thinking. You are almost merged with that feeling and become one. There's no more subjective/objective. Rest there, relax there.

Rinpoche ended the meditation by dedicating "the merits, whatever healing energies we have created, to all other beings."

After reviewing the benefits this type of meditation can provide, Tulku Thondup

Rinpoche concluded by discussing how to incorporate this practice into everyday life:

If you have felt any good things about the meditation, please carry it with you and bring that again. You can do the meditation again and again if you want, but you don't have to do the whole thing. You may do just what parts you like. The whole goal is to feel peace, joy, strength, whatever it helps. That is according to Buddhism, according to, I'm sure, any religion. It is a healthy thing to do, and you should try to do it whenever you like. You don't have to have a guru. A support system is always helpful, but you don't have to have one to do this meditation.

Buddhism and Psychotherapy

Ron Leifer, M.D.

WHILE BUDDHISM AND WESTERN PSYCHOTHERAPY SHARE the common aim of transforming the suffering of negative emotions into clarity and happiness, the approaches and techniques employed tend to be quite different. Dr. Leifer, a psychiatrist in private practice in Ithaca, New York, addressed this seeming paradox in his workshop. He examined questions related to the titular issue as well as cultural differences in defining values and setting priorities and their impact on the contemporary quest for happiness. Using Buddhist concepts such as the three principal aspects of the path, the three poisons, and the four noble truths, he discussed ways in which Buddhism and psychotherapy share common ground. Through directed visualizations and meditation, he also demonstrated Buddhist approaches to working with anger.

In 1964 Dr. Leifer met Agehananda Bharati, a Viennese-born Hindu monk, who gave him his first meditation lessons. Since that time he has been studying Eastern traditions. He became a student of Khenpo Karthar Rinpoche at the Karma Triyana Dharmachakra Monastery in Woodstock, New York, in 1980. The Dalai Lama established Namgyal Monastery Institute of Buddhist Studies in Ithaca, the curriculum of which involves the study of language, epistemology, philosophy, and debate, as well as traditional meditation practices, Shamatha, Vipassana, and Tantra among them. Since its founding, Dr. Leifer has been both student and teacher at this institute.

Dr. Leifer is among the few psychiatrists to integrate his understanding of Buddhist thought with his practice, at times causing his approach to be discredited as "heretical" by some of his more Western-oriented colleagues. The results of this work, however, attest to the wisdom inherent to his form of practice, and in *The Happiness Project,* his forthcoming book, he attempts to integrate Buddhist and Western thought.

Having studied psychiatry for many years, I found myself dismayed and eventually bored by what psychiatrists have to teach, and I've thrown myself more completely into the study of Buddhism and Buddhist psychology. Not that I've ignored Western thought at all, but I have come to think of my patients and work primarily from a Buddhist point of view. And I'd like to share with you how I view that, to give you a flavor of how it's possible to be a Buddhist practitioner and a psychotherapist in a way which is seamlessly integrated.

You heard Bob Thurman say that Buddhism is a form of psychotherapy.* And during the sixties, in a little book called *Psychotherapy East and West,* Alan Watts observed that when you look at the Eastern religions, they're more like psychotherapy than religion in the sense that their aim is the transformation of consciousness. When you look at Western approaches to psychotherapy, they look more like religions—there is a kind of dogma, there are charismatic leaders like Freud, and there are rules of deportment, rituals, and heretics. (I'm one of those heretics who, were it three hundred years earlier, would probably have been burned at the stake. But it was sufficient to have been expelled from academic psychiatry for my heretical views.)

There are some obvious similarities between Buddhism and psychotherapy. First, the aim of Buddhism is to relieve our suffering. That

is, Buddha was inspired to inquire in the direction that he did, which led to his discoveries, which have become the Dharmic teachings, by his observation of the four sights—a sick man, a dying man, a dead man being readied for cremation, and a monk meditating serenely. This state of suffering struck Buddha to the heart, and he resolved to himself that he would find the solution to the problem of suffering. So this is the motive for the whole Buddhist path.

His first teachings were the four noble truths, the first of which is the fact of suffering—that's where Buddhism begins. The aim of Buddhism is to help us deal with our own suffering. You can talk about the aim of Buddhism being the achievement of nirvana, but that's sort of nonsense for us Americans. Nobody here is going to achieve nirvana. Bob Thurman gave, I thought, a very good sign as to whether a person has achieved nirvana or not: Put a plastic bag over their head and see if they try to take a breath. A buddha doesn't care whether he breathes or not, but the rest of us are going to struggle for breath. So it's a good idea to forget about nirvana. It's a tremendous distraction, because we're either going to set ourselves on the path toward something we're never going to be able to achieve, or else we're going to think it's hopeless and give up right at the beginning.

The aim of Buddhism is to help us with our own suffering, step by step, bit by bit. If each day we can help ourselves to be a little more comfortable with ourselves, that eventually puts us in a position to help other people. That, of course, is the second princi-

* See Prof. Thurman's keynote address, "Toward an American Buddhism," pages 450–68.

pal aspect, or aim, of Buddhism. The first aim of Buddhism is called renunciation, and that's the language for a monk, who renounces secular life. I asked one of the lamas: What does renunciation mean for us guys, who are out there struggling and trying to make a living and support some people and meet our responsibilities and pay our taxes? He said it's just giving things up little by little. Maybe you don't need so much luxury; maybe you can give away a portion of what you make; maybe you don't need to grasp after fame or success quite so much. It's just a little bit of pulling back on our ambitions, on our selfish desires. I've come to a definition of maturity—the gradual giving things up. And the more gracefully we can give things up, the happier we're going to be.

It's counterintuitive. The yuppie slogan is "He who dies with the most toys wins," which is cynical and reveals its own futile desperation. But, really, the key from the Buddhist point of view is, the more you can give up, the more peace of mind you're going to have. So the first step is basically taking care of ourselves—taking care of ourselves so that we're not a burden on other people—as Trungpa said, we're not a nuisance to other people. We're able to manage for ourselves. We're able to face life and its difficulties, and also to find a degree of calmness and serenity in the doing of it.

Once we've become self-reliant to that degree, then we're in a position to take the second step, which is helping other people. And that is the key to happiness. We're all looking for the secrets of happiness, and these secrets are glamorized, like Ponce de

Leon's Fountain of Youth in Florida. But from a Buddhist point of view, a secret is not something held from us by someone else, who knows but isn't telling, and it's not something written in a book that is difficult to understand. Basically secrets are things we hide from ourselves. So the secrets to happiness, from the Buddhist point of view, are self-secret. To discover these secrets, we have to look into ourselves with a certain degree of honesty and courage. When we do, we find the very disappointing and unpleasant truth, that the path to happiness doesn't come from maximizing our own situation; it really comes from helping other people. That's a truth we have to learn for ourselves; our parents teach us that when we're very young, and we ignore it. The ministers will preach it to us on Sundays, and we ignore it. Otherwise, we don't hear much about it, but it's the essence of the Buddhist path.

The third principal aspect of the path is coming to some understanding of the nature of reality, of the nature of phenomena, and the nature of ourselves. From the Buddhist point of view, we have to come to terms with three facts of existence, and the first is the fact of suffering—that we're all going to suffer and we have to deal with our suffering. There's no way out of it and there's no way around it, but there is a way through it. We can magnify our own suffering or we can minimize our own suffering, and that's a skill we can learn with the Buddhist approach.

The second fact of existence is impermanence—that everything is changing. Much of our pain comes from trying to hold things constant and stable. We're all looking for stability and security, and that's a tragic project, because there is nothing that is stable and secure. How can we be secure when we don't know what's going to happen in the future? And we can't control other people.

I've been doing psychotherapy for thirty-five years and I've never changed anybody. I can't change anybody. I can hardly even change myself. That's a massive task for me, and it's going to be a massive task for everyone. This is not to say that people don't change in psychotherapy, but if you're working psychotherapy properly, you create the conditions in which a person can change themselves.

The third fact we have to face is that of emptiness; nothing has any substantial existence. As the Dalai Lama says, there's no table in the table, there's no flower in the flower, and there's no Ron Leifer in here— there ain't nobody inside. I was once with Jamgon Kongertul Rinpoche at a meeting of psychiatrists. He sat in front of them, he smiled a little bit, and said, "Let me ask you a question, since I'm from Asia and haven't been in this country very often. You're all psychiatrists. You're scientists of the mind. What is mind?" Well, there was an embarrassing two minutes of silence, because none of the psychiatrists could answer the question. And nobody can answer that question, because it can't be found.

So these are truths that we have to come into relationship with in order to discover the secrets of relieving our own suffering. Buddhism is a path that faces these secrets, these facts of existence, directly. And psychotherapy is also. I don't view the peo-

ple who come to see me as mentally ill at all—*ever*. I think of them as sufferers, as I think of myself as a sufferer. The word *patient* is derived from the Greek *pathos,* which means "to suffer." And *patience,* and being a patient, and the words *pathology* and *pity* all come from the same root, namely suffering. A patient is one who suffers, and we're all patients in that sense, so there's a common ground between Buddhism and psychotherapy: The aim of both is to help us to understand and relieve our suffering. That, to me, is such a significant common ground as to join the two at the heart.

One of the first things we're taught when we go to see a lama is what's called the ordinary foundations, or the four thoughts which turn the mind inward. One of those thoughts is that secular life is inherently unsatisfactory. That is, happiness is not to be found in the secular world. Happiness is not to be found through the acquisition of wealth. It's not to be found through fame or success, or through the acquisition of social power. It's not even to be found in relationships. (Although I would say of all of those, it's through relationships that we are going to find the greatest joy, but also be vulnerable to the greatest pain.) From the Buddhist point of view, the path to happiness is a journey within, and the Tibetan word for Buddhist is *nang-ba. Nang* is a reflexive which means a "self-person," "a person who goes inward." So the path to happiness is going inward into our own minds in order to understand our minds, wherein lie the causes of our own suffering.

That, at least in spirit, is the aim of psychotherapy, although it's not always practiced that way. But psychotherapy is therapy of the mind, and so a good psychotherapist will focus on the mind—How do you feel? What do you think about that? In cognitive psychotherapy, the aim is to transform the person's thinking with the idea that if our thinking about the nature of our life situations is distorted or erroneous, then those errors are going to lead us into conflicts which we're not able to resolve. As Bob Thurman said very articulately, if you pit yourself against reality, you're going to lose. Because reality is stronger than we are. So we have to adjust ourselves to the outer situation.

Now I wholeheartedly endorse an American Buddhism that is an engaged Buddhism, that is not a solipsistic or narcissistic Buddhism in which we're just preoccupied with our own inner state, although we believe that the causes of the suffering we impose on ourselves and others are to be found in the mind. Nevertheless, that does not mean that we're not to engage with each other in order to improve social conditions, in order to promote social justice, in order to protect the environment from the effects of heedless, mindless, and greedy use of resources, which is damaging to all of us and to future generations. Those are a part of the Buddhist mission as it's being defined in this country, but that has to be understood in context—that being able to make those transformations requires us first to work on ourselves.

Now, the third common ground of Buddhism and psychotherapy is a common interest in science as the valid approach to knowledge. This is a very big subject. It's so important that we understand the conflict between science and religion properly. Otherwise, we're either going to look down on religious teachings as unscientific and lose something very precious, namely a tradition of guidance for life, which is what religion provides and science cannot.

Science and religion both have a power and they both have a weakness. The power of science is that it gives us objective knowledge of the world—or more properly, rather than "objective," we use "intersubjectively verifiable"—upon the basis of which we are able to construct and invent medicines which help keep us alive, and automobiles, computers, all kinds of material things that may make the conditions of life more comfortable. Of course, all of these things come with the hazard that we may develop the false idea that our happiness is to be found through these objects. But the fact that our happiness is not to be found through these objects does not mean that these objects are not valuable and important in contributing to our comfort and to our ability to help each other to live more happy and productive lives. But science, by the rules of its own evidence, cannot prescribe a course of life for us. Science cannot prescribe an ethical path, and an ethical path is absolutely essential for the achievement of happiness.

If there is one quality that the Buddhists associate with the achievement of happiness, it's virtue. Virtue is an extremely obscure and complex term these days, because the

Judeo-Christian tradition has tended to define virtue in terms of specific acts, like not having a same-sex lover (which is such a ridiculous ethical precept). To talk about virtue involving people's private sexual activity is a self-crippling notion of virtue.

The Tibetans are a very odd people: Among them, you can do anything you want sexually, basically, but you can't be violent or aggressive. The reverse is true here. You can hate as many people as you want, but there are certain people you can't love or make love to. So we have this craziness about sex and we permit and glamorize violence. Our nation is rife with violence and we're crazy about sex. It's entirely the opposite from the Buddhist point of view, whereby you don't offend other people, you don't assault other people, you don't attack other people. If you want to go off and make love to someone, nobody's going to pay any attention.

As I understand it, as Chögyam Trungpa was leaving Tibet under the Chinese occupation, he invited a nun up to the roof of the monastery, and he said, "We're going to make love tonight, and out of this love-making is going to come my heir." They made love that night, and it was a beautiful full moon, and he never saw her again. The child was indeed born to her and he became the current Osel Mukpo, who is the head of the Vajradhatu. (I hope that's a true story. Even if it's not true, metaphorically it's true.)

A lot of Tibetan lamas and other Buddhist teachers get accused of having sex with their students, and there is something unethical about that and something that should be viewed with a critical eye, especially when the teacher has power over the student. I'm not approving of any of those kinds of dalliances. On the other hand, from the Tibetan point of view, it's not that important and they don't quite understand why we make such a big deal about that.

But the point is that the path to happiness is through virtue. The reason we need both science and religion is, as Einstein said, "Science without religion is lame, and religion without science is blind. And together they are like a man who can't walk, sitting astride the shoulders of a man with no eyes. Together, they can see and walk." So science gives us intersubjective truth about the world, and religion provides us with guidance for life. We need both of these; we need a religious view which is able to accept all scientific facts as true. The Dalai Lama has specifically said, if there is a Buddhist teaching that is contradicted by scientific fact, we have to reevaluate that Buddhist teaching.

When you study Buddhist logic in the monastery, they talk about valid cognitions—valid ideas. From the Galukpa point of view, which is a very specific point of view, the path to nirvana or to happiness is to be found through the appreciation or realization of the truth, and the realization of the truth is basically found through three techniques: valid cognitions, which are observations; valid inferences, which are logical deductions; and traditional teachings from masters (about which there can be some fuzziness and authoritarian dictates, which may or may not be true, so one has to have some critical perspective). But the path to happiness lies through correct seeing, and correct seeing is basically scientific seeing.

I'd like to focus now on the three poisons, which is a vast subject. The four noble truths are basically divided in two [pairs], and the first two noble truths deal with what are called the afflictions, or the poisons—suffering and the cause of suffering. The second two noble truths deal with a cure—the possibility of redemption from suffering and the path of redemption from suffering, which is *marga,* or the eightfold path, the ethical prescriptions. By following them, we are able to achieve some inner peace.

The three poisons are part of the second noble truth (the causes of suffering) and are often named lust, hatred, and ignorance; or greed, aggression, and illusion. Usually we'll say to ourselves, "Well, lust, hatred, and ignorance, they don't really apply to me. I don't have that much lust, and I'm not that much of a hateful person, and I'm well-educated. So it must refer to someone else. I don't really know what they're talking about when they're talking about these three." When you take a look at what the Buddhists mean by lust, hatred, and ignorance, something very different appears, like a holographic image that you have to stare at properly for a period of time before the image reveals itself. What was revealed to me by studying the three poisons intensively was this: Basically the three poisons can be divided into a pair—what I call desire and aversion—and a third member, ignorance.

Peter Matthiessen* got into a little trouble when he suggested that we were animals. I hope nobody here is offended by that idea. Those who are offended, I presume don't need bathrooms—or lunch for that matter. We are physical, biological organisms, and we can't escape that fact. When we study biological organisms from the point of view of Western science, what has been discovered is a very fundamental truth, namely that organisms behave on the basis of two fundamental motivations, which are the basic principles of behavioral psychology: Organisms seek pleasure or that which enhances well-being, promotes the perpetuation of the species, and promotes well-being and, on the other hand, avoids painful situations that may be deleterious to the perpetuation of the species, and may lead to death. These are the basic principles of behavioral psychology: We are motivated by the desire for pleasure and the aversion to pain. Well, these are two of the three poisons—our desires for sensuous pleasure (the pleasures of the eyes, the ears, touch, taste), but also, in humans, a higher and sublimated form of pleasure, which needs to be understood.

Do you know what sublimation means in psychoanalysis? Sublimation is a metaphor taken from physics, where it refers to the transformation of a solid into a gas. That is, the transformation of something apparently solid and substantial, into something more

---

* Dr. Leifer refers here to Peter Matthiessen's keynote address, "The Coming of Age of American Zen," which is excerpted on pages 396–406.

subtle. Its root is subliminal—"below the levels of perception."

In humans, in orthodox psychoanalytical terms, sublimation refers to a transformation of consciousness, which we all experience as we're socialized, as we move from childhood to adulthood. As children, we're oriented toward our bodies, toward sensuous pleasure, toward being physically comfortable, toward being warm, toward being fed, toward being hugged and nuzzled. As we grow older, we learn that we've got to distance ourselves from our parents and instead relate through language, so that our desires become sublimated. Instead of grabbing food with our hands, we learn to dine. Instead of having sex with every creature of the opposite sex that looks desirable, we have rules of courtship, and rules of kinship relationship, and incest taboos, and marriage, and kinship moieties, which are basically rules governing the use of our body. These are of a higher level of consciousness than those that govern animal behavior.

One of the things that happens when we move from childhood to adulthood is that our desires for instant gratification are transformed into desires for future happiness, what I call happiness projects. Our behavior is motivated by our desire to be happy in the future. So we go to school, we save our money, we go on vacation next year or next month rather than taking tomorrow off to stay in bed because we don't feel good. We become future-oriented and our desires become future-oriented, but so do our aversions.

Now animals (and we, ourselves, as animals), are interested in feeling good and avoiding feeling bad. We're interested in sensuous pleasure, avoiding physical pain, long life. We're interested in avoiding death. We have all of these projects and plans and hopes and desires and fears and phobias and worries. After all, what do our worries consist of? The possibility that we may not be happy in the future. And that is what our mind is constantly doing. Sometimes I'll talk to someone who is spaced out, and say to them, "What's going on?"

"Oh, I was just thinking."

"Well, what were you thinking about."

"I don't know."

From the Buddhist point of view, that is a cause of suffering. That endless churning of the mind, what's been called supratentorial chatter, or the inner newsreel, is an inner dialogue constantly spinning through our minds, so we don't know which way we're going. One of the functions of *vipassana* meditation is to watch your mind. You'll find that your mind is circling your whole life sphere, circling the drama of your life, trying to find a way to solve a problem so that you can have more happiness, more of what you want, and trying to find a way to avoid all of the infinite possibilities of disaster. That's what we're thinking all the time. How can I avoid? How can I pay that bill? What if I don't pay that bill? What if my kid gets sick? What if I don't please my boss? What if I can't do this paper? What if I can't get there on time? The three poisons. How can I get what I want and be happy and avoid what I don't want and avoid my unhappiness? Me. I.

What we want is for our lives to work our way. We've got our ideas of what's going to make us happy today, tomorrow, next week, and next year, and we try to ally ourselves with people who are going to help us in that project. People who get in our way become our enemies. So our main project is to make my life work my way according to my vision of what I would like to be and make myself into. The desires and the aversions are the primary motivators.

What are our desires and our aversions? Some of us may want to be well-liked by other people. We want to have smooth relationships with our children, parents, and spouses. We want to have jobs we're happy in. We want to make enough money to pay our bills. We would like to get a new car, we would like to go on vacation soon. We'd like to have enough money to retire at fifty-five. We've got a lot of plans! And things pretty much need to fall together quite well for all of that to work, and by and large, it doesn't work. That's the essence of our worries: *my happiness projects may not work.*

The word ignorance is a translation of the Sanskrit word *avidya. Vid* means "I see;" *video* means "to see." The *Vedas* are books of wisdom, because wisdom is presented in metaphors of seeing. So the *Vedas* mean to see, which means to see the truth, to see the truths of our lives, to see the truths of existence. *A* is a negating prefix, so *avidya* is the failure to see, or ignorance. This is not only a failure to see, understand, appreciate, and live by—to realize—the three facts of existence, it's also the projection onto the world of something that is not there, which is why it's also called illusion.

That projection onto the world of something that is not there is the assumption that objects are real and have some substantial identity. If I were to sit on this table, would that make it a chair? I have a dog who eats on my chair. Does that make the chair a table? These things are objects by conventional definition. We define these objects and then take them as real. They have no substantial existence in themselves; if we were to take that table apart, we would have some legs and the tabletop. And if I took an ax and chopped them all up, we'd have bunches of wood. Well, where is the table? There's that bunch of wood, but where is the table? And if I throw it into a fire, and it all goes up into smoke, we have carbon dioxide and all kinds of volatile chemicals, but where is the table?

A meditation called analytic meditation is prescribed for excessive attachments. So if you go to a lama and you say, "I'm in love with this woman, and she has left me," the lama will ask, "What are you in love with? Are you in love with her hair? her skin? her eyes? Imagine all of her parts, and lay them out on the floor, and you've got a bunch of hair there, and some bones there, and some muscles there, and some intestines there. What is it that you love?" The meaning is that what we love is a construction in our own mind, which we project onto the object, take it as real, and then relate to it as if it's real.

We do the same thing with ourselves.

We take ourselves as real and substantial, as the most precious thing in the world, that which is to be defended and promoted. We act in that way, motivated by our desires for pleasure and happiness and our aversion to pain, unhappiness, and death, and that's what we're all about. That very nexus of self is the cause of the pain that we impose on ourselves and others. And that's the heart of the Buddhist understanding of suffering. If we want to understand our suffering, we have to understand what we want, what we're averse to, and our own selfishness.

Now, this is very far from conventional psychiatric thought. You go to a psychiatrist now and you're going to be told you have a chemical imbalance. I feel sorry for the American public being exposed to this kind of hoax, which is not to say that psychiatric drugs don't work. They may work—I have seen them work, and I use them. However, that does not mean that the cause of the suffering is a biochemical imbalance.

For example, we may be depressed for one reason or another. Perhaps we think we're depressed because we've lost our job. From the Buddhist point of view, we're depressed because we want the job that we've lost. If we lose a job that we don't want, we're not going to get depressed about it. But given the absence of that job, and our feeling that we can't be happy and move forward in our lives without that job, our bodies are going to get bogged down. And one of the things that's going to happen is we're going to experience stress, and

when we experience chronic stress, our neurotransmitters become depleted. Indeed, Prozac may give us a jump start and help people with the depression. But we are sadly misguided if we think that the cause of our depression is biochemical and that the cure or the treatment of the depression is *solely* biochemical. The pharmacotherapy may help, but it's not going to get to the root of the matter and there's not going to be any new learning in it, and one is going to be subject to the same vicissitudes over and over again.

[A participant brought the discussion back to Dr. Leifer's saying that patients aren't mentally ill, asking him how he considers bipolar disorder (previously known as manic depression), or OCD (obsessive-compulsive disorder) "...where now you can visualize on PET scans what's happening in the brain. Is there really such a duality there?...In a way, it doesn't sound respectful of science to say that all those labels are just completely wrong, or that there's no truth in them."]

Dr. Leifer: I wouldn't say that there's no truth in them. On the other hand, the truth in them is relative truth, which depends not only on the relationship of the observer to the observed, but the mind of the observer in relationship to the observed.

I think bipolar illness is one of the hoaxes being perpetrated on the American public, which is not to say that there aren't some people who become hypomanic and the momentum of their energy is such that it becomes a physical state rather than something that they can voluntarily control. There's no question about the fact that lithium or some other mood stabilizer will help such people. But there is no such illness. It's just a name that is ascribed to people who behave in a certain way.

I was one of the organizers of the Buddhism-Psychotherapy Conference in 1987, where I made a few statements like this, and it was a total disaster because people are not able to hear this. It sounds so heretical, it makes people so angry. People have built their lives and professions on the idea that there is mental illness.

[This discussion persisted for several minutes, clearly raising several sensitive issues. Dr. Leifer used the emotional tenor it had taken on to segue into the final part of his workshop, which consisted of a guided visualization and meditations for dealing with anger.]

Anger is a form of suffering; it's not possible to be happy when we're angry. Anger takes a number of different forms. In its most obvious form, it's hot and full of energy, it's aggressive and it's physical. But anger can also be very subtle. I have seen situations where, when introducing one person to two other people, I know that person A likes person B but is angry at person C. Just in their tone of voice, you can hear the anger. You've probably heard this from your spouse or children, too. When they're angry with you, it may not be hot, it may be just a little withdrawal of warmth, a little reserve, a little less loving-kindness, a cold tone in the voice. So anger

can take all of these forms, and it can also manifest as depression.

[Dr. Leifer prepared the audience for the meditation on anger with a brief period of shamatha *meditation—]*

also called "calm abiding," or "tranquilizing" meditation, which refers to calming the mind so it's not busy with its hypermentations, with the thinking. When the mind is calm and clear of these extraneous thoughts, these worries about our lives, then we're able to turn our attention onto our own mind and examine it. The main point of *shamatha* meditation is to bring your mind into the present moment, because the busy mind is either in the past, thinking about what we wish had been, or in the future, thinking about what we hope for or are worried about. When we're in the present, the mind can't think because the present's going by too quickly.

[Directing the participants to focus their attention on the breath, Dr. Leifer explained that, after about two minutes, he would clap his hands as a cue to "imagine as vividly as you can the last time you were angry, or a significant moment in your life when you were angry with somebody close to you." He would then take them through an analysis of the anger, identifying the desires, the frustration to the desires, and the feelings of helplessness, vulnerability, and anxiety associated with not getting what they want. The participants would see how anger obliterates those feelings.]

Try to visualize vividly and experience a moment of your own anger. Visualize the situation and the person that you were angry at. Now draw your attention into your own mind, and ask yourself: In that situation, what did I want that I was not getting? Or what was being imposed upon me that I did not want? Now try to identify the obstruction—what prevented you from getting what you wanted? What prevented you from avoiding what you didn't want? That combination of wanting something we can't have, or having imposed upon us something that we don't want, is frustration. When we feel frustrated, we feel helpless, vulnerable, and frightened. In fact, helplessness is nothing other than not getting what we want.

That feeling of vulnerability, helplessness, and fear or anxiety, is experienced as a threat to the organism. It may be physical—we want to stay alive and our life is threatened, or we want to be free of pain—but more likely, we want to get there on time and somebody ahead of us is driving slowly, or we want a little quiet and the kids are making noise, or we want to go to the movies and our mate doesn't, or somebody stole some money from us and we wanted that money. Fill in your own life experience. They're all experienced as a threat to our organism, just as if we were prey being chased by a predator, and the response is the fight-flight reaction—a physiological reaction which is part of our animal nature. It is automatic and therefore part of the autonomic nervous system, which prepares the body for muscular activity.

How does it prepare the body for muscular activity? The muscles need a blood supply for activity, so the heart beats faster; the body needs oxygen, so the respiration's increased. When the muscles are being used, it generates heat, so we sweat. This combination of rapid heartbeat and respiration, tense muscles, sweating, and a menacing and threatening posture is very much like chimpanzees and apes posturing in anger against each other. We try to intimidate the world, intimidate other people into giving us what we want, or avoid their imposing upon us what we don't want. The function of our anger is to reduce our feeling of helplessness. But since the anger very rarely works, it's a pseudopower. Anybody who feels anger is feeling helpless, and the helplessness is at the core of the anger. So the question is how do we deal with our anger?

There are two ways out of anger. One is to try and get what we want or to avoid what we don't want. There's nothing wrong with that if we can do it without being harmful to ourselves or others. It follows the prescription of the Serenity Prayer: "Give me the courage to change what I can, the serenity to accept what I can't change, and the wisdom to know the difference." We apply that maxim to our own anger.

Try and reflect on your anger and think, Is there a way I might have been more diplomatic? Perhaps if I asked for what I wanted. Perhaps if I offered something in exchange. Perhaps if I thought of another approach or I was more patient. Is there a way that I could have gotten what I wanted or avoided what I didn't want? That's the first step: trying to think of some practical means for getting what you want. If it's not harmful to ourselves or others, there's nothing wrong with getting what we want.

It's more than likely, however, that we won't be able to think of something like that, so we have to develop the serenity to accept what we cannot change, and the key to developing that serenity is a Buddhist approach: One must be willing to experience helplessness, which is very difficult to do. Men have more difficulty with it because we're trained in macho. *Macho* is derived from the Latin word for "might" or "power," so we are not manly if we're experiencing helplessness, which is why men brutalize women. If a man is with a woman who isn't doing what he wants, he feels helpless, and if he can't stand that feeling of helplessness, he's going to feel his power at the woman's expense. Domestic violence, in my view of it, is the result of selfish men wanting what they want when they want it, demanding it from their wives who, if they have some sense of dignity and autonomy, are not always going to be at the service of their husbands.

So what's the solution for men? We're helpless most of the time, so we've got to learn to feel helpless. We didn't choose to be born—I'm just floating along trying to stay out of trouble, because I'm in control of hardly anything. It took me a long time to realize that. I thought I was in control and I said, Well, if I'm in control, how come things are going so badly? Maybe I've had a few more problems than you have, but in that

sense I've been lucky, because without those problems, I would have had nothing to work on. I pity people whose lives are smooth and easy, because they're not going to learn anything. We've got to learn to get into touch with our feelings of helplessness.

[A woman related this attempt to let go of anger to that of letting go of ego—"before you can let go of ego, you have to have ego to let go of." In terms of anger, she observed, "so many patients who come to us quite helpless need to learn to gather their anger before they can let go of it."]

Dr. Leifer: I agree wholeheartedly. We have to become full human beings in order to become enlightened or to move on the spiritual path. To be a full human being means to have a rotten ego. Not only that, we have to grow up and become individuals before we can experience the kinds of troubles and problems we need to work on for our spiritual development and advancement. Some people are raised in such intimidating circumstances that they have never been able to experience their anger. They need to learn how to get angry before they can come to this point. So for some people, the advice would be: "Are you feeling angry? Maybe you should express it and let it out," while for others it's: "Now wait a minute. You're angry, and that's too much for anybody to handle. Maybe you need to bring yourself under control." So both contradictory forms of advice can be right in different situations.

Now, here's why Peter Matthiessen's

advice that we have to view ourselves as animals is so vital. If we don't, we're blinding ourselves to a part of our nature with which we can never come into harmony or realistic relationship, nor can we gain any control over it. But the fight-flight reaction prepares the body for muscular activity—fight is physical and flight is physical. Animals who are threatened are going to fight or flee. But where the threat is somebody saying, "You're a jerk," or a letter in the mail saying you owe $60 for a traffic ticket, what is there to fight or to flee from?

Usually the danger we are responding to is our perception that our happiness projects are threatened. Then it doesn't make any sense—there's nothing to fight and nothing to flee from. So what happens? Well, we're stuck with our bodies; we get tense. Muscular tension is always a part of anger and it's always a part of anxiety; it is the hallmark of the fight-flight reaction, and this is what stress is: the fight-flight reaction muted into muscular tension and a hyperactive adrenal system, which eventually wears out the body and can promote physical illness.

The antidote to this state of muscular tension is relaxation. So here's the path to serenity. This is an experience that you can train yourself to be good at, which means training yourself to develop serenity in frustrating situations where you're not getting what you want or you're getting what you don't want. First one must identify the anger; recognize that one is angry. It's surprising how often people will act angry, and I'll say, "It seems to me you're angry."

They'll say, "No I'm not, I'm upset." I've developed a list of synonyms for anger. Now I have forty synonyms for anger and "anger" is the least frequently used. They'll say, "I'm upset," "I'm disappointed," "I was really turned off," "I was unhappy at what they did," "I was pissed"—all kinds of euphemisms. We have to be able to identify that we're angry.

Next we must identify that feeling of helplessness and relax the muscles while focused on the feeling of helplessness. So visualize that anger situation, feel that feeling of helplessness. I'm going to take you through a relaxation exercise, which is the antidote to tension. It's what Jon Kabat-Zinn teaches.* It is physiologically sensible; a key to serenity and to all the higher states of consciousness. This state of relaxation is an antidote to fear. While visualizing that helplessness, focus your attention on your bodies.

[Dr. Leifer noted that to "appreciate this feeling of relaxation, it's necessary to have a contrast with tension." The relaxation exercise began by participants pressing their toes into the floor or clenching their fists to feel how the effort creates tension. Upon letting go of the tension, they could then feel the relaxation.

Using this feeling as a guide, they then let go of the tension. Beginning with the muscles in the bottoms of their feet, they let go of the effort, then progressed up through the musculature of their bodies, letting go of "the effort as if you're letting a taut rubberband come to its natural state." Dr. Leifer suggested they "have the image of your own helplessness in mind— I'm helpless and I'm just going to be helpless and not do anything about it," as they progressively let go of tension. When they reached their upper body, he noted that, "by quieting our arms and hands, which are the instruments of our action and self-defense, we relax into our state of helplessness—the true state of our being at the moment."

Moving on to relaxation of the mind, he instructed the audience to do shamatha by simply focusing on the breath: "Relaxed muscles, relaxed mind." Asking the people to visualize the angry situation they were dealing with earlier, he said, "Just visualize it while relaxed and accept it, acknowledge it, look at it, welcome it, disarm it. This is transcendence."

Dr. Leifer then related the experience of anger to the practice of patience, one of the six paramitas, or transcending virtues, which he defined as "the ability, the skill, to suffer without aggression." He used the story of Job—"the Old Testament teaching on patience"—to make this point. "He endured his suffering without aggression, and that's what we have to do. Developing patience is one of the paths to happiness."

Finally, Dr. Leifer demonstrated one other exercise, which derives from Tong Len practice and the slogans of Atisha.[†] Your first reaction to this exercise will be, "This is absolutely ridiculous. I'm not going to do this.

"But as you practice it, you realize, "My

God, it's changing me." It's called Tong Len, which means "giving and receiving."

We'll start with your favorite person, then go to a stranger, then to an enemy. The exercise is a slogan in the Lo Jong: Train to give and take alternately; mount them both on your breath. Close your eyes and just imagine the person you love the most. On your out-breath, imagine yourself giving to this person all the benefits and blessings you have: your health, your wealth, your love, your property, your everything. On the in-breath, take from them, onto yourself, all their troubles, their sorrows, their debts. Give everything you have, take back the suffering from the person you love the most.

Now, visualizing a stranger, somebody you don't know, repeat this process. Then, finally, pick your worst enemy and imagine that you're giving to your enemy everything you have—all your health, your success, your beautiful family, the love you have, your bank account—and take from them all their trouble, their debts, their conflicts, their health problems.

[At the end of this exercise, a woman asked for clarification of how to understand taking away the other person's burden "Is it taking away and putting it in a bag?" Dr. Leifer responded that one took the problems of the other person on oneself.

Choosing leprosy as an example, the participant asked to what purpose one would take that on. "To transform our selfishness into compassion." Dr. Leifer replied.

The next question revisited the issue of depression and anger.]

---

* Jon Kabat-Zinn's work with Buddhist meditation techniques as a means of relaxation therapy is described by Dr. Kabat-Zinn in "Toward the Mainstreaming of American Dharma Practice," pages 478–528.

† Judith Lief dealt with the Tong Len practice at length in her workshop, "Cultivating Loving-Kindness Through the Slogans of Atisha," pages 7–23.

When we have hope that we can change a situation, we're going to get angry. When there's a sense of hopelessness, that we're not going to be able to be happy in the future, the combination of helplessness and hopelessness is experienced as depression. Depression means we're not getting what we want, or we're having imposed upon us what we don't want. We feel frightened, which is why anxiety is always a component of depression, and why anger may be a component of depression, because we may vary in our perceptions of whether there is any hope in the situation or not.

When we think there is hope, we're going to be angry; and when we feel there isn't hope, then we have no motivation to move on in our lives, and depression is that amotivational state. That's when people become suicidal, when they do not feel the possibility of happiness in the future, and if you can help somebody to see that possibility of happiness in the future, that's the way to help them out of their suicidal mood.

[A member of the audience asked how the feeling of experiencing helplessness relates to being able to live in a world that's often violent and aggressive—"being able to experience that helplessness and yet not becoming completely vulnerable to everything around you."]

Dr. Leifer: First of all, if we can understand our own anger and aggression, we can understand all the anger and aggression in the world. Let's take the Israeli-Palestinian situation right now: Isn't it clear that the anger and aggression comes from the fact that each side wants what they want and they're not going to give anything up? Isn't that also the source of domestic violence? Isn't that the source of crime? People want money and they are going to take that money no matter that it's not theirs and no matter if there's resistance. Then they become violent because they want the money and they don't want to be arrested and confined.

All that violence comes from desire, which is promoted by our culture. When you watch television, it's stimulating your desire. Buy this and buy that. You'll be happy if you use this toothpaste and you have this car and you have these sneakers and you're able to go to this game and you have a svelte figure. The entire economy, the gross national product, depends upon the stimulation of desire, and the stimulation of desire is what promotes violence.

What can we do? Well, it's a matter again of that Serenity Prayer. Distinguish what we're able to do from what we're not able to do. We can lock our doors at night, put bars in our windows, but we are vulnerable. When you're vulnerable, you have two choices: You can close up and protect yourself, relating to the world in that way. You may feel a little bit safer, but you won't actually be any safer, and the price of that is being crippled inside. Because we've armored ourselves and built a up wall, we can no longer relate to other people.

The other way is to open yourself up and get hurt. That's where the courage comes in. Open yourself up to life and allow yourself to get hurt, and then experience the pain. At least you'll feel alive. Do what you can to protect yourself—I don't mean walk out into a gunfight—but don't over-armor yourself out of fear of the world. The world's a dangerous place and none of us are going to get out of it alive.

[Bringing the discussion back to the common ground between Buddhism and psychotherapy, a man asked Dr. Leifer "Do you now feel that you can help somebody who refuses to see their suffering as spiritual?"]

Dr. Leifer: They don't need to see it as spiritual. In my office I have a shrine, so when people come in, they see a whole deck of buddhas, but I never talk about religion or Buddhism or spirituality unless they're interested in it. If they're interested, there'll be more and more discussion about it. I asked Khenpo Karthar Rinpoche what he means by spiritual, and he said, "Anything having to do with mind." I like that definition of spiritual.

[A woman observed that "some very particular cases—indignant anger, anger that arises when you see something unjust happen— could possibly be an exception to the model." She noted that "one of the most dangerous things is when someone is acting out of anger that they believe to be justice, delivering justice to the world, but not recognizing that it's coming from somewhere else. Do you think it's possible, first of all, that there can be a constructive anger? And secondly, how can you recognize in yourself when that anger is actually arising from something that is unjust for whatever reason?"]

Dr. Leifer: That's an excellent point. There are historical situations in which anger has been extremely useful. For example, during the civil-rights movement in the sixties, my black friends were very angry. Had they not been angry, there never would have been a civil rights movement. However, while the anger motivated the movement, the wise leaders at that time would not let the most angry people out onto the streets to demonstrate, because they would provoke the opposition that would bring down the repression on the movement itself.

There are no hard rules, but the key is this: If the anger is going to be helpful to other people, then it's good, positive, constructive anger. If it's going to be harmful to other people, then it's bad and destructive. So the key is whether it's helping people or hurting people.

[The final question of the session brought the discussion to the issue of doing away with perceiving oneself as the center of the universe. The participant observed that women, in particular, "tend not to have a hard time not having [themselves] be the center." This can present a conflict: "Sometimes you can feel or pursue or feel obligated to the happiness of others at the sacrifice of yourself. And when you don't, then you say, 'No, I have a right to be happy,' there's this incredible conflict with the happiness of others."]

Dr. Leifer: Wonderful point. There is a teaching on generosity, which is one of the six *paramitas*. Now generosity has two flaws:

One is stinginess, and the other is giving away things that are harmful to yourself or to which you're attached. Khenpo Karthar Rinpoche once gave this teaching on generosity, he said, "People want to see me all the time. They want me to help them solve their life problems. If I were to see everybody who came to me, I'd be seeing people seven days a week, twenty-four hours a day. At the end of two weeks, I'd be dead and I couldn't help anyone else. So my office hours are on Sunday from 2:00 to 4:00 and on Wednesday from 2:00 to 4:00."

You have to learn how to take care of yourself, but that means finding a middle ground, because learning to take care of ourselves can slide over into selfishness. On the other hand, being unselfish can turn into a kind of guilt, where we're giving things away that we don't want to give away, and then we're angry at the people we're giving to, and we become depressed because we're not good people—"I should be able to give without being angry"—and this becomes a tremendous internal conflict. You've got to find that middle ground. I'll leave you with a story about the path to happiness. It's a Hassidic story.

In the olden days, the rabbis used to go from house to house, teaching. At the end of their teaching they would get a meal, and at the end of the meal the head of the household could ask a question. And so a Hassidic rabbi went to a house, gave a little teaching, and got a meal. At the end of the meal, the master of the house asked, "Reb, how can we best please God?"

The question, How can we please God? means How can we be happy? If we please God, God will reward us with happiness. So the question is What's the path to happiness?

The rabbi said, "I can't answer you directly, but I'll tell you a story. In the olden days, they used to have trial by ordeal. If somebody was accused of a crime, they would undergo an ordeal. If they survived, that was God's verdict of innocence, and if they died, if they failed, that was God's verdict of guilt. So two men accused of theft were brought to a chasm across which was laid a log they had to walk across. The first man walked across the log, and the second man yelled, "How did you do it?"

The first man said, "All I can tell you is, if you lean too far to the left, lean back to the right; and if you lean too far to the right, lean back to the left."

So give until you feel you've given too much, then pull back. Take care of yourself. Then, when you feel you've overdone that, begin to give again.

Feeding
the Demons

Tsultrim Allione

CONTEMPORARY WESTERN ATTITUDES CONCERNING OBSTACLES in our path, such as sickness, obsession, addiction, etc., generally take on a tone of confrontation. We speak of "fighting" disease, or "conquering" our fears. We may "destroy" an opponent, and "recover from" an addiction. The Tibetan Chöd practice, however, takes a quite different approach to encounters with these difficulties: Its practitioners "feed" their demons. While we Westerners are urged to "face up to" troubles, Chöd, in essence, encourages us to become one with them. We meet them in order to understand them and their needs. Then we devote to them an abundance of whatever it is they need and demand to the point that they are fully satisfied. Having no more need to torture us, they depart.

Tsultrim Allione* led a day-long workshop in which she explained and demonstrated the principles and technique involved in this aspect of Chöd practice. As she explained, her "ideal with teaching this workshop was to extract the essence of what takes place in Chöd practice, so that the principal of it can be used without necessarily doing Chöd practice." Once comfortable with the process of feeding one's demons, it can become an important and useful part of day-to-day practice because it lends itself to on-the-spot work with issues that rise up to daunt one. For example, Chöd has been found to be helpful to alcoholics beset by the demon of an addiction. Tsultrim's application of this process arose from her work with people who are HIV-positive, who have also found much benefit from its use. But, since everyone has their own specific demons—from nagging worries and anxieties to life-and-death concerns—this method is based on each individual's own development of her or his own visualizations and feeding regimen.

---

*Biographical information about Tsultrim Allione accompanies her keynote address, "Relationship and Intimacy as Path," pages 274–85.

I'd like to teach you what I've come to understand about the nature of demons, and a method of working with the demons that I have seen to be effective in a wide variety of ways. The most dramatic and clear result that I've had working with this has been with people with AIDS. It's a way that I've been able to see how concrete the results of this practice can be.

In our *sangha* is someone named Fred, who was actually an old friend of mine. He had met the Dharma, practiced for some years, then drifted away until he discovered that he was HIV-positive. He then came back as a refuge from his fear and with some hope of finding something in the teachings that might help him with his HIV situation. He came to a Chöd retreat I was doing in the Bay Area about seven or eight years ago and he was learning Chöd. In the process, we learned to feed the demons. In this exercise, you identify your demon, and you give it a clear form, which makes it conscious, and then you feed it to complete satisfaction. When Fred started to do this, he asked if he could work with me. "What do you want to work with?" I asked him.

And he said, "Well, I don't really know."

That's the first thing that happens, usually. Our biggest demons are so big that we don't even dare to name them.

He was going to work with some kind of little side thing that wasn't his real demon, which was too scary and too embarrassing. And yet to anyone it was obvious that his main demon would be his HIV status. So eventually he decided to work with his HIV demon, which he saw as huge; it was as big

as a house. And it was green and yellow, and it was sticky, and had hands and legs and a huge mouth.

In this exercise, we ask the demon what it's wanting, and we do it out loud. You say, "What do you want?" and you visualize this in front of you, the demon. Then you switch places and you become the demon, and from that place, of the demon, you answer that question, *What do you want? What are you needing?* His demon said that it wanted his life, and it wanted it slowly and painfully; it wanted to take his beauty and take his health and slowly reduce him to death.

Next you offer the demon exactly what it wants. Of course, the greatest fear is to actually give it what it wants. But magically, you are able to manufacture an infinite amount of whatever it is that the demon wants, so that you give up the struggle—the "no you can't have"—which is actually what the demon eats: the struggle, that energy.

Fred began to feed his HIV demon, and he learned Chöd practice as well. He took it home and practiced every day for some time. The main characteristic of Fred's demon was fear, so he began to feed it, and gradually it started diminishing in size. Meanwhile, he was in the control group of a drug study, where he wasn't getting AZT. He wasn't taking anything; he wasn't doing anything special—no special diet, no special anything—and all of his friends who were HIV-positive were being terribly careful about what they ate and how much they slept. Every time they'd get a cold, there was this incredible paranoia, living with this kind of fear. But Fred just kept doing his practice. He went for his tests every month, and after a year the hospital said, "There's something funny happening here. Your T-cells are going up. What are you doing?"

He said, "I'm doing some meditation."

And they said, "Well, whatever it is, keep doing it."

So he kept doing it, and his T-cells kept going up. It has now been seven, eight years that Fred has been doing this—he's not doing anything else—and his T-cells have stabilized. Sometimes they start to drop, when he stops doing Chöd, so he'll start again.

This has occurred for other people as well, with other kinds of illnesses. It was interesting for me because it was such a clear, concrete indication of how Chöd and this practice of feeding the demons actually work. It's not just a theory. The other thing that was interesting is that, in Tibet, they predicted that, because of the extent of disease and darkness that's around, this would be the time in history when Chöd practice would become widely spread and used.

It was used in Tibet for disease and epidemics. The Chöd practitioners were the ones who were called in when there was an epidemic, like cholera or smallpox, in Tibet. The Chödpas would go in and deal with the bodies—bury people or whatever kind of funeral they were doing—because they wouldn't get the sickness.

There are two principles in what we're going to learn: One is that we need to become aware of what our demons are, and what we want to work with, and then to give that a form. So the process of first becoming

aware of it—and it can be just fear; or it can be self-hatred; it can be a substance problem, tobacco or cocaine or heroin or alcohol; it can be an illness; it can be your fear of success; it can be your fear of failure; it can be abandonment issues, anything. The varieties of the forms that our demons take are limitless, and we don't have just one, obviously.

I've noticed that (and the way it is explained in the teachings also) it is usually a hope or a fear. In America, we don't think of hope so much as giving rise to demons. We think you have to have hope; that's part of the principle. But in fact, hopes are the other sides of our fears, and those two things keep tension going.

Recognizing the demon also means getting a clear picture of what it looks like—real details. What color is it? What texture is it? What do the eyes look like? What kind of feeling do I get? All kinds of that type of detail, where you just think, I'm just making this up. And we are just making it up, really. But at the same time, when you do it, suddenly it's there, and it's extremely clear.

The second important principle is feeding it to complete satisfaction, so that the struggle is over and the demon can feel taken care of. Because these are parts of ourselves that we've split off and said, "I'm here and you're there. And I don't want you. And would you please get out of here. Would you please leave me alone." We just don't want to deal with these parts of ourselves. They become like little kids that aren't getting attention: obnoxious. The more we try to get rid of them, the more obnoxious they become, until they start to take over our lives. And at a certain point it seems like we *are* the demon; we are the disease. If we're an alcoholic, we become the alcohol demon. Even if it hasn't reached that point, it's still on its way in, taking a greater and greater toll on our energy, on our life force, on our sense of well-being, and so on.

In the practice, we feed them to complete satisfaction, which is different than giving the little kid a cookie or throwing the dog a bone. By feeding them to complete satisfaction, it's actually turning around and saying, "What is it that you need? What is it that you really want?" and paying full, complete attention to it. That's probably the first time that you've ever done that. You can have a life-threatening disease and never actually look it in the face. It's always this thing that I'm trying to get away from, trying to eliminate. Yet it's so *there*, obviously, but we don't want to look it in the face.

In our culture, we live in the paradigm of slaying the monster. We're going to kill it—kill the disease, kill the demon, get rid of the enemy. Cut it off. This is the hero's journey: Slay the dragon. When we have a problem, we think we've got to get rid of it. So this is a really amazing shift, to say, We're not going to try to get rid of the dragon. We're going to see what it needs, what it wants. What it eats. Why it's coming around. We go from destroying to nurturing and come full circle into a completely different view. When we do that, we let go of duality. We're no longer trying to kill the ego.

You know that story of Milarepa when he's in his cave and gets attacked by demons? He tries all of his mantras and the demons just get happier and bigger. Finally, he looks at them and he says, "You are none other than the nature of my own mind," and he actually enters into that state—and they disappear.

It's so simple; so obvious. And yet, this is not what we do and it's not what we're taught, and it really works. That's why I feel it's so important to teach this, and for people to know about it. For me personally, it has made a huge difference in my life. One of my big demons was the fear of abandonment, and whenever I would get into a relationship, I would always be afraid of being left or being abandoned. There would always be this little voice saying, "Well, it's probably going to happen pretty soon. This looks pretty good, but it's not going to last." So then I would make it happen, and at the end the demon would say, "You see? You have me. I'm still with you. But forget that." So this became a kind of pattern in which I thought I'm just always going to have to live with this.

Then I began to understand. I did this practice for a long time before I understood this. It's very easy to do practices but not really understand them in terms of your own life. When I started to use this understanding of demons for what was actually happening in my life, that's when I really started to understand it, and understand what is the real nature of demons. That they're not little Tibetan gargoyle creatures, but these are my hopes, my fears, my illnesses. So I started to feed my abandonment demon—who looked like a small girl with vampire teeth—every day when I did my Chöd practice, and slowly her teeth started to change, and she started to get littler and she started to get happier. I'd still call her up and feed her, but she didn't look the same anymore, and suddenly this issue was gone from my life. I don't have it anymore. And I had thought, You're just always going to have to live with this one. We don't, but the reason that we think we do is because we've been trying to get rid of them, and that's not what they need. They need attention, they need our presence, they need our love, they need our nurturing—the opposite of what we tend to give them. A lot of times in our teachings everything has to be turned around to the opposite of what we think we need to do.

I've also used this with my own sicknesses, although I haven't had life-threatening things, but just when the flu is hanging on and on and on, and then suddenly I realize, Oh, maybe there's something happening here. I had that experience once with a relationship that had ended. It was fine that it had ended, and I accepted it, no big deal. But then I got sick and just couldn't get better. Finally I went inside and worked with the demon, saw the demon of the illness, and it told me it was grief about this relationship that I had thought I didn't really have feelings like that about, because consciously it made perfect sense that it had ended.

These are the relative aspects of the practice. On the absolute level, there is no demon, there's no one feeding the demon, and there's no feeding taking place. So there's the relative and absolute that we always have to hold.

In the Chöd practice, after you do the feeding of the demons, then "the offerer, the offering, and the offered are all dissolved into the *Dzogpa Chenpo*, into the *dzogchen*, into this great perfection—aaahh—and then there's a gap, a silence. What it's saying is that after we have this experience of feeding the demon, there is the experience of emptiness: There is no offerer, there is no offering, there is no offered to. That comes in and you rest in that state, which happens very naturally, very spontaneously.

But what usually happens, or what would happen if we weren't practitioners and were just using this as a sort of psychological method, is that as soon as we feed the demon and experience space without the demon, then we want to fill that gap in. The minute the gap is there, we need to fill it up again. Who am I without my problem? My problem has been so big and I don't have it anymore. Got to fill that in with something else. But in the practice, that's when you actually enter into the *dzogchen* state or the *mahamudra* state or the absolute state. It's only through recognizing and paying attention to the relative that you can experience that.

The fundamental demon of them all is the demon of "self-clinging" (in Tibetan). In Western translation that's ego, usually, which is incorrect. In a psychological sense, we need the ego, we need that sense of continuity, of a "self." But what we don't need is self-cherishing or self-clinging, which really means egocentricity. That's another big mistake that happens in Western Buddhism, this confusion of translation, thinking we have to get rid of the ego, not really even understanding what that is. Really it is self-cherishing or thinking: *I—me*—as the center of the universe, the most important one. That's the primary demon.

The View—the way that we look at or hold the world—is *the* most important thing. It's the key. It's what we're operating out of in terms of how we see reality. What is happening here? What are we doing here? We're each having a different experience sitting in this room. We each have our View of what's happening here. We have our View of what this building is. We're not all having the same experience.

And if an ant was walking across the floor, the ant would be having its View of reality; or if a dog came in, it would be having its View of this exact same space. The same thing is happening, but because each of us is different, we're having a different experience. From a Buddhist point of view, we all start out with the wrong View. We're not actually seeing things correctly because we're seeing it from the View of self-clinging. So when I look at George [a participant], I'm not actually seeing George, I'm seeing my View of him. What could he give me, or how could he threaten me? Or maybe he doesn't even matter, he's not important to me. If I look at this room in the same way, I don't simply experience the molecules and the space and what this room actually is. I'm not seeing that. I'm seeing an illusory version of it based on my own incorrect, illusory View.

Because we're human beings and we live in this culture, we share certain Views, to the extent that we can actually start to create this kind of hologram of illusion, where we're all believing. It's like watching the news: You watch the news, and then you believe this is what's happening in the world; this is what's important that's happening in the world, and this is the way we should view what's happening in the world. So we start to get this collective illusion happening as well. Other countries have their own collective illusion, but right now, the American-TV cultural illusion is starting to dominate and go into all these little countries on CNN.

So there's this incredible, complex overlaying of views of what is real, which happens within families. It goes down to the microcosm as well. We're all in a family and everyone thinks that they know what's happening in that family, and that's what's real—whatever each particular person thinks is real, or whatever the dominant person in that family thinks. But actually, it's incorrect. This is not what's happening. There is a reality of what's happening, which is what we try to reach in practice, to be able to drop all of the illusions so that we can actually perceive reality, and that's why sometimes enlightenment is called the experience of reality.

All practice, in some way, is about trying to cut through that illusion, relax that illusion —open up our space, open up our hearts, open up our being to experience what's actually happening. When we're not doing that, it hurts. That was what the Buddha said. The first noble truth was that all conditioned existence is suffering. We condition our existence by our self-clinging.

Machig Labdrönme, the woman who founded Chöd teachings in the eleventh century, was an amazing yogini. (Her name actually means "the one mother." She was a physical woman, a physical manifestation, but on another level she is *the* Great Mother.) Machig was the founder of the Chöd teaching, which is a teaching that was practiced by all lineages in Tibet.

In her youth she was a nun, and as she got older she began to have different teachers. She kept going beyond each of her teachers, and they would say, "I can't teach you anymore. You have to go to so and so." At a certain point, she met Phadampa Sangye, who was one of her main teachers. She asked him, "How can I help sentient beings? What can I do?" It's kind of like going to your teacher and saying, "I don't know what to do. What's really the key? What's the most important thing for me to do?" The first thing he said was,

Confess all your hidden faults.

[That's hard to do, because they're hidden; it's like coming to terms with the shadow aspect of our psyche.]

Approach that which you find repulsive. Whoever you think you cannot help, help them. Anything that you're attached to, let go of it. Go to places, like cemeteries, that scare you. Sentient beings are limitless as the sky. Be aware. Find the buddha inside yourself.

Then he asked her what her understanding was. When she told him, he said, "Well, you have a good understanding, but it's still intellectual." And then he told her the most important thing to realize is,

If you do not grasp with your mind, you will find a fresh state of being. If you let go of clinging, a state beyond all conceptions will be born.

That means that we have to let go of all those little cords we've got out there. Then, when the cords are gone, the vastness of our being, the vastness of our consciousness, is present. It's not that it's not present now, but because of the cords we have going out, we can't feel it. We can't experience it. So when we say let go of clinging, what we're really letting go into is our vastness, our wholeness. It's not like we will be in freefall. When we let go, then we can actually be here, and we can actually be here with each other—in relationship with each other—because right now we're just in relationship with our illusions.

Then the fire of the great prajna will grow. [Prajna is the wisdom that discovers primordial wisdom—*shes rab* in Tibetan, profound knowing.] Dark, self-clinging ignorance will be conquered. The root of the teaching is to examine the movement of your own mind very carefully. Do this.

Machig returned to her meditation and began to read through her teachings. During her reading, she read about demons, and she began to understand what that really meant. And the whole understanding of the word "demon" was the core of her teaching. She understood that self-cherishing, or egocentricity, is really the root of all of our demons, either our hopes or our fears.

Shortly after that, she and some friends received initiation with her lama. During a Tibetan initiation, there's a point where you receive wisdom—you receive the wisdom deity into your own body—and when that happened, Machig's body raised above the ground and she did the twenty-four dances of the *dakinis* (the feminine wisdom energies), and then she passed through the wall of the shrine room, then went up into a tree that was supposed to be inhabited by a demon. The people in that area were so scared of this tree they wouldn't even look at it. Below the tree was a pond, and in the pond there was also a demon.

So this tree-pond demon—a *naga,* or water spirit—called up an army of demons, and they came to Machig. They were outraged. This was a moment like the Buddha's enlightenment under the bodhi tree—the moment of total attack. And she offered them her own body. Here they come to get her, and she offered them her own body, so there was no battle; there was nothing for them to attack. She wasn't there. On that basis, they offered themselves to her.

Metaphorically, the tree (in most cultures) symbolizes individuation. Still today, in Siberia, shamans go up into trees for their initiation ceremony and for their receiving of

power. And you'll see a lot of shamanic roots in the actual practice as well. In Siberia, they go into birch trees and speak with the spirits, and then come down to enlighten people.

When I was reading about this, I was also reading some Jungian psychology, and I read a book called *The Feminine in Fairy Tales.* It talked about a boy—and this is a true story—who was becoming schizophrenic and was sent out into the country to live on his uncle's farm. When he got there, he climbed a tree and refused to come down. His uncle, being kind of a simple guy, didn't think too much of it. He gave him some food, and the boy started to establish a little perch up there, and ended up staying for a month in this tree. When he came down, he was completely healed.

And von Franz says about this, "Sitting in a tree therefore means retreat from reality and retiring into what is threatening." This is what Machig did: She went into what was threatening when she went up into that tree. It is as though instead of avoiding a thing that threatened, one retired into it. One trusts that thing. The danger is a complete loss of connection with reality, and the advantage is that the threatened content becomes a second womb out of which rebirth can take place. The tree also has a maternal-spirit quality, something from which one can fall like a fruit. It represents the process of spiritual rebirth. In many countries there is a superstition that children come from trees. Climbing up a tree and climbing down again is a process of spiritual rebirth. The process of going into a tree symbolizes a change in reality from normal to magical; the change of View, the altered state.

When Machig offered her body to the demons, she went beyond the View of self-cherishing. She did the opposite of what the View of self-cherishing would do, of what we hold most dear, which is our body. And she offered that. Because she had no fear, the demons could not eat her. It's like a keyhole and a key; there has to be a fit for the whole thing to take place. She didn't offer any kind of keyhole as they were attacking. She reversed the whole process, and then they became her servants, her guardians. It's the same way with us, with our demons. They will become our guardians. They will become our allies instead of our enemies. So her fearlessness really came from her holding the correct view.

The next morning they came out of the shrine room to look for her, and she came down out of the tree, naked. Again, we find this metaphor that she was in naked mind; she was just there. And her friends said, "Oh, Machig, I'm sorry you missed the initiation." Then her teacher said, "Actually, you missed the initiation! Machig received the ultimate initiation." So we get caught by our hopes and fears, and this completely confuses and trammels upon and messes up our lives. With the Chöd practice and working with the demons we can begin to untangle those knots of our hopes and fears, and learn how to work with them.

I was traveling in Tibet, going to Mount Kailash, which was an incredible journey with eighty-eight people—eighty-eight anar-

chists—anarchist Buddhists! During this time the trip got very rough at certain points, and one day I saw a woman from Hawaii, and she was crying. I went and sat next to her and said, "What's wrong?"

She said, "I'm under attack. I feel completely like I will never get out of this attack from my mother. I'm thirty-five years old and nothing has changed. I feel this attack every day. And I hate it. I hate my mother. I don't want to live anymore."

So I said, "Well, let's try feeding the demons."

She'd never heard of it, and I explained a little bit. She visualized this creature who was sort of the demon of the mother, and she fed this demon that was attacking her. The whole experience with her mother relaxed from that moment on and never has come back.

Now, it doesn't always work like that. Usually our demons come back and we have to continue to work with them. But probably because it was such an extreme situation for her, and this was such a shift, once you can really see it work, then it stays. But for her that shifted completely and her life has been different ever since.

[Tsultrim invited all the participants to experience this process in a visualization. With their eyes closed, each person took a moment to determine what was "eating at" them. They did this by bringing forth the "negative voices" they heard and what they might say to the individuals. She explained that the thing that was bothering them "could be a hope or a fear or an ill-

She then proceeded to guide the partici-
pants in visualizing their demons and feeding
them.]

Take whatever you've decided is eating at you, and give it a form. Sometimes it helps to go into the part of your body that it manifests—if it manifests somewhere in your body, in your stomach or in tension in your shoulders, or headache, or some skin problems—wherever it manifests in your body, and find it there. From there, turn it into a monster. Give it a form. If it's just a concept, or you can't find it in your body, turn that into a very clear form, and put it in front of you. What color is it? How big is it? Notice details: What is the texture of the skin? If it has arms and legs, how many does it have? If it has eyes, what do they look like? Particularly notice the feeling that you get from it, and feel that feeling coming from it. Get a really good sense of the presence of it. Make eye contact with it if you can.

Now ask it what it wants. What is it that it eats? What is it that its needing? Internally ask that question: What do you want?

Now, become the demon for a minute. Imagine that you can leave your body and go out there and turn around, take the body of the demon, and from that position, answer the question, looking at yourself, looking at your body. But first take a minute and really become the demon. You might think you know what the demon wants, but before you answer, just take a minute and really

become it. Then answer the question, What do you want? What do you, the demon, want? What are you needing?

Come back into your body, but continue to see the demon in front of you. Now that you know what it wants, imagine that you have an infinite amount of whatever it is that it wants; that you magically can manifest this, an infinite amount of whatever, even if it's your life force or it wants to eat your body. Imagine that, just for the moment, you have the power to produce a million bodies or a million of your life forces, or whatever it is that it needs; an infinite amount of love. Feed it that. It might take it in through its mouth, thorough its skin, through its whole being. Just imagine that you're feeding it an infinite amount, that nothing is being held back.

As you're feeding it, begin to notice what's happening to it. Does it look different? Is it changing? Don't hold back anything. Feed it to complete satisfaction. See what it looks like. Notice how you feel now, how you feel with it. Is it still there? Notice the difference in the sensation that you have now and what you had when you began with it. Rest in that space. As you open your eyes, notice how you feel.

[A woman asked how long to continue to "be"
the demon, when one took on that form in
order to answer the question of what it wants.]

Tsultrim Allione: You stay there as long as it takes to know what that fear needs. A lot of times you think you know what it wants, but when you actually switch and become the demon, it's not what you thought it was that the demon really wants. That's why it's important to actually shift and take that position. You just stay there as long as it takes to get what it feels like. When you've got that, then you shift back.

[Another woman brought up a question about going into the process with the predetermined thought that what one wants to do is get rid of the demon. She suggested that one could then "get caught up again in the cycle of hope and fear and wanting to get rid of something."]

Tsultrim Allione: That's a good point. To experiment with that, I've done it with people without telling them what should happen or what I think is going to happen, and just asked, "What is happening?"

I did this with one woman who had an incredible amount of self-loathing, self-hatred. She said the self-hater was always there and she was really obsessed by this. She didn't know what was supposed to happen. I just took her through the process. At a certain point, she started laughing, and I said, "What's happening?" And she said, "It just put up a big sign on the door—it said GONE FISHING—and left!"

So I think what you're asking two things: One, since you think you know what's going to happen, it's like a self-fulfilling prophecy. The other part is, Isn't this just another way to sort of get rid of them? In a way it is a way to get rid of it. But really, it's a way of paying attention. It's like nurturing this part of ourselves. It does relax.

But it's like saying, "Because your kids will relax if you take care of them, does that mean you shouldn't take care of them because then you're just trying to manipulate them in another way?"

[A male participant noted that "the particular demon that I had did not go away. It was much more like one of these myths in which this terrible demon turns into somebody who's been under a spell and is sort of released like a dryad, or this beautiful shape coming out in a transformation." Tsultrim reminded the group that "you never know quite what's going to happen. Everybody's experience is so different, doing the exact same thing."

When asked if one should focus again on the same image if doing this visualization the next day, Tsultrim answered:]

No. You can do whatever. It helps me to somaticize, actually to find it in my body, but you don't have to do that. I try to find where it is and from there give it a form. So I actually touch back in with myself, rather than just getting a concept. When I was talking about my abandonment demon, that's how she looked in the beginning, but then every day I would go back in and say, "Okay, what does she look like today?" It changes.

Part of this is taking the time to look at it—to pay attention to it—and that's part of the process. Say you're HIV-positive, and you're going to work with that every day. Every day you have to go in and ask, "Okay, where is it? What does it look like?" Get that form, without thinking. Maybe it will look the same, maybe it won't. But take that time to be with yourself enough, to touch in enough, to feel it and then put it in front. Making it conscious is a big part of the process, and giving it the form is a big part of making it conscious.

In a lot of indigenous cultures, they feed the demons. In Bali, little plates are put out every morning and every night and bigger ones on special days, but it's incorporated into the culture, a form of feeding the demons. In our culture we don't have that, and so the demons are starving, going crazy.

[A participant mentioned that he "noticed a feeling of real sadness and almost shame of having misjudged and mistreated and pushed and fought this entity. He really is a very different entity, whom I've neglected."]

Tsultrim Allione: There's a line in the Chöd that says that the gods and the demons (which are the hopes and the fears) continue to arise, but with love and compassion they evolve. So that sadness is compassion. It's that kind of soft spot, heart opening. It's like when you see somebody suffering— "Oh, I didn't notice. This has been right in front of me and I wouldn't even notice." Also, don't expect this is never going to arise again—I've done this, so it's never going to arise again—because these are pretty ingrained habits, and usually they will arise again. With love and compassion, they evolve, and that's what we're doing. We're giving them love and compassion. That's the essence of practice.

[Tsultrim had with her a drum, a bell, and a thigh-bone trumpet. She demonstrated their use and explained their place in Chöd meditation as well as some of the symbolism involved.]

The drum is the heartbeat. It goes with the rhythm of the heart, and then the bell goes with it. The drum and the bell are both symbols of the feminine in the Tibetan practice, which is the wisdom aspect.

The thigh-bone trumpet is played when the actual offering takes place. It's a human thigh-bone. In India, people lived in the cemeteries. They didn't have the thing about corpses that we have. The corpse was a subject of meditation, and using the bones was part of meeting your fears, part of meeting your greatest paranoias. There are whole practices, like eating out of a human-skull cup, that keep this constant reminder of impermanence. So it was a way of meeting that place between the worlds. Chöd was often practiced in cemeteries—where the fear is.

The practice is also sung, so when you're singing it, you can't really hear anything else. I've done this in dark, scary places, making so much noise. It's sort of like being in the shower, where you can't really hear if somebody's coming in or what's going on. So this fear comes up because you're making so much noise in such a quiet, scary place. That's the whole idea of Chöd: You're actually invoking problems. You're not trying to subdue everything and make it all quiet. You're actually stirring things up. Again, that's very different than most Buddhist practice, where we're trying to settle it down, calm it.

[A question regarding the connection between Vajrayana practice and Chöd brought Tsultrim to explain the role of the Black Dakini and to describe the four feasts.]

Tsultrim Allione: The connection with Vajrayana practice is through the Blue-Black Dakini, or the Black Dakini. In the practice, your consciousness exits through the top of your head and you become the Black Dakini—the wrathful goddess. She presides over the Chöd.

In the Chöd practice, you exit, you become the Black Dakini, your body is then a corpse. You're dead. Your consciousness has exited. Then the *dakini* takes her *dakini* knife and cuts around your skull and creates a cup, which is expanded. Then the rest of your body is put into the skull cup and placed on a tripod of three skulls, which symbolize the three *kayas*. Then all the body's in it and there's a fire under it, and that fire transforms and expands and purifies the corpse. It becomes a magical substance that satisfies all beings, and from there everybody comes to eat.

In the Chöd practice, there are four different feasts: the White Feast, in which all the buddhas and bodhisattvas come, and they eat what they like. You see them eating rose-petal ice cream, or rice, or what you think buddhas would eat. Then there's the Red Feast, which is for the protectors and the guardians, and they eat what they like. To the Black Feast, which is what we have been

working with, the obstacle-makers, the karma-indebtors, and the disease-bearing beings come and eat. And each time, the substance inside the skull cup changes to be whatever they need. Then the fourth feast is the mixed feast, and that's when we feed all sentient beings.

So, your physical body has become the substance by which all beings are satisfied. That's the real core of Chöd practice, and that's why it's shamanic, because in Shamanism there's always that process with the shaman initiation of having to go through a descent into darkness, and being devoured. Then those things that devour you become the things that you can then heal or cure. In the same way that an alcoholic is really the only person that can heal another alcoholic, because they've been devoured by those demons, and they know what that is. So in this case, what we have been devoured by is our ego-clinging or our self-cherishing, which leads to our hopes and our fears and all of our demons.

[A participant asked for further explanation about the demon becoming an ally.]

Tsultrim Allione: I looked up the word *demon* in the dictionary. It descends from the Greek word *daimon*. And *daimon* means the "in-dwelling god or goddess;" "the in-dwelling divine." It means also the "soul given by the mother." During the Middle Ages, when the patriarchal culture really completely took over, this in-dwelling *daimon*, which came from the mother, became the demon. So, in some way, we're taking back ourselves; we're taking back the soul, or the in-dwelling being that's gotten split off in some way.

In the Roman Catholic exorcism, they talk about demons. Twice they say to "get out;" twice they say to "retire;" four times they say to "go out;" six times they say "depart;" and seven times they say, "give way." But they never say, "What do you want?" Our culture is built on this split, on this fear. There's the devil, the demon, the little guy with the red tail, so there's this constant dance that we're doing of the split between good and evil. We live in this completely unintegrated state, where we're always trying to push something away that is always going to be present. It's exhausting. And it turns into fanaticism and the madness that we experience in our culture.

Because Buddhism says that the root of all demons is mind-clinging, or ego fixation, then we step out of that split of God and Satan, or good and bad. That's something that's really unique in this practice. It's a very different shape that we hold our being in, when we can hold both those things, and not feel like we're trying to be all good and get rid of all the rest, which is impossible. It creates a continual sense of failure and imbalance and being split off. If you look at the whole puritanical thing, sexuality getting split off into the devil and a negative thing, and then what kinds of perversion and weirdness that created because our sexuality is so totally part of ourselves. Now we accept that more, but there's still so much about who we are that we don't accept,

which leads to that same kind of perversion, and ill-at-ease feeling, and lack of self-esteem, because we could never be all good.

[When asked if she thought this process could ever become too overwhelming for the individual to bear, Tsultrim answered in the negative.]

I think it becomes overwhelming when we don't. It becomes much bigger when we don't. I think that's a really legitimate fear (which is why we run away from them all the time): If we actually turned around, it would take over and be too big. And if we asked it what it wants and give it what it wants, what's going to happen is it's going to get bigger because it's going to be fed. That's logic.

But what happens is the opposite: When we run away from it, it gets bigger. If you think about it more as you would about sexuality, I think that helps. You can see how if we lived in a culture where sexuality was completely repressed, how huge it would get, and it would seem absolutely frightening, that this evil thing was going to get in somehow and we had to keep making bigger and bigger walls. But when sexuality is just part of everything else, part of our lives, it's not bigger than anything else. It's in balance with everything else.

When we *don't* look at it is when it gets bigger and starts to take over. Think of alcoholism. The way that alcoholism lives is through denial. The main symptom of alcoholism is denial. Why? Because if it was actually faced, it couldn't be as big as it is. The bigger it gets, the bigger the denial gets. So,

Sharing ideas carried over into the conference luncheons

when we face it and say, "What is this? What are you needing? What do you want? What is this about?" then it begins to relax.

Basically, it's trying to get our attention. And that tension of the split is what it eats. That's how it gets bigger and bigger and bigger. That tension of not seeing, which meanwhile drains our life force. You can see when somebody's getting completely taken over by a demon. Dealing with alcoholism is a good example. You begin to feel that this person is not my friend or my parent or me. And it's *not* that person anymore; the demon really has moved in to take over. But the way that that happens is through denial, or through trying to split it off or not to see it or to ignore it or to get rid of it or to battle it. We

can do it all of our lives, and it's still not going to work.

[After answering questions that had occurred to participants during the lunch break Tsultrim began the afternoon portion of the workshop with a demonstration of a method of working with a partner in this practice. She explained that the role of the partner is mainly to keep the person who is feeding the demon on track, or in the present. A temptation is to turn to the partner and go off on an intellectually based tangent, "which is another way to escape from it."

For this approach, you choose an object —a piece of clothing, a second chair, a cushion—that then represents your demon. You can decide how close you want to get to this object, which is intended merely to give the demon a placement. It is set up opposite you in order to permit you to visualize the demon in a place.

Following is an excerpt of the exchange between Tsultrim and the woman who volunteered to do the visualization with her:]

Tsultrim Allione: Do you know what you want to work on?

Participant: I'm afraid of being enlightened.

Tsultrim Allione: Okay. I'd like you to close your eyes, and locate that fear in your body, if you can find it. Go into that place in your body, and just feel that sensation for a minute. And now take that sensation and turn it into a form. Give it a form. Now, imagine it in front of you in the chair. Can you describe it to us?

Participant: It has large red eyes. It looks somewhat like Yamantaka, the Lord of Death—human body, head of a bull. The appendages can elongate like tentacles, and can consume and devour. Its emotional state is one of intense fury. Horns.

Tsultrim Allione: Does it have a size?

Participant: It pervades the universe. Huge.

Tsultrim Allione: Any color?

Participant: It's black with red eyes. And fangs!

Tsultrim Allione: Okay. Hold that. Get the vision as clear as possible. See it in front of you. Feel it in front of you. Feel its energy. Now ask it out loud, "What do you want?"

Participant: What do you want?

Tsultrim Allione: "What do you need?"

Participant: What do you need?

Tsultrim Allione: Now change chairs; you can keep your eyes closed. Take a minute and become the huge, bull-like form. Feel the question—and answer that question, "What do you need, what do you want?"

[The participant paused for approximately half a minute. When she spoke, her voice had altered slightly. Where it had had a tone of self-confidence and strength, it now took on something of a tremble. It had also coarsened perceptibly.]

Participant: I want a buddha-nature. Everybody's got one but me. So I'm just going to consume everything in sight. Destroy. I just want to destroy. I want to have the buddha-nature. Nobody loves me. I can't become enlightened. I can't free myself from suffering.

Tsultrim Allione: Do you want love?

Participant: I'm too arrogant for love.... But yes, I do.

Tsultrim Allione: Secretly.

Participant: I lie even to myself.

Tsultrim Allione: Now, come back. Come back out. Change chairs, become yourself again, and see the demon in front of you. Take a minute and go back to seeing it in front of you. This huge, desiring need for eating all good things, all buddha-nature. Needing love. See it in front of you. You're you, and it's separate. Now imagine that you have the capacity to give it what it needs; to feed it. There's an infinite amount of what it needs, and it can have as much as it wants. It's completely taking it in to complete satisfaction. It's completely satisfied.

Participant: It transformed into a baby buddha, suckling at the great breast of the great mother. I was orphaned at birth in an ambulance during the war and I was aware of this. So there's always been that primordial struggle of abandonment and rejection.

Tsultrim Allione: A lot of times there's actually another thing under the first thing that we think we're going to work with. You can allow that to happen and allow yourself to see that what's behind the first layer is not always what the real demon is or what's actually going on. As you go into it, it will reveal in other layers. That's how it happens in our lives, too: Something starts as one thing and then it takes on these different masks and shapes until you don't know what it is anymore.

Once [my partner] was there, she was very present in her body. You could feel how she was really embodied. This was not an

intellectual experience for her. It was really in her body that she was experiencing what happens. The more you can really feel it— and feel the demon, when you become the demon—then the deeper level the whole thing happens on.

Also, once she got going, it happened almost instantaneously. It doesn't necessarily have to take a long time. It seems like it should. It's such a big thing that has been there forever, or for so long that it seems impossible that it could actually be gone that quickly, but sometimes it is.

If you find yourself stuck and your demon is not getting satisfied, then *imagine* that it does, because there's a part of us that doesn't want it to. It's as though we're somehow attached to the battle with it because we've had that for so long. You can always go back to having it be unsatisfied but, just for a moment, imagine or see it being satisfied and then feel that in the body. Feel how you feel after that's satisfied. Check in with yourself at the end.

[Now that this two-person method had been demonstrated, the group divided up into pairs and worked with identifying, visualizing, and feeding their individual demons. This was followed by questions occasioned by the experience.

A man asked if there was sometimes a long lag time after assuming the form of the demon while the person tries to discern what the demon wants, "or is that just another way out, another form of escape?"]

Tsultrim Allione: It's another way out. What helps at that point is to, as physically as you can, become the demon and feel in your body as the demon, in the same way that you felt in your body as you contacted the demon. Try to really enter into the experience of the demon rather than the concept of what you think it wants. The more you can drop your ideas and enter into feeling, the easier it gets.

[The participant continued: "So once you're embodying this demon, you drop what that demon originally represented?...I had a certain fear that I would lose my demon.... Should that drop, too, and I just become this big, red form with a large mouth?"]

Tsultrim Allione: Yes. Drop your concept and just allow yourself to feel. Of course, that concept's always there in the background. This exercise is really the embodiment of this whole thing. It's like creating a map of something. The way that the demons get so confusing is that we can't see them. We don't know what they look like. They're just these vague things, even if you're dealing with such a big thing as, say, alcoholism or HIV or cancer, it still has a vague, spacey quality. The more we can give it form, and then actually enter into the feeling tone of it, then the easier it is to deal with.

[One participant had come upon an insight into the reason for the existence of the demon with which she had worked. She wanted to know if that was an important aspect of the practice or "just rationalizing it."]

Tsultrim Allione: Sometimes you will get insights into things and also, perhaps, an understanding of what's under what. For example, [with my partner earlier in the session], under the fear of the buddha-nature and wanting to develop buddha-nature was actually a longing for love. That's fine that you get these insights, but that's an intellectual spin-off. When you're doing it, it's important because this is what we do a lot. We conceptualize and have discursive thought, and we can analyze until the ends of the earth, but part of why I like Gestalt as a method is that it's not intellectual; it's very somatic. It's about the body and being in your body and staying with that process. So, even though it's a concept in the sense that we're feeding demons and so on, it's not conceptual in the sense of one thought spinning off into another one. It's very experiential.

[Tsultrim led the workshop in another visualization and meditation, in which each participant worked by himself or herself, switching places with their individual demon after it took on its form, questioning what it wanted and needed, then feeding it to satisfaction. As the workshop came to a close, she presented some observations on ways this technique and practice has been used to great effect.]

Some therapists are using feeding the demons for multiple personalities—beginning to say *What is it that you need? What is it that you want?* to the different personalities instead of trying to get rid of them. By doing this, people with multiple personalities are beginning to integrate these parts. In a way, these demons are like our little multiple personalities that are split off. In some ways, the saner we become, the less split-off we are, the more we're able to own all of our parts. So we begin not only to become whole as beings in the sense of nondual (nondual in the sense of not split), but when you come back, once the feeding is over, there's an experience of vastness and space where there's really nothing there, what they call in Buddhism "emptiness" or "nonduality." We work toward this always in meditation: that experience of nonduality.

Just by doing this meditation we fall into that and then can go into it from there. In sitting practice, sometimes I sit down and I've had some kind of encounter or conversation or gotten a letter or I have something on my mind and I don't deal with it. This will remain there through the whole meditation and become an obsession. So I might do this Chöd practice to get to the point where I can just sit.

You can do this with relationships as well. Say you're having a problem with someone that's really bugging you. Then you can imagine that you're feeding them. If somebody's really mad at you or really dislikes you, but there's nothing you can really do about it in an outward way, or there's nothing that you really should do about it in an outward way, you can imagine that they're feeding and you can feed them in the practice in this way. When you do this meditation, what often happens, in my experience, is the relationship shifts. We hold cords with people all the time and our enemies are just as linked to us as our loved ones.

The Tibetans say that you're going to be reborn with your friends and your enemies because they're all our karmic cords that we have going out.

When I first moved to Italy, I used to get furious in the traffic, the way the drivers would cut you off. I would just get furious and it built and I would get madder and one day I jumped out of my car and started screaming at somebody and then I thought, Wait, do I want karmic links with all these Italian drivers? So I realized that I was just creating this whole karmic network that looks as bad as Italian traffic.

Another time, I was married to an Italian and was getting divorced. You know what divorce is like. I think a lot of us have experienced it—there's all this stuff going on, all these tensions and cords and anger. My husband wouldn't let me leave Italy with my son, which they can do in Italy. You can leave but your child has to stay unless you get the permission. So I was stuck there and I did Chöd and fed my ex-husband what he wanted and gave him all the love and the feeling that he would get if my son were to stay there. The next day he came over and said, "I don't know why, but I changed my mind. I really understand your point of view." A few weeks later he signed the papers. It's almost as though the battle has a life of its own and it starts to feed on negativity. We can really get into this thing with each other in our lives and then we get completely caught in those tensions. So you can use this in many different ways when something's on your mind.

The point also is not to manipulate; this is not used to get what you want. The motivation always must be for the benefit of all beings. This is really what should happen. In practice, always the primary thing is *What is my motivation? Am I doing this for the benefit of all beings?* Then, at the end, to dedicate the accumulation of positive energy to the benefit of all beings. They say to have a complete practice you have to have the motivation in the beginning, the refuge, the practice, and then the dedication of the merit afterward. This is not just a psychological technique. It is an abstraction of a very profound practice and I've given it to you so that you can use it and apply it in your lives, but always to hold those two things when you do it, that my motivation is for the benefit of all beings and then the dedication of merit, which means we take all the positive accumulation we've generated together and spread it out for all beings everywhere, especially where it's really needed, all the people suffering with illness, war, famine. And this substance that we have generated goes to them, supports them, and links with them.

The Great Work
of Life and Death

Patricia Shelton

TO ASSIST A DYING PERSON'S CONSCIOUSNESS TO BECOME ONE WITH THE LIGHT is a compassionate act of great import. In 1971, Trungpa Rinpoche told Patricia Shelton that her life's work lay in assisting others at the moment of death. With the encouragement of Zen Master Seung Sahn, with whom she has been engaged in koan study since 1975, Ms. Shelton founded the Clear Light Society in 1977, with the intention of helping the dying to make the transition from life to death. Based on her wide experience ministering to dying people of diverse religious backgrounds and belief systems, she developed and pioneered the use of the Clear Light practices. She has also trained hundreds of people in other aspects of this practice, including emergency training for relatives of the dying, Moment of Death workshops geared to people in the helping professions and hospice workers, and long-term training in the complete Clear Light work for Buddhist practitioners so that they may assist the dying of all religious persuasions.

The Clear Light Practice for the Dying cuts through the confusions of mind that may be heightened by illness and medications. It provides a means to meld the practitioner's consciousness with that of the dying person and other family members, resulting in a powerful, clear unity flowing inexorably toward the moment many consider to be life's greatest spiritual opportunity—the moment of the great light of death. This practice is nonsectarian and of universal applicability. As such, it accommodates to, and blends easily with, meaningful segments of the family's religious tradition, making it the family's "own" practice.

Ms. Shelton, who has taught an introductory course in Zen practice at Boston University for eleven years, offered a day-long Moment of Death workshop at the Buddhism in America conference. Out of respect for the participants, this workshop was not taped and is not included here. What follows are excerpts from Ms. Shelton's later talk, "The Great Work of Life and Death," in which she described the advent of her work with the Clear Light practice.

When you are born, where do you come from? When you die, do you know where you go? Life is like a floating cloud which appears. Death is like a floating cloud which disappears. The floating cloud itself, originally, does not exist. Life and death, coming and going, are also like that. But there is one thing which always remains clear. It is pure and clear; not dependent on life and death. "If you can only realize that the Buddhist teaching has no words, then the lotus will blossom in your mouth." So said the Great Master Hui-neng of China, the Sixth Patriarch. So what is that one pure, clear thing? He already said the Buddhist teaching has no words— but if you do open, be very careful.

Sweater is black. The carpeting is red and gold. The chandelier lights are on. These are not matters of opinion or theory or doctrine or dogma or like or dislike. The draperies are red and gold. Great Master Huang-po said, "That which you see before you, is *it*. Begin to reason about it, however, and you at once fall into error." That is our job. That's the great job of life and death. We must take that evolutionary leap from the thinking mind, the conceptualizing mind, the mind of logic and reason into the before-thinking mind, which is the realm of wisdom. (But even saying "the realm of wisdom," one deserves to have one's mouth washed out with soap.)

So here we are. We must make the leap to the realm of wisdom. That is our job. As practitioners, if we do that, we die the great death. That is we die to the attachment of I, me, and mine. My opinions and my ideas and my hopes and fears. Me. That's the great

death, dying to that. Then, that which you see before you, is it. It's no longer, I, me, mine.

So you and I, are we the same or are we different? If you say same, you're attached to emptiness. That deserves thirty blows. If you say we're different, you're attached to name and form. That deserves thirty blows. So how can you respond with the before-thinking aspect of mind? Not with the conceptualizing mind. Can you do it?

The living and the dying are same or different? Again, if you say "same" or say "different," many blows. How can you respond fittingly with the before-thinking mind? Many years ago, Eido Roshi said, "I understand you work with the dying? Well, you know, there are two kinds of dying. What kind do you work with?" How would you answer that? What's your answer? You don't know? Well, that's good. That's better than a lot of opinions and a lot of words. As Great Master Fayen said, "Don't know is the closest thing to it." So don't fear don't know. Make your home in don't know. Wisdom comes out of don't know. It is that which you see before you; begin to reason about it and you at once fall into error. Then you're in very ordinary mind.

So we go along, all of us, practicing. We start out, maybe once a week. We go week to week. At some point we practice, perhaps, day to day and we sit every morning for a little, practicing day to day. We continue on and then we're practicing perhaps hour to hour. That is every once in a while during the day, there's a little bit of clarity. Then if we continue on, we're practicing moment to moment and that moment-to-moment practicing is redolent of Hui-neng saying, "If you could only realize that the Buddhist teaching has no words," and Huang-po saying, "That which you see before you is it."

So this is inspiring your practice and you're far away from opinions and ideas and distinctions, divisions, and schisms and all the rest. You just don't know yet. Wonderful. Then in this moment-to-moment practicing, all of a sudden that which appears before us, is, perhaps, someone very ill. Perhaps, someone dying. Perhaps someone very close to us—a parent, or a sibling, or a mate, or a child, or one's best friend, or one's lover. What do you do, in this moment, right now? What do you do? Would you know what to do? It's important. Everyone should know what to do. One person in every family should know what to do. If one person knows, the whole family can be swept in beautifully, magnificently.

I was in that position in January 1971. That was twenty-six years ago, when it was very clear that my friend, whom I was visiting at the Beth Israel Hospital, here in Boston, was dying. I simply knew it. He was an old and dear friend. I had a deep relationship with him for over nine years and ended up marrying someone else, but he was always very dear and precious to me. My husband and I would go to visit him in the hospital. On one of these visits, I simply knew that within twenty-four hours, he would be dead. I left, telling him that I would return in the evening and I went home.

Home at the time was the East–West Center in Boston, where people could come and study yoga and Buddhist philosophy and meditation. We were doing meditation practice according to the instructions of Trungpa Rinpoche, at the time, which was based on following the breath. That was essentially what we were all doing. That evening, when the group came to meditate, I had had some hours to think about my friend Paul at Beth Israel Hospital.

I said to the group, "You know, I've been preoccupied for the last few hours because I have a dear friend who is dying. I would love to help him, but I don't have the slightest idea what to do. But some things have been arising in my mind these last few hours, and I don't know if there's anything to them or not, but these are the things. First of all, I have read that teachings can be communicated verbally, through symbolic gesture, or mind-to-mind. I don't know if this is true, but this keeps rising in my mind. It's like someone knocking on my door saying, 'Pay attention to this.'

"Another thing that arises is that mantra embodies certain qualities of enlightenment and the Mantra of Great Compassion comes to mind. I don't know if this is true or not. I don't know if it embodies compassion. I have never done anything with this mantra, but putting these two things together, it's occurred to me that, if you're willing to do so, perhaps, we could all recite this *mani* mantra together, aloud, for a while. Perhaps, ten minutes or so and then continue silently reciting the mantra, each one of us for, perhaps, twenty minutes or so. Doing all this with the idea that, perhaps, in some way which we couldn't possibly understand right now, this will help my dying friend. If you're willing to."

They said, "Well, why not? Of course. Let's do it."

So, not having any sense of whether this was really worthwhile to do, we did it, because we we're doing something and we had the right intention. Our hearts were open to helping him in some way. But beyond that, we were really proceeding in ignorance. So we recited it, rather haltingly and clumsily, together for ten minutes or so, then we continued on our own silently.

I was doing my OM MANI PADME HUM silently, when all of a sudden, as if an inner TV was switched on (my eyes were closed), I perceived a great golden Buddha, which immediately disappeared, and then I saw a long, single line of people of both sexes from all traditions and countries and eras, dressed in national dress. This was a single file of people and it just went on and on and on, thousands of people, and the last person in the single file, was my friend as I knew him in this lifetime, with his right arm up over his head and his face contorted in agony. It was given to me to know at that moment, that I was seeing all the lifetimes of my dying friend. I just saw them simultaneously and yet one at a time. Then that disappeared and I had thoughts arise. These were thoughts with great authority. They weren't Patricia Shelton thinking about what can I do to help Paul. Great authority as if it was coming from someone else, but I was not hearing voices. It was just thinking: When you wrap this up,

get over to the hospital and this is what you're going to do and say and you will stay with him until the end, and this will help him. So, that took all of maybe a minute or so for all of this to happen.

I just sat there. I opened my eyes and looked around, everyone was just sitting there with their eyes closed and reciting the *mani* mantra. After twenty minutes or so, I rang the bell and asked people how they found that. People had different experiences with the mantra. Then everyone left and I went to find my husband to say that we've got to get over the hospital. On the way over to the hospital, I told him what happened. "What do you think about that?"

He said, "Well, Trungpa Rinpoche tells us not to look for sounds or sights or anything sensational."

I said, "I know that, but I wasn't looking for anything. I just wanted to help Paul and this is what happened."

"Well, I don't know what to tell you. You'll have to ask Trungpa Rinpoche. Who am I to make a comment on that?"

We went up to the intensive-care unit together and the door leading into the unit had a round window. Richard looked through it and he said, "Oh, my God!"

I said, "I know exactly what you're seeing Richard. You are seeing Paul with his right arm up over his head and his face contorted in agony and there are a lot of doctors around him."

He said, "Yes, that's exactly what I'm seeing. Patricia, you have seen truly."

I was filled with great confidence and

was very inspired to just do whatever I could do to help him. I felt quite assured that it would help him. It's as if, all of a sudden, I became someone else. So, one of the nurses came out and said, "Things are in a very difficult stage, as you can see. There are a lot of doctors here. There's a lot of internal bleeding and they can't seem to stop it. About an hour ago, he kept pulling his right arm up over his head and we had to switch the transfusion to the left arm. It's really bad."

I said, "Yes, but this is his life and his death and he should certainly have something to say about this. Please go in and speak to the doctor in charge and tell him, I'm here and that I could come in to speak to Paul." Paul was from Cuba, so I said, " I could go in and speak to him in his own language and reassure him. He must be terrified with all these doctors around his bed. Ask the doctor to ask Paul. This should be Paul's decision. I certainly won't create any difficulty for anyone, but I think I'll help Paul just by being there. If he could just see me and perhaps I could just say a few words to him."

The doctor said, "Yes, that's fine. Do come in."

We had already arranged that, once he got better, Paul was going to come home with us, so we were acting as his family at that point.

Paul really was terrified, but also very glad to see me. I spoke to him in Spanish. I said, "This is very, very serious. It's very important that you listen to me. Do you know that?" He couldn't speak, just nodded.

"All right, I'm going to say some things. Just close your eyes and just listen. Just listen." We proceeded that way in Spanish until the doctors were finished and then the doctor in charge said, "What I'm going to do is this. I imagine you want to stay."

"Yes I do."

"Well, all right. You and doctor so-and-so will stay and you can each be in the room for twenty minutes with Paul and then you change places. So someone will always be here with him and if he needs any medical assistance, then doctor so-and-so will be on the scene and will be able to provide it. Otherwise, you'll be able to be here with him and I can see it means a great deal to Paul to have you here."

He asked if I was prepared to stay all night. I said, "If necessary, yes, of course."

So that's how we left it. The doctor and I took twenty-minute turns, hour after hour after hour. I would speak in English and in Spanish to him. It seemed to help him, just my being there. He wasn't alone in this intensive-care unit far from home. About four o'clock, when the nurse was doing something for him, he kind of gestured. She said, "Oh, you want to write something." So, she brought pencil and some paper and he couldn't write. He tried. Tears rolled down his cheeks. He couldn't do it. She said, "You want to write something to Patricia?" He nodded.

I said, "It's all right, heart-to-heart is better. It's all right. As a matter of fact, I have to go home and take care of my daughter." I was nursing my child at the time. "I will be back. Don't fear. I'll be back. I'll be with you."

I was sure that he wouldn't die before I got back. It was strange how positive I was about everything, how confident. I did go home and take care of my daughter and by the time I got back, the nursing shift had changed, so the new nurse said, "While you were gone, the doctors met and agreed that they were keeping Paul alive way beyond the point that they would have struggled to do for anyone else, because he was such a beautiful man. They finally agreed that they couldn't help him. So, he's in there slowly bleeding to death. They removed all life support systems and sedated him a little, so he wouldn't be too frightened and there he is. I imagine that you would like to go in."

I went in and spent the next two hours with him, speaking to him in Spanish and in English, and this is what I was reciting again and again and again for him. This is the "Clear Light Meditation for the Dying," which came to me during that recitation of the *maṇi* mantra:

A vast, boundless ocean of light.
A vast, boundless ocean of light.
An infinite ocean of radiant light.
An infinite ocean of radiant light.
The light is everywhere.
The light is everywhere.
All is light.
There is only light and it is light exhaling into light.
It is light dissolving into the great light.
It is light merging with the great light.
It is reunion with the great light.
It is reunion with the vast, boundless ocean of light.

I went on and on in English and Spanish. Every once in a while, just to reassure him, I identified myself and said, "I'm with you. We shared so much in the past and we are sharing this now. Just listen. Just listen."

At some point, I had the thought, Oh, it would be so nice if he could open his eyes and we could have one last visual exchange. This person, who had been so dear to me. So kind. The compassionate man that I've known in this lifetime, outside of my teachers. Good to everyone. I thought, if we had one last exchange, that would be wonderful, but thought, well that's selfish, just continue on. So, at a certain point, his eyes did seem to open, but had nothing to do with me or him or anything. His eyes opened wider and wider and he was looking out into space and he started smiling and the smile grew and grew and grew and grew. He was in ecstasy. And all of sudden, it was as if every cell in my own body was plugged into high-voltage electricity. I knew what it was. He was right in the great light. He was right there. He was ecstatic.

At that point, I switched over to the instructions in the *Book of the Dead* about the light being himself.

That which you see before you is it, and if what is before you is the great light, that's what you are in that moment.

He was in ecstasy. That went on ten or fifteen minutes and then it faded off. About that time, the nurse came in and said, "I think we're just about at the end."

I said, "That already happened."

She said, "Oh, I didn't know if you were aware of it."

It transformed me. *That which you see before you is it.* He was before me in ecstasy. When the mind is clear, it's like a mirror, so you are what is being reflected at that moment. It was very wonderful for us both. I hope you can all have that kind of experience with someone. I went on to have that with my mother and many, many, many people. After my mother, I felt that my life has borne fruit. I was able to help my mother—my mother who suffered so greatly, in so many ways, during this lifetime—and she was able to die so beautifully.

I wrote a poem at the time about Paul's death. It's called "Paul's Death."

Paulino.
Beautiful Paulino.
Dying young in an intensive-care unit of a
    Boston hospital. All the curtains drawn
    round.
Dying far from home. It's a long way to
    Havana.
Paulino of the noble bodhisattva heart.
No desire for yourself; only for all beings.
Paulino dissolving in each exhalation into
    the vast, boundless ocean of light.
With each exhaled aaahhh—dissolving into
    the vast, boundless ocean of light.
Light dissolving into light.
Light exhaling into light.
Light merging with the light.
Light in the ten directions.
Vast, boundless ocean of light.
Paulinito, donde estas? Where are you?
Eyes, staring out into space. An ecstatic smile.
Blood-stained crucifix on a white sheet.
Twelve noon in Beth Israel Hospital.

Another question for you: "When the four elements disperse, where do you go?" This is a koan used by Zen Master Tosetsu Juetsu.

In our own practice, we must bring our minds to that place that Hui-neng talked about. He said, "The Buddha's teaching has no words, so practice has to bring us there." When working with a dying person, we want to bring the person there, where there is no thinking at all.

Then, as Huang-po says, "That which is before you is it." So, if the dying person's mind is clear when the light arrives—and it always does, inexorably, although for most people it's gone like that; but if you've been working with someone for hours, days, weeks, months preparing them for this moment—the mind will be clear. The mind will have cut through all the medications, the suffering, pain, thoughts, and everything. The mind will be clear, so it will be the light.

You'll be doing an incredible service, because the moment of death offers the greatest opportunity, spiritually, in a given lifetime. Very few people know this and very few know how to effect this. We can't depend on ourselves then; we may be filled with medications and pain and so on, so we really need someone there to help us.

I saw Trungpa Rinpoche two weeks after Paul's death and he said, "Oh, this is absolutely wonderful. Who could have imaged this would happen in America? In America, they don't know what death is because they don't know what mind is. If you want to know what death is, you must know what mind is. Don't read anything here about death. They don't know anything here. Just continue. You've been given a great teaching —a mind treasure. I just want you to keep practicing and we'll speak about this again in the future." About a year later, he said, "Now you must start, you must help other people."

I said, "Well, we're not in Tibet. We have no tradition here." (Remember, this was in 1972.)

He said, "That's right, so you have to find your own way."

"Will you help me?"

"Certainly not," he said. "I have my own job to do. That's your job, but you will sit with many thousands, as you did with Paul. You'll help other people to help others and so on. That's your job, and how you do it, well you'll have to work it out."

So, it has been sort of like Milarepa's house for me—trying this and trying that and that didn't work and this didn't work and so on. But gradually we had practices coming together, starting with this one.

He said also, "Don't be too attached to me because you'll have other teachers coming along and they will all help you in this work. Don't be attached."

He was right. He said about the *Tibetan Book of the Dead,* "We're not trying to transplant Tibetan practices for the dying here, because those are strictly for Tibetan Buddhists. America is made up of Christians, Jews, Muslims, and everything—non-believers. You must develop a whole repertoire of practices that will help any person whatsoever in America, without imposing any doctrinal element on anyone."

So, we have done that over the years.

We have a whole body of practices actually and we can go and sit with anyone. Although, our work is based on Buddhist mind, the mind that Hui-neng and Huang-po and all the other great masters are pointing us to. Still, if we're working with a Jewish person, we do it in English or in Hebrew. If we're working with a Catholic, we do it Latin or in English. We have a whole repertoire and we infuse their own practice with elements from their own tradition.

I also did some work with Kalu Rinpoche, who felt I should have the *phowa* initiation, which occurred in 1974, but I met Zen Master Seung Sahn in 1975 and found that the koan practice was for me. I've been with him ever since. In 1977, he encouraged me to found the Clear Light Society. To multiply myself. To train other people and so on. Offer services to dying people.

"I just have one bit of advice to give you on this," he said. "When you've trained someone, before you allow them to go out and work with anyone, they must answer the cat koan."

Master Na-ch'üan, a very marvelous Chinese master, who never lost an opportunity to teach, one day looked out the window and saw that the monks from the east hall and the monks from the west hall were in some sort of altercation about a cat. So he went out and he lifted the cat up by the scruff and said, "You monks, who can save the cat's life?" In the other hand, he had his precept's knife. He said, "If no one can speak, I will kill this cat." They couldn't say anything, so he killed the cat.

That evening, when Chao-chou, his number-one disciple returned from visiting outside the monastery, he went to the master's room to pay his respects and let him know he had returned to the monastery. Master Na-ch'üan told him what had happened with the cat.

He said, "Now if you had been there, what would you have done?"

Chao-chou (who was later to become one of the great masters himself, but at this point was very young) took off his grass slippers and put them on his head and walked out of the room. The Master said, "Ah, if you had been there, I could have saved that cat."

So how do you save this cat? What can you shout out? It doesn't take much—two or three words—but they have to be the right words. This is a great-compassion koan. Just feeling sorry for the cat won't save the cat. You must have great compassion. Here you have to move beyond just talking about great compassion and shout out the right words. Then you can go work with the dying. And you should respect the dying enough not to rush out. If you want to help someone, really prepare yourself; it's very worthwhile.

Here's another question for you from Master Tosetsu Juetsu: *When you die, how will you then be reborn?*

Let's come back to Huang-po: *That which you see before you is it. Begin to reason about it, however, and you at once fall into error.* There is one thing which always remains clear. It is pure and clear, not depending on life and death. What is that one pure and clear thing?

And Hui-neng saying, *If you could only realize that the Buddhist teaching has not words. Then, the lotus will blossom in your mouth.*

From my heart, I wish that for all of you.

Being with Dying

Joan Halifax

BUDDHISM TEACHES THAT NOTHING CAN BE CONSIDERED CERTAIN except the fact that everything dies as a part of life. Yet, though we all die—and we all know we shall die—death is probably our greatest source of fear and suffering, especially in Western cultures. The combination of the certainty of death, and the suffering brought about through our concerns regarding it, place death and dying firmly at the center of much Buddhist thought and teaching. In fact, every session presented at the Buddhism in America conference at least touched upon some aspect of human death and its central importance to the way we live life. Two speakers in particular—Joan Halifax and Patricia Shelton—dealt primarily with issues attendant upon dying.

Joan Halifax is a Dharmacarya in the Tiep Hien Order of Thich Nhat Hanh and has worked with dying people for more than twenty years. As an author and anthropologist focusing on cultural ecology, she has also worked with indigenous peoples in the Americas, Asia, and Africa, and has taught on the faculties of Columbia University, the New School for Social Research, the University of Miami School of Medicine, the Naropa Institute, and the California Institute of Integral Studies. In 1978 she was appointed honorary Research Fellow of Medical Ethnobotany at Harvard's Peabody Museum. The following year she established the Ojai Foundation, an intercultural educational center in southern California, for which she served as president until her departure in 1991, when she founded Upaya, a Buddhist study center in Santa Fe. Among her books are *Shamanic Voices, Shaman: The Wounded Healer, The Fruitful Darkness, The Human Encounter with Death* (with Stanislav Grof), and her forthcoming *Being with Dying,* which gave the name to this workshop.

Ms. Halifax writes: "In being with dying, we can see death and know life in terms of compassion and awakening." Her day-long workshop (an abbreviated version of a program she leads at Upaya, geared toward caregivers, dying people, and others committed to being with dying) helped the participants begin to develop an approach to death that is kind, open, and dignified, and to learn to care for the living and for life itself.

W e've come together to touch the most important event of our life: the event of our death, which is more than an event. It's something that informs every out-breath.

I'd like us to remember our mortality, the inevitability of our death. I'd like us to remember that we have no idea when we will die. It could be in the next minute. Those of you who might be diagnosed with a so-called terminal illness, a life-threatening illness, perhaps you won't die of that; we don't know really what will give rise to our deaths.

That quality of immediacy that comes from being with dying, I'd like us to bring into the room. It's a quality of immediacy that is effortless. We could call it presence. When you listen to the last words of a dying person, you don't know if it's their last words, but you listen with that quality of care and attention. I'd like us to bring that care and attention forward, using this day as a day of practicing devout listening, in the spirit of Avalokiteshvara, the bodhisattva of compassion—Kanzeon, the one who hears all the sounds of joy and of suffering in the world.

I'd like us to listen not just with our ears, but with our hearts, with a heart that we could call deep heart; that is, deeper than our suffering, but opened by suffering; without prejudice or judgment. And when the critic, the judge, the intolerant one sounds inside of us, I'd like us to turn toward that one with compassion. Do not practice intolerance toward our intolerance.

I'd like us to actually use the few experiences of formal practice in the way of craft, recognizing that the practice of meditation itself is enlightened behavior. That this practice is what we will call forth, whether we're changing a bed pan, giving a sponge bath, cleaning a wound, sitting with someone who is distressed beyond measure. I'd like us to hold that quality of openness and practice mind. The actual details of meditation practice point to the quality of mind we're calling forth in being with dying.

[Ms. Halifax informally polled the audience to find out something of its demographics. Predictably, the group ranged from beginners, with little or no meditation experience, to long-time followers of various Buddhist traditions. She also asked for an idea of what sorts of religious backgrounds were represented by the participants, finding that they were widely varied as well. Finally, she queried the group regarding how recently they may have lost someone close to them, who present worked in a caregiving profession, etc., then remarked, "I'm glad that a beginner is sitting to my right. I'm glad that we're not all Buddhists. Most of us who work with dying people will never help a Buddhist die. But all of us who work with dying people hopefully will help buddhas die. So this is a kind of keynote, an edge that we want to explore. Who we perceive to be dying."

Ms. Halifax then led the workshop in a classical meditation that is particularly useful in working with dying people. Focusing on the breath, she suggested that they use a simple verse—"I calm body and mind," on the in-breath; "I smile, dwelling in the present moment," on the out-breath. After the medita-

tion period, she continued with a few observations about this technique.]

When we begin, it's helpful to consider why—what is our motivation? What brings us to this practice? And to cultivate a heart that is really awake, really alive. In Buddhism, we call this *bodhichitta,* which means "awakened heart." I often equate *bodhichitta* with the neurosis of falling in love, but instead of having just one love object, you love all beings, and you love unconditionally, as a mother would love her only child. But in that same spirit, a mother often finds it difficult to differentiate herself from her child—that quality of nonduality; in the spirit that Thich Nhat Hanh talks about, "being peace." A healthy mother doesn't say, "I love you." It's the feeling that flows from her that brings her and the baby together. So it's that quality, the sense of real connectedness, that we often begin by opening toward just one other person.

Sometimes it's difficult to open our heart to the world. It's a little general. It's like the bodhisattva vow, "I vow to attain enlightenment in order to save all sentient beings." Two daunting tasks. But how about, "I vow to be fully present with my father, who is so old. I know he won't be here in so many years." It's a quality of immediacy, not a sort of generalizing.

Cultivating *bodhichitta*—understanding why we're doing this—is very important. Most of us who have come to practice have come because we're suffering, and most stay because they're suffering and have seen a way.

So this practice, very simple though it is, is informed by a very deep sense of commitment and motivation. It's not so much that we can take a person's suffering away or create a context for enlightenment for anyone. But we're called in the simplest way, courageously to be fully present, and to attend to that for which we are not present.

Motivation is really essential, and in perfect motivation, we have two things. First is the awakening of *bodhichitta,* the fostering of an awakened heart, which often means that we touch our own suffering. The second is refuge: That we have a sense of coming home to the possibility that we can be free of suffering. This is one of the keys in working with dying people. It is changing your perception of a person who has a diagnosed illness as a sick person to that of a person who has within them the possibility for freedom. You don't deny or disavow the suffering. You hold its relative truth, being present in an individual's life. But you don't refer to "the colostomy in room 564"; he's the *buddha* in room 564. You change your perception of each being from an aggregate of pathology to looking through that suffering to the place where that being is free.

In Buddhism, we have the three refuges. You take refuge in the Buddha, you take refuge in the Dharma, you take refuge in the *sangha.* Taking refuge in the Buddha, in the outer sense, means taking refuge in a teacher who had some extraordinary insight and taught about that. But fundamentally, taking refuge in the Buddha means to take refuge in the capacity for each being's freedom. Can you imagine, if we looked at each other and instead of seeing a man or a woman, a gay person or a straight person, a black person, a Native American, we saw a free person? A person free from suffering? We have this way of holding double vision, double sight. We perceive the suffering, and we perceive also their original nature. Our job as sharers in compassion, as caregivers, is to be able to see the suffering and also the capacity within the individual for freedom from that suffering, and to have no expectations; no gaining idea. So taking refuge in the Buddha means to take refuge in the nature of awakening of each being.

Taking refuge in the Dharma means not just the teachings of the Buddha—that's the outer sense—but it really means taking refuge in truth, in reality, this moment. Being able to see the relative nature of this world and to respond, seamlessly. To be awake in this world, at the same time being able to look deeply to the absolute, to the ultimate.

The *sangha* is not just a Buddhist club that practices together. When we take refuge with a *sangha,* we take refuge with each being. We are practicing together. It's a whole quality of recognition. Many times in working with dying people, you're not necessarily with somebody whose personality you find easy to be with. Not everybody is dying the death you would like them to. Dying often makes people very irritable. Moreover, when you're diagnosed with an illness, many people become their own medical-research project. Not everyone, but some people just go in the opposite direction and their life can

become very self-centered. Maybe you don't feel so resonant with this. Why should we not offer the same quality of love to this one as to our own mother? our own sister? our beloved? When we talk about equanimity, that's what we're basically referring to. Can we not be partial? Not have, "I like this one better than that one," but really hold an open heart to all beings? Our best teachers become the people for whom it's *most* difficult to be fully present.

We do the practice, then, and we consider three levels of the practice. The first level has to do with calming, stilling the mind, and also noticing what comes up. The next level has to do with the development of compassion, really opening in the heart of *mahayana* to the suffering of all beings.

When he learned about the work I was doing, one teacher asked me, "Do you have a willingness to be sick like each person you're working with?" When he asked me the question, I happened to be working with a man who had AIDS-related lymphoma, and as I sat with him, I really asked myself. The tumors in his groin were in my groin, the tumors in his neck were in my neck. It's something that we would say if this person was our beloved. We hear it from many relatives of dying people. The husband whose wife is dying of breast cancer, who says, "I would just do anything if it were me, not her." Do we have that kind of willingness? We can only really have it if we're able to accept suffering and death in our own lives. So this work is a strong call in the truth. I can't say that I fully realized my ideal, but i'm aware of the difficulty from my own experience.

Another level that we cultivate in our practice is of absolute spaciousness, equanimity: a mind that is called forth, that is stable, radiant, open, present, able to be with anything. Then, at the end of practice, we dedicate the merit. We don't say, "I'm doing this as a self-improvement course." We further cultivate compassion by saying, "May whatever good that has arisen in the course of this practice be given away to beings everywhere. And most especially to so-and-so and so-and-so, who really need it."

Finally, the third phase is really the translation into our everyday lives of our practice, our vowing mind. Nurses, doctors, social workers, psychologists, relatives, friends—compassion in action; enlightened activity.

So we have view, which is informed by *bodhichitta* and refuge; we have the meditation practices of stilling, compassion, and spaciousness; and then we have the translation of these activities into our everyday lives. In Buddhism, many of you will know the *paramitas,* the perfections: of perfect generosity, complete generosity; of perfect virtue; of absolute wholesomeness; of patience; of energy and enthusiasm; of concentration and wisdom. These become activities, ways we express our freedom.

In the practice of listening (which will be an activity that is very key to our practice of being with dying, to contemplative care of dying people), the listening is not only to the dying person, nor to the community of caregivers, but also to oneself. In the lineage of

Thich Nhat Hanh, there is a wonderful series of invocations of the bodhisattvas. The bodhisattvas are beings who are awakened, who've chosen to come back to earth to help other beings. They're archetypal, they dress really nicely, they have great hairdos, beautiful jewelry, and in that manifestation, they actually represent qualities, we could say, of our adornments of emptiness; qualities of our own heart and mind. So Avalokiteshvara is not somebody out there; it's each one of us. Manjushri, the bodhisattva of penetrating wisdom, is you. You are Samantabhadra, the bodhisattva of effective action. And you are Kshitigarbha, the bodhisattva of the earth, who perseveres. Here is a short invocation of Avalokiteshvara:

We invoke your name, Avalokiteshvara. We aspire to learn your way of listening, in order to help relieve the suffering in the world. You know how to listen in order to understand. We invoke your name in order to practice listening with all our attention and open-heartedness. We will sit and listen without any prejudice. We shall sit and listen without judging or reacting. We shall sit and listen in order to understand. We shall sit and listen so attentively that we will be able to hear what the other person is saying, and what is being left unsaid. We know that just by listening, we already alleviate a great deal of pain and suffering in the other person.

[In this spirit of listening, Ms. Halifax asked each member of the workshop briefly to say their name and tell why they had chosen to

take part in this session. Following that, she went on to give some details of how she, herself, became involved in working with people who are dying.]

I've asked myself over the years why I've gotten into this work, and it really wasn't until about two years ago that I suddenly remembered that my grandmother had created some of the most beautiful of the gravestones in a graveyard in Savannah, Georgia, and that she sat with dying people, and that she not only sat with dying people, but she often, after a person was dead, fixed their hair and dressed them and did that part. I was raised partly in Savannah, and my memory of my grandmother was of being in her bed a lot, curled up in her arms, as she talked about what she did with her life. That thread kind of disappeared until about two years ago, and I suddenly realized that I'd been somehow made a little bit more comfortable around dying and death through being a granddaughter.

But it was actually not until I began to practice Buddhism in the mid-1960s that death became a subject of interest to me. I was a young anthropologist and my practice pointed to something that exists in other cultures that is not very present in ours: rites of passage that allow individuals to encounter death formally as part of our experience of culture and life. I worked in a medical school as a medical anthropologist, and as a cultural broker—somebody who works on the interface of systems—the traditional healers in the southern-Florida area, of which there were many different kinds, and being a

bridge for those people into the conventional medical systems.

What I saw in the conventional medical systems was a pretty hard situation in 1970. I was on the faculty of psychiatry and pediatrics. Happily, the dean was a very innovative person. He was new, and he really decided to turn the medical training on its head. So students had patient contact the first day in medical school. (Conventionally, it's not until the third year.) But the adebration or the echo of uninformed medical training, which still goes on in this country in terms of its impact on doctor-patient relationships, was really disturbing for me, and I saw that typically death was a failure. Dying people were kind of shunted to the side. Hospitals were not good places to die. The idea of palliative care was not present in 1970, or minimally so. It was a disturbing experience for a young person.

I then married the psychiatrist Stanislav Grof, and we did a very interesting project together: LSD psychotherapy with people dying of cancer. These were laborers and physicians and everybody in between, of all educational backgrounds, genders, races, and so on. They were there with full knowledge after they had been referred by physicians into our program. We did this as a double-blind study, so that half the patients received LSD, half didn't. It was a very profound experience. I was just thirty at this time, and I wasn't prepared in any way by my psychology, by culture, by anything, for the depth of the psyche when the defenses were lowered using this powerful substance.

It was a contemporary rite of passage.

All of the people with whom we worked either were suffering from intractable pain, difficulty with medical management, severe depression, or severe anxiety. So our population was a population, so to speak, of people who were undesirables. We also had people who were self-referred into the project, who'd heard about the project—just ordinary people, not hippies, per se.

While Stan was taking notes, I was generally on the couch holding the person who was dying, sometimes up to eighteen hours a day. And it was really different than what I'd seen in the medical school. We talk about intimacy and relationship; I learned a lot in that particular situation. Being a quite tender person, one of the big questions that I had was, Would my closeness with this individual create a countertransference problem, or the professional-boundary discourse that, needless to say, has to go on. This person's whole psyche is exposed, as if their skin is gone—it's just the flesh of their soul that you're with—and what's it going to be like for them and for me?

Every notion I had was wrong. I thought that they would be more dependent on me. In fact, the relationship, because it was fulfilled, not frustrated, by therapeutic distance, made them more filled. The mothering and the love that I gave them worked, and it worked for me, too. The people I didn't have that kind of intimate relationship with are still on my heart, in a not entirely healthy way.

The second thing was, we already knew that this was beneficial. The people went through a very profound experience of dying and being reborn, in a kind of religious context

that was set in place by the relationship with Stan and me or the other therapists, where the kind of music that we played, the preparation for the patients, the quality of attention, the relationship of trust, all allowed people to let go in such a deep way that many of them went through a very profound experience of death, which could look pretty scary from the outsider's point of view—like a bad trip. But happily, on the other side, for most people, was an experience of rebirth, which had a profound effect on their final days.

Having been an anthropologist, I'd worked in Africa, I'd done cross-cultural anthropology in the lab at Columbia, so I'd looked at a lot of things conceptually. I'd looked at things culturally, but I never realized how rich the human psyche is, and how we've deprived ourselves out of fear of death, literally. So when our marriage came apart, we both continued to work with dying people, I without the psychedelic drugs. And it's twenty-five years later, and this is one of the jobs that one has.

About four or five years ago, after first moving to Santa Fe, I became a—a pastoral person. But it wasn't as though my congregation was where I was. Sometimes I'd fly to Seattle, and then to somebody in Brooklyn, and then to somebody in Los Angeles. Thank goodness I settled in Santa Fe, and some of the local caregivers saw what I was doing, and they said, "Show us what you're doing. Teach us." So we started this program. It's wonderful, because it's not just about the professionalization of caregiving around dying. It's about training professionals—we have a whole program for that—but also this is the care that villagers need to do with each other. We are each in a village, and it has to do with community development, and it has to do with what we want at the time of our death, which is probably not to be isolated or not to be simply attended to by professionals. But to be in a community that has both professional skills and the skills that come with being a family member, a community member, a villager. So in Santa Fe, we have this educational program for professionals, we've got an educational track for people like us, and then we have a service program, and so on.

It has been interesting for me, having been in the "death business" since 1970, to watch it ebb and flow in the past twenty-five years. Now it's becoming popular again. I think that what we're seeing is an outcome of very important work that was done in the 1960s by Dame Cecily Saunders of St. Christopher's Hospice, whom I happily had the opportunity to spend time with in 1972. St. Christopher's Hospice was just a dream! It was a slightly hospital setting but it was really like a house, with a living room, and cocktails, and people smoking in bed. And Dame Cecily Saunders would go around and sit on people's beds. It was a very intimate, warm atmosphere.

Pain care was not a problem, like it has been in this country. One of the big things I've seen in working around this area of death and dying, with those people who have diagnosed illnesses, and the rest of us, there's fear of death, but often there's an even greater fear of pain. So what we're beginning to see are pain-management

strategies that make the dying process for many people less oppressive psycho-physically, and what many of you attend to—what I attend to—is not the complex situation around tremendous pain, but that around the psychological, social, and spiritual issues related to death and dying.

[Here, Ms. Halifax asked the participants to divide up into groups of four or five people in order to explore a critical question: How do you want to die? What's the picture of your ideal death? What's the setting, who's there, who's not there, what are the physical and psychological conditions? She asked each person to imagine that they knew that they were going to die tomorrow and that they could have things exactly as they wanted them. How would that be? She continued: "I ask for you all to bear witness, basically to do this as a counsel, to speak as deeply and truthfully as possible. To not speak with inhibition, feel that there is a spiritual expectation of you.

"Practice sets our being into a track. It creates a path inside of us. In Buddhist psychology, Thich Nhat Hanh often talks about watering the wholesome seeds. By telling your story of how you ideally want to die, you are setting a template, a pattern, in place for yourself. That probably will change over time, but you're also inviting others to bear witness to this. I ask you not to consider this a game, but a prayer."

This exploration lasted about half an hour, after which several members of the group shared their reactions and feelings, one of which brought Ms. Halifax to observe that "there are levels of mind engaging around the experience of dying, and the actual gateway of

*death, that we can only intimate." She suggest-
ed that, regardless of the nature of outward
appearances to people in touch with the dying
person, we cannot know just what that experience is to that person. Referring to* The Death
of Ivan Ilyich *and noting that she doubted
Tolstoy had read* The Tibetan Book of the
Dead, *she observed that "what arises for
[Tolstoy] is luminosity."]*

Years ago, I gave a lecture in a small group
called "Mind and Life," which is basically six
scientists sitting with the Dalai Lama for six
days, each of us giving a lecture of some
hours in the morning, and then, in the afternoon, discussion. Mine was on near-death
experiences, and I kind of knew what was
going to happen. I was really excited, because
the question is, Is this like what's described in
the *Bardo thödol?* I went through very
detailed explanations from all the different
researchers of all the different stages and
experiences, and I began to look at a near-
death experience as an extraordinary adap-
tive mechanism to a catastrophic situation,
and what a divine thing the human mind is.

My experience with dying people has
deepened over the years, in sitting with
dying, and becoming more and more
respectful and interested in the basic teachings of the *bardos.* And the call for us, if it's
not our path, is not to get jangled up into
trying to figure out the *bardo* system, but
actually to develop a quality of presence and
simplicity and strength that allows us to be
present for whatever it is that will arise.

For those who are intensively involved
in the investigation of the science of con-

sciousness, the Tibetan teachings are
extremely interesting, as are other systems.
But there are very simple things that we, as
Western people, can do to prepare ourselves, that do not require conceptual training at that level.

Also, to realize this genuineness, who we
truly are in the deepest nature, some of us
will require a certain kind of medicine, others of us will require another kind of medicine. As one teacher of mine said,
"Enlightenment is an accident. Practice makes
you accident prone." So it's not to say that
people who've done a lot of practice are
guaranteed a perfect exit, but the odds are
on your side a little bit.

However, if we take *The Death of Ivan
Illych* as a possibility for every person—here's
someone with no spiritual training, in a completely dysfunctional situation, who you could
say was liberated at the moment of death. I
think it's very important for us to hold both
of these possibilities. It doesn't necessarily
look like liberation from the point of view of
the outsider. We don't really know what's
happening from the point of view of another
person's internal experience. But we are
aware that a certain view, and certain practices of stabilizing the mind and awakening
love and compassion can actually create a
greater possibility for a death that is more
dignified, whether it's instantaneous or arising
from a chronic illness. Those practices are in
all of the traditions.

*[Before the lunch break, Ms. Halifax led the
group in another period of meditation, asking
the participants to bring their attention particu-*

larly to their out-breath. "Our out-breath is the last breath. Imagine that we are exhaling into radiance. We are exhaling into luminosity, and we're following that breath into light. How precious this out-breath, this release. And allow a sense of bliss, or kindness, or the smile to accompany that out-breath."

She then asked that each member of the workshop practice a change in perception: "As you move through the hallways and into a restaurant or wherever you're going, and as you're encountering people, if you could perceive them as buddhas. If you will perceive them as free. If you will look through their suffering, not past it, to the place where they are free. We are so culturally conditioned to perceive people both superficially and also in terms of negative categories. The invitation is to look deeply, and see how that looking medicines you." This provided a topic of discussion in the afternoon portion of the workshop.]

The *gatha* I introduced this morning is one I use with dying people:

[breathing in] I calm body and mind.
[breathing out] I smile, dwelling in the present moment. This is the only moment.

Saying "Dwelling in the present moment" is quite helpful for people who are particularly in pain. This moment of pain might not be the same as the next moment of pain.

There are two *gathas* that I have found to be especially helpful in my own practice, for giving to people who are sick or sad. This breathing in is a real medicine. It's the medi-

cine of calming, but it's also the medicine of bringing the mind and the body together. Breathing in: "I calm body and mind." You feel that in the inhalation, drawing the body and the mind together as you draw in the breath. And then breathing out, "I smile." The smile is medicine. A lot of us have a very pious relationship to our spiritual practice, but we really want to nurse the seeds of happiness, even when our situation is not happy.

Not always do we feel happy when we're practicing, but we're doing this as a practice. In cry therapy, your therapist will tell you, "Go boo hoo hoo hoo," and after a while, from the frown and from the sounding, tears actually come up. Well, this is the same thing. Just raise the edge of those lips and watch what happens to your inner attitude. This is a quality we're developing, a serene, sustaining presence you will be asked to turn to others as well as yourself.

The other *gatha* I want to teach you comes from the *Mahasatipatthana-sutra,* or the *Sutra of Mindful Breathing.* I actually use this a lot in my own practice, when I've lost touch with the present moment. It's very simple. There's one word for each inhalation, each exhalation:

in—out
deep—slow
calm—ease
smile—release
present moment—only moment

I've done this with a lot of sick people. Staying right with the breath; speaking very quietly. But almost every time I do sitting practice to gather myself in and to remind myself of where I am, I do this *gatha* also.

These are Zen verses called *gathas*, and for me they're prayers. This is one of the ways that I, as a Christian-born Buddhist, pray. I think prayer is something that most of us in the West really understand. We're brought up with prayer. We have ways of saying prayers that we don't even know.

At dinner parties, a person like myself often finds the chair on either side of them empty. It's like the story of Jumping Mouse. Remember when Jumping Mouse fell into the river and he went back to his people, and they went, "Oh, gosh, he's wet. Must have been in the mouth of an animal and didn't want to eat mouse because mouse is probably poison." Well, that's one of the things that people who work with dying people experience. You are interworld entities. You work between the worlds, and it's like dirt is matter that is out of place. You might think that you're kind of heroic working with dying people, and you deserve a little bodhisattva button; and because people will think you're so brave and wonderful and kind and compassionate. But there's something in the unconscious in many people that will find you dirty, contaminated, because you've been in the presence of the mystery.

These are little clues along the way, like look at everybody as buddha. Or, guess what, not everybody's going to look at you like you're buddha, because you are in contact with sickness, suffering, death, and decay.

If there's not some sense of physical revulsion, often you'll experience a kind of fear [other people may have] of you.

[Ms. Halifax asked the participants to tell of their experiences during the lunch break as they tried to regard all beings as buddhas, as free. Many had forgotten to do so; others had tried briefly but, finding it too difficult, gave up. Some who had tried, found that they needed to make eye contact with people, which could present its own difficulties. A woman who mentioned that she lives near abortion clinics, told of trying something like this with protesters she often encounters as she walks by.]

Participant: I live near several abortion clinics, and I've lately begun to do that there, because I don't usually think that that's the way to spend your time, parading outside with those pictures. But every time I walk by, I stop and I say hello to these people, and once in a while they say hello back. And when they smile and say hello back, they just look like regular people instead of who I imagine they are, and it actually makes me feel very good to be there.

Joan Halifax: Great. This is about reconciliation. This is working with dying. Not just at an abortion clinic or with veterans. This is fundamental reconciliation work, and a lot of times the reconciliation comes between caregiver and dying person, because we feel we have to defend our hearts: If we allow recognition to happen, we'll be just devastated by loss, or betrayal.

[Responding to the panoply of experiences, Ms. Halifax brought them into focus by bringing up the concept of going beyond thought.]

What we're asked to do is to go deeper than thought, beyond language. To not be in the reflex of the thoughts; to not be caught in the language in the world of descriptions. Can we let go, relax, concentrate, stabilize ourselves so that we are in what we would call primary mind? A mind that recognizes everything but doesn't name it?

At a creation point in practice, you discover that thoughts are actually getting in the way of your practice, because they're so conditioned. And you want to see more directly, perceive truth as it is. So that's what one sort of practice is about: stilling the mind to the point where it is like a mirror. It reflects things just as they are, and one does not go into a description in relation to that. Things just as they are. That's one of the primary purposes of Zen practice.

The discursive mind, when it is based on clear reasoning in response to the world, can produce a great set of engineering plans, a fantastic insight or description of emptiness. The discursive mind can compose a piano concerto. But in this work, because thought in a sense is thinking about the condition of a dying person, when we join with the dilemma of this dying person, hopefully thoughts are not between us and the dying person. We've relaxed to the point where there's no mind chatter going on; where we've opened our whole being to this one before us. And the experience is of nonduality, of not a self

and another. One is completely present for this one, as though there is not another.

So that is one of the realizations of this kind of contemplative care, where the distinction between you and me disappears. That's not to say thinking isn't important and rich and fun and difficult. But this kind of practice, this kind of work, requires that we actually let the discursive mind go. When I walk into the house or the room of a person who's dying, I try to walk in with as little baggage as possible. I try to leave my ideas in the car, outside the door. I literally pause before I cross the threshold. I gather my mind up, that is, the strength of mind, planted in my spine. I remember why I'm doing what I'm doing. It is because of love. And then I remember I'm entering into the field of mystery. I honestly don't know what's going to happen. I've been doing this work since 1970 and I can say that every moment is a kind of surprise, a teaching for me.

[Next, Ms. Halifax had the group divide into pairs. Sitting across from each other, each member of the couple gazed into the other's eyes, "without personality," for a period of time. She gave the following directions.]

Practice actually staying bold or courageous in the act of perceiving that person as a buddha, or free, or perceiving through to their liberated nature. I'd like to know how it feels for you to be in that experience of intimacy. Can you look into the eyes of a dying person, imagining the truth there, that we're all terminal? Can you bear to be perceived for the freedom that is inside of you? See them as fully awakened. Imagine that indeed their buddha-nature is fully present, blooming, so that you are able to see. Don't pity them because they can't see, and don't run a riff about that. See through the story into essence. And do it as a practice, recognizing at the same time that you are being perceived with the same direction, the same admonition.

[While doing this, each person was to try to pay attention to two things: How it feels to be perceived free, liberated from your suffering, and how it feels to perceive others that way. And to take note of "transparency, intimacy, permeability; look at the resistance."

After a period of gazing, each pair talked with one another about their experience and the issues Ms. Halifax had raised, then all participants discussed it as a group. Responses were widely varied, from acute discomfort to visualization of glowing light surrounding the partner. Ms. Halifax pointed out that this is not something one would do with a patient, it was an exercise used to help discover "how can I open myself up and respect the other person's personal boundaries? How can I change my perceptual frame of reference so I'm not perceiving them racially, in terms of gender or story or soul scars. Can I look through to their essence? Will they let me? And if they don't, can I still?"]

Joan Halifax: In the clinic, so to speak, a lot of what you're going to do is what is done in Japan—"see with your belly"—that, in fact,

many people who are dying don't want to be seen at all because they don't like the way they feel or look. And frankly, our work is not about stripping people naked. It's about profound respect.

You always let the person lead. When I enter the room of a person I've not met before, I'm very shy and very humble. Not, "Hey, how're you doing!" Or, "Gosh, it's *really* good to meet you." I enter very shyly and humbly. If I'm with Native Americans or certain Asian peoples, I'll actually bend over a little bit and bring myself low. You make yourself small, in a certain way, and tender, which then invites forth the contact.

It brings to mind the quotation from St. Francis of Assisi, "What you're looking for is what is looking." Sometimes when we're looking from within our experience, when looking for the divine, or freedom, God, out there, it's so hard. But when we intend to see God in each other, or freedom, or liberation, or radiance within each other, we discover our own.

The other thing is to imagine this was not the face of a friend or beloved, but the face of death into which you were looking. The face of death for each of us probably has a particular personality, a history with it, characteristics. It can be perceived personally and archetypally. We're also asked to look through the face of death to the place where death means freedom. These practices are about awakening, about freedom, and I ask us to consider what it means to look through the face of death into freedom.

This awakened heart that is the supreme elixir that overcomes the sovereignty of death.
It is the inexhaustible treasure that eliminates poverty in the world.
It is the supreme medicine that quells the world's disease.
It is the tree that shelters all beings, wandering and tired, on the path of conditioned existence.
It is the universal bridge that leads to freedom from unhappy states of birth.
It is the dawning moon of the mind that dispels the torment of disturbing conceptions.
It is the great sun that finally removes the misty ignorance of this world.
This is *bodhichitta,* the supreme elixir;
Our awakened hearts, this is *bodhichitta.*

Metta practice, the practice of loving-kindness, is a very skillful way that we can work. There are actual, wonderful strategies that are used in *metta* practice that are very easy to learn and very easy to teach. In our training for people who train others to work with caregivers and dying people, this is maybe one of our most popular offerings. But let's face it; not that many people are going to learn how to do consciousness transference at the time of death, *phowa.* Not that many people actually have the will, and even the subtlety, to settle down to do mindfulness practice. But this is easy, because

it reminds us of something that's very familiar to all of us, and that's prayer.

In classical *metta* practice, one works beginning with the *brahma-viharas* and the four immeasurable states of mind. You do actual practices that generate loving-kindness, one of the abodes; that generate compassion, another abode. Loving-kindness is that feeling that a mother has for her child, that a father has for his child. It's very tenderhearted, nondual love. Compassion is the deep desire that this one be free of suffering, and a willingness to actually experience the suffering of another. Then joy, the third abode. This is wonderful, because this is joy in the well-being of others. Finally, equanimity, which is the fourth abode, and which is the deepest *dhyana,* the deepest form of concentration, where we, without any sense of partiality, any sense of specialness, offer love to all beings equally. Mao Tse-tung, Hitler, whomever.

In Buddhist psychology, these adornments of emptiness are seeds within the continuum of our consciousness. These practices water these seeds; they strengthen these qualities. I feel it's very important for us to touch our suffering, but we don't need to practice suffering. Most of us need to practice more wholesome states of mind so that we can face our suffering with strength, not without courage. And this is one of the things that we will embody as caregivers of dying people. Our relationship with a person in an extreme state of suffering points to a relationship that they can have within themselves toward that suffering. The more able we are to accept the person's pain, the person's fear, just as it is, simply to be present for it, the greater possibility of their accepting their pain, their physical suffering, and being present for it. The more we try to fix and pity, or contract around the difficulty, that exemplifies a negative relationship within the individual. It's important to practice these skills. We are strengthening the muscles of love, compassion, joy, and equanimity. Everybody was born with these features within their mind-ground.

Also, with violence, hatred, aggression, jealousy, pride, envy—our culture waters these unwholesome seeds. Just turn on your television if you want to have the seeds of fear and violence watered. You don't even have to go to the Fox channel. Just watch CNN; the news. So often, we water the seeds of unwholesomeness within us before we actually have the strength to face the suffering in the world; to face suffering, period.

We're a kind of Peace Corps, and we're going to places in the world that are in danger. We need to go with skills and strength. You are a place that is in danger. You need to go to those places with skill and strength. We are with each other in danger and suffering. We need to be with each other with skill and strength—and love. That's why practice is important, and that's why a community that supports that in any denomination is important, because it's rather difficult for us to support ourselves, as what happens in the course of practice.

Loving-kindness practice brings up a lot of hate in us, often. The opposite often happens. We think we're courageous, we have our eyes open and we're looking into each other's eyes, and then we're asked to look deeply into each others' buddha-nature, and we experience fear, because of the culture we're from, because of our past experiences. We are here to reflect and to support. A community is very important. Being with dying is about a community. It might be a community of compassionate strangers, or it might be a family and professionals, but it's really important to acknowledge the aspect of community development in our work, and to water the wholesome seeds, and to support each other, and to be courageous about calling the caregivers together, and enjoy a period of silence or do a *metta* meditation. A young guy who died of AIDS a couple of years ago and I were walking down Madison Avenue. He said, "You know, I just got out of the hospital. Thirty, forty, fifty people came, asked me almost the same questions. Nobody sat in quietness with me, and that's what I really wanted, somebody just to really be with me."

One of the worst ways and most unloving ways that we distance ourselves from a dying person is to do what we think is courageous: "How are you doing?" It's like that's the question that seems to want to be asked, but behind that question is really the call for love.

The emphasis in this practice is on balance—the balance between opening one's heart endlessly and at the same time, of accepting the limits of what one is able to do. The balance between compassion and equanimity. Compassion is the trembling or the quivering of the heart in response to suffering. Equanimity is a spacious stillness that can accept things just as they are. The balance of compassion and equanimity allow us to care and yet not to get overwhelmed; not to be unable to cope.

[Ms. Halifax led the workshop in two types of metta practices—a group for caregivers, and then a series for dying people. The meditation for the first is as follows:]

[in-breath] May I offer my care and presence unconditionally.
[out-breath]… knowing it may be met by gratitude, indifference, anger, or anguish.

[in-breath] May I find the inner resources
[out-breath]… to truly be able to give.

[in-breath] May I offer love
[out-breath]… knowing I cannot control the course of life, suffering, or death.

[in-breath] May I remain in peace
[out-breath]… and let go of any expectations.

[in-breath] I care about your pain
[out-breath]… but I cannot control it.

[in-breath] I wish you happiness and peace
[out-breath]… and I cannot make your choices for you.

[in-breath] May I see my limits compassionately
[out-breath]… just as I view the suffering of others.

[As the workshop began to draw to a close, Ms. Halifax presented some important elements of being with dying that might be thought of as "pointers" for the person who is considering this sort of work. A number of these dealt with "the shadow in this kind of work—the downside, the traps." She observed that "spiritual care, contemplative care of dying people, sounds very romantic. And it isn't. I like the practice for it, I like the training for it, but it's life."]

One of the most obvious things is, if you want to see yourself, if you really want a good look at yourself, go sit with dying people. The work for a contemplative caregiver is not coming in, doing a procedure, and leaving. It means sustained presence, and sustained presence can mean positive projection and negative projection; positive and negative countertransference. Which is to say, you can be looked at as a god or goddess incarnate—the great savior of the person in the family situation—and your ego can get incredibly involved in this plus. You can start feeling really useful, and you might even be really useful. But the minute you start feeling any kind of inflation or pride or self-importance, you'd better go talk to somebody. Pride goeth before a fall.

When the patient is projecting all these wonderful images on you, because you're so spiritual and you're dealing with all the deep issues, it can as easily flip into negative transference, which means that you can be actively disliked for penetrating into the unknown, and you can as easily as not be asked to leave—permanently. Being found ineffectual is a very upsetting situation, so you have to be very equanimous, not only with the person but with your own responses. Check your ego at the door.

Countertransference. There are some people you really love because they're dying a great death, and you feel somewhat responsible for it, and everybody loves you. But then there's the person you have trouble with. How did I end up with this profane grouch? Somebody who's not only grouchy, but indifferent. Scowls at you when you come in the room. What are you going to do with that? Check your ego at the door. That's where you really need your sense of humor. This is not work for people who don't have humor. The most profound respect is called forward in you, but a lot of humor is needed. For those who get through the great ego dash that most of you will go through, or have gone through, humor will be what really brings you a lot of solace. And it's good humor between you and the dying person. Sometimes it's possible to actually smile around the corner of an absolutely impossible person and situation with them. Again, equanimity is really important. Any signs of inflation or hyperdeflation, get yourself into a support group quickly. Talk with your *sangha*.

We work with what we call "partners." Contemplative care requires such transparency, so much presence. And you don't have techniques to hide behind; you're not doing something to anybody. You're just there. It's often easier for two people to be there than just one person. Sometimes we've got a whole group of people. A woman who had breast cancer wanted to meditate with a group of women in our community, so ten women came over and sat with her, not to overwhelm, but just sitting around the bed, doing practice.

It's not so easy to do this work alone. We discourage it. Check out each other's perceptions—it's easy to fool yourself. And having supervision: somebody who's back home, who's inside but outside of the circle, who can help through what will inevitably be difficult situations. Dying is not always an epiphany, as we would like it to be, and incredible problems arise. You can get on the dying person's side but have their family totally down on you. The family wants to give big doses of medication to the dying person who's acting out. You realize they're snowed; they've got the doctors on their side. What are you going to do? The dying wife wants to have her husband euthanized—taken to Holland and given deliverance; physician-assisted suicide. A dying person presents themselves as having cancer, when all they want to do is commit suicide; they don't have cancer. These are true stories.

Drama: If you're a drama queen, go and do something else. This is not your job! Because the theater around dying is often just right out there on the edge. You're not on the periphery of this work, you're in the heart of this situation.

You think you've got all the skills, so, from the family that feels overburdened from taking care of a dying person, you basically take away all the good jobs. You're the pastoral expert, giving succor, and the family's sitting out there looking like idiots. That's not your job. Your job is to get the community involved and get out of the picture. You're not there to mediate God to the person; you're there to bring the presence of God into the room, through everybody in the community. This is an inclusive practice.

Hours: You have to know how long to stay and when to leave. I've had eighteen-hour days and felt great at the end of them. I've had six-hour days and felt like I was going to die at the end of them. I've done hours when I should have left in forty-five minutes. You learn when it ceases to be nourishing and sane. Heroics are just what you don't want to do. You want to be able to engage the network—the entire family system and the professional caregiving system—in setting up a sensible schedule.

You can be a ray of hope, or you can foment absolute chaos. Often your work is actually to straighten out a schedule. Get everybody together in a meeting. I had this fantastic gay woman who had lymphoma, and she had these twenty-five women who were taking care of her, but nobody knew when, how, where, what. So the job was bearing witness, and then listening to everybody, putting a schedule in place, and then saying, "Go for it."

You're not going in there as a Buddhist, you're going as a human being. You're not lay-ing meditation or God or Jesus Christ on anybody. You're finding out what their job or their care is about; what their tradition is about. Just because they don't go to church doesn't mean they haven't got something. It's really important to always let the patient lead. We really have to get your expectations, desires, and prejudice out of the way. And if you want to see them get in the way, just put yourself in this situation.

A lot of times you're doing nothing for hours. You think, Why am I sitting here? There's this something lying in a bed called a dying person, and it's not dramatic at all. What are you going to do? Read *Redbook* or something? No. Your thoughts are not your thoughts. These practices that we pointed to today are practices. We ask you to cultivate a mind that dwells on loving-kindness, think good thoughts, because your thoughts are not your own. If you start to have 1,300,000 stray thoughts coming in, take a leave. People in comas, dying people, they're on their trip, but often they have incredible sensitivity to what's going on at a very subtle level—your fear, your impatience.

[A participant noted that he frequently finds that the patients with whom he works "need permission to go," and that that is a way in which the caregiver can help both the dying person and the family. He pointed out that it is "not certainly to wish them away," but that the dying person and their loved ones face "a very great hurdle...in just letting go. There's not much to keep; they just can't let it go."]

Joan Halifax: That's the complement. How can you create a setting where the family feels good about letting the dying person go? How can you create a setting where you don't wish, or they don't wish, the dying person away? Equanimity. Willingness to stand in the fire of a tremendous amount of confusion, where nothing might make sense. The only thing that will make sense is your openness to just being led by the deepest truth in the situation.

[Another participant mentioned that people who are dying "know exactly how to push your buttons in various ways when you're doing your best. Simply put down a glass of water for your father there, and he says, 'Don't put it there; put it there!' And what comes up in terms of how you feel after some time of that kind of treatment." He further observed that, involved in the situation with family are issues external to the dying process, such as the parent recognizing that they no longer control the person they may still regard as their child, but who, as an adult, has become independent.]

Joan Halifax: This is a real call to your practice, and when you lose it, when you just see aversion or impatience arising, turn toward yourself with compassion, and to this one with compassion. If you're leaking, leave the room and calm yourself. Most of the people I've worked with aren't that interested in me, or my situation, or my problems, or even my responses. They're interested in themselves. And it has not been my experience that self-disclosure in this situation conduces to more

honesty. I really need to work my stuff out and not expect that this person is going to get into some kind of clearing process with me.

[One of the participants was a doctor, who mentioned that the real pitfall for him "is referable to one of the points of the guided meditation that says, 'I can't have any control over your pain, or your dying process.'" He pointed out that it is easy for a physician to feel that, through the use of procedures and medications, "there are tools to at least bend" the pain. He explained that it was very tempting "to think that one can alter this process, because you seemingly can, or you can keep someone alive, and you can still their pain with big drugs or, in miraculous cases, even with homeopathic remedies. So how [can one] be an interventionist without intervening somehow, without being the doer."

Ms. Halifax told him: "Our little under-the-breath prayer is, Doing the best that I can."

The discussion focused on the issue of easing others' pain, bringing the doctor to observe that "this should get into medical training... early on in the experience for medical students. The projections onto a doctor as being a savior or a goat is supported even on rounds: Who died in your service? Why did they die?"

His remarks prompted another member of the group to say that "that's a problem not just for the physician, but for the family, too. They feel if their relative's dying, they've failed....I work in a rehabilitation hospital, with physical therapists and occupational therapists, and nurses, and they give the most loving care to patients who are dying. Then we do a support group for them, and they say they feel like a failure. Because our whole model in Western life is to fix it. And in some ways, the way not to feel ineffectual is not to try and be effective. You're not going to lose; we don't keep score here. I see the families struggling, too, to keep their relative alive."

Ms. Halifax recounted the experiences of a fellow anthropologist, who has wide experience with non-Western attitudes and practices surrounding death.]

A friend who's an anthropologist lived with a tribe of Indians for many years, and she told me a story that I think is very relevant here. When she first got into this Indian village her first time, she brought a lot of medical supplies, and after she'd been there for a few months, a family showed up, a mother and a father, an infant and a number of children, and the infant was very sick and seemed to be neglected. She said to the parents, "Well, what's with the baby?"

They said, "The baby's going to die."

"But why aren't you taking care of it?"

"Well, the baby's going to die, lady!"

She said, "Give me the baby."

So she washed the baby, fed the baby, put new clothes on the baby, and that night she went to bed with the baby in her arms. And she woke up in the morning; the baby was dead. And everybody laughed.

They said, "We told you the baby was going to die."

And she told me, "You know, it's twenty years later, I'm married to an Indian, I have six Indian children, I live there most of the year. If I had it to do all over again, I wouldn't do any differently."

There's a quality of heart and mind around the value of human life that, regardless, we're all going to die—very soon or later. And so what is it that we want to bring into this precious human life at this time. And can we develop people, healers, in our society, each of us, because we all need to assume that role in some place in our world, where it's not about curing, but it's about healing.

This has to do with a real reformation of professional training, of health-care professionals, where death is seen as a natural part of the life process. When it's not, incredible distortions arise, producing end-of-life scenarios that are our worst nightmares. And the health-care costs of that—you all understand what this means, not just spiritually, psychologically, socially, but economically.

These questions about, for example, physician-assisted suicide or pain control with high doses of morphine, are pretty interesting to me as a Buddhist in being with dying people. For example, many Buddhists felt that somehow obscuring the awareness would be a detriment to the moment of liberation at the moment of death. Around pain, compassion would only say that we should bring the best that we can—pharmacology and drugs—to alleviate pain. I asked His Holiness the Dalai Lama about this very issue. I said, "What about substances that actually seem to mitigate awareness?"

He said, "That's not the level of mind that's relevant."

He said that what would be a detriment is the pain. That, in fact, the greatest act of compassion would be to alleviate the pain, and even though the level of awareness that is obscured is that which we would interact with, that's not the level of mind that comes forward or is engaged at the moment of death. This is a very deep level of mind.

One lama, when asked this question, responded something like, "Compassion, please! Why, it's a miracle that we're living at a time when a certain amount of physical pain can be mitigated."

It's time to draw to a close what we've done today. I'd like to do that with two things. One is a quote from Rilke:

Love and death are the great gifts that are given to us.
Mostly they are passed on unopened.

I thank you for opening the gifts of love and death. And I would like to conclude with a poem. by Thich Nhat Hanh. It's called "The Old Mendicant."

Being rock, being gas, being mist, being mind, being the mesons traveling among the galaxies at the speed of light, you have come here, my beloved. And your blue eyes shine so beautiful, so deep, you have taken the path traced for you from the nonbeginning to the never ending. You say that on your way here, you have gone through many millions of births and deaths. Innumerable times, you have been transformed into firestorms in outer space. You have used your own body to measure the age of the mountains and rivers. You have manifested yourself as trees, grass, butterflies, single-celled beings. And as chrysanthemums. But the eyes with which you look at me this morning tell me you have never died. Your smile invites me into the game whose beginning no one knows, this game of hide and seek. Oh, green cater-pillar, you are solemnly using your body to measure the length of the rose branch that grew last summer. Everyone says that you, my beloved, were just born this spring. Tell me, how long have you really been around? Why wait until this moment to reveal your-self to me, carrying with you that smile so silent and so deep? Oh, caterpillar, suns, moons, and stars flow out each time I exhale. Who knows that the infinitely large must be found in your tiny body? Upon each point on your body, thousands of bud-dha-fields have been established. With each stretch of your body, you measure time from the nonbeginning to the never ending. The great mendicant of all still sits there on Vulture Peak, contemplating the ever-splen-did sunset. Oh, Gautama, how strange. Who said that the udemorra flower blooms only once every two thousand five hundred years? The sound of the rising tide, you cannot help hearing it, if you have an attentive ear.

Joan Halifax gasshos to a workshop participant

4

Mindfulness and Compassion

Socially Engaged Buddhism
in the West

The Coming of Age of American Zen

Peter Muryo Matthiessen

INTERNATIONALLY KNOWN FOR HIS WORKS OF FICTION AND NONFICTION, Peter Matthiessen (Muryo Sensei) has devoted his life and work to pursuing sane and sensible approaches to the environment and social justice. While many of his books are informed by his Zen practice, *The Snow Leopard, Nine-Headed Dragon River,* and *East of Lo Monthang* have specifically Buddhist orientations.

The Buddhist underpinnings for Sensei's practice initially comprised studies in Rinzai Zen under the late Nakagawa Soen Roshi and Eido Shimano Roshi. He then began studying Soto Zen with the late Taizan Maezumi Roshi, then Baisan Tetsugen Glassman Roshi, who gave him transmission as a teacher in 1984.

Matthiessen delivered the opening-night keynote address at the Buddhism in America conference. One may argue that an opening talk is most effective when it poses questions and presents ideas that then arise and are discussed and challenged throughout the proceedings that follow. By such standards, Sensei's address did not disappoint, and many of his observations and propositions provided points of departure and talking points at many other workshops and discussions to follow. While some conference attendees balked at, or stumbled over, certain ideas they found disturbing, others pushed them further and held them up like prisms through which blossomed myriad ways of looking at the role of Buddhism in North America and the numerous permutations it now takes. Matthiessen's address also sounded a note that would be heard, to greater or lesser degree, in more than half the presentations during the weekend: the central role that engaged Buddhism is taking as Buddhism develops its new roots in the West.

I'm very honored to be in this position, with so many really wonderful teachers at this conference. I've only once given a keynote speech, with mixed results. I'm not sure what a keynote speech is! I think I'm supposed to tell a joke, and give you boilerplate once over lightly. I'm not going to do that. When I heard about doing a keynote I thought, My God, I better think up a Buddhist joke. But I couldn't think of one. So, I think I'll do my best to talk to you. I have a captive audience—a big advantage.

The idea of Buddhism in America interests me, particularly the ecumenical quality we have here. I speak as a Zen student, but there are so many strains and flavors here. Some of them have been here for a long time—as long as Japanese Zen. My lineage, of course, is Japanese Rinzai and Soto Zen, which itself is a composite of, basically, Hinduism and the Tao, Confucianism, etc. That's what's happening here, we're forming this new amalgam. Of course, there is a strong Korean Zen tradition here, under Soen-sa-nim, and Tibetan Buddhism is probably the strongest element of all right now. Many other Mahayana and Hinayana groups are represented, and many of them have been affected in a very positive way by American Indian teachings, maybe more than we realize. So, I think we in America are grounded in that in a certain way.

We also shouldn't forget the religions in which most of us here are grounded, those murderous old troublemakers the Christians, Muslims, and Jews! Those traditions are very, very powerful. We seem to have turned toward the East, but I think many of us see the Western traditions in a new light. We see that the essential teachings are very close to Eastern teachings. In fact, in my lineage, we have a number of Christian monks and nuns, some who have even had Dharma transmission. This is happening more and more as time goes on.

So, all of these strains are coming together, and what we are trying to look at is, what is going to happen here in the West. In American Zen, with Maezumi Roshi's death, in a sense the great era of Japanese Zen teachers began to draw to a close. There are still some here, but that was, to me, a benchmark, an indication that the Dharma is being left in our hands now. I think we are going to make a shift toward a less hierarchical practice with less finery. This has always been true, that any reformation movement simplifies things again to get back toward what the original teaching was. The Japanese teachers, to their great credit, wanted us to do that. They always encouraged us to form our own Zen, to not be so dependent on them.

I had three Japanese teachers, all very strong, and I owe them an enormous amount. Of course, the way we think of it in Zen practice, they aren't gone. Everything is right here, now, and they are a part of us. So, let's not forget what we owe the bringers of these wonderful teachings, no matter which sect or group we happen to be in.

I thought of a metaphor I'd like to relate to you. For the Amazonian tribes, the fundamental dish is called a "pepper pot," a loose term indicating a very large pot in which anything is thrown in. That pot is never watched, but it's always on the boil. In other words, everyone who comes into the Indian camp can feed out of it; it's always ready.

What I love about this is that it's such an old tradition, one wonders what is lurking at the bottom of the pot—maybe a slab of musk ox from the Bering crossing? You don't know, it may still be down there! But the pepper pot is always fresh, always its own thing, and yet never different. An embodiment of the idea of not two, not one—a wonderful thing for us.

So, I'd like to see a great pepper pot made out of American Buddhist strains, but how can we work together and yet keep our own special flavor? We may say we are after the absolute, but finally our life is led in the relative, and those tastes of life are wonderful. We would not want to blur everything together.

So, what is this American Buddhism going to be, and where is it going to go? It seems to me that our common ground is social action, social justice. Thich Nhat Hanh wrote a few years ago:

Should we continue to practice in our monasteries, or should we leave the meditation halls in order to help the people who are suffering? After careful reflection, we decided to do both. To go out and help people and to do so in mindfulness. We called it "engaged Buddhism." Mindfulness must be engaged. Once there is seeing, there must be acting. Otherwise, what's the use of seeing? We must be aware of the real problems of the world, and then with mindfulness, we will know what to do and what not to do to be of help.

I think that's sensational. I've always felt that way, and in fact quarreled rather bitterly with one of my Japanese teachers, who said it is ridiculous to talk about going out and helping people when you aren't enlightened. What he said kind of shook me up, as he wasn't entirely wrong.

There are many, many perils of social activism. It's a wonderful way to get off the hook and pretend you're doing something, your ego is pumped up, etc. I worked for a long time with Cesar Chavez and saw this happening—the pride people took in social action. The pride of helping other people can really get in the way and do a lot of damage. So, I understood what this roshi was telling me, and even my teacher, Tetsugen Roshi,* wasn't into social action when I met him. But he made a shift, and today is probably one of the most socially active Buddhist teachers in America. In fact, I think that all of American Buddhism has made a shift in this direction. I love *zazen,* but somehow sitting on that black cushion and straining toward the absolute while in the relative world, where there was so much misery and poverty, didn't make sense. I don't think Americans were ever really geared for sitting only, and I think there was always a schism between American students and Japanese teachers for this reason.

---

*Tetsugen also spoke at the conference. See his workshop "Instructions to the Cook," pages 427–39.

Way back in the eighth century, Master Hua Jang said, "If you keep the Buddha seated, this is murdering the Buddha." This is a slightly different teaching, in that he is talking about quietism. To sit in the perfect *zazen* of a frog or a hen is not quite what we have in mind in terms of bodhisattva practice. Clinging to the form of sitting rather than to the essence and spirit behind it is a mistake. There we can hearken back to our first teacher, Shakyamuni Buddha, who spoke about the four noble truths, suffering, and the human condition. After we study the four noble truths, we go on to the three pure precepts, in my tradition. The third precept is basically doing good for others. This is a very ancient teaching; this isn't something new.

In America, Robert Aitken Roshi was one of the very earliest ones to work with engaged Buddhism. Also Gary Snyder, toward the end of the sixties, wrote about the Buddhist approach to individual transformation in combination with social justice. Today we have the Buddhist Peace Fellowship, a very effective organization. I suspect that most American Buddhist teachers are now involved in some type of social action—maybe prison work, working with homeless or sick people, etc. Tetsugen Roshi, whose group works with homeless AIDS patients, feels that we should start with the people who are most oppressed and defenseless, and I feel that's absolutely correct.

Mohandas Gandhi said: "To see the universal and all-pervading spirit of truth face to face, one must be able to love the meanest of creation as oneself. That is why my devo-

tion to truth has drawn me into the field of politics, and I can say without the slightest hesitation, and yet in all humility, that those who say that religion has nothing to do with politics do not know what religion means." I suppose I'm saying that engaged Buddhism approached mindfully is not different from the way I envision American Buddhism to be.

So how do we incorporate social activism into our practice without losing the spirit of the practice? That seems to be the more difficult issue, as the practice came from a meditation background—from the view that at least a glimpse of the absolute is necessary. Without this experience, our life is relatively stunted. This is hard for all of us, no matter what our profession is.

I did want to mention something that is very important to me. It came out of an extraordinary trip that Tetsugen Roshi organized to Auschwitz. Tetsugen, for a number of years now, has led these street retreats, and Rick Fields and I were on the first one. We weren't seriously pretending to be homeless persons. (You can't fake that.) The idea was that, since we were working with homeless people at that time, it seemed hypocritical not to have at least a taste of what their life was like: how they were treated in the streets, how they got their food, the compulsory church services, and so forth. So, this experience was very powerful.

Then, Tetsugen had this idea to spend a week at Auschwitz. I had just come from Hawaii and didn't really want to go, but it turned out to be one of the great experiences of a lifetime. One mysterious thing happened that I've been struggling to get to the bottom of. Now, the Polish countryside in November is very gloomy and rainy. We arrived at a hostel, which is right up against the fence at Auschwitz. You look out of your window right into the camp, there's no getting away from it. I remember thinking, Do we really need this?

The next morning we went to the Auschwitz Museum, and it is really a shocker, no question. Piles of worn-out shoes, human hair, baby clothes, and the like on such a scale that you wouldn't believe without seeing it. What place in the human spirit does the creation of a death camp like this come from? To pretend it was a few evil people is unrealistic. We can't get away with that. There were thousands and thousands of people deeply involved, as we all know. In the afternoon, we walked out to Birkenau, about a half-hour walk from Auschwitz. We went there and did our meditation all day for the next six days, right on the selection platforms, and then during the walking meditation we would go to the crematoriums and make offerings, sing, and chant and then go back and sit some more. We got names from the Holocaust Museum and chanted about thirty thousand of them in the snow. It was immensely moving.

From the first or second night, there was a strange feeling in this group of about one hundred forty people, of four faiths (Christians, Jews, Buddhists, and Sufis), from about ten countries. The retreat was set up so that the attendees could give testimony at night, which was extraordinarily powerful. Rabbi Singer was singing, and eventually it turned into dancing. Some people were shocked when the dancing started, but it happened so naturally. Rabbi Singer started to move, then took people's hands, and we all formed a circle and went around the auditorium. It was very exhilarating and joyful. Later, we had a clergy meeting, and discussed what had happened. Everybody felt very guilty about this exhilaration. Why were we happy at Auschwitz, representing the very worst that humankind is capable of?

So I went back out to Birkenau and sat every day, and I grieved for everybody. Not just the grief from the camp, but grieving for the human condition. The conditions at these camps tended to knock away masks. People, from the beginning, were very open with each other, like they had known each other forever. I thought that was why I felt such enormous happiness and opening up, but somehow it seemed something was missing in this explanation.

Many of us have read books that paralyzed us because they were so sad. In my case, it would be Dostoevsky's *The Idiot*— incredibly sad book, and yet absolutely exhilarating, because it's so true. Dostoevsky doesn't back away from the truth, and I think that all great art has that quality. So I starting thinking, when I returned home, about what truth I could have possibly seen at Auschwitz that turned the sadness I originally felt there into such exhilaration.

What you see at Auschwitz, in a shocking way, demonstrates what Goethe, the

German writer, meant when he said, "I have never heard of any evil or crime of which I personally am not capable." He was able to see clearly into his own humanity. It's not a matter of Germans and Jews as much as the nature of homo sapiens, this primitive and primal species.

I think there are three truths which we find very hard to face. One is that we are an animal—a very, very big, hungry animal. Another is that we are going to die. Everyone knows it, but a part of us doesn't accept this truth. The third truth we don't face is that man has always been capable of extreme brutality, and we're still doing it.

When we gathered together at Auschwitz, I asked the representatives from ten countries whether they could say their country was never guilty of genocide. The United States certainly has been. So, how can we pretend we are any different than the Germans were? Yes, the Germans have to face what they did, as every country does, but that isn't the underlying problem.

I think what we have trouble facing is that we will never make progress, we are not going to change the nature of our species. We think we are becoming more civilized, and it's true that our technology becomes more advanced. We're tool users, like chimpanzees. Certain birds are tool users, too. That's not such a great accomplishment. Our tools get better and better, but the animal behind these eyes isn't changing. We have our encounter groups, religions, Buddhist conferences, and other lovely ways of covering up this fact. For instance, when we went

into Kuwait to safeguard our oil, we killed 250,000 people!

So, in my opinion, we're very naïve if we think we're going to change this, which does not mean that there's nothing to be done. I think one reason it's so difficult to get anything done is that we all say, My God, look at the leadership. No wonder we're not getting anywhere. We've got people like...." (I won't name them because we'll get into a political hassle here, but we have these third-rate people running every country, as far as I can make out; not very wise people or very courageous people or anything.) "But when we get this straightened out, when we get our party in there, things are going to be different."

Even if you don't agree with me that we still hope that the human being is perfectible, that we can grow, we can become more civilized, I think we secretly still think that—at least I did until Auschwitz.

Instead of always making excuses for our condition, why don't we just say: This is who we are. I'm Peter Matthiessen. I have weak eyes. I have glasses. I have funny-looking ears or hair or something like that. I'm six-feet-two; I have a zip code. These are the facts I'm stuck with, I have to deal with, and we'll say the same thing about our species. This is who we are and so we have to institute controls. We cannot let the world get to the point where it is now, where there's an enormous growing inequity between rich and poor pushed very hard by our so-called leaders. These guys have got it made and more and more the poor people all around the world are being deprived. It can only lead to more fights, more genocide, more pollution, more environmental damage, which is very much associated with poverty. You can't separate these things. The days of environmentalists who do sort of grand things and conserve parks and so forth are over. You have to work with poor people if you're going to protect the environment. You have to do things. These things are all coming together. We talk about Indra's net. It's all one. It's all this oneness if we can accept who we are and recognize this is a very dangerous side of our nature and we must control it.

Somebody challenged me at the talk I gave last night and said, "What's your solution to this?" I really haven't got one, but I think we can't start without recognizing this quality and then, in our own way, as Buddhists, how do we take care of this? That's what concerns us here. I'm not an economist and I don't really have a political solution, but I think we begin by doing exactly, in a sense, what we've been doing all along, what our teachers have told us forever.

First of all, I want to accept this truth cheerfully. This is what caused, I think, the exhilaration, that there was no more fooling around, that this was it. If you didn't get it after Auschwitz, you're never going to get it. I suspect that this is what underlay that excitement and everybody felt it. I've had four letters from people who were at Auschwitz and I thought it was only me who was kind of crazy. One of them is a wild-scrawled postcard from this woman in Warsaw; she's a psychoanalyst, and she said, "My voice is still vibrating with the names.

My heart is still echoing with love." And another person wrote from Paris, "Nothing, I might add, is what it was since the naked rightness of Auschwitz." This is the tone, so it's not just me.

Well, I think, as Buddhists, we deal with this simply by asking, what is our teaching? What is our only real teaching? Our only real teaching is being in this moment, this paying attention to this moment, moment after moment. This is where our life is. This is where the thusness is. You know, we talk about the past and the future being ghostly areas and it's right now, step after step, moment after moment.

May I suggest that we approach this truth—if it is a truth, and it may not be; I may be totally deluded; we have a very good word in our practice, *delusion,* and we may be looking at it right now—but may I suggest that we approach this truth cheerfully and with exhilaration because it seems to me that it's liberation to free ourselves from the hope of fundamental change in the species and to face the Buddhist truth, the American Buddhist truth, that spiritual actions can only be taken from a place of oneness with all sentient beings and only be taken each moment, one moment at a time. It's from this place of clarity and oneness that perhaps American Buddhism can make a contribution and a difference.

Seeing this, the first step may be exhilaration or whatever, and then liberation, and then freedom. If we truly see this, and that means really accepting it, then we're free to act, we're free to do something about it. So we do it, and we do it in the best way that

Peter Muryo Matthiessen addresses the conference

each of us can. This is something I learned from Chavez. People always say, What can one little person do? This is what too many Germans said. This is what too many people everywhere have said throughout history and will always say when things get rough. What can one little person do?

Now Cesar Chavez was one of the really great Americans. He had no education at all, no money, no resources of any kind. He had the whole establishment against him, the state with Governor Reagan in charge a lot of the time, the railroads, the Catholic Church, all the growers, the agribusiness, and he did it. He did it by doing what I'm talking about. He did it with this oneness of things. He just went step by step. He knocked on doors if needed. He got people to help him. He did it single-handedly without one single resource. He said, "I don't want to hear people saying what can

one little person do. One little person can do a lot." And he made the point that, if everybody did something—not just talked about it—but *did* something for the common good, we could turn this whole thing around in very, very short order, no matter what our true nature is. Because the good side is there, too, right there, ready to jump in and help.

So, this is my theory. We just take care of life, breath after breath. We just take care of it.

I'm going to end on a wonderful, short poem that I love and, in a way, urges us on. It's by Antonio Machado, a Portuguese poet:

One shining day the wind called my soul with an odor of jasmine saying,

I bring the scent of jasmine which will take away the odor of your roses.

And I said, I have no roses. All the flowers in my garden are dead.

And the wind said, Then I'll take the withered petals and the yellowed leaves,

And the wind took them.

And I wept, saying, What have I done with the garden that was entrusted to me?

So a great garden has been entrusted to us. Let's take care of it. Thank you.

[Though this was a keynote address, Matthiessen Sensei responded to a number of questions and comments from the audience. In particular, two aspects of his talk drew remarks and spurred questions: his comment concerning "the Hitler in us all," and his referring to

humans as animals. Following are excerpts from some of the audience observations and Sensei's responses.]

Participant: Twenty-two years ago, when I was nineteen years old, I traveled to Dachau with my German boyfriend, much to the distress of my parents. I met him in Israel. He was doing restitution work instead of being in the German military and it was a really hard thing to find Dachau. Like, there were no signs saying where Dachau is, but I really wanted to go. So we went and [it's], you know, surrounded by the barbed wire and those guard towers. It was one of those January, German, ashen days, and we stood there and the crematoriums were there, and we just wept and wept....And it occurred to me what a beautiful and horrible place the world was.

This was about ten years before I discovered Buddhadharma, and it was quite healing. I was taught as long as I can remember that Germans were "them" and we were "us," then that was that. Many years later, after I discovered Buddhadharma and began to study and meditate, I was at a Yom Kippur retreat and there was a discussion group on...a prayer about all of our sins...and I made the comment that there's a Hitler in all of us. I was never invited back. One person became absolutely incensed and there were a few people interested in what I had to say but I noticed that I never got called again.

I was thinking about the whole aspect of the shadow, like the Hitler in all of us, in terms of right action in the world and

Buddhism in America...[and] how we can really be effective in the world if we don't understand that we are capable of doing what Hitler did, and how we can use the practice and the study and Buddhism itself in America in the twentieth century to awaken ourselves to that without drowning in it?

Peter Matthiessen: I don't think we can be effective until we recognize that we've tried everything. Some of the religions that have come and gone are truly noble, including the ones we've all forsaken. They have a great nobility about them. Tremendous yearning and tremendous learning and tremendous art have often been associated with religion. We have tried all that and now I think there are so many people that it's really almost out of control. The solution has to be worked out.

I do what my heart tells me and the beginning of the solution is to pay attention and for all of us—each person—to take responsibility. We're still going to do dark, bad things. We're still going to be mean to our child or be selfish to somebody in the street or be pushy. We're all going to be human beings—that's who we are—but if at the same time we were doing something else and making a contribution, I feel this would be growing, just like throwing stones in a pond, and circles will start to spread and it may be by this increased accumulation of energy and force that something can actually happen.

Participant: Do you have a vision of human beings beyond the animal?

Peter Matthiessen: Beyond the animal? No, I like our animal side.

Participant: Would you think...Buddha [to be of a] more animal nature or did he show a different side?

Peter Matthiessen: Well, Buddha was a great teacher. Jesus was a great teacher. There are many, many great teachers. There are some in this room, tonight, but the animal part of you is just a fact. I could take myself in lateral sections and all my organs and bones and I can show you an animal right down to the smallest detail of physiology. Homo sapiens is all one, no matter where you live or what color you are or where you're coming from. We are one animal and we are an animal very closely related to another animal called a chimpanzee, even to the degree that people speculated that we could breed with them. So we can't get away from it. Every function we have is very animal.

Participant: My...understanding of a basic principle is impermanence—that everything changes.

Peter Matthiessen: Do you mean the permanence of the species? If you understand the nature, you do have that sense of evolution or whatever. Species don't really evolve. A species forms, and if it works it sticks around. A shark has been around for we don't know how many million years. Most species on earth which we now see have been around far, far longer than we

have and they presumably work, because they're still here. I think the jury is still out in our case. I don't know if we work or not. If another species comes along with a man-like appearance, as we did with the poor old Neanderthals, they're going to say, Look at these guys. They attack each other. They're greedy. They've spoiled everything. They pollute. They're completely untrustworthy, rapacious. And they'll exterminate us, probably. That's it. We won't change. We'll mend our ways, but the species will always be there. That's what we have to accept. It would be there even if we do mend our ways, even if we make a wonderful Earth—which we're capable of doing; we're capable of anything—I don't think we're capable of it unless we face the side of us that has to be brought under control. Even the hard way.

Participant: The Dalai Lama had indicated that a path to set us on this road to healing would be to compose a secular ethic which would be guidelines cutting across all religions, races, creeds, nationalities, lines, but guidelines to teach our children to live by. No matter how many times I ask this question, nobody knows. Nobody can come up with an idea. This is the closest that I have seen to the possibility of beginning to form a secular ethic based on these teachings. How do you see that we might arrive at a such a place?

Peter Matthiessen: What concerns me is the beginning. Where do we start? I have no great pronouncement to make about it at all. I'm working my way in a very primitive side, after my animal fashion, toward some clarity on this point. I think it's possible. I'm sure that if we go back to that word *exhilaration,* I think that's where the exhilaration came from. People just recognizing the dark truth, the truth liberates us, but recognizing a dark truth by itself, just that, is really not enough. There must have been an implication that if we can seize this and face it and be brave about what we see and really deal with it, then we have a starting place.

I've always felt that we've been treading on mush. I've been working on the environment and social action for fifty years. I wrote a book about American Indian land cases and religious abuse. Of about ten of them, eight were defeats, utter defeats. Two we so-called won, and both of those have been overturned since, both defeats now. And yet, you don't give up. You keep on doing it, moment after moment.

That's what I'm getting at. You just take care of what we can take care of, what we can reach. But the point is that if all of us do that, it isn't one little isolated, so-called do-gooder group, or some religious group, or whatever. If everybody is doing that out of their animal nature, we speak of operating enlightenment out of delusion. We are deluded. All of our acts are deluded. Out of our delusion, we still act in kindness. It's not

New Year's resolutions anymore. It isn't politics anymore. We're getting nowhere with that stuff.

Participant: This is going to sound really strange, but I was brought up as what is considered a pagan today....We were brought up to love nature, to love our fellow people. Is there any way possible through buddha-nature that we can love individually and also unconditionally and remove the animal side of us?

Peter Matthiessen: I don't believe we can, nor would I want it. For example, life would be far less beautiful if we all lived forever. If we were all wonderful people, boy, would that be boring. I would really hate it. It's the tension between good and bad, between dark and light, that makes things extraordinary and beautiful. That's why art occurs, why art begins. So I want to recognize our animal nature, but to control it where necessary. Something as crude as the UN peace force should be on duty all the time, and there are many sanctions you can bring against people who are committing genocide, economic ones bringing the biggest and most immediate results. There are ways to do it. That's for the leaders to work out. But I don't think we're going to get over the animal nature and I don't think that it's a desirable thing that we do.

Engaged Buddhism and Diversity

AN AMERICAN PERSPECTIVE

Bill Aiken

Soka Gakkai International (SGI)

IN 1995, DAISAKU IKEDA, PRESIDENT OF SGI, PRESENTED A SPEECH entitled "Peace and Human Security," in which he made observations concerning the diversity among modern-day Buddhist practitioners and the importance of compassion in the inner life of the individual:

Our task is to establish a firm inner world, a robust sense of self that will not be swayed or shaken by the most trying circumstances or pressing adversity. Only when our efforts to reform society have as their point of departure the reformation of the inner life—human revolution—will they lead us with certainty to a world of lasting peace and true human security....Confusing knowledge for wisdom is the principal error in the thinking of modern man....The consistent intent of Buddhism is to develop the compassionate wisdom which is inherent in the depths of life....By focusing on the deepest and most universal dimensions of life, we are able to extend a natural empathy toward life in its infinite diversity. And it is a failure of empathy....that in the end makes violence possible.

Soka translates as "value creation" and *gakkai* as "society. Soka Gakkai, the Japanese branch of SGI, is a lay-Buddhist association founded upon the teachings of Nichiren. Members of SGI strive to find ways in which they can cast their individual lives in sympathetic harmony with those of other sentient beings, regardless of their beliefs, racial or religious heritage, gender, etc. The following essay, which did not result from a presentation at the Buddhism in America Conference, was written for inclusion in this volume. It is very much in keeping with ideas and the spirit of engaged Buddhism and its contemporary practice, as discussed at the conference.

The coming of the twenty-first century coincides with the end of a decade of particularly harsh political and cultural dissension fueled by a free society that is also a captive audience for a multitude of influences from dissonant lands, religions, philosophers, and social engineers. Though many Americans acknowledge some vague notion of shared primordial roots, a turbulent history of human relations among diverse people has led to a social discourse stricken with paralysis. The simple courage required to engage in open, constructive dialogue has succumbed to a fearful attachment to the wounds of past and present injustices. Lamentably, a menacing undercurrent of opposing interest is all too real.

Opinion leaders now scrutinize ways to quell what has become known as "culture wars," as popularized by sociologist James Hunter. These serious cultural conflicts cut at the root of America's civic vitality, born from a sense of individualism turned to factionalized, competing ethnic and interest groups. Indeed, when it comes to relationships among the differing cultures in America, not all encounters are amicable.

Conflict and disharmony are constantly in our national dialogue, our news media, and therefore our national consciousness. The differences among people in American society are coming into sharper focus. Witness the often-polarized reactions of blacks and whites to the Million Man March or the O. J. Simpson verdicts. Or consider the disparate responses of men and women to gender-related issues.

Clearly, the fissures between races, eth-

nicities, and classes are widening as a sense of "tribalism" engenders associations of people banding together as they seek to hold on to their homogeneity. Some fear that attachment to difference will lead to a withdrawal among respective tribal camps from which each will glare at the other across ever-widening chasms of mistrust and misunderstanding.

How can we, as Buddhists in America, cause the light of compassion, courage, and wisdom to shine on the challenges and conflicts of America's diversity? Some see in Buddhism a sleeping giant capable of leading America's factionalized groups down the path toward common ground. Indeed, Buddhism holds the key to hope for peace with its promise of self-mastery through seeking inner reformation, discourse through seeking sustained dialogue, and understanding through seeking spiritual renewal.

Getting Engaged

The U. S. branch of the Soka Gakkai International (SGI), a lay-Buddhist organization in the Nichiren tradition, is perhaps unique among American Buddhist groups in that its membership roughly reflects nationwide diversity. As Professor Jan Nattier of Indiana University writes: "The Soka Gakkai is unusual, for it has a substantial percentage of African-American, Latino, and Asian-American members, in addition to those of European-American ancestry. The Soka Gakkai is the only Buddhist organization with a substantial black membership."

Every month, our members gather to

recite and study the Lotus Sutra in places that range from inner-city projects to suburban homes and everywhere in between. The diversity of our *sangha* is a source of great joy and hope. It also is a tremendous challenge, and we are still working on the answers. But our own struggle to face up to the difficulties and conflicts that arise from the issue of diversity has given us both experience and insight into the problems and benefits of this challenge. It has also fueled our determination to demonstrate that the principles of Buddhism can provide a pathway to resolve one of the world's most pressing problems.

Soka Gakkai (literally "value-creating society") is centered around the teachings of the thirteenth-century Japanese Buddhist reformer Nichiren. As Tina Smith, a Washington, D. C.– based trainer/consultant who has practiced Buddhism with the U. S. branch of SGI for twenty-two years, says:

American culture teaches people to blame others for their unhappiness. Parents blame children. Children blame parents. Government blames the people. The people blame the government. Spouses blame spouses. And races blame one another. But Buddhism teaches that if you are unhappy you must look within your own life and seek the wisdom, courage, and confidence to change your unhappiness. As an African–American, when I experience a racist incident, I use my Buddhist practice to make causes that will bring about a different effect in my environment.

In the crossfire of the culture wars that

plague America, the idea of peace and genuine coexistence eludes most individuals. It is too difficult, generally, for each individual to see how he or she can take significant steps toward lasting and meaningful change within society. Still, as human beings, we do have the power to wonder—to imagine—and to ask over and over again, How can I make a difference? And when the question How can I contribute to society? sustains itself in people's hearts, it is transformed from a mere question into a true quest, echoing the Buddha's words:

At all times I think to myself:
How can I cause living beings
to gain entry into the unsurpassed way?*

As Buddhists, we aspire to a peace that goes beyond the suppression of conflict. We seek to create a condition of peace that begins in the human heart and extends outward. In other words, we strive through practice to conquer our own demons and delusions, and to open the inner treasure of our enlightened nature in order to nurture, within our surroundings, such values as common good, wisdom, self-cultivation, and creativity. The important question, then, is how to bring these values to bear on the issues of race and diversity that confront America.

Part of what our experience has taught us is that, rather than looking for a single

---

*The Lotus Sutra, Burton Watson trans. New York: Columbia University Press, 1993, p. 232. All quotations from The Lotus Sutra in this article, are reprinted from this translation and edition.

solution, or trying to impose a certain order, we should take our first steps by engaging in a peace process based on the eternal Buddhist principles of hope, sustained compassionate dialogue, forbearance, wisdom, and self-reformation. This is a process we've been pursuing not only in addressing the issues of interpersonal harmony, but in making our organization more responsive to and reflective of our diverse membership as well. Perhaps this process, or some variation on it, is not simply a way of doing good as Buddhists, but constitutes the very path to our own enlightenment as well.

Hope: The Engine That Drives the Engagement Process

In *Prophetic Thought in Postmodern Times,* Cornel West writes:

To talk about human hope is to engage in an audacious attempt to galvanize and energize, to inspire and invigorate world-weary people....For some of us there are misanthropic skeletons hanging in our closet. And by misanthropic I mean the notion that we have given up on the capacities of human beings to do anything right. The capacity of human communities to solve any problem.

Humans have an almost mystic capacity to imagine something better for their lives, to hold on to that vision in the name of hope, and to act upon that hope in the name of betterment. Shakyamuni, Nichiren, and countless others entered into the Way, burning with the "hope" that they could find the

solution to human suffering and then alleviate that suffering. Hope could be said to constitute the spiritual driving force needed for any type of human progress. Thus, if we are to undertake the process that leads to a genuine peace within society, we must first establish within our hearts the hope that our efforts can and will make an important contribution.

Buddhism, however, does acknowledge the reality of the *saha* (mundane) world. There are times when the evidence of the size, scope, and intractability of the problems of race, gender, or ethnic relations can prove overwhelming to even the best-intentioned, leading to violent outbursts, resignation, or detached pity. From the standpoint of our tradition, we view this tendency toward spiritual fatigue as just part of what it means to live in the Latter Age—a period marked by a decline in the Buddha's teachings—and the general impurity of life itself. But a tendency does not necessarily define the end; for us it provides the tension from which we can begin.

The Lotus Sutra contains the parable of the phantom city, in which a guide leading his charges across a barren landscape to a place of immense treasures is confronted with the peoples' weariness and their unwillingness to continue any farther. In response, he conjures up a fantastic city where the travelers can rest, refresh themselves, and regain their resolve for the remainder of the journey. Within our American Buddhist movement, numerous experiences arise where mistrust and anger are transformed into trust, compassion, and mutual respect—often after a rather intense process during which all the poisons first percolated to the surface in order to be clearly perceived, then discarded.

Sustained Compassionate Dialogue

These good men and good women should enter the Thus Come One's room, put on the Thus Come One's robe, sit in the Thus Come One's seat, and then, for the sake of the four kinds of believers, broadly expound this sutra.

The Thus Come One's room is the state of mind that shows great pity and compassion toward all living beings. The Thus Come One's robe is the mind that is gentle and forbearing. The Thus Come One's seat is the emptiness of all phenomena. (*The Lotus Sutra,* p. 166)

These words of the Buddha give us a clear guide for how to engage with others, whether for the sake of teaching Buddhism, resolving our personal differences, or reforming an institution.

Another important lesson taught by experience is that the first step toward building genuine understanding and peace among people is that they must first attempt to engage with one another in the spirit of genuine compassion. This is what it means to "enter the Thus Come One's room." We invite them into a compassionate life space, warmly embrace them, and discuss life as equals. We learn from one another as fellow human beings, and together we strive to improve our lives. The very act of engagement, the willingness to reach out and open a dialogue, is itself the most significant step

forward, as writer and news commentator Patricia Elam-Ruff's experience illustrates:

When I first starting practicing [Buddhism] about nine years ago, the leaders in my area were all white, and I had a lot of anger toward the white race. I thought, Why am I in a group with all white people, me of all people? I was very angry about it and I'm sure they knew it because I had an attitude all the time. But through Buddhist practice—through working with them and getting to know them and seeing their compassion for everyone; for example, the fact that they came into the black community almost all the time and had no problem with that—well, in time I really came to appreciate them. They really reached out and wanted to know what my concerns were....There were things we disagreed on, of course, but I saw sincere compassion in their life through the practice and that was a very important realization for me. I think that also just practicing and really understanding the Buddhahood in everyone has made me open up so much in terms of how I view people.

From an organizational viewpoint, we have been trying to emulate the Thus Come One's room by creating compassionate spaces where members can engage in a free and open dialogue on the issues they feel to be important. This has taken the form of diversity committees at both the national and local levels, whose role is to consider the needs and viewpoints of those whose voices had not been clearly heard in the past. This process has led us to identify certain inconsistencies and injustices within our own movement, such as the racial and gender makeup of our leadership, or the visibility of minority cultures and viewpoints in our publications. We have also conducted workshops in various cities, where the issues of racial, gender, and ethnic differences have been addressed from a Buddhist point of view.

A Mind That Is Gentle and Forbearing

Dialogue on a sustained basis with anyone different from oneself takes courage. Sustained dialogue may require a willingness to listen to the pain, and sometimes the anger, that the other person is feeling. This is the point of practice where one is challenged to cast off their attachment to the lesser self, and to see the other person's suffering—the other person's truth—with the eyes of the compassionate Buddha.

As an example of such forbearance, Nichiren called on his followers to emulate the spirit of the Bodhisattva Fukyo (Bodhisattva Never Disparaging), who appears in the twentieth chapter of the *Lotus Sutra*. Not particularly devoted to reading or reciting the scriptures, this bodhisattva would bow to each person he met—monks, nuns, laymen, or laywomen—and speak words of praise to them, saying "I would never dare treat you with disparagement or arrogance. Why? Because you are practicing the bodhisattva way and are certain to attain buddhahood" (p. 266). For this he was regarded by many with a mixture of suspicion and

abuse. For years he would carry out this practice, and for years he would be cursed and vilified. But at the point of his death, having expiated his karma through his lifetime of practice, he had a striking breakthrough, whereby he attained "great purity of vision and purity...of the six faculties,...the power to teach pleasingly and eloquently, the power of great goodness and tranquillity." (p. 267). He was thus able to extend his life and lead untold numbers of people to the state of buddhahood.

Buddhists in particular need to consider the cultivation of such forbearance to be of paramount importance if they are to touch the lives of those they encounter and enable them to grasp the Dharma. Our experience has shown that only when someone feels that you have clearly understood *their* truth, no matter how painful it may be, will that person's heart be open enough to grasp the truth that you have to offer.

Cultivating the Buddha Wisdom

To sustain encounters and dialogue, one must possess rich spiritual reserves of vitality, creativity, wisdom, and selflessness. From this standpoint, to "sit in the Thus Come One's seat" could mean to awaken to the Buddha's unrestricted compassion, courage, and wisdom through Buddhist practice.

It has been the experience of many practitioners that the process of engagement and dialogue leads to a sometimes painful awakening to the reality of their own delusions. It's easy to believe that we have freed ourselves from attachments to race, gender, or ego while we are sitting in a peaceful room with few disturbances. It's when we are engaged with others, especially those who are very different, that we open ourselves up to a very enlightening, often humbling, view of how far we have progressed and how far we still have to go. In a sense, the process of engagement serves as a catalyst to bring these impediments to our attention, just as the process of forging steel brings all of its impurities to the surface. When confronted, we may be inspired to redouble our efforts in practice and thus break the chain of suffering.

It is in fact our fusion with the buddha-wisdom that enables the real breakthrough in dealing with "others." The wisdom of Buddhism enables us to break the confines of *shoga* (the lesser self), the private and isolated self held prisoner by its own desires, passions, and hatreds. It is the emergence of buddha-wisdom that enables us to see each other, not through the narrow prism of our differences, but rather through the broad lens of human solidarity, which is rich with differences and distinctions.

When we really see others, we open our own lives to the great textures and colors of the human tapestry and begin to enjoy the benefits of our diversity. Consider the experience of R. Marion Woods, a writer and editor of European ancestry:

I was raised in an upper middle class family where prejudice was an unwelcome visitor. I cried as a child when I heard a bus driver ask our maid to sit in the back. But when I embraced Buddhism in the seventies, I had difficulty relating to the group's diverse membership. I was told to practice with the people in my group, rather than shop around for a "more sophisticated" group with whom I could homogenize. Later, I was surprised to find that I'd developed a deep and lasting bond with a reformed street-fighter from the countryside.

When I moved to Chicago to get my degree, my new Buddhist leader came to pick me up for a discussion meeting. I found out later that the landlord had looked out the window, saw an African-American, and refused to open the door. I was horrified beyond words during the ride to the meeting, but my leader said, "She's just scared. She doesn't understand." That year, I learned so much from the members of my *sangha,* all of whom were African-American. I used to whine about my family and friends "persecuting" me for being a Buddhist in a Christian country. But I came to realize a depth of courage I'd never seen in other people. I realized if anyone knew about prejudice and persecution, it was my new African-American Buddhist friends in Chicago. Through their practice, they had garnered an unshakable confidence in their lives—completely unaffected by the opinions of others and by the sometimes gritty circumstances of real life. I saw first-hand a courage, an ability to take the high road, that until then I'd only witnessed among the characters I met in story books, and it has deeply inspired me.

The Process Is the End

As I stated in the beginning, even those of us who come from racially diverse *sanghas* have not found all the answers. We continue to struggle with the myriad of problems that derive from both individual and institutional racism. I do believe, however, that we have come a long way in finding the process, and through that process, we have made important steps forward in creating an atmosphere of trust, appreciation, and understanding. Furthermore, our experience has deepened our belief that, for our nation and the world, the wisdom and compassion of Buddhism is in fact a sleeping giant and can do much more to banish the suffering and conflict that so often accompanies "otherness."

But in order for the spirit of Buddhism to have any real impact on this very real problem, it requires that real people—you and I—engage ourselves in the task of seeking out those who are suffering. It requires that you and I travel to neighborhoods very different from our own and meet with people very different from ourselves. It requires that we listen—really listen—to their truth, and open our own hearts in dialogue, sharing the wisdom and compassion of the Buddha. I'm convinced that this process will not only contribute to the "solution" of mutual respect and understanding, but will be a genuine transformative experiment, capable of leading America's factionalized groups down the path toward common ground. Indeed, Buddhism holds the key to hope for peace with its promise of self-mastery through seeking inner reformation, discourse through seeking sustained dialogue, and understanding through seeking spiritual renewal.

Mindfulness and Compassionate Action

Joan Halifax

MANY PEOPLE AT THE BUDDHISM IN AMERICA CONFERENCE posited a similar conception of what eventually will prove to be the great contribution of Western, or at least North American, Buddhism: the practice of social action in light of Buddhist precepts. Dubbed "engaged Buddhism," or more generally "engaged spirituality," it has manifested itself in a panoply of types of outreach. The Buddhist Peace Fellowship, for example, has helped inform the peace movement with Buddhist tenets, while it also helps Buddhists see how their lives and practices can serve various social and environmental concerns. Other Buddhists are on paths that are more personally oriented, where their work is of a person-to-person nature, such as working with people who are homeless or ill, or helping the dying make their great transition.

Thich Nhat Hanh wrote: "People might be used to distinguishing between contemplation and action, but I think in Buddhism, these two cannot be separated. To meditate is to be aware of what is going on—in yourself and the world. If you know what is going on, how can you avoid acting to change the situation?"* What becomes clear on even the slightest investigation is the myriad ways in which Western Buddhists are engaged with practices intended to improve those worlds of which they have become aware.

Three speakers—Roshi Bernard Tetsugen Glassman, Rev. Kobutsu Malone,† and Joan Halifax††—presented workshops that dealt specifically with aspects of engaged Buddhism. In her session, Ms. Halifax presented the basic underpinnings of this element of practice exemplified so simply and eloquently by her teacher, Thich Nhat Hanh.

---

*East West, January 1990, page 80.

†See Tetsugen's "Instructions to the Cook: Zen Lessons in Living a Life That Matters," pages 427–39; and Kobutsu's "Prison Zen Practice in America: Life and Death on the Razor's Edge," pages 440–47.

††Biographical information about Joan Halifax accompanies her workshop, "Being with Dying," pages 373–93.

In mindfulness meditation, the actual posture and the craft of the practice points to the qualities of mind that we're developing. We can look at the meditation practice as medicine, for when we're doing this practice we're realizing the Buddha. The Buddha is present—literally and figuratively in our midst. And why not? Why not be a buddha? It's much more practical to be a buddha than anything else, actually. So when we're doing this practice we're entering into that vow together, and that vow carries with it a great sense of verticality; a capacity to uphold in the midst of conditions; a sense of conductivity and flexibility. We're describing the condition of the spine— strength, uprightness—and also we're in contact with the earth. Our legs aren't crossed, really shutting out our instincts, but we've exposed our guts, our belly, our generative organs, our heart.

This practice is about openness, and if we're going to bring it into the world we want to be able to have a strong sense of verticality and of openness simultaneously. We call it a strong heart. A heart that is so tender that it can't sustain being in the presence of suffering. It's not a heart that will want to go out into the world, so our practice is a call to develop strength. It's also a practice that calls us into a quality of attention and, at least in the beginning, it can be very refreshing. In the middle it can be very upsetting, and in the end it can be very ˟ refreshing. Being a student of Thich Nhat Hanh's, it's very wonderful that we bring to the actual experience of practice this half-smile, which is an actual display of buddha serenity, just as the postures display Buddha's body, speech, and mind—or Buddha's body, silence, and mind.

[Ms. Halifax led the group in a brief period of meditation, after which she told them:]

The first image that came to me while sitting here was of a man called Jerry, whom I sat with in the process of his dying quite a few years ago. After he died his friends and partner chose to bathe him at home and to take care of his body in an appropriate manner and to lay him out for three days. So we had the opportunity to spend time with Jerry in this very peaceful environment of the home. Jerry had been a very successful businessperson and was always worrying and making deals, but he actually died a very peaceful death. It was wonderful, from my point of view, to see somebody who had been so concerned with the material world die so peacefully so that it helped us who were around him.

I always felt that he had a slightly worried look on his face. No matter what was going on, it was like he was always making a deal. I walked into the room where he was laid out—people had left petals on his bedspread and there he was—and Jerry was smiling. A lot of us don't really smile until we're dead, we're so busy saving the world and doing good things. Jerry reminded me that our natural state, when we let go of everything including the body, is of this smile. Because I've sat with quite a few bodies, I remembered suddenly this kind of flow of smiling faces, and I thought, Can we just think of ourselves as dead? We've lost it all. Avanindra said, "The glass is already broken"—we're already dust. The future is in the present.

My friend Issan Dorsey (there's a wonderful book about him called *Street Zen*) was a man who put his altar in the street. He was a crossdresser, he was gay, and in his gay, crossdressing community he was the one who tried out all the drugs. Issan started something called the Hartford Street Zen Center. He was a student of Suzuki-roshi and then Baker-roshi and he was really sweet. I had the good fortune to teach with him over the years. (In his final years, as he was dying of AIDS, he'd come down to Ojai and we'd do sesshins together.) Just before his death, when he was barely ambulatory, Issan was recognized as a roshi and properly honored, and his transmission poem had a line in it which has really stayed with me: "Abiding in ultimate closeness." It's lived inside of the place in my spine that is behind my heart. It really is what holds my heart up, because I feel this work we do as engaged Buddhists is not about doing something for someone else, but it is, literally, compassion—abiding in ultimate closeness.

One of the great traps that we can experience with compassion—and this is Buddhists, Christians, Jews, anybody—is that it can actually separate us from the other. It can foster a sense of dualism, of self and other. Issan's transmission poem points to what I feel is compassion as a verb, and it is

about ultimate closeness, about fundamental nonduality.

I think one of the shadows that we face in engaged spirituality is turning it into social work and into a context of service that implies an "other." I'm really concerned that engaged Buddhism, that compassion in action, engaged spirituality, will not be based in a view that is sufficiently realized through practice, and that we'll bring our Judeo-Christian, lower-level dualistic perspective into our engaged spirituality. Because I've been in this field a long time, I've made a tremendous number of mistakes, perpetuated a view in my work that I feel has not been true. And so instead of snowing you with invoking the names of the bodhisattvas right off, I just want to say "Wake up call, American Buddhists." I really would like to help you avoid the profound errors that I have made as a Christian Buddhist woman in America at this time.

So that's the piece: abiding in ultimate closeness, intimacy. When we say "practice," we're talking about training. There's a tremendous amount of conditioning that we are subject to in this culture. This is an incredible culture that we live in—*multicul*-ture, because there are many cultures represented here. But the democratic idea of the self-determining individual, the sense of equal rights, equality, equal but different. It's so strange that in a culture where equality is so important, a constitutional right, we have a great intolerance for diversity, sadly enough. I'm not speaking just about racial or ethnic diversity, I'm talking about crazy people and homeless people and dying people and everyone else who is marginalized because it's just too hard to look at. So the call is for us to actually engage in a practice that cultivates precisely those qualities about which I was speaking in the little introduction to mindfulness practice. How can we uphold ourselves? How can we really be strong? How can we face it and be open, transparent, permeable? This heart, this feeling being? How can we really be in touch? This is a very big question.

What does a practice look like for Westerners, for laypeople—most of you and me—who have sex lives, and jobs, and children, and have parents to take care of when they get older, and have complicated relationships in our vocation, have peer groups. What do we do? What kind of practice? I'm putting this out as a question to you.

I went to the Soviet Union and was interviewed by very highly trained women architects who were renovating and restoring old Orthodox churches, and they said How do you do it? How do you go shopping, cook the meals, take care of the children, go to work? How do you manage it? We're exhausted! It's exhausting! This is a life of nothing extra. One of the things that I think a lot of us fail to realize is we have lives of a lot of extra. But many women don't exactly feel that way. My friends who have children are involved with childbearing and rearing, cooking, educating, caregiving of all different kinds.

And I see the lives also of people who have less money, where there's not so much extra. These are the lives that I feel a tremendous concern about. How can we create a context of training—that is, practice qua training—to train ourselves away from a view that is profoundly dualistic? Where self and other are constantly reified; where people and supposed nonsentient beings are objectified? You see the objectification of women, of dying people, of poor people everywhere. How can we reclaim this boundless self? How can we come home to a sense of communion that includes all beings? I don't know. But I know that Buddhists are trying to find a way where this can happen and a way for laypeople to realize this.

I think it's one of the reasons why, in the United States, or in the West, Buddhism has entered our lives in a very strong manner. We want to know how to bring contemplation, mindfulness, and everyday life together. And because of the Judeo-Christian ethics of service, of helping others, of natural altruism, of natural generosity, in a certain way we're prepared by the virtue of our cultural backgrounds, to actually be in a movement that is engaged in bringing our everyday lives, our vocations, and our spiritual practice into a unity. Bernie Glassman is exploring the edge of it, Thich Nhat Hanh is exploring the edge of it; Mahaghosananda, a man who invites us to bear witness to suffering in Cambodia, is doing it his way, as are Sulak Sivaraksha and Joanna Macy.

We have a really important assignment before the end of this millennium, and that is the revaluation of vocations, the fostering of new vocations. Vocation actually means "how we send our voice in the world." What's our song? What are the new professions, the new vocations? What are vocations going to look like in the twenty-first century? Are we all going to be natural healers? Are we going to change this perception of alienation, transform it through training or some form of illumination or education, and understand that what we eat is medicine and what we do is healing? Or are we just going to continue to extract and poison?

This sounds a little moralistic but it doesn't feel very moralistic when you work in a health-care system, or when you spend time with people from Clinton's administration who are involved with environmental policy. How are we going to feed ourselves in fifty years, forty, thirty years? There are some really important questions. Why do we have to wait to be a buddha? Why not now?

[Ms. Halifax asked the participants to give brief insights and ideas into their "sense of what the world is going to look like in twenty years, in thirty years. And what can we do now for those who come after us?" She wrote them on a board as they were offered and the group arrived at a long list of issues, among them stopping over-consumption, developing a new sense of economics and economic justice, and fostering community and the community-development process.

Having created this list, Ms. Halifax then suggested they try to "find the common features between old vocations reformed and new vocations on the horizon." Suggestions included

breaking down the hierarchy, connectedness or interbeing, nourishing, active engagement, process orientation, authenticity, mutuality, mentorship, listening.

Using the ideas that arose, Ms. Halifax said: "The question is, how many of us have really considered this list we just put together in terms of our current vocations and how they affect them. We see a lot of need on the landscape, and we're also aware of a lot of the dysfunctionality of how we bring our professions into healthy being."]

The threefold training is *sela, samadhi,* and *prajna. Sela* refers specifically to precepts, vows, and it's interesting to look at what the Buddha asked his disciples to carry on, just before he died. It wasn't the teachings of the Buddha, it was, basically, the precepts.

What's so important about the precepts for us as Buddhists? Superficially the precepts are basic rules of conduct that help protect us and other beings from harm. They're a kind of code of nonharming. Or, we could say they're rules of love. They're how a buddha would live, if we were choosing to live in such a way. From a very deep sense, the precepts are actually ways in which we stabilize our mind; ways in which we don't enter into behaviors that create a sense of agitation, of grasping, aversion, of guilt, of shame, of lies that harm beings.

Thich Nhat Hanh just did a very important shift of the five wonderful precepts, and the fourteen precepts of the Tiep Hien Order are now called mindfulness trainings. This is very different than the Ten

Commandments and the superordination of a system of rules by which we are to abide; if we don't…big problem. In most Buddhist lineages, those precepts—originally called the five grave precepts having to do with body, speech, and mind—were about not killing, not stealing, not engaging in sexual misconduct, not engaging in harmful speech, and not taking alcohol. But Thich Nhat Hanh has done something quite interesting with the five grave precepts: He first changed them to the five *wonderful* precepts, then he elaborated on them in a very prescriptive way, which a lot of people really like and some people don't like because they feel that it gives too much of what we're supposed to engage and not engage. But Thich Nhat Hanh's rationale in this is very clear: that Western society is going through a very profound change, where our values are crumbling, and where some things just need to be laid out.

[Ms. Halifax read and commented on the five mindfulness trainings:]

Aware of the suffering caused by the destruction of life, I vow to cultivate compassion and learn ways to protect the lives of people, animals, plants, and minerals.

This is a very profound invitation for all of us, about developing compassion, and then it's proactive. It says, "And I'm going to *learn* ways." So much of what we talked about on the list was basically proactive—it's about education. It's not just about picking up the messes, it's literally about creating the context where people can find wholesomeness. The first precept concludes with:

I'm determined not to kill, not to let others kill, not to condone any act of killing in the world, in my thinking, and in my way of life.

Now who here in this room doesn't have a piece of leather on their body? Thich Nhat Hanh wears his little clogs. There is no way that we can abide by this precept in the strict sense. If we look at our lives, what we see is that we not only need to turn compassion toward the cow who provided our shoes, but also toward ourselves, because there is no way that we can live without harming other beings.

One of the most important elements of this work that we're doing has to do with intolerance and tolerance. Inclusivity as different from exclusivity. The minute we say the guy who executed so-and-so is a bad guy, or Qaddafi is a bad guy, or that Hitler isn't inside of us, that we don't have this seed of violence, aggression, and ignorance within us, we're deluded. So these mindfulness trainings are in essence a path of compassion, in a very fundamental way, of recognizing that there is no way that we ourselves can live so virtuously. But the precept says that I am aware of doing this. In Vajrayana practice, meat is the food of compassion. When you take a bite of your steak, you want to generate compassion for the being who you are now eating, and really recall the suffering of that one. The second precept:

Aware of the suffering caused by exploitation, social injustice, stealing, and oppression, I vow to cultivate loving-kindness and learn ways to work for the well-being of people, animals, plants, and minerals. I vow to practice generosity by sharing my time, energy, and material resources with those who are in real need. I am determined not to steal and not to possess anything that should belong to others. I will respect the property of others, but I will prevent others from profiting from human suffering or the suffering of other species on Earth.

This is a very deep call to look into our lives. I've been given many beautiful Buddhas for our center, Buddhas from around the world, and most of them have come from countries that are war torn. I'm sure most of those Buddhas have been stolen. We can look at every part of our lives and say, Where did this come from? in this sort of continuum of interbeing. How many mahogany dens meant the end of how many species in rain forests? How many of us wear clothing made by children in countries where child labor is happening? This is not to make us feel bad. It's a call for us to bear witness to not just somebody over here who's stealing or oppressing. We, too, steal and oppress in the continuum of interbeing as things are.

Aware of the suffering caused by sexual misconduct, I vow to cultivate responsibility and learn ways to protect the safety and integrity of individuals, couples, families, and society. I am determined not to engage in sexual rela-

tions without love and a long-term commitment. To preserve the happiness of myself and others, I am determined to respect my commitments and the commitments of others. I will do everything in my power to protect children from sexual abuse and to prevent couples and families from being broken by sexual misconduct.

I teach often to young people. That's a hard one for them to do—"I'm young…I'm just exploring"—but imagine, if we had seen sexuality as a kind of sacrament; if sexuality had not been devalued in our society, trivialized in the way it has. Imagine how that would have affected our relationships. Imagine a world in which that would be possible.

So responsibility is a deep call. You notice he doesn't say "marriage," he says "love and a long-term commitment." You know what a long-term commitment is when you know what a short-term one is. Nothing's permanent. We're talking about this precious human body. Those who are sexual beings are called actually to move not just to value the property of others, to value living beings or beings everywhere, from mountains and lakes to you and me, but to value the act of love, sexual communion, between us.

The fourth precept is probably the hardest for people our age to keep:

Aware of the suffering caused by unmindful speech and the inability to listen to others, I vow to cultivate loving speech and deep listening in order to bring joy and happiness to others and relieve others of their suffering….

What if we looked on speech as a healing practice? What if we had a quality of being able to still ourselves so deeply in our practice of listening that others could truly hear themselves? That mindful speaking and deep listening are proactive in the sense of an actual practice of healing in society. The fourth precept continues:

Knowing that words can create happiness or suffering, I vow to learn to speak truthfully, with words that inspire self-confidence, joy, and hope. I am determined not to spread news that I do not know to be certain, and not to criticize or condemn things of which I am not sure. I will refrain from uttering words that can cause division or discord, or that can cause the family or the community to break. I will make all efforts to reconcile and resolve all conflicts, however small.

Each of these mindfulness trainings is talking about a behavior that is fundamentally healing in our world. Finally, the fifth precept:

Aware of the suffering caused by unmindful consumption, I vow to cultivate good health, both physical and mental, for myself, my family, and my society by practicing mindful eating, drinking, and consuming. I vow to ingest only items that preserve peace, well-being, and joy in my body, in my consciousness, and in the collective body and consciousness of my family and society. I am determined not to use alcohol….

From Thich Nhat Hanh's perspective, all of these mindfulness trainings—precepts—

inter-are, so alcohol gives rise to speech that is unwholesome, gives rise to aberrant sexual behavior, gives rise to oppressiveness, to killing and violence.

…I'm determined not to use alcohol or any other intoxicant or to ingest foods or other items that contain toxins, such as certain TV programs, magazines, books, films, and conversations….

This has been such an interesting precept for me to work with. The more practice you do, the more sensitive you may become, and at a certain point what is a toxin for you is different for someone else, perhaps even to the point that the more practice you do, nothing remains a toxin.

…I am aware that to damage my body or my consciousness with these poisons is to betray my ancestors, my parents, my society, and future generations. I will work to transform violence, fear, anger, and confusion in myself and in society by practicing a diet for myself and for society. I understand that a proper diet is crucial for self-transformation and for the transformation of the world.

At the level of our lay practice, the five precepts really provide an edge that teaches us constantly. From the Buddhist perspective, *sela*—the precepts—are a way in which we settle down. We allow our nervous system to cool, our heart to cool—not to be cold—to gentle, we could say. In this state of gentleness, we then are able to begin to realize the second part of the threefold training:

samadhi, concentration. Often I call it communion. It is coming to a place where you and all of this are really one.

We start with our concentration rather intimately with our breath and as our practice develops, the concentration opens so that it's deeply inclusive. But in the beginning of our practice, we're bringing the mind and the body together. Mindfulness practice is a basic practice—very simple, very nonsectarian—that allows for mind and body to come into integration. Mindfulness practice means "being in touch with the present moment," *this* moment, in each thing we do. So *samadhi,* deep internal steadiness, stability, allows for wisdom to arise; for understanding to be relatively pure, not impeded by doctrines, theories, thoughts, concepts, conditions.

In Buddhism, wisdom is not about lowercase "knowledge." It is actually understood as a mind that has steadied down into such internal stillness that it reflects reality just as it is. Often the image used is a mirror, and that practice is polishing the mirror, the great jeweled mirror of the mind. Out of that understanding the precepts naturally arise. One begins to live the life of a buddha and a bodhisattva. Then, living that life, concentration deepens, *samadhi* becomes more fulfilled, and out of that deep sense of communion, of nonduality, the wisdom mind appears.

I bring in the threefold training because, in working with the professions, the core elements of the new vocations, and the shadow elements, we're looking at the question What is engaged spirituality? What is compassion in action? What is our world view? What is the world view that has been transmitted down through the generations from our ancestors? What is the world view that arises when we stop and go deeper than our conceptual mind? What do we see?

That view comes to a couple of things that are important for us to be aware of. One is the presence of suffering, not only in our lives, but in the world. Another is the presence of change, impermanence, the transitoriness of this relative world in which we live. Even our sun is going to extinguish itself.

A very profound realization is that you and I are not separate, that the sun is in my body as heat mediated through many things—petroleum, heating the building, the food I've eaten—all of the elements are here. This notion of interbeing that Thich Nhat Hanh developed is very important We see that we are not a separate self-identity, but in fact, if we look at our condition, our situation, we discover that we inter-are with everything. We're full of everything; everything is full of us.

Tetsugen [Bernard Glassman] used the image, if my right hand is bleeding, my left hand is going to do something about it. If Michael has cancer, I'm going to be there—I have cancer. Somebody mentioned burnout from too much empathy, but many of the compassion practices that we do in Buddhism actually are realization practices of nonduality, where we do not hold ourselves separate from the suffering of other beings. One of the precepts in the Tiep Hien Order is *Do not avoid suffering.* Thich Nhat Hanh once was visited by a rather affluent couple whose marriage was coming apart, and they asked, "What can we do?" He said, "I beg you to go to work in a leprosarium." Peter [Matthiessen] talked about going to Auschwitz, that he had been so depressed, and then suddenly the depression broke, it literally shattered—just like Avalokiteshvara shatters into a million pieces, his depression shattered into a million pieces—and many beings are now touched by his experience, his exhilaration. Go someplace where the suffering is greater than you. Enter into the suffering of other beings and watch compassion generate out of you. Often feeling sorry for ourselves is not a very satisfactory condition, but really feeling the sorrow of the world is medicine for us.

[A participant asked if a distinction is made between feeling sorrow for the world and feeling sorry for the world?]

Joan Halifax: *Absolutely.* Sorry for the world is an enemy of compassion because you and the world are separate. Compassion means that I am one with the world. Some of the compassion practices in Buddhism also are about allowing that suffering to touch us deeply, to transform. One teacher said that Buddha, too, was wounded. There's almost no Buddhist I know who is a Buddhist because they wanted to get enlightenment. Like [Roshi Bernard Tetsugen] Glassman said, "I had an addiction to the self." They went there out of misery. We went there because we were suffering.

Here's a little story: A particular roshi who was giving a lecture kept saying, "Everything's okay. Everything is okay just as

it is. Just as it is, everything is okay. Just as it is." Somebody said, "Is that really true, that everything's okay just as it is?" The roshi says, "Wait a minute, that's a tough question." Then the person who asked the question wrote this poem:

Everything, just as it is.
As it is, as is.
Flowers in bloom,
Nothing to add, nothing to reduce.
The entire world.
Hiroshima.

"The entire world / Hiroshima." Our challenge is not to be entrapped by the absolute, the ultimate. Our challenge is to be able to, like a shaman, walk on the threshold of the relative and the absolute; to be deeply in touch with suffering and joy, and seamlessly responsive in the world, not quietistic; not "everything's okay, this is all a dream."

It's a dream until you get a diagnosis that is catastrophic; until your eight-year-old child is killed. Finding that balance between the absolute; a true view of spaciousness. It's something I experienced—as someone who was born a Christian—in a Russian Orthodox church in 1988, when the churches were just opening. I felt the numinous. I felt the presence of God through the lights and the music and the devotion in this church. I had a *kensho* experience, my heart broke open. I felt no separation from the decades of suffering of all the peoples in that church, and the presence of God. Can we have that heart present in us? It is a kind of shamanic equilibrium that we're called to in this work of compassion and action. "The whole world / Hiroshima."

[Ms. Halifax opened the session up to questions and observations, one of which dealt with inclusion and prejudice among Buddhist practitioners. While this concern presented itself in various guises throughout the conference, the woman speaking at this point articulated her thoughts in a way that wrapped together a number of elements. Deeply moved, she said:

"The thing that comes up for me when I'm in conferences like this is that there are so few minorities. I was at a retreat with Thich Nhat Hanh and I was one of three out of eight hundred people. I have my own judgments, conditioning, baggage, and yet here is this very rare opportunity to engage about something that I need to talk about."]

Joan Halifax: You have pointed out to us what is true. There are not that many people of color here. Perhaps we could explore the reasons and at the same time explore our impoverishment by that absence as a truth.

This practice, this view, is a treasure, and not to take it to the street is off. I think your call is for us to be proactive, to translate this vision of Buddhism into forms that can nourish not just people who have some degree of affluence, or people from, not a racial culture, but an economic and social culture that is particular.

[Thanking the participant and Ms. Halifax "for the courage that you just demonstrated in say-

ing these things," another member of the group said that similar issues frequently come up for her in Dharma circles.

"While I am extremely thankful for gatherings like this that bring together people from so many different traditions, and I think that's one of the wonderful things about being a Dharma practitioner in the West, having that diversity—at least ostensibly in the traditions, maybe not in the participants. I'm thankful for it but, at the same time, how much did this conference cost? A lot, and I'm lucky that I was able to have the resources to do that, but it was so prohibitively expensive that many of my own friends didn't feel that they could come."

She suggested that future conferences address this issue by creating a scholarship fund or other means to help those who were not able to attend due to financial considerations. Continuing from there, the participant brought up the issue that, while this may be the status of Buddhism in America at this time, and people have to be patient and recognize that that's part of the transmission process, "At the same time [we should] not sit back and be complacent and say that I don't have responsibility for that transformation, and that I don't have a responsibility to bring more people of color into this wonderful view and wisdom that we all find so valuable in our lives."

To close the workshop on mindfulness and compassionate action, Ms. Halifax conducted a short service in which she invoked the names of the bodhisattvas…"for each one of you carries all of the qualities of all of the buddhas and the bodhisattvas. Do not forget who you really are."]

We invoke your name Avalokiteshvara. We aspire to learn your way of listening in order to help relieve the suffering in the world. You know how to listen in order to understand. We invoke your name in order to practice listening with all our attention and open-heartedness. We will sit and listen without any prejudice. We will sit and listen without judging or reacting. We will sit and listen in order to understand. We will sit and listen so attentively that we will be able to hear what the other person is saying and also what has been left unsaid. We know that just by listening we already alleviate a great deal of pain and suffering in the other person.

We invoke your name Manjushri. We aspire to learn your way, which is to be still and to look deeply into the heart of things and into the hearts of people. We will look with all our attention and open-heartedness. We will look with unprejudiced eyes. We will look without judging or reacting. We will look deeply, so that we will be able to see and understand the roots of ill being, the impermanent and selfless nature of all that is. We will practice your way of using the sort of understanding to cut through the bonds of ill being, thus freeing ourselves and other species.

We invoke your name Samantabhadra. We aspire to practice your way, which is to act with the eyes and heart of compassion.

We vow to bring joy to one person in the morning and to ease the pain of one person in the afternoon, and we vow to practice joy on the path of service. We know that every word, every look, every action, and every smile can bring happiness to others. We know that if we practice wholeheartedly, we ourselves may become an inexhaustible source of peace and joy for our loved ones and for all species.

We invoke your name Kshitigarbha. We aspire to learn your way so as to be present where there is darkness, suffering, oppression, and despair, so that we may bring light, hope, relief, and liberation to those places. We are determined not to forget about or abandon those who are in desperate situations. We will do our best to establish contact with them when they cannot find a way out of their suffering and when their cries for help, justice, equality, and human rights are not heard. We know that hell can be found in many places on Earth and we do not want to contribute to making more hells on Earth. Rather, we want to help unmake the hells that already exist. We will practice to realize the qualities of perseverance and stability that belong to the Earth so that, like the Earth, we can always be supportive and faithful to those who need us.

May the merit of this practice penetrate into each thing in all realms and benefit all beings.

Instructions to the Cook

ZEN LESSONS IN
LIVING A LIFE THAT MATTERS

Roshi Bernard Tetsugen Glassman

SPEAKERS AT THE CONFERENCE WHO DEALT WITH DAY-TO-DAY ISSUES and concerns faced by contemporary Western practitioners of Buddhism often noted that Buddhists in the West, and particularly in North America, comprise a very large percentage of laypeople, who must juggle the requirements of family and work along with maintaining active and fulfilling Buddhist practice. Roshi Glassman is an example of how one can live a life firmly routed in Buddhist teachings and ideals while building on that foundation in the secular world of commerce.

Along with being spiritual leader of the White Plum Sangha and Abbot of the Zen Community of New York and the Zen Center of Los Angeles, Roshi Glassman is an aeronautical engineer and an entrepreneur. He is also a social activist, in which role he founded the Greyston Mandala of social service organizations in Yonkers, New York. In the course of his wide-reaching work, he has established a profitable gourmet bakery to create jobs in the depressed area of southwest Yonkers, built supportive housing for homeless families, led a retreat of more than 150 Buddhists who came to bear witness at Auschwitz, and is now building housing and a day-treatment center for people with HIV/AIDS.

According to Roshi Glassman, one of the most useful metaphors for life is what happens in the kitchen. In his book *Instructions to the Cook*, he writes: "Zen masters call a life that is lived fully and completely, with nothing held back, 'the supreme meal.' And a person who lives such a life—a person who knows how to plan, cook, appreciate, serve, and offer the supreme meal of life—is called a Zen cook." This metaphor extends to what he calls the five main courses of a complete meal: spirituality, study, livelihood, social action, and relationship and community.

After a brief period of meditation, Roshi asked the members of the group to speak out with brief questions and concerns they wished to hear him address. He made a list of these, and tailored his talk to the interests and needs of his audience.

Nowadays, when I meet new folks, we spend time telling our stories and who we are. That would be impossible here, but for me that's the biggest joy. So I'll tell a little bit of my story, and then ask you to ask me a question on a subject you would like to hear about. Mozart? I don't care. And it won't be where you ask a question and I answer. I hate to answer. I like questions. I used to remember all of this, but now I have a pen and a piece of paper and my glasses because I can't read what I write. I'll mark down many of the notes, then with maybe twenty or thirty such threads, we'll weave a story integrating those themes and threads and go from there.

I was born in Brooklyn a little before the beginning of the Second World War. I'm an addict, and I'm addicted to myself, as I think all of us in this room are. About forty years ago I fell upon a recovery program called Zen that has helped me to deal with my addiction to the self. It took a lot more years before I realized that that addiction wasn't going to go away. It's somewhat related to what Peter Matthiessen* was saying about the recognition of our ingredients, one of which is our animal nature. In Buddhism we have a theory of the six realms (one of which is the animal realm): that we're constantly transmigrating out of each through each, at every instant. So essentially, as far as our abilities of recognition, we're in each of those six realms all the time.

*See Peter Matthiessen's keynote address, "The Coming of Age of American Zen," on pages 396–406.

I felt it was a very important step to come to the realization that I wasn't going to get out of those six realms and now wind up in some perfectly sober state, or buddha state. But I was addicted to the self; that's part of what I am, as a human. I am an animal, and I do have the Hitler within me, the Nazi within me, because everything I see is me. So it's not getting to some place where it's all over. I think that was very important for me, as it is in the Alcoholics Anonymous program, to come to that first realization that, yes, I am addicted and I don't have control to where I can say: "Oh, I am good, and I have practiced for these many years and know what compassion is, and I will take care of everything, and I'm at some end." No, I'm just at the beginning. I'm on the same path that everyone in this room is, and I don't have control.

What does control mean? In a sense, it means I know something. I know how to do it. But I *don't* know, and when people ask me how, I don't know; I have no answers.

The second step of my addiction process was having faith in something which I didn't understand. I call it the Buddhadharma, but I don't know what that is. It really is having faith in the path. And third, having determination to follow that path. I have that. I'm not content to sit on the cushion and come to peace, whatever that means. I am determined to do the path and to work for every aspect of myself, which I see as the whole universe.

So I was lucky forty years ago to stumble onto this recovery path I call Zen. I'm still on it. I'm working the steps. And through my years I've moved through different ways of manifesting my life. I've been many things and probably will be many things.

I don't like the word *practice*. This room is filled with many people with many ideas of what that word means. When I say "practice," I really mean "live." I'm not negating meditation: Many times when I say I want to use the word *practice* for living, people think that I say you don't need a regular regime of sitting. I don't think that. For me, practice is living, which doesn't negate certain things that go on in living like breathing, eating, peeing, doing meditation. Those are parts of my daily life.

But for me, the joy or the excitement is to find the right question. I have no interest in answers. For me, the world of life or practice is the search for the questions, and the questions have power. The questions that we don't even know that we have, those inner questions that haven't surfaced yet to our consciousness, those are key questions for us. So the practice is, How do I find out those questions that are within me, that I don't allow to surface? Why? Maybe I'm afraid for them to come up. Maybe I'm not ready—my system somehow isn't ready for those questions. Whatever the reasons, I know that there are a lot of questions within me and within us as a group, which is another form of me, that need to surface.

You can feel them: Some are funny; some have power. There's an excitement about the questions. The answers are not so interesting. That's why I do a lot of what I do. I go to places where I hope questions that

I've been avoiding will arise. Maybe that's a crazy life, seeking questions, but that's what motivates a lot of what I do. Places that are very familiar become not so interesting. You could say I'm just a pleasure seeker and that could certainly be a problem, but I wanted to let you in on what motivates me.

Having said that, I'll try to address some of the things that came up for me in your questions. One that really struck me was the question of listening: How do you listen to pain without having answers? When you said that, I thought of Avalokiteshvara, the bodhisattva of compassion, who has many different forms and manifestations—Kwannon, Kanzeon. Many times Avalokiteshvara—Kanzeon—is translated as the "the listener of the sufferings." *Kan* means "to contemplate." So when we say "Avalokiteshvara listening," it means fully embodying listening, not with the ears, but listening with the pores of the body, with the hairs on the head, with the feet, listening and fully becoming. *Ze* is the word for the earth, and *on* is the sounds. So literally, Kanzeon is the bodhisattva that fully listens to all the sounds of the earth, which many times is translated as the sufferings, but literally, it's all the sounds.

So Avalokiteshvara—Kanzeon—takes on this vow to bring an end to all the sufferings, or to raise the bodhi mind of all the sounds of the earth. Not just the people, everything, all the people, including you and me. When Kanzeon took on this vow, she/he/it didn't have any answers and was put into the position of listening to all this stuff and having no answers. Kanzeon was really listening to all of it, but had no answers. Do you know what happened? *Burst!* into millions of pieces. Then all those pieces came back together—now we have thousand-armed Kanzeons—and each hand held a different implement. One had a pen, one had a sword, one had a hoe, one had a flower.

Now Kanzeon is doing the work. He's listening, still having no answers, but is doing everything in every sphere where she/he appears, doing the things that need to be done in that sphere. No one hand is more important than the other. So in a sense, without having the mental answer, the physical answer was that those millions of pieces were made whole as one being, with the recognition that each piece was the whole being. Not that I was making myself whole by bringing everything into me, but recognizing that everything *is* me and that each thing, as it is, is me, and that everything as it is is what it is. Each thing had many complicated questions, but the Kanzeon is not looking for the answers. It's asking what needs to be done now.

The book I wrote, *Instructions for the Cook,* has as its main theme that the ingredients are right in front of us. We each have our ingredients and with those ingredients we need to make the meal. For me it was such an obvious thing that I didn't think it was the main theme. It was just a statement. I guess what's not obvious is that you shouldn't be so concerned with the ingredients that you *don't* have. Each of us has a certain set of ingredients. It's like going into the kitchen when I'm really hungry. I go into the kitchen

and open the refrigerator and there are things—maybe some bread, some cheese, peanut butter, steaks. I could open the refrigerator and say, "Oh, look what's missing. I don't have pepperoncini. (I love pepperoncini.) I'm not going to eat." I'm starving. I could say I'm not going to eat. Then I could wait longer and open the refrigerator again. "Oh, look what's missing. I don't have such and such. How can I go on? I won't eat." You can't do that forever. You'll die.

The message in the book is take those ingredients, make the best meal possible with them, and now, if you want, go get the things you don't have as your next thing. Do what you can—make your supreme meal—out of what you have. As humans, we have all these questions. Take all these questions and make something of them. How do you listen to the sufferings without having answers? It is much, much better to listen without having answers.

For us as Dharma teachers, at least I've found, nobody really, really wants me to answer them. What they want is for me to listen to them and, as a human and probably (I don't know if this is a stereotype, but I'm going to say) as a male, I tend to want to help or solve the issue. They have these little quotes in *Newsweek,* and this guy said that he had learned that when his wife is in pain, the best thing he can do is just be quiet. I'm always trying to resolve my wife's pain or the issue. He was 103 and she was 100. He said that when somebody asked him how he lived so long, he'd say, "I got to realize that when my wife was in pain I should just be quiet." So listening is really key. That listening Avalokiteshvara does is not a bland listening. It's becoming, really *being*, with the person. That's part of my street work, or what I call "bearing-witness" retreats, the Auschwitz work, it's a listening. I go to places to listen. For me, the listening is the learning, the teaching.

How do you deal with somebody who's crazy? I have a friend, a Korean who studied in Korea, was a teacher in Korea, then went to Japan for a while, then came to this country for a while, and then went back to Japan. He worked with mentally retarded youth, which wasn't an accepted role for him as a Korean teacher in Korea. When he worked with mentally retarded youth, he was not trying to change them. He actually ordained them and they lived together in a temple as buddhas. He said to me, "In the eyes of the Buddha, we're all retarded." So he had no intention for them to be anything other than what they were. He honored them as buddhas as they were.

I have some friends who are street people. By that, I mean that they've lived the majority of their lives in the streets, having chosen to do that. I remember once a conversation with a man named Bernard Isaacs, who is the king of the mole people. He lives in tunnels in Manhattan and has been living underground in tunnels for maybe twenty years now. He's called "the king of the mole people." The mole people have gone through ups and downs, like most civilizations. There are many different communities. I think the largest population recorded by survey is about seven thousand people living that way. Now, I think, the numbers are smaller, but it's hard to tell because there are maybe ten different levels of places to live underground and sometimes they go further down. There are some people that live way down and never come out. They have runners and are very organized; in some sense more organized than street people that live in the streets. The structures are very set. Bernard Isaacs is highly respected.

I met another man in street retreats, who had been head of a shanty village under the FDR Drive in Manhattan, who also basically has been living in the streets since Vietnam. Now, however, for maybe two years he has not been—he moved into our house in Yonkers and is doing other things and, of course, having slippages, as we all do. But once I was with the two of them listening to a conversation. Many of us would call the conversation "crazy." They were talking about things that happened ten thousand years ago. You might have smiles on your faces listening. They were not denying each other. They were treating everything that the other person said with dignity. I remember that moment very distinctly because it was a tremendous learning experience.

We listen to each other talk and, believe me, it has the same validity as their talk. We believe what we're saying, the worlds we're living in, whether you believe you're all screwed up because you don't know anything or you believe you're not screwed up because you know something.

Whatever you believe, that's what you believe, but that's got 100 percent validity in my system. What they were saying had 100 percent validity in their system.

Would I take what they were saying and buy stocks on it? That's a different world. I take what they're saying as what they mean, as what they feel, as what they were saying. I don't know what to call crazy or not crazy. That's getting beyond listening. Listening is just listening. I can't call what I'm hearing crazy or not crazy, good or bad, this or that, unless I have answers. If I have my set of knowledge, then I can say, "Oh, yeah, what they're talking about, how can that be?"

In a wonderful book called *Survival in Auschwitz*, Primo Levi describes bodhisattvas. He doesn't call them bodhisattvas—I'm not sure what he calls them, to tell you the truth; maybe survivors—but he describes some people that were around him in the camp. He describes this guy who was a dwarf. Let's say he was Benny the Dwarf. The paragraphs in which he talks about Benny the Dwarf are just so beautiful. After describing him, he says that if a camp was liberated and Benny was in our society, there were only two places he could be: a mental institution or a maximum-security prison. But here in Auschwitz he was a leader because he knew how to live moment to moment. Many of the people who were dying in our society would have esteemed roles and would be called very sane, but they did not know how to live moment to moment, and they would fall apart immediately.

We know that we each have our own societies. We may have what we call our Buddhist society and we say or may think that Buddhist society is somehow better than Christian society or Jewish society, and definitely better than capitalist society or whatever. We have all our societies and within each of those that we construct—these societies don't create themselves, we create them—we as humans are creating the elements that fit and don't fit.

One of the powerful thinkings of Gandhi was that he did not want to work for a society whose construct required that there be a class that was going to be stomped on. We've created societies where that's a part, and we can work with people to move them from out of that into other elements, but we need that part—we need some group there. If you look through all the ways that societies were built, that's inherent in the system. Gandhi was trying to work to create a system, a society where that wasn't the case.

Well, it's not so simple. I had a student, a Maryknoll sister, who made a very important statement. She said that if you work within the system to try to take care of the aspects that need taking care of, then the society will compliment you and reward you, like a Mother Theresa. But if you try to change the system, they'll kill you. And they do. It happens all the time.

If you're truly listening, a lot of what we're talking about falls away, and what's left? Doing something; doing something with what you're hearing, with what you're feeling. That became the main theme of my book. People around the book tour kept coming up to me to say that from the system we've created, they couldn't do anything until they were fully enlightened, or at least 75 percent enlightened. I'm sure this is true for 90 percent of this group and 90 percent of the group in the big hall. That's what we think, that we can't do things, can't run around like chickens without our heads, without knowing what we're doing because we're going to create a bigger mess. I felt that way. Now I just create a bigger mess. My feeling is that you have to do something with the ingredients you have, and I'm part of my ingredients.

At the very same time, I am also personally convinced that I have to keep becoming more and more open, more and more aware of the questions that are hidden within me. I'm constantly practicing, bearing witness to myself and to others. I think they both have to go on at the same time and then it becomes so simple. You get the practice that feels right for you, that's most appropriate for you, and don't worry if it's the best one. Practice. Take all of the things that you feel and do something with them. Don't give yourself the liberty of saying, Well, I don't have the right ingredient. It's amazing. Whether it's hospice work or working with children or working with homeless people, learn, listen, listen from the people, listen from the kids, listen from the people dying.

The Peacemaker Order that we're starting is based around three tenets. The first tenet is penetrating into the unknown; the second is bearing witness; and the third is peacemaking or healing. In the tradition in which I was trained, Soto Zen, those three are called the three pure precepts. The first one is ceasing from evil—I call that penetrating into the unknown, getting rid of all the answers, all the attachments to the knowledge. It doesn't mean doing a lobotomy, it means starting from the place of saying, I don't know. Really being in that space, with all of what you know, starting with that phrase. Now bear witness, truly hear what's going on in this situation. Out of that will come the practices of peacemaking or healing.

I'd like to talk about these three in terms of a famous koan: Why does the Western barbarian have no beard? The Western barbarian is a name for Bodhidharma, who lived in India and is somewhat famous in Zen. There are many statues and many drawings of him and he's always pictured with a big beard. So the question is, Why does Bodhidharma have no beard?

Koans try to drive you into a place of bearing witness, so what I just said as the three tenets, in some sense, are a description of koan study. For koan study, you first have to drop what you think you know, so you have to go into being, listening, bearing witness to Bodhidharma, becoming Bodhidharma, forgetting, letting go of the fact that you know Bodhidharma has a beard. It's got nothing to do with that. Being in that state of Bodhidharma—you can feel the food caught in the beard; you can feel the maggots crawling around; you could feel the snot falling into the beard. It's all there. And what happens when you fully listen, when you fully become Bodhidharma with the beard, when you've done this penetrating into the unknown and then bore witness and now really are Bodhidharma and can feel all this? What happens? You might take out a comb and comb out the stuff, you might wash it. The healing practices will come out of that state. You don't have to run around for solutions to what to do with the beard. You don't have to run around for solutions of whether there is one or not. It's all irrelevant. You *are* there.

Your hand starts bleeding. For somebody to pose the question to you: Is that emptiness or not? What's the difference? It's bleeding. If I'm bearing witness to who I am and this thing is cut and bleeding, I don't ask questions. I *am* it. It's easy to see because this is part of me, but I am it. You're a nurse but you don't have my bandages with you. Do you say, "I don't have bandages. I won't do anything." Maybe I have a handkerchief, a shirt. Maybe I take a piece of paper that's dirty, but that's what I have. I do something with what I have, because it's me. I don't ask the question, What do I do? That's because I've borne witness to me.

So those are the three practices we'd like to work out of. If you want to do work with children, that's great. From our tenets' standpoint, what does it mean? The situations are completely different. I don't know if you're talking about children with legs, without legs, with this, with that, black, white. Bear witness to the situation. Learn from the kids. *Be* the kids, and then out of that will come stuff. Then read everything and see what everyone has written in regard to what you've experienced.

So the Peacemaker Order is not an order of knowing anything, but of promoting people to do those things and to be active; not just to be in conferences about it, but to get out and do things, and to do things with the ingredients that they are working with.

[Opening up the session for discussion, Roshi brought home the point that the ingredients are what each person has to work with herself or himself when a participant began his question as follows:]

Participant: If we use your ingredients for cooking up…

Roshi Glassman: No, no, you use *your* ingredients.

Participant: *Our* ingredients in cooking up a…

Roshi Glassman: No! You've got to use *your* ingredients.

Participant: If we use my ingredients for cooking up American Buddhism…

Roshi Glassman: No. Say, "If *I* use *my* ingredients for cooking up…."

Participant: Okay, if I use my ingredients for cooking up an American Buddhism, given the ingredients I have…in this room, I get a pretty tasty American Buddhism. I get some Euro-Americans, and black Americans, and Latino Americans, and Asian Americans, and I like that stew….I see as the second part of that, as other people use their own ingredients to cook up an American Buddhism stew using those same ingredients...

Roshi Glassman: No. Everybody has different ingredients.

Participant: A lot of people are starving with their own ingredients. Do you have suggestions for how we can talk better to each other so that we can work together in sharing?

Roshi Glassman: By listening to each other. We don't get together to hear each other, we get together to tell each other how to do things right, or "my" way. Get together to listen. To learn to listen is hard.

[Another member of the group asked Roshi to address the source of awakening—does it necessarily have to result from sitting or meditating? Could it perhaps arise from an experience in the world?]

Awakening comes from awakening, and it can come in many ways. I'm sure we would have different definitions of what we mean by awakening. The word *buddha* means "to awaken," so that's got to be an important element of what we're doing. The way I was trained, it's of key importance so that's something we work toward, but I don't personally like to talk about it or to put the worry of getting attached to it. I'd rather one gets into the right kind of practices and then, as Hakuin Zenji said, if you're doing the right kind of practice, those things are "natural arising." When he was in his eighties, he said

that he had had dozens of major *kenshos*—*ken* means "to see" and *sho* is "true nature"—and innumerable minor *kenshos,* and he said, Now I'm first starting to learn to live in accord with that.

I've seen too many people trying to aim toward some experience they had, to re-create or to do something, and that's a major trap. (We call it the "cave of the devil.") I think it's extremely important. That's what the word Buddhism means and it should not be something that you're concerned with.

[Another participant asked how one can bring individual mindfulness to function as a mechanism for mindfulness in a greater society. This concern brought up an important theme that would continue through the balance of the workshop: the importance of taking action—"doing something"—if for no other reason than it is in human nature to take up and follow or emulate things that work.]

Roshi Glassman: It's very important what you're asking, and the importance has got to do with what Muryo Peter [Matthiessen] was saying about the importance of each person. Our Congress consists of senators and congresspeople, and however you think of them, they're voting on different things and they're creating laws and budgets, etc. They're people. And, as people, the ones from New York are concerned with what's going on in New York. What they need are examples; they need cases that work. If you do something and it works, they want to know about it and out of that comes a model for how things will work in the whole country.

So if you ask me how can the various communities of mindfulness create change, first of all, if they're doing something that's meaningful, it will be copied. If they're not, they shouldn't be copied. I sort of trust in evolution.

Jonas Salk did a little Zen practice when he had his institute in San Diego and he sat a little with us at the Zen center in Los Angeles. He said, if there's a healthy cell in the body, it replicates. That's how you deal with disease. Looking at Zen in those days, he said, "I think this is a healthy cell and that it will replicate in this society."

If we create healthy communities— whatever you want to call them, mindful, awakened—they will be cloned, they will replicate. If we don't, others will come to gobble them up because it's unhealthy. So it really comes back down to each one of us creating the best meal.

A friend and I were on a street retreat five years ago and it was a day in which there was an annual, wonderful feast done by one of the churches in the Bowery—a meatloaf meal, but they had a lot of other things around it. Rick's a vegetarian, and we were at the back of this long and very wide line outside, sort of moving up. Everybody's pushing a little bit—it was not the most polite group—but there was a great meal being offered. A few blocks away on Bowery Street was a station wagon that came from a church in Harlem with great barbecued-chicken meals. These three guys came, who

had just eaten some of the barbecued chicken, and one guy said, "Watch," and he says out loud, "Hey, they've got some great barbecued chicken up on Bowery at the...." Rick heard that, his ears popped up, and he took off running. He was vegetarian, but based on your ingredients, if you make the right meal, they will come.

I think that's what you've got to worry about, not how you're going to get them all together and how you're going to get people to come and duplicate what you're doing. Who knows you got something good? Serve the meal and if it's good, they will come.

Participant: I'm a little confused about the ingredients. I heard you say make the best meal possible with the ingredients that you have, and then once you've had that meal, if you see this other meal and you don't have the ingredients, then go out and get those ingredients. At what point do you know that you're satisfied with the meal you have and come to a point that you're ready to get those other ingredients?

Roshi Glassman: That's what's great about life: We keep getting hungry. At every moment, you've got to create a meal. Sometimes you're creating the meal to eat it; sometimes you're creating it to serve it. But no matter how many times you eat the meal, believe me, you'll want another one at some point. The metaphor, of course, is that at every moment these are my ingredients and this is what I'm going to do.

When I first started working with the

homeless, I got a lot of static from a lot of people who were advanced Buddhists. They were telling me that I shouldn't be doing what I was doing, I should be teaching enlightenment to those homeless folks—you want to teach how to fish, you don't want to give fish. Wasn't I screwing things up by doing the things I was doing? They really believed what they were telling me and were coming at it as real good Buddhists, because we know that the only real thing is enlightenment. And I said, "Okay, you're starving. Stop. Get in the place of starving. You're doing koan study. You're starving. What do you want from me? Do you want me to teach you how to sit right now or do you want a meal? And then having the meal, now what do you want?" Now's the next moment—now what's the need?

So if I take out of the ingredients of this moment, if I'm starving, I need food. Next moment, what are the ingredients? I'm not starving. That's not one of my ingredients anymore. Now I could do another meal. Knowing what the ingredients are is so important. How do you hear those? How do you know those? That's in some sense what I'm saying our practice should be, to see more and more clearly what our ingredients are—how to listen, how to bear witness, how to be this moment—so I can see the ingredients in front of me. It keeps changing and every instant I'm making another meal.

[Referring in particular to Roshi's Auschwitz retreat and to what he had referred to earlier as "the Hitler in ourselves," a man asked what one was to do about taking responsibility for those people who, while claiming to be enlightened, are actually hurting many others. Roshi began by saying that he always has to keep coming back to himself to determine what he can do. He then discussed aspects of the Auschwitz retreat.]

We actually had about 153 people, and probably about 153 different ingredients. People were there for different reasons. We had about 25 to 30 from Poland, whose whole understanding of why they came changed during the five days. Some of the Polish folks found out that they were Jewish when they were in their late teens or early twenties because their parents had hid it from them because of the anti-Semitism that was still there in Poland. They didn't want their kids to grow up under what they had.

In the Peacemaker Order, we have different kinds of villages associated with us. There's one in Poland, and the mother of the man who was coordinating it was a Jewish intellectual and his father was a Catholic intellectual who was killed in the camps. His mother hid during the war. She was a writer so she helped the places where she was hiding in trying to improve their lot, but she would write letters on their behalf that didn't sound like farmer's letters, so eventually the Gestapo would come and they'd have to run to another farm.

Andre was a baby, but he does remember once his mother grabbing him and going where all the cows were and hiding under the cows and black boots circling around, looking, then right after that his mother picking up and moving to another place. Well, one day, he was about fourteen or fifteen, in Poland, walking down the streets and Polish people started to yell at him, "You dirty kike," and all kinds of things like that, and to hit him. He went home to his mother and said, "What's going on? Why are they yelling at me for being Jewish?" That's when he found out he was Jewish. So he was at this retreat for one reason, and there were a number of people like him.

Every morning we had small groups of about eight people divided by language. In the evening we all met as a big group, sharing stories of what was happening, with translators for five different languages. The first night, the Polish group met as a group and they were angry, Andre said, because they didn't know exactly why they were there.

The German people that were there were talking a lot about how to deal with their feelings of guilt. Many of the German people had parents or grandparents who worked the camps and were part of the system. They were dealing a lot with guilt. There were a lot of Jewish people there and they were dealing with a lot of anger.

But, the Polish people were saying, Why are we here? This is our country, but it's not our thing. It's a little like things I hear in Westchester County. Why is the inner city our problem? It's the black problem. We all do this. I don't believe that any of us take ownership of the issues that are us. We say it's somebody else's issue. That's why the world goes on the way it does. Well, they were dealing with that: It's somebody else's issue. The Germans came and built the camp here, and all these people got imported here, but they just happened to pick Poland. Nothing to do with us.

By the next night, their ingredients had shifted a lot from sitting all day, being part of everything that was going on, people from many countries, many nationalities, religions talking. It was a very powerful retreat so I said, We'll do this as an annual retreat, but we'll only do it if the Polish group would be the hosts. This will be your offering. The first year we'll support you—because it was a very complicated logistical thing—but it will be your offering, your meal, and we'll work with you in making the meal.

I keep coming back to that same thing. I take my ingredients and make my meal. I want people to take their situations and figure out what to do with them. When somebody asks about studying with me, I'm not going to tell them what I think, in a sense. I'm going to ask them to do something about their situation: You raised it so it's your ingredient. You can't say it's somebody else's ingredient. It's your ingredient. Now do something with it, don't put it aside, don't think it's unimportant. It's an ingredient of yours. Do something with it.

[The final issue raised concerned listening to so-called crazy people. Hearkening back to Levi's story about Benny the Dwarf, a woman asked Roshi to "look at the mentally ill person who wants to live in that kind of condition? Right now, if you want to live in [an institution], you're

not allowed in. It's only if you don't want to be there, that you're placed there. Would you say that this person who wants to be there should be living in the moment elsewhere or...if he wants to be there, he should be allowed to be there?"]

Roshi Glassman: I want to take all the things you said because they're all very important for me. I don't listen to a crazy person, or a homeless person, or a this, or a that. I listen to people. I don't know what they are. You've already prejudged what they are because they're in this institution or because they're talking differently. I was saying that when I listened to Bernard Isaacs talking to this other gentleman, Larry, for me it was two people talking. They may be judged by others in some way or another, but I don't want to do that. I want to hear. I don't want to tell Bernard Isaacs where to live or Larry where to live. Larry is now living with us in Yonkers. Is that better? That's up to him.

Another person I really admire is a man from Cameroon. He was an activist Marxist and was in prison as a Marxist, an educated man. After he was released, he was told that if he didn't leave the country he would be killed, so he fled and he went to France. He went to the Sorbonne and got a degree in anthropology, then he came to this country. Pretty much from the time he got to this country, he saw homelessness and couldn't believe that we had homelessness. He's been living homeless since that time, mostly in shelters in Harlem, and has been working in creating different kinds of job situations and various things.

After I started the Zen Peacemaker Order, he came up to me and said, "Is it okay if I steal what you're doing and create a Peacemaker Order in Harlem?"

I said, "You can't steal it. It's yours."

So he has created a Peacemaker Order in Harlem and has a newsletter already. We're creating an interfaith center called House of One People and he's already creating one in Harlem. But he lives the way he wants to live. Are you going to go to India and tell the mendicants they're not living right?

Again, listen to what or who you're working with and what the people want. I'm not trying to change people, I'm trying to learn. I'm trying to hear the questions within me that I'm avoiding and I think by doing so, things change. But I have no interest in telling somebody what or how they should be doing. The only thing I can say is listen in your situation and make your meal.

It's complicated. Don't worry about it being complicated. Don't worry about being frustrated about not knowing what to do right now. Make your best meal, that's all.

Prison Zen Practice in America

LIFE AND DEATH ON THE RAZOR'S EDGE

Rev. Kobutsu Malone

WE ALL FACE DEATHS—OUR OWN AND THOSE OF OTHERS IN OUR LIVES—but few face the experience of bearing the cruel and insistent knowledge that our death, or that of someone we care about, will take place at a given place and time. This is the exclusive province of death row.

While prisons in general, and certainly death row in particular, may seem odd locales to find Buddhism, it is just such places and situations that call for Buddhist philosophy and compassion in modern-day America. In reaching out to the disenfranchised, engaged Buddhists in America may find their great work with the incarcerated and condemned.

Rev. Kobutsu Malone, an American Rinzai Zen Buddhist priest, fell into his prison work by chance, but there he found great need for Buddhist teaching and practice. Today he works with male prisoners in New York State's Sing Sing prison, where he established the Dharma Song Zendo in 1992. He serves the zendo as prison chaplain and he cofounded the Engaged Zen Foundation, which is designed to foster spirituality in prisons.

As an extension of his work at Sing Sing, Kobutsu Malone supported a convicted murderer awaiting execution by the state of Arkansas in 1996. Calling upon all his resources as a Buddhist and a caring human being, even to the point of trying right up to the last moments to dissuade from their tasks those who were about to takel this man's life, Rev. Malone brought humanity and love to a place better known for its brutality and its officially instituted denial of spirituality.

We started out working in Sing
Sing about five years ago. This
was sort of an extension of a
major crisis in my life. By heritage I'm Irish.
We tend to be somewhat thick-headed and
oftentimes our practice involves being
severely jostled out of our complacency. For
me, it was a major depression, a divorce, a
loss of job. My car broke—I broke—and
after about eighteen years of practice I finally
went running back to the monastery for
refuge. I walked almost entirely from New
York City, about 120 miles, and I showed up
at the monastery one morning at 3:00 A.M.,
totally exhausted, and fell asleep in the
sewing room downstairs. In the morning, a
bunch of students came down and they
dragged the abbot down. "There's this weird
guy downstairs asleep in the sewing room."
The abbot came down and he took a look
at me and started laughing.

During the period of time that I stayed
there and got my life back together, I came
to the realization (and this was through the
assistance of another monk who was, at the
time, dying of AIDS) that for me my practice
and my work involved being of assistance to
others. During that period it gelled solidly in
my mind that this is the direction that I was
to take.

Sing Sing came along. People often ask,
Why are you working with those sleazeball,
no-good criminals? You could be working
with young kids. Well, no one came and said,
Hey, there's a bunch of young kids that need
your help. Somebody came along and said,
Hey, there's this prison and these guys would
like to learn about meditation. You want to
do it? I said sure. If somebody had come
along and said, Hey, there's some old folks in
a nursing home, I'd have done that too. It just
happened. According to the abbot though,
it's all Dharma. He says, "Kobutsu, you belong
in prison."

We started in. It was a little unnerving
for me at first because I've spent a lot of my
life avoiding prison, actively. Sing Sing is the
second oldest correctional facility in New
York State and it's a pit. You wouldn't want
to live there. Nobody would. We started out
with a group of men who had formed what
they called a meditation group. They had a
bunch of fellows that had formed committees and when I walked in they showed me
a flowchart with the organizational squares
and lines. There was a sergeant at arms and
a director and I said, "Wait a minute. How
many guys have you got here?"

And he said, "Oh, eight."

Well, we finally wound up, by the time
I'd finished with them for about a month,
with one. There were some clashes and I
made it clear that I was there for one purpose and that was to serve as a conduit for
the transmission of Rinzai Zen practice. That
was precisely what we were going to do. We
were not going to set up outside corporations. We were not going to put ads in the
newspaper requesting people to send in
money. Some of the schemes were quite
creative.

We began sitting in a small room in the
hospital that was essentially a storage room.
We started sitting on a bunch of blankets

that one of the boys stole out of the laundry, ratty old prison blankets. We had a very difficult time getting cushions in. Our credibility with the administration was tenuous at best. They saw this bald-headed Irishman walking in in a robe and they didn't quite know what to make of it. They couldn't figure out if I was bringing in dope or smuggling guys out in my robe. It was difficult educating them in terms of our needs. Getting them to recognize the fact that we had a religious group took about two years. One of the first things that I requested was permission to bring in donated cushions to sit on and we were told that you can't bring those in. Those are articles of worship. I said, "We don't worship the damn things, we sit on them."

We finally had a group of about five men who were seriously involved in practice and at that point, since we were getting nowhere in our requests to be recognized as a religious group, we got ourselves involved with an attorney and things changed quite drastically as soon as the attorney stepped in. The bottom line was recognize us as a religion and avoid court because we'll win. And they did.

At this point in time, Sing Sing and the New York State Department of Corrections are very proud of the programming we have running there. It doesn't cost the state a dime. We have quite an assortment of men involved in the program. There's a core group of perhaps three or four very dedicated practitioners, perhaps a dozen not-so-dedicated practitioners, and a few hangers-on and peripheral-type people, very much like out here.

Sing Sing is a particularly unique prison in that a good portion of the population is transient. These guys are brought in and immediately processed through Sing Sing and sent to other facilities. Most of the people that I deal with are doing long time. You don't get into Sing Sing unless you've got at least three or four years and the vast majority of my students are doing on the order of twenty-five to life. Generally what we found in other facilities is pretty much this same thing. Guys that are in for a short time tend to want to just do their time and get the hell out. Guys that are looking at doing twenty-five to life are also looking at themselves, because they're realizing, I'm going to be here a *long* time. In that sense, they have a distinct advantage. They have almost a greater advantage than people in the free world approaching their practice.

I received a letter last week from a man who has a Ph.D., is a former federal law enforcement officer, and is currently doing time in Fort Leavenworth. How fortunate. This guy is writing to us. He wants to receive information; he wants to receive books. He's very excited about his practice and quite sincere about it. But had it not been for prison and whatever happened to him that brought him to that point, he may not have made the connection.

Frankie Parker was in the same situation. In the early eighties, Frankie was heavily involved in coke and any other drug that could be snorted, injected, inhaled, whatever, running with motorcycle gangs, drinking heavily. He wound up committing two murders and wound up in prison. Frankie came into our lives in March of this last year in the form of a letter that was really quite remarkable. I pick up the mail every morning and invariably there are inmate letters. I remember receiving this one—it had one of these kid's stickers on it with happy birds with hearts and things around them and it said, "Put a smile in your life." I opened it up and the return address is Death Row, Arkansas. And then he mentioned that he was completely out of appeals and expected to be executed shortly. Receiving that letter was pretty heavy. Dealing with teaching *zazen* and running a little zendo in the prison was one thing. I had always delivered a verbal message, Oh yeah, I'm opposed to the death penalty. Now I can say, "I am opposed to the death penalty." Back then it was just projection.

We normally don't give out our telephone number to incarcerated people, for obvious reasons. In Frankie's case, since he had so little time and the content of his letter really touched me, I gave him our home phone and told him please call collect. Over the next few weeks and months we developed a very cordial relationship. He had a great sense of humor and told some great jokes, yet he was quite cognizant of what was going on around him. He knew that he was coming down to the wire. He'd spent twelve years on death row.

It's interesting the crisis that came to him after committing two murders, after being sentenced to death. He responded for the first four years of being in prison as

many people do, and that is aggressively. One of the attitudes that people adopt when they go into the prison system is, "Move on me and I'll kill you." It's a defense mechanism. It's a shield. For many people, that's the only thing that they can grasp hold of and it's a pretty tough environment. No matter what anybody thinks and hears about country club prisons and how great and how easy it is in there, that's bullshit. It's not. The incidence of violence and rape is phenomenal in prisons. The brutalization that takes place between prisoner and prisoner and guard and prisoner is appalling.

Frankie wound up fighting guards and one day they dragged him off down to the hole, the maximum security cell, where they lock up these guys when they cause trouble. Threw him in there. During the daytime they take out the bedding so you can't sleep it off. So you've got essentially a cell with a concrete floor and a commode and that's it. He got in there and he pissed off and cussing and throwing himself at the door and finally looked around and surveyed his condition and realized there was no Bible in there. Now, the one book they let you have in the hole is the Bible. He pounded on the door, "Give me my friggin' Bible!" The guard came back to the door and opened it up and threw something in and slammed the door behind him and went off. He said, "Here's your stinking holy book, asshole." Frankie kicked it around a little bit, screamed some more. Finally got tired, sat down and read the book.

The first thing he read was this: "Mind is

the forerunner of all actions. All deeds are led by mind, created by mind. If one speaks or acts with a corrupt mind, suffering follows, as the wheel follows the hoof of an ox pulling a cart." Something happened in that cell that day in Arkansas—that change, that instant, wherein the mind folded in on itself and realized the nature of contemplative practice.

He changed, drastically, to the point that guards were bowing to the man. In Arkansas! And I have never seen an inmate in a facility treated the way this man was treated. He was given the name Si Fu. Some guy saw some kung fu movie. For many people in prison and for many of the guards, this is their only connection, what they've seen on TV. So Frankie got the name Si Fu and eventually adopted it, took it on as his legal name. Seeing these guards saying, "Oh, Si Fu," was pretty remarkable.

We conducted a five-month-long campaign, a letter-writing campaign and a publicized campaign, and urged people to write to the governor and request that he commute Frankie Parker's sentence from death by lethal injection to a sentence of life in prison without possibility of parole. The net result of five months of very, very intense activity was that he was scheduled to be executed on August 8. Toward the end of that month of July, the beginning of August, my wife Lizzie and I flew down to Arkansas and visited with Jusan—at that point his name was changed to Jusan. I had given him *jukai*—which is (perhaps a good term is) "lay ordination"—on a prior visit. The first visit

we went, he was scheduled to be executed in, I believe, four or five days. The day we arrived in Little Rock, he received a reprieve and the following day I did a *jukai* ceremony for him and my abbot Eido Shimano Roshi had given him the name Jusan, which means "mountain of eternal life." One of our friends had made him a *rakusu* and Roshi had done calligraphy with his new name on the back.

When we went down the second time, we pretty much knew that this was going to be it. The governor was brand new. He was not an elected official and had assumed the position of governor because the prior governor had been convicted of two federal felonies and had to leave office. Unfortunately, that man still had the notion that he was going to hold onto power because the day he was supposed to resign he informed the state legislature that he wasn't going to resign, he was simply going to take a leave of absence. At that point, the capitol was in total chaos. This was probably one of the reasons that he did not grant clemency to Frankie, because he didn't recognize the fact that his political career was over. Anyway, the new governor was a fundamentalist-Baptist preacher and his first act in office was to change Jusan's execution date: He issued a proclamation that cut six weeks off Jusan's life. That was his first official act.

The last day was probably the most difficult day of my life. We spent the day in what is known as a "quiet cell," which is a very small cell. The regular bars are covered over with an expanded steel screen which has innumerable coats of paint on it to the point where it's almost impossible to see through. All of our communication had to take place through a food slot. The ambient temperature was on the order of 95+ degrees. We were under constant observation. There were officers in and out all day involved in what they call the death watch, and that involves a logbook wherein every so many minutes—every five minutes, every fifteen minutes—every time anything changes within the situation, it's all noted down. "Inmate uses toilet." Noted down. "Toilet is flushed by...." You cannot flush you own toilet in these cells. Buttons for flushing the toilet and supplying water are on the opposite wall, so the guard or whoever is there has to do it. This is to prevent the inmate from drowning himself prior to execution.

We spent the day dividing up his personal possessions. We did *zazen* as we were able. He wrote letters. He tied up his personal correspondence. He spoke with people on the telephone. He spoke with Eido Shimano Roshi. He spoke with Philip Kapleau Roshi and he spoke with Lama Tharchin Rinpoche and numerous friends and relatives. During the time that Jusan was using the phone, I was at liberty to walk in the short hallway and speak with the guards, essentially to allow him some privacy on his telephone calls. I spent some time speaking with the guards who were actually going to be taking part in the execution process and I went to each one of them and formed some kind of a one-on-one relationship with them—"Hey, how you doing? Man, this sucks.

Have you done this before?" Blah blah blah—and finally imparting the message that, Hey, you don't have to do this. This is wrong. This is murder. This is not cool. Just that.

One of Jusan's things was that he loved to do origami. He had three fingers on one hand because one of them had been shot off, and he'd sit there doing this and next thing you know, out would come this three-dimensional folded cage or a box or cranes or snails. Really remarkable. And he spent a good portion of his last day on earth teaching the guards how to make the folds in the paper so they could go home that night and show their children. And they were grateful and he was grateful to be able to do it for them. This is what the guy wanted to do. He was a born teacher.

There is no doubt in my mind that this man was a realized being. I remember on the phone with him one day, we were talking about this, that, and the other thing and I said, you know, some off-handed comment, "Hey, man, there's nobody home." And he said, "Oh, I know *that*," and it was clear he knew that. Both Kapleau Roshi and Eido Roshi made the comment "This guy was impressive." When he spoke with Eido Roshi, he said, "Well, Roshi, today's my last day."

He said to me at one point, "I hope you like Mexican food."

"What do you mean, Mexican food?"

He said, "Well, that's what my last meal is going to be and I've asked you to join."

Oh, man, I hope somebody's got some Di-Gel in here. In the afternoon his last meal did arrive, and it was Mexican food, and there were huge amounts of it. I joined him for Mexican food. In the newspapers they reported the amount of Mexican food that this man had consumed for his last meal: twelve enchiladas, sixteen tacos. It was unbelievable. This guy should have died from overeating.

Later on, the assistant director of correctional services came in and said, "Okay, in a few minutes the tie-down team will be arriving." At that point, I put on my robe—I'd been sitting there in my kimono all day because it was so hot—and my *kesa* and my *zagu*. Jusan and I had really choreographed his death. The state had their choreography and we had ours and our choreography involved our chanting the three refuges:

I take refuge in the Buddha.
I take refuge in the Dharma.
I take refuge in the Sangha.

And we were going to continue this chant for as long as we could. That was it.

At 8:47 in the evening, there was a commotion outside the access door to the death cells. The door opened and the tie-down team burst in. There were about six of them initially. They were helmeted, they had body armor, they had ankle boots. Two of them came in with full-body riot shields. They pinned Jusan at the back of his cell. All the time

I take refuge in the Buddha.
I take refuge in the Dharma.
I take refuge in the Sangha.

They chained him. They chained his ankles, they chained his waist, they chained his hands to his waist, and they brought him out of his cell. They had asked me to walk ahead of Frankie and lead him to the execution chamber, and I told them no way was I going to lead anybody to any execution chamber. I will walk next to him. They wouldn't allow me to do that so they led me, by my elbows.

There was a short hall, about fifteen feet long, that we entered to go to the execution chamber, and they had this hall lined with officers, shoulder to shoulder, same gear, riot helmets, full-face shields, body armor, gloves, the whole nine yards. In the hall, we had constructed a small shrine that we'd arranged with the administration to be present and it was a cardboard box with a piece of felt and a small Buddha on it. We approached the shrine. We bowed to the Buddha. He bowed to the Buddha. We continued our chanting. We turned to each other. We bowed three times.

I take refuge in the Buddha.
I take refuge in the Dharma.
I take refuge in the Sangha.

At that point we were facing each other. Our chanting stopped. I looked at him. He looked at me. I saw a single tear roll from his right eye down the inside of his cheek, over the corner of his goatee, and disappear into the bottom of it. I could see every hair in his goatee—I can still see every hair in his goatee, every pore in his skin, every breath he took. We embraced, and he said in my ear, "I love you, my brother. Thank you so much." We again placed our hands in *gassho* and made one final bow, accidentally touching forehead to forehead, as in lamas greeting each other within the Tibetan tradition.

I was guided out a side door. He was guided into the death chamber. I exited the building and the hearse that we had arranged to be present to remove his body was waiting. I continued to chant and I was directed around the perimeter of the building to the entryway of the viewing chamber. Behind me was a white van with the state witnesses in it. There were numerous correctional officers in the area. I continued the chant. My voice was weakening somewhat. I was experiencing incredible temporal dilation and everything had turned very, very psychedelic.

After a few minutes the door to the viewing chamber opened. I stepped in and positioned myself at the front of a very large picture window that had a curtain drawn behind it. The witnesses filed in. They didn't know what to make of it—here was this Buddhist monk chanting out loud. They were shocked.

They were seated. A few minutes passed. The curtain opened. The room flooded with brilliant white light. Jusan was strapped to a gurney, both arms coming out diagonally. There were plates that retained his head. There was a strap over his forehead. He was wearing his *rakusu*. They had draped a sheet to about breast height to attempt to hide the fact that he had a *rakusu* on, but we had threatened them with lawsuits if they did not allow him to wear his vestment. They wouldn't allow him to wear his robe.

Four days before he died, he asked me, "Do you think I am ready to become a monk?" I couldn't answer that and I said, "Absolutely. We'll do the ceremony right now." A lot of criticism came from that, and a lot of people were real happy that it happened. "Do you think I'm ready to become a monk?" Four days to live.

On the corner, on the strap of his *rakusu*, just above where the sheet had covered it, he had paperclipped a picture of His Holiness the Dalai Lama, who had written a letter on his behalf to the governor, and I could just see the top of His Holiness's head peering out from under the sheet.

An announcement was made. It was inaudible because of the chanting. Some other men came into the room, one of whom had a stethoscope. They announced, and at that point I knew, that Frankie had been executed. He had remained on the table with his eyes closed, perfectly still, for four minutes. I know what was going through his mind.

I take refuge in the Buddha.
I take refuge in the Dharma.
I take refuge in the Sangha.

A warm farewell on a frigid day

5

Buddhism in America

Toward an
American Buddhism

Robert A. F. Thurman, Ph.D.

In his keynote address, Robert Thurman recalled a talk by Gadjin Nagao, noted Japanese historian of Buddhism, on the subject of "the five peaks of Buddhism." Nagao explicated each of the first four peaks and their various times in painstaking detail, but when he arrived at the fifth, he simply and briefly stated that there is no fifth peak, nor will there be unless it occurs in America, from which its spirit could, in turn, experience a transmission back to Asia.

Prof. Thurman devoted a sizable part of his talk to explaining why Nagao's observation is probably correct. He showed that, through its history, Buddhism has almost always been a countercultural phenomenon, in that—with the exception of seventeenth-century Tibet—cultures that have fostered a Buddhism-based religion have done so counter to the prevailing religious, governmental, and cultural institutions.

Prof. Thurman contrasted the militaristic model of "fighting an enemy" with the Buddhist battle against the egocentrism that is rife in modern thought and attention. He defined Buddhism in a nonreligious way, showing how the Dharma can—even should—live side-by-side with one's culturally founded religion and lifestyle. Warning against a too-easy Western adoption of Asian forms and practices, he demonstrated the necessity of one's locating Dharma in the midst of one's own life, rather than approaching it in reverse in order to reposition one's self in the midst of a predetermined set of circumstances that one labels "Buddhist."

As in "Being Free and Enjoying Life," his workshop, this address was liberally peppered with fascinating, potentially controversial asides and bursts of great energy and humor. In sum, Prof. Thurman provided a means of viewing contemporary Buddhism in the West that is at once understandable and readily examined in the context of everyday life.

---

*Biographical information about Prof. Thurman is included with the introduction to his workshop "Being Free and Enjoying Life," page 216.

I'm very honored to talk with you here tonight. There's quite a lot of you here, and most of you are practicing Buddhists, I'm sure for many years, and one has the feeling of sitting in front of hundreds of thousands, if not millions, of man- and woman-hours of meditation time. Therefore, one really should be weighing every word, since it is resonating like a deep bell in minds that are open and receptive or completely incredulous—one or the other. So, it's a real honor to address you about Buddhism and the future of Buddhism in America, if there will be such a thing. Will there be such a thing? That's the question.

In talking about this, I have four parts to what I want to talk about. The first part is: What is this thing called Buddhism that we're talking about? That we think might take place here in America—that *is* taking place in America—and that might take another kind of place or more place in America at some point.

Second is, What is it doing here, or what could it do to America and through America to the planet, in relation to its own history, once we have some sense of what *it* is?

Third, how will it be doing it, and how can it do it, and in this light, what is the contribution of the Asian Buddhist traditions, in their own sort of cultural matrices and/or in various forms deriving from their own cultural matrices? And what would be an American contribution to that?

Then, last, some sort of vision of the future or some speculations about the future. Will in fact there be a success? Will Buddhism here succeed in the goal of Buddhism? The same goal that Buddhism has

had everywhere, in all of the countries that it has been? That it has spread in the past, and also disappeared from, in other times. We have to remember that, even in the country where Buddhism originated, its overt presence has more or less disappeared. In the last thousand years, even. So we have to realize that Buddhism doesn't only come but Buddhism also goes, and how will that be connected here in America?

First let me give a preview of my overall thesis here. I worked on this subject and did four lectures in San Francisco early last year, which is where I first got to the thought, and I startled myself in the middle of that series of lectures, because I came to the idea that Buddhism will not actually be able to succeed in its mission here in America, unless it is able to perform that mission without being Buddhism. That's sort of the short form; that's a preview of my thesis. In other words, Buddhism has to go beyond being Buddhism in order to do the work that Buddhism wants to do, wherever it is. Okay, so it's Buddhism without Buddhism. That's my title. Very Zen, don't you think?

I was a bit startled by that in San Francisco. And some of the local San Francisco Buddhist centers were a little bit irritated by that. And there are many Buddhist centers represented here, I'm sure, of different kinds, and I don't want anybody to take it personally, please. I think they overlook the fact that this is within the framework of American religious pluralism—and in some sense, Buddhism has the profile of a religion—and therefore, all Asian Buddhisms are utterly welcomed in America and they are wonderful in America. We all love them, we've all benefited by them. And they won't be disappearing, because religions will not be disappearing. But, the reason I say Buddhism has to not be Buddhism to really accomplish its mainstream service for America, is that I'm defining Buddhism as something *other* than these different religions, although not excluding them.

So what is Buddhism, then? Let's look at that. Buddhism, of course, first and foremost probably, is a therapy. It's a therapy that Buddha elaborated for demented human beings. And it's helped also divine beings actually. The language about how humans are the best is a little exaggerated. The Buddha also taught the gods quite a lot. He used to hang out in different heavens, and his mother was in one heaven, and he went and gave her a long teaching, poor thing. She was up there relaxing in the heaven of Indra, called the Sudarshana heaven, where they have really quite nice villas, and he comes up there and gives her like a three-month course in the Abhidharma. Poor woman, really; after bringing him to birth and everything.

But it is a therapy for demented human beings such as us—or such as myself. I never would say "us," because you all may be enlightened, and one should always remember that. When we say this and that about "us," assuming everybody else is not enlightened, we shouldn't. Other people may be enlightened, actually. We always have to know that. So I'll just say such as me.

And fundamentally, it's a therapy about selfishness. About the fact that we are still saddled with a kind of programming from our previous existences, as less than human beings, or too much more in the wrong way than human beings, where we are still too focused on ourselves. And this focus on ourselves makes us sick and makes us miserable, and then we of course help make others miserable. And it doesn't work. So the Buddha, when he figured this out, developed this therapy.

I should spend a few minutes doing this first, how I see this, just to make it really simple, so it connects to my mainstream definition of Buddhism. People say that Buddhism is the four noble truths. But the four noble truths is not some sort of a dogma. The four noble truths is a therapeutic recipe. It's a diagnosis of the unenlightened state, which is going to be unsatisfactory. If you're unenlightened, you're going to have a rotten time, basically. It isn't that everything is having a rotten time, and it isn't that Buddha is having a rotten time. Buddha is having a *great* time. And it isn't that Buddha thought everyone has such a rotten time that Buddha left the planet or left existence or obliterated himself in some sort of an existentialist manner. The Buddha is present everywhere, and enlightenment is a state of infinite life, boundless incarnation, boundless existences everywhere. Buddha didn't go anywhere—Buddha exploded everywhere. So there's no disappearing in Buddhism, there's no way out of this mess, except to become enlightened and then enjoy it.

So the four noble truths is this recipe. The first one is suffering: If we are unenlightened, we're going to have a rotten time. The second is the cause of why we're having a rotten time, and why we're having a rotten time is that we wrongly think that we are the center of the universe. (You all know this, but it's always worth going through. I love to do it in a group of people. Makes them so uneasy.) Everyone here in this room thinks they're the main thing in the room. Every single individual here thinks, *I'm it*, in the room. Right? Even if you're sitting way over at one corner, it's the center of the room where you are. And each of us thinks, I'm the main thing here. And, then everyone knows, of course, that everyone else thinks that. Although we normally don't think about that. But we uneasily know that this fool sitting next to me thinks that he or she is the main thing.

And so, although we're comfortable here in a Dharma setting—we may even be married, for that matter—still, each of us at some deep level has a contradiction with the other one. They disagree. You think you're the center, and she thinks she's the center, so when you get down to some really life-and-death issues sometimes, there can be conflict. More fundamentally, when we think we're it in the universe, and the universe is just the other opposed to us, we're in a losing battle with that other. Isn't it simple? If you fight the universe, because you're it, and the universe doesn't agree, then who wins? You lose. Sooner or later, even God lost. Everyone loses. Because there are so many other gods, you know.

And so that was Buddha's big insight: As long as I think I am it—and I'm Siddhartha

and I've got to do some big thing—then I'm never getting enough. And I never get it done, and the world is overwhelming me. And suddenly, I see through the delusion of being Siddhartha as the only real thing. And instead, I see Siddhartha as an interconnected thing with all the other things…Siddhartha as the eccentric Siddhartha who's interconnected—not the center, but *part* of everything with everybody else. And that's all enlightenment is.

Once we realize that—really viscerally, through every level, realize it, and I really mean viscerally, according to the Buddhist definition—Siddhartha, a being who is a buddha, does not need to draw the next breath egocentrically. So I can rule myself out anyway. I can hold my breath for a while, and then I'll turn purple, and then I'll gulp the air, even if it's filled with noxious fumes. Even if I'm drowning—I'll gulp it even if it's not air, but water, because the involuntary reflex of grabbing this thing for me, I can't resist.

But a buddha can resist that. A buddha does not need to breathe for any selfish reason, because a buddha is not identified with the body that is drawing the air and the oxygen. A buddha is the life that is beyond the confines of any particular body, although it can be totally invested in their body. So that's a very rigorous definition. If you want to check it out on any enlightened guru, or anybody, or yourself after you've had a big blinding-light experience or something: "Am I enlightened?" Just hold your breath for a while. Or put a plastic bag over guruji's head and see how long he lasts. If the guy is clawing and choking for air in a little while, then he's cool, he's still a good guru, maybe, but he's not buddha.

The third noble truth is the fact that it is truly possible to understand this simple thing. It would be easy if we took a nihilistic misinterpretation and thought that the Buddha's big news was simply that everybody doesn't exist—it's not that you're not the center of the universe, it's that you don't exist. That's not what he taught. That would be stupid. That wouldn't be enlightened. Some guy jumping up in India under a Bodhi tree or in front of a stupa and saying, "Hey, nobody's here." Thanks a lot. Do be quiet, then.

He didn't say that either. It's more complicated. It is: We're not the only absolute thing, and we're not some sort of absolute nonexistence. We are a relative, vulnerable, interactive, interconnected, sort of vague-boundaried thing that is there as part of, interconnected with, and yet somewhat individually responsible in relation to the entire universe. Which is much more subtle. A very small exaggeration to diminish therefore. We are here, each of us, but we're here ex-centrically, not absoluto-centrically. That's it.

The truth of cessation of, or freedom from, suffering comes from that recognition. And Buddha was so happy when he realized that. He said, "Wow, peaceful, happy, elixir of immortality." Remember, he was really flipping out. Of course, there are different versions of what he said, but in any version he was just happy as a bee. He even said, "I'm not going to go teach people, they'll never figure this one out."

And then, God—Brahma, that is, who they thought was God in India in those days—came and said, "You'd better teach." He came down and said, "This guy has figured it out, he'd better teach. I'm tired of people blaming me." The problem is their deluded egocentrism. So Brahma brought him the Wheel of Dharma, and said, "Go out and teach."

Then the fourth truth, the path, is all of the methods of his doing that, and they divide into three basic things. They divide into ethical methods: Change your lifestyle to reflect your interconnectedness rather than that you're the absolute one, who can eat whatever, do whatever, take whatever, etc. Change your mental function, by meditating, by developing control of the deeper layers of your mind instead of being just driven compulsively by habits that are plugged in there from your former lives, from your genes, from your culture. And then, gain wisdom, which is, of course, the central of all of those. The wisdom is simply that understanding about the self; that understanding about how the self is relative and not absolute.

Therefore, what are those three things? The ethical thing is like a religious thing, it's a social thing. The meditational thing is a psychological thing. It can be also a religious thing. The wisdom thing can be religious and psychological, but more, the wisdom thing isn't really religious. The wisdom thing is scientific. The wisdom thing is technical. It's like you understand who you really are, and not some sort of big religious thing, that I really am something that's going to be really an angel or something. No, you understand technically how you're constructed, that there's no solid core in your construction; that there's no absolute, sort of little platinum you, a little homunculus that is sort of you pulling the strings. That's sort of absolute. Realize that that's not there, although we feel that it's there, and realize that it isn't there in others, although it seems to be there in others, and realize that the table doesn't have it, and the planet doesn't have it, and the atoms don't have it, and that's a scientific realization. People say about Buddhism that Buddhism is a therapy. So that's the fundamental therapy. Relativity being the main insight.

Then, based on that, with the ethical thing, it's the social thing also, not just the religious thing. Based on his own shift-over from being miserable to being ecstatically happy, the Buddha founded basically a social revolution. He started a revolutionary process that goes on to this day. And it totally transformed India, no matter what you may read in some sort of Tao or neo-Brahmin histories, or Western materialist histories that think the history of the world is just military history. He socially transformed India completely by this insight. Because the culture of society, to which this insight has never occurred, is a culture that somehow tries to control and balance people without ever questioning this internal delusion that I'm it. So we try to be polite with each other, pretend that we're not thinking that we're it. Therefore, you go through the door first. I know I should, because I'm it, but I'll let you go through. I'll

let you go through because that's courtesy, that's manners, it's our cultural custom.

Cultures that don't have this fundamental insight are based on just trying to restrain all these things, and of course they work very poorly and very imperfectly, because basically everyone is seething with the opposite of all the things they are restraining themselves to try to do. And as soon as you press on that culture, as soon as you have starvation, a riot, some sort of dreadful situation, then people start behaving like absolute monsters, as we've noticed on this planet.

It's not any particular people. It's not true that any one group of people is particularly like that. They're all equally like that. That includes us. We're particularly rough—we have been in our history. So in founding this, what the Buddha did was, he said this is the main thing that everyone is born for. This is the purpose of your life—not only your life, but all of your millions of lives. Imagine how you would feel if you had the vision the Buddha did. And he looked at another person, his brother, his friend, and he saw this person as a being who had been struggling infinitely, for billions of lives. The individual being had been through all of Carl Sagan's movies, you know. Up from Precambrian slime, crawling around, eating weird things, snuffling around, snufflupagussing, and everything. Finally, they got to be a human being; and as a human being they're looking into the nature of their experience and trying to improve it. And yet they're still driven by this illusion that I'm it. And being driven by that, they're going to lose the human life at some point fairly soon, and then they might go back to being a snufflupagus. If you saw people like that, you would say, Hey, wake up. Use your time, your precious moments. You are at a point in your evolution, you are at a cross-road, where you can actually take your heart and peel a horrible shell right off it. And open it in a certain way, and turn it inside out, and really enjoy your world. Forever. And after that you can help other beings do that. You become finally—instead of the worm in a cocoon that you've been crawling around as—you become like a butterfly, who flies around and showers other beings with the possibility of becoming a butterfly.

If you saw that, you would get a bit intense. You'd decide, Hey, let's create something. But then what do you do? There's no school for that. There is no place. So you have to say, Well, let's have a sun god. People would come and they would say, I take refuge in you. I like this. This is good. They would feel enfolded; they had never met a person who felt that their life was as impor-tant as his own life. We only meet other people who think they're over there, being them, the real one. And they see us over here, being us, the real one. And we sort of reach out from inside these little shells and we say, We'll be nice—Hello—good morn-ing—Good-bye. We have never met any-body who feels that we're just as alive as they are, and actually is so bored with them-selves, having been hanging out with them-selves, that they think we are more interest-ing than they are.

So people liked the Buddha. They said,

I'm coming too. He said, "Hey, *bhikku,* come here." And then immediately their hair flew off—he had this fabulous haircut machine—their hair would fly off and they would change their couture, immediately. And then they would focus their life on transforming themselves from this human state, which is already nearly transformed, from his point of view, into a being that has no longer any dis-sent, no longer any blind or compulsive movement within evolution. Death is no problem whatsoever. Death is just a doorway opening to a bigger kind of embodiment; a bigger being.

Each one of us can do that in this life, in a relatively short period of time. Buddha saw that. He had to set up an institution. He called it the *sangha.* Monastic—why not? Because you don't want to waste any time, you know, having families, having sex, running around worrying. Why bother?

Why not take all that energy and put it into this major transformation? You're not giving anything up. Nobody who joins that feels like they're losing anything. It's not called "ordained" in Asia—coming under some order. That's a Western monastic term. You're coming under the boss, you're being ordained, getting ordered. In the East, it's escape. When you become a monk or a nun, you're getting free. Imagine a woman in India, with her thirteenth childbirth, four of them living, some boring husband she was married to by social arrangement, who doesn't know the first thing, never read Masters and Johnson, or even the *Kama Sutra*—some old fuddy-duddy who bought her from the parents, and so forth. And then she hears, I can be a nun and educate myself. I don't have to cook for this guy, I don't have to bear children. You think that's giving something up? Whoopee! Let me out of that household!

That's social revolution.

And it's amazing that he chose India, or India was the only possibility where this happened. Maybe different buddhas tried this in other countries, but in India it happened because it was loose enough, open enough, intelligent enough that they let it happen, which was amazing. Thousands of women and men ran out and became nuns and monks, but then these were monks and nuns who were not really religious. They were not being "professional" monks and nuns.

A monk or a nun was like a soldier joining an army to go to war. You don't do it to become a professional soldier, you're sort of drafted by the force of the intensity of your objective, and you just drop all unnecessary sideline things. You shave your head to put on some sort of a uniform and you train to do these things to accomplish an objective, as a soldier does. You lose all fear. You're ready. You sort of live beyond life and death, because you could be killed at any time.

So the monk thing is like that, but counter to the soldier, the monk is not attacking other beings. The monk is attacking this hard shell of egotism in the center of the heart. The monk is attacking the inner enemy of *I'm it*—I'm the great one, who is greedy, who hates others who don't agree, who is deluded. So, it's a war. Being a monk or nun is to go to war with the inner enemy as a life-or-

death matter. It's not a routinizing thing. Of course it became routinized later, but originally it was not.

Then furthermore, in founding that, the Buddha founded the root of an educational movement that continues to this day. There was no university in his time; there was no liberal arts college; there was no notion of educating yourself for liberation. You were an apprentice to your parents and the different trade or craft or priest or whatever they might have been. He was an apprentice to his father, who was a king. And so he founded something where people go not to learn to do something productive for the collective, but where people go as individuals to open their hearts—to declare war on the closed heart, the iron-curtained heart of the ignorant person.

Then Buddhism became a counterculture, because there was still the official culture of the brahmins in India, of the kings, of the merchants, and this was a kind of counterculture, where people would escape from that official culture. And it maintained itself as a counterculture the whole time in India, although it became incredibly powerful as a counterculture, and it totally transformed India as a counterculture. But at the brink of becoming a mainstream culture, fifteen hundred years later, toward the end of the first millennium, India was unfortunately invaded by outside Westerners, violent militarists, and culturally it was thrown back centuries, a millennium, and Buddhism was wiped out. So that counterculture was wiped out, and that's why Buddhism did disappear in India, because it remained only countercultural, the way that Buddhism is here in America now—countercultural.

Then we hear about Buddhism as a way of life. And Buddhism did become a way of life for those within within that counterculture in one particular country, then in Tibet, which was sort of approached by the poor Buddhists who were persecuted out of India. They looked around for where to go, with all their incredible techniques of changing the human heart. They were being wiped out in India, they saw, and they looked up there and saw these poor, unsuspecting Tibetans, up there with their yaks, who were pretty fierce at the time. They used to fight, they had armies and they used to conquer everybody. They weren't like the mild-mannered Tibetans now.

And these Buddhist masters in India, these great adepts, looked up there and they said Aha! We think we see a good hideout for a millennium or so. And they went up into Tibet, and they laid it on the poor Tibetans, and the poor Tibetans, within three of four hundred years, completely transformed their whole culture. That country, the first in Buddhist history, I think you can say, became mainstream-cultural Buddhist. But it took a thousand years to fully do that. It came there in the seventh century. By the seventeenth century only did Tibet really disarm its army. And that is the measure—if you understand the thesis about Buddhism —that Buddhism is the counterforce in history to militarism. Buddhist monasticism, educationalism, heart transforming, declaring

war on your own egotism. This is the historical, only major, multinational counterforce to the one apparently dominant multinational force in the world today—militarism. And the Tibetans were the only country that completely abandoned their army, finally. They gave up being armed. They unilaterally disarmed their army. People will argue, "No, they had few a troops here and there," but give me a break. Look what happened to them in the twentieth century. They had no army, basically, from being a country that had a major army of conquest before that.

That's what I call a mainstream-Buddhist nation. The criterion is to abandon the military. For America, for example, to become a mainstream-Buddhist nation, we would have $300 billion dollars a year to spend on the *sangha*. My friend Surya Das mentioned to me—and it's a good idea—that all of these closing military bases would be Dharma centers. They wouldn't be religious, so they wouldn't freak out the people in the churches and the synagogues and the this and that. They would be just centers, like educational centers. We'd have Jon Kabat-Zinn out there in front, shouting about how this is not religious and this isn't Buddhism. I'll join him. So it's separation of church and state. This is just people doing stress-reduction and relaxation programs. Can you imagine what our country would be like if we had $300 billion dollars' worth of stress relaxation. We would actually, genuinely become civilized from the Buddhist perspective, finally. We would join Tibetan monks.

But this happened in Tibet. Therefore

it's conceivable—it's shown itself historically—Buddhism can become a mainstream
civilization. It did not in Japan. It did not in
Southeast Asia. I don't mean there weren't
great Buddhists in those countries, and
great Buddhist orders, and great Buddhist
moments of imperial patronage, and so
forth. But what I mean is, that the emperors, the kings, etc., kept their armies. And
when Buddhism got a little too uppity and
had a little too much land, they confiscated
it, and they put the money back into funding their military machine. And that means
that it remains countercultural.

Then, of course, Buddhism is a world religion. That was a Western invention, their
concept of world religion, because at the
beginning of this century, Buddhism was still
the majority world religion. There was over a
billion, maybe a billion and half, Buddhists in
the world. Now there's only two or three
hundred million nominal Buddhists and out
of those, how many ... how many people in
this room? There are very few real Buddhists,
in a sense. There are a lot of nominal
Buddhists—a few hundred million—but
they're third or fourth in the role of world
religion. In our century, there's been a massive Buddhist holocaust, everywhere, due to
communism and materialism and other
things.

Finally, Buddhism is simply a contemplative
discipline. This is sort of the therapy level. I
like to define Buddhism as an evolutionary
sport. That's my favorite definition. It's a

sport, like hockey, lacrosse. And it's an evolutionary sport. You realize that life is play, and
you realize that what you do affects your
evolution. Every little thing that you do, even
everything that you think. And so, you want
to play this game really well. You want to
evolve positively. You don't want to risk falling
into a negative trend of evolution in any way.
And then you become Buddhist when you
really realize that. You become completely
focused on that, no matter what else.

Coming back to history, I was in Mount
Baldy Zen Center twenty years ago, and we
had one professor from Japan with us, who
was a noted Japanese historian of Buddhism.
He was the professor of Buddhism in Kyoto
for years, Gadjin Nagao. And he was giving
this series of lectures on Buddhist history
that was testing all those Zen students' abilities to stay awake to the absolute core. But
then everybody suddenly woke up toward
the end where he said that there are four
peaks in Buddhist history. And the first great
peak in Buddhist history is the time of the
Buddha, of course. The second great peak in
Buddhist history is the time of the rise of
Mahayana, in India, and when it then spread
through central Asia. And Mahayana and
Theravada also spread to Southeast Asia.
Then the third great peak is the time of the
T'ang dynasty, he said. And the beginning of
Buddhism in Japan, and he left out the Pala
dynasty and Gupta dynasty in India and Tibet.
But that's an East Asian sort of thing, and I
quickly corrected that. (He was scared of the
Pala dynasty in India and Tibet and this sort
of thing because he's scared of Tantra.

Mahayana Buddhists do tend to be a little scared of Tantra, all those women, all those nude women, running around. It's a little worrisome: Is that really the Dharma, all these really beautiful female buddhas?) So we fixed that up.

And so the third major one is about the seventh century of the Common Era, when you have Tantrayana, when you have all these adepts and these amazing characters, and Zen really gets its birth in China around that time. The fourth one is the time of the great Pakmodrupa renaissance in Tibet and the Kamakura era in Japan. He called that the fourth great peak.

And then people were waiting for the fifth one, because the lecture was entitled "The Five Peaks." So where's the fifth one? Everyone was waiting. He looked up at this point, and all Zen students were desperately trying to stay awake, and he said,

There will be no fifth peak, unless it happens here in America. This is the only place where there could be a fifth peak in the history of Buddhism, a fifth great renaissance in Buddhism, and it can only be created by you. Then, if you did it, it will reverberate back in Asia where Buddhism was, where people have the forms of Buddhism. But it will not be able to originate there in Asia. It will only happen here.

He didn't elaborate too much exactly why, but I will elaborate.

Consider the definition of Buddhism that I all-too-quickly gave, of Buddhism's great moments being when people start to live outside some sort of regular, binding, routinized cultural and mental rules of their own, and people begin to see that it's a life-and-death issue for them, and that if they die unenlightened and still absolutist and still selfish, that they're in great danger. (The terror part is important. I apologize—I know everyone is escaping from Jonathan Edwards in Protestantism in American Buddhism.)

This needs people to be healthily respectful for it. When you want to be a relativistic being, not an absolute being, you want to be connected. We all talk today about being connected and relational to the world. That relationality has to be infinite. You can't leave out of that relationality someplace where you're going to drop out just automatically, because you're going to be annihilated at death. Then you've already got a negative nirvana. What do you care about anything, finally, if you let yourself off the hook like that?

You have to have a relationality where what you do, every little gesture, good or bad, has infinite future effect. You're tied in not only to infinite past, but to infinite future. You can describe it any way you want. You don't have to call it "rebirth," "reincarnation," if you don't like that. You're going to be reborn in a computer at Harvard or something, or at MIT. I don't care. But you have to feel connected to the future infinitely, so that what you do is infinitely significant. There's no sort of black hole that your deeds and your thoughts can fall into.

This gives a degree of intensity of commitment about the quality of thoughts and deeds right now that is irreplaceable. Without that degree of intensity about the thoughts and the deeds right now—the degree of intensity coming only from infinite interconnectedness, infinite consequentiality—then you don't have the energy coming both from enthusiastic joy about how you can be the most unlimitedly magnificent being, and from sheer terror that you don't want to be some kind of really miserable being, way beyond any form of human misery.

The combination of this intense joy and terror is the kind of energy we need to really turn around these deeply encrusted inner, instinctual habits. We're not just talking about surface intellectual habits, we're talking about deep, instinctual habits of the heart. Deep like the genes and the nervous system that we have to turn around to become enlightened.

Once someone gets that vision of enlightenment, then there's no other purpose in life. Everything else is irrelevant to that purpose. Even making others happy, because you realize that you can't really make others happy unless you have created this shift in your own heart. Even if you do something for another, when you're really thinking, I'm the one. Aren't I nice to do this for them, it doesn't really help them that much. Only when your heart opens does it really help others.

Besides, what is helping them? Giving them just a home? Giving them another meal? They're going to be hungry later. Really helping them is helping them with their evolutionary question: What can I get done toward transforming my being and wrenching open this egocentric heart before I die? Which could be anytime. And when you help someone with that, then you really help them. Then they have woken up to their great evolutionary opportunity and great evolutionary responsibility.

So when people begin to do that, there becomes a movement that goes from heart to heart by morphic resonance. I love that concept—it's like mind-to-mind reverberation, without even words or communicating or Internet or anything. It's the mental Internet between living beings, between the modem wetwares that we have stuffed in here. So when your own heart opens, this creates a resonance where other hearts will open. They don't perceive it as coming from yours, but it does. And then when they open some, this resonates back to you. So that's how a movement starts.

Buddha's routine thing was to be a king. He was a bad guy. He was supposed to take care of his wife and his child; and his poor father was trying to retire. "Oh, I'm going to get enlightenment," this kid says. In Indian culture, the father gets to retire when the kid takes over the throne. The kid is all trained up and ready to be the king, and his father says, "Here's the throne, son."

He says, "Sorry, Dad, I'm going to get enlightenment. I'm going to go to the woods."

Dad says, "*I'm* going to the woods! I'm going to Florida. You take the kingdom!"

He says, "Tough luck, Dad. You have to hang on. Wait until my son grows up."

And he leaves them all. Buddha did

something wrenching, in terms of his culture, because he had a vision living beyond routine life and death. And that's what *real* Buddhism is. It's not a religion—it's all of those things—but the basic thing is that the individuals, one by one, person by person, begin to live beyond life and death. And then this catches, and then they patch up institutions, because what do you do with a bunch of people who are living beyond life and death? They're sort of wandering in the street, they get in the way of traffic, they forget this and that, they lose track of their i.d. cards, so you begin to create different kinds of institutions.

At the time of Mahayana in India, at the time of Buddha in India, at the time of the Tantrayana and the T'ang dynasty, Chan and so forth in China, at the time of Kamakura and of the great Tibetan masters in Tibet, and the great monastic explosion in Tibet and Mongolia—these peaks have all come when so many people just said, To hell with it all. I'm not taking orders from anybody. I am a human being. I made myself this kind of human being by my own bootstraps, over millions of lives. And I still don't know quite how to control it. I don't know how to really use this fabulous brain that I have. I don't know how to open this incredibly sensitive heart that I have. And there's nothing else worthwhile in life but opening that heart and that brain, and it isn't even that hard, if I really put my effort into it. So that's what I'm doing, period. And don't tell me, You're being mean. Stay home. Cook. Because the food I cook when I actually hate your guts because I'm really self-centered and I'm having to cook for you is not really even good for your health. But when I have opened my heart and my brain, the dinner I will make will really flip you out. And don't worry, I'll be back. But I'm not cooking a bunch of crap for you under this bad mind. I'm getting rid of it.

Then, suddenly, we need air force bases. The Tibetans basically turn over their air force bases. Surya was kidding, but why shouldn't we turn over those dumb air force bases? What are we doing with them? Flying missions here and there, like carrying eggs of destruction, and flying them around to make ourselves feel important and spending billions of dollars to drop them on who? For what reason? And then encouraging morons like the Chinese dictators and any other would-be dictators in Russia and other places, too, or in Baghdad or wherever, to get some of their own? Why shouldn't we turn over those bases and have people get out there and do stress reduction instead? Send out that vibe? Then we could parachute in stress-reducers everywhere.

And Maharishi has a point! I'm sorry. The guy has got a point. He wanted to throw in 40,000, but he didn't have the troops, the poor guy. He wanted to throw in 40,000 meditators in Bosnia. That would have been good.

So that's why I think Nagao said that we could have this renaissance here in America only. Because in America, Buddhism is not a routine thing for us. For those of us who have encountered it, it was like leaving our routine things, like the Buddha did. Some of us may

have re-routinized it by becoming re-accultur-
ated as an Asian. I did at first. I went and tried
to become a Tibetan monk. Shaved my head,
put on a robe, ran around and sort of developed a way of cringing. I spoke the language
really well, because I'm like a parrot. Then,
only twenty-five years later, my daughter looks
and says, "Oh, look, Daddy looks like Henry
Miller in drag!" when she saw the picture. I
had these sunglasses on and a shaved head.
That would have been all right in the nineties
probably, but in the sixties it was ridiculous.

So the point is, we approach it so we
can get stuck back in an Asian cultural routine, but the real thing we bring is some non-
routine thing where we're going to the pulse
of life itself. We're going to the core of the
heart itself. Without labels of "Buddhism," or
"not Buddhism," or any such thing. Don't tell
me Buddhist practice is going to this and
that center, sitting on this or that pillow.
Buddhist practice is when you want the
same ten-dollar bill that he wants, and you
are just jumping for it, and you just stop
yourself. And you say, "Let him have his ten-
dollar bill." "All right, here; here's another ten-
dollar bill." (Just to punish yourself!) "Take
another one!" That's Buddhist practice, right
there. Now, you may need years of meditation to let go even of ten cents. But that's
the practice. And the living practice is just as
much in those ethical self-transcendings as in
meditational self-transcendings, as in wisdom
self-transcendings of developing the stability
and the insight to see through yourself.
Which is, of course, enlightenment.

But remember, when you see through

yourself, what do you see? You don't see a
nonself. You see everybody else. If you look
through yourself and you became transparent, the invisible man, what has he got to
see? He sees everybody else only. He can't
even see himself unless he puts on that
weird pair of socks and the pipe and the
weird scarf, or raincoat.

So this is how we can do this in
America. If we can keep from re-routinizing
over-much; if we can keep de-routinizing and
we can keep going from heart to heart. This
is why we're coming to this stage now, in the
nineties. And it's very fitting that we do it. Do
we think we're doing it because we're better
than everybody else on the planet? I sometimes almost get to feel that way. That is, of
course, a bad mistake. It's most likely that we
have come to this because we are more dis-
satisfied, we are more freaked out about it.

In the sixties we were totally anxious
about it, not because we were better, but
because we were worse. Why do I say we
were worse? Well, we have the pursuit of
happiness in the Declaration of
Independence. We have "democracy." We
have opportunity for all, etc.—b.s.—and I
don't mean Buddhist studies.

Our genocide of the Native Americans is
the most horrendous genocide in the history
of the planet—more than any of Genghis
Khan's particular slaughters; more than the
Germans; more than the Chinese are doing
presently to the Tibetans; more than any
genocide ever—so that is in our national
consciousness, and every one of us knows it.
Even certain people I know who think it's a

great idea, unfortunately—not in my party, but some other party—they're still deeply struck by it, deeply horrified by it, really.

And then, we still have the most horrible military machine in history. We're a big power, they say. It's absurd. We are starving our own people in all of our own cities, and we are busily taking more at the top, and chopping back more. Welfare: "Oh, we'll cut back." Reinstating capital punishment. Idiot politicians showing themselves in commercials going *clang!* on some jail door. And still keeping up our $300 billion overt defense budget, much less the indirect one, which doubles the ongoing investment.

So why, therefore, are we so unhappy in our routines? Because we've become crazy as a culture. We have brought the planet to the brink of destruction. Not the Chinese. Not the Indians. Not the Africans. We did it. The Euro-American honkies—of course, not all of you are those—so, especially me; I'm the mainly guilty one. And therefore, when we grew up, we felt highly anxious. When we went to Exeter and stuff, and they said, "Oh, you're the elite and you're going to run this and that corp." We felt, Maybe we don't really want to run that corp. It's like trampling up people's lives. Maybe we're not doing the world any service. And we sure look like we're destroying our own water and air and earth and food chain.

The food chain, we have destroyed. It's inedible. Filled with antibiotics and pesticides and that's why everyone is sick with this and that. Because we eat poison. We live in poison. We're more anxious. We're more freaked

out. So we realize that the egocentric routine magnified into the tribal national routine is a bad routine. Because we have realized that, we have the opportunity more than those who are still a little comfortable in some vestige of a culture. We have the opportunity to generate a tremendous renaissance—*tremendous*—in this living beyond death.

Of course, if we try to do it on a religious basis—"We're going to save you all with Buddhism"—it's a hopeless project. It's even a bad project. To go out and tell them, "Hey, we're going to convert everybody to Buddhism; it's so much better," even if we think so, is a really bad idea. Because then that will simply stimulate total religious war, and other religions will say, "Well, who are these aliens, what are they doing?" It will be very, very bad.

Besides, it isn't even true, because it isn't just owning up, changing a bunch of slogans. I love the Dalai Lama. People run up and say, "I want to be a Buddhist, your Holiness." He says, "No, thank you. Be a good Jew. Be a good Christian." But then later he says, "Well, yes, if you want to do some meditation or you want to do this or that later, that's fine." But the idea of people bringing a certain fanatic, egocentric, authoritarian personality structure and lining that up behind Buddhism and saying, "I am a Buddhist," is frightening. It's the last thing we want.

Buddhism more or less avoided that throughout its history, and remained anti-authoritarian everywhere it was, more or less. And that's why it doesn't have any massive crusades or jihads on its record. It has little struggles and little problems, but nothing massive, compared to the other religions that make religions out of the egocentric complex that Buddha was trying to cure. You can see why. Making a religion out of something like, you're not an absolute ego, but there is one absolute ego that tells you you can behave like one on occasion when he wants you to destroy some opposing temple. That's most religions, unfortunately. They're part of cultural routines rather than working against cultural routines. There are always individuals *within* those religions who try to work against the absolute ego, and look what usually happens to them. They get done in—and then some people make a thing out of them getting done in—basically, they got done in.

So Jon Kabat-Zinn's thing is brilliant and is essential, and we shouldn't fear that it will somehow erode Buddhism or that it's like taking out and marketing or medicalizing our precious Buddhism that should only be kept within this Tibetan cultural framework or this Japanese cultural framework or this Burmese cultural framework or whatever it is. *No!* He is making this service to the human heart, which is all that Buddhism has ever been, available to people who couldn't do it with the labels Buddhism, with the Burma, with the Thailand, with the Tibet, with this kind of thing. And we have to think of more things like that to do. We have to do that on the medical level. We have to do that on the sports level. We have to have Buddhism as a sport taught in a gym in school—meditating. Or doing it in a moving thing, like a martial

art defense. Or maybe figuring out how to do Buddhist lacrosse. That way, you begin to teach sports people that through this way of opening the heart, even they'll be better at the sport than they are with this stupid kill-the-enemy type of thing.

If you look at Shakyamuni Buddha's time, the other major institution that was founded at that time was world-conquering militarism. That was founded around that time. The Achaemenid empire in Iran, the Indian Magadha dynasty, the Proto-Han dynasty (although the Chinese were behind the pulse there), and Alexander the Great emerged a little later, but these things were beginning at that time. And Buddha founded the counter movement, which was war on egotism, war on ignorance; the monastic movement, which then moved into religion: Christianity; Jainism; it was not in Hinduism until Buddhism left India, but then it went into Hinduism. Taoism adopted it from Buddhism. He started this counterforce movement.

Now Protestantism, you note, which led to the greatest militarizing of the northern-European peoples, that led to the conquest of the planet that we are enjoying today, still—I use *enjoying* advisedly—that happened when Protestantism shut down all monasteries in northern Europe. I don't know if you noticed. That was the big thing about Protestantism: "We don't need no monasteries!" So that means the kings can have all the land, and all the produce, and all the wealth. Then what do the kings want it for? Well, they want productivity out of people, and they want soldiers, and they want conquest.

And then they went out and conquered the whole planet.

However, the vestige of that counter-force, the monastic force, is still here in our schools and universities and high schools and prep schools. Those are really all monastically derived institutions, although they look far from it today. They're even co-ed! But they originated out of monasteries, all the Western universities did, just like the Buddhist universities in India came out of Buddhist monasteries.

Now, one other "counter" example: Buddhism was very powerful in China for a thousand years. It brought about a tremendous transformation in China. Anyone who tells you that the Chinese are inscrutable, and radically different, and they're all so different, and we can't deal with them like other people, and they're blah, blah different—a sort of subtle, subconsciously racist attitude that you'll hear from people about the Chinese, which I absolutely don't agree with—is ignoring the fact that Buddhism was a non-Chinese thing. It came from India, and had a major impact on the Chinese heart over thousands of years. They loved it dearly, even though they called it the barbarian religion, and they made pictures of Buddha as a hairy guy with a weird beard. But in China, Buddhism always remained countercultural. Buddhism never somehow connected, formally in any way, to the mainstream educational institutions of China. They remained Confucian and state-dominated. Therefore, when the neo-Confucians suppressed Buddhism, it sort of died out in China.

We can look at all these examples from history. We cannot be content with remaining countercultural only, because we cannot do the service for our fellow Americans that we want to do, which is not make them recite some chant with us in the morning. Let them go "Hail Mary. Mother of God." Who cares? Fine. I love Mary. She's Tara. Or Tara is Mary, if they like. I don't care. They can pray to Jesus or Mary or Moses, it doesn't matter. But the heart has to be able to relativize the sense of self-absoluteness. The heart has to open. They have to find pleasure in life. They have to find happiness through the happiness of others. That's the service that we need to offer them, and you can't do that by demanding that they adopt a whole bunch of cultural things from Japan or China or Tibet or any such thing. You can only do that by serving them in the place where they look for that service.

Everyone looks for that service from educational institutions. They go to college to be liberally educated; to develop decency, sensibility, sensitivity, and intelligence. And they get shoddy service. Nobody breathes a word about decency. They join a football team and they're told to go out and kick butt. Sensibility—for art history, they go in and learn which is Renoir, which is Gauguin, but nobody really makes them sit and contemplate Gauguin or Van Gogh for six hours in a Gauguin sesshin, until even the crows are flying in spirals. So they don't get a real opening of their sensitivity. And intelligence, they just get how to manipulate words so as to run corporations, and to trick people, and write crappy memos, and find tax loop-holes. They don't get intelligence of under-standing their own heart. They don't get training in the gym of how to let an emotion go by and not identify with it when that rage jumps up which is going to break down three marriages for them in their life as a rich executive, and they're going to beat women, and they're going to be nasty to their children and be alienated from them, and then they're going to have a heart attack and a pacemaker at forty-six. Instead of the university helping them learn to let that anger just go out of the solar plexus and visualize it as a cosmic fire, burning up all the negativities in the universe, instead of that, they're trained to be more angry at the other team and go out and kick butt!

So without talking about Buddhism, we can challenge our schools. Danny Goleman has done this beautifully. In his "emotional-intelligence" thing, he doesn't breathe a word about Buddhism, and it's in the California schools; it's all over the place. People are reading it. And all it is is mindfulness about the emotions and how to help young chil-dren become mindful. But does he say something in there about I love Joseph or I love Buddha in his dedication? No. And that's not bad, he shouldn't say that. Then they will all read it in those schools. So he is offering —in the terms of the institutions that are there, mainstream institutions—the service of helping the human heart. We have to think of more ways to do that. The education system is *primary*. It's good to have alterna-tive-education things. That's okay, and we

should do those, and they should be rein-forced and strengthened, but then we should make a bigger effort to deal with the regular educational institutions and challenge them within their own framework. Wait until you have tenure, though! Don't try it before you get tenure, or that will be the end of you! Wait until tenure, and then do the challenge.

Another thing I think we should have would be some new universities that are not formally Buddhist at all—not connected to any particular Buddhist sect or anything—but are based on that principle. We should have some sort of university of light—university of the open heart—joining with religious people and mystics and sufis from other tra-ditions, so it's not perceived as some single religious group. Universities that emphasize the meditative, the inner science on the intellectual level, and really do a proper job. We need that pressure on the regular uni-versities. Their notion of the curriculum of reading a bunch of white males. So we would need a place with a curriculum that's focused on enlightenment, and that says that to be educated you have to be enlightened —not necessarily a perfect buddha, but some degree of enlightenment, some degree of reversal of this heart knot. Some loosen-ing of that knot, where the heart kind of goes flutter putter when it's about to blow up in some way, and you begin to realize that your heart itself is not just some absolute thing. It itself is interconnected with the universe, which is what the Buddhist experience can convey, can it not? The heart opening, or the face falling off, the ability to identify with the other viscerally, even glimpses of that. No one should get a B. A. or a B. E.—Bachelor of Enlightenment; Bachelor of Arts and Sciences of Enlightenment—until they have had some kind of experience like that. Otherwise, no license to run those corporations, no license to go around and to say, "I'm educated." So that's what we really need.

I'm very honored to have addressed all of you, and as you go out and accumulate another million hours of meditation time and rack it up on your rosary or your scoreboard or wherever you keep it—and you should keep score, by the way. I will share from my beloved Tara Tulku, the late teacher of mine: You should count the hours. It's like you count the mantras that you perform. Because if you've clocked a million hours, you should be proud of yourself. You should rejoice. How are you really going to learn to overcome jealousy about the great accomplishments of others, jealousy which is the one great thing that prevents us from working as a group to really accomplish our objectives—rivalry and jealousy—how are you going to overcome that if you don't truly appreciate your own good deeds? So it's a great yoga to count your hours. Get your certificate. Don't be shy about it. "Oh, I meditated, but I never noticed how long I was there." Don't do that. If you meditate months and weeks and years, rack them up. Notch your sword, whatever it is. And be proud of yourselves.

And as you go on with that, try to think on every level—like Kabat-Zinn is doing, like Goleman is doing, like others are doing—what can I do also on the mainstream level to reach out to people who indelibly think of themselves as Christians, Jews? How can I unthreaten them? How can I help them open their hearts in the terms of their own teachings, their own charisma, their own rituals? And you will come up with such creativity and such wonderful things in the next million hours of meditating that it will be a joy to behold in the next century, in the next millennium. Let's all pray for that, and please all do that.

How the Swans
Came to the Lake

Rick Fields

IN HIS BOOK *HOW THE SWANS CAME TO THE LAKE: A Narrative History of Buddhism in America,* Rick Fields quotes a passage attributed to the Buddha:

> 2,500 years after I have passed away into Nirvana, the Highest Doctrine
> will become spread in the country of the red-faced people.*

If "the red-faced people" are taken to be Native Americans, when we consider the frequently quoted statistic that Buddhism is the "fastest-growing religion" in the United States, it would seem that the perpetuation of Buddhism in America is right on schedule.

In his book and the talk based on it that he presented at the Buddhism in America Conference, however, Rick Fields shows that an avid American interest in Buddhism and its philosophical approach to spirituality is not new. In the nineteenth century, Ralph Waldo Emerson and Henry David Thoreau both studied Buddhist texts and teachings. Henry Steel Olcott pursued knowledge of Buddhism when traveling to India and Ceylon, then brought back his ideas of the Dharma and published them in widely read articles and books. The 1893 Parliament of World Religions brought many renowned Asian Buddhist delegates to Chicago, causing one C. T. Strauss, a Jewish businessman from New York, to take the three refuges, thereby becoming the first person to "become a Buddhist" in the United States.

In essence, both the book and the talk trace the lineage of American Buddhism directly from Shakyamuni Buddha. It is this perpetuation of the Dharma in the Americas, right into the present day, that Mr. Fields emphasizes.

In addition to his history of American Buddhism, Fields has published *Chop Wood, Carry Water* and *The Code of the Warrior.* Formerly editor of *The Vajradhatu Sun,* an international journal of Buddhism, he is currently editor-at-large of *Tricycle: A Buddhist Review.*

---

*From a 1931 translation of Bu-ston's *History of Buddhism.*

ince this is a Buddhist conference with a lot of Zen influence, I guess we'll start on time. One of the big differences among American Buddhists may not so much be in terms of meditation but in terms of time of starting. If you're a Zen American Buddhist, you start on time and you get up very early in the morning. If you're a Vipassana American Buddhist, you spend a long time sitting at one time, often. And if you're a Tibetan American Buddhist, you're on something called Tibetan time.

My own teacher, Trungpa Ripoche, was habitually late for talks. Once I was going to hear him speak about twenty miles from where I was living. Knowing how late he was, I didn't leave St. Johnsbury until 2:00 (when he was supposed to start), and on the way there the water hose in the car broke, so I had to hitchhike back to St. Johnsbury, get a new water-hose line, hitchhike back and install it. I'm not a very good mechanic so it probably took twice as long as it should have, and I got there just as he was beginning the talk anyhow.

So this is just to say that there are many different styles of Buddhism in America. America is in a very interesting position. In this country right now, it seems to be very extreme, kind of a melting-pot situation, so for various reasons we have this embarrassment of riches as far as Buddhism is concerned.

Let me backtrack a little bit. Quite a few years ago, I embarked on a project to write a book on Buddhism in America and at that time there weren't quite so many groups

and not nearly as much information. The Buddhist groups that did exist were fairly spread apart. This was just in the beginning of the Tibetan invasion and somewhat at the tail end of the Japanese Zen occupation, and I was going to write kind of a field guide to Buddhism in America. My idea was that I was going to travel around the country and visit different Buddhist groups and write about them, and students who were interested in studying could have this book and go to different places.

So I started. I worked on that project but I quickly found that this really wouldn't work. For one thing, if I tried to come into a Buddhist group and say, "I'm a journalist. I'm writing this book about Buddhism in America," the people in those days would look at me a little bit skeptically, to say the least.

So I found out that I would have to spend some time in each group, sitting with them and getting to know them so that they would realize I wasn't just trying to do something really superficial and rip them off in some way. If I went to the roshi and said, "I'm writing this book on Buddhism in America. What is Buddhism?" If it was Soen-sa-nim, he might hit me with his stick.

Sasaki Roshi said, "Tell Rockefeller that I want all his money. Why should he give his money to all those other people? I need it more."

They would sort of play with me and I wouldn't get a straight answer.

Or maybe someone would say, "Who is asking this question?" and ring that bell.

I went to visit the people up in Barre,

Massachusetts, who were just starting the Insight Meditation Center—Joseph Goldstein and Jack Kornfield, whom I had known and first met at the first session of Naropa Institute in Boulder. They said, "Well, if you really want to know what we're doing, why don't you come and sit this three-month silent retreat with us?"

When I went to see a Tibetan lama, he would say there are four noble truths. The first noble truth is this. The second is that, and then there's the eightfold path, and then there's the fourteen different Tantras and I would get this very complete but basically meaningless (to me) elucidation of all the kind of a scholastic Indian tradition of teaching the Dharma.

Or even scarier, they would say, "Well, if you really want to learn about Tibetan Buddhism, we have this three-year, three-month, three-day retreat that you can do, or perhaps you'd just like to do *ngöndro* and start with 100,000 prostrations and then come back and I'll talk to you."

So I figured out that that wasn't going to work. Of course, by then I'd already spent the money from the advance for the book which was—I won't even say what that was in those days! But I did find that when I asked, "Well, Roshi, how did you come to America?" or "What brought you here?" or talked to Jack and Joseph about how they had become teachers, just in those stories it seemed that the truth of Dharma emerged. It seemed that the indirect approach was much better than a head-on assault on the question. So, I started discovering these stories, and for a writer, stories are gold.

Let me back up again, because this book is really about my continually backing up. Having figured out that what I was going to do was a history, I began to look at what traditional Buddhist histories are.

All traditional Buddhist histories in whatever tradition start with the story of the Buddha. Often, in the Zen tradition, they'll start with the Buddha holding up a flower to Mahakashyapa, who smiled, which was the beginning of the lineage of Zen Buddhism. And isn't that great, a lineage that begins with a smile and a flower? Not with some incredible enlightenment experience or vision of the systematic vision of the world or theory of anything.

So I thought a history of Buddhism in America, just like a history of Buddhism in Tibet, should begin with the story of the Buddha. I wrote a first chapter, which is a story of the Buddha. Then I got to the end of that chapter and I wondered, Well, now what happens? Or what happened?

I tried to sort out a little bit what people think happened a couple hundred years after the Buddha, when followers started arguing with each other. I think it was Ananda who, when the Buddha died, said, "You have to follow the major rules of the *vinaya* but not the minor ones. The minor ones are more relative and you can adapt those to the times." So after the Buddha's *parinirvana,* Ananda told people that and they said to him, "Well, which ones did he mean to be the minor ones?"

And Ananda said, "Oh, I forgot to ask him. You know, I was distracted, he was dying...."

So people, of course, started discussing that and you could say we're still discussing it. Gary Snyder says that Buddhism is a 2,500-year dialogue about the nature of mind, and to me that's one of the best descriptions of what Buddhadharma really is.

I don't think of it as a religion, frankly. I think of it as kind of a corrective to religion that's masquerading as a religion and that might hopefully save the world from religion, allowing the other religions to do their beneficial things when they're beneficial.

But, basically, my feeling in working on this book was that this was something very valuable that was coming to America. It was not just another alternative in a smorgasbord of groovy, different approaches to the question of the divine and all that. But rather it was something crucial, something very radical, something radical in the sense that it goes to the root of the problem of being human, which is really, I think, what Peter Matthiessen* was talking about. We need a radical look at this question of being human that nice religions have not solved.

And since America seems to be playing something of a pivotal role in the world these days, because of its technology and power, it's doubly important that we have something like Buddhism to temper this Wild West of a country. This country really began with genocide—we came here as if there was nothing here. Well, that's a lie. This was

*See "The Coming of Age of American Zen," the keynote address presented by Peter Matthiessen (Muryo Sensei), pages 396–406.

fully populated with a very wonderful and sophisticated variety of peoples.

So what we're doing is important. Everybody's saying, Wow, this is really important. This is the time that it's all happening and this is the moment and we're really at the center of this moment. And to a certain extent that's very true. Right now, Buddhism seems to be in some ways more popular than it's ever been and we tend to think like this is a first-time occurrence. But what I had discovered in researching this book, which became like a detective tale for me, was that American Buddhism has a long history. Buddhism in the West has a long history. So even though this seems like we're the first ones that are doing this, it's not at all the case.

I thought I'd pick up some highlights from my book, *How the Swans Came to the Lake*. One of the things that had moved me in doing my research was that I believe I was able to trace an unbroken lineage from Shakyamuni Buddha to America right now. In other words, all Buddhist history is really the history of lineage, of the Buddha holding up the flower and Mahakashyapa smiling. In some form or the other, that's the way Buddhist history goes. That's how Buddhadharma has been handed on. It's handed on from one human being to another human being. There are exceptions—people who had direct experience of *Sambhogakaya* buddhas or various things, but still, they always pass that on to another human being.

So that's how it's happened, and the miracle is that it's come to us directly from the Buddha, through various teachers, from countries in Asia. Buddhists in Japan and Sri Lanka had very little knowledge of each other or experience of each other's practice merely a hundred years ago. It was an American, Henry Olcott, who actually was one of those who brought them together for the first time.

Since we're in Boston I'd like to talk a little bit about Emerson and Thoreau, who were some of the first people to translate and to read Buddhist texts and to sort of mix it with Western thought. Here's a section from Thoreau.

Sometimes, in a summer morning, having taken my accustomed bath, I sat in my sunny doorway from sunrise til noon, rapt in reverie, amidst the pines and hickories and sumachs, in the undisturbed solitude and stillness, while the birds sang around or flitted noiseless through the house, until by the sun falling in my west window, or the noise of some traveller's wagon on the distant highway, I was reminded of the lapse of time. I grew in those seasons like corn in the night, and they were far better than the work of the hands would have been. They were not time subtracted from my life, but so much over and above my usual allowance. I realized what the Orientals mean by contemplation and the forsaking of works.

To me, Thoreau is sort of like the Taoists were in early China—somebody who had this kind of very natural appreciation of contemplation and nature all as one. In his book

A Week on the Concord and Merrimack Rivers, he writes,

I know that some of you will have hard thoughts of me, when they hear their Christ named beside my Buddha. Yet I am sure that I am willing they should love their Christ more than my Buddha, for the love is the main thing.

That's a great attitude, I think. He wrote later,

There is an orientalism in the most restless pioneer, and the farthest west is but the farthest east and every man's brain is the Sanskrit. The Vedas and their Agamas are not so ancient as serene contemplation. Why will we be imposed on by antiquity....And do we but live in the present?

The first Buddhist scripture that I could find in America was a translation of a section of the *Lotus of the True Law,* the *Lotus Sutra,* and Thoreau had translated it from the French from Burnouf, who was one of the first Pali and Sanskrit scholars at that time. So in that way, Buddhism came into this country as something valuable, as something interesting.

The next thing that happened was a connection through Bronson Alcott, who had a vegetarian, free-thought commune out in Concord, Massachusetts. Among his group was Edwin Arnold, an English poet who had been in India. The English had colonized India and Arnold had begun to learn Sanskrit. He wrote a book called *The Light of Asia,* which was the life of the Buddha in verse, and he ended up bringing the book to America, publishing it, and really promoting it just like people promote books these days. I just have one little snippet here I'd like to read:

…He is one with Life
Yet lives not. He is blest, ceasing to be
OM, MANI PADME, HUM! The Dewdrop slips
Into the shining sea.

This was Edwin Arnold's version of nirvana. It's a little Hindu-y, a little Christian, but basically he got the story very much accurate. He titillated his readers with detailed descriptions of Siddhartha's palace life, where delicate dark-browed ministers of love fanned the sleeping eyes of the happy prince, and brought tears to their eyes in a scene in which Siddhartha bids his son and wife farewell. That book in America went through eighty editions and sold between half a million and a million copies. We're talking 1878.

So we're not the first ones to come across this, and I think it's good for us as American Buddhists to realize the whole Buddhist history, but also to begin to find out about our own Buddhist history.

The next phase that I want to jump to is a chapter that I call "The White Buddhists." The White Buddhist was a name given to Colonel Henry Steel Olcott who was, along with Madame Blavatsky, founder of the Theosophical Society. Now we're talking around 1890.

I won't go into too much detail about the Theosophical Society but people probably know that Madame Blavatsky was one of the great forerunners of what looks like New Age thought now. She was investigated at one point by the Psychic Society in England and they said, Well, we don't think she's really in touch with these masters and we don't think she's a total fraud, but she's certainly one of the greatest imposters that the world has ever seen.

But the person I'm interested in is Colonel Henry Steel Olcott, who met her in America and joined up with her in forming the Theosophical Society. She and Olcott went to Sri Lanka, or Ceylon as it was called then, and they actually took refuge in the Buddha, Dharma, and *sangha,* thus becoming the first, as far as I could tell, Americans to actually take that step. They didn't do it here in America. The Sinhalese at that time had been colonized, first by the Portuguese and then by the English, and the English had virtually outlawed Buddhism. You couldn't be married as a Buddhist and if you wanted to go to school, you had to go to English schools, and Olcott became very involved in the struggle of the Sinhalese Buddhists for freedom, as Blavatsky did in India, in terms of reviving Indian pride in their tradition and fighting for independence.

So early on there was a kind of joining of American anticolonialist tendencies with the anticolonial struggle in Asia. And Henry Olcott, among other things, in Ceylon wrote a book called *The Buddhist Catechism.* (To show you how karma works, a gentleman here named Fernando, who works with Jon

Kabat-Zinn, came up to me. He also works with the Theosophical Society here in Boston, where they have a copy, a very old copy—he's also a book collector—of *The Buddhist Catechism*. It's dated 1910. This is the forty-third edition of this book, which is still in print and is still a pretty good book.)

In the introduction to the Catechism, Olcott suggested that the word *Buddhism* itself was only a Western term. "Buddha Dharma," he said, "was the best name for it." Nor should it be thought of as a religion. "The Sinhalese Buddhists," he wrote,

have never yet had any conception of what Europeans imply in the etymological construction of the Latin root of this term. In their creed, there is no such thing as a "binding" in the Christian sense, a submission to or merging of self in a Divine Being.

Unlike Blavatsky, who looked to India and the masses for inspiration, it seems clear that Olcott had begun to view the world through Buddhist eyes.

By the way, when Blavatsky and Olcott sailed from America to India, they left the Theosophical Society under the care of Abner Doubleday, the founder of baseball— a more American thing you could not imagine! So I just wanted to show you that this has been a part of our culture and continues to be.

In Sri Lanka, Blavatsky and Olcott met a person named Dharmapala, who was a young, revolutionary Sinhalese who had been

thrown out of school and whipped for taking off Wesak, the day of Buddha's birth, as a holiday. He had responded to his English schoolmasters by memorizing almost the whole Bible and coming up with Buddhist arguments against it.

He was an amazing man and he came to the World Parliament of Religions in Chicago in 1893, which was another big watershed in American Buddhist history. He was a very handsome layperson, and called himself Anagarika, which means "homeless." He had long black hair and a black beard and flashing eyes and all the ladies fell in love with him. He was a very effective speaker. He said,

Now history is repeating itself. Twenty-five centuries ago India witnessed an intellectual and religious revolution which culminated in the overthrow of monotheism, priestly selfishness, and the establishment of a synthetic religion, a system of life and thought which was appropriately called Dharma, philosophical religion. All that was good was collected from every source and embodied therein and all that was bad was discarded. The tendency of enlightened thought of the day all the world over is not toward theology, but philosophy and psychology. The barque of theological dualism is drifting into danger.

This was his sort of challenge. Well, it turned out that somebody in the audience heard him speak, a man named Strauss, a New York businessman. He received the three refuges—which is more or less what marks your becoming a Buddhist, taking refuge in Buddha, Dharma, and *sangha*—in Chicago, in 1893 and, as far as I can tell, that was the first time on American soil that somebody had become a Buddhist.

At that same conference there was a monk from Japan, Soyen Shaku, who was a very great Zen master. He had read for them a talk that he had written which had been translated back in Japan by D.T. Suzuki. It was a talk, interestingly enough, on cause and effect in Buddhism, one of Buddhism's crucial tenets.

Also in Chicago was a man named Paul Carus, who was a publisher in Illinois. He heard this talk and got to know Soyen Shaku. Paul Carus then wrote a book called *The Gospel of Buddha* and invited D.T. Suzuki to come to Illinois to work with him in his publishing house.

Through that connection you can see the lineage being handed on: D.T. Suzuki arrived in Chicago around 1911 and spent many years in Illinois translating books. He did a translation of the *Tao Te Ching* and began his career as the foremost interpreter of Buddhism in America.

I want to just close up with the 1950s and the whole Beat movement—people like Gary Snyder, who went to Japan to study, Allen Ginsberg, and Philip Whalen, who [became] active Buddhists. And Jack Kerouac, because for me the book that he wrote called *The Dharma Bums* totally ruined my life. I could have been a lawyer.

The day after *The Dharma Bums* was published, Kerouac, Ginsberg, and Peter Orlovsky were on their way to an elegant penthouse party in honor of Kerouac's new novel, when Kerouac stepped into a phone booth and called up D.T. Suzuki. Kerouac said he'd like to stop by for a visit and Suzuki asked when he wanted to come by. "RIGHT NOW!" Kerouac yelled into the receiver, and Suzuki said "O.K.."

Kerouac, Ginsberg, and Orlovsky (Suzuki was teaching at Columbia at this time) all trooped over to the brownstone on West 94th Street that Suzuki shared with the Okamuras, a Japanese-American family he was staying with.

"I rang Mr. Suzuki's door and he did not answer," Kerouac wrote in a reminiscence published in the *Berkeley Bussei,* the magazine of the Berkeley Buddhist Association, in 1960.

—suddenly I decided to ring it three times, firmly and slowly, and then he came—he was a small man coming slowly through an old house with panelled wood walls and many books—he had long eyelashes, as everyone knows, which put me in the mind of the saying in the Sutras that the Dharma, like a bush, is slow to take root but once it has taken root it grows huge and firm and can't be hauled up from the ground except by a golden giant whose name is not Tathagata—anyway, Doctor Suzuki made us some green tea, very thick and soupy—he had precisely what idea of what place I should sit, and where my two other friends should sit, the chairs already arranged—he himself sat behind a table and looked at us silently, nodding—I said in a loud voice (because he had told us he was a little deaf) 'Why did Bodhidharma come from the West?"—He made no reply—He said, "You three young men sit here quietly & write haikus while I go make some green tea."—He brought us the green tea in cracked old soupbowls of some sort— [They were probably like priceless T'ang-dynasty teabowls.] He told us not to forget about the tea—when we left, he pushed us out the door, but once we were out on the sidewalk he began giggling at us and pointing his finger and saying, "Don't forget the tea!"—I said, "I would like to spend the rest of my life with you."—He held up his finger and said

"Sometime."

So anyhow, it goes on and on. This book is filled with the humanity—the story of Buddhism which is, after all, the story of people practicing.

This new edition contains a kind of new ending where I talk about the disillusionment that Buddhism seemed to be going through. During the sixties, when people started meditating, perhaps under the influence of LSD and other things, there was the idea that you could have this explosive enlightenment experience and that would pay all the bills. After that everything would be fine and you wouldn't have any problems.

Many of us in the years since have discovered that it doesn't really work like that. It's actually much more interesting! So that kind of disillusionment, I think, is part of the maturing of the Dharma that is already going on—realizing that it is really about living life in a different way as a Buddhist, or as a full human being. There are all these different forms of Buddhism in this country and everybody's saying, What is American Buddhism going to be like? Is it going to be a combination of everything?

One of the things that I said in the end of the new edition is that whatever the shape taken, the shining, well-worn goal of the Buddhist teaching remains the same, the four noble truths, the fact of suffering, its origin, cessation, and the path and the practice that puts it all into practice again and again and again.

Toward the Mainstreaming of American Dharma Practice

Dr. Jon Kabat-Zinn

IN 1979, JON KABAT-ZINN AND HIS COLLEAGUES FOUNDED the Center for Mindfulness, Medicine, Health Care, and Society at the University of Massachusetts Medical Center in Worcester, Massachusetts. This program is based on the use of meditation and Dharma practice by people who are ill or in need of help with coping with the stresses and difficulties in their lives. With the American medical profession often closed-minded about "nontraditional" approaches to healing, Dr. Kabat-Zinn first designated the clinic a "stress-reduction and relaxation program," but, from its inception its key medicine has been Dharma practice and meditation.

Throughout the Buddhism in America conference, speakers and workshop members made reference to the work of colleagues. Few names arose as often as Jon Kabat-Zinn's, in part because of the longevity and recognition of his work, but also because his work at UMass Medical Center crosses over into so many different areas of contemporary life, whether social or spiritual, and affects thousands of individuals. As Lama Surya Das said: "Jon Kabat-Zinn is an example of an American Dharma-farmer...bodhisattva or something very, very special....We can rejoice that there are people like him around, fearlessly taking the Dharma out into the world for the benefit of all....That is what Jon is doing with this work: taking this pure, pure, pure teaching—Dharma teaching; practice teaching; heartfelt, altruistic, service-oriented, spiritual teaching—out of the Buddhist ghetto, out of the Buddhist languages, out of the highest religious context...[and] spiritually contributing to the world. And not just to the world (all beings), but to individual people at...places where people with real suffering, not just our leisure-class sufferings, go."

In addition to his work at UMass Medical Center, Dr. Kabat-Zinn is author of the widely read books, *Full Catastrophe Living* and *Wherever You Go, There You Are*. His most recent publication, written in collaboration with his wife Myla, is *Everyday Blessings: The Inner Work of Mindful Parenting*.

W hat I'm most interested in is the use of Buddhist meditative practices, as opposed to spreading Buddhism, if you will.* There was a time that I considered myself to be a Buddhist, but I actually don't consider myself to be one now, and although I teach Buddhist meditation, it's not with the aim of people becoming Buddhist. It's with the aim of them realizing that they're buddhas. There's a huge distinction, and so I prefer to think in terms of Dharma as opposed to terms of Buddhism per se, because it generates a lot of confusion. The sense is that Buddhism, as I understand it, particularly through its meditative practices, is pointing to something that has to do with the fundamental nature of being human. And it doesn't have anything to do with where you were born, or what color your skin is, or what your belief system is.

I think that's one of the reasons that Buddhism is becoming such a major force in the Western world. I was leafing through Christopher Titmus's book *The Green Buddha* and found that he had dedicated it to the welfare, happiness, and liberation of all beings. But interestingly enough, he has a whole list of people who said something or other about Buddhism. I'll just cite a few. H. G. Wells said, "Buddhism has done more for the advancement of world civilization than any

other influence in the chronicles of mankind." Arthur Schopenhauer the philosopher: "If I am to take the results of my study as the standard of truth, I should be obliged to concede to Buddhism the preeminence over the rest." T. S. Eliot: "I am not a Buddhist, but some of the early Buddhist scriptures affect me as parts of the Old Testament do." Carl Jung said, "As a student of comparative religion, I believe that Buddhism is the most perfect one the world has seen."

Of course these are all opinions, and as Buddhist practitioners, we all know what we can do with opinions. Albert Einstein said, "The religion of the future will be a cosmic religion"—remember that this is Einstein speaking; he has a very, very special place in the domain of science—"The religion of the future will be a cosmic religion. It should transcend a personal god and avoid dogma and theology. Buddhism answers this description. If there is any religion that would cope with modern scientific needs, it would be Buddhism."

Aldous Huxley said, "I shall say again and again that between Buddhism and modern science there exists a close intellectual bond." I was so struck by that, I thought I'd just open the talk with it.

My work at the UMass Medical Center, in the stress-reduction clinic, started in 1979. I was there doing molecular genetics and gene cloning and muscle-development research for three years before that—in another lifetime. But I was looking for a way to bring my meditation practice and my work together: right livelihood. I felt like there was a sort of balance in family life, balance in relationships at that point in my life,

---

*The first day of the conference, Dr. Kabat-Zinn worked with a group of participants in a day-long workshop. He later presented a keynote address; both sessions dealt with his work at the Center for Mindfulness, Medicine, Health Care, and Society. Since the keynote sketched an outline that was fleshed out in the workshop, text from the keynote here precedes that from the workshop.

but there was a deep yearning to bring my practice into my work in such a way that, as I put it at the time, they would pay me to meditate all the time. That has backfired to some degree.

But, the surgeon general's report in 1979 noted that, among other things, as much as half of U. S. mortality in 1976 was due to unhealthy behavioral lifestyles; 20 percent to environmental factors. Around the same time, René DuBois observed that human health transcends purely biological health because it depends primarily on those conscious and deliberate choices by which we select our mode of life and adapt creatively to it's experiences. And the key word here is *adaptation*.

I'm telling you these things because I'm going to try, in painting this picture, to give you a sense of how the Dharma perspective might influence some aspect of mainstream—in this particular case, science, medicine, health, and health care. I am looking for an opportunity or an interface and a connection between languages, so that some kind of larger connection might become apparent and both a need and an opportunity for something to emerge, for something to happen, for a receptivity that might not have been seen before.

One of the themes of my talk is going to be that, if you are interested in bringing Dharma not simply into the unfolding of your own daily life—which is a huge enough undertaking, costing not less than everything—but in some way bringing into the domain of right livelihood a social action, working with what I call the full catastrophe

of the planet or of the world, then we have to take a certain level of responsibility that I think is exactly what Peter Matthiessen was pointing to yesterday—the importance of taking individual responsibility for the totality. Meditate locally and then act globally.*

John Knowles, who was president of the Rockefeller Foundation, then became chief of Massachusetts General Hospital, noted about the same time, in 1979, that the next major advances in health of the American people will come from the assumption of individual responsibility for one's own health, and a necessary change in lifestyle for the majority of Americans. Well, you know that meditation practice is the biggest lifestyle change that is really possible. It transcends diet, it transcends exercise, it transcends everything. Because it influences everything. But to just plunk your body down and spend an hour every day practicing nondoing, in terms of lifestyle change for the mainstream, is fairly un-American. There's a fundamental lifestyle change, and I believed back then and still do, that it actually is catalytic for all sorts of other secondary, or second-order lifestyle changes, like diet and exercise and so forth.

I quip with Dean Ornish—he has his people on that 8-percent-fat diet to reverse coronary artery disease and of course they practice meditation and yoga—and I like to say, Well, they would have to practice meditation and yoga to stay on an 8-percent-fat diet in the United States. Because when you

---

*See Matthiessen's keynote address, "The Coming of Age of American Zen," pages 396–406.

practice, then you know why you're doing it, and it's not just to reduce your coronary artery blockage. That might work for a little while but there are far more fundamental yearnings and motives that can be tapped through meditation practice.

I want to a make a connection between the words *stress* in English and our general concept of it in this society, and the Buddhist concept of *duhkha*. If you want to teach meditation in the mainstream, you have to find some kind of pull. If you created a clinic for Buddhist meditation, it's not very likely that you'd reach the people that you wanted to reach. And it's not very likely you'd get to do it in the hospital or any other institution in mainstream society. But if you call it stress reduction and then you practice Buddhist meditation, there's no problem at all.

Now, people ask, Well, what do you do in a stress reduction? Oh we meditate, we do some yoga. That makes sense. But if you called it the Yoga Meditation Clinic, every-body would laugh and throw you out. So, it's not like there is some fundamental reason that these things can't be done.

I've always used the term *meditation*. I teach Buddhist meditation—then I put in parentheses "without the Buddhism." That's for people who don't know anything about Buddhism. For people who know something about Buddhism, I just say I teach Buddhist meditation. The cultural and ideological over-lays, and the historical elements of it, beauti-ful and honorable and wonderful as they are, are not necessarily the heart of the Dharma, which transcends them. Therefore, this offers an opportunity for us to tease out, or invite,

the emergence of what we might call American Dharma.

We have no idea what that would be, but the chances are it's not going to be Buddhist, in the small-minded idea of Buddhism. I think what the people Christopher Titmus quotes are saying is that there's something about Buddhism that is fundamentally different from the other reli-gions—leaving aside Hinduism and the yoga tradition—that is so profoundly universal because it speaks to a lawfulness that is as lawful as $e = mc^2$; or Newtonian physics. That it is verifiable for oneself and you don't need to believe anything, you just need to try it— a condition of complete simplicity costing not less than everything.

So, you have to have a big, wide funnel, and stress pulls people. We have signs up in the hospital saying *Stress Reduction*, with an arrow, and people kind of follow them in a hypnotic trance. "I could use that, you know." "Oh, stress reduction, what is that?" It's not just the patients; it's everybody who works in the place.

And then we tell people that it's stressful to take the stress-reduction program, but that seems to be okay. You can work with paradox: "You want stress reduction? Well it doesn't come in pill form." A lot of people think they don't have time. A lot of the resi-dents say this because they don't have any time—they don't have any life—they're working all the time, staying up all the time, treating patients after thirty-six hours of not sleeping. So they ask, Just give me the essence. Give it to me quick, because I don't have any time. And we say, Well, there is not a magical pill that can do this for you and if there were, clearly it would be illegal and you couldn't even write yourself a prescription.

So we have come to call what we do mindfulness-based stress reduction. We did not call it that at the beginning, but now we're in our eighteenth year of doing this, and so we're trying to move the bell-shaped curve along, and our vocabulary changes as the world changes. This whole talk is basically the product of a very small number of people working extremely hard because of a commitment that goes far beyond the fact that we're employees of the UMass Medical Center. In fact, I like to say that I'm a nonemployee of the UMass Medical Center. I work for Dharma, but they just happen to cut my paycheck. But I don't make a distinction between "they" and "Dharma"—it's all one, and so things unfold, and in interesting ways.

I don't do this work alone, as I was saying. I have a wonderful group of very fine and committed colleagues who do a great deal of the teaching and research, the professional training and so forth. When the Moyers program featured our clinic, although they filmed a lot of other people, in the editing process they made it look as if I just did everything by myself. And so it's very hard sometimes to get the media to understand that this is not a one-person operation. And rather than focusing on the person, what we will really want is for people to understand that the focus is on the practice in the deeper sense of the word.

That's on-going and it requires an awful lot of work to shift things so that they stop making some person into the focus, which is a major problem in all of this kind of work. Whether you're focusing on the Buddha or Mother Theresa, the Dalai Lama, or projecting onto this lama or this guru, it means big trouble for Americans. And I don't want any part of it, but you have to be ready to deal with all sorts of projections, when you put yourself out there in a certain way, and say Yes, we do this stuff. It happens with the patients all the time. I work overtime and so do my colleagues to sort of reflect all those projections onto us. He's so calm—Mr. Stress Reduction. Mr. Relaxation. That's horseshit. It's just not true, as my children or my wife could tell you.

Over the course of the past eighteen years, this stuff has actually spread, through various ways. People have become inspired from what a small number of people who are deeply, deeply committed to practice have done. I don't even ask and I don't know whether my colleagues—and there are about twenty people who work in the Center for Mindfulness—are Buddhist or not. I've never even thought to ask them. All I want to know is that they are deeply grounded in Buddhist meditative practice, particularly in mindfulness practice. We have ways of finding out how deeply grounded they are, but it's hard to measure—it's not something where it's just your chronology, or history, or where you sat on retreat. It has to do with something far deeper and more intangible in order to be able to stand in any place and convey the heart of Dharma practice in a way that someone else, who's not particularly on your wavelength, could hear.

This has been spreading out, and I like the image of Indra's net—Peter Matthiessen mentioned that yesterday, too. We actually have put out a newsletter among the professionals who are doing this kind of thing, called "Indra's Net." We took the logo from an Italian group that also has a magazine called *Indra's Net.* The notion is that there's no center. That it's just a kind of web of interconnectedness, which is actually a reflection of the deepest universal web of interconnectedness that the scientists, the quantum physicists, speak about and also that Buddhists understand through direct experience.

So the heart of the work that we do is mindfulness. And it's not like we're trying to disguise Buddhism and sneak it in. We're not talking about Buddhism, we're talking about mindfulness. It happens to be that mindfulness was most finely developed and refined on this planet, in this era, in the Buddhist tradition. There's an enormous domain of wealth and wisdom and understanding and topological maps for cultivating mindfulness and for understanding something about the mind. Now you might think about mindfulness, as we do, sort of casually, as moment-to-moment awareness.

I like to make the point that meditation is really about paying attention. There's nothing particularly magical or mystical about it—everybody is capable of paying attention—only it's gotten a bad reputation because when you stare out the window in the second grade, and the teacher catches

you at it, what does she yell at you? So, we have to begin again with our understanding of tension.

[Showing a slide of a Buddha statue] This comes out of the Buddhist tradition, but people might be interested to know that in some fundamental way, this statue or other artistic representations of a similar kind, don't actually represent the deity, although in some traditions they're spoken of that way. But the fundamental representation here is of a state of mind, and that state of mind is best characterized by this word: *awake.* All of a sudden everybody goes, "Oh, I didn't know that. Well that makes sense," and there's no more barrier.

So what do we mean by this? "I'm awake." Well, in the view of the meditative traditions, what we call our everyday state of mind, waking mind, the meditators consider that to be a profound state of sleep—that we're sleepwalking through life—robotlike, more hypnotic-trancelike than awake. And when you begin to really attend the on-going emergence of moments and mind, body formations and thought formations, it's moment to moment. You realize that we are just virtually not at home a great deal of the time. Even as you sit here listening to me. Buddhists are not immune to that. In fact, Buddhists might be more at risk for that, because it's so hard to be in touch with beginner's mind. So, the potential is that we can actually go on automatic pilot—as you all know from meditation practice—and for years at a time, decades at a time, have children and not even see them. Be married to somebody and wake one day and say, How did I get here? Who are you? It's the wrong question to be asking. So we can be quite unconscious and the implication of that is that you may never be where you actually are. When you realize this, it can be a hell of a rude awakening, no matter how old you are chronologically.

Blaise Pascal said—and I like to evoke authorities from the Western culture in talking about this so that it's not just seen as some kind of subtle way of turning everybody into some kind of Asianphile—Pascal said in *Pensées*, "All of man's difficulties are caused by his inability to sit quietly in a room by himself." So the idea of asking medical patients who are under a great deal of stress or pain, or who have cancer, heart disease, AIDS, chronic pain, to just be still is a huge thing to ask of somebody. And of course you can't force somebody to be still, so you have to ignite some kind of passion in them for stillness.

Now Pascal was like a genius of the second order, so he really understood this. A genius of the first order is described by Feynman, who was himself a genius of the second order, as somebody that you get the feeling you would be just like if only you were a tiny bit smarter, or stayed up later at night. But a genius of the second order, there's just no contest. You don't even think about it. And, of course, the Buddha is like that.

And then you realize that that's true for all of us. Actually that is our true nature. And the impediments to that emerging in the unique way that is each one of ours—there's a unique aspect to our true nature, we're not just all one and all the same—what those impediments are is part of the work of liberation. To actually see that we create them, for the most part, for ourselves. We create them for our children as well. It's not necessary to do that, and by practicing non-doing—just nonharming, noninterfering—that genius can emerge. That's the orientation we take toward our patients—Oh, another genius has arrived. Well what form do you come in?

Thoreau said in *Walden*—and if you haven't read *Walden* recently, go back and read the whole thing; it's a rhapsody of mindfulness—"I went to the woods because I wished to live deliberately, to front only the essential facts of life and see if I could not learn what they had to teach, and not when I came to die discover that I had not lived." That's that risk of being on automatic pilot: You think you know what you're doing. You think you know what you're doing and have got a tremendous rationale for it all. And sometimes, late at night, or when things have just reached an impasse, or you're just on the verge of breaking down, you *will* break down and you'll say Yeah, I don't know what the fuck is happening. I have no idea what's happening. And I've been so unconscious that even the good things that I've done are tainted in some way by the fact that I don't even know. That's a wonderful place to touch, because then we can begin to be honest with ourselves.

That's what the practice is really about. It's clear seeing, clear understanding, clear comprehension, bare attention, and naming things as they are to the extent that we're capable of it, in this moment, and then moving on. And if we ever hope for the future to be different, the only time that we ever have to fool around with the future is now, because this is the last moment's future. So if we want the next moment to be different, the only way we can have it be different is to stand in this moment and hold it in a way that is more seeing, more knowing, less imposing, and less caught up in thinking and opinions.

In the *New York Times*, when Martha Graham died at age ninety-six, they had this wonderful obituary. She said "All that is important"—speaking about dance—"all that is important is this one moment in movement. Make the moment vital and worth living. Do not let it slip away unnoticed and unused."

When I give this kind of talk to a medical audience, they have moments, just like everybody else. A surgeon: Oh, I don't have moments; I'm just a surgeon. Nonsense! They have bodies; they have feelings. Everybody is the same in that regard. And no one's paying attention to the store, to the apparatus. It's one of the Buddha's great gifts, and yoga's great gifts. Start paying attention to the apparatus. If you want to play the violin, you have to tune it.

And meditation is everywhere. It's in bubble-gum wrappers [reading from a bubble-gum wrapper]:

—"What are you up to, Mort?"
—"Practicing meditation. It fills me with inner peace. After two minutes, my mind is a complete blank."
—Gee, and I thought he was born that way.

It's a totally erroneous view of meditation, and it's very, very common. You sit down, you make your mind completely blank, you know, it's cheaper than a lobotomy, and then you're there. A totally erroneous view of meditation, but it's out there. It's out there and it can be worked with.

And then so is yoga. The eight-year-olds know all about it. Jung said, speaking about Zen, "All the same, the psychotherapist who is seriously concerned with the question of the aim of his therapy cannot remain unmoved when he sees the end toward which this Eastern method of psychic healing, 'i.e., making whole,' is striving."

So back in 1979, the question was: If we set up a clinic based on relatively intensive training in Buddhist meditative practices, would anybody come? Would it be acceptable? Could we even pull it off in the hospital? Would it make any sense to people who are suffering from a wide range of things? But, what's a better place to teach Buddhadharma than in the hospital? The best places to go are the places that function as *duhkha* magnets in the society because Buddhist meditative practices have something to say about holding *duhkha* and using it, if you will, to participate in the potential for healing and for transformation. Taking individual responsibility and at the same time understanding the sanghic perspective and the collective mind and the collective heart is an extraordinary opportunity.

So the question is, Is this going to fly? You say, who knows? So we try it. We started it two days a week and I did everything—

phone calls, talking to doctors, everything—and then taught the class. So would it be acceptable to mainstream medical patients, to doctors, to hospital administrators? Would insurance cover it? At that time there were no HMOs, but now the big thing is can we get the HMOs to pay for it? Would it work for other ethnic groups? Or for people who are at the highest stress levels in this society. People who have the least, and who are exploited the most in our highly materialistic society that tends to discard people right and left—elderly, immigrants, minorities, women? Those were all questions that emerged over time.

We originally called it the stress-reduction and relaxation program, or SR&RP. In the Vipassana tradition, they speak about meditation courses—you go on a ten-day course or retreat, or a hundred-day retreat, or a thirty-day retreat—but they're spoken of as courses and they have certain elements that look like courses—teachers, and teachers teach, and they're residential. But, it occurred to me—actually it didn't occur to me, it came to me in a flash one afternoon sitting at IMS in the eleventh day of a retreat—that actually this model of a course on mindfulness could be used in other places. Instead of having people just live there, which is a great model, but for people who are busy and have children and hold down jobs and everything, maybe coming to a once-a-week course and having homework would be a good model.

So, in the stress-reduction clinic or a stress-reduction relaxation program, there's a clinic in the form of a course, and the course lasts for eight weeks. The commitment is to come to class once a week for two and a half or three hours at a time. There are thirty to forty people in the class and there's homework. This is the most stressful part. Aside from the lifestyle change of getting yourself to the class, to the hospital once a week, what's really stressful is this lifestyle change. You have to carve out a minimum of forty-five minutes a day, or more like an hour, to practice, at least six days a week. And we say we give you one day off for good behavior, recognizing that the mind's always going to play games: Well, I don't think I'll do it today. So we say, okay, there's one day you'll not do it. Even if you want to, don't do it. But you have to decide in advance what day that's going to be and stick with that, and then you do it, whether you like it or not. You don't have to like this, you just have to do it. And at end of the eight weeks, you can tell us how it was. But in the middle, if the mind says this is bullshit, I hate it, and I'm more tense than ever, or I'm not seeing anything, or my skin itches more, or I hate sitting still, we don't care. We just don't care. Just stay with it. (And I'm just speaking for myself; my colleagues do it their way.) There's no one way to do this and there are plenty of wrong ways to do this, but there are plenty of right ways to do it, too. People love to be challenged in that way.

Then there's an all-day session, which is in the form of a seven- or eight-hour silent mediation retreat on a Saturday or Sunday.

And there are individual interviews. So we speak with everybody at least twice: once before the program, once after the program. They're modeled on Zen interviews—although we don't call them Zen interviews; we don't sit in robes—but they are an opportunity to really be mindful. We try to create a culture where, from the moment you call a patient on the phone and someone answers and says, "Hello," that's when the teaching starts. And it doesn't matter whether you're a secretary, or an interviewer, or whether you're the greatest teacher in the world, or whether you're a researcher, you hold that present moment and the sacred quality of that interaction, or you're not doing your job.

The whole idea is that the work and practice are not two; and life and practice and work, they're not three. It's all one whole. And that's a high standard to hold oneself to. But it seems to me that there just is no other way to do this work. To use any other way would be dishonoring the true nature of both yourself and the other person, and what's the point of working in the domain of the buddha fields or mindfulness if you're not willing to hold that? Of course you forget and mess up right and left, but that's not a problem, as long as you're willing to come back and to own what's happening.

So it's a clinic, as I said, in the form of a course, and the foundation of the course is mindfulness practice. It's not to make people into good meditators or turn them into Buddhists covertly or overtly. The unifying theme is cultivating mindfulness in daily living.

In other words, transforming the quality of the day. In fact, Thoreau said in *Walden*, "To effect the quality of the day, that is the highest of arts." And the next-to-the-last line in *Walden* is, "Only that day dawns to which we are awake." So it's not to make people into good meditators, although that's an occupational hazard, or a side effect, of getting involved in this kind of work, but what we're really shooting for is being more present in one's life, no matter what's happening.

The context of the course, the language that we use, because you can't use a Buddhist vocabulary for this, is how to take better care of yourself; how to live more skillfully and more fully; how to move toward greater levels of health and well-being. And of course, no one knows how to do that, so it's an exploration, but we know something about it.

And it's a complement to medical treatment, not a substitute for it. So if you have headaches, we don't let people come to the stress clinic to meditate away their headaches without getting a full neurological medical workup. We're not into meditating away your brain tumor. We do work with people with brain tumors, but they have to go through the medical system first. We're not the front-line treatment, if you will. But we're a vital complement to what's possible in health care and in the hospital.

I like to point out that there's a very unusual model. The medical and psychiatric model, and rightfully so, is based on years of scientific research and the careful attempt to move away from voodoo and witchcraft and spiritualism and all sorts of things that have no basis in the scientific framework. So they have spent years developing specific biologically based treatments for specific problems. And then these Western medical doctors send their patients to a stress-reduction clinic, and what do we do? Whether you have headaches or chronic pain, AIDS or heart disease, gastrointestinal problems, high blood pressure, coronary-bypass surgery, or just general levels of stress, panic disorder, we put everybody in the same room and do one thing with them. Now, from the medical/ psychiatric model, that's insane—I just want to name that—because you have to be willing to take responsibility for being crazy to do this work.

Which reminds me of a story about Sahn Sunim, whom I studied with for a while. Someone once came to the Zen center and asked a question—and you know, there are a lot of people who come to the Zen centers and the various meditation centers, and they're maybe a little more unbalanced in life than other people who might not be coming to the Zen center. That's not to say that everyone who comes to the Zen center is that way! But he looked at this guy after he asked the question—I don't remember what the question was—and he sort of rubbed his bald head, and said, "You're crazy! You're crazy!" And he was right! But everybody's like, Whoa, what a socially incorrect thing to say! And then he said, "But you not crazy enough!" He had this wonderful Korean way of speaking. "You not crazy enough!" And I think that's a good teaching for us medita-

tors, that we have to be willing not only to be crazy, but to be really crazy. And really crazy might actually approach sanity in an insane world.

So we don't cede the high ground to people who are in trouble or who are experiencing *duhkha,* because there is not one of us that is not experiencing *duhkha,* not living right inside it. And if we say, "Oh, no, that's for the people over there, the patients, they have the problems, I'm okay; I'm just a great meditator." Horseshit. And the problem isn't the "great meditator" part, the problem is the pronoun "I." When you connect them up, there's a definite problem.

So in the mindfulness-based stress-reduction model, we take mixed groups and we work with them all, doing one thing. But we're paying attention to what they have in common, which is they all walk in breathing. It's amazing, there's not one single person that comes in that's not breathing; there's not one single person that comes in that doesn't have a body; there's not one single person that comes in that doesn't have feelings; there's not one single person that comes in that does not have thought formations that appear in the mind. Well, those are the four foundations of mindfulness. We can work with that. And it doesn't matter what the body is, how old it is, what it's ravaged by, whether it's missing an arm or a leg or a breast, or whether it comes in a wheelchair or whether it's paralyzed from the neck down. Because we work with the one thing that is in some way the final common pathway of what it means to be human. And that's, I think, why Buddhism is so fundamental—it points right there.

It's very hard to talk about, to put it into words. But we try. And to put it into words that don't depend on some 2,500-year-old tradition whose vocabulary is not appropriate in the setting that you're working in, and may actually be a barrier to your own understanding, because if you're using other people's words, you still haven't got it!

But we do pay individual attention to people and try, as best we can, to listen to where people are in their lives. That's not just like an assembly line. You don't just come on in and we just make you into a meditator and we don't care what's the matter with you. That sometimes happens in the meditative tradition. They don't want to hear about the drama, don't give me your melodrama, don't give me your story. I don't want to hear it. Just breathe in, breathe out, let go. What's the matter with you? Can't let go of that one? Can you hear the violence in that?

But that has a current. We need to look at the dark side of our own attachments to our traditions and everything else. And all of us, all the time, it's not like it's something you get over as you get older. So we really try to listen. And as much as possible, we make suggestions for how they can work with the practice individually so that it's sculpted, tailored to what their needs are. Of course, everybody can't do yoga. I mean, if the back doesn't work, there's lots of things you can't do. Sometimes sitting for forty-five minutes is absolutely impossible.

We start people lying down on the floor. Sacrilege! You can't meditate lying down! Look at all the Buddha statues that are lying down. Well, he's different—he's the Buddha. Of course, falling asleep is an occupational hazard if you're lying down.

Now, we see meditation as a way of being. *Not* as a technique. That's another thing in this society, in the mainstream: They think meditation's a technique. It's like relaxation. You meditate, you get into The Meditative State, and then you're home free. Your mind's a blank, or you're just cosmic love or compassion, or whatever it is. Like, throw the switch, you're there. No problem. That's so far off!

Meditation is a way of being. It's a way of life. Practice is not like a rehearsal. This is not a technique. This is always the performance, this life. And in Western medicine and psychotherapy and psychology, a lot of people are trained: See one, do one, teach one. So you go through a little workshop for five days or three days, you learn the technique, then you do it on other people for the rest of your life. Do you do it yourself? No, I don't need it. I've got it. I don't need it. I only practice my breathing when I'm stressed.

You see, one of the other things that Buddhism and Taoism and yoga really contribute is the notion of the way, of a path, of a life path. It's not like we're doing this because we're stressed, or we're doing this because we're upset, or we're feeling panicky so we attend to our breathing. We do it because we're alive. And because it's interesting to ask what it means to be human.

Whether we're feeling good, bad, ugly, indifferent, old, young, fat, thin. Doesn't matter. Because we're alive.

Now, if you relate to somebody that way, can you feel how they get right away that you don't care that they're fat? It's just irrelevant. Who are you? Who *are* you? Not for me; I don't care who you are. Do *you* have any idea who you are? I'm busy enough trying to find out who I am. So we've all got our work cut out for us. And no one's higher than anybody else. When people hear that, they say, God, I feel like how did I find this place? (Our practice is to walk out of the hospital at five o'clock at night or whenever it is, with at least as much energy and freshness as when you walked in. That's part of the practice.) But you hear these stories, and they're just unbelievable. And I like to say to people, "I don't know if this will be of any use to you at all. On the other hand, I think you've come to the right place." Because at least here we're willing to work. And we're willing to work if you're willing to work. Otherwise, go someplace else. Most people say, Okay, I'll roll up my sleeves, and I'm going to do it. Without any attachment to outcome.

So having said that meditation's not a technique, of course, then we are free to use techniques, and we do—three formal meditation techniques, one of which is the body-scan sitting meditation (Hatha yoga). And we don't leave them on their own. There are guided audiotapes that they use as part of their homework, so that we gradually bring them up to forty-five minutes of silent sitting.

And we let them sit on chairs. They don't have to sit on zafus, but there are plenty of zafus if they want to sit on the floor. And since Moyers, we've made the interesting observation that more and more people coming to the first class get right down on the floor on the zafus. They don't want anything to do with the chairs. So I'm left to sit on the chair.

[Showing a slide of SR&RP group at UMass Medical Center] The first four men in this row are actually Catholic priests. We offered programs for the Worcester diocese for two years and there were enough priests that really wanted to do it, we said, "Fine, we'll do a class for you all by yourself." Which we usually don't do. We just throw everyone in together. But they came to the all-day session because it's silent, so even if their parishioners were there, no one could talk. So it worked out okay. But after eight weeks, they didn't want to stop, so we actually went eight months with the priests for two years. It was very, very moving, because, in the seminary, in the Catholic tradition, they spend so much time learning stuff that's not at all related to spirituality. Very often they get out of there and they just haven't been nourishing their own tradition and, interestingly enough, find this path in through Buddhist meditation practice taught by a nonbelieving Jew from New York, and a renegade Catholic.

[Showing another slide] This is an action shot of the body scan. Hatha yoga at night in the orthopedic corridor when we've got more classes going than we have spaces. We

just take over the orthopedic corridor, which seems quite fitting. And we do the Hatha yoga as a form of mindfulness practice. So these people are actually practicing just as if they were sitting. Moment to moment, what is going on in the mind and the body; with the breath; with, say, sensations in the hip or the back of the knee or the back of the neck or shoulders. Not trying to break through or get beyond your limit, but to actually attend to the full range of impulses, sensations, thoughts, feelings, at that place, and dwell there for a little bit of time with a certain amount of discomfort, if that's appropriate. Tremendously powerful.

Hatha Yoga, tai-chi, and chi gung are all consciousness disciplines—unbelievably powerful—and they provide tremendous tools for us to bring into the mainstream, because people don't even have a clue that we have these kinds of methodologies for accessing the deepest aspects of what it means to be human and, I might say, to retune the systems, the natural homeostatic pathways and mechanisms in the human body and the mind-body connection, for healing and for transformation and deep seeing. So you can have the experiences of transformation, deep seeing, at night, on the floor of the orthopedic corridor in the hospital. And people do.

This is in the inner-city clinic, directed by Fernando des Torrijos, and the Spanish-speaking class. Most of these people do not speak English, and it was interesting for us to ask, Is the cultural barrier too great to actually offer this kind of thing to people who don't speak English and who come from an entirely different culture? The answer is No. If it's taught right, if it's taught in a language that people can understand, they love it.

Many doctors, after they've been referring patients to the stress-reduction clinic, refer themselves and their families. And so we're having the ripples go out. You don't have to advertise, it just happens when something has a certain kind of authenticity and honesty and taps into something as powerful as Dharma. Do I have to use the word Dharma? You don't have to teach morality in the kind of Buddhist formulation. You just embody it, and everybody understands. It comes out of the practice, then it spills over—and we emphasize this enormously in the curriculum—into everyday life. That's what it's really about. In how you pour yourself a cup of coffee and how you say good morning and how you pass the butter and how you do the dishes. Whether you make eye contact with your children. And how you touch.

So the whole practice is being in touch, right through the day. And people get this, they just get it in spades, and it's very, very impressive. I never tire of seeing it. I've been doing this for eighteen years and my jaw is constantly dropping; I am just amazed that people will do this. It's got nothing to do with me or my colleagues—we're not doing this to them or for them—it's the Dharma unfolding, at least that's the only way I can express it. It's everywhere and in everybody, and when you create the right conditions, it emerges and "does itself" as long as you're willing to collaborate, to practice.

And it's taken its place in one of those emergences. When we started out in 1979, this field called behavioral medicine was just coming into being. I don't like behaviorism, behaviorist, any of that stuff, but it seemed like there was an interface in what they were saying and what we were saying. So now, in the late nineties, it's become mind-body medicine, and there's a field called mind-body medicine within medicine, and meditation has a huge place in it. People are getting more and more of an understanding that meditation is not relaxation. It's not a little breathe in, breathe out, left nostril, right nostril, etc. It's about the deepest aspects of understanding that are possible, and compassion, and self-compassion. People come out of the stress-reduction clinic saying, "Wow, I just thought I was coming to get a little relaxation, to learn a little how to deal with my stress. I had no idea. This is the deepest thing I've ever experienced." I just like to smile and say, "Well, isn't that interesting."

We also do research. We're doing studies on healing and the effect of the mind on healing. [Showing slide] This chart concerns psoriasis; the meditators seem to be clearing a lot faster, which is a cost-saving because they're reducing their treatments by a factor of about a third. And that's true for two different kinds of ultraviolet-light treatments. We're looking at cost-effectiveness, at fundamental mechanisms, at the breast (women with early-stage breast cancer). We're collaborating with the MacArthur Foundation Mind-Body Network to look at fundamental neurobiological, neuroendocrine, and immune changes with mindfulness-based stress reduction in the work setting.

But make no mistake about it. None of those things are what it's really about. Those are just side effects of the deepest aspects of practice. When you teach, as best you can, from those deepest aspects of practice, which means teaching out of your own experience, out of your own practice, and not out of some ideas or some book—that's the authenticity that's required. Then we let the results, whatever they are, take care of themselves. And we practice, as best we can, nonattachment to outcome, nonstriving. Otherwise you're going to get interested in raising and lowering your blood pressure or raising and lowering your T-cell count, and that's delusion.

[Showing a slide with a circular diagram] In the past two years we've formed the Center for Mindfulness in Medicine, Health Care, and Society. It has a patient-care aspect, a research aspect, and an outreach (or education) aspect. Notice that mindfulness is at the heart of it, and then there's an administrative ring, and then there's emptiness. I like that formulation. This is a take-off on the *kalachakra* mandala. We're basically talking about what happens in the room. I try to use this as a teaching tool for health professionals, that the name of the game here is to get people into a room. That's the whole idea of the stress-reduction clinic. That's why you have secretaries and telephones and doctors that refer, and the health care system, and the hospital, and the whole *duhkha* field, and the whole buddha field—and going on to society and world, universe, employers, corporations, insurance, HMOs.—the whole idea is to get people into a room. Then there's a certain work that can be done in that room. If the people who take responsibility for it are up for it, and the invitation is the correct invitation, out of that things start to oscillate in every direction, and the whole world rotates in consciousness, in small ways that are not detectable but that are fundamental. If you allow anything to unfold or to become a tiny bit freer, less contracted in itself, the entire universe is already different. And when you hold that as part of your work and your practice, it tends to have its repercussions in the world.

So these are a few repercussions, aspects of Indra's Net. The ripples are going out now because we've stayed in one place for so long, just doing the one little thing that we do. A small number of highly dedicated people, who are dedicated more than anything else to their own Dharma practice and their own deep learning, part of which is the work with other people.

[In response to enthusiastic applause] The whole point of this talk is not to applaud this, although I appreciate the sentiment very much, but it's the notion that if each one of us took responsibility in a very small way for what we most yearn to do with our practice, can you imagine what the consequences of that would be? And that is already happening. We are doing it. So I think the applause is really for all of us. And I appreciate it very, very much.

[In the day-long workshop led by Dr. Kabat-Zinn, the participants explored many of their own personal reasons for their practices and the directions that they take. The morning session began with a brief period of sitting meditation, during which Dr. Kabat-Zinn directed the group.]

As you sit here, become fully embedded in this present moment with its myriad of aspects, perhaps grounded in the body and a sense of the breath moving, the sounds near and far, novel and familiar, perhaps of thoughts moving through the mind, perhaps more of expectation and excitement about being a part of this amazing, wonderful, calling process that this conferences is pointing to. In this moment of sitting here, with the meaning that it has for you in your life, and here in this room in this moment, what is it in its essence for us? And how might this in some way or other be introduced or presented to someone who has no relationship to this particular orientation toward life? What is understandable in all this? What is transmittable? What are the conditions for entry, for clear seeing, for dwelling in the unfolding of present moments with equanimity, with dispassion, with some degree of acceptance and self-compassion? How could you talk to your mother, father, brother, friend, or a stranger so that, if this might be of some value to them—and that's a big if—that the heart of it might be communicated? What would be skillful? Where would your blind spots most likely emerge? Where would your attachments to outcome lie?

What would the quality of your intention and motives be were you to try to communicate your love, your excitement for this way of being, to someone who may have no particular interest in meditation or sitting still or isms of any kind, but who may be hurting, lost, adrift, or out of touch?

Something propelled us to come here, and I'm very interested in that something because I don't think any of us are here by accident. There's a sense of some kind of calling or longing behind getting a body to go anywhere—and some of you have come from long distances. It gets us places where things may possibly emerge that might not emerge in that time and place if we're not there. We're constantly making decisions of this kind, so here we are. Wonderful.

I'm making some assumptions. I think it would be good to ask so that we have a sense of this, but I'm assuming that most people who would come to participate in a Buddhism in America conference already have a deep connection to what the Buddhists call practice. How many of you feel that you have a deep connection to practice? If you don't, that's not any less wonderful, it's just another feeling. But for me, it's exciting to participate in something where I get to work with people who come already with that feeling of a deep connection to practice, because usually I work in fields where people don't have that. They haven't the slightest idea what we mean by those words and part of my job is to try to ignite a certain kind of passion for silence, for still-ness, for reflection, for embodiment, for self-compassion, for wisdom.

This workshop is called "Toward the Mainstreaming of American Dharma Practice," so there are a bunch of problems right off the bat. What does mainstreaming mean? What does American mean? What does Dharma mean? What does practice mean?

We probably all have different ideas about that, so that's why this is a collective exploration. And it's not the mainstreaming, it's *toward* the mainstreaming, so there's a sense that something is happening, that we are in process. I may see this conference romantically, maybe erroneously, as a very important reflection of the something that's happening and in some way a marking of it, a celebration of it! This coming together in this way would not have happened twenty-five years ago. So something's happening and we're all part of it.

It's actually that we're all part of life and the celebration is not just Buddhism in America (because one is in a very dangerous territory to say anything about Buddhism). If you know anything about Buddhism you realize that as soon as you say something that draws a line, that differentiates this from that. Like, say, meditators—if you think, or if sometimes it happens that you find yourself thinking, as a meditator, then you no doubt think there are people who are meditators and people who aren't meditators. Or you might think, Well, there are Buddhists and then there's everybody else. You have to be very careful about those kinds of things because you could make distinctions that have some value, but you could get caught in them, get attached to, "I am a Buddhist." There's a very big problem with saying those words—not with the "Buddhist," but with the pronoun "I."

So what is the movement toward the mainstreaming of Dharma practice in America, and is Dharma practice the same as Buddhism? My own sense is that that is a very important and fundamental question to ask. The word *Dharma,* to me, is pointing to something that really is universal. The Buddha and others happen to penetrate deeply enough into experience of reality that they perceive certain relationships that just are— just like $e=mc^2$—just part of the way the universe presents itself. So is it, for instance, that desire itself contains the seeds of suffering? Is that Buddhist? Is it that if you're a Buddhist, desire creates suffering? Or is it just that desire has inside it a certain element of inevitable separation and suffering? I think that's really worth collectively exploring.

Part of my interest in being here is because I've had the absolute pleasure and privilege for the past eighteen years to work at trying to bring my sense of what Dharma practice means into various domains which, for lack of a better term, I'm calling mainstream. But these terms are very fluid and what was mainstream in 1979, when I started doing this kind of work, may not be mainstream today. People are suffering everywhere in one way or another and people are experiencing joy everywhere in one way or another. I'll put my prejudices right out

here in the beginning. There's some very, very deep value for more and more people on the planet to stop, ponder, be still, and look deeply into what it means to be human. That's my bias, and I think that I've not encountered anything more powerful in that process than what we call meditation.

Meditation is a vast term itself, but it is the pathway into the experiencing of life unfolding in the present moment and everything that comes out of that. I believe it to be incredibly valuable in our society and something that is literally a matter of life and death on an individual and social level. That's why I do the kind of work that I do. Understand that dialogue is, in some way, the outward collective manifestation of what we usually think of as individual meditation. So dialoguing together can itself be meditation. We can just hold the space together, and the thoughts, instead of coming up in one mind, will be coming up in one hundred minds. And when we hold these thoughts and watch them and relate to them in the way that is fearless and also selfless, we can step back a tiny bit from our positions, but still let the ideas flow.

I would like to start by having a dialogue that inquires about what we're doing here, who we are, and what it was that inspired us to be here for these three days of the conference. What is it? How does this fit with what you're doing, with your life, with your practice, with your values? Let's be honest and never mind whether we're being politically correct—Buddhistically politically correct or whatever! Let's just be who we are and see how that goes.

Participant: I work in a nursing home in a very, very conservative area with very conservative people....I teach there and tried doing a lecture on mindfulness meditation. It's a little teeny step. I brought in a speaker, also. I didn't tell anybody exactly what he was going to teach as I wanted to spread this message without alienating people.

Jon Kabat-Zinn: I tend to stay away from the word *spread* because it has inside of it something of an evangelical or messianic kind of connotation. Language is always a reflection of thought and what the thought process is. Sometimes I find writing is a fantastic meditation because you see this stuff go up on the screen and it's almost like you're meditating, but it's coming up on the screen of your mind and you're saying, My God, is that in there too? All the words individually make sense but then you ask, What's underneath this? What am I trying to say? And then you begin to see that the words—every one of them—stink. They're loaded. They have a certain odor to them. So we have to continually watch ourselves when words come up such as "spread the Dharma." Watch out! That's like an early warning signal, a great early warning signal. Is it I've got some great thing and now I'm going to spread it around?

This is not a criticism of you. This is a part of that collective inquiry, if you will. But we need to look at our words—I do it all the time. Now, if the Dharma is no-thing,

then spreading it is not possible. See, the Dharma already is everywhere so we don't need to spread it. That takes a lot less energy. If we're spreading something that doesn't need to spread because it's already there, then we're not doing the right work.

As we go along, if you don't mind, in a sort of playful spirit I will mirror back certain words so that we can selectively, in our dialogue/meditation, begin to see the ways in which the very thoughts that we have, however highly positive or sincere the merit behind them, come out of something much deeper—which is our own practice. So the only time that this work can be authentic is when it's coming from deep, deep within yourself, and you'll have to continually be suspicious. Otherwise we can get into various aspects of spreading, and it's done all the time in Buddhism.

One of the reasons I stopped being a Buddhist at a certain point was because I didn't want to be a lieutenant or a lieutenant colonel in a particular lineage, a particular Buddhist army, and because I understood Buddhism as being something much larger that was pointing to finding your own path. And sometimes, as part of your own path, you are part of armies or whatever, but sometimes not. So at different points we have to make decisions—as the Buddha himself said, be a light unto ourselves.

Participant: I do think the other side of the coin is to be aware of the larger picture. For example, I work with ethnic people in Chicago and go wherever I can to help them, as well as letting them know that I am involved in Buddhism. I think that political action for Buddhists is important without losing the core of the practice. We have to realize that we can also become a force, just as the Catholic Church has become, and this is very important for us to do because we're a humanist religion.

Jon Kabat-Zinn: I agree with you and I think there are an infinite number of paths for us to follow. Part of this inquiry, as far as I can see, is finding the path that is our own. Very often people that are like-minded will get together and move in a particular direction and that's unbelievably powerful. And other people will see it differently and move in other directions. Since the world is so multi-faceted, what might work in Chicago in the Asian immigrant population might not work in New York City with a Puerto Rican population. But if we're talking about Dharma as opposed to Buddhism, then how you show it, how you hold it, would in some way have to do with your awareness of what your ultimate commitments are and what is skillful in terms of working with them.

Participant: Before you can find your own path, don't you have to have some sort of training to start off with?

Jon Kabat-Zinn: In my own life trajectory that's one of the most staggering parts of this whole thing. It wasn't until I came in touch with Buddhism that I began to understand that life could actually be looked at as a jour-ney. That's in all the traditions, so there are many, many different ways to hold that, but the notion of a practice in which one could actually cultivate certain aspects of the mind and body came from Buddhism. I'm referring to mind in the Buddhist sense, the largest sense, which includes heart, spirit, and soul.

There's a certain kind of inner work that needs to be done and it's kind of like farming or cultivating and it takes a long time. It's not the usual American sort of thing where you just take a pill and you've got it. Or you go to a weekend workshop and whammo, it hits you and you've got it! This is long, hard, inner work with forces in one's own mind and life that are very often humiliating. Let's face it, it's just absolutely humiliating how much stuff is in there that seems to be exactly what we *don't* need. Nevertheless, it's there and we can admit it to ourselves.

So how could you possibly do this kind of work—let's say teach meditation? After going to a weekend workshop you could say, "Oh, yeah, I got it. I was with a Zen master for fifteen minutes and now I'm out there teaching." It's very seductive because that's a great job, being a meditation teacher! Everybody thinks you're terrific and they come and they bow to you in one way or another. Then you just say crazy things and everybody thinks it's fantastic. (I'm just joking, but it's true.)

What you're pointing to is extremely important. You can't possibly do this without standing in it yourself in some way that is not just making it up. It's coming out of a deep, deep tradition that passes on a way of being that requires training and that some people are very, very skilled at helping other people to develop. So we have to continually ask ourselves, What are we capable of doing *at this point?* And that's an absolutely essential part of the practice.

In psychology or in medicine there's an expression: *See one, do one, teach one.* OK, I've got it. Of course, you wouldn't want somebody to be operating on your heart the first time they'd seen one and then done one, but there is this notion that you learn the stuff and then you do the stuff on other people. This is very far from the Dharmic understanding, which is that first of all there is no end to the learning process and the only way you can work with anybody else is by working deeply with yourself. That takes years and years to understand. It's not like, "Oh, yeah, I used to meditate when I was under stress or when my life was a problem, but now I got that and I just teach it to other people because it's a useful skill." This treats meditation like a technique that you just plug in and do when you have a problem.

But the Dharmic view is that meditation is a way of being. It's not something you pull out when you're in trouble; it's a way to live. Yes, it can be very helpful when you're in trouble, but it also can be helpful at every other point in your life. That was entirely new to me, that there was actually a way of being that had an architecture, a topology, that had been mapped out in large part by other people, but that you had to verify for yourself. There was no taking any of it on somebody else's authority. You have to walk

the path and verify it for yourself. It's not head understanding or what you read in books. That makes for a very different kind of working.

Participant: I work in a factory setting where I teach people the sort of basic understanding about what it is to meditate and it's been incredible how much people have resonated with it. I have these rooms filled with people who, when they're not making golf balls, are meditating! I'm a neophyte and yet I know the reason I came here is because what I can do with these people is limited because of my own limitations…so I really hope to get something to enable me to take myself further and to therefore be more helpful to others.

Jon Kabat-Zinn: I think your insight is absolutely right on. We do not know what is possible but we do know the limits of what is possible, the most limiting aspect of which is the way in which we limit ourselves. So the cardinal principle is continual cultivating and deepening of our own practice, whatever that means. It doesn't necessarily mean that you have to go on a retreat for three years and then go back to the golf ball factory. To me, practice could include your work. If work is practice, then what is practice? When I sit over there in the morning, that's practice, but then when I go to work, then that's work. The reason I created my job was because I wanted my job to be my practice and it seemed easier to do by making it from scratch. But the principle applies no matter what your job is. You live it.

Participant: I'm a great example of twenty years of practice at having my practice and my job separate and I've just come to the conclusion that they need to be the same thing. I'm a management consultant and I do business and technology strategies for big companies. I'm here because I've made a decision to respond to what I see in my client. My observation is what organizations need to do to make profits seems to alienate the human beings in those organizations from growing in ways that get in the way of the organization achieving what they need to achieve.

Jon Kabat-Zinn: And do they know that?

Participant: I don't think so, although I'm heartened with the golf ball folks.

Jon Kabat-Zinn: I think they do know that. Many, many corporations are beginning to understand that.

Participant: I'm hoping they are and as I've been reading and thinking about this, I'm beginning to see that there are a lot of people who are. So I'm changing my professional practice at some point to try and bring spirit into the workplace, and I haven't a clue what that looks like. I'm trying to find a vocabulary. I'm trying to find ways to work with organizations that I think will be more important to them.

Jon Kabat-Zinn: We're talking about mainstreaming the Dharma. Do you know what that really means? That means completely revolutionizing the society. It means moving the entire bell-shaped curve although we're not moving it by pushing or forcing. We're intending for it to move, and since we *are* it, if we move, it moves. It's not possible for it not to. So I would say, in anybody's case, the best way for you to change the organization is to hold yourself in a particular way within the organization, then it's already changed. Just like a crystal. If one atom inside the crystal is changed, the entire crystal has, in some way, to rearrange itself to accommodate you. It's often subtle, very subtle, so you wonder How long, oh Lord, before "they" get it and part of that is like dualism—making "they" distinctions.

I got a call not too long ago from a $4 billion consulting company that is behind reengineering a corporation. I'm sitting there on the line and this high-level business consultant is saying to me, "We now know why reengineering the corporation was a failure in America."

First of all I say, "Oh, it was a failure in America?"

And I'm seeing casualties of it right and left, of all the downsizing and just a horror show of what it was doing to people's lives all in the spirit of having preserved their dividends for the shareholders. They're just killing off the workforce.

He says to me, "We know what was the matter with the fatal flaw with reengineering and downsizing the corporation, and that was that it had no mindfulness, that it really was heartless."

The next big thing in corporations is not going to be changing size—that's not most fundamental—it's exactly what you're saying. It's pointing to the heart of what work is and who does it. When people understand work and what the work of the organization really is, then you tap into sort of the nuclear-type power of people and you generate creativity and production and happiness in ways that are just not possible otherwise. So these heavy-duty corporations are saying "Mindfulness is the answer." Well, that's terrifying. What's going to be the answer after mindfulness fails?

Participant: One of my pet theories is that consulting in itself, if it isn't integrated, brings very, very little value to the client.... I've just discovered in the last day or two that one of the fractures between myself and some of the consultant team that I'm a part of is that...there's a headlong rush to get to the desired state, to get to the place where oftentimes the consultant believes that they know where the company or the corporation needs to be. So there's a headlong rush into the transition state and it's extraordinarily jarring. But my job is to integrate that and to help my clients. We're being paid to get the company the hell out of there.

Jon Kabat-Zinn: I think it's so true of so many things in the way we live and work. What it means to me to embody mindfulness or to have your practice be your life in some way rather than something you do every morning, is really to work at not get-

ting caught up in forcing goals. But it's difficult to understand the notion of unfolding with intention and to allow yourself to be present all the way along with enough room and openness for things to unfold. So we're working constantly and worrying constantly about making this happen as opposed to getting comfortable with how it actually is right in this moment, which includes the flowing movement toward the next moment.

It's only if we can hold this moment that we can influence the quality of the next moment, because this moment is last moment's future. So if we want the future to be different, there's only one way to make the future different and that is to hold the present in the way that you are suggesting. If people understood how to apply that to organizations, the whole culture would rotate fairly rapidly. Now, that's a fairly difficult thing to do. It's easy to say, but that's what practice is about.

And there is a huge dark side to it in that it's not just some sort of sense of a messianic thing where we're going to spread this wonderful Dharma. It's very, very hard and often we wind up being lost or confused. We may be trying to help other people become more balanced and the more we help other people become balanced, the less balance we feel in our own lives. There's something wrong with that picture and we have to be able to hold it and own it without having to try to immediately correct it. That's hard because it's terrifying and it's very, very painful.

If anybody has not read David Whyte's

The Heart Aroused who's interested in bringing Dharma or bringing soul or bringing mindfulness into work settings, you should definitely read it.

All organizations ultimately are made up of people, just the way our bodies are made up of cells. You need the cells to be healthy and when the cells stop being healthy, they stop listening to the control mechanisms that are built into the biology of being. When the cell doesn't have that is when they start taking off on their own, and that's called cancer.

Organizations develop cancer just as much as individuals develop cancer. There has to be a continual nourishing of the feedback loops that keep things in balance so that the whole can continue to emerge and manifest. Whyte has a wonderful poem in that book —he goes into corporations, large corporations, and he does poetry because that's his path. He has been a Zen student for many years but he does poetry to ignite the same kind of passion that I was talking about around meditation. I don't see them as two different things. Many poets and artists work in the domain that is deep reflective space underneath thinking—deep, deep, deep underneath thinking. He had some people write at (I think it was) AT&T and one woman wrote the following—talk about the dark side, and speaking one's truth—she wrote: "Ten years ago I turned away for a moment, and it became my life." Can you feel that? "Ten years ago I turned away for a moment, turned my face for a moment." You know how many times we do that? We shy away from something, we turn, we close off,

we tense up, we contract. "I turned away for a moment, and it became my life."

Participant: About three years ago I decided to work where I would take groups out for a week at a time in southeast Alaska and instruct them in Zen meditation. Most of the people who are coming on the trips are not meditators but they're self-selecting. They're people who are drawn to the idea of meditation. It tends to be people who feel a real hunger and a response to that hunger.

For me, the challenge is that I'm not a meditation teacher, but as I get into this work I'm realizing what an amazing opportunity it is and responsibility on me to take people out to very, very remote places and ask them to be quiet, sometimes for the first time in their lives. So the combination of those elements is very powerful and sometimes frightening but I realize that I am doing something. I've created a job for myself that is exactly what I want to be doing and exactly where I want to be doing it....So that's why I'm here, to see how other people are working with the same kinds of problems.

Jon Kabat-Zinn: I find that very moving. I think that we can take responsibility for certain elements of the teaching without necessarily having to be meditation teachers, especially if you're in a kayak in southeast Alaska. The silence, the mountains, the waters, everything collaborates to bring you into the present moment. I think that the Dharma itself, that the instructions for practice, are so simple that when you just come to them

with beginner's mind you can, in the right circumstances, give that as a gift to somebody
else. When the mind wanders, you don't
have to believe it. When it goes off here,
notice that it's not here and bring it back.
That's an incredibly powerful gift to give to
somebody. A few little hints like that, and
that you can use the breath in a particular
way while you're looking at a mountain or
sitting or standing next to a tree, tiny little
suggestions that might come out of your
Zen experience or Vipassana practice or
Tibetan practice or whatever it is.

This stuff is so powerful that even if
you're doing it on the very, very elementary
level, even if you're just sharing the rudi-
ments of practice, the practice itself is not
either beginner or advanced. It just is. So
when you give part of that in a way that has
integrity and that can be heard, I think it has
an amplifying effect that is awesome. I never
feel that I'm actually doing anything when I'm
teaching. What I'm doing is just putting out
the possibilities and simple suggestions for
reflection, for observation, for attending, for
paying attention. Then I just watch the genius
of people connect with the genius of
Dharma and then something else happens.

Participant: In most respects I feel really
confident and comfortable with what I'm
doing and I'm grounded enough in my practice that I feel comfortable introducing basic
meditation. But I sometimes feel a little nervous that I'm not a psychotherapist, and
sometimes people come to these kinds of
things not knowing how much pain they're

sitting with. Now, I'm a half-hour boat-plane
trip away from the nearest person or the
village, and so far it hasn't been a problem
but I'm afraid I could get myself in over my
head.

Jon Kabat-Zinn: That may be a big problem,
though. It always seems like what you're not
is just what you need! I just might as well tell
you this. I have no training in the formal sort
of medical or psychological sense to be
doing what I'm doing in the hospital. My
Ph.D. is in molecular biology and I've never
had a course in psychology or group process
or anything like that in my life. I don't have
an M.D. and sometimes, in the old days, people would just sort of scratch their heads
and say, How is this guy, who has no credentials whatsoever, running a wildly successful
and very, very deep outpatient psychiatry
clinic?—which is what it looks like to them,
although it's not a psychiatry clinic or in the
department of psychiatry. It's stress reduction
and it's in the department of medicine.

Nevertheless, health insurance pays for
it. It's embedded within medicine and almost
none of my colleagues have any credentials
to be doing that, either as psychotherapists
or as anything else.

And you all know this from your meditation practice, that anything can come up.
Absolutely anything can come up in this
work. But probably if you didn't have any element of Zen or mindfulness in your kayaking
trips, that would be just as true. When you
get out there in the wilderness, anything can
come out and we freak out and there ain't

nobody to back you up and so it's up to you.

So it's perfectly wonderful that you're nervous about it, and certainly we all are at times. I think it's important to name that and know that, but there's something about the authenticity of practice that I believe is responsible. In other words, when something is required, you're capable of that response, of responding in the appropriate way—because that's what practice is—and you do your best, as you say. You're there and you're willing to be there with whatever comes up.

Now, that is part of the job description of being a meditation teacher, a willingness to be there with whatever comes up, with no gaining idea whatsoever, including success or failure. That's hard work. So we do need the support of our collective *sangha,* in the very largest sense, to know that we're out there on those edges and we're playing with things that from a certain point of view seem not only dangerous but perhaps even irresponsible. The interface between irresponsible and responsible has everything to do with how you hold the willingness to have anything come up, and then how much it pushes your buttons so that you react in a way to make it worse instead of open in a way that will, in fact, be healing. It's huge, huge work and it's something that requires constant refining.

How many of you are parents? How many of you have children? What's that all about? It's the same thing. Is it not true that in a family just about everything comes up—or is it all sweetness and light in your family? And being a parent is like the same calling in some way. The question of how you hold this and provide for the unfolding of being when we've got all these fears and all these desires and we want the children to turn out a certain way. It's another part of practice, making life practice.

The stakes are very high with parenting, but we tend not to see it that way. I think the best way to teach children or to let children grow into all they can be is to do your own life with integrity—that you do the practice. Not teach them to be meditators, but use parenting as its own practice, moment by moment. And I like to let the kids be as little Zen masters that grow, that don't stay little, but that can actually provide all of the opportunities for the deepest spiritual teaching.

If not parenting, then work. And if not work, then solitude. Or if not solitude, then sports. There is no human activity that can't be used as part of the reflective practice. The Buddha said in one sentence the entirety of the practice, of all of Buddhist teaching: *Not holding onto anything and making it "I" or "mine."* That's a huge challenge.

Participant: I'm involved in community outreach programs. It's a self-selecting group, much like the one you work with. My fiancée...works with the mentally ill who have become the crazies who ask me for a dollar when I'm parking the car.

Jon Kabat-Zinn: A lot of people that you're describing as "crazy" come to Zen centers to check out what goes on there, kind of like a magnet, a *duhkha* magnet. All meditation centers are *duhkha* magnets. They draw people. One of the reasons that I wanted to bring this work into a hospital is that it's even more of a *duhkha* magnet.

There has to be a willingness to meet the craziness, without having any kind of onus associated with it, and just dance there. All of a sudden you can help ground the person. Well, what grounds a person more? When you watch your mind, you find that everything's in there. You've got Adolph Hitler and Eichmann and every conceivable horror show that humanity is capable of. I've got news for you—it's all inside, buried someplace or other. It's not socially respectable to admit it, but your kids know it. They've seen it. I'm not saying we're bad people. I'm saying we're human. Well, isn't it very comforting to know that when you have a really crazy thought that can often express itself as really crazy behavior, that you see it as an event and you don't buy into it as "I," "me," or "mine"? And you know that it's a thought and not the truth? That it's possible to let it be, all of which is completely embedded in the most elementary instructions for meditation practice. That's a life saver. That's a lifeline to ground you back into something you can trust.

What can you trust? Well, if nothing else, you could trust that this breath is coming in. Yeah, I've got all these crazy thoughts but this breath is coming in. This breath is going out, and right now I can feel my body sitting. I can feel my butt on the chair. That's incredibly grounding for somebody who tends to be completely off in this, that, what

they did to me, ruined my life, all those types of things.

My life is ruined. That's not true. That's just a thought. But when you believe that it's the truth, then you've got a whole kit and caboodle of things that go along with it. And liberation, what this whole practice is about, is not *not* having thoughts like that, it's knowing what those things are and not getting caught in them. So I think there's infinite room for working with people in that particular place in their lives by giving them back the gift of their own sanity. Only it's not the previous sanity they had when they were working in the corporation and being driven crazy in another way. It's a larger sanity that can hold even that craziness. Again, it's a challenge to do that because you have to hold it in yourself.

Participant: Do you feel comfortable teaching meditation?

Jon Kabat-Zinn: Within a holding context that's appropriate for what's going on. That's part of the practice—knowing how to create the context that's appropriate. For instance, say we wanted to teach meditation to a bunch of people that came into the room. We'd say, Okay, the first thing we have to do is sit like this. Let's just get into the full lotus and then we can talk or be silent. Well, that's not very skillful, is it? This is a very good thing, but it's not necessary. We start people off meditating lying on the floor. A lot of people think, Well, that can't be real meditation. That's diluted, lying on the floor.

Everybody will fall asleep. But when your body is in a lot of pain or you're incapable of sitting still for five seconds, no less forty-five minutes, there's something to be said for getting people on the floor in a comfortable place and then maybe they can touch the breath in a new way.

We're having a dialogue with a hundred people. Some people feel this group is too big. So you have to create contexts that are appropriate for having everyone's needs met. Our classes in the hospital tend to be quite large because the assumption that we're making is that people don't need to get close to the teacher; they don't need to know who the teacher is. Their job is to know who *they* are and if we're all doing the "know who I am" or "know something about myself," then something happens where all of a sudden the room gets so much bigger, it doesn't matter whether there are twenty people or thirty people. But when it matters, it really matters, so you have to create conditions where people feel like they're not going to run screaming from the room because they have to do something that they can't do.

Participant: What about the issue of material payment to the teacher?

Jon Kabat-Zinn I know in the Vipassana tradition they make a huge thing about that. It may be that that's only bound by one or two generations. In the monastic cultures, money wasn't necessarily part of the bargain because it was a monastic culture and the monasteries were entirely supported by the communities.

But, there's another issue, too, which is money and then attachment to money. So when Buddhism goes from one culture to another, it very often adopts a good deal of what is present in the culture that it's landing in. Well, if we're known for anything in this country, it's money—that money is the coin of the realm, so to speak. It is the measure of value, in some ways, but it is also very complicated and money may be disappearing. It's all becoming plastic and electronic. So it's got a real abstraction to it.

Nevertheless, we charge for the stress-reduction clinic and yet we believe it to be Dharma teaching. We hope that it is Dharma teaching. It's not some watered down anything. It's just a different venue. All the retreat centers charge for room and board, and then there's this notion of Dharma, that money is given freely to the monastery, to the teachers for the teaching, but it's never asked for. It's not required. So it's the notion of a free exchange.

But in this society, what do you do about that? If you want to integrate into medicine, for instance, you've got to be able to charge the insurance companies for this. Otherwise it won't be integrated into the system and, in some way, it won't survive. If you write a book, you're going to get royalties. Now, you can give the royalties away but you also have to raise your children and send them to school and put food on the table. So there are all these complicated issues that come up around Dharma.

I've been talking about this a lot with the meditation teachers that I know. It's one of the dark areas people don't want to go anywhere near, because it brings up I, me, and mine like nobody's business: *I* wrote that book. It's *my* money. Well, it's kind of funny to hear a Buddhist say, "I wrote that book," because even there it's like a big abstraction. You can't actually say that you wrote a book because who is the *you* that wrote that book? And if you're honest, it's a mysterious process of emergence. A pronoun could claim it, and it's true you put your name on it, and it gets sold by corporations that tend to be really big and then you get some part of it because you are the author. I think what we need at this point in time is dialogue. We need to be naming those kinds of things and inquiring and hearing.

There has got to be exchange for anything to happen between human beings. So the fundamental notion here is what is exploitative? And what is the inner motive for doing it? For instance, what if you pay for a tape that teaches you about meditation and the money for that tape goes to further the work of someone or to help the teacher to live or to buy health insurance.

When a lot of the American Dharma teachers learned this stuff over in Asia, they were like Peace Corps people in their early twenties, who went over there, became monks or nuns, came back, and now they're in their fifties, and soon they'll be in their seventies, and should they not have health insurance because they're not attached to material things? Somebody's going to have to pay for that, for taking care of them in some way. So if you don't have children, maybe you can be a hippie in the same way as when you were twenty, but if you have a family, children, responsibilities, then in this society you do need money to make that happen, and it's very different from a monastic-based society where you could live as a renunciate, if you will, and work things in a different way.

Participant: I'm a recovering lawyer who doesn't practice law anymore....I've also worked with corporate America and felt like I couldn't be there until I was free. And then what I heard you say about walking the path, doing what you're doing—not trained in it but then ending up in a medical community. For me it's about how do I integrate this for my work...because the dream I have is to have a roomful of attorneys meditating.

Jon Kabat-Zinn: That's actually happening. We are at a point in history where things are really beginning to rotate in a colossal way. I was in a huge Boston law firm not long ago talking with some of the top partners and they're interested in mindfulness. They said, "One of our biggest problems is the junior lawyers, the people who are trying to become partners. They get bonuses every year, huge bonuses, and you know what they call those bonuses? They call them 'no-life bonuses' because in order to make partner, in order to 'get ahead,' they have completely sacrificed all balance in their lives to do this work." Then, of course, it's litigious and adversarial. And talk about judging, they're constantly trying to discern advantage and then do that kind of thing.

I've run programs for judges and it's very interesting that the job description for a judge—what's the verb that's used?—is a *sitting* judge. There's a connection here. How do judges get to be judges? They get appointed. They're political appointments for the most part. What kind of training do they have in sitting? None. What kind of training do they have in what the mind does while they're sitting up there on the bench? None. In order to be a judge, you have to know something about judging. You have to be able to observe judging and you also have to be able to suspend judgment. Otherwise you can't hear anything because it all comes through the filter of what you already think, or your opinions.

Well, doesn't Buddhism have something to say about that? Can you see the sort of natural connection? So when I was teaching these judges, they were absorbing it like a sponge because it's what they do. They have to sit and they watch a parade of the most horrible things that people do to each other. Talk about a *duhkha* magnet. They see absolutely the most horrible things that people do to each other and they can't bring it home and tell their husbands and wives about it. There's no place they can unload it and it's all going in and they don't have a relationship to it based on practice. That's a hell realm.

This was maybe ten years ago. And it turns out that the judge in that case was in my class. At the time I didn't know that, but we were practicing and when he gave the charge to the jury, he said to the jury, "I want you to listen with 100 percent of your being and I want you to listen without making any judgments or coming to any conclusions about what happened whatsoever. Just be present and see if you find that your mind is wandering or that you're pulled into thinking about this or that and just notice that's happening. See if you can't use your breath to bring you back into your body so that you can really be in the jury box."

Well, it turns out that one of the defense lawyers is a Vipassana meditator and he's standing listening to the judge saying this, and saying to himself, "What the hell is going on in this courtroom?" He goes up to the judge afterward and says to him, "I've seen you give charges to the jury a thousand times. I've never heard you say anything like this." And the judge says, "Well, I'm taking this stress-reduction course at the UMass Medical Center and it just occurred to me that this might be a really good idea for the jury to practice being present."

Now you could say, Just be present. That's another encapsulation of all the teachings. Just be present; just be aware. You know how helpful that is? It ain't very helpful. One person in a million, in a billion, will hear *Just be present,* and go right into it, develop a mind that clings to nothing. Hui-neng, the Sixth Zen Patriarch, was enlightened when he heard some monks chanting the *Diamond Sutra,* but there aren't a lot of Hui-nengs floating around at the turn of the twentieth century. So to say *Just be present* isn't enough. It helps if you give a few instructions.

That's just what the judge said. He's no Dharma teacher, but the Dharma was there in some way that didn't ever have to be named as Dharma. The outcome of a trial is always a function of the minds that are willing to be present and to attend, then to discern—and then when it's time to weigh evidence and decide, then you do so. But when it's not time, you suspend judgment. So a judge should really be called a "suspend-judgment" judge. That requires huge training.

When you finish medical school, they usually invite some august person in to give a talk and they talk about compassion, empathy, humility, all those great things that doctors are supposed to have picked up along the way. But usually the first they hear about compassion, empathy, and humility is at graduation! And that's going to be the last they're going to hear about it, too. In the Tibetan tradition, if you want to develop compassion or empathy or humility, well, you train hard for maybe fifteen, twenty, or thirty years. It doesn't just grow on a tree. So this notion of practice, of life being training and of mind states being aspects of life that we could actually know something about and develop into a fine art, that's a new addition to our society in some ways, although it's been a very old current as well.

Thoreau teased it out of all sorts of Oriental literature a hundred years ago. It's been around in this society, too, and T. S. Eliot, in the last stanza of the *Four Quartets*, wrote the words:

We shall not cease from exploration
And the end of all our exploring

Will be to arrive where we started
And know the place for the first time.

The Zen circle. Right back into the marketplace, only totally different, awake. Later on in that stanza it says: "Not known, because not looked for."—we're not attending, not knowing, because it's not looked for—"but heard, half heard, in the stillness/Between two waves of the sea." Beautiful isn't it? Just like the space between two thoughts. The waves and the stillness need each other. They're part of the same thing. You can't write those words without knowing something about stillness. Then he says:

Quick now, here, now, always—
A condition of complete simplicity
(Costing not less than everything)

Does that sound like doctors to you? How did T. S. Eliot get that? I called up a friend of mine whose father is a world-renowned Eliot scholar as well as a professor of English at a big university and I said to him, "How did T. S. Eliot get that? This is as articulate an expression of enlightened mind as I've ever seen."

He said, "Well, he was very influenced by Buddhism when he was younger."

But ultimately you've got to walk the path that's not influenced by Buddhism. You can't arrive there at that kind of ability to give voice with words to something that's wordless, that's far beyond words, without having in some way visited. That does not mean that T. S. Eliot's life was totally together, either. I think it was a mess. But the work of

Jon Kabat-Zinn and participants in his workshop enjoy a light moment together

an artist, the work of a poet, sometimes is this very, very deep work in solitude, in silence, of just this same kind we're talking about.

Rilke is another one with a deep connection to Buddhism in his own way and he has a wonderful poem (it's in David Whyte's book) that has in it that same image of the stillness between two waves of the sea. Only he's talking about music, which, of course, is not just notes, but also the silence in between the notes. It's the whole. Rilke was writing about that and said: "I am the rest between two notes that are somehow always in discord"—he doesn't say they're

somehow always sweetness and light and beautiful and warm and fuzzy. "I am the rest between two notes which are somehow always in discord because death's note wants to climb over. But in the dark interval reconciled, they stay here trembling and the song goes on." An unbelievable affirmation. Eliot's next line after "costing not less than anything" is "and all manner of things shall be well."

So, at this point I'd like to focus a little on the work we do, taking the example of the stress-reduction clinic itself. We call what we do mindfulness-based stress reduction. That's a term that we came to in the past four years. We used to call it just stress reduction, but as it's become more and more known, and as it moves more and more into the society, it seemed adding "mindfulness-based" described it more accurately.

One of the things we practice in our program is yoga. This picture, if you think about where it is, is amazing. We're taking over the medical center, the dean's conference room, which is the largest room in the building, and logging millions of person hours of mindfulness practice in it, literally. I like to think that those vibrations affect everything else that goes on in the hospital. And you know what? It does, in a lot of different ways: partly through the media, partly through books, partly through the fact that this is reimbursed by health care, and partly the patients going back to their doctors and saying, "Thank you for sending me. That was the best thing you've ever done for me."

It's a clinic in the form of a course, and the course lasts basically ten weeks, one week of which you're seen individually at the beginning and then one at the end. In between, eight weeks of classes, groups sized between thirty and forty, one instructor. You come to class once a week for two and a half hours. Sometimes it's three hours. Then there's an all-day session.

We also teach in the inner city. We teach the program entirely in Spanish. The population in the inner city there is almost 50 percent Hispanic: many recent immigrants, many people who immigrated a long time ago and never learned English. So it's quite a jump to go from the Caribbean-rim culture, or Latin Central American culture, to Buddhist meditation in North America, in Worcester, Massachusetts. And yet, when it's articulated in the way that people in the program articulate it, the basic feeling is that although it's not for everybody, the people that it's for take to it like ducks to water. They recognize it because of its universal spiritual aspect. They know that really well because it's deeply embedded in their cultures.

It's called the City Campus Stress-Reduction Clinic and this is part of a neighborhood health center as well. All the referrals come out of this neighborhood health center. There's also a Vietnamese population growing in Worcester and the ultimate thing would be to find a teacher to teach in Vietnamese. Many of these people are Buddhists, so you can imagine they're coming full circle in a way, but we have not reached that point yet.

Now, I'm also working with a number of school teachers. So this is beyond the medical center, but over time, with *Full Catastrophe Living* and *Wherever You Go, There You Are*, I sort of connected up with a whole bunch of people who have the same kind of inspiration, that they want to bring this into their work. In the case of this school teacher in the Salt Lake City area, she came to me and said, "I want to do this in the public school." I said "Don't do it. You'll be massacred." I mean, in a 90-percent Mormon community doing Buddhist meditation! Of course, she didn't listen to me, which is the sign of a really good student.

Every day, a different child rings the bells and they have a period of quiet sitting—the child decides how long—but they're not allowed to sit more than ten minutes because they've got to get to other parts of the school day. But they actually sit quiet for ten minutes. And they know what they're doing. I've visited these kids, and they're not just robotlike imitations—they are actually practicing. These are fifth graders. They do it every day and they chose to do it. She has them decide at the beginning of every year, and for the past six years she's been doing this.

Now they have a reputation spread through the whole school. The sixth-grade teacher in this school is a Mormon bishop, and the kids convinced him he had to learn it and teach it, too. The kids were the driving motivation behind this happening after a while and the parents were reporting very positive effects of this at home.

It looks from what I've shown you as though she's brought the formal meditation practices into the classroom. She has, but that's the least important and least interesting thing of what she's done. She has actually redone the entire curriculum from the point of view of meditation and mindfulness. She went to the Utah board of education founding statement, which said education should have four aspects to it: an intuitive aspect, a somatic aspect, an affective or emotional aspect, and a cognitive aspect. She said, Well, holy cow, I've been in the school system for years and never knew that, and no one ever does that. They just do the cognitive. So she's now using the meditation to cultivate the intuition, feelings, sensation, and thought all as one whole. She's integrated mindfulness into geography, mathematics, science, poetry,

English; the entire curriculum is mindfulness-based.

This is her genius. I could never have done that. She is an extraordinary teacher with a deep, but not a long, understanding of practice. She's now a student of the Zen teacher Charlotte Joko Beck, but when I met her, she had just picked this up in this stress-reduction clinic at Latter Day Saints Hospital at Salt Lake City, which was modeled on our program. I went out there and visited with their graduates of this program for a day. It's a Delta Airlines hub and a lot of the people there were air traffic–control people, airline pilots—high-stress level, high-performance people—and they were talking, unbelievably, about how this experience of meditation had influenced their lives. If I'd just closed my eyes it would have sounded just like our own patients. That's one of the ways that I know how good the teaching is. I don't have to see the teachers teach. All I have to do is see the students.

It's the same for the children. There was one boy in the class who was the most hated kid in the school. He had started kindergarten and just got more and more hated because he had ADHD [Attention-Deficit Hyperactivity Disorder] and no one could handle him. No one could relate to him. He was extremely smart but couldn't sit still for thirty seconds. He was never on task. Drove all the teachers nuts.

Well, he got into the practice, first lying down, doing the body scan, doing the yoga, which takes energy and is more interesting. Then he gradually learned to sit and by the end of the first year, he could actually sit still for five minutes. By the end of the second year, he could sit still for ten minutes. I went out and visited the school after he had been doing it for two years, I think. I could only be there on a Saturday. The kids value this so much, they actually brought their parents to meet me. We had two or three hours together, and I had the kids guide various meditation practices. This boy sat next to his mother and guided a fifteen-minute sitting, most of which was silence, and he didn't move. Every once in a while he made the correct, appropriate, guiding instructions. His mother said to me, "This is a different boy." And he's gone from being the most hated kid in the school to just a regular boy.

I showed these slides at Duke University, and the person who was editor-in-chief of a journal called *Attention-Deficit Disorder* asked me if this could have some relevance to attention-deficit disorder. I said that, from a Buddhist point of view or from a meditator's point of view, the entire society has attention-deficit disorder. Meditation is all about paying attention and the first thing you discover is we don't know anything about paying attention. So he asked me to write an editorial to that effect for the journal.

For the past four years we have developed a program at the request of the Massachusetts committee on criminal justice to go into the prisons and deliver mindfulness-based stress reduction in the prisons. [*Showing a slide*] This is Norfolk Prison, where I taught originally and then many other people taught, including a fellow who had been a helicopter pilot in Vietnam, then,

when his tour of duty was up, he became a monk, spent fifteen years in Thailand, then was a monk in England for another five years. Then he saw the Bill Moyers show and wound up working for us. He came out from California and wound up working for us in the prisons for a number of years. This is sitting in one of the prisons. By the way, this is a men's prison and it's a woman teacher.

Think for a minute. This is a woman meditation teacher, lying on her back, guiding a body scan in a room full of incarcerated men. That takes a certain amount of courage and centeredness. Lots of people want to come and work in the hospital and teach in the hospital, and we used to quip, "Well, okay, first you teach in the prisons and if you come out alive, then maybe you can teach in the hospital." They know within fifteen seconds whether you're putting out bullshit. Their bullshit detectors are on the highest possible gain because they're bullshitting each other all day long. What goes on in the prisons is very, very heavy and very scary and so the majority of prisoners appreciate authenticity and they know the opposite immediately. It really is a challenge for a do-gooder, middle-class meditation teacher to walk in there and have something to say to these people. You only get about five seconds before you lose your credibility, so it's a huge challenge and a very good training program for people who want to be Dharma teachers.

[*Showing a slide of a newspaper headline:* YOGA FOR CONVICTS] Then, at a certain point last year, this was the headline in the *Boston Herald*. For four years it cost the University of Massachusetts Medical Center a lot of money to run this program. On the other hand, we saw a tenth of the prison population every year, so there's no question that they were getting their money's worth, and people were finding changes, and it was run as a research project.

The reporter actually did a fairly credible job with the story but the editors put a volatile headline on it and in an election year, with the governor [Weld] and Senator Kerry running for the Senate seat, they couldn't compete fast enough to vilify the other about how prisoners should be treated with punishment and not rehabilitation. So within thirty seconds that headline killed any chance that our program would be refunded.

We had many friends in the prison system, because we were not just teaching the inmates, we were also teaching the prison staff, including the commissioner of public safety. That went all the way up to the top and people loved it, but we didn't have a friend there who would say anything in our favor two hours—one minute—after this thing hit the stands. You have to be willing to be political, and this was the editorial:

Of all the bizarre waste of federal funds, meditation classes for Massachusetts convicts takes the cake.

There's also a cartoon. "We've found a much cheaper way of curbing violent behavior in prisoners than the $900,000 yoga and medi-tation program. The V chip." "They're watching "Mr. Rogers."

So you have to be prepared to do battle—Dharma combat, if you will—around these issues. We were very prepared to do it and a yoga teacher at Interface wrote a beautiful editorial to the *Boston Globe* about the whole thing, suggesting that they were out of their minds to cancel this program, which was probably the best thing that was going on in the prisons in terms of reducing recidivism, hostility, and violence. Not to mention the cost it takes to control and contain inmates and the cost to society when people who have been just brutally treated go back out onto the streets.

We've also entered into the world of world-class as well as collegiate sports training because everybody in sports knows that usually the mind is much more important than physical conditioning in terms of performance, or winning and losing. Everybody is extremely highly trained and physically conditioned but the mind requires a similar kind of training and conditioning. Now that's accepted and well-known, so back in 1984 I trained the U. S. Olympic rowing team in meditation. Went to the Olympics with them.

Then George Mumford and I connected up with Phil Jackson a number of years ago and George Mumford has been going out and training the Chicago Bulls for the past three years. First, when Michael Jordan left, that was a big stress on the team, to lose the best player that's ever played in basketball. So they worked with the team in Michael's absence. Michael came back and everybody's meditating, including him, now. The whole team is practicing mindful yoga and mindfulness meditation now.

How much do they do it? Do they do it every day? Who knows and, in some ways, who cares? They're doing what they need to do. These are multimillionaires and yet they understand that there is something here that's very deep. It's more than just a competitive edge. They know that while they may be getting millions now, they're not going to be getting millions once their bodies break down. So they understand impermanence and there's a strong motivation to bring wisdom to how you handle the life cycle.

I think that's one of their motivations for practicing this, not just performance, but I will point out that last year they had the best record ever in basketball and, as of today, they've won thirty-three games and lost four, so they're on an even better trajectory. And they have one of the oldest groups of players in the National Basketball Association. Kind of interesting. I'm not saying that meditation is the reason why they're doing so well—obviously that's not true—but every little aspect counts in terms of bringing everything to completion.

[Dr. Kabat-Zinn concluded the morning portion of this workshop with a period of meditation, during which he said the following:]

One of the beauties of this practice is having countless opportunities to take nothing for granted—encountering each moment in its total uniqueness, in its freshness, each breath. And each time you take your seat in this way, beyond thinking of it as meditating, just sitting, here and now, not letting the past and the history of your relationship to sitting practice color your ideas about what you're doing; rather, dwelling in the spaciousness of total presence with nothing holding. Rejecting nothing, pursuing nothing. Fully awake with the entire field of awareness, allowing that to be as large or as narrow as feels appropriate. Putting out the welcome mat for whatever arises. Beyond expectations that anything at all needs to happen. Knowing where your mind actually is from moment to moment, from breath to breath.

Bringing the Dharma more into your life, more into your work, more into your world in a way that reflects both your unique place and the uniqueness of your being and the seamless wholeness of it all, the seamless wholeness of the Dharma, the part that's beyond name, beyond form. That aspect of it that is unchanged and unchanging. That is contained in Buddhism but that is larger than Buddhism. What is it for you? Even in the tiniest emergence, intention, just holding that question. Not even trying to answer it. Just holding it in awareness.

[The afternoon continued much as the morning had, with participants bringing up personal concerns that often brought out ideas from Dr. Kabat-Zinn.]

Participant: I teach courses in contemporary Buddhism. One of the first questions that students ask when I ask a similar question to what you just asked is whether I'm a Buddhist. It raises some of the things that we talked about this morning, about whether the label is skillful or unskillful when we use it or choose not to use it. It seems that in our discussion this morning, we were talking about mindfulness, meditation, Dharma, and practice as descriptions of what we do, and you said that some years ago you stopped calling yourself a Buddhist. I think the slides helped me to understand how in many of the things you do, that might get in the way. But I wonder if this is a stealth religion or a stealth movement that we've got going here and whether we're kind of making it up as we go along? For instance, in the discussion about money, most of us don't have a clear idea about what historical and traditional Buddhism was really like. We think that it involves renouncing money and not accepting or giving. In each area that we talk about, there are heavy traditions involved that we, as Americans, may just not really want to know about.

Jon Kabat-Zinn: Not want to know about because they're irrelevant, or because we just enjoy being ignorant?

Participant: Or because it might interrupt our liberal view of how society or individuals should be. I'll just share one thing that shocked me in my class this fall. I'm using a book by British anthropologist Anna Grimshaw called *Servants of the Buddha.* She describes the very harsh conditions with the nuns as they serve and prepare food and do virtually everything for the monks who live on top of the mountain basking in sunlight and chanting and meditating and doing ritu-

als. It's so shocking that there are really two societies and they are truly serving the Buddha and acting mindfully. They chose to live this life whereas some of the monks, in fact, were set up for that life by their families and weren't particularly suited for it. One of my students is a mainland-Chinese graduate student and he said, "You know, this book is used by the Chinese government as a defense for its takeover of Tibet. They liberated the nuns so that women did not have to do that kind of work." So that's an aspect of the tradition that maybe we don't understand in this society.

Jon Kabat-Zinn: I'm glad you brought that up. I said earlier that we should visit the dark side plenty. There are dark aspects to everything and the real problem is when you can't name them because it's taboo. For myself, that's one of the reasons why I want to make the distinction between Dharma and Buddhism.

I really don't care about Buddhism. It's an interesting religion but it's not what I most care about. What I value in Buddhism is that it brought me to the Dharma. Now, within Buddhism as I understand it, being fairly ignorant, there are an awful lot of injustices of one kind or another, some of which you're describing, and there are plenty of others, exploitation of all sorts, some of which also involve gender exploitation. But I'm really talking more about introducing Dharma or furthering the Dharma possibilities within the society. Buddhism will have some relationship to that, and Americans don't know everything about the traditions.

Secondly, it may not be appropriate for the traditions, whatever they are, to perpetrate themselves here, and it may be that there's something much deeper going on that is in some way going beyond religion as we know it—perhaps a merging of religion and science and native understanding, multiculturalism, all sorts of things, and there's a new something emerging that none of us are really capable of holding in our consciousness.

So yes, we're faltering and kind of cute in our little ignorances and sometimes transgressions and everything else. But the question is, Is there some way that we can collaborate and bring our own innocent integrity to it, our own envisioning something new and yet taking from what's old, as appropriate, where it seems useful? What feels to me like the possibilities of fueling a renaissance at the turn of the millennium that, in many ways, is far beyond the scope of the renaissance of Europe in the fourteenth to seventeenth centuries. Far beyond it in terms of its global capacities, in terms of going beyond art and architecture, and that would not just be the sacred quality of one tradition—the Catholic Church—but something that embraced all of humanity.

If we could begin to understand and live according to those principles—whether you want to call it the Tao or the Way or the Dharma or something else—it would be amazing. It's not the name that's important, but the level of understanding which really appreciates indigenous cultures, science, religion, spirituality, and medicine, allowing for the infinite possibilities of being human.

Participant: You were just saying that there is the fundamental multicultural aspect to the principles of the Dharma. I had come to recognize from my own study and practice that all cultures have the Dharma within them. It's just a question of what place you give them within a particular cultural position at a particular time....A very fundamental point is that we sometimes have some emotional investment in a kind of an elitism that's leaving out a large portion of the world because we don't want to see that everybody has it. It's just a question of what the opportunities are for them to be exposed, and so forth.... What does it take to create these kinds of programs when people are acting out of frustration and anger? How does one turn that energy into a form of constructive, creative empowerment?

Jon Kabat-Zinn: The interesting thing is that something actually requires our participation and it's part of us anyway. It's doing us and we're doing it and we don't want to do somebody else's work on the planet. That seems to be rule number one.

So the question is, What is my work on the planet? That's a really good life koan: What is mine to do? And I mean "mine" in the sense of it's true we all share the same buddha-nature. Can we use the vocabulary that in some fundamental way we're all aspects of buddha-nature and is that aspect of buddha-nature beyond form, and therefore universally the same? But it's also true that we're all different. So we don't want to say, Okay, we're all the same, same, same, same. Only one, one, one. We understand one, but if we're just attached to one then we don't understand two. But we don't understand what Buddhists might call the ten thousand things. So how do we hold the one and the ten thousand things at the same time? And then each one of us is unique and there are things that we can do that no one else on the planet can do. So what is your calling? Where can you contribute?

I showed you the slides about the children in part because the teacher knew what the apparatus was because she *was* the apparatus. I didn't know. I just looked at her and saw a nice roley-poley person that may be a great fourth-grade teacher, but how could she bring the Dharma into this? It's all my own prejudice—she's only been sitting for six months—all my own prejudice. She tapped into her genius and also the calling, if you will, of the Dharma. This is in the service of something very large and very deep, but without making it heavy and moralistic and ponderous.

Well, how do you hold that? It seems to me that's a very, very large part of the practice. Aside from just sitting still and being still, how to use this energy that we are given that's called a lifetime. The Buddha was very clear that life is precious, fleeting, and extremely rare. A human life. A human body. How can we make use of it?

There's a wonderful line in a poem by Antonio Machado, the last line of which is: "I said to myself what at a certain point is life? I said to myself what have you done to the garden that was entrusted to you?" Think for a minute: What are the gardens that are entrusted to you? It's a sacred trust, whether you believe in God or not, whether you're a Buddhist or a Taoist or a Jainist. Sacred trust.

How about the body? That's a good place to start. What have you done with the garden that is entrusted to you? How many people on the planet abuse the apparatus just mindlessly? Of course, that makes for great difficulties in living the journey because if the body's not willing, then it just makes that full of that much more *duhkha.*

What about the breath? They say that in Eskimo languages there are hundreds of words for snow. Well, how many years have we collectively been watching our own breath? How many words do we have for the differences that we might see in the breath? Not too many, but they're there— thousands of them, different breaths.

What have we done with the garden that's been entrusted to us? Do we even know we have gardens entrusted to us? What about parents? What about our children, those gardens? What about our relationships? What about our colleagues or our Dharma gifts? So I don't know the answer to that. That's the big koan. That's the huge koan. Can we collectively start asking those kinds of questions? Then, not necessarily having to know where it's all going, but from the heart putting one foot in front of the other, knowing that this foot is here now.

Participant: I wanted to go back to a word that always stops me in my tracks—*elitism.* Part of my childhood experience was sometimes things happen and they're good things and I'm a lucky guy; and when they're not so good, then I'm an angry guy and this stuff happens. I guess I continued to study and I realized that a lot of what I was calling bad or lucky or good had a lot to do with my interpretation of what I was going through.

The neighborhood that I grew up in, although it was not a Buddhist area at all, was very supportive of that attitude; had that old Protestant work ethic—take responsibility for your own life and you're set. But then I will run into people who grew up in areas that are different. This term *elitism,* when I think about it, I don't even know how to deal with it. That's because, from my experience, there are certain life paths that are going to be more conducive to embracing Buddhism and there are going to be certain life paths where it would be very easy to look for saviors or somebody else who would relieve us of the pressure that goes on in life.

Jon Kabat-Zinn: I heard the term *elite* and it really just had to do with this sense of exploitation in some way, that you're in some way dominating somebody else, either in your own mind or in the actuality of what's going on. And it's well-documented that that kind of stuff happens. It seems to me that the whole notion of elitism just has duality built into it. It's just us and them, and either we're the elite or they're the elite. My understanding of what true practice is about is just dropping that kind of thinking, and not being pulled into the actions that that kind of thinking leads to, either by omission or commission.

The reason the morality is stressed so much in Buddhist circles is you're not just the meditator. You're cultivating various kinds of moral qualities. It's because it's not possible to do this work if you're out there raping and pillaging all the time. Yes, that would predispose you to not really be able to find that space between the two notes or the stillness between the two waves of the sea because you're feeding the choppiness of your own mind.

So there's some kind of way in which, if you hope to achieve any kind of clarity or any kind of stillness in life, you have to stop creating all of that kind of karma. Sometimes I've heard sitting described as not making more karma. If you sit and it's a good thing, just don't make more karma. Just sit there. Because you're making a certain kind of karma but you're not making it as bad karma.

Participant: Have you ever had a person or persons look at your own lifestyle and what you've done that you're sharing and not really understand how you have gotten where you are? And they say, "Sure, this is great to talk about enlightened stuff in a hotel room. I'm on second shift putting bolts on here."

Jon Kabat-Zinn: Well, everybody does that in one way or another. We're constantly projecting onto other people about them. If you take on, or are given, the mantel in any shape or form of meditation or Dharma teacher, the projections that come at you are just fantastic and very problematic. If the practice is about knowing yourself, then what is all this projecting onto other people?

So I work overtime to deflect all of those projections that are coming from my patients—*I know he knows, and he will give it to us, and then we'll know;* or, *We'll do the same hard work that he did,* or some variation of that—instead of, No, there's a work that's uniquely mine to do and I have to do that and we'll do this in parallel and he is no more special than I am. Maybe there is an elite, but it's everybody—we're all part of the elite. If it's true that a human incarnation is a very rare and wonderful event, then whether you're working at a carburetor plant in South Boston or you're sitting on top of one of those sixty-story skyscrapers with a cigar in your mouth and your feet on the table, it's all the same.

Then the question is how we choose to live. We noticed in the prison work right away that there are people in prison who seem to be far more evolved than the people that we see who are running the hospitals, for instance. You see things in India, in any third-world country, that you'd never see here. I don't want to make fast generalizations, but my sense when I first went into old Delhi was that people look a lot happier here than they do in New York City and they have a lot less than even the poorest in New York.

So a lot of it is a question of how we understand this. The way I see this whole thing happening is that we're beginning to look at the whole, perhaps for the first time on the planet, and ask fundamental questions about what is of value in what humanity has come to see in the past five thousand or fifty

thousand years. Certainly a very, very important part of it is Dharma and how it is going to manifest in the world. And there's no attachment. If the Dharma went underground for the next six thousand years, it wouldn't shed a tear about itself. So in some ways it's up to us. That's a calling that involves a lot of responsibility, that if we know something we can actualize it in ways that influence society, that reduce suffering.

Participant: I'd like to put out the idea of looking at our responsibility to the Dharma. We can say that it was born in India, that it grew in China, and then it flowered in Japan. I wonder if it could possibly rot in America? I'm not a Buddhist (although I practice Vipassana and different things), but my commitment is to Dharma, universal Dharma. Coming from a yoga tradition, I notice what's happening to yoga in America and that becoming extremely mainstream, it seems to be becoming very different—leaving out the essence of what yoga is. So I'm wondering, if people are focusing extensively on the concept of mainstreaming, that possibly over time it can dilute the Dharma or dilute the teachings.

Jon Kabat-Zinn: You're asking the absolute fundamental question: What is our responsibility here, and what is our understanding? Because, as we established in our discussion before, you can't do anything that's beyond your understanding. So can we deepen that understanding and can we really take responsibility as best we can? Each one of us is finite and the Dharma is infinite, so articulating and embodying it in ways that are not a dilution or a distortion is very difficult.

I think that's the challenge of the era, to tell you the truth, and things are so time-accelerated. It took hundreds and hundreds of years for Buddhism to move into China and into Tibet. It was long, slow work over the generations and passed from disciple to disciple. They didn't have the Internet or multimedia. Everything is instant, now, so it's like we're working in an entirely new buddha realm or buddha field. As I can see, although we can all help each other and reflect each other, we're in the business of making new models. Taking what's best from what is already known and holding it in a way that is really willing to face the unknown. But some fundamentals are unchanging: The human mind is the human mind. It's pretty much the same as it was in the Buddha's time. The human body is pretty much the same body although maybe taller and healthier.

I think we can be in touch with the essence of Dharma without diluting it at all, but in some way we have to help each other to do that and to stay honest at it. That's why the talk around it is important. I like to call what we're doing now "talk yoga," and it's just as, maybe more, important than standing on your head! Some people get attached to silence—"We should just sit and not talk"—but sometimes talk is really important and I think that's one of the values of this kind of conference. Maybe there are more of us on the planet than we thought, and maybe that in itself is some kind of a force for healing or for transformation.

Participant: I'm fairly recently on a spiritual journey. I'm a medical doctor...actually a pathologist. I think there's a tremendous opportunity with the Dharma. Our population is aging and I see a tremendous opportunity to apply what we've learned from our practice, merging it with all this incredible stuff that's happened scientifically. To me this is a tremendous challenge, and that's one of the reasons I'm here, to see how that actually can be done.

Jon Kabat-Zinn: Not to be flippant about it, but if pathology is your field, then how can you bring this domain and that domain together, given that they really never were separate. If it is really all one seamless whole, then it's more a matter of seeing it and teasing it out in relief rather than that you have to put two things together that weren't together. Think for a minute about what's happened since the Industrial Revolution. What was the Industrial Revolution? Well, we figured out that you could actually boil water and make the steam turn something. Out of that came railroads. And what did railroads do? They connected points that weren't connected before, allowing for the transport of goods and information faster and much more effectively.

Then we discovered gasoline. If you burned gasoline and made cylinders go up and down by exploding them and igniting them, you could actually also turn wheels. Then you have cars and they go someplace else. Then someone figured out they could devise ways in which electric current would go through wires, so then you have electricity.

You have light bulbs. You have computers, you have telephones, you have all sorts of technological advances that enhance connectivity.

And what is meditation about? It's about perceiving connectivity, really. So the outside world is dealing with all of these things that make connectivity and interconnectedness more and more palpable. Meanwhile, if we're not doing the inner work in understanding connectivity, then there will be no wisdom in our use of the railroads or cars or anything else. So we need to develop, if you will, the inner technology and the inner science to hold the outer, and then understand that inner and outer are not separate.

When I was working with Soen Sunim, at one point he decided that some of us should become Dharma teachers. I said, "I don't want to be a Dharma teacher. I'm coming here to learn from you. You're the Dharma teacher and I'm the student." But he had it in his mind that he had to bring people along by making them teachers, a little bit the *see one, do one, teach one* mentality. There was a lot of wisdom behind it actually, because when you are up there and you've got to say something, it elevates you in a way, calls you to do it.

I said to him, "Soen Sunim, you're the Zen master. I don't know anything." And he scratched his head and he said, "You only talk about area you understand. Don't talk about area you don't understand." It was useful advice.

Participant: I'm a writer and in doing a book which took many years, I became a kind of voracious consumer of other people's descriptions of their inner experiences. It became very clear to me, what you pointed out in the beginning, that there are words we can use to describe the experience and there are other words that we can use to point toward the experience that we can't describe. I am always on the go for those words and it's an interesting thing to try and translate silence into a book.

I'm a pretty severe critic of myself when I write and I feel...that the best way to operate is to figure that no one wants to read anything that I write and it really has to be authentic. When it comes to the subject of working with the dying and bringing in spiritual issues, which can quickly become watered down and sort of turned into New Age sewage, it's very difficult.

I found your books...very helpful. When I sent in this manuscript, I got a call from my editor...and she said, "We love the manuscript but it would be great if you took the word *Zen* out of the subtitle and we do see it cropping up here. We're concerned about that." All I can say is it's been kind of helpful to hear people say in a number of ways how important it is to find your own language.

Jon Kabat-Zinn: I'm so glad you brought this up—maybe what it's calling on you to do. You live in a Zen center, you're working on the Zen hospice project, but you're not allowed to use the word *Zen* in your writing. What is going on here?

One way is to just get frustrated, exasperated—"Ah, they're no good"—but another way to look at this is it's actually the next dose of training that's required to drop down underneath and ask what is really going on? Perhaps there's something missing, and what occurred to me when you were talking is that there's something missing and there's no blame for it. If we understand the situation and there is something that needs a slight turning, then with the slight turning everything all of a sudden falls into place. I'm sure you've had experience of that many, many times.

So the question is, Can you use the word *meditation?* People are asking me that all the time. "Do you use the word *meditation* with the doctors?"

And I say, "Mm-hmm."

"Do you use the word *yoga* with the doctors?"

"Mm-hmm."

But when you were speaking, I had this thought that, because you're so close to Zen, maybe there's a sentence missing or a paragraph missing that the editors have not gotten that, when they get it, all of a sudden using the word *Zen* won't be a problem.

When I teach meditation, or in writing, no matter what audience I'm working with, what I'm going for is: *Oh! Is that what it is? Of course. That makes perfect sense.* That it be commonsensical, that the understanding be so available that all of a sudden there's no more resistance because there isn't anything to argue with.

I spent quite a number of years formally training in the Korean Zen tradition, and at a certain point I came upon the notion that *Zen* is just this fantastic word that peaked people's interest and that Zen means absolutely nothing at all. You want to get

someone into the tent, and your job is to be the barker, so you do certain kinds of things to peak people's interest, like wearing robes or shaving your head. And you say things like, "Up is down," or whatever. And people go, "Whoa, fantastic!" and they sort of wake up for a moment or two. And then you've got them. Then you say, "You should see what's inside."

Now, if there's some way to translate that, your editors are going to say, "Oh, that's what it is." Then you've established what Zen is in the first paragraph and you can use Zen in every paragraph after that and nobody will bat an eye. If you don't do that initial translating, then it's like you're in your own club, and that makes for separation. Hopefully that's done in a way that you're not disrespecting everybody who spent their lives over the past 2,500 years practicing Zen. It's not meant to be flippant or disrespectful, but playful in the sense that we know that if Zen is nothing, it is playful. And it can laugh at itself and, in fact, Zen is nothing. Just look at all the koans—What is Zen?—and the various responses to that and all those things like, well, "Zen is Buddha." There are all these stories where someone comes in and says, "What is Zen?" Zen is Buddha.

The other student hears it and he tries it out. "What is Zen?" Zen is Buddha.

"No!"

"What? The other guy just came in and said Zen is Buddha!"

"Yeah, when he said it, that was correct. When you say it, it is not correct. What is Zen? Give me one word of Zen."

"You know, I've been sitting for twenty

years and I've heard all these words of Zen. What is it? It's worthless, absolutely worthless, and just completely frozen in time. And then, right there, all of a sudden in the garden some frog jumps off a lily pad and he hears the plop. And he just says that,

> Still pond
> Frog jumps in.
> Plop.

Ah!

So if you can take that energy and put it into words, you can sell Zen on the street corner and every one of your editors will be there with you selling it.

I went to Kyoto myself at a certain point, the only time I've been to Japan. *Full Catastrophe Living* came out in Japanese and they invited me to talk on mindfulness at an international congress of psychology. But I had friends in this country and friends in Japan who had invited me and I said I wanted to meet with a Rinzai Zen master when I was over there. So they arranged for me to meet with this fellow named Morinaga Roshi in Kyoto actually at a small Zen temple inside of Ryoan-ji, which is a huge Zen temple where the most famous rock garden in Japan is.

It turned out that the only time the Zen master could see me was the day after I flew over. So I get into Tokyo, drop my bags, knowing no Japanese at all, find my way to Kyoto on the bullet train, and then wind up in this eighth-, ninth-, tenth-, twelfth-century setting, which is my absolute dream of nirvana—a Zen temple with the cypress trees,

the stork in the water, the tatami mats on the veranda, and the Zen master serving little rice cakes. It was amazing. To boot, in Japan Zen masters can marry. So he had a daughter and his daughter married a man who was a full professor of Far Eastern studies at Princeton, who was absolutely fluent in Japanese. So I had a translator.

I was in total seventh heaven and I knew I was going to get to see this guy and all my Japanese friends, who are psychologists, were saying, "What are you going to talk to him about? He's going to eat you alive. This is the Rinzai school. It's not Soto, where you can just breathe in, breathe. What are you going to say?" Which just shows you that they have tremendous fear, absolutely zero understanding, from what I could see, about what Zen really is. Tremendous respect for it, tremendous fear, and tremendous ignorance.

So I said, "Well, actually what I want to talk to him about is the work we're doing in the hospital and what his ideas are around how to teach Zen in the secular setting, as well as the question of whether it's even skillful to use the word *Zen* or to tell Buddha stories, which we don't do. We don't go and tell stories about Hui-neng and rice pounding and the Buddha and Shariputra. We just talk about the breath coming in and breath going out and various other ways that we try to bring the practice alive."

I had sent him a copy of *Full Catastrophe Living* in Japanese, so he at least had some sense of who he was going to talk to. I don't know how it got arranged that I met with this guy, because he wasn't meeting with anybody and actually the monastery was closed.

So I arrived in this amazing setting and we're chatting, and one thing leads to another and I'm kind of setting him up for this big question. He was about seventy-two years old at the time. (He died a couple of years ago, but from what I heard, he was a real hard line–conservative, old-style Rinzai Zen master, who might not want to hear about bringing this stuff into the mainstream in America.)

So I told him what we do. That was established, and I said, "If it becomes necessary in that kind of a setting for the doctors and the patients to really understand the heart of meditation practice, if it becomes necessary to abandon the terminology like *Buddha* or *Zen,* what should I do?" I watched as the translator framed it in Japanese and I watched the Zen master very carefully.

Without a moment's hesitation this old guy said, "Throw out Buddha. Throw out Zen."

And I said, "Yes! It's true. It's like that." It was like my test of him in some way. That's exactly what he said, with no hesitation! His Japanese colleagues would never have guessed he would say something like that. I mean the psychologists never had guessed that he would be that free, that unattached to a thousand years of tradition in Kyoto. So I felt this incredible reassurance that all the stuff I'd been reading and practicing had been a kind of living manifestation.

I think that very often the impediments that we run up against are our own fear and our own inability to make ourselves understood by somebody else. Those aren't problems at all. Those are indicators of the next

place that we need to put our attention. So who isn't your teacher? What occasion is not an opportunity for a deeper seeing, a deeper kind of understanding, a deeper kind of realization? And if we approach life like that then, yeah, the shit is always hitting the fan and our expectations are always being thwarted, and that's either a drag or it's great.

There's a wonderful image in the yoga tradition of the rapidly spinning grindstone—life, *samsara,* rapidly spinning grindstone. If you stick your hand in a rapidly spinning grindstone, you're not going to have a hand and it's going to create an enormous amount of pain. But that does not mean that a rapidly spinning grindstone is bad or of no use. If you know how to use it, you can take a scissors or a knife and make something useful out of it. But you have to know how to position yourself up against that interface in a way that is safe and fearless. When you do that, all of a sudden, the world collaborates in moving through the notion of obstacle to the notion of it's all here for our understanding, including the stuff that is really the most horrible.

So as far as I can see, our purpose in being here is no joke. It's not some kind of congratulatory, all the Buddhists getting together to congratulate ourselves on how wonderful we are and how great Buddhism is or where it's going or anything like that. This is the razor's edge. This is life or death. That's what practice is all about, how we deal with life and death—and they're not two. They're right in our face all the time and, if we're not aware that they're in our face all the time, then we're living in delusion. If we're terrified all the time because of that, then we're also living in ignorance.

The question is how to live. It's like the Buddha was a great scientist. He said, "I looked, I observed, and this is what I observed and it's for you to test it empirically. Don't believe me. Test it out." And I think it's reaching the point where that's filtering into the society enough so that part of our work is testing out certain aspects of it. We're doing very elaborate studies on healing, for instance, on how the mind influences healing and its fundamental basic biology of consciousness and a relationship of mind to body. That's new stuff at the absolute cutting edge of science. It's happening in a lot of different places in medicine, and that's only one small field. There are millions of fields and each one of us, I believe, actually represents many different fields.

Our yearning, our longing is to know that fields are ours to play in. So the buddha fields are infinite and we have the opportunity to be at play in them in some way that is furthering of, let's say, a healing or an understanding of what it means to actually reside on this planet for the brief moments we call lifetimes, and what it means to be of some use and actually what it means to be human.

I sometimes like to begin talks that I give by quoting from Joseph Campbell, who did that series with Bill Moyers on the power of myth. After listening to him talk for a quite a while, Moyers said to him at a certain point: "Joe, I think I understand now why myth is common to all culture."

And Campbell said, "Why is that?"

Moyers said, "Because myth embodies the deep meaning of the culture, and what we're all looking for in life is meaning."

Campbell said, "Well, people say that what we're all looking for in life is meaning, but I don't think that that's really what we're looking for at all. I think what we're all looking for or yearning for is an experience of being alive."

He might be right, and it's terrifying to think that you could live decades of your life and miss it entirely.

Our view in the stress-reduction clinic is that as long as you're breathing, there's more right with you than wrong with you. So no matter what you're coming in with—AIDS, cancer, heart disease, chronic pain, or whatever—our view is that right now, in this moment, there's more right with you than wrong with you. We're willing to work with anybody as long as they're willing to work. We can't do the work for anybody, but there are certain sorts of characteristics that you do have to have, and one of them is the breath has to be moving in and out. We do not have a good track record with the dead. The Tibetans may, but we don't. But if the breath is moving in and out, then there is the possibility.

Let's say you're eighty years old and you feel like you made a mistake in your twenties and that your whole life is a waste. People do feel that sometimes. Like, I didn't marry that person and it's colored my whole life; or, I did marry that person and it colored my whole life. Very often this happens in parenting. I had these children and then I didn't see them for thirty or forty years. I lived with them but I never saw them. Why? Because I never saw anything except my own idiocies, my own imagination, my own sweet-talking myself into how I was doing or where I was going and what my ambition was.

Well, you start to do mindfulness-based stress reduction and talk to people about what goes on in their minds and their lives, and the levels of grief at what's been missed are unbelievable. The potential for greed, hatred, and ignorance in human beings is absolutely colossal. And there is true potential built into all of us, into our genes, to transcend greed, hatred, and ignorance. So what else is there to do on the planet? What other jobs might there be? That's the way I see it and that's why I do this work.

Participant: I think, in addition to the fact that Buddhism really works and is therapeutic and prophetic and all of the things that we've talked about, is the fact that Buddhism offers us the opportunity to praise the tradition within the settings of the *sangha*. That's an element that I don't think we've talked much about—the refuge taken and the bowing and the lighting of the candles and the incense. The placing of the offering before the image is a way of saying thank you to this particular tradition that we've been talking about, whatever we choose to call it on the outside world.

Jon Kabat-Zinn: Well, we're very careful in the hospital—and it's very hard work not to bow to each other—because it doesn't look so good in the hospital. But we do kind of do it. I'll just do it to a patient. Usually I'll hug them but sometimes I will bow or I will say, "I bow to you."

But I want to say, since you've sort of brought it to the devotional level and the level of *sangha,* I try to look at *sangha* non-linearly and nondualistically, so the *sangha's* everybody, as far I can see, and it's not just the Buddhists. When a patient comes into our office, the Dharma practice of that moment is to be fully present with that patient because they're the Buddha and you're the Buddha. To be that present without any thoughts of You're the Buddha, or I'm the Buddha, but just being there. That is a sacred trust. All doctors know that it's a sacred trust, but they're not trained to hold it as if it were sacred and really breathe life into it that way.

Very often a doctor-patient relationship is somewhat less than ideal because neither person is in the room. The patient refuses to be in the room because they don't trust the doctor and the doctor's too busy or whatever. So you can see that this has enormous potential because the *sangha*—if you're willing to have the *sangha* be everybody—includes dogs and cats and raccoons with three legs as well as trees and mountains and rivers. Then where is there not an occasion for a life of deep connectedness, a life of deep appreciation, a life of sensitivity, a life of awareness, a life of compassion?

I asked you in the first guided meditation of

the morning, to think of somebody that's close to you who is suffering, who might actually benefit from some aspect of Dharma practice, but who is never going to hear it the way you hear it—never. Is there some way to touch what's deepest in it for you in such a way that's like hitting the bells. The resonances would go out and actually begin an oscillation in the other person that would look like common sense, or a sympathetic resonance, or a kind of, Oh, is that what it's about? Or, I feel that. There's not a separation here. It's like the invitation to the possible in oneself. So much of the time we feel hopeless and helpless and project that out onto everybody else.

There's a wonderful poem in David Whyte's book *The Heart Aroused*, by David Wagoner, which I'll recite if you don't mind. A lot of it has to do with standing and has to do with the heart of practice. It's from the Native American tradition, not from a Buddhist tradition. Sometimes poems can be useful in helping people understand practice on a heart level and perhaps motivate them to do something as peculiar as standing with no purpose other than to be present. There's no elevator. There's no bus. Just standing. We're not waiting but we are attending.

The poem goes like this. It's what an elder might say to a seven- or eight-year-old girl or boy who would come asking, What do I do when I'm lost in the primordial forest? And of course, we often get lost in our lives. People have spoken about being in touch with the path, but sometimes we're not in touch with the path or it seems higher,

and we're in touch with grief or we're in touch with fear or we're in touch with just a feeling of confusion. What do I do when I'm lost in the forest? It's not just for a little kid. This is what the elder says:

Stand still. The trees ahead and the bushes
    beside you
Are not lost. Wherever you are is called Here,
And you must treat it as a powerful stranger,
Must ask permission to know it and be
    known.
The forest breathes. Listen. It answers,
I have made this place around you.
If you leave it, you may come back again,
    saying Here.
No two trees are the same to Raven.
No two branches are the same to Wren.
If what a tree or a branch does is lost on you,
You are surely lost. Stand still. The forest
    knows
Where you are. You must let it find you.

I want to thank you for your being and for the energy that you brought here and for the fact that you brought yourself here and we shared time together. Whether you spoke or didn't speak is not important. But you're here, we're here together. And I think perhaps that if we've just even scratched the surface of the questions that brought us here or the intentions that brought us here, it's not bad for a first meeting. This has been an absolutely marvelous day for me to be here with you and to share in some way our collective passion and our collective *sangha* and our collective Dharma. I'm just filled with gratitude for the opportunity to have this time together. It truly feels like a rare event in that this conference has the potential to be a truly historical moment, and momentous in the sense of signaling and celebrating something that, as far as I'm concerned, is truly unnameable and goes way beyond anything we could possibly think. Perhaps it is the most exciting movement of energy on the planet as we approach the odometer change of the century and the millennium.

Buddhism in the Media

A PANEL DISCUSSION

with Rick Fields, Wes Nisker, and Helen Tworkov

FEW PEOPLE CAN HONESTLY SAY THAT THEY LIVE A LIFE UNTOUCHED BY THE MEDIA. With the seemingly minute-to-minute advances in communications technology, other people's thoughts, words, opinions, teachings, and needs are placed before us in a dizzying panoply that is difficult to ignore. While just the word *media* automatically conjures up worrisome issues of manipulation, cultural decline, and least-common-denominator thinking, it is important to recognize the valuable contributions for which the media can be instrumental in bringing about.

At the sole panel discussion at the Buddhism in America conference, three people who are deeply involved in the publication of Buddhist periodicals spoke about the perceptions of Buddhism that are presented by the mainstream media as well as what they, in their capacity as editors and writers, try to present. Two of the panelists had already presented workshops in other aspects of Buddhism in the Wes. Wes Nisker (see "Breaking Out of the Shell of Self," pages 245–65) is cofounder and editor of *The Inquiring Mind*. Rick Fields, who spoke on the rise of Buddhism in America (see "How the Swans Came to the Lake," pages 469–77), is the editor of *Yoga Journal*. They were joined by Helen Tworkov, founder and editor-in-chief of *Tricycle: The Buddhist Review* and author of *Zen in America*.

Mr. Nisker, acting as moderator, introduced his colleagues, then asked members of the audience to raise questions the panel could address. Each panelist spoke for a few minutes about his or her work in the media and how they came to work in that field. They shared observations about Buddhism's treatment by the media and other related issues. The discussion was then opened up to include audience members' opinions as well.

Wes Nisker: Welcome to this panel workshop on Buddhism in the media. To my left is Helen Tworkov, the founder and editor of *Tricycle* magazine and author of *Zen in America*. To my right is Rick Fields, editor of *Yoga Journal* and author of *How the Swans Came to the Lake*. I'm Wes Nisker, cofounder and editor of *Inquiring Mind* and author of *Crazy Wisdom*. We all work with Buddhism in the media.

I am the moderator of this panel, chosen at random, not based on the circulation of our respective journals or anything like that. We decided that we are not going to simply talk about how Buddhism is treated in the mainstream media, but also how it is treated in Buddhist media and whether or not Buddhism can be adequately represented in any medium. We thought we would begin by each of us talking a little bit about our own history in media and some of our stories, but in order to partially begin to weave in some of your questions and concerns into our story, we thought we would ask what you would like to know or what issues you would like to raise in this workshop and then, as we tell our stories, we might be able to touch on some of those.

Participant: To what extent do you think the media acknowledges that there's now a uniquely American Buddhism and therefore a new chapter in the history of world Buddhism?

Participant: I'm interested in how you perceive your audience. Who do you perceive your audience to be and how do you reach them?

Participant: To what extent is Buddhism kind of a media phenomenon thrown into the mix with the New Age label and how are you trying to distinguish yourself from that label?

Participant: I'm interested in the presentation of Buddhism in American media within the context of the political situation in Tibet.

Participant: Since Buddhism is sort of an enlargement of American culture, how do you maintain the revolutionary quality of Buddhism?...

Wes Nisker: How does Buddhism maintain its revolutionary quality—transformative quality—as it becomes more mainstream and the media begin treating it as an "in" thing or the fashionable thing to be?

Participant: The traditions that are growing in this country that are part of American Buddhism but may not always be covered in the media.

Wes Nisker: A perspective on some of the schools of Buddhism that are not so generally covered in the media, such as Nichiren.

Participant: My perception of the mainstream-media account is that they cover the mainstream religions rather shallowly and I just wondered if you're concerned about how they would cover Buddhism.

Participant: You all are editors of Dharma periodicals rather than mainstream ones. I would like to have a discussion of issues of editorial responsibility and perhaps how you make your decisions.

Rick Fields: I'm just trying to think of the first writing that I did in the Buddhist field. I think maybe it was for the old *Whole Earth Review,* which then became *Co-Evolution Quarterly.* I had been working on this book, *How the Swans Came to the Lake,* which ended up being about a five-year project, and in that time I was traveling around the country seeing a lot of books. I was lucky enough to be in San Francisco when Suzuki Roshi was there and a lot of stuff was going on.

I remember my first meeting with Suzuki Roshi. I had been in Golden Gate Park getting stoned with somebody and they said, "Hey, you want to go over to the Zen Center and sit?" So we went down to Bush Street in Japantown and sat *zazen* in the old synagogue they were then using. I had never seen or met Suzuki Roshi and really didn't have much idea of what was going on. After sitting, just out the door, was this little guy, Suzuki Roshi, with this stick. He would bow to each person as they went out and since I didn't know he was there, I had the experience of walking here and, bam, you know, he just looked right through me. I wasn't there. Something happened and that was sort of one of the first transmissions that I had.

I met Stuart Brand at the time, so I guess I wrote something about Buddhism in America or access to Buddhism in America

for the *Whole Earth Review* and became, for one or two issues, their religion editor.

That was my beginning. As part of writing my book, I went up to the Rochester Zen Center and wrote a piece on Kapleau Roshi, which *New Age Journal* published. Then I started writing pieces for *New Age* on Buddhism, and became kind of like their Buddhist expert. Trungpa Rinpoche described Buddhism as being like a crocodile—you get a little bit in and the crocodile's teeth keep you from getting out. So I was in the crocodile's mouth! I was a Buddhist even though I was writing about EST and rebirthing and making my living as a journalist.

The only place I could write about Buddhism was the alternative media, because my tone wasn't cynical enough for the mass media at that point. I was able to have this open, yet skeptical view of the subject and also be a participant in the subject, which to mainstream journalism is kind of like the thing with LSD: If you don't take LSD, you can't really write about it because you haven't experienced it. But if you *do* take it, you can't write about it because you're brain dead! Or if you go to a workshop and have some experiences and write about it, then you're brainwashed. But to me, as a journalist, if you don't have the experience, it's just not as much fun or as accurate.

So I worked with New Age journals off and on and then I became the editor of a newspaper in Boulder, the *Vajradhatu Sun,* which was run by my root lama, Trungpa Rinpoche. The *Vajradhatu Sun* was trying to report on Buddhism in general and

Rinpoche had a particularly wide view and appreciation of various forms of Buddhism, which is one reason I studied with him. The *Vajradhatu Sun* was, in his mind, going to be like the *Christian Science Monitor* of Buddhism. The *Christian Science Monitor* has a viewpoint of Christian Science, but at different times it's a trustworthy, real newspaper. I took the job because I felt that it was one way that I had of working with him as a teacher, as the normal way of being a good student and doing the things you were supposed to do didn't seem to work for me too well.

After a couple of years of working with that newspaper, I know I published some of Helen's first writings that became her book, *Zen in America.* I think there was a piece about Kwong Roshi and we weren't paying anybody anything at all. I decided that since we could only pay people ten or twenty-five dollars an article, that this was just an insult, so it was just cleaner to say we don't pay. This is merit. This is pure merit you get for writing for us.

After about five years of working there and freelancing at the same time, the situation arose where there was a kind of scandal in the Vajradhatu community and I felt that we had to publish something about it because I was going on this *Christian Science Monitor* model and I was a journalist. It turned out that the publication was published by the *Vajradhatu* board, and so I had my first experience of an editor-publisher situation. Basically, they kept stalling and I said I'll wait for x-amount of time before doing something because it's a very difficult situation and I agree we have to figure out what

we're going to say. And while that was going on the *New York Times* came out with a story and so I said, Well, you know, now it's out there and you really have to say something, but they still didn't want to. So I said that in that case I have to resign; it's the only professional, ethical thing I can do.

After this a small newsletter grew up in our community, called *Sangha,* that started publishing other stuff. At that point, Helen and I became involved in discussing putting together an independent Buddhist newspaper.

Helen Tworkov: Well, there were a couple of journalists talking about an independent journal from the early eighties—Rick and myself and Andy Cooper, who is at *Ten Directions.* But somehow the timing wasn't right. Rick had just finished *Swans* and he wanted to go back to Boulder to be close to Trungpa Rinpoche, so he went to do the *Vajradhatu Sun.* And so it didn't come up again until Rick separated from the *Vajradhatu Sun.* It really brought home the lack of any forum for Buddhists to be writing about dilemmas in their own communities. There was simply not anyplace to do that.

The mainstream media has actually done a pretty good job in many cases and in particular around this. We have not seen, for example, revengeful, malicious views that we might have at some point expected. But what we did see was Buddhism being talked about in a context that was not particularly sympathetic, so what are we going to learn from this? We're committed to Buddhism. It's here to stay. We're not about to say I'm never going to practice again because this bad thing happened or whatever happened. How are we going to investigate it? How are we going to learn from it? How are we going to use it? And there was really no place to do that because there was really no discussion going on.

Now, something else curiously happened in the eighties because in addition to the problems of Trungpa Rinpoche's community, there were problems in other communities—a situation with Baker Roshi at San Francisco Zen Center; Maezumi Roshi in Los Angeles; some problems in the Vipassana community. So the sex, money, alcohol—whatever they were—scandals were hitting across the board. I think until that happened people didn't know a whole lot about each other's communities, but there was a sense that they had the best one, that Vajrayana students would interpret the perfect teachings in the most literal way; the Zen people always had a sense of being very special about being Zen students; Vipassana students thought perhaps that theirs were the earliest Buddhist teachings.

So one of the things that happened during the eighties with all these scandals was that things really got leveled out. Suddenly, we were all in the same boat and it didn't matter whether we were Tibetan students, or Zen, or Vipassana. It was pretty much of a mess and none of us knew what was going on.

One thing that happened is that we understood that as Americans new to Dharma, the obstacles that we were confronting gave us a lot in common with other Buddhist sects. And what that allowed for was the possibility of a magazine that could

Helen Tworkov during the media panel discussion

be addressed to Buddhists of all different kinds. Until then I think perhaps you couldn't have made it work. Just financially, there wouldn't have been enough people to buy it. So I feel that the scandals were a great kind of leveler. I think they allowed for the possibility of having a nonsectarian journal, which may not have happened until then.

In 1990, when we started talking about *Tricycle,* there were two possibilities or intentions: One was to create a forum where Buddhists from different lineages could talk to each other and be in touch with each other, and the other was that, by that time, it seemed as if we could successfully create a common language. Sometimes a Vajrayana student cannot read Zen language or a Zen student cannot read English Vajrayana language. So if we could create a way of talking through a nonsectarian Buddhist-communication medium, we could create a language at the same time that could also address non-Buddhists in the world at large. The risk was whether it could work financially or not because we've never had any foundation or institute or major funder behind us.

When we started, we certainly counted on drawing subscribers from the Buddhist community. In our case it meant people new to Buddhism, who were involved in some exploration, some investigation, of what this tradition was about and what it meant to them and the practice community. The first reader survey we did showed, us much to our surprise, that 50 percent of our readers were not Buddhists and were not calling themselves Buddhists. So we see that there's a tremendous amount of interest in Buddhism that's not necessarily coming from practitioners, that there's a great deal of interest in Buddhism as a view, as a philosophy, as a kind of a fresh perspective on one's own life in the society and that it's possible to be interested in these things without necessarily being engaged in practice.

I'd like to talk a little bit about the first issue because one of the things that happened as *Tricycle* went on is it became very common for me to hear, "Oh, the last issue of *Tricycle* was the best one ever." This happened steadily for about ten issues in a row. And actually I always thought the first issue was pretty great but there are so many spelling errors and it's so bad visually that I can barely open it up. The very first issue of *Tricycle*—it was the year of Tibet coinciden-

tally—we asked Spalding Gray to interview the Dalai Lama. That caused a big stir and a lot of people were very, very offended by it. Immediately they defined *Tricycle* as the *People* magazine of Buddhism. It was going to be too secular. It was going to be too popular.

He was in one of these huge hotels and below the Dalai Lama's room was a swimming pool with all these young California beauties with little bikinis. So Spalding Gray asked him something about what did he think about when he sees these young women. Many people found the question extremely offensive. It didn't phase him in the least.

One of the reasons we asked Spalding Gray to interview the Dalai Lama was because at that time, even in 1990, the Dalai Lama had been interviewed so often. I must have read a hundred interviews at that time. So how do you interview somebody and not get the same old interview? What we wanted to do with *Tricycle* was to establish a guideline that said, If you can read it somewhere else, it's not for us. That was true with a lot of things we covered, and it's true even now.

Somebody raised the question of Tibet, which is really interesting in terms of the media for this discussion. When the media comes in, it is covering so much. Can we give it another angle? Can we cover something about the Clinton administration's Asian Buddhist funding that the *New York Times* isn't covering? Could we do it better? I don't think so. We don't have that kind of money to send reporters in. But do we have another way of looking at it? I'm not sure we do. When we think we have another way of looking at it, we'll try to find that way. So in the case of the Dalai Lama, when you have somebody who's been interviewed that much, I think we hired the right person because Gray asked questions that nobody had ever asked him, not just about girls in bikinis.

He asked, What do you do when you get up in the morning? What do you do? You're in this hotel and you get up, what do you do? You meditate. Well, how long do you meditate? Where do you meditate? Do you meditate on the floor? Do you meditate on the bed? He engaged the Dalai Lama in a kind of questioning that, in fact, people don't do with him. So we got a very unique interview, which is what we wanted.

Now, interestingly enough, for all the criticism that we got at that time about being very popular, the people who were very critical did not seem to notice what I thought was terrific about the first issue, that we put the Pali canon on the newsstands. Nobody talked about that. So in the criticism that we received, I saw that the people that were going to be very vociferous about Spalding Gray were not going to talk about the Pali canon. The Pali canon to them was not as sexy and it was not as juicy and it didn't have as much play. So that brought up this whole question of what kind of mix can you work with and how do you introduce Buddhism in this culture?

Here's one of the things that was very helpful to me. Years ago when I was living in the Zen community of New York with Bernie Glassman, I was working on my book Zen in America and was having very cold feet. I think in the middle of working on this book, the

Zen scandal started to hit and I thought I just might as well take this book and throw it in the fireplace, just forget about it. I don't remember exactly what we were talking about, but one day I said to him, "I just feel that I'm going to do something to violate the Dharma." Without batting an eyelash, he looked at me and said, "Don't worry. You can't." And it was a great teaching, especially for the kind of work that I'm now doing and have done. What he showed me in two seconds was that I had a monumental, egocentric confusion about my relationship to the Dharma. I can violate myself. I can't violate the Dharma. The Dharma cannot be violated.

I also don't mean to introduce that as a way of creating irresponsibility, or [an attitude of] Whatever I do, it doesn't matter. That's not true either. But I do think it illustrates this discussion of not only what I'm doing with Tricycle but also the mainstream media. There is a lot of concern that, whether it's with Tricycle or other magazines or the mainstream media, somehow the Dharma will be diluted. It will be. I take that, at this point, to be completely inevitable.

When I first got involved with Buddhism, about 1965, I felt very protective of the Dharma. Everybody did. Every time the word Buddhism was mentioned in the mainstream press, you sort of cringed, hoping that they were going to get it right, that they weren't going to call us a cult. My feeling now is that Buddhism is here to stay and it will get diluted and that's the nature of it and that's going to be the nature of any kind of cultural evolution. It has to be. It has to become secularized.

And what does that mean? My own hope is that you disseminate the Dharma and deepen the Dharma at the same time. I don't see it as two separate processes where you can just go deep and then you go deep and deep and then at some magic moment you say, Well, we've really seated this tradition deep enough so that now we can spread it. Or we say, Well, the teachings are so deep that nobody in this country can get it anyway, so let's just kind of spread it out thin for the next three hundred years and then we'll go really deep. There are all kinds of ways of understanding that.

My own understanding is that it's kind of a false separation in a way. Each one of us is capable of very different kinds of practices and kinds of lives with Dharma. And some people want to figure out how to secularize it with the good intention of helping many people. Some people think that maybe living in a monastery is the best way to help many people. As far as I can figure out, both of those things are accurate and true. So I think that you create a lot of different kinds of venues and some of them may be perceived as disseminating Dharma, some may be perceived as going deep with the Dharma, but they're all part of the same process.

So I no longer have any fears about the mainstream media and how they're going to get it all wrong. We all get it all wrong a lot of times, no matter who we are, who we're writing for, and what we're doing. You see all these stories coming out about Catholic priests. Well, the Church is not about to collapse, for better or for worse. It's here to stay and I feel the same way about Dharma. I don't feel

afraid of anyone getting it wrong. It's going to ride out whatever miscommunications or misguided statements might be made.

Wes Nisker: I'll just jump off from that with a little response actually to one question and also to your question.

Bringing up the Dalai Lama again, I always used to try and separate Buddhism from the New Age until I read, or somebody told me, that the Dalai Lama was asked whether he was fearful that Tibetan Buddhism would be lumped in with the New Age. He said, "Oh, no. We all be happy to have new age." That sort of cut through.

I just want to tell a little bit of my story, as I entered Buddhism in the media through a different medium. I was working in radio in San Francisco in the late sixties. I was a radical newscaster on an underground radio station and Scoop was my name. Later I went to India and found a Burmese Buddhist teacher. One of the most difficult things I experienced when I first sat down to meditate was the fact that songs kept coming up in my head and, having worked in a radio station, it was insidious. Since we played album sides on the radio, a song would come up and it would track through the whole side. And sometimes a song would come up and I'd go back to my breath for fifteen seconds and then fifteen seconds later the song would come back and it would be fifteen seconds later in the song.

I came back from India in 1971 filled with inspiration and enthusiasm for the Dharma and I thought, I'm going to take it to the radio. I'll turn the world on. I'll turn all the hippies in San Francisco on because this is the real revolution! I got a job back at the same radio station doing little features and started putting on spots about Dharma. It was a real lesson because I would be listening to myself and the radio station would be chugging along with rock-and-roll music and the deejays and then my little piece would come on and the energy would just drop right out of the whole. And, of course, a few weeks into it the station manager said, "This isn't working very well. You have to either start smoking dope again or we can't have this on our airwaves. It's a tune-out."

I think that incident is actually very instructive in terms of presenting Dharma through electronic media. I think there is a real conflict in presenting Dharma through electronic media, which is very different from print media. Print media is more personable in the sense that it's a mass-media forum and electronic broadcasting is very difficult to get anything in depth across.

In 1981 I was asked by a few Vipassana teachers if I wanted to start a journal for the Vipassana community, so myself and a partner, Barbara Gates, started *The Inquiring Mind*. It started out as a four-page little newsletter and is now, as you know, forty-five pages with a big mailing list. It's been very exciting watching it grow. We try to maintain our independence from any particular point of view, offering a forum to all the different voices within the Vipassana world as well as some voices outside of the Vipassana world, the Theravada world, whatever that world is that I live on.

There are always disputes. You just can't please all the people all of the time, it seems. For instance, we will put in an article—say, an interview with Jane Tillman about how Jungian archetypal psychology fits or doesn't fit with Buddhadharma—and we will get letters from orthodox Theravadans saying this is "West Coast" Dharma. They label us as West Coast because we publish in the Bay area, and there often seems to be an East Coast–West Coast dichotomy in that the more conservative folks are here on the East Coast. Anyway, we'll get letters about that and people saying we aren't really putting in enough about the actual practice, that this should just be a journal of practice and we shouldn't have articles about how improvisational theater might have some resonance with Dharma practice. So we run into those conflicts all the time.

Rick Fields: With Buddhist fundamentalists basically?

Wes Nisker: Yes, yes, absolutely. Buddhist absolutists. We're always walking that line between following our own interests and what we think serves the Dharma ultimately, which, from my point of view, has a lot to do with integrating other aspects of life and parts of American culture that do seem to have some kind of resonance with the Dharma. It's not only putting Buddhism out there but bringing things into Buddhism. And, as Helen says, I'm not so worried. I think it's going to get diluted and there will be people who love the diluted form, whatever it turns out to be, and whatever they call it, and there will be people who stay with the purity of the Asian way of doing it and that will be one stream of the Dharma in America. There'll be many streams and then we'll have an ocean, eventually. I'm not so worried about that either.

I'm also not so worried about how the mainstream represents us. Somebody mentioned here something that I was thinking about this morning. Look at how they represent Christianity or Judaism. It's very shallow the way the media represents most everything, including politics. So how can we expect them to treat Buddhism in any depth when they can't even treat a presidential election campaign with any depth? Why should we even concern ourselves as long as they mention us, as long as they don't forget us?

Rick Fields: What do you think about the recent celebritization of Buddhism? It seems in America for anything to be taken seriously, a movie star has to do it. Richard Gere is vocal about the Dalai Lama, so then people say, Oh, well, then maybe there's something to this.

Wes Nisker: In fact, right now all of you are missing hearing Robert Thurman, who *Time* magazine called the number one Buddhist in America, I think. So what are you doing here?

Participant: At lunch they were saying how that's because he's Uma's father.

Participant: If she were there, we'd be at that workshop.

Participant: Richard Gere and Uma Thurman are movie stars, but it seems, reading our publications, that we also are creating a star system. I think this is happening and I want to know how comfortable you feel about it.

Rick Fields: When I was editing the *Vajradhatu Sun,* which was a newspaper that also went to a lot of other places, we also found, as Helen did with *Tricycle,* that a lot of our readers were not connected with the Vajradhatu community. There were people who lived out in Kansas and different places and the people in the community didn't actually read the newspaper that much because they knew all the gossip. They knew everything way before our versions got out. And they were practicing; they were in the middle of this whole Buddhist thing. They were reading *People* magazine when they were off, or something else.

But I was trying to bring in various new ideas, so I started something called "Media Watch" in the *Vajradhatu Sun,* where anytime there was a mention of something having to do with Buddhism in the mainstream media, we would mention it ourselves or reprint it. This was often about some celebrity or other. I find it interesting because I think that those celebrities are our culture's archetypal figures.

In *Yoga Journal* we cover Buddhism, but we had this core audience of people doing yoga. As you know, Jane Fonda came out with a videotape because there's this sort of Hatha-yoga boom, which has to do with fitness, partly. All of sudden, instead of doing aerobics, people are doing yoga. So Jane Fonda comes out with this videotape and I really like the way we played that. To me, it was news. It was emblematic of yoga entering the larger culture. The purists all said, That's her; that's ridiculous. We're not even going to pay attention to that. To me, it meant something that the aerobics queen of the world had switched to yoga. There was a certain irony to the whole thing.

But then we did an interview with Jane herself on the telephone and she said, "Look, I'm doing this. I'm not a super yoga expert. I admit it." And we also interviewed her yoga teacher. So we went a little further than just the mainstream media, which was just where the news was, that Jane Fonda did yoga, and we went into the story a little deeper.

One of the reasons we're like *Tricycle* and, I think, unlike *Inquiring Mind,* is that we're a newsstand publication and we actually don't take any grants. *Yoga Journal* is the most commercial publication represented here. We exist purely on ads and subscribers and newsstand. So I wanted to be able to have "Jane Fonda Does Yoga," or something like that on the top of the cover.

Wes Nisker: Or Sting on the cover.

Rick Fields: We put Sting on the cover doing yoga because I want to draw people. It's a way of drawing people in. So, again, I'm not afraid that because Sting is doing yoga that that's going to destroy yoga.

Wes Nisker: I just want to make one quick comment on that question. Just like there's truth behind cliché, there's a reason why often the same people are featured in all of our journals, and that's because some of them have the most interesting things to say. Helen and I have had this discussion often, of looking for good writers to submit articles that we can trust. There aren't that many, so we use the same people commenting on certain issues because they have the most original, interesting things to say.

Helen Tworkov: One thing [to consider] is, are you creating these superstars? Well, certainly the kinds of circulation that any of us have don't make a dent in creating Richard Gere or anything like that. We can't add significantly to the stature of these people. I think a lot of it comes down to intention— what you're trying to do—and clearly *Tricycle* is in a situation where, in addition to ads and subscriptions and newsstand sales, we also depend on contributions, because we're not self-supporting yet. I hope we will be. We have to sell magazines.

And even before the Hollywood community got involved, when we were first talking about starting *Tricycle,* we knew very clearly that there were a certain number of well-known, major writers, such as Peter Matthiessen and Gary Snyder, that we sought for articles.

Now, of course, we're talking about practitioners and, frankly, in the interview I did with Richard Gere, he identified himself as a practitioner. There's a lot of holier-than-thou discussion of the media stars, as if just because they're famous they become people who cannot be serious about Buddhism. I think that that's not quite on target. I don't think they should be judged more harshly or by any other standard than we should judge ourselves. And we could go on endlessly about the merits and demerits of commenting on other people's practice.

I think in the case of Tibet, it becomes much more complicated because given the current political situation, just about the only weapon that they have available to them at this time is public media attention. They've got nothing else to rest on, whether that means endless interviews with Richard Gere, or Richard Gere talking about Tibet on the Academy Awards show. It gets attention. The more stars the Tibetans have on their team, the better, because that is the only shot they have. So to then come back to the Buddhist media and say, Oh, you guys are just pumping up certain cases. Sharon Stone had twenty-two Tibetan monks playing at some party. However else we judge it, there's the possibility that those very situations and the media attention they get could potentially help stop this holocaust that's going on in Tibet.

So I think a lot of it comes back to an extremely basic Buddhist principal, and that has to do with intention. What is the intention? Are you trying to sell magazines and, if so, why? What's the intention behind trying to sell *Tricycle*? What's the intention behind trying to create even more media attention for Richard Gere or to report on Sharon Stone's private musicians? What is the intention? I think in the case of Tibet you're into an extremely special situation.

Participant: I've been tracking the Tibetan issue, and many of my experiences have touched on getting the Tibetans to use the film media to get a lot more attention for their cause. The Tibetans get a lot of attention when the Dalai Lama comes to the United States, but as soon as he leaves, there's no attention whatsoever.

Helen Tworkov: You have the same problem in Christianity or Judaism or any of the main religions. You don't have a story unless there's some dramatic scandal or some problem.

Participant: The *New York Times Magazine* did a wonderful piece years ago on meditation.

Wes Nisker: There are a few.

Helen Tworkov: But generally, it's my understanding that that's a problem among religious-news editors.

Participant: I'm somebody who works in mainstream press covering religion. Just two points that I'll make. One is that what you're saying here is what I hear from every religious group that I come in contact with: Nobody understands us. Nobody can portray us. And that's all true because what you're talking about can't be put into words. Unless you've experienced it, you don't understand it.

On the other hand, I write for Religion News Service, which is a national syndicate. We're independent of any particular group and we're picked up by several hundred newspapers around the country. Primarily what I write about are what we call the minority religions, minority meaning not

Protestant, not Catholic, fewer in number. So I write a lot about Judaism, Islam, Hinduism, and I cover the Dalai Lama a lot when he's in Washington and things like that.

We have a New Age columnist as well as having an evangelical-Christian columnist. I am constantly amazed at the play that our New Age columnist gets in Catholic publications in Saskatchewan, Canada. You just would not expect it. I'm surprised at the play my stories get in Birmingham, Alabama, or Salt Lake City, where they will use big spreads.

And they're not putting their spin on it. It's the spin that we send out. They may mislabel a headline. They may chop a part out of it that we think is important for explanation, but there's a growing interest out there among mainstream-media people; they may be behind the curve but they see the curve changing. They see their readership changing and they want to stay in business. They want to relate to what's out there. So don't give up on it and I think you should all try and work more with it.

Rick Fields: I get lots of calls from people in the media saying, This is happening. What can you tell me about it? And I find that basically the reporting is pretty responsible and sympathetic on the whole.

Helen Tworkov: I have, too. In fact, I think it's been amazingly sympathetic. I think before it was sympathetic, it didn't exist at all. I think the Dalai Lama has played a particularly huge role in all of this—who knows about Buddhism, what they know about it, and how the media has handled it. If my memory

serves me correctly, this started about a year or two before the Nobel Prize. The *New York Times* was giving unbelievable coverage to the Dalai Lama and with enormous sympathy following one devastating article in the magazine section by a pair of husband-and-wife journalists who went to Tibet. But it's almost as if that came out and then every article for the next three years was trying to counteract that. I've been very astonished at how sympathetic it's been.

Participant: I was going to go back to a form of a question that was asked earlier that was talking about making stars. What I was hearing was that, within the Buddhist world of publications and so forth, we have stars coming out there. Not Richard Gere stars or whatever, but stars in the Dharma world. And I'd just like to ask you how you relate to that decision-making process. I know there are certain Dharma-teacher names that are popular and if you put them in there, people are going to be more likely to pay attention to the magazine. But, at the same time, you don't want to create a kind of little, exclusive clique where new, fresh ideas can't fit in. How do you go about making that decision?

Wes Nisker: Well, it's kind of a matter of chicken and egg. In the Vipassana journal, we pay attention to the major Vipassana teachers and we call on them for comment and interview, when we have a theme, because they are the ones who are thinking very deeply about a lot of things. We try to give voice to people, other people who come along who we think really deserve to have a forum, that either are expressing an approach to Dharma or their own vision that really deserves it. It's just a matter of intuition and trusting our own judgment. That's where our own practice sort of becomes "the medium is the message." So as the people who filter, we have to be as pure as we can or as open as we can.

Participant: How about the other argument that a person is well-respected because they've been covered a lot?

Rick Fields: One of things that people forget, I think, is the mechanics of publication. When I took this job at *Yoga Journal* (and I should say that I'm a contributing editor at *Tricycle*), people would say, What's your vision for the magazine? And I could make up some bullshit, but the truth is that I've got to fill this magazine every two months and I want to have a certain mix of things in it. It's not like I have millions of dollars and lots of time and sit there with some great strategic master plan! It's what's available!

It may be that somebody's a fantastically interesting teacher—somebody like, say, Toni Packer. She would be a star. Here's somebody who's published a couple of books of talks, but if we wanted to do a story about Toni Packer we would have to get a writer to go and do a story about Toni Packer. It's not so easy to find that person. So then a publisher publishes a book about Toni Packer by a student of hers who happens to be a writer. And Helen gets the book, hopefully enough ahead of time, and looks at it and says, "Wow, I can use this. It's already done. It's already written. I'm going to use it." It's not like anybody's plotting to make a star out of Toni Packer.

Helen Tworkov: I can't think of one example in *Tricycle* where we contributed to somebody's reputation. I think we are very dependent on unsolicited material and, of course, a lot of the people who send us material are the students of people who have had contact with those teachers because they're attracted to their teachings through other people or through books. So it can be a closed system. I'm aware of that and it can be a problem, but I used to, and I still, wish I had more money for editorial; that I could actually call somebody and say, Will you cover this? Could you do that? We don't have that kind of money, but there's something good about that, too, as I think it keeps the material very responsive to what's out there. If it doesn't come in, it's not out there. Now, there are times when it's true that I would like to have the money to go get it but, by and large, if there's some interest out there, it finds its way in. So there's a kind of a reality check to just seeing what comes into the office.

Wes Nisker: And hopefully it comes into my office before it comes into her office.

Emergent Trends
in Western Dharma

Lama Surya Das

MANY OF THE PRESENTERS AT THE CONFERENCE DISCUSSED WAYS in which Buddhism in the West has diverged, and must continue to diverge, from aspects of more traditional forms of practice and belief. Lama Surya Das* noted that, throughout its history, Buddhism has both changed the cultures that have taken it on and has been changed by them. While steeped in the traditions of Tibetan Buddhism in particular, Surya Das recognizes the importance of the Dharma's speaking to practitioners in their languages and in the light of their own cultural backgrounds. Otherwise, no matter how profound or moving the inherent message, it will fall upon deaf—or at least dampened—ears and spirits.

In this, his keynote address, which was the closing event of the conference, Surya Das looked carefully and deeply at how the Dharma has been affecting the West, North America in particular, and how these effects are changing the lives of those people who are willing to let them in. He presented a ten-point prescription for characteristics that he feels must determine the nature of the Dharma for it to take firm root in America. Many of these would probably be considered to be quite foreign to Asian forms of Buddhist practice.

Lama Surya Das concluded his talk—and, hence, the conference—by leading the audience of more than six hundred people in the chant of Kuan-yin Avalokita Chenrezi, OM MANI PADME HUM. At first he was joined by only a handful of participants, but the deep, resonant sound grew and grew, until it engulfed the hall, then gently died away to pure quiet. This was an eloquent demonstration of the profound possibilities inherent to the blending of ancient with contemporary as Westerners come into their own practice of the Dharma.

---

* Biographical information for Lama Surya Das is included in the introduction to his workshop, "We Are All Buddhas: The Joy of Meditation and the Natural Great Perfection," page 202.

T his has been a wonderful weekend here in the Back Bay of Boston— Bodhgaia on the Charles as some wise man called it—where one of, perhaps the, oldest Western Buddhist-practice centers in America was founded in the midfifties and still remains—the Cambridge Buddhist Association—and many other ancient connections, ever since Thoreau and Emerson were here talking up the Dharma and nonsectarian dharma—Hindu and Buddhist, etc.—until now.

I think it's very appropriate that this should transpire here in the Back Bay. Buddhism is always a little bit in the back, where it belongs. Not pushing forward, but quietly contributing; not converting others, but quietly contributing. When I called the hotel on Thursday to confirm my reservations, I talked to a woman at the desk who spoke with even more of a non-Boston, foreign accent than myself, and she said, "Oh, the buddha convention?" As a conference organizer and a person who likes to get together with other people, I hadn't really thought of this as a convention, but I thought, Yeah, right, it's the *buddhas'* convention. The buddhas are gathering. America the buddhaful. American Buddhas awaken: Throw off your chains, your concepts. Then I wondered, will they distribute hats? Like conventions hats?

I'm sure if Buddha were alive today and reteaching the eightfold path that he would have an extra inning, the ninth inning, called "good humor" or "right humor." Very important, especially for American Dharma and contemporary Dharma for us all, lest we take ourselves too seriously. I myself have fallen prey to that vice, I assure you. My old girlfriend used to call me "Serious Das." So, be warned that this talk also might veer in that direction. If it does, too bad.

I was thinking, what actually is our common ground that we share here? Is it, as Peter Matthiessen said, social action? social activism?* I think not...exactly. If we step back a little further, where is that coming from? I think that our common ground is really in the enlightenment experience, in practice, in spiritual awakening. Whether we think of where Buddhism comes from—and I don't mean in the East, India; there's no East or West in buddha-nature after all–where does Buddhism come from? It comes from something that happened under the Bodhi tree. It comes from an awakening; an enlightenment experience. Not just *his* enlightenment experience, not just *the* experience, but the awakenedness, the wakefulness, enlightenment awakeness itself, which we also participate in right now. That's where Dharma comes from and must come from if it's going to be living Dharma. A real Dharma transmission. A contemporary Dharma. A living flame of Dharma. Not just old rumors from the past.

So, the common ground that I see and enjoy myself, which is after all, what counts for me, the Dharma, is a very personal, individual intimate affair, I hope. Not just an institution or some kind of -ism with all the schisms that come along with it, but that

---

*See Matthiessen's keynote address, "The Coming of Age of American Zen," pages 396–406.

awakenedness experience, that innate wakefulness, that's where the Dharma lives and that's our common ground, as I see it.

Some people would say that meditation is our common ground or sitting is our common ground, whatever school we're in, whatever practice we're doing. That's fine, but I think even deeper than sitting, it's the awakeness itself that is our common ground and where it's happening right now. Let's not overlook it. And we participate in that. That's why the teachings say we are all buddhas by nature. We only have to awaken to that fact. That's what "awakening" means. That's what "satori" or "breakthrough" means. That's what enlightenment experience is: awakening from the dream of delusion—delusion about ourselves and others; delusion about reality. We are all buddhas by nature. Don't take my word for it. It says so in the *Hevajra-tantra,* in the Dzogchen tantras, in many other places. We are all buddhas by nature. It's only momentary obscurations which veil that fact.

Some of us are more like sleeping buddhas than awakened buddhas. Some of us are like sleepwalking buddhas. Still, we all participate in this innate wakefulness, this luminous awareness, or whatever we call it. All words fail. All words are weak translations, and yet that's our commonalty, I think, in Western Dharma. Everywhere actually, but as the subject today is Western Dharma and our conference here is Buddhism in America, I think that's our common ground today.

We hear many times about sitting or meditation. I think we've taken meditation up and that's very good, but that's only one of the three trainings of Buddhism—the three higher trainings: ethics, meditation, and wisdom (or awareness) training. So let's not just emphasize sitting or meditation or quieting our minds, but the heart of that, the luminous heart of Dharma; inexpressible, yet summed up in these weak translations: wakefulness, awakeness, awareness, presence, attention. Pay attention, it pays off. So, here, if we're talking about a Western Dharma—contemporary Dharma, American Buddhism, as Bob said, *toward* an American Buddhism,* a Western Buddhism—we really must consider that there may be more than one American or Western Buddhism.

Maybe we should throw out American Buddhisms. Here in New England, I think we might notice we have a distinctly New England–flavored Buddhism. It's a little different than in Europe or in California. Around New England, we've taken up the religion of sitting. Elsewhere people are doing other things that are also Buddhist, that are not just sitting: building temples and stupa shrines, chanting, publishing, and many other things. But I think here we've taken up the very rational form of Buddhism based around meditation practice and we see some of the most long-lasting meditation centers here, like the Vipassana Center in western Massachusetts, one of the bestpractice places in the world, not just in the Western World.

So, I think it's important that we realize that all of the sitting is a means to an end

---

*See Robert Thurman's keynote address, "Toward an American Buddhism," pages 450–68.

and that mediation is not just something we do, it's a way of being. It's not a doing, it's a way of being; it's a way of wakefulness. And not fall into mere techniques or mere positions or even into mere Buddhism. I think the commonality here, whether we talk about social action or getting enlightened for the sake of all beings, as we often hear, is the heart and mind. Awakening the mind, opening the heart. The balance of wisdom and compassion, truth and love. Not just any technique. Not just concentrating or quieting our minds. Not just any one piece of it, but all of it. Every piece in all of it and all of it in each piece.

Maybe we're parents and we don't have time to sit, to go to these bachelor retreats for weeks, months, and years. Maybe parenting is the most difficult bodhisattva practice. Waking up every night at two in the morning to burp the colicky baby, who barfs on your head to give thanks. That's much harder than getting up at five in the morning and going off to the zendo with your friends and chanting the *Heart Sutra* and drinking tea in a beautiful, elegant shrine room and being proud of ourselves. So, who talks in the West about family practice? That's social action. At home, social activists talk about "think globally, act locally." How about family practice? That's social activism, right there. Maybe the real family people don't have time to go on pilgrimages to Auschwitz. (Excuse me, Roshi. He challenged me to go there, last night. I'm definitely afraid to go there, so this is my getting back.)*

So I think our common ground is this awakeness, this buddha-nature. Even calling it buddha-nature makes it too foreign. It's not buddha-nature, it's *our* true nature, it's "you-ddha" nature. It's our true nature and we hear all beings are endowed with buddha-nature. All beings have buddha-nature. It's like a catechism. It's not even true. It sounds like we all have this buddha-nature inside. It's like a needle in a haystack. We have to find it. Buddha-nature is *every* needle of hay in the *whole* stack and the ground that it's on also. That's why spending a lot of time looking for that needle may have no purpose at all. It's just one more thing to do—which we may enjoy, then do it, enjoy it, but it's not much better than any number of other things people are doing in life. In fact, it's exactly the same as what everybody else in life is doing, which is seeking happiness or whatever.

So, why should we become Buddhists, when we can become buddhas? This is the gospel, the good news of Dharma. We can all be buddhas. We are buddhas by nature, we can all awaken to that. It's not so far from here to there. There is here. The word *here* is in the word *there*. It's not so far. We may have to try, make an effort, go around the world, sit on mountain tops, seek gurus or teachings. We may have to go there, but as T. S. Eliot said, we may have to go around the whole world to arrive back where we started and know it "as if for the first time." But that's where we're headed. Of course, that's we're we are. *It* is always here, right here—*IT*, with a capital *T*—*we* are elsewhere.

---

*Here Lama Surya Das refers to Roshi Bernard Tetsugen Glassman's Auschwitz retreat, which he described in his workshop, "Instructions to the Cook," pages 427–39.

That's the problem. It's always right here. We are usually elsewhere, or so it seems.

So the whole practice is here. It's right beneath our feet, beneath our bottoms. It's right here. It's not even beneath the surface. It's all surface anyway, and this is what we're doing. This isn't just something that transpired 2,500 years ago in the East. This isn't just something that the Dalai Lama or Mother Theresa or Christ or Lama Surya Das can do. Who are they? Who do they think they are? The Dharma, the truth, is for everybody—whoever loves it, wants it, practices it. That's who it belongs to. It doesn't belong to anyone. It belongs to whoever loves it, practices it, enjoys it.

Can you remember what brought you to the path? to the Dharma? to seeking? Was it a book? Was it a spiritual friend? Was it an illegal-substance experience? There are many gateway portals to the Dharma. What brought you here this weekend? It's too simple to say there's nowhere to go and nothing to get. Since we're still searching and seeking, let's be real. Let's not cut off our spiritual life, paralyze ourselves with some nondual claptrap, some rationalizations. *There's nowhere to go. There's nothing to do. I read it in a book.* Why were you reading the book? *Because I'm looking for something to do and somewhere to get,* etc. So, let's be very honest with ourselves—at least that's what I'm trying to require of myself, and I assure you it's not easy—honest, authentic, and genuinely ourselves. That's the way.

I remember somebody asked one of my old lama friends in the seventies—in

Darjeeling, in Kalu Rinpoche's monastery on a hillside in Darjeeling, in the Himalayan foothills—asked another old lama, "How did you manage to walk out of Tibet, across the snow mountains, all the way here, escape the Chinese, all the way here on foot at your age?" No down jackets, no maps, nothing. No Northface sleeping bags.

He said, "One step at a time."

I think that's my inspiration, or my battle cry: one step at a time. Right now the path is beneath our feet. It's up to us to keep reviving it every moment, every day, and to recognize also that it's not just a path to get somewhere else, it's the path that arrives right home, here. So, we deserve to enjoy it right now, every step of the way.

One day Ananda asked the Buddha, "Lord Buddha, is it true that the *sangha*, the community, the spiritual friends are half of the holy life?"

Buddha said, "No, Ananda. The *sangha* community is the whole of the holy life."

Spiritual friends, spiritual friendship, or just friendliness is the holy life. It's life. It's our life. We all have the Buddha. The Buddha is around everywhere. The Buddha means "enlightenment" or "wakefulness." We all have millions of Dharma books, Dharma teachings, Dharma workshops, Dharma conferences, Dharma farmers everywhere, like us, trying to bring up the crops of bodhi, Dharma farmers—*Dharma*cists, not just Buddhists.

We have the Buddha and the Dharma. We have the truth and the teachings about reality, but do we have *sangha* in the West? Where is the *sangha* that can support this wisdom work? Of course, the whole community, the whole circle of beings does in a way, but sometimes it's a little subtle, isn't it? You feel like you're going upstream. Everybody is headed for the mall on Saturday and you're heading to the mountains.

Traditionally there were different kinds of *sanghas*. I think emerging in the West today we see mostly the lay *sangha*. Actually there are three *sanghas*, I think, emerging today: the lay *sangha*, which is most of us; the monastic *sangha* (the ordained monks and nuns); and the third, the in-between *sangha*, or the Tantric *sangha*. As Suzuki Roshi said, "You Westerners, you're not exactly householders, but you're not exactly ordained, celibate monks either. You're a new breed." That's where most of us are. Those are the three *sanghas* today and any one of them can help support us at different stages of our life. We can practice with them in a contemplative community, monastic *sangha;* or in a lay way, in our own community or family *sangha;* or in a Tantric way, in an in-between way, where we're laypersons, but devoting most all of our time to the spiritual practice.

You know, in the West, in America at least, there are an estimated one to five million Buddhists. Probably one million "converts," like most of us are (I hate the word. I'm only Jewish on my parents' side, anyway… in this life)…but one million of us converts and five million all together, including the ethnic Buddhists from Cambodia and Vietnam, etc., who found a new life here. Fortunately! I'm glad to have them and that they could get here. With roughly half men and half women—there are a little more women—but we have a fairly gender-equal situation here in Western Buddhism with half the teachers being women also, more or less, which is a step forward from how it was in Asia.

Many people find that they have many spiritual friends here, more than one would think. People are always asking me, Where can I find a place to meditate, or Who can I do this with in remote Boise, Idaho, or Kansas? Of course these places are everywhere, but we have to seek them. We have to find them. Put a little effort, a little bit of ourselves into it—as Jon Kabat-Zinn said the other day, quoting T. S. Eliot in the *Four Quartets*: "not found, because not sought." Who has to do that seeking? Who is that up to? Who shall do it? Who wants to do it?

Today, from the East we've inherited three great traditions—just talking about Buddhism basically—the Theravada, Mahayana, and Vajrayana Tibetan Buddhist traditions, which have been essentialized, distilled, come down to us in America, in the West, mostly as the Vipassana, coming out of Theravada tradition; the Zen and some other schools like Pure Land and Nichiren from the Mahayana traditions; and the Mahamudra Dzogchen from the Vajrayana traditions. So these Vipassana and Zen and Mahamudra Dzogchen are distilled things that we can practice, that embody all of what went before. We've been transmitted all of this ancient wisdom. This is the transmission to us from the East, from the past, from the Buddha, and so on.

Now we're in the phase of transformation, as the Dharma enters a new culture, as it moved from India to other cultures, it historically has always undergone transformation. It has changed and affected, hopefully for better, the countries it has entered. It's also been changed and affected, integrating the cultures it has entered. So you see how different it is in Tibet, or China, or Japan, from how is it in Burma and Thailand. So it's very traditional that this is happening now in the West.

Our melting-pot karma here in the West is one Dharma, I'm sure. This is the first time all the extant schools of Buddhism have existed together and rubbed shoulders so closely in one place, at one time. In the East it would never have happened, and it never did. Many of us have practiced or are practicing with teachers and practice centers of different traditions, and this is very much out of karma to work out and work through. It has its down-sides. We might fall into dilettantism, or never really go deep, always withdrawing before we follow through. But it has it's up-sides also, many up-sides.

Where I come from, and my teachers of the nonsectarian, practicing lineage of Tibet —the Rime lineage, we call it, nonsectarian practicing lineage, not-studying lineage—I think this practicing lineage is what we have here today. People want to meditate. They want to get something out of it. Don't we? Talk about all beings, but why are we here, really? Let's get real. For the three jewels: me, myself, and I. Most of the time. So any American Buddhism or contemporary Dharma has to relate to the fact that this is a melting pot and we're all getting osterized together and that's the beauty of it, as well

as the conundrum and the frustration of it all. And the Rime outlook of Tibet, which was really a renaissance, didn't mix everything together. It preserved everything in it's own way, so we can actually practice the different things as they were meant to be, and yet they're all complementary to each other. They help us round out our spiritual lives, outer and inner lives, and this is a contemporary Dharma.

So, Buddhism has already, in a few short decades, greatly influenced a few fields in the West. Maybe you've noticed the great influence that our meditationist Dharma has in the fields of therapy and psychology. In the fields of death and dying, in hospice work, really bringing it through in the mainstream more and more; in the fields of mind-body medicine and the healing arts. In the creative and performing arts. Even in sports—the top of sports—the Chicago Bulls or Baggio, the Nichiren practitioner who is the greatest soccer player in Europe, on the Italian team. Dharma has had great effect in the human-rights, nonviolence, and social-service movements. Maybe you've noticed that among the last five or six winners of the Nobel Peace Prize were two Buddhist leaders, international activists: the Dalai Lama of Tibet and Aung San Suu Kyi of Burma. Let's not forget her, she needs us to remember her and help her over there.

Buddhism had a great effect and is still having an effect, just beginning, I think, in the fields of right livelihood and ethics in business and so on. "Right livelihood" has become a little buzzword. It's good. Everybody is seeking it these days. I don't know how it's going to work out, but at least it's provoking some kind of deeper searching for our vocation so we can make a life, not just a living. Deep ecology, another effect of Buddhist thinking, an interfaith dialogue in ecumenical understanding. Very important for our shrinking planet.

So, what I really wanted to talk about today, is what I defined as these ten trends in Western Buddhism or American Dharma.

First: Dharma without dogma. Of course, there are vestiges of that within our own minds, but basically a Buddhism without beliefs. A Dharma that's less doctrinaire and dogmatic and belief-based, one that is much more inquiring, skeptical, and rational and finding-out-for-ourselves-based.

Second: extremely lay-oriented (of course, with room for monasticism and other intermediate forms), but lay-oriented with the three *sanghas,* and so on.

Third: meditation-based and experiential, rather than academic, theoretical, esoteric, study-based, and so on. If you talk Buddhism these days, people think about meditation first, I would say.

Fourth: gender equal, as I already mentioned and did want to mention again, because this weekend I felt a lack of discussion of women in Dharma. This is something we could talk about at our next conferences, gatherings, or just on the way home in the car or train today. This is a very important issue. I'm a feminist myself, having been trained by one, and I think it's very important, especially, that men speak out. It's hard for the minorities to speak out for themselves, so it's important for the ruling classes

and the exploiters, the dominators, also to speak out for those underfoot.

We may not be able to change our behavior, but at least we can try. It's hard to change. Isn't it? Let's face it. Yet change is inevitable. So, let's allow for that, too.

Buddhism in the West is much more gender equal. If you've been in the East, you know what I'm talking about. Half the teachers in the West are women. In fact, some of the best teachers whose workshops I went to this weekend were the women. I can hear from men anytime; I can hear my own thoughts anytime about enlightenment from the eyebrows up—mind training, education, clarity, wisdom. But how about being grounded in our bodies? How about emotional intelligence? The logic of the emotions. How about having an honest-to-god feeling once in a while, you men? It's not that easy, is it? (I don't know why. It's not that hard, really.) So, gender equal and supportive of women. Equal-opportunity employers in Dharma, Inc. Very important.

Fifth: nonsectarian, eclectic, ecumenical, inclusive. A sort of amalgamated Dharma. Again, not just mushing everything together and losing all the fine tastes and distinctions, but a real beggar's banquet, a wonderful feast table all laid out nicely so we can taste everything itself as it is. Nonsectarian, not fundamentalist or dogmatic.

Sixth: extremely essentialized, simplified—not oversimplified, hopefully, although that is always a danger. It's so easy to oversimplify. Huston Smith said recently, when asked, Buddhism in America seems to be becoming mostly a mixture of pop psychology and New Age stuff. I thought that's a lit-tle bit critical, but it's also not untrue. And that's also fine. That's our karma, to make something new. To discern what's vital from what's extraneous and to help be part of the reshaping of the living Dharma in the West. Reshaping ourselves, as well as the Dharma, since we are *that*.

Simplified, demystified. For example, Vipassana is a very simplified, essentialized distillation of the entire Theravadan tradition in the East. They don't exactly have those ten-day meditation retreats in the East, nor could women and laypeople go to those monasteries until just the last hundred years in Burma and places like that. So, in the West, simplified, essentialized, demystified—not the-ological, cosmological—and a little bit pop and so on, but that's okay. Let's face it, we all like the idea of instant enlightenment. You know, add hot water—poof. Or take it in a pill. We've all tried that; that doesn't work, at least not for long. It's easier to get enlight-ened that way, than to stay enlightened.

And demystified: In the West we've left the churches and their Latin masses, most of us, the high churches and the things that we don't understand in seeking something that we can sink our teeth into and our postmod-ern, rational, skeptical, scientific way. So, that's good. It might have a little down-side—we have to be careful not to throw out the bud-dha with the bathwater—but it's extremely helpful in that we will actually find out for ourselves. And I think we are. As the Buddha said, his last words: Walk the path yourself. Walk the path with diligence. Work out your own way. The teacher only points the way.

You choose if you want to walk it, and you walk it. Every step of the way is the way, so don't wait around until you get somewhere.

Seventh: Egalitarian, democratic, nonhier-archical. Not so top-heavy and institutional-ized. This is also very Western, modern, democratic, American, Jeffersonian, delightful, I think. Not so class oriented. Not so theo-cratic or feudal. More egalitarian. Sitting in circles, rather than with one person on a throne and the rest below. Circle, rather than pyramid. Circles of *sangha,* rather than pyra-mids of evolution, and so on.

Eighth: a Dharma that is psychologically astute and rational; practice-based. Of course, with room for faith and devotion—and some of us, our hearts open very much that way, it opens the other side of our brain, the intuitive side. But generally, most of us in the West, I think, would agree, if you're looking at Vipassana or Zen or the Mahamudra Dzogchen traditions, and the self-inquiry movements and so on, they're psychologically astute. It's not based on beliefs or received knowledge. It's skeptical and inquiring; it's very practical.

We want to do it and we want to know how to do it and we're determined to do it. It's a kind of do-it-yourself Dharma. That is exactly congruent with the Buddhist teachings —do-it-yourself Dharma. There's nobody else that can do it for you. Of course, others can help on the way—spiritual friend, *kalyanami-tra,* teacher, elder, friend, supporter can help on the way—but still, we each walk ourselves and that's healthy. That's no problem. That's the good news. The bad news is, nobody can do it for us, but that's also the good news.

As somebody asked Chögyam Trungpa Rinpoche once, Does grace have any place in Buddhism? Trungpa, who was a genius, said, "In Buddhism, grace is patience. When you're patient, things come to you." He didn't just say that yesterday; he said that twenty years ago.

Ninth: Our Western Dharma is emerging as experimental, innovative, inquiry-based, exploratory, skeptical, and so on. It's very forward looking—present and forward looking—rather than preservationist. ("If it's in the past, it must be good.") It doesn't mean we have to throw it out right away, but also, we might question it. For the living Dharma to be true, it has to be old wine, yes, timeless old wine, but in new bottles.

I think that's what we see happening today as we have new generations of teachers here—not just the first wave, who came from the East, the Asian-born teachers, and the second-wave generation of people like myself, who trained with the Asian teachers in the East or even here. Now the third-wave generation is here of Western teachers trained by Westerners in the West, carrying forth the living flame of Dharma, of truth, of wakening. Transforming the transmission—being transformed in new ways, in new practices, beyond practice, beyond the old forms, and so on. Of course, still having recourse to the old forms.

Last—and I'm putting this last to tie up the weekend, since Peter Matthiessen started with the Friday first—is Dharma in the West is very much more than before socially active, socially informed, and engaged. Informed citizens; not reclusive or withdrawing, but much more integrated Dharma. Integrated, rather than introverted and reclusive and insular. Integrated with daily life, and our inner life and outer life being merged, so that family life, the workplace, the yoga of relationships as a spiritual path, and so on, all have a place in the mandala of practice, the buddha field of practice, here in America the buddha-full.

The Dalai Lama said, "What is important? The past is past; the future is important. We are the creators...." (The future is in our hands now. Even if we fail, no regrets. We have to make the effort. We know what to do. We have to make the effort. Even if we fail, no regrets.)

"To contribute to others, rather than to convert others. Motivated always by the altruistic *bodhichitta*..."—this awakened heart-mind; this wisdom and compassion mind; this unselfish, heroic, spiritual, awakening mind—"...motivated always by this altruistic, luminous, radiant *bodhichitta,* be creative in adapting the timeless essence of the Dharma to your own cultural times and circumstances."

That's an empowerment. You've heard about Tibetan Buddhism empowerments and initiations. That's an empowerment. Have your head on straight and your eyes pointed forward, as the Zen master said. That's all we need. The Zen master said, "Walk, run, sit, but don't wobble."

So, in reflecting upon where we've arrived at in the West, I was thinking about what brought us here, what brings us together, what brought us to the path. How to keep renewing it everyday so that it's actually a living, spiritual life now, for us; authentic, genuine, living spirit. Not necessarily religious, but spiritual, mystical even. Let's reflect for a moment upon what brought us here and what were our expectations? What were we looking for? And what shall we bring away from this conference? You see, you're all members. You're all buddhas already. The hotel has you registered that way.

If I were you, I'd take it home, before it fades. Reflect upon what will help us as we go home. What can we bring home? Is there something to bring home? Can we just keep our eyes peeled every step along the way and notice that what is here, is also there? Did we make some new *sangha* connections or learn some new Dharma perspectives or have a good time? Did we gain a little feeling of more friendliness to others and to ourselves also? A little connectedness? A feeling of belonging to something greater than ourselves, maybe? Maybe we came from afar to meet some other, likewise kindred spirits here. That is beautiful; may it continue to be so. Let's do this *sangha*-making wherever we are. Maybe we can put together half of this affair in our own town and be host to others who are looking for it. Not just guests—hosts. As the rabbi said a long time ago, I think it was Rabbi Hillel, "If not you, who? And if not now, when?"

I think I'm going to close here. If not now, when? That's my kind of escape clause. I consider this a great privilege to get together to address you, to take an hour of your time, to explore these things together. Life is precious. An hour is a lot. Six hundred of us getting together for a weekend. It's amazing.

Monks begin work on the Medicine Buddha Sand Mandala, which was completed by the conference's end

There's a lot of reverberations on many levels, seen and unseen.

I would like to ask you to join me, join us, join yourself, if you wish, in a little closing ceremony. Of course, this being a contemporary Dharma. Very simplified, distilled, dedication, sharing the positivity and the merits. Sharing what we've gained here with all. Including all in our practice. Embracing them in our hearts. Elevating our aspirations to include all. Not just to selfishly hoard it, as if it's something we can lose. It's increased by sharing and by giving it. Not missionarizing, but openly radiating and sharing the blessings.

Please join me in chanting this beautiful chant and hymn of the female Buddha of love and compassion, Kuan-yin Avalokita Chenrezi: OM MANI PADME HUM. We haven't really developed our good English soul music yet, so we're chanting in these funny languages, but I'll leave it to some of you to take the next step—rap music or whatever the next step is going to be—for chanting the *Heart Sutra* or our own prayers in English, or French, or German, or Spanish, or whatever. OM MANI PADME HUM, the Sanskrit chant of love and compassion. Radiating from our heart, sharing the merits, sharing the blessings. Radiating from the sunlight heart within us. Warming up. Extending our embrace to all, who are not that different than us. Who want, need, aspire to more or less the same things we do. For we're all interconnected anyway. All beings seen and unseen, human and otherwise, throughout all possible universes.

Mantras are not usually chanted for their meaning, but this means "the jewel is in the Lotus," or "the Buddha—love and compassion—is within our own spiritual blossoming"—like the lotus blossoming. Love and compassion is within our own spiritual blossoming, so we water this flower with these chants, these prayers, these moments of mindfulness or presence. And these flowers are beautiful, even half-blossomed, even unblossomed. Growing out of the mud of our base nature, blossoming in the sun, which is really the alchemical transformation, transmutation, that Tsultrim* was talking about this morning in her talk about tantra. Transformation.

So, please join in when you're ready OM MANI PADME HUM. The national mantra of Tibet; the Dalai Lama's mantra; the mantra of my own teacher, the late Kalu Rinpoche, and many others. OM MANI PADME HUM. Bring it out from the depths. This is a Buddhist prayer. Don't be afraid to move your body; we're not wood yet. Try it if you haven't yet,

just try it. From the heart; heart radiating, heart overflowing, heart opening; chest opening; breath opening. Visualize the warm-sun in your heart radiating, warming you up, radiating out in all directions at once.

May all beings be happy. May all be peaceful and fulfilled. May all beings be awakened, liberated, free. Radiating light in all directions at once, touching all beings; light rays reaching out. Illumining the darkness. Reaching out and blessing all beings; radiating blessings. Share your blessings, share the merits with all. Don't be stingy. Compassion for all equally. Loving-kindness for all beings. Forgiveness for all; accepting all. Love for all—love unconditional.

Loving yourself, bring it all back. Accepting yourself totally. All the light rays comingback to you. Forgiving yourself, accepting yourself, loving yourself, embracing yourself. Open yourself to love; receive love. Soften up, open to it. Soaking-in love, feeling your love. You deserve it. Gently melting, dissolving—dissolving in inner light, love, and joy. Resting in that light. Being that. OM MANI PADME HUM

Let go totally; just be present, natural, complete, at home, at ease in the great perfection.

May all beings everywhere be awakened, liberated, fulfilled, and free. May there be peace in this world and throughout all possible universes, and may we all together complete the spiritual journey. Homage to the Buddha within. Don't overlook her.

Good night everybody. God bless.

---

*See Tsultrim Allione's keynote address, "Relationship and Intimacy as Path," pages 274–85.

Afterword

Al Rapaport

Many conferences take place today, which makes for no lack of places to spend our money and our time. But the fact that nearly eight hundred people elected to gather together on a cold winter weekend in Boston to discuss the future of Buddhism made this conference a unique event, the experience of which surpassed most attendees'—and certainly the organizer's—expectations. As one person wrote on the post-conference evaluation form: "My difficulty has been that there was too much happening...but it's great to tap into different teachings and teachers...to dialogue and bring it home."

In fact, bringing it home is what this conference was about. Participants came from all walks of life; among them were doctors, lawyers, and architects as well as priests, monks, and nuns. As a doctor stated, "I wasn't sure what to expect, but I learned a lot, and I gained tools that I'm sure will assist me in my spiritual growth and in my medical practice with patients."

In other cases, it was the sense of community, or *sangha,* that the conference engendered that most impressed attendees:

I especially appreciated gaining this sense of the larger *sangha* and the cross-pollination of traditions....I thought it might be just one general talk after another, and as such, not very useful. But actually the sense of community was quite helpful and encouraging, as was meeting a variety of teachers and a great many practitioners.

As conference organizer, what amazed me most was the caliber and attitude of the participants. Evidently this also impressed those attending: "The presence of so many wonderful teachers combined with that of warm, intelligent attendees, was remarkable," said one person. Another "loved the friendliness and openness of most people. Over and over I'd speak to someone who at first seemed remote and we would have a great 'meeting.'"

Nor was this attitude lost on the personnel of the Boston Park Plaza Hotel, for a staff member told me: "It was an incredibly nice crowd and the staff keeps remarking how much they enjoyed serving them. Everyone was so respectful and grateful for even the littlest thing....It made our job easy."

However, from a "practice" point of view, probably the most important result of the Buddhism in America Conference was the effect it seemed to have on the spiritual quest of many attendees, as witnessed by the following comments:

I planned a weekend of observing, sharing, learning, and socializing—and that all happened because of the great teachers and the dynamic atmosphere. I didn't expect to do a lot of "personal work," but I did. It transformed me.

This was a fantastic experience for me. It renewed my commitment to my practice, which is perhaps the most valuable gift someone can receive!

I found my first (official) teacher at the conference, and I will always be grateful for this.

I came to the conference with no expectations—only excitement, since I am only a beginner to practice. However, I left with a heart full of joy and a hand full of new friends as well as a teacher who is in my nearby area.

In the course of a fairly long and busy professional life, I've attended many conferences on many topics. This was one of the very best, on any subject. It's early to be sure, but I now believe that those three days in Boston clarified and solidified my commitment to practice.

The metaphor of the diamond net of Indra is a popular one in Buddhism. This net is made up of countless gems, each of which reflects every other gem. Thus, each facet's effect extends for eternity. On a practical level, we can see our life as this net, with every action we take affecting the entire universe. In terms of the dissemination of Buddhism in America, while the results of this conference may be difficult to ascertain now, they may become more apparent in the future. In a way, it has opened up a whole new avenue for Buddhists to express themselves.

Glossary

The terms included in this glossary have been culled from the presentations included in this book. The definitions are geared toward the specific uses and approaches of the presenters as they spoke during the Buddhism in America Conference. Many Buddhist terms have rich, ages-old overlays of meaning and interpretations. The reader is encouraged to seek out additional sources for more in-depth and practice-specific interpretations.

Words enclosed between < and > are defined elsewhere in the glossary.

anapanasati (Pali)   meditation on the breath; the basic practice for most schools of Buddhism

anitya (Skt.)   lit. "impermanence"; the condition of mutability, flux, or transiency, which characterizes all things

Atiyogayana (Skt.)   *See* Dzogchen

avidya (Skt.)   ignorance; *avidya* is considered to be an all-encompassing trouble, or "disease," that afflicts the impure mind. Its cure is enlightenment, or *vidya* (wisdom; knowledge)

bardo (Tib.)   lit. "in-between state"; a state of being that exists between death and rebirth

bhikshu (Skt.)   generally, a Buddhist monk; specifically, a monk in the <Mahayana> tradition

bhikshuni (Skt.)   generally, a Buddhist nun; specifically, a nun in the <Mahayana> tradition

bhikku (Pali)   generally, a Buddhist monk; specifically, a monk in the <Theravada> tradition

bhikkuni (Pali)   generally, a Buddhist nun; specifically, a nun in the <Theravada> tradition

bodhi (Skt.)   enlightenment; awakening

bodhichitta (Skt.)   lit. "mind of enlightenment"; the decision or determination to become enlightened or awakened

bodhisattva (Skt.)   lit. "enlightenment being"; a person striving to attain enlightenment

brahma-viharas (Pali and Skt.)   lit. "divine states of dwelling"; the four immeasurable (or virtu-ous) states: kindness, compassion, sympathetic joy, and equanimity

Buddhadharma (Skt.)   lit. "Buddha teaching"; generally, teachings intended to lead to enlightenment; specifically, the teachings attributed to <Shakyamuni Buddha>

bushido (Jap.)   lit. "the way of the martial scholar"; the samurai code of honor and morality

Ch'an (Chin.)   Chinese school of <Mahayana> Buddhism; Ch'an derives from <*dhyana*> in India and became <Zen> when brought to Japan.

chakra   lit. "wheel" or "disk"; basis of meditation on points of energy in the human body, which result from left and right energy channels wrapping around a nexus, affecting energy flow; particularly prevalent in forms of Tantric practice. Also the Buddhist symbol of law

chintamani (Skt.)   the wish-fulfilling jewel; symbolic of several individual buddhas and <bodhisattvas>

Chöd (Tib.)   lit. "cutting off"; Tibetan practice in which one visualizes an obstacle in one's path (e.g. sickness, pain, a fear) as a demon, then feeds this demon all of what it wants until it has been sated; a practitioner is a Chödpa

dakini (Skt.)   female buddha; great teacher in
    <Vajrayana> and Tantric Buddhism

Dharma (Skt.)   a complex, necessarily ambiguous
    word that encompasses many meanings,
    depending on the context and the speaker's
    intent. Among the more-frequently encoun-
    tered uses are (1) "the one ultimate reality"
    (i.e., natural laws to which all beings are sub-
    ject); (2) the direct teachings of <Shakya-
    muni Buddha> as put forth in the sutras;
    (3) the object of thought; mind.

dharmakaya (Skt.)   lit. "the body of the law"; the
    embodiment of pure buddha mind; the unity
    of the Buddha with everything that exists

dharmata (Skt.)   the nature of all things

dhyana (Skt.)   meditation or concentration; more
    generally, any state derived through absorbed
    attention. ("jhana" in Pali; "ch'anna" or "ch'an"
    in Chinese;" zenna" or "zen" in Japanese)

dorje (Tib.)   lit. "lord of stones"; the symbol of the
    essence of reality, the basis of everything. In
    Tibetan Buddhism the dorje is the masculine
    symbol of the path to enlightenment. See
    also vajra.

duhkha (Skt.)   pain, suffering, distress, sorrow; the
    nature of human existence

Dzogchen (Tib.)   lit. "great perfection"; medita-
    tion practice predicated on the concept that
    all appearances are creations of the mind,
    therefore purity of mind is always present,
    needing only to be recognized. Closely asso-
    ciated with Nyingma school of Tibetan
    Buddhism.

eightfold path   the fourth of the <four noble
    truths>; the path leading out of suffering. It
    consists of right understanding, right thinking,
    right speech, right attitude, right livelihood,

right effort, right mindfulness, right concen-
    tration.

four foundations of mindfulness   See satipatthana

four noble truths   the basis of Buddhist teaching;
    they are (1) the truth of suffering (see
    duhkha); (2) the truth of the origin of suffer-
    ing; (3) the truth of the ending of suffering;
    and (4) the truth of the path that leads out
    of suffering i.e., <the eightfold path>.

gassho (Jap.)   lit. "the joining together of the
    palms of the hands"; <Zen> gesture of
    greeting, gratitude, recognition, or veneration

gatha (Skt.)   lit. "thread"; a song, verse, or poem;
    often included within a <sutra>

Hinayana (Skt.)   lit "the lesser vehicle"; Originally,
    a path that split from the <Mahayana> tradi-
    tion of Buddhism; Hinayana emphasizes the
    striving for liberation of the individual, rather
    than the more-inclusive enlightenment of all
    sentient beings. Hinayana emphasizes teach-
    ings and practices the aim of which is the
    removal of mental afflictions in order to
    achieve <nirvana>. Frequently referred to as
    <Theravada>, which is the only Hinayana
    tradition still practiced today.

kalyanamitra (Skt.)   lit. "noble friend"; someone
    who shares wisdom and teachings of the
    <Dharma> with one or more others who
    have progressed less far along the path.
    Often used as a term for teacher.

karma (Skt.)   lit. "deed"; conduct; an act that has
    moral significance—be it for good, evil, or of
    neutral effect—arising from the universal law
    of cause and effect

karuna (Skt.)   compassion

klesha   lit. "trouble, defilement, or passion"; a defilement that is overcome through training. The ten *kleshas* are greed, hate, delusion, pride, false views, skeptical doubt, rigidity, restlessness, absence of shame, and lack of conscience.

koan (Jap.)   An object of <Zen> meditation used for attaining enlightenment. A koan is a phrase from a paradoxical story, <sutra>, or question-and-answer construct upon which one meditates. ("kung-an" in Chinese; "kong-an" in Korean)

Madhyamika (Pali)   one of the two primary schools of <Mahayana> Buddhism. The focus of Madhyamika is the demonstration of emptiness, or <*shunyata*>, which leads to ultimate liberation.

mahamudra (Skt.)   lit. "great seal"; In the Tibetan Kagyu school of Buddhism, *mahamudra* refers to the Middle Way. This meditative system recognizes the position of the individual relative to the existence or nonexistence of reality. The meditator dispenses with visualizations and rituals of <tantra>, instead maintaining a focus on the natural state of mind, which is the union of luminosity and emptiness <*shunyata*>.

mahasiddha (Skt.)   generally refers to an ascetic master of the <tantras>, who is recognized through certain magical abilities that demonstrate his or her enlightenment. More specifically, Tibetan Buddhism was greatly influenced by the eighty-four *mahasiddhas*, men and women from all walks of life whose examples set ideals for individual enlightenment.

Mahayana (Skt.)   lit. "Great Vehicle"; with <Hinayana> one of the two primary schools of Buddhism. While both approaches emphasize the historical teachings of <Shakyamuni Buddha> as revealed in the <sutras>, the primary emphasis of Mahayana is on the path and practices of the <bodhisattva>, which necessarily strives for the liberation and enlightenment of all sentient beings.

maitri (Skt.)   benevolence, loving-kindness, friendliness ("metta" in Pali)

mandala (Skt.)   lit. "circle"; a diagram or symbolic representation that encompasses the cosmos, representing the residence and attributes of the buddha, <bodhisattva>, or other deity who is the focus of meditation. The mandala is important in <tantra> as a meditation reference point.

mantra (Skt.)   a sound or very brief sequence of sounds that bear(s) power in the utterance and hearing. Mantra is manifested by the meditator as a focus of attention and a calling-forth of certain cosmic elements or attributes of the buddhas. Sometimes misconstrued as chant.

maranasati (Pali and Skt.)   mindfulness of death

marga (Pali)   way or path; any method that leads to enlightenment

metta   See *maitri*

Mikkyo (Jap.)   lit. "the secret teaching" or "the esoteric teaching"; mystic teachings that arose in India after the <Hinayana> and <Mahayana> and were brought to Japan by Saicho, founder of the <Tendai> school and Kukai, founder of the <Shingon> school. ("Mi-tsung" in Chinese) mudra (Skt.) lit. "seal; sign"; a codified physical posture or gesture of symbolic character. In Buddhist art, the mudra employed by a buddha or deity is freighted with iconographic meaning. In <tantra>, the mudra confers specific power and mystical import upon the meditator who assumes it. Mudras assist the meditator in establishing and maintaining a direct connection with the buddha whom they are visualizing in a meditation.

nirvana (Skt.) lit. "extinction"; the final liberation from the cycle of rebirths, or <samsara>, and deliverance into a wholly new mode of existence. This is the ultimate goal of Buddhist practice and is attained by ceasing all desire and being in the complete absence of all desire.

one-pointedness the focusing or concentration of mind on a single point or object. See also samadhi

phowa (Tib.) lit. "change of place"; a practice of particular importance to those who work with the dying and to one who is dying him- or herself. Phowa allows the meditator to remove the consciousness to a pure buddha-paradise at the moment of death.

prajna (Skt.) lit. "wisdom"; transcendental insight or wisdom attained through enlightenment

Pure Land Buddhism school of Buddhism in Japan and China that centers on the quest to be reborn in the Pure Land—the last rebirth prior to attaining <nirvana>. Its founder, Honen, held that transitional paths to enlightenment—e.g., meditation, ritual, and the precepts—did not lead to enlightenment; salvation was attainable only through reliance on the power and compassion of the buddha Amitabha, who vowed to bring to the Pure Land all beings who devote themselves to this quest. Today, Pure Land Buddhism, or Jodo-shu, has the largest number of adherents of any school in Japan.

Rinzai (Jap.) With <Soto> Zen, one of the two schools of Japanese <Zen> still active today. Its primary emphasis is on <koan> practice.

Ritsu (Jap.) lit. "discipline"; a school of Japanese Buddhism that stresses a strict observance of the <vinaya> rules of discipline and the <Theravada> ceremony of ordination

samadhi (Skt.) lit. "make firm"; concentration; a state of <one-pointedness> of mind that one attains through meditation

Sambhogakaya (Skt.) lit. "enjoyment body" or "body of delight"; the divine or celestial form of a buddha who is in her or his paradise and may enjoy the truth that she or he embodies

samsara (Pali) lit. "always moving" or "wandering together"; the cycle of rebirths. One is dragged from life to life until one has become free of hatred, greed, and delusion, at which point one enters <nirvana>. Since all beings are trapped in this cycle until they attain enlightenment, samsara has come to be interpreted as fate or destiny.

sangha (Skt.) In its most general use, sangha refers to a community, thus the community of Buddhist believers. Within Buddhism, however, there are many different levels of community so, depending on the context, sangha may refer to the community of Buddhist monks and nuns, or to all those who profess certain practices, or even specifically to the individuals who sit together at a particular <zendo>.

satipatthana (Skt.) lit. "four foundations of mindfulness"; a basic meditation practice of the <Theravada> tradition of Buddhism. In sequence, the four foundations are mindfulness of body, of sensations, of mind, and of mental objects.

satori (Jap.) enlightenment; in certain schools of <Zen> Buddhism, satori refers to a moment of nondual awareness

sattva (Skt.) a sentient or conscious being; a living organism that plainly seeks to avoid pain and strives for happiness

seiza (Jap.) lit. "sitting in silence"; the posture traditionally adopted in <Zen> practice. It differs from the half- or full-lotus in that the sitter kneels, then sits upon his or her heels while holding the back erect.

sensei (Jap.) teacher; title of respect in Japan

sesshin (Jap.) lit. "gathering one's thoughts"; in <Zen> practice, a period of especially intensive and strict practice

Shakyamuni Buddha the historical Buddha, who, prior to his enlightenment, was known as Prince Siddhartha

Shamatha (Skt.) lit. "dwelling in tranquillity"; the meditative practice of calming the mind; frequently coupled with <Vipassana>. ("samatha" in Pali; "chih" in Chinese)

Shikantaza (Jap.) lit. "only sitting"; <Zen> meditative practice in which no particular object (e.g. the breath, a visualization, etc.) is used as a focus of concentration. According to

Dogen Zenji, the highest and purest form of <zazen>.

Shingon (Jap.) lit. "sect of true words and spells"; a mystical school of Japanese Buddhism, brought to Japan by Kukai in the ninth century. Its is characterized by elaborate rituals, deep learning of two particular <sutras>, and the contemplation of <mandalas>..

shunyata (Skt.) lit. "emptiness"; the fundamental Buddhist conception of ultimate reality: All beings and things are essentially void of self and are impermanent. ("sunnata" in Pali; "kung" in Chinese; "ku" in Japanese)

siddha (Skt.) a person who has attained perfection

Siddhartha See Shakyamuni Buddha

Soto (Jap.) With <Rinzai> Zen, one of the two schools of <Zen> still active in Japan today. Its primary emphasis is on the practice of <shikantaza>.

stupa (Skt.) The stupa originated as a burial mound, which later led to its use as a shrine to hold relics of deceased holy figures. Over time, it became a sculptural or architectural structure used to house sacred objects, including texts, such as <sutras>, and images.

sukha (Skt.) bliss or joy; happiness or peace

sutra (Skt.) In <Theravada>, the sutras are the direct teachings of <Shakyamuni Buddha>, which were passed down verbally among his followers, until ultimately they were committed to writing. In <Mahayana>, the canonical sutras also include some nonhistorical sermons, such as the Heart Sutra and the Lotus Sutra. ("sutta" in Pali) tantra (Skt.) lit. "continuum"; in narrower sense, a text that passes on a specific aspect of the wisdom of <Shakyamuni Buddha> (c.f. sutra). More generally, as a basic element of <Vajrayana> practice, tantra can include chanting and visualizations, among other approaches.

tathagata (Pali and Skt.) lit. "thus-gone one'"; an epithet for buddhas, i.e., one who has gained enlightenment in the course of his or her quest for truth

tathagata-garbha (Skt.) lit. the "seed of the thus-gone one'"; the <Mahayana> belief that each sentient being holds within itself the seed or germ of enlightenment, though it may be unrecognized or unacknowledged by that being or those beings among which it finds itself

Tendai (Jap.) Japanese form of <T'ien-t'ai> school of Buddhism. After its transmission to Japan by Saicho in the eighth century, elements of <Zen> and esoteric practices also became blended with T'ien-t'ai.

Theravada (Pali) lit. "the way of the elders"; the only remaining school of <Hinayana> Buddhism today; it is most widely practiced in Southeast Asia. Emphasis is placed on right practice and right conduct, with the <four noble truths> and the <eightfold path> being of primary importance.

three refuges, or three jewels the Buddha, the <Dharma>, and the *<sangha>*

threefold training the three elements of training that, together, comprise all of Buddhist teaching. They are (1) training in moral discipline; (2) mind training; and (3) wisdom training.

T'ien-t'ai (Chin.) Chinese school of Buddhism that holds primarily that enlightenment is not to be achieved through the elimination of attachment to illusory phenomena, but rather is discovered as innately given. The doctrine, based in the Lotus Sutra, is concerned with the rejection of all such phenomenological realities as the philosophy of *<shunyata>*. T'ien-t'ai was developed in China by Chih-i in the sixth century. See *also* Tendai.

Tong Len (Tib.) lit. "sending and taking"; a Tibetan mind-training stemming from a slogan of Atisha: *Sending and taking should be practiced alternately; these two should ride the breath.* In this practice, one takes in negative qualities from outside oneself and sends out positive qualities that counter that which is taken in. (E.g., if one takes in the suffering of another, then one would send out kindness, healing energy, or well-wishes to others.)

tulku (Tib.) lit. "transformation body"; one who is recognized as the reincarnation of a deceased Buddhist teacher; a buddha appearing in human form

upaya (Skt.) lit. "skillful means"; a key ability of <bodhisattvas> and buddhas, who adapt their approach to teaching <Dharma> to the needs and interests of their student(s). Manifestations of *upaya* may be of any sort, including <koans>, straightforward discourse, or even deception or tricks that cause students to grasp the point being taught.

vajra (Skt.) lit. "diamond"; symbol of the
immutability of ultimate reality, or
<*shunyata*>. See also *dorje.*

Vajrayana (Skt.) lit "Diamond Realm"; developed
primarily in Tibet, a form of practice that
emphasizes <*tantra*>.

vinaya (Pali and Skt.) lit. "that which leads away
from <*samsara*>"; the discipline inherent to
the Buddhist precepts, or rules of conduct;
the code of behavior for monks and nuns

Vipassana (Pali) form of Buddhist practice that
emphasizes insight meditation. Its coupling
with <Shamatha> meditation is necessary
for the attainment of enlightenment.
("vipashyana" in Sanskrit)

yana (Pali and Skt.) lit. "vehicle"; means or
method by which one moves toward
enlightenment; practice. The three primary
yanas are <Hinayana>, <Mahayana>, and
<Vajrayana>, the last of which holds that
one may practice any or all at once.

yogi (Skt.) a man who has "yoked" himself to the
Divine; a great teacher or saint

yogini (Skt.) the feminine form of <yogi>; See
also *dakini*

zafu (Jap.) lit. "sitting cushion"; cushion on which
one sits during <Zen> meditation

zagu (Jap.) lit. "sitting thing"; mat or cloth on
which a <Zen> monk sits or prostrates himself or herself

zazen (Jap.) lit. "sitting meditation"; seated meditation, which, in <Zen>, is seen as the most
direct path to enlightenment

Zen (Jap.) lit. "meditation"; meditation in which
all distinctions and dualities are eliminated.
See also *dhyana*

zendo (Jap.) lit. "meditation hall" or "meditation
room"; place in which *zazen* is practiced;
<Zen> monastery or school

Selected Reading

The following books were written and/or recommended by presenters at the Buddhism in America Conference. Except where a presenter specified a particular edition of the work, the most recent edition is cited.

Classic Buddhist Texts

The *Flower Ornament Scripture: A Translation of the Avatamsaka Sutra.* Thomas Cleary, trans. 3 vols. Boulder, Colo., and Boston: Shambhala, 1984–87.

The Holy Teaching of Vimalakirti: A Mahayana Scripture. Robert A. F. Thurman, trans. University Park: Pennsylvania State University Press, 1976.

Mahamudra Teachings of the Supreme Siddhas. Sherab Dorje, trans. Ithaca, N.Y.: Snow Lion, 1995.

Thurman, Robert A. F., trans. *Essential Tibetan Buddhism.* San Francisco: HarperSanFrancisco, 1995.

The Tibetan Book of the Dead: The Great Liberation Through Hearing in the Bardo by Guru Rinpoche According to Karma Lingpa. Francesca Fremantle and Chögyam Trungpa, trans. Berkeley, Calif.: Shambhala, 1975.

Tsong Khapa's Speech of Gold in the Essence of True Eloquence: Reason and Enlightenment in the Central Philosophy of Tibet. Robert A. F. Thurman, trans. Princeton, N.J.: Princeton University Press, 1984.

Contemporary and Related Works

Aitken, Robert. *The Dragon Who Never Sleeps: Verses for Zen Buddhist Practice.* Berkeley, Calif.: Parallax Press, 1992.

Allione, Tsultrim. *Women of Wisdom.* London: Routledge & Kegan Paul, 1984.

Aoyama, Shundo. *Zen Seeds: Reflections of a Female Priest (Utsukushiki hito ni)* Patricia Daien Bennage, trans. Tokyo: Kosei, 1990.

Arnold, Edwin. *The Light of Asia; or The Great Renunciation (Mahabhinishkramana), Being the Life and Teaching of Gautama, Prince of India and Founder of Buddhism (as Told in Verse by an Indian Buddhist).* Wheaton, Ill., Theosophical Publishing House, 1969.

Batchelor, Stephen. *Alone with Others: An Existential Approach to Buddhism.* New York: Grove Press, 1983.

———. *The Awakening of the West: The Encounter of Buddhism and Western Culture.* Berkeley, Calif.: Parallax Press, 1994.

———. *Buddhism Without Beliefs: A Contemporary Guide to Awakening.* New York: Riverhead Books, 1997.

———. *The Faith to Doubt: Glimpses of Buddhist Uncertainty.* Berkeley, Calif.: Parallax Press, 1990.

Becker, Ernest. *The Denial of Death*. New York: Free Press, 1973.

Bercholz, Samuel, and Sherab Chödzin Kohn, comps. *Entering the Stream: An Introduction to the Buddha and His Teachings*. Boston: Shambhala, 1993.

Buddhadasa Bhikkhu. *Anapanasati: The Sixteen Steps to Awakening*. Bhikkhu Naga-sena, trans. Bangkok: Sublime Life Mission, 1971.

Carus, Paul. *The Gospel of Buddha According to Old Records*. Tucson, Ariz.: Omen Press, 1972.

Chögyam Trungpa. *The Myth of Freedom and the Way of Meditation*. John Baker and Marvin Casper, eds. Boston: Shambhala, 1988.

Dilgo Khyentse Rinpoche. *Enlightened Courage: An Explanation of Atisha's Seven-Point Mind Training*. Padmakara Translation Group, trans. Ithaca, N.Y.: Snow Lion Publications, 1993.

Dorsey, Issan [Tensho David Schneider]. *Street Zen: The Life and Work of Issan Dorsey*. Boston: Shambhala, 1993.

Glassman, Bernard Tetsugen, and Rick Fields. *Instructions to the Cook: A Zen Master's Lessons in Living a Life That Matters*. New York: Bell Tower, 1996.

Goleman, Daniel. *Emotional Intelligence*. New York: Bantam Books, 1995.

Goldberg, Natalie. *Long Quiet Highway: Waking up in America*. New York: Bantam Books, 1993.

Grof, Stanislav, and Joan Halifax. *The Human Encounter with Death*. New York : Dutton, 1977.

Gunaratana, Henepola. *Mindfulness in Plain English*. Boston: Wisdom Publications, 1993.

———. *The Path of Serenity and Insight: An Explanation of the Buddhist Jhanas*. Delhi: Motilal Banarsidass, 1985.

Halifax, Joan. *Being with Dying* (audio cassette). Boulder, Colo.: Sounds True, 1997.

———. *The Fruitful Darkness: Reconnecting with the Body of the Earth*. San Francisco: Harper SanFrancisco, 1993.

———. *Shaman, the Wounded Healer*. New York: Crossroad, 1982.

———. *Shamanic Voices: A Survey of Visionary Narratives*. Harmondsworth, Eng. and New York: Penguin Books, 1980.

Japanese Death Poems Written by Zen Monks and Haiku Poets on the Verge of Death. Yoel Hoffmann, comp. Rutland, Vt.: Tuttle, 1986.

Jaynes, Julian. *The Origin of Consciousness in the Breakdown of the Bicameral Mind*. Boston: Houghton Mifflin, 1990.

Kabat-Zinn, Jon. *Full Catastrophe Living: Using the Wisdom of Your Body and Mind to Face Stress, Pain, and Illness*. New York: Delacorte Press, 1990.

———. *Wherever You Go, There You Are: Mindfulness Meditation in Everyday Life*. New York: Hyperion, 1994.

Kabat-Zinn, Myla, and Jon Kabat-Zinn. *Everyday Blessings: The Inner Work of Mindful Parenting*. New York: Hyperion, 1997.

Leifer, Ron. *The Happiness Project: The Three Poisons That Cause the Suffering We Inflict on Ourselves and Others*. Ithaca, N.Y.: Snow Lion Publications, 1997.

Levi, Primo. *Survival in Auschwitz and The Reawak-ening: Two Memoirs.* Stuart Woolf, trans. New York: Summit Books, 1986.

Levine, Stephen. *Healing into Life and Death.* Garden City, N.Y.: Anchor Press/Doubleday, 1987.

Ling, Trevor. *Buddha, Marx, and God: Some Aspects of Religion in the Modern World.* London: Macmillan, 1979.

Matthiessen, Peter. *At Play in the Fields of the Lord.* New York: Vintage Books, 1987.

———. *East of Lo Monthang: In the Land of Mustang.* Boston: Shambhala, 1995.

———. *Nine-Headed Dragon River : Zen Journals, 1969–1985.* Boston: Shambhala, 1987.

———. *The Snow Leopard.* New York: Penguin Books, 1987.

Nisker, Wes "Scoop." *Crazy Wisdom.* Berkeley, Calif.: Ten Speed Press, 1990.

———. *If You Don't Like the News—Go out and Make Some of Your Own.* Berkeley, Calif.: Ten Speed Press, 1994.

Nyoshul Khenpo Rinpoche and Lama Surya Das. *Natural Great Perfection: Dzogchen Teachings and Vajra Songs.* Ithaca, N.Y.: Snow Lion Publications, 1995.

Olcott, Henry Steel. *A Buddhist Catechism.* Boston, Estes and Lauriat, 1885.

Packer, Toni. *The Light of Discovery.* Boston: Tuttle, 1995.

———. *The Work of This Moment.* Boston: Tuttle, 1995.

Rhie, Marylin M., and Robert A. F. Thurman. *Wisdom and Compassion: The Sacred Art of Tibet.* New York: Tibet House and Harry N. Abrams, 1996.

Rumi. *Delicious Laughter: Rambunctious Teaching. Stories from the Mathnawi of Jelaluddin Rumi.* Versions by Coleman Barks. Athens, Ga.: Maypop, 1990.

———. *One-Handed Basket Weaving: Poems on the Theme of Work.* Versions by Coleman Barks. Athens, Ga: Maypop, 1991.

Seung Sahn. *Only Don't Know: The Teaching Letters of Zen Master Seung Sahn.* San Francisco: Four Seasons Foundation, 1982.

Shaw, Miranda. *Passionate Enlightenment: Women in Tantric Buddhism.* Princeton, N.J.: Princeton University Press, 1994.

Snyder, Gary. *Mountains and Rivers Without End.* Washington, D.C.: Counterpoint, 1996.

Sogyal Rinpoche. *The Tibetan Book of Living and Dying.* Patrick Gaffney and Andrew Harvey, eds. San Francisco: HarperSanFrancisco, 1992.

Surya Das. *The Snow Lion's Turquoise Mane: Wisdom Tales from Tibet.* San Francisco: HarperSan Francisco, 1992.

Suzuki, Shunryu. *Zen Mind, Beginner's Mind.* New York: Weatherhill, 1988

Tenzin Gyatso (14th Dalai Lama). *The Meaning of Life from a Buddhist Perspective.* Jeffrey Hopkins, trans. and ed. Boston: Wisdom Publica-tions, 1992.

Thich Nhat Hanh, with Robert Aitken, et al. *For a Future To Be Possible: Commentaries on the Five Wonderful Precepts.* Berkeley, Calif.: Parallax Press, 1993.

Thoreau, Henry David. *Walden,* and *A Week on the Concord and Merrimack Rivers.* (Library of America) New York: Literary Classics of the United States, 1985.

Tulku Thondup. *Enlightened Journey: Buddhist Practice as Daily Life.* Harold Talbott, ed. Boston: Shambhala, 1995.

———. *The Healing Power of Mind: Simple Meditation Exercises for Health, Well-Being, and Enlightenment.* Boston: Shambhala, 1996.

———, trans. *The Dzog-chen Preliminary Practice of the Innermost Essence.* Brian C. Beresford, ed. Dharamsala: Library of Tibetan Works and Archives, 1982.

Tworkov, Helen. *Zen in America: Five Teachers and the Search for an American Buddhism.* New York: Kodansha International, 1994.

Wallace, B. Alan. *A Passage from Solitude: Training the Mind in a Life Embracing the World: A Modern Commentary on Tibetan Buddhist Mind Training.* Zara Houshmand, ed. Ithaca, N.Y.: Snow Lion Publications, 1992.

Watts, Alan. *Psychotherapy, East and West.* New York: Vintage Books, 1975.

Whyte, David. *The Heart Aroused: Poetry and the Preservation of the Soul in Corporate America.* New York : Currency/Doubleday, 1994.

Wu Kwang. *Open Mouth—Already a Mistake.* Cumberland, R.I.: Primary Point Press, 1997.

Zopa Rinpoche, Lama Thubten. *Transforming Problems into Happiness.* Ailsa Cameron and Robina Courtin, eds. Boston: Wisdom Publications, 1992.

To order copies of The Buddhism in America Conference audio tapes, contact:

Sounds True Catalog

P.O. Box 8010

Boulder, CO 80306

(800) 333-9185

For a complete catalog of Buddhist related books from Tuttle Publishing, contact:

Charles E. Tuttle Co., Inc.

RR1 Box 231-5

North Clarendon, VT 05759-9700

(802) 773-8930 or Toll-fee (800) 526-2778